Spanish for Life

M. Carol Brown
California State University, Sacramento

Kathleen C. Moore
California State University, Sacramento

HH Heinle & Heinle
Thomson Learning

United States • Australia • Canada • Denmark • Japan • Mexico • New Zealand
Philippines • Puerto Rico • Singapore • Spain • United Kingdom

The publication of *Spanish for Life* was directed by the Heinle & Heinle
College Foreign language Publishing Team:

Wendy Nelson, Senior Acquisitions Editor
Stephen Frail, Marketing Manager
Esther Marshall, Senior Production & Development Editor Supervisor
Jennifer Aquino, Developmental Editor

Also participating in the publication of this program were:

Publisher: **Vincent P. Duggan**
Associate Marketing Manager: **Kristen Murphy-Lojacono**
Senior Manufacturing Coordinator: **Mary Beth Hennebury**
Photo Researchers: **Jeff Freeland, Bénédicte Ferru, Judy Mason**
Project Manager: **Kristin Swanson**
Composition: **Greg Johnson, Art Directions**
Interior Designer: **Sue Gerould, Perspectives**
Illustrator: **Len Shalansky**
Cover Designer: **Ha Nguyen**
Cover Illustration: **Christie's Images/Superstock**
Text Printer/Binder: **Quebecor World**

For permission to use material from this text contact us:

Web: **www.thomsonrights.com**
Fax: 1-800-730-2215
Phone: 1-800-730-2214

Heinle & Heinle Publishers
20 Park Plaza
Boston, MA 02116

UK/EUROPE/MIDDLE EAST
Thomson Leaning
Berkshire House
168-173 High Holborn
London, WCIV 7AA,
United Kingdom

LATIN AMERICA
Thomson Learning
Seneca, 53
Colonia Polanco
11560 México D.F. México

JAPAN
Thomson Learning
Placeside Building, 5F
1-1-1 Hitotsubashi, Chiyoda-ku
Tokyo 100 0003, Japan

AUSTRALIA/NEW ZEALAND
Nelson/Thomson Learning
102 Dodds Street
South Melbourne
Victoria 3205 Australia

ASIA (excluding Japan)
Thomson Learning
60 Albert Street #15-01
Albert Complex
Singapore 189969

SPAIN
Thomson Learning
Calle Magallanes, 25
28015-Madrid
España

CANADA
Nelson/Thomson Learning
1120 Birchmount Road
Scarborough, Ontario
Canada MIK 5G4

Library of Congress Cataloging-in-Publication Data
The Library of Congress has assigned the following Library Congress
Catalog Card Number for the student textbook:
99-76679
CIP

ISBN: 0-8384-0711-0 [Instructor's Annotated Edition]
ISBN: 0-8384-0702-1 [Student Textbook]

Printed in the United States of America

1 2 3 4 5 6 7 8 9 03 02 01 00 99

Preface to the Instructor's Edition

Introduction

The **Spanish for Life** program was written to address student needs that are not met in mainstream introductory Spanish courses. Non-majors, adult learners, professionals learning Spanish for its career benefits, students with language learning disabilities, and other segments of the student population are requesting courses tailored to their specific needs. In many programs, Spanish classes may only meet once or twice a week. Increasingly, educational institutions have been offering a variety of course options for students:

- conversation track introductory Spanish
- reading track introductory Spanish
- occupational Spanish courses
- Spanish for Non-majors

These courses have been appearing across the country at a rapid rate. As enrollments continue to climb in Spanish courses, the demand for materials that are flexible, need-specific, and easy to use is expected to increase. It was for this reason that the **Spanish for Life** program was written.

As the name of the program suggests, **Spanish for Life** was written with the intention that it could be used by learners at all phases of life. Students, adult citizens seeking to learn the language of their Spanish-speaking neighbors, and professional businesspersons, law enforcement personnel, or health professionals can all benefit from the **Spanish for Life** program.

Whatever the needs of your curriculum, **Spanish for Life** can be adapted to meet them. The streamlined textbook can be used in one- or two-semester courses, as the main text or as a supplement, and the accompanying worktexts and audiocassettes can be used to address the needs of occupational Spanish courses, conversation track courses, reading-track courses, Spanish for non-majors, or even traditional Spanish courses. Each worktext follows the same scope and sequence as the **Spanish for Life** textbook, but with content-specific vocabulary, functional language, and communicative practice layered upon the grammatical syllabus. Used together, the textbook and worktext can accommodate a variety of teaching and learning styles, and grammar can be emphasized (or de-emphasized) according to the needs of the course.

Program Components

The complete Spanish for Life program includes the following components:

Spanish for Life
- Student textbook with *Atajo: Writing Assistant for Spanish*
- Instructor's Edition

Worktexts and Audiocassettes
- *Spanish for Life* Worktext (Spanish for everyday use)
- *Spanish for Life* Audiocassettes
- Health Worktext
- Health Audiocassettes
- Business Worktext

- Business Audiocassettes
- Law Enforcement Worktext
- Law Enforcement Audiocassettes

Additional Components

- *Test bank CD-ROM:* one test per chapter, one quiz per lesson, two in-class midterms, two take-home midterms, and two final exams. The test bank also has a test tape for the listening comprehension activities, and a sample vocabulary quiz and comprehensive final exams for the *Spanish for Life* Worktext.
- *Spanish Transparency Bank:* 100 four-color transparencies, thematically correlated to chapters in the core text as well as in every chapter of each worktext.
- *Spanish for Life home page on the WWW:* **http://spanishforlife.heinle.com** contains self-quizzes that can be scored on-line and emailed to instructors if wished, or printed out and submitted as hard copy.
- *Atajo: Writing Assistant for Spanish:* included free with every *Spanish for Life* textbook, this Spanish language word-processor and spell-checker contains a hyper-linked dictionary with the pronunciation of over 11,000 words, and several helpful databases: a full grammar reference, a vocabulary index, and a phrase book. This indispensable tool can be used by learners for years to come, whenever they have occasion to produce a Spanish-language document. It is correlated directly to the *Querido Diario* integrated at the end of each chapter in the core text.

Spanish for Life in the Classroom

Though you may elect to use **Spanish for Life** in a way not outlined here, we offer the following possible methods for adapting **Spanish for Life** for different course objectives.

Conversation-Track Beginner Courses (Also Spanish for Non-Majors or Continuing Education Spanish Courses.)

- The **Spanish for Life** textbook, the Spanish for Life Worktext, and the Spanish for Life Audiocassettes can be combined to create a program that emphasizes communication in class. The grammar presentations in the textbook are clear and straightforward so that students can read them out of class, while freeing up class-time to be spent on the communicative activities and listening activities found in the worktext.
- Alternatively, the Spanish for Life Worktext and Audiocassettes can be used in brief, introductory level conversation courses that wish to de-emphasize grammar.

Occupation Spanish Courses

Courses that focus on preparing students for specific career purposes have several options with the **Spanish for Life** series, with more options planned for future publication. The career-based worktexts that accompany the **Spanish for Life** textbook are designed to provide the career-specific vocabulary, functional language samples and communicative practice over the grammatical syllabus defined by the **Spanish for Life** textbook. Used together, the worktexts and the textbook provide students with both a solid foundation in the structures of the language and a set of practical language applications they can use immediately in their jobs. Worktexts can also be used independent of the textbook when grammatical accuracy is not a principal focus of the course.

- *Spanish for Life* Textbook + Spanish for Life Worktext and Audiocassettes

  This worktext prepares the student for and helps develop practical and useful communication. With three real-world dialogues in each chapter presenting new vocabulary in context while adhering to and practicing the grammar points of the core text, the Spanish for Life Worktext fosters a fun, interactive and realistic environment for your student to learn and use the Spanish language. **Notas culturales** and **Expresiones idiomáticas** correlate to the country profiled and the the theme of each chapter. Each **Síntesis** section concluding every chapter focuses on reading (**A leer**) with pre-reading activities, vocabulary expansion (**Expansión de vocabulario**), speaking (**Expansión oral**), translations (**Traducciones**), cultural tie-in with website links (**Enlace cultural**) and spelling and pronunciation (**Hablemos mejor**).

- *Spanish for Life* Textbook + Spanish for Business Worktext and Audiocassettes

  The Spanish for Business Worktext was written for business professionals seeking practical Spanish they can put to immediate use in their jobs. This worktext provides realistic, everyday situations and relevant business conduct codes and vocabulary for businesses operating domestically or internationally. Special features in every chapter such as business etiquette, (**¿Sabía Ud. que... ? en los negocios...**), translations of business documents (**Se necesita traductor/a**), negotiating in Spanish over email and voicemail (**Contestador automático; Correo electrónico**), and preparing presentations on the themes/topics of each chapter (**Presentaciones como en los negocios**), and country-specific business tips and facts (**¿Sabía Ud. que... ? en España...**) prepare students for the real-world situations they are bound to encounter in any business setting.

- *Spanish for Life* Textbook + Spanish for Health Worktext and Audiocassettes

  Ideal for anyone working in hospitals, private practices, volunteer associations, or any related medical context which serves Hispanics, the Health Worktext provides accurate translations of medical terms, diagrams, and recent articles on major health issues. **Notas culturales** and **¿Sabía que... ?** follow every dialogue in each chapter of the Health Worktext. Both provide specific facts, support and/or advice to the student relating to the theme and country profiled in each chapter. Special features in the **Síntesis** section of each chapter, include **A leer** with pre-reading activities, **Correo electrónico**, **Contestador automático**, **Traducciones**, **Mi agenda**, and **Para discutir**.

- *Spanish for Life* Textbook + Spanish for Law Enforcement Worktext and Audiocassettes

  Designed for those professionals working as police officers, prison employees, firefighters, court clerks, etc., this worktext gives students ample exposure to appropriate vocabulary and terms while placing the student in real-world contexts and situations.

When there is a prerequisite for matriculation in an occupational Spanish course, the worktexts may be used independently for a one-semester course. General Spanish for the Professions courses, where there is focus on more than one career, may use more than one worktext in the class, as they follow a consistent format and the same scope and sequence.

SFL Teaching Strategies

General Strategies

To help students get the most from their study of Spanish, it is important to explain both the text and your classroom procedures very clearly. Familiarize them with the various sections of **Spanish for Life: Lecturas**, grammatical explanations, ¿**Sabías?**, **Practiquemos**, dialogue bubbles, **A ver si sabes** (self-test), and **Querido Diario**. Point out the vocabulary lists at the end of each chapter and the glossaries at the end of the book. Encourage them to compile their own personal vocabulary lists of words and expressions that particularly interest them.

Three of the chapters of **Spanish for Life** are considerably shorter than the others. The *Capítulo preliminar* presents information about the Spanish speaking world at large, greetings, introductions, farewells, identification of cognates, the alphabet and its pronunciation, colors, a section on the accent in Spanish, a self quiz and a journal entry. Most importantly it serves as an introduction to the format of the book and can continue to serve as a reference later in the course.

Chapters 17 and 18 are also very short. It is not anticipated that any but the most exceptional groups will be able to finish them. The grammar they present are lower frequency forms and forms which typically are among the last to be acquired by learners and can be left for later study. However, in order to complete their familiarity of the countries of the Spanish-speaking world, it is recommended that students read the **Lecturas** and ¿**Sabías?** sections of those chapters.

All grammar explanations are presented in English throughout the book This gives the instructor the opportunity to spend most of the time in class speaking Spanish. From the Preliminary Chapter through Chapter 4, the instructions to the **Practiquemos** activities and the ¿**Sabías?** readings are presented in English. However, starting in Chapter 5 the instructions and ¿**Sabías?** sections are in Spanish. It is expected that, at first, students may experience some difficulty and need some help, but that should pass quickly and they should soon be accustomed to most things being presented in Spanish.

Listening Strategies

For students studying a second language in an area where that language is not spoken, it is especially important that they hear as much of the language as possible in class. For that reason, it is crucial to conduct the class in Spanish, using it as the medium of communication, not just as a specimen to be dissected. Make sure that all classroom commands are given in Spanish. Converse with the students about every day matters in the language. The reading passages may be read aloud. You may want to hand out the reading(s) with blanks where words are missing (cloze) and have students listen and fill in the blanks.

To give students more practice, bring supplementary listening activities to class. Commercial audio and video tapes are available, CD-ROM disks with listening practice are becoming easier to obtain, and through cable, Spanish-speaking television is quite readily accessible. Music in Spanish is widely available in the large book and music stores or on the Internet. It is fun to tape common commercials and ask students to identify the product or service before it appears on the screen. They might also be asked to identify words or situations in a short newscast.

Read your students stories or legends, or, if you can find them on tape, play the tape so students hear other voices and other accents. Invite guest speakers, parents, exchange students and the like to give short talks about subjects of interest. There are many ways available to enhance students' listening experience. Your imagination is the limit.

Speaking Strategies

It is extremely important that language students begin immediately to apply what they are learning through oral communication. Each lesson is designed to give students the opportunity to use the language actively from the first day of class. The dialogue bubbles and instructor's notes provide a variety of ideas and communicative prompts to guide students in developing their speaking skills. Transparency icons appear frequently throughout the chapters. These can be used as advance organizers to stimulate conversation, questions and answers. Have students personalize their observations using the vocabulary and structures that they are learning.

Many of the written activities are ideal for role-playing prompts as well. Have students substitute their own names or names of friends and family members in the dialogues, using the topic as an idea to develop their own conversations.

Role-playing the dialogues and incorporating the dialogue bubbles into daily lessons allows students to build their confidence and demonstrate their auditory memory, control of pronunciation, vocabulary and linguistic structures.

The *¿Sabías?* selections can also be used effectively as prompts for discussions. Have students summarize orally what they have read, give their opinions and ask further questions on the ideas presented.

Reading Strategies

In order to help students to develop their reading skills in Spanish, have them go through the steps for pre-reading first. They should read the title of the passage and see what they already know about the topic, trying to predict the contents. Then ask them to identify vocabulary and linguistic structures that are familiar, to look for cognates and to distinguish between content words and function words. Have them apply these text decoding techniques which will help them to strengthen their reading comprehension.

After the text has been read and studied, ask them how the passage differed from their initial expectations. Use the comprehension questions that serve to guide the student in making the appropriate connections with the ideas and facts presented. Certain questions require higher level critical thinking skills by asking for application to real-world personal situations and seeking opinions on what was read. The comprehension questions may be done independently or as a whole class activity allowing students to develop their answers orally by using the vocabulary and structures that they are learning. The reading questions may also be used effectively as writing prompts, thus giving students further opportunity to explore and develop interesting topics found in the readings.

For further development of the reading skill, provide students with authentic materials in Spanish such as newspapers, magazines, cartoons, legends, ads and short stories; there is a wealth of real-world materials available which will serve to augment what is given in the text and provide further practice.

Writing Strategies

The old adage says that in order to learn to write, you must write. This is as true in a second language as in the first. And students need to write more than one or two words to fill in a blank. *Spanish for Life* presents many opportunities to practice writing, but a useful supplement can be provided by students' keeping a daily journal which you assess holistically, reacting to the content and questioning only what is incomprehensible. They can write something about themselves using the Spanish they know, starting with the preliminary chapter. If they write one sentence each day, they can turn in five to seven sentences a week.

If you read journal entries globally and react to the content only, then reading time is not prohibitively long and you can learn interesting things about your students. It is important that both you and your students concentrate on the message and not on the form. There are plenty of occasions when grammar, spelling and punctuation are the focus.

Student may enjoy communicating on the Internet with a Spanish-speaking person or with one of their classmates. One class of students may correspond with another class, writing them notes or letters. As they advance, students may write short reports on events in Spanish-speaking countries using information they find on the Internet or in the library or bookstore. The reports could be prepared by groups or individually.

Whatever students write and whoever reads it, the important thing is that they keep writing.

Sample Semester/Quarter Lesson Plans

Syllabi	Semester System	Quarter System
Week 1	Begin Preliminary Chapter	Begin Preliminary Chapter
Week 2	Finish Preliminary, begin Chapter 1	Finish Preliminary, begin Chapter 1
Week 3	Finish Chapter 1	Finish Chapter 1
Week 4	Begin Chapter 2	Begin Chapter 2
Week 5	Finish Chapter 2, begin Chapter 3	Finish Chapter 2, begin Chapter 3
Week 6	Chapter 3	Chapter 3
Week 7	Finish Chapter 3, begin Chapter 4	Finish Chapter 3, begin Chapter 4
Week 8	Chapter 4	Chapter 4
Week 9	Finish Chapter 4, begin Chapter 5	Finish Chapter 4
Week 10	Chapter 5	Review and Exam
Week 11	Finish Chapter 5, begin Chapter 6	Begin Chapter 5
Week 12	Finish Chapter 6	Chapter 5
Week 13	Begin Chapter 7	Begin Chapter 6
Week 14	Finish Chapter 7	Finish Chapter 6, begin Chapter 7
Week 15	Review and Exam	Finish Chapter 7
Week 16	Begin Chapter 8	Begin Chapter 8
Week 17	Finish Chapter 8, begin Chapter 9	Finish Chapter 8, begin Chapter 9
Week 18	Finish Chapter 9	Finish Chapter 9
Week 19	Begin Chapter 10	Begin Chapter 10
Week 20	Finish Chapter 10, begin Chapter 11	Finish Chapter 10 and Review
Week 21	Finish Chapter 11	Begin Chapter 11
Week 22	Begin Chapter 12	Finish Chapter 11, begin Chapter 12
Week 23	Finish Chapter 12, begin Chapter 13	Finish Chapter 12
Week 24	Finish Chapter 13	Begin Chapter 13
Week 25	Begin Chapter 14	Finish Chapter 13, begin Chapter 14
Week 26	Finish Chapter 14, begin Chapter 15	Finish Chapter 14
Week 27	Finish Chapter 15	Begin Chapter 15
Week 28	Begin Chapter 16	Finish Chapter 15, begin Chapter 16
Week 29	Finish Chapter 17, readings Chapter 17	Finish Chapter 16
Week 30	Readings from Chapter 18, Review	Readings from Chapters 17 and 18, Review

Practiquemos/¿Comprendes? Answer Key

Capítulo preliminar

Practiquemos

A. ¡Hola!
1. Buenas tardes. O: Hola, ¿qué tal?
2. Hola, ¿qué tal? O: ¡Hola, chico(a)!
3. Buenas tardes. O: Hola, ¿qué tal?
4. Buenas noches. O: ¿Qué tal?
5. ¡Hola, chico(a)! O: ¿Qué tal, chico(a)?

A. Nuevos amigos
1. Memo, quiero presentar al profesor López.
2. Silvia, quiero presentar a Julián y a Marta.
3. Buenos días, clase. Quiero presentar a la señora Lora.
4. Tori, quiero presentar a Carlos.
5. Chicos(as), quiero presentar a mi amigo, Roberto.
6. Señorita Salazar, quiero presentar a Lorena y a Susan.

B. Presentaciones
Answers will vary.

A. Despedidas
1. Buenas noches, Sr. (Sra., Srta.) García. Hasta mañana.
2. Adiós, chicos(as). O: Chao. Hasta pronto.
3. Buenas noches, hasta luego.
4. Buenas noches a todos (everyone). Hasta mañana.
5. Buenas tardes, señor(a), señorita. Hasta luego.
6. Adiós, primo(a) (cousin); hasta pronto. o; Chao, Pablito (Juanita). Hasta luego.

A. Palabras afines
art, auto, baseball, brilliant, Chilean, combination, condiment, culture, doctor, examples, especially, student, extrovert, famous, football, football player, generous, giant, (gigantic), history, influence, melody, mural, nation, notable, part, simplify, television, timid, traditional, vanity, variety, zoological

A. Equivalentes
1. department
2. tranquility
3. approximately
4. compartment
5. nation
6. extension
7. nationality
8. comprehension
9. especially
10. creation

A. Al comienzo...
1. inaction
2. predestined
3. reconstruct
4. prehistoric
5. posthumous
6. remodel
7. inaccessible
8. postgraduate
9. demonstrate

A. Mis ojos
No answers.

B. La pronunciación
No answers.

A. ¿De qué color?
Answers will vary.

A. ¡Correcto!
1. fácil; to indicate the stressed syllable
2. botón; to indicate stressed syllable
3. sofá; to indicate stressed syllable
4. examen
5. familia
6. ciudad
7. tesis
8. precaución; to show that two contiguous vowels do not form a diphthong
9. teatro

B. ¿Diptongo?
1. envía
2. continúa
3. mío
4. tardío
5. asistencia
6. ministerio

¿Comprendes?
1. Spanish is spoken on four continents.
2. Venezuela is the Spanish-speaking country that has the largest area.
3. Mexico is the Spanish-speaking country that has the largest population.

Capítulo 1

Practiquemos

A. ¡Hola!
1. tú, because your cousin is a member of your family
2. usted, because you want to show respect to your boss
3. ustedes, because you want to show respect to your boss and his or her family
4. vosotros, because your buddies live in Spain and you know them
5. tú, if you are at the same level and know each other well
6. ustedes, because that is the only plural form used in Latin America
7. usted, because you want to show respect to your Spanish instructor
8. tú, because that person is a member of your family

B. Después de clase
1. yo, because you use I to talk about yourself
2. tú, because he is her friend and the person spoken to
3. ellos, because they are spoken about
4. ellos, because they are spoken about
5. él, because he is a man who is spoken about
6. nosotros, because she is talking about herself and someone else
7. usted, because she wants to show respect and he is the person spoken to
8. ellos, because they are spoken about
9. ella, because her mother is a woman who is spoken about.

10. ellos, because they are spoken about
11. ustedes, because there is more than one person
12. nosotros, because she is talking about herself and someone else

A. Son así.
1. es
2. son
3. eres
4. es
5. son
6. soy
7. sois
8. somos

B. Yo soy...
1. eres
2. somos
3. es
4. son
5. soy
6. es
7. son
8. somos
9. sois
10. son
11. es
12. somos

C. La clase
1. es
2. eres
3. somos
4. son
5. es
6. es
7. sois
8. es

A. El diccionario
1. feminine, cockroach
2. masculine, orangutan
3. feminine, hen
4. feminine, giraffe
5. masculine, fish
6. masculine, elephant
7. feminine, butterfly
8. masculine, dog
9. feminine, snake
10. masculine, monkey

B. Otro
1. libros
2. señoritas
3. noches
4. estudiantes
5. señores
6. días
7. profesores
8. chicos

A. ¿Masculino o femenino?
1. la
2. el
3. las
4. los
5. las
6. los
7. el
8. la

B. Nombres
Answers will vary.

C. El señor profesor
1. el before title
2. not necessary before name
3. la before title
4. not necessary before name
5. el before title
6. la before title
7. not necessary before name
8. not necessary before name

A. Interesantes
1. alto
2. guapa
3. activo
4. inteligentes
5. bonitas
6. peruanos
7. simpática
8. tímidas
9. delgada
10. tradicionales

B. ¡Magnífico!
1. extrovertido
2. activa
3. simpático
4. inteligentes
5. baja
6. gorditos
7. alegres
8. buena

C. ¿De dónde?
1. Mi amiga es mexicana.
2. La profesora es española.
3. Los chicos son puertorriqueños.
4. La estudiante es chilena.
5. Julio y Lisa son salvadoreños.
6. Elena es panameña.
7. Los señores son colombianos.
8. Raquel y Claudia son cubanos.

D. Así son.
1. La señorita es simpática.
2. (El) papá es alto.
3. Los chicos son tímidos.
4. La profesora es introvertida.
5. Marta y José son alegres.
6. La clase es tradicional.
7. Las mamás son delgadas.
8. Martín es gordito.
9. Nosotros somos inteligentes.
10. La fiesta es buena.

A. Nacionalidades
1. Es de México.
2. Es de Colombia.
3. Son del Perú.
4. Es de El Salvador.
5. Son de Chile.
6. Es de Argentina.
7. Es de Puerto Rico.
8. Son de España.

B. Muy durable
1. El diccionario es de papel.
2. La computadora es de plástico y metal.
3. El boli es de plástico y metal.
4. La calculadora es de plástico y metal.
5. El cuaderno es de papel (y metal).
6. La pluma es de plástico y metal.

C. ¿De quién?
1. El diccionario es de Raquel.
2. El cuaderno es de Isabel.
3. La calculadora es de Fernando.
4. El papel es de Francisco y Elena.
5. El boli es de Lorenzo.
6. La mochila es de Marcos.
7. El lápiz es de Susana.
8. El libro es de la profesora.

A. Números de teléfono
1. cinco cinco cinco - siete uno dos cero
2. nueve ocho dos -seis uno uno cero
3. cuatro uno cinco - cero cero siete siete
4. ocho cuatro cuatro - nueve dos tres siete
5. tres dos uno - cuatro tres siete seis
6. seis cinco cuatro - nueve nueve cero ocho
7. ocho cero cinco-cuatro tres dos uno
8. cinco uno cinco – ocho siete seis dos

B. ¿Cuántas cosas?
1. veintiún libros
2. diecinueve chicas
3. quince mochilas

4. diez bolígrafos (plumas)
5. veinticinco chicos
6. treinta sillas
7. una profesora
8. catorce calculadoras

C. ¡Problemas de matemáticas!
1. 19 + 3 = 22 diecinueve más tres son veintidós
2. 20 - 10 = 10, veinte menos diez son diez
3. 30 - 9 = 21, treinta menos nueve son veintiuno
4. 16 + 5 = 21, dieciséis más cinco son veintiuno
5. 4 + 12 = 16, cuatro más doce son dieciséis
6. 17 + 6 = 23, diecisiete más seis son veintitrés
7. 25 - 14 = 11, veinticinco menos catorce son once
8. 12 - 2 = 10, doce menos dos son diez
9. 28 + 2 = 30, veintiocho más dos son treinta
10. 13 - 9 = 4, trece menos nueve son cuatro

A. ¡Quiero presentar… !
1. Quiero presentar al señor.
2. Quiero presentar a María.
3. Quiero presentar a la chica.
4. Quiero presentar al profesor.
5. Quiero presentar a Ramón y Lucía.
6. Quiero presentar a la señora Martínez.
7. Quiero presentar al amigo de María.
8. Quiero presentar a la clase.
9. Quiero presentar a la señorita Pérez.
10. Quiero presentar a mi amiga.

B. ¿De quiénes?
1. Los cuadernos son del señor Gómez.
2. El boli es de la profesora Galán.
3. Las calculadoras son de los estudiantes.
4. El libro es del profesor Muñoz.
5. Los papeles son de las chicas.
6. El diccionario es del profesor de español.

A. Riesgo
1. ¿Cuándo es?
2. ¿Quiénes son?

3. ¿Cómo es?
4. ¿De quién son?
5. ¿Quién es?
6. ¿Qué es?
7. ¿De dónde son?
8. ¿Cuándo es?

B. Diálogo
JUAN: qué
JUAN: Quién
JUAN: Cómo
LOURDES: Cuándo
JUAN: De dónde
JUAN: De quién

¿Comprendes?
La influencia mexicana
1. It is evident in the popularity of foods like tacos, burritos, tostadas, and salsa.
2. "Tejana" music, a mixture of Mexican and country-western.
3. *Answers will vary.*

Los hispanos en los Estados Unidos
1. About 30 million Hispanics live in the United States.
2. People who come from or whose relatives come from Central or South America or the Caribbean are "Hispanic".
3. They have two different cultural heritages.

Hispanos muy conocidos
1. Sammy Sosa, Pedro Martínez, Mary Jo Fernández, as well as many others.

Capítulo 2
Practiquemos
A. ¿Qué tal?
1. estamos
2. está
3. están
4. estás
5. estoy

A. ¿Dónde?
1. está
2. están
3. estamos
4. está
5. están
6. estoy
7. están
8. están

B. ¿Estamos todos?
1. está
2. están
3. estoy
4. están
5. está
6. estás
7. está
8. estamos

C. ¿Está cerca?
1. Santiago de Cuba está lejos.
2. Santa Clara y Santo Domingo están cerca.
3. Guantánamo está lejos.
4. Matanzas y Cárdenas están cerca.
5. Isla de la Juventud está cerca. *(could be considered lejos)*
6. Nosotros estamos lejos.
7. Manzanillo está lejos.
8. San Francisco y Los Ángeles, California están lejos.

A. Artículos de la clase
1. unos
2. una
3. un
4. unos
5. un
6. unas
7. unos
8. una

B. Familiares
1. un
2. unas
3. unos
4. una
5. un
6. unas
7. unos
8. una

A. Actividades
Answers will vary.

B. Muy inteligente
1. hablar
2. llegar
3. comprender
4. celebrar
5. vivir
6. leer
7. beber
8. aprender

C. Destinos
1. Yo
2. Tú
3. Usted / Mi mamá
4. Marcos y yo / Nosotros
5. Susana y Carlos / Ellas

A. Vacaciones
1. van
2. vamos
3. va
4. voy
5. van
6. va
7. vamos
8. vas

B. ¿Adónde vas?
1. Voy al trabajo.
2. Voy a la clase de español.
3. Voy al cine.
4. Voy a la casa de mi amigo.
5. Voy al centro.
6. Voy a la oficina.
7. Voy a la biblioteca.
8. Voy al café.

C. Después del trabajo
1. Isabel y Alfredo van al cine.
2. Yo voy a la casa de Norberto.
3. Hortensia va al gimnasio.
4. Norberto y yo vamos a la clase de español.
5. Ustedes van al teatro.
6. Mi esposo y mi mamá van al centro.
7. Mi papá va al doctor.
8. Tú vas al mercado.

A. Esta noche
1. Lucas / Fausto va a mirar la tele (TV).
2. Alicia y yo vamos a la clase de español.
3. Tú y Rita / Mis padres van a comer en un café.
4. Yo voy a aprender mucho.
5. Tú vas a descansar.

B. El sábado
1. Mi papá va (a ir) a trabajar.
2. Quique y Sara van a mirar televisión.
3. Abuelita Carmen va a escribir cartas (letters).
4. Mamá y Araceli van a cocinar.
5. Mi novia y yo vamos a salir.
6. Mi abuelo José va a leer.
7. Mis padres van a caminar.
8. Tú vas a estudiar.

C. Lugares distintos
Answers will vary.

A. En el trabajo
1. tienen
2. tiene
3. tengo
4. tenemos
5. tienes
6. tienen
7. tenemos
8. tienen

A. ¡Qué familia!
1. Aurora de la O tiene dieciocho primos.
2. Juan y Joaquín Montes de Oca tienen veintitrés sobrinos.
3. Mi hermana y yo tenemos diecinueve tíos.
4. Tú tienes trece primas.
5. Ustedes tienen doce hijos.
6. Yo tengo siete hermanas.
7. Florentino y Ana Castellán tienen treinta nietos.
8. Berta Ruiz tiene veinte sobrinas.

B. Yo tengo…
Answers will vary.

A. ¡Quejas!
1. Papá tiene que trabajar.
2. Yo tengo que estudiar.
3. Mis hermanas tienen que practicar el piano.
4. Mi hermano y yo tenemos que correr.
5. Mi mamá y mi papá tienen que dormir más.
6. Y tú, ¿qué tienes que hacer?

B. El fin de semana.
1. Mi esposo tiene que trabajar.
2. Mi hijo y su amiga tienen que salir.
3. Mi hija Martina y yo tenemos que cocinar.
4. Yo tengo que descansar.
5. Mis hijas tienen que estudiar.
6. Y usted, ¿qué tiene que hacer?

C. De negocios
1. Alberto Coto tiene que ir a Madrid, España.
2. Yo tengo que ir a Buenos Aires, Argentina.
3. Verónica Llano y Horacio Luna tienen que ir a La Habana, Cuba.
4. Tú y Marcela tienen que ir a México, D.F., México.
5. Gilberto Márquez y yo tenemos que ir a Lima, Perú.
6. Tú tienes que ir a San Salvador, El Salvador.

A. Aquí
Answers will vary.

B. En la clase
Answers will vary.

A. Nuestras familias
1. nuestro abuelo, our grandfather
2. tus hermanos, your brothers (and sisters)
3. sus padres, your, his, her, their, parents
4. mi primo, my (male) cousin
5. su sobrina, your, his, her, their niece
6. nuestras hijas, our daughters
7. tu madre, your mother
8. nuestra familia, our family

B. ¿De quién?
1. Son nuestros bolígrafos.
2. Es su casa.
3. Son sus libros.
4. Es tu computadora.
5. Son mis papeles.
6. Es su oficina.
7. Es su trabajo (vuestro trabajo).
8. Es nuestra clase.

C. No comprendo.
1. Son los libros de Carlos.
2. Es la oficina de Alicia.
3. Es el carro de Mario y su hermano.
4. Son los papeles del señor González.
5. Son las sillas de mamá y papá.
6. Es el cuaderno de Juanito.

A. A practicar
no key

B. Problemas
1. 53 + 24 = 77, cincuenta y tres más veinticuatro son setenta y siete
2. 66 + 30 = 96, sesenta y seis más treinta son noventa y seis
3. 89 + 11 = 100, ochenta y nueve más once son cien
4. 71 + 7 = 78, setenta y uno más siete con setenta y ocho
5. 49 + 4 = 53, cuarenta y nueve más cuatro son cincuenta y tres
6. 35 + 60 = 95, treinta y cinco más sesenta son noventa y cinco

7. 93 + 4 = 97, noventa y tres más cuatro son noventa y siete
8. 29 + 3 = 32, veintinueve más tres son treinta y dos

C. Inventario
1. Hay treinta y cinco lápices finos
2. Hay ochenta y dos bolígrafos azules (blue)
3. Hay cincuenta y una plumas
4. Hay noventa y seis bolígrafos rojos (red)
5. Hay cuarenta y un libros de arte
6. Hay setenta y siete lápices rojos
7. Hay noventa y nueve cuadernos
8. Hay cincuenta y ocho paquetes (packages) de papel

¿Comprendes?

Cuba
1. Ninety miles.
2. In Miami, Florida.
3. Because there are so many Cuban Americans who live there.

Los turistas en Cuba
1. La Plaza de la Catedral, el Capitolio Nacional, la Isla de la Juventud, theaters, restaurants, clubs, la Plaza de la Revolución
2. Answers will vary.

La familia cubana
1. It is very close knit, and also an extended family.
2. Answers will reflect personal opinions. Many American families are also close knit, but few are extended families. In many American families, the generations don't party together.

José Martí
1. He was a freedom fighter and a poet.
2. The line of poetry refers to Cuba, the Caribbean, the tropics, etc.

Capítulo 3

Practiquemos

A. De México
1. practico
2. desayunan
3. desayuno
4. deseo
5. Trabajo
6. prepara
7. cena
8. miramos
9. bailamos
10. trabajas
11. Tocas

B. Mi rutina
1. trabajo
2. hablo
3. llama
4. hablamos
5. prepara
6. escuchamos
7. bailamos
8. visitan
9. cenan
10. descansamos
11. miramos
12. miras

C. Los fines de semana
EDUARDO: pasas
BEATRIZ: tomo
  toco
  canto
EDUARDO: escuchamos
  bailamos
  mira
  trabajo
BEATRIZ: visito
  ceno

D. Un día típico
1. llamo
2. soy
3. estudiamos
4. deseamos
5. desayunan
6. preparamos
7. llega
8. termina
9. tomamos
10. terminan
11. descansan
12. descansas

A. ¡La lotería!
1. cuatro mil pesos
2. sesenta y seis mil
3. un millón novecientos ochocientos cinco
4. nueve mil cuatrocientos cincuenta y dos
5. cincuenta y cinco mil

B. ¿Cuántos boletos?
1. veintitres mil
2. un millón cuatrocientos setenta y siete mil ciento veinticuatro
3. noventa y ocho mil quinientos cuarenta y cuatro
4. cinco millones de boletos
5. ochenta y nueve mil seiscientos cincuenta y siete

A. ¿Cuánto tienes?
1. contamos
2. cuento, novecientos setenta y nueve pesos
3. cuenta, novecientos ochenta y seis pesos
4. cuentan, mil veintisiete pesos
5. cuenta, mil quinientos ochenta y cinco pesos
6. cuentas

B. Vamos a jugar.
1. juego
2. juegan
3. juega
4. jugamos
5. juegan
6. juega
7. juegan
8. juegas

A. Actividades típicas
Answers will vary.

A. Meses y estaciones
1. julio, verano
2. febrero, invierno
3. septiembre, verano
4. febrero, invierno
5. enero, invierno
6. diciembre, invierno
7. marzo, invierno
8. octubre, otoño
9. septiembre, verano
10. Answers will vary.

A. Fecha de nacimiento
Answers will vary.

B. Fechas memorables
1. h, el dieciséis de diciembre de mil setecientos setenta
2. g, el dieciséis de septiembre de mil ochocientos diez
3. f, el treinta y uno de agosto de mil novecientos noventa y siete
4. c, el veintiuno de julio de mil novecientos sesenta y nueve
5. b, el seis de marzo de mil ochocientos treinta y seis

6. e, el nueve de abril de mil ochocientos sesenta y cinco
7. a, el cuatro de julio de mil setecientos setenta y seis
8. d, el catorce de mayo de mil novecientos noventa y ocho

C. ¿Cuándo?
1. el dieciocho de febrero de mil novecientos ochenta y dos
2. el catorce de julio de mil novecientos noventa y tres
3. el primero de diciembre de mil novecientos setenta y dos
4. el veintiséis de abril de mil novecientos sesenta y nueve
5. el doce de agosto de mil novecientos cincuenta y siete
6. el quince de enero de mil novecientos veintinueve
7. el veintitrés de septiembre de mil novecientos cuarenta
8. el cinco de mayo de mil novecientos treinta y ocho

A. Un día típico
1. comienza
2. comienzan
3. comienzan
4. comenzamos
5. comienza
6. comienzo
7. comienzan
8. comienza

B. En la clase de español
1. empieza
2. cierra
3. comienza
4. piensan
5. recuerda
6. recuerdo
7. encontramos
8. recuerdas

A. ¡Me gusta!
Answers will vary.

B. Es mi favorito
Answers will vary.

C. Mis actividades favoritas
Answers will vary.

A. Los Pérez
1. una clase
2. discos
3. la guitarra

4. su trabajo
5 el desayuno

A. La clase de español
1. –
2. –
3. a
4. –
5. –
6. a
7. –
8. –
9. a
10. a

A. ¡Qué tiempo!
Answers will vary.

B. ¿Y tú?
Answers will vary.

C. ¿En qué estación hace...?
Answers will vary.

D. ¿...y en Chicago?
Answers will vary.

¿Comprendes?
Sobre México y los mexicanos
1. Many people of Mexican heritage live in the southwest: California, Arizona, Texas, Colorado, Nuevo México, as well as large cities like Chicago and Detroit.
2. The geography of Mexico is varied, much like the United States.
3. *Answers will vary.*

La ciudad de México
1. It has everything: museums, theaters, cinemas, exhibition halls, the Palacio de Bellas Artes, centers of learning, good restaurants of all kinds, and commercial and business centers.
2. It is a plaza in the center of Mexico City.
3. The ancient Aztec capital of Tenochtitlán.

La salud mexicana
1. The Mexican people are very conscious of maintaining good health.
2. It's not serious because it is a play-on-words on three very important foods in the Mexican diet: tacos, tostadas, and tortas.

La geografía y el clima de México
1. The geography of Mexico is varied: there are mountains, coasts, plains, tropical jungles, and deserts.
2. The climate will vary according to the season of the year: humid with much rain in the spring and dry in the fall and winter.

Capítulo 4
Practiquemos
A. ¡A leer!
1. leen
2. leo
3. lee
4. lees
5. leemos
6. lee
7. leen
8. leemos

A. Los deberes
Answers will vary.

B. Algo nuevo
1. aprende a
2. aprendemos a
3. aparenden a
4. aprende a
5. aprenden a
6. aprendo a
7. aprendemos a
8. aprendes a

C. Una carta
1. comprendo
2. aprendemos
3. aprendo
4. come
5. beben
6. debo
7. leo
8. corremos

A. En mi clase...
1. asistimos
2. dirige
3. escriben
4. describo
5. discuten
6. escribes

B. ¿Y tu dirección?
Answers will vary.

C. Típicamente...
Answers will vary.

D. ¿Qué vamos a hacer?
Answers will vary.

A. Una carta a casa
1. veo
2. aprendo
3. sé
4. Asisto
5. conozco
6. doy
7. salgo
8. regreso
9. veo
10. Llego

B. Cada día
1. comprendo
2. veo
3. conozco
4. doy
5. sé
6. venzo
7. salgo
8. vengo

A. ¿Qué oyen?
1. oyemos…
2. oigo…
3. oye…
4. oímos…
5. oyes…
6. oyen…

B. ¿Oyes algo interesante?
Mi madre oye…
Yo oigo…
Mi esposo oye…
Mis compañeros oyen…
Tú oyes…
Nosotros oímos…
Mi amigo oye…

C. ¿Qué pasa?
1. incluye
2. instruyen
3. oigo
4. construyen
5. destruyes / construyes
6. construímos

A. ¿Qué saben de la RD?
1. sabemos
2. sabes
3. sé
4. saben
5. sabe
6. sabe
7. saben
8. saben

B. ¿Qué saben hacer?
saben…
sabe…
saben…
saben…

sé…
sabes…

C. Nuevos estudiantes
1. conoce a
2. conocen
3. conocen
4. conocen a
5. conozco
6. conoces al
7. conocemos
8. conoce

D. Buscando información
1. sabes
   sé
   sabe
   conozco a, sabe
2. conoces a
   conozco a
   sabes
   sé
   sabe
3. conocen
   conozco
   Saben
   saber
   conocer

A. ¿Qué hora es?
Son las seis de la mañana.
Son las dos y media de la tarde.
Son las doce o Es mediodía.
Son las tres y veinticinco de la tarde.
Es la una y veintiocho de la mañana.
Son las doce de la mañana o Es medianoche.
Son las cinco y cinco de la mañana.
Son las cinco menos cuarenta y cinco de la tarde o Son las cuatro cuarenta y cinco de la tarde.

B. ¿A qué hora?
Answers will vary.

C. Horarios
LINDA: es
SAMUEL: Son las nueve y veinticinco.
SAMUEL: A las dos de la tarde
LINDA: A la una
LINDA: A las ocho de la noche
LINDA: a las siete y veinticinco
SAMUEL: a la una
LINDA: a las nueve de la mañana
SAMUEL: Son las nueve y treinta y cinco. (Son

las diez menos veinticinco.)

A. ¿Qué te gustería hacer?
Answers will vary.

B. ¡Me gustería!
Answers will vary.

C. Preferencias
Answers will vary.

D. Sobre Cabarete
Answers will vary.

¿Comprendes?

El deporte más popular
1. Baseball is more popular than soccer.
2. Many American baseball players play in the Dominican Republic in the winter.
3. Pedro Martínez and Sammy Sosa are well-known baseball players from the Dominican Republic.

El alcalde de Santo Domingo
1. Johnny Ventura is the mayor of Santo Domingo.
2. He is also a musician.
3. He directs the city and directs his orchestra as well.

La naturaleza en la República Dominicana
1. There are so many things to see such as the national parks, forests, and many bodies of water.
2. One can see many types of sea creatures, trees, lakes, lagoons, and a variety of plants and animals.

Sammy Sosa, un gran dominicano
1. He is a great baseball player.
2. He does a lot to help his people and donates money for social causes.
3. "Altruistica" means to have unselfish concern for the welfare of others.

Cabarete, pueblo encantador
1. Cabarete is on the north coast of the Dominican Republic.
2. Cabarete offers many types of water sports, typical

music, and popular
rhythms of the island.
3. *Answers will vary.*

Capítulo 5

Practiquemos

A. La invitación
1. puede
2. pueden
3. podemos
4. puede
5. puedes
6. puedo

B. ¿Vamos a comer?
1. cuece
2. huele
3. muerdo
4. duelen
5. muere
6. volvemos, cuecen

C. Un accidente
RITA: tuerces, puedes,
     duele
CARLITOS: puedo, duele
RITA: pueden muere
CARLITOS: duele
RITA: duermes, cuezo
RITA: vuelvo

A. A ver
Answers will vary.

B. El menú
Answers will vary.

A. Muchos idiomas.
1. entiendo
2. entendemos
3. entienden
4. entiende
5. entiendes
6. entiendo

B. ¡Ay! Lo siento
Answers will vary.

C. Un caso triste
1. viene
2. pierde
3. miente
4. tiene
5. defendemos
6. perdemos
7. prefiere
8. entiende

D. En la Casa Colón
Answers will vary.

A. ¿Qué vamos a comer?
1. pide
2. piden
3. pedimos
4. piden
5. pido
6. pides

B. La despedida
1. despedimos
2. sigue
3. consigue
4. sirven
5. repiten
6. ríe
7. dicen
8. despedimos

C. El Restaurante El Dorado
RAQUEL: quiero
NORMA: entiendo, sugieres,
     puedes?
DANIEL: tiene, quieres,
     eliges, pido
NORMA: seguimos
RAQUEL: entiendo.
RAQUEL: pienso.
NORMA: pedimos, muero

A. Borinquen
1. es
2. es
3. está
4. es
5. es
6. está
7. son
8. son
9. está
10. está
11. es
12. está
13. es

B. Turistas
1. están
2. es
3. están
4. es
5. son
6. son
7. está
8. es
9. es
10. están
11. es
12. son

C. La invitación
MAMÁ: Es
ANITA: está
MAMÁ: está, Son, está,
     están
ANITA: está

MANUEL: es, es
MAMÁ: está
MANUEL: está
PAPÁ: está.
SARITA: está, está
MANUEL: está
MAMÁ: es, es
MANUEL: es

D. En la tienda de artesanías
JORGE: es
JORGE: está
DEPENDIENTA: Está
JORGE: es
DEPENDIENTA: es
JORGE: Es, es
DEPENDIENTA: es
JORGE: es

A. ¡Qué comida!
Answers will vary.

A. Mis amigos
1. Lorena es más que ocupada que sus amigos.
2. Elvira es más entusiasta
   que Juan.
3. Tú eres más baja que el
   profesor.
4. El libro de español es más
   corto que el libro de
   biología.
5. El postre es más grande
   (mayor) que la ensalada.
6. Maribel es más vieja
   (mayor) que Nené.

A. Comparaciones
Answers will vary.

A. Países bonitos
1. La República Dominicana
   es tan bonita como Puerto
   Rico.
2. Puerto Rico es tan interesante como la República
   Dominicana.
3. La República Dominicana
   tiene tan buen tiempo
   como Puerto Rico.
4. Puerto Rico no es tan
   grande como la República
   Dominicana.
5. Puerto Rico tiene tantas
   playas bonitas como la
   República Dominicana.
6. La ciudad de San Juan no
   es tan vieja como la ciudad
   de Santo Domingo.

A. El Caribe
1. Béisbol es el deporte más
   popular.
2. Puerto Rico es la isla más
   pequeña.

3. Las islas tienen las playas más bonitas.
4. Las playas tienen la arena más blanca.
5. Santo Domingo es la ciudad más antigua.
6. Cuba es la isla más cerca de Miami.

A. Más comparaciones
Answers will vary.

B. Orgullo borincano
1. hermosísimo
2. buenísimo (bonísimo)
3. simpatiquísimo
4. interesantísimo
5. riquísima
6. preciosísima

A. Novios
JULIÁN: algo
MÓNICA: nada
JULIÁN: alguien
MÓNICA: nadie
JULIÁN: siempre
MÓNICA: también, Nunca

B. En el café
MARTA: ni ni.
CAROLINA: nunca
MARTA: algunos (unos)
CAROLINA: alguna
MARTA: ninguna
CAROLINA: algo
MARTA: nada, No, nada
CAROLINA: tampoco

C. ¡Contradicciones!
PABLITO: nunca, ningún
PABLITO: ni, ni.
JUANITO: Nadie
PABLITO: nunca
JUANITO: tampoco

¿Comprendes?

Puerto Rico Estado Libre Asociado
1. Puerto Rico es un Estado Libre Asociado de los Estados Unidos.
2. No necesitan pasaporte, pueden votar en elecciones locales, sirven en las fuerzas militares, no tienen que pagar impuestos.
3. Muchos puertorriqueños están satisfechos, pero otros quieren libertad o ser estado de los Estados Unidos.

Sabor a Puerto Rico
1. Son típicos arroz, frijoles, habichuelas, carne, frutas y otras comidas.
2. Es necesario cocinar los plátanos, comemos las bananas crudas.
3. Porque tiene muchas frutas, verduras, arroz y frijoles.

San Juan
1. San Juan está en la costa norte.
2. Es una ciudad amurallada, tiene calles de adoquines, las calles son angostas, tiene edificios coloniales, tiene una fortaleza.
3. Age will vary with year—current date minus 1500 years approximately, e.g. 21st Century – 15th Century = approximately 600 years.

¿Es latino Puerto Rico?
1. Creen que Puerto Rico es más americanizado que otros países.
2. Tienen mucho orgullo de su patria.
3. Answers will vary.

Capítulo 6

Practiquemos

A. El sábado por la mañana
1. está jugando
2. están preparando
3. está mirando
4. estoy trabajando
5. está practicando
6. estamos hablando
7. están bailando
8. estás estudiando

A. ¿Quién puede... ?
1. está escribiendo
2. están leyendo
3. estás haciendo
4. está oyendo
5. está comiendo
6. estoy bebiendo

B. ¡Visitas!
Answers will vary.

A. ¿Qué están haciendo, Mami?
1. están poniendo
2. está repitiendo
3. están pidiendo
4. estoy friendo

5. estamos riendo
6. estás durmiendo

A. ¿Cómo se dice?
1. b, because progressive only refers to the current moment in Spanish
2. a, because progressive only refers to the current moment in Spanish
3. b, because this sentence refers to the current moment
4. a, because progressive only refers to the current moment in Spanish
5. b, because this sentence refers to the current moment
6. a, if we are talking about right now; b, if we are referring to the future

B. ¡Ay! Es Águeda.
1. Mamá está haciendo la comida.
2. Papá y José están viendo un (el) partido de fútbol.
3. Susana y Roberto están estudiando.
4. Mi amiga y yo estamos leyendo revistas.
5. La tía Eva estea barriendo en el garaje.
6. Yo estoy oyendo música latina.
7. El tío Mario y Raúl están cortando el césped.
8. Papá está comiendo papas fritas

C. El lunes por la mañana
Answers will vary.

A. No puedo ver.
Sí, la veo.
Sí, las veo.
Sí, lo veo.
Sí, los veo.
Sí, sí, la veo.

B. ¡Con salsa!
1. Las
2. Los
3. Las
4. La
5. Lo
6. Las
7. Lo
8. Los
9. Lo
10. La

C. ¿Quién lo hace?
Answers will vary.

D. En mi familia.
Answers will vary.

A. La fiesta
1. compra
2. escribe
3. arregla
4. busca
5. pide
6. habla
7. lee
8. ve
9. llama
10. prepara

B. Mucho que hacer
MAMÁ: di
MAMÁ: sal, haz, Ven
MAMÁ: pon, ten, vé, pon
MAMÁ: Sé, ten

C. Mensajes.
vé, saca, lava, pon, llama,
Pon, haz, come

A. ¡Ten cuidado!
1. tomes
2. bebas
3. escuches
4. salgas
5. vayas
6. comas
7. tomes
8. seas

B. En clase
1. habla, no hables
2. bebe, no bebas
3. come, no comas
4. copia, no copies
5. abre, no abras
6. está, no estés
7. duerme, no duermas
8. sale, no salgas

A. Actividades
1. está estudiándolos, los está estudiando
2. están mirándolo, lo están mirando
3. Están comiéndola, la están comiendo
4. estás escuchándola, la estás escuchando
5. está lavándolos, los está lavando
6. estamos escribiéndola, la estamos escribiendo
7. está haciéndolos, los está haciendo
8. estoy preparándolas, las estoy preparando

A. Más quehaceres
1. va a lavarlo, lo va a lavar
2. va a sacudirlos, los va a sacudir
3. va a sacarla, la va a sacar
4. va a cortarlo, lo va a cortar
5. va a ponerla en orden, la va a poner en orden
6. va a barrerla, la va a barrer
7. va a limpiarlos, los va a limpiar
8. va a prepararlo, lo va a preparar

B. El viaje
Answers will vary.

A. Limpiando la casa
1. Bárrelo
2. Límpialo
3. Ponlos
4. Pásala
5. Sácala
6. Sacúdelos
7. Córtalo
8. Termínalos

B. Una amiga enferma
1. Ciérrala, no quiero cerrarla
2. Bébelos, no quiero beberlos
3. Cómela, no quiero comerla
4. Prepáralo, no quiero prepararlo
5. Tómalas, no quiero tomarlas
6. Llámala, no quiero llamarla

A. ¿Qué dice tu amigo?
1. los pongas
2. la sacudas
3. las hagas
4. lo llames
5. la laves
6. la saques

B. La dieta
1. no la comas
2. no las bebas
3. no fumes
4. no lo bebas
5. no la comas
6. no lo bebas

C. El examen
1. Quiero mirar la tele, no lo mires ahora
2. Quiero leer una novela, no la leas ahora
3. Quiero escribir cartas electrónicas, no las escribas ahora
4. Quiero salir al cine, no salgas ahora
5. Quiero escuchar música, no la escuches ahora
6. Quiero llamar a mis amigos, no los llames ahora

¿Comprendes?

Mirando hacia el futuro
1. Por la guerra civil de los años 80.
2. Están construyendo pozos, consejeros de otros países están aconsejando a los salvadoreños en la educación, la salud y la agricultura.
3. *Personal opinion will determine response.*

¿Quiénes son los salvadoreños?
1. Porque hay mezcla de sangre india con sangre europea. Los indios son los mismos. (maya, Olmeca. tolteca, pipil).
2. Los dos países tienen diferentes grupos étnicos. *(Answers will vary with personal opinion.)*

Disfruta de El Salvador
1. La Catedral Metropolitana, el Teatro Nacional, el Jardín Botánico.
2. Está al norte y al oeste de San Salvador y está muy cerca de Guatemala.
3. *Answers will vary.*

La Isla Montecristo
1. Por la naturaleza pura, los animales, y la rica vegetación.
2. *Answers will vary.* Galapagos Islands, Madagascar, etc.

Capítulo 7

Practiquemos

A. En la cocina
1. La señora Martínez preparó la comida.
2. Manuel habló con sus amigos.
3. Luci y yo limpiamos.
4. Germán y sus amigos jugaron fútbol.
5. Mamá llamó a papá.
6. Pamela y yo tomamos café.
7. Pamela y Norma lavaron los platos.
8. Yo cociné la carne.

B. El viaje
1. empaqué
2. viajó
3. compraron
4. pagó
5. llegamos
6. visitaron
7. saqué
8. preguntó
9. Comenzaste
10. contestó, comencé

C. Antes del viaje
1. Recordaste, recordé
2. Pagaste, pagué
3. Reservaste, reservé
4. Sacaste, saqué
5. Empacaste, empaqué
6. Compraste, compré
7. Llamaste, llamé
8. Buscaste, busqué

A. Congreso internacional
1. aprendió
2. bebieron
3. asistí
4. viste
5. escribió
6. comimos
7. describieron
8. oímos
9. recibimos
10. salieron

B. Correspondencia electrónica
1. aprendí
2. asistimos
3. discutieron
4. oí
5. comimos
6. bebimos
7. leyó
8. salimos
9. vimos
10. escribí

C. Ayer
1. Por la mañana Elaine estudió sus lecciones.
2. Rob y Jane trabajaron.
3. La señorita Arrabal escribió sus planes.
4. Anita leyó un reporte.
5. Yo hablé por teléfono con otros estudiantes.
6. Laura y Martha oyeron cintas.
7. ¿Tú preparaste (la) tarea?
8. Peter y yo comimos en la cafetería.
9. Yo busqué artículos en la biblioteca por mucho tiempo.
10. Por eso yo llegué tarde a la clase de español.

D. Otro fin de semana
Answers will vary.

A. De regreso
1. le
2. me
3. te
4. nos
5. les
6. nos
7. le
8. les

B. Esta mañana
1. me
2. les
3. te
4. nos
5. le
6. nos
7. me
8. les

A. Juanito, por favor
1. Prepárales el almuerzo a tus hermanitos.
2. Pídeles dinero a tu padre.
3. Dile tus planes a tu madre.
4. Pregúntales la tarea a tus profesores.
5. Léele un cuento a tu hermanita.
6. Escríbeme una lista de tus actividades.

A. De viaje
1. Estamos escribiéndole una carta. Le estamos escribiendo una carta.
2. Van a prepararnos una comida especial. Nos van a preparar una comida especial.
3. Puedo conseguirle una visa de estudiante. Le voy a conseguir una visa de estudiante.
4. ¿Vas a comprarme la guía? ¿Me vas a comprar la guía?
5. Puedo decirles el itinerario. Les puedo decir el itinerario.
6. Están sirviéndonos un café especial. Nos están sirviendo un café especial.

B. ¡Magnífico!
1. A Susana y Jorge les gustan las cervezas colombianas.
2. ¿A usted le gusta el ajiaco?
3. A Alicia le encanta el Monserrat.
4. A nosotros nos gusta el jardín botánico.

5. ¿A ti te gustan los museos?
6. A mí me encanta el Mercado de las Pulgas.

A. Un mensaje
1. hice
2. Fui
3. hablé
4. dijo
5. Fue
6. di
7. compré
8. hice

B. ¿Y ayer?
1. La señora Menéndez fue a la agencia de viajes.
2. Robert y Cecilia hicieron sus quehaceres.
3. Tía Rosa y yo dimos una vuelta por el parque.
4. El señor Menéndez hizo unas llamadas telefónicas.
5. Princesa, la perra, fue a la oficina del veterinario.
6. Abuelita Carmen hizo un pastel.
7. Yo fui al supermercado.
8. Todos dijeron: «Fue un buen día.»

C. Un fracaso
MANUEL: fueron
ELENA: Fuimos
MANUEL: fue
ELENA: Fue
MANUEL: pareció, Dijeron
ELENA: Fue, resultó, Dio, dio, fue

B. Esperando
1. ¿Cuánto tiempo hace que la familia Alarcón espera? Hace dos horas.
2. ¿Cuánto tiempo hace que Ernesto y su novia esperan? Hace veinticinco minutos.
3. ¿Cuánto tiempo hace que yo espero? Hace una hora y veinte minutos que tú esperas.
4. ¿Cuánto tiempo hace que Silvia y su mamá esperan? Hace cuarenta y cinco minutos.
5. ¿Cuánto tiempo hace que tú esperas? Hace media hora.
6. ¿Cuánto tiempo hace que Hector y yo esperamos? Hace diez minutos.
7. ¿Cuánto tiempo hace que Javier y tú esperan? Hace tres horas.

8. ¿Cuánto tiempo hace que los socios del Club de golf esperan? Hace una hora y media.

B. ¿Cuánto tiempo hace que... ?
1. Raúl, ¿cuánto tiempo hace que conduces tu carro nuevo? Hace un mes que conduzco mi carro nuevo.
2. Gloria y Ester, ¿cuánto tiempo hace que Uds. asisten a la Universidad de Bogotá? Hace un año que asistimos a la Universidad de Bogotá.
3. Fernando, ¿cuánto tiempo hace que lees las novelas de Gabriel García Márquez? Hace un semestre que leo las novelas.
4. Profesor Guzmán, ¿cuánto tiempo hace que Ud. enseña en la Universidad de Bogotá? Hace diez años que enseño en la Universidad.
5. Margarita, ¿cuánto tiempo hace que recibes cartas por correo electrónico? Hace dos semanas que recibo cartas por correo electrónico.
6. José y Lulú, ¿cuánto tiempo hace que van frecuentemente a Cartagena? Hace muchos años que vamos frecuentemente a Cartagena.

A. ¿Cuánto tiempo hace que... ?
1. Hace... que hice las tareas de español.
2. Hace... que fui a una fiesta.
3. Hace... que hablé con un miembro de mi familia.
4. Hace... que vi una buena película.
5. Hace... que comí algo.

B. ¿Cuántos años hace... ?
1. ¿Cuánto tiempo hace que los estadounidenses llegaron a la luna? Hace ... años que los estadounidenses llegaron a la luna.
2. ¿Cuánto tiempo hace que Gabriel García Márquez recibió el Premio Nóbel? Hace ... años que Gabriel García Márquez recibió el Premio Nóbel.
3. ¿Cuánto tiempo hace que Fidel Castro tomó control del gobierno cubano? Hace ... años que Fidel Castro tomó control del gobierno cubano.
4. ¿Cuánto tiempo hace que los EE.UU. proclamaron su Independencia? Hace ... años que proclamaron su Independencia.
5. ¿Cuánto tiempo hace que tú naciste? Hace ... años que yo nací.

¿Comprendes?

¡Viajamos a Colombia!
1. Colombia es el único país del continente sudamericano con costas en el Pacífico y Atlántico.
2. Cultivan café, caña y azúcar.
3. En la capital de Bogotá, los sitios son el Museo del Oro, la Catedral de Sal y también la oportunidad de ver el ballet folklórico.

Los chibcha
1. Alonso de Ojeda fue compañero de Cristóbal Colón.
2. Los indios chibcha vivieron de la agricultura, produciendo maís, papas, manioca y otros productos.
3. Los vencieron porque los cinco caciques de los cinco grupos de chibcha no se unieron en su defensa.
4. Aspectos de la cultura chibcha perduran en la cultura colombiana y los colombianos consideran la aportación de los chibcha un aspecto muy importante de la historia del país.

Gabriel García Márquez, autor extraordinario
1. Tiene setenta y un años. (Depende del año.)
2. Ejerció la carrera de abogado también.
3. Sus obras tienen temas como el nacionalismo latinoamericano. También nos lleva a diferentes planos de la realidad e irrealidad. Los orígenes y tradiciones latinoamericanos son importantes también.
4. Es uno de los autores más famosos de Sudamérica y ganador del Premio Nóbel de Literatura de 1982.

El Dorado
1. No fue un mito porque los indios cubrían el nuevo jefe de la tribu de polvo de oro.
2. "El Dorado" que buscaron los españoles fue un país de oro y piedras preciosas.
3. Las expediciones dieron forma al norte de América del Sur.

El café en Colombia
1. No, es una planta nativa de Colombia.
2. Tienen tres o cuatro años.
3. El agricultor cosecha los granos y los trabajadores los lavan, los tuestan y los mandan al mercado. Compramos el café en el supermercado y lo molemos. Después agregamos agua caliente.

Capítulo 8

Practiquemos

A. El terremoto
1. hubo
2. quisieron
3. pudieron
4. estuvo
5. pusieron
6. fueron
7. tuvieron
8. supieron

B. ¡Un buen restaurante Guatemalteco!
1. trajo
2. pudiste
3. anduvieron
4. vino
5. no quiso
6. conduje
7. estuvimos
8. Hubo

C. El accidente
1. b
2. c
3. a, c
4. b
5. a, c

D. De vacaciones
Answers will vary.

A. Mis vacaciones
Answers will vary.

A. La comida
1. llegó, sirvió
2. frió, hirvió
3. siguieron
4. sirvieron
5. pidió
6. repitieron
7. divirtió
8. despidieron, sintieron

B. Ayer
1. Los estudiantes repitieron las palabras nuevas.
2. Nosotros seguimos las instrucciones del profesor.
3. Yo sugerí la actividad nueva.
4. Paco durmió toda la hora.
5. Tú reíste a toda la clase.
6. El profesor divirtió a los estudiantes.

C. ¿Quién mintió?
Yo dije: Asturias nació en 1946.
Tú mentiste.
Roberto dijo: Asturias recibió el Premio Nóbel en 1968.
Roberto no mintió.
Mónica y Arnoldo dijeron: Asturias fue agricultor.
Mónica y Arnoldo mintieron.
Nosotros dijimos: Asturias escribió poemas.
Ustedes no mintieron.
Tú dijiste: Asturias murió en 1968.
Yo mentí.
Ustedes dijeron: Asturias estudió medicina.
Nosotros mentimos.

A. Dámelo
1. Pásame la calculadora. Pásamela. — Ya te la pasé.
2. Dame el diccionario. Dámelo. — Ya te lo di.
3. Pásame los bolígrafos. Pásamelos. — Ya te los pasé.
4. Alcánzame las cartas. Alcánzamelas. — Ya te las alcancé.
5. Dame el memo del jefe. Dámelo. — Ya te lo di.
6. Pásame la pluma. Pásamela. — Ya te la pasé.

B. Promesas
1. Nos los diste.
2. Elena me la regaló.
3. Emilio y José te la escribieron.

4. Yo te lo leí.
5. Pepe nos la preparó.
6. El jefe nos lo dio.

C. La comida cooperativa.
1. Cecilia me las trajo.
2. Elena y Paco te la hicieron.
3. Jorge y Memo nos los mandaron.
4. Tú nos la cocinaste.
5. Yo te los serví.

A. El viaje
1. Consíguesela.
2. Prepárasela.
3. Compráselos.
4. Búscasela.
5. Resérvaselos.
6. Empácasela.
7. Tráeselas.
8. Mándaselas.

B. ¿Quién lo hizo?
1. Yo se las compré.
2. Gerardo se lo mandó a Ud.
3. La señorita Flores nos los organizó.
4. Su esposa nos los mandó.
5. Nosotros se las hicimos a Ud.
6. Usted nos lo dió.

A. ¿Cuándo?
1. Me la escribió anteayer.
2. Nos (Se) los dieron esta mañana.
3. Se las dijimos el viernes pasado.
4. Te la pintaron el mes pasado.
5. Se lo compraron el lunes.
6. Nos lo mencionó la semana pasada.
7. Te lo expliqué ayer.
8. No se lo trajiste nunca. (Nunca se lo trajiste.)

B. En la oficina
1. Sí, se la va a escribir. Va a escribírsela.
2. No, no se lo puede comprar. No, no puede comprárselo.
3. Sí, se (nos) la puede preparar. Sí, puede preparársela. (preparárnosla)
4. No, no se los tenemos que escribir. No, no tenemos que escribírselos.
5. Sí, se lo van a traer. Sí, van a traérselo.
6. Sí, se las puedo mandar. Sí, puedo mandárselas.

A. ¿Qué tienen?
1. tengo prisa.
2. tiene miedo.
3. tienes sueño.
4. tiene hambre.
5. tienen calor. Todos tienen sed.
6. tenemos suerte.
7. no tiene razón.
8. tiene ganas de

B. ¿Cómo respondes?
1. Tú no tienes razón.
2. Tú tienes sueño.
3. Tú tienes hambre.
4. Tú tienes que estudiar. Tienes miedo.
5. Tú tienes sed. Tienes calor.
6. Tú tienes sed.
7. Tú tienes éxito.
8. Tú tienes suerte.
9. Tú tienes paciencia.
10. Tú tienes prisa.

C. En el café
ANTONIO: tengo sed
CAROLINA: Tengo sueño
ISABEL: tengo hambre (prisa)
ANTONIO: tienes prisa
CAROLINA: Tiene suerte
ISABEL: suerte
CAROLINA: Tengo hambre.
ANTONIO: tienen frío
CAROLINA: tienes razón

D. Una clase típica
1. tengo prisa; ¿Cuándo tienes prisa?
2. tienen hambre y sed; ¿Cuándo tienes hambre y sed?
3. tenemos éxito; ¿Cuándo (no) tienes éxito?
4. tiene sueño; ¿Cuándo tienes sueño?
5. tengo ganas de; ¿Cuándo tienes ganas de jugar voleibol?
6. no tiene razón. (tiene prisa); ¿Cuándo no tienes razón?
7. no tienen ganas de; ¿Cuándo no tienes ganas de cometer errores?
8. tienen celos; ¿Cuándo no tienes celos?

¿Comprendes?

Rigoberta Menchú
1. Ella se dedicó a mejorar la condición de su gente escribiendo libros donde

expuso la corrupción de los líderes guatemaltecos.
2. *Answers will vary.*
3. *Answers will vary.*

Miguel Ángel Asturias
1. Vivió 75 años.
2. Asturias escribió sobre temas sociales, los mayas y el destino del país.
3. Rigoberta Menchú, Gabriel García Márquez

Los mayas
1. El sistema maya se basa en 20.
2. Un códice es un libro hecho de la corteza de un árbol.
3. Protestó los abusos de los indígenas.
4. Los mayas son similares a los griegos porque inventaron un sistema matemático, un sistema jeroglífico de escritura y estudiaron los astros.

El Popol Vuh
1. Significa libro de la comunidad.
2. Muchas personas dicen que el Popol Vuh es la Biblia maya porque describe como los dioses crean hombres y por qué.
3. Nos ayuda a comprender la civilización fascinante de la gente maya.

Capítulo 9

Practiquemos

A. Fuera de la oficina
1. se baña
2. se levantan
3. te lavas
4. se peinan
5. nos ponemos
6. se afeita
7. me acuesto
8. se duermen

B. Al campamento
1. levántate, me levanto
2. báñate, me baño
3. péinate, me peino
4. ponte, me pongo
5. lávate las manos, me lavo las manos
6. acuéstate, me acuesto

A. ¡Qué hermosas!
Answers will vary.

A. ¿Reflexivo o no?
1. se
2. (not necessary)
3. se
4. me
5. (not necessary)
6. se
7. se

A. En el hospital
1. La enfermera lavó a la Sra. Peña. La Sra. Peña se lava.
2. El enfermero afeitó al Sr. Gómez. El Sr. Gómez se afeita.
3. El enfermero te peinó. Tú te peinas.
4. La enfermera despertó a las niñas. Las niñas se despiertan.
5. La enfermera me vestió. Me visto.
6. Los enfermeros acostaron a los hermanos Herrera. Los hermanos Herrera se acuestan.

B. El orden
1. José se pone los calcetines.
2. Yo me pongo el suéter.
3. Paulina y Susana se ponen los pantalones.
4. Tú te pones la blusa.
5. Norberto y yo nos ponemos la chaqueta.
6. Tú y Enrique se ponen los zapatos.
7. Ernesto y Sandra se ponen el reloj.
8. Elena se pone el collar.

A. Apagón
1. se puso alegre
2. me puse triste
3. se puso enojada
4. te pusiste triste
5. se pusieron contentos (alegres)
6. nos pusimos contentos (alegres)

A. ¡Me encanta Perú!
1. a
2. De
3. a
4. de
5. con
6. en
7. En
8. En
9. sin
10. sobre

B. La rutina diaria
1. con
2. sin
3. a
4. en
5. de
6. sin
7. en

A. ¿Qué ven?
1. lejos de 2. Antes de 3. encima de 4. Cerca de 5. enfrente de

B. Mi dormitorio
Answers will vary.

A. ¿Con quién?
1. migo
2. ellos
3. tigo
4. nosotros
5. ellas
6. ustedes
7. ella

B. Contestando preguntas
1. de él
2. de ustedes
3. a ellas
4. a nosotros
5. sin ella
6. sin ellos
7. contigo
8. conmigo

C. ¿Qué llevas?
Answers will vary.

A. ¿Cuál?
1. Este reloj
2. Aquellas blusas
3. Esa falda
4. Estos zapatos
5. Esas camisetas
6. Ese traje
7. Esta corbata
8. Esos calcetines

B. Comprando regalos
SILVIA:	esa
DEPENDIENTA:	Esta
SILVIA:	esa
DEPENDIENTA:	aquellos
SILVIA:	esta
DEPENDIENTA:	aquellas
SILVIA:	estos, esta

A. Colores típicos
1. amarillo
2. roja, blanca y azul
3. verdes
4. blanca
5. grises
6. anaranjado

7. marrón (café)
8. negro
9. violeta
10. azul marino

B. En la tienda
1. esos
2. esta
3. ese
4. este
5. esas
6. esta
7. esos
8. esa

A. ¡Qué bonito!
1. ese, éste
2. Ésta
3. Éste
4. ese, Éste
5. Éste
6. Éstos

B. Dame, dame
1. esa, ésta
2. ese, éste
3. esos, éstos
4. esos, éstos
5. esas, éstas
6. ese, éste

A. ¿Qué es?
1. aquello, aquello
2. esto, eso
3. eso, esto
4. aquello, aquello
5. eso, esto
6. esto, eso

¿Comprendes?

Los peruanos
1. Los ricos tienen ropa elegante, trabajan en bancos, tiendas y oficinas, compran en supermercados o pequeñas tiendas, y van al cine o a conciertos o dramas. Los pobres viven en casas de cartón o no tienen casas, y venden cosas en la calle o son criados.
2. La vida del campo es tradicional, la gente tiene ropa tradicional, trabaja en el campo o en el mercado. En la ciudad, la gente viste ropa elegante y trabaja en oficinas, bancos, tiendas, etc. Las diferencias entre los ricos y los pobres no son tan evidentes.
3. *Personal opinion will determine answers.*

4. En los dos países, hay diferencias entre los ricos y los pobres y los dos países tienen muchos grupos étnicos. En los Estados Unidos, la gente no vende chicle en la calle. Los indios norteamericanos viven en reservaciones y no libres en las montañas.

Mario Vargas Llosa
1. *Opinions and answers will vary.*
2. *Opinions and answers will vary.*

Los tesoros del Perú
1. Artefactos de oro, plata, cerámica, turquesa, piedras preciosas.
2. Answers will vary. (Tikal, Chichén Itzá, Uxmal, etc)
3. Los Andes, el Amazonas, desiertos, selvas, animales, plantas exóticas.

Los incas
1. Sobresalieron en adaptar las invenciones de otros grupos.
2. Nuestros edificios tienen cemento, no tienen piedras tan grandes y no duran tantos años.
3. Machu Picchu es un centro religioso de los Inca. Ahora está en ruinas.
4. El sol es el dios principal.

Capítulo 10

Practiquemos

A. Las vacaciones de verano
1. visitaba
2. nos levantábamos, desayunábamos
3. montaban
4. hablaba
5. jugábamos
6. preparaban
7. tocaba, cantaban
8. pasabas

B. Hace cinco años
Answers will vary.

A. Los sábados
1. hacíamos
2. Teníamos
3. barría
4. sacudía
5. debía (tenía que)

6. prefería
7. escribía
8. hacían
9. salíamos
10. comíamos
11. nos divertíamos
12. creíamos

B. Hace diez años
Answers will vary.

C. La señora Perón
1. reconocía
2. defendía
3. Recordaba
4. sentía
5. defendía
6. consideraba
7. pensaban
8. gobernaba
9. compartía
10. servía

A. Los cuentos de abuelito
1. era
2. era
3. éramos
4. era
5. íbamos
6. Veíamos
7. era
8. era
9. veía
10. iba

B. Mi niñez
Answers will vary.

A. ¡Buenas noticias!
1. no quería, sabía, tenía
2. no podía
3. pudo
4. conoció
5. sabía
6. tuvo
7. Supo

B. Escritor
1. conocía 2. sabía 3. conoció
4. sabía 5. tenía 6. pudo
7. sabía 8. pudieron

C. En el gimnasio
CATALINA: Tuve
MÓNICA: conocí
CATALINA: conociste
MÓNICA: conocí
CATALINA: pudiste
MÓNICA: supe
CATALINA: quería
MÓNICA: quise
MÓNICA: supo, quiso

A. ¿Qué te pasa?
Answers will vary.

A. Gustos
Answers will vary.

B. Somos diferentes
Answers will vary.

C. Problemas
1. me molestan 2. le falta
3. nos encanta 4. nos gusta
5. le importa 6. le fastidia
7. le molesta

D. Respuesta
Answers will vary.

E. Después del accidente
1. le dolía
2. le fastidiaba
3. le dolían
4. le fastidiaban
5. le encantaban
6. le interesaba

¿Comprendes?

"No llores por mí, Argentina"
1. Juan y Evita Perón hicieron mucho para su país. Evita inició muchos programas sociales, luchó por los derechos humanos y los derechos políticos de las mujeres. Junto con su esposa, Evita, Juan inició muchas reformas económicas.

El laberinto literario de Jorge Luis Borges
1. El tono poético, el carácter filosófico y el esceptisismo caracterizan las obras de Jorge Luis Borges.
2. Tenía un carácter muy fuerte y tenía ganas de continuar su trabajo.

Una carta de Argentina
1. Son dos ciudades de estilo europeo, cosmopolitas, muy grandes
2. Es famoso por sus cataratas.
3. Fueron a los Andes porque les gusta esquiar.

Capítulo 11

Practiquemos

A. Explorando la ciudad
1. se levantaron
2. Desayunaron
3. se fueron
4. llegaron
5. tomaron
6. se encontraron
7. llevó
8. fueron
9. almorzaron
10. tuvo
11. salieron
12. se divirtieron

B. ¿Qué aprendieron?
1. nació, murió
2. asistió a, se educó
3. fue
4. Inició, autorizó
5. dirigió
6. fue, regresó
7. mató

A. Una noche en Tegucigalpa
Answers will vary.

B. La escuela
Answers will vary.

C. ¿A qué hora?
Answers will vary.

A. Protección del planeta
1. el aire
2. el oxígeno
3. el dióxido de carbono
4. el combustible, el pesticida, el herbicida
5. la capa de ozono
6. mantener el ecosistema
7. la química, el pesticida, el herbicida
8. los insectos
9. prevenir el calentamiento global
10. *Answers will vary.*

A. Una visita
LAURA: pasó
PABLO: pasó
LAURA: era, leía, sonó, Contesté, habló
PABLO: llamó
LAURA: estaban, decidieron, invitaron, divertimos
PABLO: invitaste, hice

B. Una historia romántica
1. trabajaban
2. iba
3. hacía
4. almorzaba
5. volvía
6. se sentían
7. era
8. necesitaban
9. tomaron
10. bajaron
11. Se saludaron
12. entraron
13. se vieron
14. comieron
15. esperó
16. invitó
17. dijo
18. comenzó

C. Una diferencia
1. Fue—focus on completion of actions
   Iba—focus on repetition of action
2. Estudié—focus on completed time period
   Estudiaba—focus on continuation of action
3. leyeron y escribieron—focus on completion; two sequential, completed actions
   Escribían mientras leían—focus on simultaneous continued actions
4. supiste—focus on beginning of knowing (finding out)
   sabías—focus on continuing state of knowing
5. Tuvimos—focus on end of condition; had to study and did; obligation fulfilled
   Teníamos—focus on continuing need; no indication of end of obligation

D. Eloísa
Answers will vary.

A. Nuestros compañeros
1. la serpiente
2. iguana
3. los pájaros, los perros, los gatos
4. cerdo
5. los loros
6. los peces
7. los pájaros
8. los conejos, las vacas, las gallinas, los cerdos
9. la ardilla
10. el caballo
11. la cabra
12. el tiburón
13. el león
14. la jirafa
15. la gallina
16. las vacas, las cabras

A. Recién llegados
1. acaba de
2. acaban de
3. acaba de
4. acabamos de
5. acabas de

6. acababan de
7. acaban de
8. acaba de

B. Visitando Tegucigalpa
1. acabábamos de
2. acababa de
3. se acabaron
4. acabaron con
5. acaban de
6. acabamos

¿Comprendes?

Costa Rica y un líder sin igual, Óscar Arias Sánchez
1. Costa Rica es un país democrático progresista, que tiene una larga historia democrática. Es pacífica y próspera. Es el país de la paz.
2. Era un buen líder que estableció un sistema de seguros, sanidad, educación fuerte y un banco nacional.
3. Ganó el Premio Nóbel de la Paz por su plan de pacificación.

Tegucigalpa
1. Era un centro de la industria minera centroamericana.
2. «La zona viva», el Museo del Hombre Hondureño, la casa presidencial, la Universidad Nacional de Honduras, la Catedral San Miguel Arcángel

Informe: la ubicación de la nueva planta
1. Honduras tiene ruinas mayas y una mezcla de razas. Costa Rica es más homogénea y conserva menos de su historia indígena.
2. Honduras tiene más interés cultural, pero la vigorosa protección del ambiente en Costa Rica favorece el establecimiento de la fábrica allí.
3. el clima, la uniformidad de la cultura de Costa Rica

La biodiversidad de Costa Rica
1. una variedad de ecosistemas, bosques lluviosos, bosques montañosos, montañas, valles y costas
2. Costa Rica tiene especies que son extinguidas en

otras partes. Esto se debe a la protección ecológica del gobierno.
3. Tiene la colaboración de intereses privados, el gobierno y la población costarricense.

Capítulo 12

Practiquemos

A. El nuevo empleo
1. Escriba
2. Haga
3. Lleve
4. Prepare
5. Arregle
6. Mande
7. Traduzca
8. Coma

B. ¡Ejercicios!
Answers will vary.

A. En Panamá
1. Léanla.
2. Véanla.
3. Visítenlos.
4. Súbanlo.
5. Sáquenlas.
6. Mándenlas.
7. No los compren.
8. No lo gasten.
9. No las olviden
10. No los pierdan.

B. En clase
1. siéntense
2. Saquen; Sáquenlos.
3. Tomen; Tómenlos.
4. No hablen; No lo hablen.
5. Hagan; Háganlo.
6. No comparen; No las comparen.
7. No escriban; No lo escriban.
8. Lean; Leanlos.
9. Pásenme; Pásenmelos.

A. Mi opinión.
Answers will vary.

A. Los preparativos
1. llame
2. empaquen
3. lleguemos
4. compres
5. recuerde
6. termine

B. Nuevo empleado
1. hablemos
2. aprenda
3. interrumpan

4. haga
5. tengas
6. ayude

C. Examen mañana
1. vayan
2. dé
3. sepamos
4. esté
5. sean / seamos

D. Esperanzas
Answers will vary.

E. Mi trabajo es…
Answers will vary.

A. En la oficina
1. Es dudoso que la correspondencia llegue antes de las dos.
2. Es curioso que María no sepa usar la computadora.
3. Es mejor que Cintia y Pablo hagan las llamadas telefónicas.
4. Es necesario que nosotros completemos estos archivos ahora.
5. Es sorprendente que haya tanto que hacer hoy.
6. Es importante que los técnicos reparen las computadoras.
7. Es bueno que hoy sea viernes.
8. Es esencial que tú me esperes hasta las cinco.

B. El memo
1. preparen, 2. estemos,
3. haya, 4. tenga, 5. pueda,
6. reconozcan

C. ¿Qué piensas?
Answers will vary.

A. Pares
1. e
2. e
3. y
4. e
5. e
6. e
7. y
8. e

B. El nuevo apartamento
1. u
2. u
3. o
4. u
5. u
6. u
7. o
8. u

C. Al comienzo del alfabeto
1. el, las
2. la, las
3. el, las
4. el, las
5. la, las
6. la, las
7. el, las
8. la, las
9. el, las
10. el, las

¿Comprendes?

¡A Panamá!: unos consejos
1. Las atracciones de la Ciudad de Panamá incluyen el distrito colonial San Felipe con sus edificios del Siglo XVI, la Avenida Central, la Universidad de Panamá, el Parque Natural Metropolitano y el Canal de Panamá.
2. Las esclusas mueven las naves de un océano al otro
3. Respuesta libre

Violeta Chamorro y la política nicaragüense
1. Es una mujer extraordinaria porque tiene un papel importante en la política en Nicaragua. Es muy fuerte de carácter y tiene mucha experiencia política.
2. Ella logró muchos cambios económicos y reestableció relaciones con los EE.UU.
3. No es común tener una mujer como presidenta porque generalmente las mujeres no llegan a posiciones tan altas en el gobierno. Hay una tradición que los hombres tienen todas las posiciones de poder. Hay (Había) solamente una y ella ya no es presidenta.

¡Y tú vas a Nicaragua!
1. El Toro Guaco, un festival que celebra la antigua relación entre tres pueblos nicaragüenses.
2. San Juan de Oriente es famoso por su cerámica.
3. No hay respuesta fija, pero probablemente es porque Miskito es muy similar a la palabra inglesa mosquito y los ingleses vivieron en esa costa por muchos años.

La pluma mágica Rubén Darío
1. La vida temprana de Rubén Darío era muy difícil. No vivió con sus padres y era tímido y era un niño enfermo.
2. Las obras de Rubén Darío tienen muchos cultismos, palabras que él inventó, nuevos ritmos, verso libre y muchas licencias poéticas.
3. El término "modernismo" se refiere a un movimiento literario que trata de renovar la literatura moderna y fusionar las diferentes escuelas literarias.

Capítulo 13

Practiquemos

A. A Venezuela
1. empaquen
2. hagan
3. llamemos
4. mandemos
5. recoja
6. ayudes
7. lleven
8. tenga

B. En la oficina
1. lleguen
2. haga
3. dé
4. sea
5. esté
6. ayude

C. El viaje del fin de semana
Answers will vary.

A. En la agencia de viajes
Answers will vary. Suggestions follow.
1. vean
2. no salgan
3. reciban
4. pase
5. sirvan
6. tengan, diviertan
7. vuelva

B. La buena salud
Answers will vary.

C. Digo yo
Answers will vary.

A. Mi casa / tu casa
Answers will vary.

B. En mi trabajo
Answers will vary.

C. La carta
Answers will vary. Suggestions follow.
1. queremos
2. visiten
3. recomiendan
4. veamos
5. sugieren
6. pase
7. insiste
8. hagamos
9. haya
10. quiero
11. digas
12. hiciste

A. Mis metas
Answers will vary.

A. En Caracas
1. vayamos
2. empiece
3. veas
4. tengamos
5. visitemos
6. mate
7. pueda
8. mande

B. En mi casa
Answers will vary.

C. Mis emociones
Answers will vary.

A. Vamos a Mérida
1. tenga
2. sea
3. podamos
4. vayan
5. pueda
6. prometa
7. terminen
8. tengamos
9. veamos

B. Mi clase de español
Answers will vary.

A. ¿Cómo te sientes?
Answers will vary. Suggestions follow.
1. Estoy contento que tus padres viajen a Acapulco.
2. Estoy sorprendido que tu hija saque malas notas.
3. Estoy triste que no puedas ir a un concierto de tu grupo favorito.
4. Estoy alegre que tu profesor(a) de español no venga a clase.
5. Estoy contenta que tu jefe me dé más dinero.

6. Estoy desilusionado que tu familia no vaya de vacaciones.
7. Estoy enojada que tengas que trabajar más horas.
8. Estoy triste que tu mejor amiga viva en otra ciudad y no te escriba nunca.

B. En mi vida…
Answers will vary.

C. ¿Cuál es tu opinión?
Answers will vary.

¿Comprendes?

Un hombre renacentista, Andrés Bello
1. Lo que caracteriza las obras de Andrés Bello son las circunstancias de su tiempo —la fuerza independentista, la nueva cultura de América y el amor a la realidad hispanoamericana.
2. Andrés Bello escribió un libro de gramática, Gramática de la lengua española. Hizo muchos estudios sobre la lengua española.
3. Bello creía que la conservación de la lengua española en su pureza era muy importante. También creía que la lengua era un vínculo de fraternidad entre las varias naciones de origen español.

¡Viva la música!
1. El joropo es un ritmo característico de Venezuela.
2. La música de la costa central tiene la influencia africana.
3. El cuatro es una guitarra de cuatro cuerdas que se usa para tocar las melodías características venezolanas.

Capítulo 14

Practiquemos

A. Tomás
Answers will vary. Suggestions follow.
1. La mamá de Tomás dice: Dudo que la Alhambra esté en Granada.

2. Las hermanas de Tomás dicen: No creemos que los catalanes hablen catalán.
3. El hermano de Tomás dice: Es dudoso que el ceramista Lladró viva en Valencia.
4. Tomás dice: Dudo que miles de turistas vayan a Sevilla cada año.
5. Los hermanos de Tomás dicen: Es dudoso que en Gibraltar puedas ver monos.
6. Tomás dice: No creo que los españoles coman mucho arroz y pescado.

B. ¿Cómo reaccionas tú?
Answers will vary.

A. ¿Adónde?
Answers may vary somewhat.
1. Se sigue por el Paseo del Prado, se dobla a la derecha en la calle de los Madrazo, se dobla a la izquierda en la calle del Marqués de Cubas y se sigue hasta la Plaza de las Cortes.
2. Se toma la calle Carlos Tercero, se dobla a la derecha en calle de la Unión, se dobla a la izquierda en la calle Lemos, se dobla a la derecha en la calle Espejo se dobla a la derecha en la calle Mayor, se dobla a la izquierda en la calle Julio y se sigue hasta la Plaza Mayor.
3. Se sigue la calle Zaragoza, se pasa por la Plaza de la Santa Cruz, se sigue en la calle de la Bolsa, se pasa por la Plaza del Ángel, se sigue un poco a la izquierda en la calle del Prado, se dobla a la derecha en la Plaza de las Cortes hasta la Plaza Cánovas del Castillo, se dobla a la derecha en el Paseo del Prado y allí está el museo.
4. Se toma la calle San Alberto, se dobla a la izquierda en la calle de la Salud, se sigue casi derecho en la calle Galdo, se dobla a la derecha en la calle de Preciados, se sigue media cuadra y se dobla a la izquierda en el callejón de Preciados, se sigue en la calle Misericordia, se cruza

la Plaza de San Martín, se toma la calle Flora, se cruza la Plaza de Santa Catalina Donados y la Plaza de Isabel Segunda y allí está la Ópera y el Teatro Real.

B. En Madrid
Answers will vary.

C. Una tortilla diferente
1. Se pica
2. se pone
3. Se pela
4. se fríe
5. Se bate
6. se pone
7. se quita
8. se pone
9. Se agrega
10. se vuelve
11. Se cocina
12. se sirve

A. Preguntas y más preguntas
Por
Para
Por, por
por
Para
para, para
Por
para
para

B. El Museo del Prado
1. para
2. para
3. para
4. Para
5. por
6. para
7. Para
8. para
9. por
10. por
11. por
12. para

C. Una visita a Toledo
Answers will vary. Suggestions follow.
SANDRA: por fin
SUSITA: Por eso
TOMÁS: por eso
JUAN: Por consiguiente (Por eso, Por lo general)
SUSITA: Por suerte, por lo menos
SANDRA: Por eso
TOMÁS: Por Dios
SANDRA: por lo pronto (por lo general)

¿Comprendes?

Ana María Matute: autora española del siglo XX

1. Ana María Matute se considera rebelde porque expone y renuncia los valores superficiales de su época.
2. Era una niña enfermiza a quien le gustaba leer y observar a la gente.
3. Los temas típicos de sus obras son la desolación, la tristeza, la tragedia y la autodenigración.

España: Todo bajo el sol

1. En Granada, se puede ver la Alhambra y el Albaycín; en Sevilla, se puede ver la catedral, la Giralda y el Alcázar; en Córdoba, se puede ver la mezquita y la judería.
2. Antoni Gaudí fue arquitecto. Se encuentra su obra en Barcelona.
3. Se dice que los restos de Santiago, santo patrono de España, están allí. Por eso Santiago de Compostela fue el fin del Camino de Santiago, la ruta de peregrinación durante la Edad Media y uno de los tres lugares más sagrados del mundo cristiano.

España: mosaico cultural

1. Las grandes influencias culturales incluyen los romanos, los germanos, los musulmanes y los judíos.
2. Unificaron todo el país y expulsaron a los musulmanes y otros grupos no cristianos.
3. Don Juan Carlos es el rey de España.

Capítulo 15

Practiquemos

A. En el restaurante

1. Se busca cocinero que conozca la cocina indígena.
2. Se busca contador que tenga experiencia.
3. Se busca meseros que hablen varias lenguas.
4. Se busca maitre d' que sea amable.
5. Se busca gerente que planee un menú interesante.

B. Vamos a Chile

Some answers will vary. Suggestions follow.
1. Buscamos un hotel que sea lujoso.
2. Tenemos una agencia de viajes que sepa mucho del país.
3. Queremos encontrar un guía que sea muy atento.
4. Mi compañero encontró una excursión que va a la Isla de Pascua.
5. Otros compañeros tienen interés en un viaje que incluya unos días en los Andes.

C. Mi ideal

Answers will vary.

A. En mi trabajo

Answers will vary.

B. Sobre Chile

Answers will vary. Suggestions follow.
1. No hay isla donde se pueda esquiar en Chile.
2. Sí, la región de Atacama y en Tierra del Fuego hace mucho frío.
3. Los puertos Montt y Valparaíso tienen mucho tráfico internacional.
4. Sí, (No, no) necesito un mapa que enseñe la geografía de Chile.
5. Claro que se puede encontrar un libro que habla de Chile en mi biblioteca.

A. Se busca trabajo.

Answers will vary.
1. Se busca seguro de salud.
2. (No) Se busca sindicato.
3. No se busca mucho trabajo en comité.
4. Se busca un cheque semanal.
5. No se busca una historia de huelgas.

A. En Chile.

1. Se ven volcanes activos.
2. Se suben las montañas.
3. Se come comida rica.
4. Se visitan museos interesantes.
5. Se escucha música popular.

B. Fiesta familiar

1. Se mandaron las invitaciones.
2. Se invitó a la familia.
3. Se compró la comida.
4. Se contrató a los músicos.
5. Se puso la mesa.

C. La casa

Answers will vary. Suggestions follow.
1. Se lavó el coche.
2. Se barrieron los pisos.
3. Se cortó el césped.
4. Se sacudieron los muebles.
5. Se arreglaron (hicieron) las camas.

A. Pares

1. discutido y resuelto
2. escrito y leído
3. dicho y hecho
4. visto y oído
5. abierto y cerrado

B. Mis asociaciones

Answers will vary.

A. Datos sobre Chile

1. Coquimbo era cultivado por los indios diaguitos.
2. Los latifundios fueron iniciados por los españoles.
3. Las regiones altas son habitadas por las vicuñas, animales en peligro.
4. En 1973, el gobierno constitucional de Salvador Allende fue derrocado por Augusto Pinochet.
5. Patricio Aylwin fue elegido por los chilenos en 1989.

A. ¡A esquiar!

a. exactamente
b. cuidadosamente
c. tranquilamente
d. rápidamente
e. lentamente
f. felizmente
g. regularmente
h. inteligentemente
i. inmediatamente
Answers to items 1–5 will vary.

B. De joven

Answers will vary.

C. ¿Cómo?

Answers will vary. Suggestions follow.
1. frecuentemente, constantemente
2. constantemente, frecuentemente, tranquilamente

3. frecuentemente, mensualmente
4. generalmente, locamente
5. increíblemente

A. ¿En qué orden?
Answers will vary. Suggestions follow.
1. La primera cosa que se hace es leer el anuncio del puesto.
2. La segunda cosa que se hace es estudiar las cualificaciones.
3. La tercera cosa que se hace es recoger la solicitud.
4. La cuarta cosa que se hace es llenar la solicitud.
5. La quinta cosa que se hace es pedir las referencias.
6. La sexta cosa que se hace es hablar con el/la director(a) de personal.
7. La séptima cosa que se hace es hacer una cita.
8. La octava cosa que se hace es prepararse para la entrevista.
9. La novena cosa que se hace es vestirse bien.
10. La décima cosa que se hace es planear una fiesta para celebrar.

B. En el estadio
1. veintava (vigésima), octavo
2. diecisieteava, décimo
3. primera, primer
4. treintava (trigésima), sexto
5. cuarentava (cuadragésima), segundo

¿Comprendes?

Chile: un país de contrastes deportivos
1. Para esquiar, la gente va a la Isla de Pascua o al Valle Nevado.
2. La Isla de Pascua ofrece muchas oportunidades para esquiar.

Chile: país único
1. Permite que las naves eviten pasar por el Cabo de Hornos.
2. Las Islas de Juan Fernández fueron estudiadas por Charles Darwin. La Isla de Pascua tiene unas estatuas enormes de piedra.

Gabriela Mistral: tesoro nacional chileno
1. Gabriela Mistral pasó muchos años educando a la juventud chilena. Trabajaba en las escuelas primarias y secundarias más rurales. También fue a México para ayudar con su reforma educacional en 1922.
2. *Answers will vary.*

Pablo Neruda: chileno esencial
1. Pablo Neruda cambió su estilo de escribir, rompiendo más tarde la tradición poética. Usaba símbolos e imágenes personales en sus poemas espirituales, enigmáticos y sutiles.
2. Los escribió apasionadamente.

Capítulo 16

Practiquemos

A. Otra vez
1. Vamos a caminar por el sendero inca.
2. Vamos a pasar una semana en el Lago Titicaca.
3. Vamos a visitar los parques nacionales.
4. Vamos a comer platillos picantes y eschuchar música popular.
5. Vamos a comerlos y escucharla todos los días.

A. ¡Gol!
1. Gritemos mucho.
2. Sentémonos cerca de la línea de medio campo.
3. Bebamos muchos refrescos.
4. Vistámonos en los colores de mi equipo.
5. Quedémonos hasta el final del juego.

B. Vamos de vacaciones
Answers will vary.

A. ¿Casa? ¿Apartamento?
1. No alquilemos una casa.
2. No vivamos cerca del centro.
3. No busquemos un apartamento con piscina.
4. No paguemos un alquiler alto.
5. No pidamos un contrato.

B. ¿Quieres… ?
Answers will vary.

A. Mi casa
Answers will vary.

B. En el futuro
Answers will vary.

A. ¿Y hoy?
1. se ha comprado
2. ha vuelto
3. me he puesto
4. han visto
5. has conducido
6. hemos comido
7. se ha acostado
8. lo han pasado

B. Todavía no
1. no han visitado
2. no ha ido
3. no has sacado
4. no hemos hecho
5. no han asistido
6. no ha bebido
7. no han comprado
8. no ha pasado

A. ¡Ojalá!
Answers will vary.

B. Mucho que hacer
1. haya estado
2. haya podido
3. haya considerado
4. hayan tenido
5. haya ahorrado
6. haya tomado

A. En La Paz
1. había consultado
2. habías almorzado
3. había cambiado
4. había hecho
5. habíamos tomado
6. lo habían visto

B. ¡Qué mañana!
1. había salido
2. se había preparado
3. lo había recogido
4. lo había puesto
5. se había ido

A. En busca
Answers will vary. Suggestions follow.
1. Lo primero es
2. Lo necesario es
3. Lo importante es
4. Lo dudoso es
5. Lo difícil es

B. Necesito empleo
Answers will vary.

¿Comprendes?

¡A Bolivia!
1. El altiplano es una región muy alta que está cerca del Lago Titicaca.
2. Los indios trabajan en la agricultura. Producen cebada, quinoa, papas, maíz, zapallo y yuca, y crían alpacas, llamas, ovejas y ganado.
3. Los bolivianos comen yuca, papas, carne y verduras. Su comida es picante porque usan ají picante.

La literatura boliviana
1. El tema es la igualdad de la mujer y el hombre y la lucha por los derechos de la mujer.
2. Rigoberta Menchú, Gabriela Mistral, Isabel Allende, ...

Aspectos curiosos de Bolivia
1. Ambas ciudades son capitales del país.
2. Las importaciones vienen por tierra, aire o por la buena voluntad de los países vecinos.

Capítulo 17

Practiquemos

A. Nuestro viaje
1. En Malabo visitaremos el pueblo de Moka.
2. En Río Muni yo buscaré evidencia de la magia negra.
3. En Bata mis hermanos irán a la playa.
4. En Mbini tú conocerás a la gente local en los cafés.
5. En la Isla de Corisco mi esposo sacará muchas fotos de las vistas preciosas.
6. En todas partes todos harán cosas interesantes.

B. ¡Gracias a Dios que es viernes!
Answers will vary. Each sentence should contain a future form.

A. ¡Qué viaje!
1. llegué
2. comer
3. llegues
4. podemos
5. estés
6. sea
7. nos veamos

B. En Ecuador
Answers will vary.

¿Comprendes?

El ecuador; cinturón del mundo
1. Los nombres «Ecuador» y «Guinea Ecuatorial» se refieren al ecuador; los dos países se encuentran en el ecuador o muy cerca de él.

Las Islas Galápagos
1. Las Islas Galápagos sufren del efecto de los muchos seres humanos que les quitan el territorio a las plantas y animales nativos de allí.

Capítulo 18

Practiquemos

A. ¿Y tú?
1. iría
2. comerías
3. visitaría
4. exploraríamos
5. se divertirían

B. ¡Así lo haría yo!
Answers will vary.

A. ¿Cómo?
En la calle... podría Ud., podría
Me encantaría
En la tienda... podría
Me gustaría
Podría
Me encantaría

A. En un restaurante uruguayo
1. se portaran
2. comieran
3. bebiera
4. pidiera
5. fuera

B. ¿La realidad o no?
1. estudiaríamos...
2. vivieran...
3. se doctorara
4. harías...
5. ...

A. ¿Cómo son?
1. madrecita
2. pedacito, papelito
3. callecita
4. muchachón
5. panecillo
6. niñito, chiquito, hermanito

¿Comprendes?

Un cuentista uruguayo, Horacio Quiroga
1. Lo morboso, lo fantástico, lo trágico y temas de la muerte caracterizan las obras de Quiroga.
2. Hay muchos autores que desarrollan estos temas: Edgar Allen Poe, ...

Paraguay y Uruguay
1. Hay parques nacionales exquisitas y un yermo vasto.
2. Tiene una bella costa, una topografía variada de montañas bajas y seis ríos.

Spanish for Life

M. Carol Brown
California State University, Sacramento

Kathleen C. Moore
California State University, Sacramento

HH **Heinle & Heinle**
Thomson Learning

United States • Australia • Canada • Denmark • Japan • Mexico • New Zealand
Philippines • Puerto Rico • Singapore • Spain • United Kingdom

The publication of *Spanish for Life* was directed by the Heinle & Heinle
College Foreign language Publishing Team:

Wendy Nelson, Senior Acquisitions Editor
Stephen Frail, Marketing Manager
Esther Marshall, Senior Production & Development Editor Supervisor
Jennifer Aquino, Developmental Editor

Also participating in the publication of this program were:

Publisher: **Vincent P. Duggan**
Associate Marketing Manager: **Kristen Murphy-Lojacono**
Senior Manufacturing Coordinator: **Mary Beth Hennebury**
Photo Researchers: **Jeff Freeland, Bénédicte Ferru, Judy Mason**
Project Manager: **Kristin Swanson**
Composition: **Greg Johnson, Art Directions**
Interior Designer: **Sue Gerould, Perspectives**
Illustrator: **Len Shalansky**
Cover Designer: **Ha Nguyen**
Cover Illustration: **Christie's Images/Superstock**
Text Printer/Binder: **Quebecor World**

For permission to use material from this text contact us:

Web: **www.thomsonrights.com**
Fax: 1-800-730-2215
Phone: 1-800-730-2214

Heinle & Heinle Publishers
20 Park Plaza
Boston, MA 02116

UK/EUROPE/MIDDLE EAST
Thomson Leaning
Berkshire House
168-173 High Holborn
London, WCIV 7AA,
United Kingdom

LATIN AMERICA
Thomson Learning
Seneca, 53
Colonia Polanco
11560 México D.F. México

JAPAN
Thomson Learning
Placeside Building, 5F
1-1-1 Hitotsubashi, Chiyoda-ku
Tokyo 100 0003, Japan

AUSTRALIA/NEW ZEALAND
Nelson/Thomson Learning
102 Dodds Street
South Melbourne
Victoria 3205 Australia

ASIA (excluding Japan)
Thomson Learning
60 Albert Street #15-01
Albert Complex
Singapore 189969

SPAIN
Thomson Learning
Calle Magallanes, 25
28015-Madrid
España

CANADA
Nelson/Thomson Learning
1120 Birchmount Road
Scarborough, Ontario
Canada MIK 5G4

Library of Congress Cataloging-in-Publication Data
The Library of Congress has assigned the following Library Congress
Catalog Card Number for the student textbook: 99-76679
                                                                                  CIP

ISBN: 0-8384-0702-1

Printed in the United States of America

1 2 3 4 5 6 7 8 9 03 02 01 00 99

Capítulo		Grammar	Communicative Functions	Vocabulary
Capítulo preliminar: El mundo de habla española	2		Greetings Introductions Farewells Identification of cognates	The Spanish alphabet and its pronunciation Basic colors Written and spoken accents
Capítulo 1: Los hispanos en los Estados Unidos	16	Subject pronouns The verb **ser** Gender and number Definite articles Adjectives **Ser de** **Al** and **del** Interrogative words	Describe people Identify things Ask questions	Descriptive adjectives Classroom objects Numbers 1–30
Capítulo 2: Cuba y los cubanos	38	Basic functions of **estar** Indefinite articles Infinitives **Ir** **Ir a** + infinitive **Tener** **Tener que** + infinitive **Hay** Possessive adjectives	Tell and ask how people are Describe location of things Tell where you are going and what you are going to do Tell what you have to do Describe the classroom	Adjectives of condition Prepositions of location Familiar buildings and destinations Family members Common verbs (infinitives) Numbers 31–100
Capítulo 3: México y los mexicanos	60	Regular present tense verbs: **-ar** Stem-changing verbs (o→ue, u→ue) Days, months, seasons The date Stem-changing verbs (e→ie) Personal **a** Introduction to **gustar** and **encantar** + infinitive, **encantar** Direct object and personal **a**	Describe typical activities Tell the date Tell your favorite activities Describe the weather	Numbers 101– … Days of the week, Hundreds, thousands, millions Days of the week, months of the year, seasons, Formulas for telling the date Weather terms
Capítulo 4: La República Dominicana y los dominicanos	82	Regular verbs: **-er** Regular present-tense verbs: **-ir** Verbs with an irregular first person The verb **oír** **Saber** vs **conocer** **Me gustaría, te gustaría**	Discuss your daily schedule Make plans Extend, accept and reject an invitation Tell time	Entertainment and pastimes Time vocabulary

Capítulo		Grammar	Communicative Functions	Vocabulary
Capítulo 9: **Perú y los peruanos**	202	Reflexive verbs and pronouns Prepositions Pronoun objects of prepositions; **conmigo, contigo, consigo** Demonstratives	Describe your daily routine	Daily routine The face Clothes Colors
Capítulo 10: **Argentina y los argentinos**	228	Imperfect tense: regular verbs Imperfect tense: irregular verbs Changes in meaning: preterite vs. imperfect The verb **gustar** and verbs that have the same structure	Recount childhood memories Talk about likes and dislikes, aches and pains	Human body Health
Capítulo 11: **Costa Rica y los costarricenses** **Honduras y los hondureños**	246	Preterite tense: review of uses Imperfect tense: review of uses Preterite vs. imperfect The verbs **acabar de, acabarse, acabar con**	Describe and narrate in past Tell a story in the past Recount a past incident	Ecology Animals
Capítulo 12: **Nicaragua y los nicaragüenses,** **Panamá y los panameños**	264	Formal commands: **usted** and **ustedes** Present subjunctive mood; present-tense forms Impersonal expressions and the subjunctive mood Changes required by the first syllable of the following word	Ask (Order) someone to do something Express attitudes	Impersonal expressions World of work: skills, professions, duties, activities, personnel
Capítulo 13: **Venezuela y los venezolanos**	286	Subjunctive mood: verbs of volition, will, prohibition Subjunctive mood: verbs of reaction (emotion) and anticipation Verbs like **gustar** to express reaction **Estar** + adjective to express emotion	Express desired outcomes Express feelings with regard to a situation	Goals: work and money, family, personal life

Preface to the Student Edition

Introduction

The **Spanish for Life** program presents the basics of the Spanish language in a format that is easy to understand, fun to use, and completely customizable to meet the needs of students or working professionals who wish to have a working knowledge of Spanish.

Accompanying the textbook are several worktexts, each one designed to focus the practice of Spanish on the particular content area that most interests the learner: Spanish for Life (everyday Spanish), Spanish for Business Professionals, Spanish for Law Enforcement Professionals, and Spanish for Health Professionals. Each worktext comes with its own audio tape that you can use to practice Spanish in class, at home, in your car, or on the run.

Chapter Organization

The core textbook contains 18 self-contained lessons plus a preliminary chapter that present the fundamentals of the Spanish language, along with cultural and factual information about the countries in which Spanish is spoken. Each lesson culminates in a self-test that allows the learner to assess their own progress on a continual basis.

Chapter openers: Each lesson begins with chapter openers that provide maps and useful data about the country or countries highlighted in the chapter. The grammar points, communicative functions, and vocabulary to be learned are also listed on these chapter openers. The SFL web site is also referenced by icon and address in the chapter opener. This web site leads the student to exciting activities, additional information on the country profiled and up-to-date web site links.

Lecturas: Brief non-fiction readings provide a context for the grammar points being presented in the chapter. At the same time, these readings focus on cultural, historical or political information pertinent to the country or countries highlighted in the chapter. The vocabulary is carefully controlled and unfamiliar words are glossed. **¿Comprendes?** questions serve as quick comprehension checks for the readings.

Grammar presentations: Grammar is presented clearly to allow learners to move quickly to communication. Where appropriate grammar presentations are illustrated through the use of charts.

Practiquemos: Following each grammar presentation, ample practice is provided with clear instructions allowing for practical usage of the language. Communication bubbles call out opportunities for peer interaction, allowing the learner to put the language to immediate use in communicative ways.

¿Sabías que… ?: These cultural notes present country and culture specific information that is eye-opening and always fun to know and share.

¡Nota! boxes: Timely reminders regarding the grammar or vocabulary presented and language specific notes appear in these blue boxes at point-of-use for easy reference. These help students apply previously-studied information in new situations.

A ver si sabes… : A self-test at the end of each chapter allows learners to frequently check their progress, to find out what they know, and what they may need to practice more. The answers to this self-test are found in your textbook.

Querido diario: These simple writing activities at the end of each chapter pull togeth-er grammar vocabulary from the lesson. **Querido Diario** encourages students to write freely as if they were writing in a personal journal. Learners are encouraged to use their copy of *Atajo* as they complete these assignments.

Preguntas culturales: Focusing on the culture presented throughout the chapter, these questions reinforce what cultural information and facts were presented to the student in the chapter.

Vocabulario activo: The active vocabulary found in the chapter is summarized in this list at the end of the chapter, providing the learner with an easy reference. The vocab-ulary for each chapter has been carefully selected for high-incidence so students do not learn words they will only use in one chapter.

Other Components of the Spanish for Life Program

Worktexts

Those students who are studying Spanish for professional goals-such as using Spanish in business or in the health field-need more specific functions, vocabulary and guid-ance in the language learning process. *Spanish for Life* core text correlates to a vari-ety of different worktexts that meet the specific needs of these students. Each worktext closely follows the grammar scope and sequence of the core text while introducing new vocabulary necessary for speaking Spanish in the professional settings. Work-texts offer both additional practice with the core vocabulary and grammar of each chapter and, in the case of the professional worktexts, specific vocabulary for these areas. The country profiles in the core text are also featured in the corresponding chapters of the worktexts. The chapters of each worktext are organized by theme with all new vocabulary tied to these themes. Each worktext chapter begins with a dia-logue that can be heard on audiocassette

- *Spanish for Life* Textbook + *Spanish for Life* Worktext and Audiocassettes

  This worktext prepares the student for and helps develop practical and useful com-munication. Paired with the *Spanish for Life* textbook, these books are designed for use in standard conversational Spanish courses. With three real-world dialogues in each chapter presenting new vocabulary in context while adhering to and practic-ing the grammar points of the core text, the *Spanish for Life* Worktext fosters a fun, interactive and realistic environment for your student to learn and use the Spanish language. **Notas culturales** and **Expresiones idiomáticas** correlate to the country profiled and the theme of each chapter. Each **Síntesis** section concluding every chapter focuses on reading (**A leer**) with pre-reading activities, vocabulary expan-sion (**Expansión de vocabulario**), speaking (**Expansión oral**), translations (**Traducciones**), cultural tie-in with web-site links (**Enlace cultural**) and spelling and pronunciation (**Hablemos mejor**).

- *Spanish for Life* Textbook + *Spanish for Business* Worktext and Audiocassettes

  The *Spanish for Business* Worktext was written for business professionals seeking practical Spanish they can put to immediate use in their jobs. This Worktext pro-vides realistic, everyday situations and relevant business conduct codes and vocabulary for businesses operating domestically or internationally. Special features appearing in each chapter such as business etiquette, (**¿Sabía Ud. que... ?...en los negocios...**), translations of business documents (**Se necesita traductor/a**), negotiating in Spanish over email and voicemail (**Contestador automático; Correo electrónico**), and preparing presentations on the themes/topics of each chapter (**Presentaciones como en los negocios**), and country-specific business tips and facts (**¿Sabía Ud. que... ?...en España...**) prepare students for the real-world situations they are bound to encounter in any business setting.

■ *Spanish for Life* Textbook + *Spanish for Health* Worktext and Audiocassettes

Ideal for anyone working in hospitals, private practices, volunteer associations, or any related medical context which serves Hispanics, the Health Worktext provides accurate translations of medical terms, diagrams, and recent articles on major health issues. **Notas culturales** and **¿Sabía que... ?** follow every dialogue in each chapter of the Health Worktext. Both provide specific facts, support and/or advice to the student relating to the theme and country profiled in each chapter. Special features in the **Síntesis** section of each chapter include **A leer** with pre-reading activities, **Correo electrónico**, **Contestador automatico**, **Traducciones**, **Mi agenda**, and **Para discutir**.

■ *Spanish for Life* Textbook + *Spanish for Law Enforcement* Worktext and Audiocassettes

Designed for those professionals working as police officers, prison employees, firefighters, court clerks, and other law-related professions, this worktext gives students ample exposure to appropriate vocabulary and terms while placing the student in real-world contexts and situations.

Cassette Program

Audiocassettes accompany each of the worktexts. They contain the listening portions of each chapter: **Diâlogo**, **¡Escuchemos!**, **¡Hablemos!** or **Contestador automático**. This audiocassette program is ideal for use in the language lab, at home, or in the car.

Spanish for Life Web Site

The **Spanish for Life** Web site, **http://spanishforlife.heinle.com**, has additional discrete-item practice exercises as well as more communicative exercises which correlate to the core text. Moreover, it has individual links to each of the worktexts with additional situations, activities, and extensions related to each of these fields. Each chapter will also have its own links to Spanish-speaking newpapers, museums, and other up-to-date web sites.

Atajo: Writing Assistant for Spanish

Each student textbook is also packaged with a copy of *Atajo: Writing Assistant for Spanish*, a Spanish language word-processor with helpful on-line Spanish-language databases. This valuable tool for life can be used in your studies, on the job, or anytime you need to write something in Spanish and an English language word-processor won't do.

Note to the Student

Tips for Language Learning

Welcome to your study of Spanish! This textbook was written especially to meet your needs. After teaching more than 20 years, the authors wanted to apply their experience to create a new kind of Spanish text. Whether you love languages or struggle to learn them, these easy tips will improve your experiences.

- Spend some time studying Spanish each day. Repeated short study sessions are more productive than marathon sessions. Don't postpone studying until right before class or the night before a test. Keep up on a daily basis.

- Try to have contact with the language outside the classroom by listening to Latin or Hispanic music, watching Spanish-speaking TV (many cable companies carry Telemundo, Univisión or Galavisión), or, if you are lucky, talking with a native speaker. Eating at Taco Bell or petting a chihuahua probably won't help, but it won't hurt.

- Use flash cards to practice vocabulary and grammatical structures. They may be written words or drawings. Tape material you want to learn to the bathroom mirror and work on it as you brush your teeth.

- As you study, try to look up as few words as possible. Guess meaning from context and clues in the text. Don't be afraid to guess or to take chances speaking. Volunteer as often as possible. The best language learners are those who are willing to take a risk.

- When you listen to Spanish, concentrate on those things you DO understand and try to piece together the meaning based on this information. If you get flustered by the things you don't understand you will miss the next sentences that are said. When listening to a tape, listen as many times as necessary to get the meaning.

- Try to find materials in Spanish written for Spanish speakers. Newspapers, magazines or ads written in Spanish provide additional reading practice as well as a glimpse into the Spanish-speaking cultures.

- Write messages in Spanish to your classmates, either conventional notes or letters on paper or via email.

- Keep a journal in Spanish to practice writing the things you are learning to say. Try to write a sentence or two everyday. As you advance, your entries will become increasingly more sophisticated and complex. When you look back over your entries you will be able to see how much progress you have made.

- Learn songs and poetry in Spanish. This will help you with pronunciation and fluency as well as providing vocabulary and grammatical structure and more experience with the culture.

List of Reviewers

Martin H. Durrant, *Mesa Community College*
Elaine Graybill, *Tyler Junior College*
Marie Karem, *University of Scranton*
Marius Cucurny, *Orange Coast College*
Ralph Tarnasky, *Aims Community College*
Theresa Johnson, *Saint Louis University*
Patricia Moore-Martinez, *University of Pennsylvania*
Eric W. Vogt, *Thunderbird*
Michael J. Horswell, *Florida Atlantic University*
Shirley Melston, *Niagara Community College*
Paula Heusinkveld, *Clemson University*
Karen Stone, *Mesa Community College*
Christine Esperson, *Cape Cod Community College*
Domenico Maceri, *Allan Hancock College*
Nancy L. Watkins, *Mesa State College*

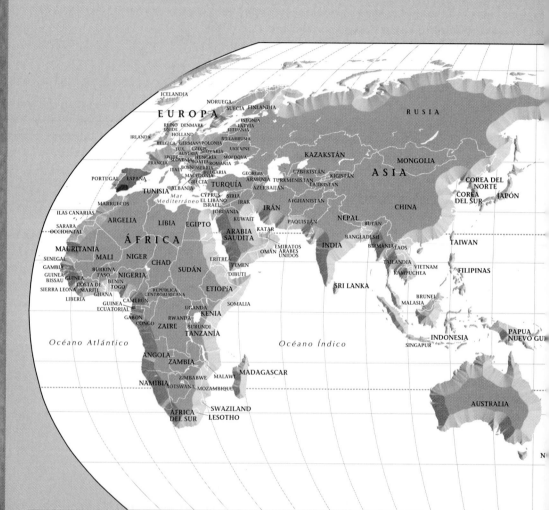

ICELANDJA

EUROPA

NORUEGA
SUECIA FINLANDIA

RUSIA

REINO DENMARK
UNIDE
IRLANDA   HOLLAND

ESTONIA
LATVIA
LITUANES

BELGICA GERMANYPOLONIA
BIELARRUSIA

LUX. CZECH
AUSTRIA SLOVAKIA   UKRAINE
SWITZHUNGRIA MOLDOVA
FRANCIA SLOVENCROATIA ROMANIA

KAZAKSTÁN

MONGOLIA

ASIA

ITALY BOSNIASERBIA
BULGARIA
MACEDONIA
GRECIA

GEORGIA
ARMENIA TURKMENISTAN
AZERBAIJAN

UZBEKISTÁN
KIGISTÁN
TAJIKISTÁN

PORTUGAL ESPAÑA

ALBANIA   TURQUÍA
TUNISIA   CÝPRUS SIRIA
Mar   EL LIBANO IRAK
Mediterráneo ISRAEL
JORDANIA

AFGHANISTÁN

CHINA

COREA DEL
NORTE
COREA   JAPÓN
DEL SUR

MARRUECOS

ILAS CANARIAS

KUWAIT
LIBIA   EGIPTO   KATAR
SARARA   ARABIA
OCCIDENTAL   ARGELIA   LIBIA   SAUDITA

IRÁN

PAQUISTÁN   NEPAL
BUTAN

TAIWAN

MAURITANIA
SENEGAL
GAMBIA
GUINEA GUINEA
BISSAU

ÁFRICA
MALI   NIGER
BURKINA
FASO   NIGERIA
BENIN

CHAD

SUDÁN

EMIRATOS
OMÁN ÁRABES
UNIDOS
ERITREA   INDIA
YEMEN
DIBUTI

BANGLADESH
BIRMANIALAOS
TAILANDIA   VIETNAM
KAMPUCHEA

FILIPINAS

SIERRA LEONA   COSTA DE
MARFIL
LIBERIA   GHANA

TOGO
REPÚBLICA
CENTROAFRICANA   ETIOPÍA

SRI LANKA

BRUNEI
MALASIA

GUINEA CAMERÚN
ECUATORIAL
GABON
CONGO   ZAIRE

UGANDA
KENIA
RWANDA
BURUNDI
TANZANÍA

SOMALIA

Océano Atlántico

Océano Índico

SINGAPUR

INDONESIA

PAPUA
NUEVO GUI

ANGOLA
ZAMBIA

NAMIBIA

ZIMBABWE MALAWI MADAGASCAR
BOTSWANA MOZAMBIQUE

ÁFRICA   SWAZILAND
DEL SUR   LESOTHO

AUSTRALIA

N

EL MUNDO DE HABLA ESPAÑOLA

Número de países: 21 (22 con los Estados Unidos)
Área: 21.363.200 km^2
Población: 389.000.000

El mundo de habla española

rtico

GROENLANDIA

ALASKA (EEUU)

CANADÁ

NORTEAMÉRICA

ESTADOS UNIDOS

Océano Atlántico

Golfo
MÉXICO de México   BAHAMAS

HAWAI (EEUU)

CUBA   REPÚBLICA
DOMINICANA
JAMAICA   HAITI   PUERTO RICO   SAN CRISTÓBAL Y NEVIS
BELICE   DOMINICA
HONDURAS
GUATEMALA   NICARAGUA   MAR DEL CARIBE   SAN VINCENTE Y
EL SALVADOR   LAS GRANADINAS
PANAMÁ   TRINIDAD Y TOBAGO
COSTA   VENEZUELA   GUYANA
RICA   SURINAME
COLOMBIA   GUAYANA
FRANCESA

ECUADOR

MÓN   KIRITOATI   SUD AMÉRICA   BRASIL

PERÚ

FIJI

BOLIVIA

PARAGUAY

ISLA DE PASCUA (CHILE)   CHILE
ARGENTINA

URUGUAY

Océano Pacífico

ISLAS MALVINAS

In this chapter you will learn:

- Greetings
- Introductions
- Farewells
- Identification of cognates
- The Spanish alphabet and its pronunciation
- Basic colors
- Written and spoken accents

I.   ¡Buenos días!

Read this conversation between Cristina and Paco as they greet each other.

LECTURA 1

LECTURA 2

❖ Para saludar

To greet someone, the following expressions may be used.

Buenos días.	*Good morning.*
Buenas tardes.	*Good afternoon.*
Buenas noches.	*Good evening. / Good night.*
¡Hola!	*Hi!*
¿Qué tal?	*How are you?*
Buenos días, profesor.	*Good morning, professor.* (male)
Buenos días, profesora.	*Good morning, professor.* (female)
Buenas tardes, Carlos.	*Good afternoon, Carlos.*
¡Hola, chicos!	*Hi, guys!*

Answers to the question **¿qué tal?** include the following:

Muy bien, gracias.	*Fine, thank you.*
No muy bien.	*Not too well.*
Regular.	*OK.*

Any of these answers may be followed by **¿y tú?** or **¿y usted?** to invite the other person to answer the question. The use of **tú** or **usted** depends on how you address the person.

To respond to someone you know well:

Bien, gracias, **¿y tú?**	*Fine, thanks, **and you?***

To respond to an elder, a professor, or someone you are not familiar with:

Regular, gracias, **¿y usted?**	*OK, thanks, **and you?***

Practiquemos

A. ¡Hola! How would you greet someone at the times provided? Note that more than one greeting may be appropriate.

MODELO: 8:00 A.M., arriving at work or school
Buenos días. o:
Hola, ¿qué tal?

> Greet two of your classmates appropriately and return their greeting. Then greet your instructor and respond appropriately.

1. 2:00 P.M., arriving back after lunch
2. 9:00 A.M., meeting a friend for coffee
3. 5:00 P.M., meeting a date for an early drink
4. 9:00 P.M., arriving at a friend's house for dinner
5. 11:30 A.M., meeting your significant other for an early lunch

II. ¡Qué gusto!

LECTURA

❖ Para presentarse

To introduce yourself, you say **Me llamo** followed by your name.

Me llamo Paquita.	*My name is Paquita.*
Me llamo Eugenio.	*My name is Eugenio.*

When introducing one person to another, these formulas may be used:

Quiero presentar a Carlos.	*I would like to introduce Carlos.*
Mucho gusto.	*Nice to meet you.*
Igualmente.	*Likewise. (For me, too.)*

Practiquemos

A. Nuevos amigos. You are introducing two people to one another in señorita Salazar's Spanish class.

MODELO: José, a Selena
José, quiero presentar a Selena.

1. Memo, al profesor López
2. Silvia, a Julián y Marta
3. la clase, a la señora Lora
4. Tori, a Carlos
5. amigos, a Roberto
6. la señorita Salazar, a Lorena y Susan

B. Presentaciones. Write introductions that introduce four friends to señor Martínez. Tell where each person is from and write a logical response for each introduction.

Introduce yourself to a classmate and then introduce that person to the class.

MODELO: **YOU:**   *Sr. Martínez, quiero presentar a Juan. Es de México.*
SR. MARTÍNEZ: *Mucho gusto, Juan.*
JUAN: *Igualmente, Sr. Martínez.*

¿Sabías?

When we think of Spanish-speaking countries, we usually think of Europe (Spain) and Latin America, but this image is incomplete. It leaves out **Guinea Ecuatorial** (Equatorial Guinea), which is located on the west coast of Africa, extends 28,050 square kilometers, and has a population of half a million.

III. Hasta luego

LECTURA 1

[1]**Sr. (señor):** *Mr., man* / [2]**Sra. (señora):** *Mrs., woman* / [3]**Srta. (señorita):** *Miss, young woman*

LECTURA 2

❖ Para despedirse

To say *good-bye,* the following words and expressions are used.

Adiós.	*Good-bye.*
Adiós, chicos.	*Bye, guys.*
Buenas noches.	*Good night.*
Buenas noches, María.	*Good night, María.*
Chao.	*So long.*
Hasta luego.	*See you later.*
Hasta mañana.	*See you tomorrow.*
Hasta pronto.	*See you soon.*

Practiquemos ✏

A. Despedidas. How would you say good-bye to people under the following circumstances?

> Say good-bye appropriately to at least four classmates at the end of class and respond appropriately to their farewells.

MODELO: your friends in the
            morning
            Chao.

1. your boss at the end of the day
2. your kids when you leave for work
3. your roommate when you go out at 9:00 P.M.
4. your family when you retire for the night
5. your teacher when you leave class in the afternoon
6. your cousin who is leaving on a trip

IV. Nuestro mundo

Numbers are not learned yet; Also, please point out the use of the period for thousands in Spanish vs. the comma in English.

LECTURA

El mundo[1] de habla española[2] **consiste** en 22 **naciones —en Europa, África, América del Norte,** América **Central,** América del Sur[3] y el **Caribe.** El **área total** es 21.363.200 **kilómetros** cuadrados.[4] Y el **número** de **personas** de habla española es 389.000.000.

---

[1]**mundo:** *world* / [2]**de habla española:** *Spanish-speaking* / [3]**Sur:** *South* / [4]**cuadrados:** *square*

¿Comprendes?

1. On how many continents is Spanish spoken?
2. Do you know which Spanish-speaking country has the largest area?
3. Do you know which Spanish-speaking country has the largest population?

■ Identificación de palabras afines

Cognates are words that have a similar meaning and spelling in two or more languages. Spanish and English share many cognates since Spanish and much of English are derived from Latin. Some cognates included in this selection are **hispanos** *(Hispanics),* **norteamericanos** *(North Americans),* **mucho** *(much),* and **millones** *(millions).*

Other cognates include the following.

radio	*radio*	planta	*plant*
lámpara	*lamp*	animal	*animal*

Practiquemos

A. Palabras afines. Scan these Spanish words and identify the cognates by naming the related English word for each.

arte	doctor	generoso	parte
auto	ejemplos	gigante	simplificar
béisbol	especialmente	historia	televisión
brillante	estudiante	influencia	tímido
chileno	extrovertido	melodía	tradicional
combinación	famoso	mural	vanidad
condimento	fútbol	nación	variedad
cultura	futbolista	notable	zoológico

■ Terminaciones de palabras

Certain endings in Spanish are similar to English endings. This can help in the identification of cognates.

-mento	*-ment*	apartamento	*apartment*
-dad	*-ty*	ciudad	*city*
-mente	*-ly*	rápidamente	*rapidly*
-miento	*-ment*	movimiento	*movement*
-ción	*-tion*	noción	*notion*
-sión	*-sion*	aprensión	*apprehension*

Practiquemos

A. Equivalentes. Give the English equivalents of these words.

1. departamento
2. tranquilidad
3. aproximadamente
4. compartimento
5. nación
6. extensión
7. nacionalidad
8. comprensión
9. especialmente
10. creación

■ Los prefijos

Likewise, Spanish and English share many *prefixes* that can also help you identify cognates.

pre-	*pre-*	preliminar	*preliminary*
pos-, post-	*post-*	postponer	*to postpone*
in-	*in-, un-*	incontrolable	*uncontrollable*
de-	*de-*	denotar	*to denote*
des-	*de-*	desodorante	*deodorant*
re-	*re-*	reaccionar	*to react*

Practiquemos

A. Al comienzo… Give the English equivalents of these words.

1. inacción
2. predestinado
3. reconstruir
4. prehistórico
5. póstumo
6. remodelar
7. inaccesible
8. postgraduado
9. demostrar

> Do you know any other cognates in Spanish and English? Are there any words commonly used in English that originally come from Spanish? Make a list and ask a classmate what the words mean.

■ El alfabeto español y su pronunciación

The Spanish alphabet is very similar to the English alphabet, but the pronunciation of some letters is different.

Letter	Name	Pronunciation	Sample word
a	a (ah)	*a* as in *car*	*Ana (Anna)*
b	be (bay)	*b* as in *baby*	*bebé (baby)*
c	ce (say)	*s* before *i* or *e*	*centro (center, downtown)*
		k before other letters	*carbón (coal, carbon)*
d	de (day)	*d* to begin words	*donde (where)*
		th as in *the* elsewhere	*Eduardo (Edward)*
e	e (eh)	between short *e* as in *set* and *ay* as in *day*	*de (from)*
f	efe	*f* as in *far*	*frente (front)*
g	ge (hay)	*h* before *e* or *i*	*general (general)*
		hard *g* before other letters	*García (Garcia)*
h	hache (ache)	not pronounced	*honor (honor)*
i	i (ee)	*ee* as in *cheeta*	*Anita (Anita)*
j	jota (hota)	*h*	*José (Joseph)*
k	ka	*k* (only found in foreign words)	*kilo (kilo)*
l	ele	*l*	*Luis (Louis)*
ll	elle (eye)	*y*	*llama (flame)*
m	eme	*m*	*mamá (mom)*
n	ene	*n*	*no (no)*
ñ	eñe	*ny*	*cañón (canyon)*
o	o	*o* as in *cope*	*Tomás (Thomas)*
p	pe	*p*	*Pepe (Joe)*
q	cu	*k*	*que (that, what)*

Point out that **c** before **i** and **e** and **z** everywhere are pronounced as *th* in Spain.

Letter	Name	Pronunciation	Sample word
r	ere	no English equivalent	pero *(but)*
rr	erre	no English equivalent	perro *(dog)*
s	ese	*s*	Susana *(Susan, Suzanne)*
t	te	*t*	tomate *(tomato)*
u	u	*oo* as in *too*	humano *(human)*
v	uve	no English equivalent	vino, uva *(wine, grape)*
w	doble uve	*w* or *v* (only found in foreign words)	water *(water closet)*
x	equis	*x*	examen *(exam)*
y	i griega	*y*	yanqui *(yankee)*
z	zeta	*s*	zoo *(zoo)*

■ The letters **b** and **v** have the same pronunciation. They are pronounced as English *b* at the beginning of words and after **m** or **n**, and elsewhere are pronounced as a softer *b*, using both lips but not closing them firmly.

■ The letter **q** is always followed by **u**, as in English.

■ The letters **k** and **w** are found only in words from other languages.

■ The combinations **ch** and **ll** used to be considered single letters and were alphabetized in separate sections in the dictionary, after the sections **c** and **l**, respectively. This changed in 1995, and now **ch** and **ll** are found within the **c** and **l** sections of dictionaries. However, since many dictionaries were published before the change, be sure to look for separate alphabetization if you cannot find a word where you expect it.

■ The letter **u** in Spanish never has a **y** sound as in English. The words **<u>u</u>niversidad** and **<u>u</u>niversal** sound like **<u>oo</u>niversidad** and **<u>oo</u>niversal**, rather than like English *university* and *universal*.

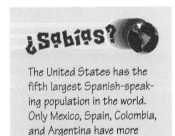

¿Sabías?

The United States has the fifth largest Spanish-speaking population in the world. Only Mexico, Spain, Colombia, and Argentina have more Spanish speakers.

Practiquemos

A. Mis ojos. In partners, practice reading the following letters from an eye chart. Check each other's accuracy.

E	L	M	B	T	Y
O	Q	W	C	U	N
A	D	V	X	P	H
R	S	LL	Z	I	G
F	E	J	I	K	A

Ask two classmates their names and have them spell them for you.

B. La pronunciación. Pronounce the lists of cognates on pages 8–9 after your instructor says them.

❖ Para describir con los colores

amarillo	*yellow*	café	*brown*	verde	*green*
azul	*blue*	negro	*black*		
blanco	*white*	rojo	*red*		

¿Sabías?

Although nearly 400,000,000 people speak Spanish, Spanish speakers represent less than 7% of the world's population.

Practiquemos

A. ¿De qué color? Write three things you associate with each of the colors. Then share your list with a partner.

1. rojo
2. verde
3. blanco
4. amarillo

5. negro
6. azul
7. café

■ El acento escrito y el acento hablado

You may have noticed that some Spanish words have written accents. These accents serve one of three purposes:

■ to indicate the stressed syllable of the word

■ to distinguish one word from another that is spelled the same way except for the accent mark

■ to indicate that two contiguous vowels do not form a diphthong

To indicate the stressed syllable of the word

Most accent marks belong to this group. If a Spanish word has no written accent, the stress is predictable: Words that end in a vowel, **n**, or **s** are stressed on the next-to-last (penultimate) syllable.

<u>ca</u>-sa	*house*	a-<u>mi</u>-go	*friend*
<u>li</u>-bros	*books*	es-<u>tu</u>-dian	*they study*
mo-<u>chi</u>-las	*backpacks*	i-<u>ma</u>-gen	*image*

Words that end in a consonant other than **n** or **s** are stressed on the last syllable.

ver-<u>dad</u>	*truth*	ha-<u>blar</u>	*to speak, talk*
na-cio-<u>nal</u>	*national*	a-<u>troz</u>	*atrocious*

Words whose spoken accent (stress) doesn't follow this pattern have a written accent to indicate the stressed syllable.

na-<u>ción</u>	*nation*	a-<u>ná</u>-li-sis	*analysis*
lá-piz	*pencil*	ru-<u>bí</u>	*ruby*
<u>Chá</u>-vez	*Chavez* (last name)	<u>tí</u>-mi-do	*shy*

To distinguish one word from another

Accent marks used to distinguish two words otherwise spelled the same include all question words.

¿dónde?	*where?*	donde	*where*
¿cuál?	*which?*	cual	*which*
¿cómo?	*how?*	como	*as, like*
¿cuándo?	*when?*	cuando	*when*
¿por qué?	*why?*	porque	*because*
¿quién?	*who?*	quien	*who*
¿qué?	*what?*	que	*that, which*

Accent marks are also used to distinguish two words with the same spelling, such as the following:

te	*you* (direct object)	té	*tea*
de	*of, from*	dé	*give* (command)
mas	*but* (conjunction)	más	*more*
el	*the* (article)	él	*he* (pronoun)

These accents must be memorized as the words are learned.

To indicate that two contiguous vowels do not form a diphthong

Accent marks are also used to "break" diphthongs. A diphthong consists of two vowels that form one syllable. One of these vowels must be **u** or **i** ("weak vowels").

| Mar<u>io</u> | *Mario* | v<u>ie</u>nto | *wind* |
| c<u>uo</u>ta | *quota* | r<u>ue</u>da | *wheel* |

Whenever the vowels **i** and **u** occur in the same syllable, they form a diphthong.

| ¡cuidado! | *be careful!* | ciudad | *city* |

When **u** and **i** do not form a diphthong with **e**, **o**, or **a**, that is, when they function as "strong vowels," a written accent mark indicates this fact.

rí-o	*river*	ha-<u>cí</u>-a	*he/she was doing / you were doing*
frí-o	*cold*	con-tin-<u>ú</u>-a	*he/she continues / you continue*
pa-<u>ís</u>	*country*	ba-<u>úl</u>	*trunk*

Practiquemos

A. ¡Correcto! Write accent marks where needed following the guidelines for written accents. The underlined syllables indicate the stressed syllable. Be sure you can explain why you did or did not write an accent mark. Note: The definitions are provided solely as a matter of interest. These words are not to be memorized.

MODELO: ve-<u>raz</u>   *truthful*
*You add no accent because the word ends in a consonant other than **n** or **s** and is stressed on the last syllable.*

1. <u>fa</u>-cil   *easy*
2. bo-<u>ton</u>   *button*
3. so-<u>fa</u>   *sofa*
4. e-<u>xa</u>-men   *exam*
5. fa-<u>mi</u>-lia   *family*
6. ciu-<u>dad</u>   *city*
7. <u>te</u>-sis   *thesis*
8. pre-cau-<u>cion</u>   *precaution*
9. te-<u>a</u>-tro   *theater*

B. ¿Diptongo? Write an accent mark where needed to indicate a stressed **i** or **u**. As above, the definitions are provided solely as a matter of interest. These words are not to be memorized.

MODELO: ma-iz   *corn*
*maíz; You write an accent on the **i** because it is stressed and does not form a diphthong with another vowel.*

1. en-<u>vi</u>-a   *he/she sends / you send*
2. con-<u>ti</u>-nua   *continuous*
3. <u>mi</u>-o   *mine*
4. tar-<u>di</u>-o   *late*
5. a-sis-<u>ten</u>-cia   *attendance*
6. mi-nis-<u>te</u>-rio   *ministry*

A ver si sabes

Use this self-test to see if you know the material presented in the Preliminary Chapter.

A. ¡Saludos a todos! Fill in the blanks with the appropriate words to complete the dialogue.

1. _____ días, Pablo. ¿Qué _____? _____, gracias, ¿y _____?
2. _____ tardes, Lupita. _____ presentar a Samuel. _____ _____, Samuel. _____, Lupita.
3. Hola, Enrique. ¿_____ tal? No _____ _____. ¿Y tú, Yolanda? _____ bien, _____.

(later in the conversation)
Bueno, adiós. Hasta _____ _____, Enrique.

Preguntas culturales
How many Spanish-speaking countries are there, and where are they found?

B. Parece familiar. Tell Elena the English equivalents of these words.

1. consideración
2. elevador
3. internacional
4. medicina
5. población
6. estudiante
7. profesor
8. hidrógeno
9. capacidad
10. generalmente

C. Juanito. Help little Juanito spell the following words correctly by supplying written accents where necessary. The stressed syllable is underlined. Then pronounce the words you have spelled and spell them aloud.

1. <u>cri</u>-sis
2. es-<u>tu</u>-pi-do
3. <u>la</u>-piz
4. o-<u>ri</u>-gen
5. vi-<u>vir</u>
6. am-bi-<u>cion</u>
7. sa-<u>bi</u>-as
8. au-<u>sen</u>-cia

Querido Diario. At the end of each chapter you will be writing in a journal, using the Spanish you have learned and consulting the **Atajo** program. In this chapter, you will write your first entry. You will greet your **Diario**, introduce yourself, and say good-bye. You may start by writing "**Querido Diario,**…"

 Phrases: greeting, introducing, saying good-bye

Vocabulario activo

Saludos
Buenos días.
Buenas tardes.
Buenas noches.

¡Hola!
¿Qué tal?
Buenos días, profesor.

Buenos días, profesora.
Buenas tardes, Carlos.
¡Hola, chicos!

Despedidas
Adiós.
Adiós, chicos.
Buenas noches.

Buenas noches, María.
Chao.
Hasta luego.

Hasta mañana.
Hasta pronto.

Respuestas
Muy bien, gracias.
No muy bien.
Regular.

Presentaciones
Me llamo.
Quiero presentar a...
Mucho gusto.
Igualmente.

Los colores
amarillo
azul
blanco
café

negro
rojo
verde

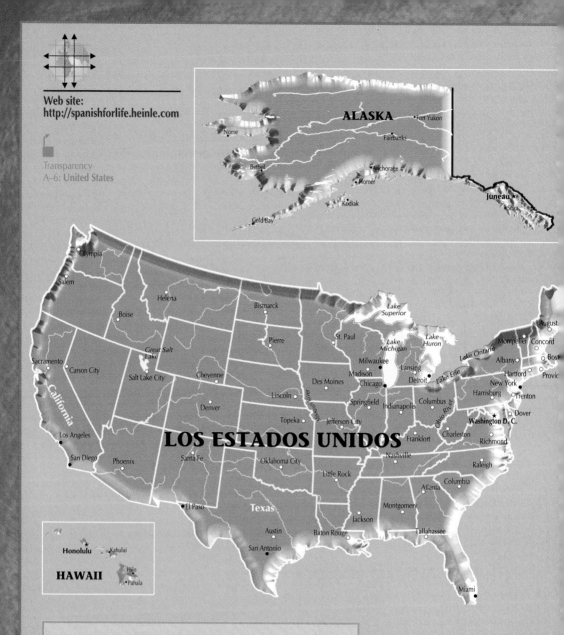

Web site:
http://spanishforlife.heinle.com

Transparency
A–6: United States

ALASKA

- Fort Yukon
Nome
Fairbanks
Bethel
Anchorage
Homer
Kodiak
Cold Bay
Juneau
Sitka

Olympia
Salem
Helena
Bismarck
Boise
Lake Superior
August
Pierre
St. Paul
Lake Michigan
Lake Huron
Montpelier
Concord
Great Salt Lake
Cheyenne
Milwaukee
Lansing
Lake Ontario
Albany
Boss
Sacramento
Madison
Detroit
Lake Erie
Hartford
Provic
Carson City
Salt Lake City
Des Moines
Chicago
Ohio River
New York
California
Lincoln
Springfield
Indianapolis
Columbus
Harrisburg
Trenton
Denver
Jefferson City
Dover
Los Angeles
Topeka
Washington D. C.
LOS ESTADOS UNIDOS
Frankfort
Charleston
Richmond
San Diego
Phoenix
Santa Fe
Oklahoma City
Nashville
Raleigh
Little Rock
Columbia
Atlanta
El Paso
Texas
Montgomery
Austin
Jackson
Tallahassee
San Antonio
Baton Rouge

Honolulu
Kahului
HAWAII
Hilo
Pahala

Miami

LOS ESTADOS UNIDOS

Nombre oficial: Estados Unidos de América

Área: 9.372.614 km^2

Población: 30.000.000 (de habla española)

Capital: Washington, Distrito de Columbia (D.C.)

Moneda: dólar

Idioma oficial: inglés

Fiesta nacional: 4 de julio, Día de la Independencia

Los hispanos en los Estados Unidos

Una cartelera en un pueblo de la California del Sur

In this chapter you will learn:

GRAMMAR POINTS

- Subject pronouns
- The verb **ser**
- Gender and number
- Definite articles
- Adjectives
- **Ser de**
- **Al** and **del**
- Interrogative words

COMMUNICATIVE FUNCTIONS

- Describe people
- Identify things
- Ask questions

VOCABULARY

- Descriptive adjectives
- Classroom objects
- Numbers 1–30

I. ¿Quién es americano?

LECTURA

¿**Yo?** **Yo** soy[1] de[2] Costa Rica.

¿**Tú?** **Tú** eres[3] de Argentina.

¿**Ella?** **Ella** es[4] de Canadá.

¿**Ellos?** **Ellos** son[5] de México.

¿**Ustedes?** **Ustedes** son de los Estados Unidos de América.

¿**Nosotros?** Sí, todos **nosotros** somos[6] americanos porque somos de las Américas.

---

[1]**soy:** *am* / [2]**de:** *from* / [3]**eres:** *are* / [4]**es:** *is* / [5]**son:** *are* / [6]**somos:** *are*

■ Los pronombres de sujeto

In Spanish, as in English, the subject of a sentence may be identified by a pronoun. These pronouns are called subject pronouns.

Subject Pronouns			
Singular		**Plural**	
yo	*I*	**nosotros(as)**	*we*
tú	*you (fam.)*	**vosotros(as)**	*you (fam.)*
usted	*you (form.)*	**ustedes**	*you (form.)*
él	*he*	**ellos**	*they (masc.)*
ella	*she*	**ellas**	*they (fem.)*

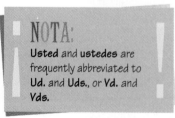

NOTA:

Usted and ustedes are frequently abbreviated to **Ud.** and **Uds.**, or **Vd.** and **Vds.**

Spanish has more pronouns meaning *you* than English. Spanish allows you to distinguish between a familiar and a formal style of speech when addressing people. This is somewhat analogous to addressing people by their first name or their last name.

Friends, family members, coworkers, and classmates are addressed as **tú**. Strangers, store clerks, bosses, professors, and the like are addressed as **usted**. **Usted** is more respectful than **tú**.

The usage here is general. It may vary from country to country and does not apply to countries where **vos** is used in place of **tú**.

When speaking directly to more than one person in Latin America, **ustedes** is the only form used. In Spain, **vosotros(as)** is used with more than one friend or family member, while **ustedes** is used with strangers or superiors. If the group is mixed (e.g., colleagues and bosses), the more respectful **ustedes** is used.

Practiquemos

A. ¡Hola! Indicate how you will address the following people, choosing from **tú**, **usted**, **vosotros**, and **ustedes**. Be sure you can explain your choice.

MODELO: your sister
tú, because she is a member of my family

1. your cousin
2. your boss
3. your boss and his or her family
4. your buddies (in Spain)
5. your coworker
6. your brothers and sister (in Latin America)
7. your Spanish instructor
8. your spouse or significant other

Point to one other student, a group of students, or your instructor, and tell how you would address each.

B. Después de clase. Carmen, Enrique, and Professor Olivárez are talking after class. In their conversation, what pronoun will Carmen use to refer to the following people? Be sure you can explain your choice.

MODELO: her friend Ana
ella, because Ana is a woman who is spoken about

1. herself
2. Enrique (to him)
3. her other classmates
4. her parents
5. her father
6. herself and Enrique
7. Professor Olivárez (to him)
8. Enrique and the other classmates
9. her mother
10. Professor Olivárez and the other professors
11. Professor Olivárez and Enrique (to them)
12. herself and the other classmates

a. **yo**
b. **tú**
c. **usted**
d. **él**
e. **ella**
f. **nosotros**
g. **ustedes**
h. **ellos**
i. **ellas**

II. La influencia mexicana

Avenida Collins en Miami, Florida

L E C T U R A

La influencia mexicana en los Estados Unidos **es** notable. El arte mexicano de murales **es** imitado en muchas[1] ciudades[2] en los Estados Unidos. Los alimentos[3] como[4] el taco, la tostada y las enchiladas **son** tan populares como[5] la hamburguesa y el «perro caliente[6]», y recientemente[7] la salsa ha llegado a **ser**[8] más popular que el *ketchup* como condimento. La música tejana, rica[9] combinación de melodías y ritmos mexicanos con influencia de la música *country western* **es** muy popular en el suroeste,[10] especialmente en Texas.

[1] **muchas:** many / [2] **ciudades:** cities / [3] **alimentos:** foods / [4] **como:** like / [5] **tan... como:** as . . . as / [6] **perro caliente:** hot dog / [7] **recientemente:** recently / [8] **ha llegado a ser:** has come to be / [9] **rica:** rich / [10] **suroeste:** southwest

¿Comprendes?

1. In what ways does the Mexican influence become evident in North American cuisine?
2. What Mexican music is heard in the United States?
3. What Mexican influences are present in your town?

■ El verbo ser

Estar will be presented in Chapter 2.

The Spanish verb **ser**, *to be,* is used to identify persons or objects or to tell when something takes place. The present tense of **ser** has six forms that correspond to the subject pronouns presented above.

ser						
yo	**soy**	*I am*	nosotros(as)	**somos**		*we are*
tú	**eres**	*you are (fam.)*	vosotros(as)	**sois**		*you are (fam.)*
usted		*you are (form.)*	ustedes			*you are (form.)*
él	**es**	*he is*	ellos		**son**	*they are (masc.)*
ella		*she is*	ellas			*they are (fem.)*

Ella **es** profesora.	*She **is** a professor.*
Nosotros **somos** estudiantes.	*We **are** students.*
Él **es** el señor Martínez.	*He **is** Mr. Martínez.*
La clase **es** ahora.	*Class **is** now.*

When the subject of the sentence is obvious from the form of the verb, the subject pronoun may be omitted. The English subject *it* has no equivalent in Spanish and is never expressed.

Soy estudiante.	*I'm a student.*
¿**Es** el señor Martínez?	*Is he Mr. Martínez?*
Es el libro de español.	*It's the Spanish book.*

If the subject of the verb is not clear from the context, a subject pronoun may be used.

¿Usted es el profesor?	*You're the professor?*
Yo no. **Él es** el profesor.	*Not me. He is the professor.*
Tú y yo somos estudiantes.	*You and I are students.*

Likewise, subject pronouns may be used for emphasis.

Ella es la profesora.	*She is the professor.*
Tú eres el estudiante.	*You are the student.*
Soy yo.	*It's me. (lit: I am I.)*

Practiquemos

A. Son así. Select the appropriate verb form to tell about these people.

MODELO: Ella (eres, *es*) mi amiga.

1. El profesor (es, somos) el señor Pérez.
2. Ellos (somos, son) estudiantes.
3. ¿Tú (soy, eres) profesora?
4. ¿Usted (es, son) la señora Chávez?
5. Tomás y Elena (sois, son) estudiantes.
6. Yo (soy, es) señora, no señorita.
7. Vosotros (sois, somos) chicos.
8. Tú y yo (soy, somos) profesores.

B. Yo soy… Match the subjects with the proper form of the verb **ser.**

MODELO: *es* él

_____	**1.** tú	a.	**soy**
_____	**2.** nosotros	b.	**eres**
_____	**3.** Clara	c.	**es**
_____	**4.** Lorenzo y Paco	d.	**somos**
_____	**5.** yo	e.	**sois**
_____	**6.** usted	f.	**son**
_____	**7.** Lisa y Pablo		
_____	**8.** Édgar y yo		
_____	**9.** vosotros		
_____	**10.** ustedes		
_____	**11.** ella		
_____	**12.** tú y yo		

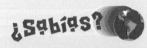

¿Sabías?

There are more Puerto Ricans living in New York than in Puerto Rico.

Pick three words that describe you and describe yourself to three other people.
MODELO:
Yo soy Anita Smith. Soy estudiante y soy inteligente.

Have students describe the other students in their group. For example: Él es...

NOTA:
The different forms of **ser** may be used more than once.

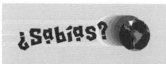

Discuss with the class the meaning of this **Sabías** and what it could mean for the future.

C. La clase. Fill in the blanks with the appropriate forms of the verb **ser** to tell what you learned about your fellow students on the first day of class.

MODELO: Enrique *es* estudiante.

1. Federica _____ mamá.
2. Tú _____ Carlota.
3. Nosotros _____ estudiantes.
4. Ellos _____ estudiantes y profesores.
5. La clase _____ ahora.
6. Ella _____ la señorita Gómez.
7. Vosotros _____ papás.
8. La fiesta _____ mañana.

■ El género y el número

El género

When talking about languages, the term *gender* refers to grammatical categories. Spanish has two genders, masculine and feminine, and all Spanish nouns belong to one of the two genders. While it is true that many words for males are masculine and many words for females are feminine, there is no direct correlation between biological and grammatical gender. The word **persona** *(person)* is feminine, no matter to whom it refers. **Ser humano** *(Human being)* is masculine whether referring to a man or a woman. Nouns which designate objects or ideas have a grammatical gender although the objects or concepts clearly have no biological gender.

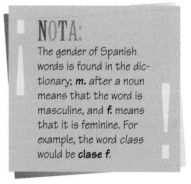

NOTA:
The gender of Spanish words is found in the dictionary; *m.* after a noun means that the word is masculine, and *f.* means that it is feminine. For example, the word class would be **clase f.**

ángel *(masc.)*	angel
víctima *(fem.)*	victim
mesa *(fem.)*	table
libro *(masc.)*	book
idea *(fem.)*	idea
concepto *(masc.)*	concept

The gender of each noun must be learned. It is helpful to know that most nouns ending in **-o** are masculine and most words ending in **-a** are feminine, but there are many exceptions and many nouns that do not end in **-o** or **-a**. The safest practice is to learn the gender of the word along with its meaning.

El número

In addition to gender, Spanish nouns have number; that is, they are singular or plural. The plural of nouns ending in a vowel is formed by adding -**s**. The plural of nouns ending in consonants is formed by adding -**es**.

> **NOTA:**
> Dictionaries give the singular as the base form (except for words like scissors, which are rarely used in the singular).

diccionario	diccionarios	*dictionary(-ies)*
calculadora	calculadoras	*calculator(s)*
profesor	profesores	*professor(s)*
papel	papeles	*paper(s)*

> **NOTA:**
> In Spanish, masculine plural is used both for exclusively masculine groups or mixed groups of masculine and feminine. For instance, **padres** may mean fathers, but it also frequently means parents. **Profesores** may mean male professors, but it is often used to mean a group of professors, comprising males and females.

Practiquemos

A. El diccionario. Look up the following words in the dictionary and find out their gender and their meanings.

1. cucaracha _____
2. orangután _____
3. gallina _____
4. jirafa _____
5. pez _____

6. elefante _____
7. mariposa _____
8. perro _____
9. serpiente _____
10. mono _____

B. Otro. You have one of the following. If you get another, what do you have?

MODELO: papel   *papeles*

1. libro _____
2. señorita _____
3. noche _____
4. estudiante _____

5. señor _____
6. día _____
7. profesor _____
8. chico _____

■ El artículo definido

The definite article *(the)* in Spanish has four forms corresponding to the two genders, masculine and feminine, and the two numbers, singular and plural.

	Singular	Plural
MASCULINE	el	los
FEMININE	la	las

Masculine Nouns

People

el amigo	**los** amigos	*the (male) friend(s)*
el chico	**los** chicos	*the boy(s), guy(s)*
el estudiante	**los** estudiantes	*the (male) student(s)*
el papá	**los** papás	*the dad(s)*
el profesor	**los** profesores	*the (male) profesor(s)*
el señor	**los** señores	*the man (men)*

Classroom Vocabulary

el bolígrafo	**los** bolígrafos	*the ballpoint pen(s)*
el cuaderno	**los** cuadernos	*the notebook(s)*
el día	**los** días	*the day(s)*
el diccionario	**los** diccionarios	*the dictionary(ies)*
el lápiz	**los** lápices	*the pencil(s)*
el libro	**los** libros	*the book(s)*
el papel	**los** papeles	*the paper(s)*

Feminine Nouns

People

la amiga	**las** amigas	*the (female) friend(s)*
la chica	**las** chicas	*the girl(s)*
la estudiante	**las** estudiantes	*the (female) student(s)*
la mamá	**las** mamás	*the mom(s)*
la profesora	**las** profesoras	*the (female) professor(s)*
la señora	**las** señoras	*the lady(-ies)*
la señorita	**las** señoritas	*the young or unmarried lady(-ies)*

Classroom Vocabulary

la calculadora	**las** calculadoras	*the calculator(s)*
la clase	**las** clases	*the class(es)*
la computadora	**las** computadoras	*the computer(s)*
la fiesta	**las** fiestas	*the party(-ies)*
la mochila	**las** mochilas	*the backpack(s)*
la pluma	**las** plumas	*the (fountain) pen(s)*

Masculine plural nouns with the masculine article may designate a group of purely masculine people or objects but they are also used to refer to mixed groups of masculine and feminine. Feminine plural nouns and articles designate groups of feminine nouns exclusively.

las estudiantes   *female students (only)*
los estudiantes   *male students; male and female students*

The definite article is used before titles in Spanish except when addressing a person directly. Titles include **señor, señora, señorita, profesor, profesora, doctor,** and **doctora.** They are not used before first names or family relationships.

> # NOTA:
> When talking *about* Dr. Sánchez, you would say **la doctora Sánchez**. When talking *to* her, you would say **doctora Sánchez.**

la señorita González   *Miss González*
el profesor Valadez   *Professor Valadez*

Practiquemos

A. ¿Masculino o femenino? Write the appropriate definite article for the words listed below.

1. _____ fiesta
2. _____ señor
3. _____ noches
4. _____ chicos

5. _____ señoritas
6. _____ días
7. _____ profesor
8. _____ mamá

B. Nombres. Write four words that match each article in number and gender.

1. el _____ _____ _____ _____
2. la _____ _____ _____ _____
3. los _____ _____ _____ _____
4. las _____ _____ _____ _____

C. El señor profesor. Add a definite article to each name if it is necessary and then explain why it is or is not necessary.

1. _____ señor Alonso
2. _____ Mario Vega
3. _____ profesora Gómez
4. _____ Alicia de la Rocha
5. _____ doctor Manzanares
6. _____ señorita Estrada
7. _____ Elena Martínez
8. _____ Horacio Laredo

> Use the vocabulary you have studied to play hangman with a partner. Be sure to use the definite article.

III. Los hispanos en los Estados Unidos

LECTURA

Muchos norteamericanos son de otras[1] naciones. Muchos son **hispanos**, eso es,[2] son de América Central, de América del Sur, del Caribe o de España. Aproximadamente treinta millones de norteamericanos son **hispanos**.

Los hispanos son **orgullosos**[3] de su cultura y de su historia, pero también son muy **similares** a los otros **norteamericanos**. Son orgullosos de los Estados Unidos. Son muy **afortunados**[4] porque[5] son de dos culturas diferentes.

---

[1]**otras:** *other* / [2]**eso es:** *that is* / [3]**orgullosos:** *proud* / [4]**afortunados:** *lucky* / [5]**porque:** *because*

¿Comprendes?

1. How many Hispanics live in the United States?
2. What makes a person a Hispanic?
3. What cultural advantages do Hispanics have?

■ LOS ADJETIVOS

Adjectives are words like *red* (**rojo**), *short* (**bajo**), *funny* (**cómico**), *difficult* (**difícil**), which describe nouns. Like definite articles, Spanish adjectives must reflect the gender and number of the nouns they describe.

■ Adjectives whose masculine singular forms end in **-o** have four forms.

	Singular	Plural	
MASCULINE	activ**o**	activ**os**	*active*
FEMININE	activ**a**	activ**as**	*active*

Other adjectives in this category include:

alto	*tall*	argentino	*Argentinian*
bonito	*pretty (people, things)*	chileno	*Chilean*
bueno	*good*	colombiano	*Colombian*
delgado	*slim, thin*	cubano	*Cuban*
extrovertido	*extroverted*	mexicano	*Mexican*
gordito	*chubby, plump*	panameño	*Panamanian*
guapo	*good looking (people)*	peruano	*Peruvian*
introvertido	*introverted*	puertorriqueño	*Puerto Rican*
pequeño	*small, short*	salvadoreño	*Salvadoran*
simpático	*nice*		
tímido	*timid, shy*		

■ Adjectives whose masculine singular form ends in **-e** or a consonant have two forms. Adjectives in this category include:

Singular	Plural	
aleg**re**	alegr**es**	*happy, cheerful*
inteligent**e**	inteligent**es**	*intelligent*
tradicional	tradicional**es**	*traditional*

Most adjectives of nationality follow the rules above, as in **argentino**, **mexicano**, etc. However, a few follow a slightly different pattern.

		Singular	Plural	
MASCULINE		español	español**es**	*Spanish*
		alemán	aleman**es**	*German*
		francés	frances**es**	*French*
FEMININE		español**a**	español**as**	*Spanish*
		aleman**a**	aleman**as**	*German*
		frances**a**	frances**as**	*French*

NOTA:
Adjectives of nationality are not capitalized in Spanish.

Adjectives occurring after the verb **ser** describe the subject of the sentence.

María es **guapa**.	*María is good looking.*
Joaquín es **colombiano**.	*Joaquín is Colombian.*
Los chicos son muy **activos**.	*The children are very active.*
Los profesores son **simpáticos**.	*The professors are nice.*

When describing two feminine nouns with the same adjective, the feminine plural form is correct. When using the same adjective to describe a masculine noun and any other noun(s), the masculine plural is the correct form.

María y Carlota son **altas**.	*María and Carlota are tall.*
María y Felipe son **guapos**.	*María and Felipe are good looking.*

Adjectives are frequently placed next to the nouns they describe. In Spanish, normal descriptive adjective placement is *after* the noun.

el señor **alto**   the **tall** man
la chica **tímida**   the **shy** girl
los estudiantes **extrovertidos**   the **extroverted** students

Practiquemos

A. Interesantes. Select the correct form of the adjective to describe the people in a Spanish class.

In pairs, describe yourselves to each other using at least four adjectives. Include words that describe both of you together and each of you separately.

MODELO: Las chicas son (delgados, *delgadas*).

1. Carlos es (alto, alta).
2. La señora es (guapo, guapa).
3. El chico es (activo, activa).
4. Los estudiantes son (inteligente, inteligentes).
5. Las señoras son (bonitos, bonitas).
6. Mario y Carlota son (peruanos, peruanas).
7. La profesora es (simpática, simpáticas).
8. Susana y Alicia son (tímidos, tímidas).
9. La señorita es (delgado, delgada).
10. Las clases son (tradicional, tradicionales).

Have students describe a well-known person (artist, musician, political figure), using at least four adjectives. After each person has been described, have the class try to guess the identity of that person.

B. ¡Magnífico! Describe a class party by filling in the blank with the proper form of the adjective provided.

MODELO: José es _____. (tímido)
           José es *tímido.*

1. Timoteo es _____. (extrovertido)
2. La chica es _____. (activo)
3. Mi amigo es muy _____. (simpático)
4. Los profesores son _____. (inteligente)
5. Mamá es _____. (bajo)
6. Carlos y Tomás son _____. (gordito)
7. Los estudiantes son ___ ___. (alegre)
8. La fiesta es muy _____. (bueno)

C. ¿De dónde? Write sentences that describe the nationality of these newcomers to the United States. Then, locate their country of origin on the map in the chapter opener.

MODELO: los profesores / argentino
           Los profesores son argentinos.

1. mi amiga / mexicano
2. la profesora / español
3. los chicos / puertorriqueño
4. la estudiante / chileno
5. Julio y Lisa / salvadoreño
6. Elena / panameño
7. los señores / colombiano
8. Raquel y Claudia / cubano

D. Así son. Write sentences to describe these people and events, using the nouns and adjectives given.

Describe your friends and family using three or more sentences.

MODELO: estudiantes / inteligente
          Los estudiantes son inteligentes.

1. señorita / simpático
2. papá / alto
3. chicos / tímido
4. profesora / introvertido
5. Marta y José / alegre

6. clase / tradicional
7. mamás / delgado
8. Martín / gordito
9. nosotros / inteligente
10. fiesta / bueno

IV. Hispanos muy conocidos

Gloria Estefan

Edward James Olmos

Sammy Sosa

LECTURA

Los hispanos de los Estados Unidos y del mundo[1] son importantes en la música, el cine, la televisión, la política y los deportes. Y **son de** muchos países.[2] En la música, Gloria Estefan **es de** Cuba y Julio y Enrique Iglesias **son de** España. En el cine,[3] Edward James Olmos y Emilio Estévez **son de** los Estados Unidos y Rita Moreno **es de** Puerto Rico. En la televisión, Jimmy Smits y Héctor Elizondo **son de** los Estados Unidos y Cristina Saralegui (presentadora del programa *Cristina,* en español y en inglés) **es de** Cuba. En los deportes,[4] Sammy Sosa y Pedro Martínez, famosos jugadores[5] de béisbol **son de** la República Dominicana. Entre las jugadoras de tenis, Mary Jo Fernández **es de** Puerto Rico, Arantxa Sánchez Vicario **es de** España y Gabriela Sabatini **es de** Argentina. Éstos[6] son muy[7] pocos[8] ejemplos de los muchos hispanos conocidos en todas partes.[9]

---

[1]**mundo:** *world* / [2]**países:** *countries* / [3]**cine:** *movies* / [4]**deportes:** *sports* / [5]**jugador:** *player* / [6]**Estos:** *These* / [7]**muy:** *very* / [8]**pocos:** *few* / [9]**en todas partes:** *all over, everywhere*

¿Comprendes?

1. Name three well-known Hispanics in the field of sports.
2. Who is your favorite Hispanic entertainer?
3. Can you think of other well-known Hispanics?

■ *Ser de*

> **NOTA:** Unlike nationalities, the names of countries are capitalized in Spanish as in English.

Origen

The verb **ser** is used with the preposition **de** to indicate where someone or something is from.

Soy de los Estados Unidos.	*I'm from the United States.*
Sammy Sosa **es de** la República Dominicana.	*Sammy Sosa is from the Dominican Republic.*
Pablo Neruda **es de** Chile.	*Pablo Neruda is from Chile.*

Material

Ser de is also used to indicate the material that something is made of.

Los CDs **son de** plástico.	*CDs are (made of) plastic.*
La Estatua de la Libertad **es de** metal.	*The Statue of Liberty is (made of) metal.*
Muchos edificios **son de** cemento.	*Many buildings are (made of) cement.*

> **NOTA:** Spanish does not use the apostrophe to indicate possession. **María's libro** has no meaning in Spanish. It is necessary to say **el libro de María** to express this information.

Posesión

Possession is expressed in Spanish by **ser de** and a noun that indicates the owner.

Son de Rafael.	*They are Rafael's.*
El diccionario **es de** María y Carlos.	*The dictionary belongs to María and Carlos.*
Los libros **son de** los estudiantes.	*The books are the students'.*

Practiquemos

A. Nacionalidades. Indicate the country of origin of these members of an English class for immigrants.

MODELO: Raúl y Tina son cubanos.
Son de Cuba.

> Have students identify these countries on transparencies.
> A-2, A-3

1. El señor Villegas es mexicano.
2. Mariana Alba es colombiana.
3. Los señores García son peruanos.
4. Gabriel Lozano es salvadoreño.
5. Anita y Clara Gil son chilenas.
6. El profesor Moreno es argentino.
7. La señorita Bravo es puertorriqueña.
8. Alma y Nicolás Santana son españoles.

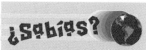

¿Sabías?

- The word **hispanos** is a form of **Hispania,** the Latin name for Spain.
- Two out of every three Hispanics who live in the United States are of Mexican origin.

B. Muy durable. Indicate the material from which these classroom objects are made.

Materiales: metal   plástico   papel

M O D E L O :   libro   *El libro es de papel.*

1. diccionario
2. computadora
3. boli

4. calculadora
5. cuaderno
6. pluma

C. ¿De quién? Identify the owners of the following belongings now in "Lost and Found."

M O D E L O :   pluma / Alberto
    La pluma es de Alberto.

1. diccionario / Raquel
2. cuaderno / Isabel
3. calculadora / Fernando
4. papel / Francisco y Elena

5. boli / Lorenzo
6. mochila / Marcos
7. lápiz / Susana
8. libro / la profesora

As an additional whole-class activity, point out a variety of classroom objects and ask students what they are made of and to whom they belong.

❖ Los números 1–30

0	cero	11	once	22	veintidós (veinte y dos)
1	uno	12	doce	23	veintitrés (veinte y tres)
2	dos	13	trece	24	veinticuatro (veinte y cuatro)
3	tres	14	catorce	25	veinticinco (veinte y cinco)
4	cuatro	15	quince	26	veintiséis (veinte y seis)
5	cinco	16	dieciséis (diez y seis)	27	veintisiete (veinte y siete)
6	seis	17	diecisiete (diez y siete)	28	veintiocho (veinte y ocho)
7	siete	18	dieciocho (diez y ocho)	29	veintinueve (veinte y nueve)
8	ocho	19	diecinueve (diez y nueve)	30	treinta
9	nueve	20	veinte		
10	diez	21	veintiuno (veinte y uno)		

The numbers 16–19 and 21–29 can be written as one word or three as shown. Most Spanish-speaking people prefer to use one word, especially in the case of 16–19.

Uno drops the final **-o** before a masculine singular noun. This is also true when **uno** is part of a larger number, as in 21.

The form **una** is used before feminine nouns. The same is true of **una** in larger numbers, like 21.

The other numbers remain the same when used in counting or before nouns.

un chico	*a boy*
veintiún cuadernos	*twenty-one notebooks*
una señora	*a woman*
veintiuna sillas	*twenty-one chairs*
tres lápices	*three pencils*
diecinueve estudiantes	*nineteen students*

The words **más** (+) and **menos** (–) are used when adding and subtracting in Spanish. When adding, the verb form is always **son**. When subtracting, if the answer is *one,* the verb form is **es**; otherwise, use **son**.

Dos **más** dos **son** cuatro.	Two **plus** two **are** four.
Veinticinco **menos** trece **son** doce.	Twenty-five **minus** thirteen **are** twelve.
Cuatro **menos** tres **es** uno.	Four **minus** three **is** one.

Practiquemos

As a follow-up activity, have students circulate around the class and write down the telephone numbers of five classmates. Numbers may be shared with the class if students are willing.

A. Números de teléfono. Write out the following telephone numbers.

MODELO: 211-6990
            dos uno uno-seis nueve nueve cero

1. 555-7120
2. 982-6110
3. 415-0077
4. 844-9237

5. 321-4376
6. 654-9908
7. 805-4321
8. 515-8762

B. ¿Cuántas cosas? Write out each number to tell how many of the following can be found in the classroom.

MODELO: 26 notebooks
            veintiséis cuadernos

1. 21 books
2. 19 women
3. 15 backpacks
4. 10 pens

5. 25 men
6. 30 chairs
7. 1 teacher (female)
8. 14 calculators

C. ¡Problemas de matemáticas! Solve the following problems, writing all words in Spanish.

MODELO: $4 + 4 = 8$ *Cuatro más cuatro son ocho.*
            $9 - 6 = 3$ *Nueve menos seis son tres.*

1. $19 + 3 =$
2. $20 - 10 =$
3. $30 - 9 =$
4. $16 + 5 =$
5. $4 + 12 =$

6. $17 + 6 =$
7. $25 - 14 =$
8. $12 - 2 =$
9. $28 + 2 =$
10. $13 - 9 =$

■ *Al y del*

Spanish has two contractions, **al** and **del**. The preposition **a** (which may be equivalent to the English *to,* but sometimes there is no equivalent in English) combines with the masculine singular article **el** to form **al**. The preposition **de** *(from, of)* combines with **el** to form **del**.

Presentamos **al** profesor.	We introduce **the** professor.
Ramón es **del** estado de Jalisco.	Ramón is **from** the state of Jalisco.

There is no change in the other definite articles: **a la, a las, a los, de la, de las, de los**.

Practiquemos

A. ¡Quiero presentar… ! Tell who you are introducing. Use the contraction **al** where necessary.

MODELO: el estudiante
Quiero presentar al estudiante.

1. el señor
2. María
3. la chica
4. el profesor
5. Ramón y Lucía
6. la señora Martínez
7. el amigo de María
8. la clase
9. la señorita Pérez
10. mi amiga

Have students make up an identity on a name tag, including a title (e.g., **señor[a]** or **señorita**), and attach it to their clothing. Then have them form groups of four and introduce each other, including the title.

B. ¿De quiénes? Identify the owners of the following items left in the teachers' lounge. Use the contraction **del** where necessary.

MODELO: ¿la mochila? / la profesora Álvarez
La mochila es de la profesora Álvarez.

1. ¿los cuadernos? / el señor Gómez
2. ¿el bolígrafo? / la profesora Galán
3. ¿las calculadoras? / los estudiantes
4. ¿el libro? / el profesor Muñoz
5. ¿los papeles / las chicas
6. ¿el diccionario? / el profesor de español

■ Palabras interrogativas

In order to ask questions, the following interrogative (question) words are used. Note that each word has a written accent.

¿Qué?	*What? (definition)*
¿Quién? ¿Quiénes?	*Who?*
¿De quién? ¿De quiénes?	*Whose? (Of whom?)*
¿Cómo?	*How? What? (you didn't hear what was said)*
¿Cómo es…?	*What is . . . like?*
¿Dónde? / ¿De dónde?	*Where? / From where?*
¿Cuándo?	*When?*
¿Por qué?	*Why?*
¿Cuál? ¿Cuáles?	*Which? What?*
¿Cuánto(a, os, as)?	*How much? How many?*
¿Cómo es Juanita?	***What** is Juanita **like**?*
¿Cuándo es la clase?	***When** is the class?*
¿Cuál es tu teléfono?	***What** is your telephone number?*
¿De dónde es Julio?	***Where** is Julio **from**?*
¿Quiénes son?	***Who** are they?*
¿Cuánto es el libro?	***How much** is the book?*

Practiquemos ✎

A. Riesgo (Jeopardy). You hear the answer to a question but you miss the question and must guess what it was. What questions do the following sentences answer?

MODELO: Es María.
¿Quién es?

1. Es mañana.
2. Son Elena y Rogelio.
3. Es alto y guapo.
4. Son de Ramona.

5. Es Miguel.
6. Es el diccionario de español.
7. Son de Puerto Rico.
8. Es esta noche.

Have students role-play the dialogue in class.

B. Diálogo. Juan and Lourdes are talking before class. Complete their conversation using the appropriate interrogative words.

JUAN: Hola, Lourdes. ¿ _____ tal?
LOURDES: Muy bien, ¿y tú?
JUAN: Regular. Oye, ¿ _____ es el profesor de español?
LOURDES: Es el señor Santana.
JUAN: ¿ _____ es él?
LOURDES: Es muy simpático y es inteligente. ¿ _____ es la clase?
JUAN: Es mañana. ¿ _____ _____ es el profesor Santana?
LOURDES: Es de México.
JUAN: Otra cosa. *(Another thing.)* _____ _____ es este *(this)* libro de español?
LOURDES: Es de Gloria.
JUAN: Gracias, Lourdes. Hasta mañana.
LOURDES: Adiós.

A ver si sabes

Use this self-test to see if you know the material presented in Chapter 1.

A. ¿De quién hablas? Give the appropriate subject pronouns to tell how you refer to the following people in a conversation in Spanish with a coworker and your boss.

1. yourself
2. you and your family
3. your coworker (to him)

4. your mother
5. your boss (to her)
6. your friends

B. Mis amigos y mi familia. Albertina is describing her friends and family to Mariano. Complete her conversation with the appropriate forms of the verb **ser**.

1. Mis papás _____ muy simpáticos.

2. Mi profesora _____ inteligente.

3. Mi amigo Ernesto _____ alto.

4. Mis amigos y yo ___ ___ guapos.

5. María y Cristina _____ delgadas.

6. ¿Tú _____ alegre?

C. ¿El? ¿La? Provide the missing article in these sentences about class.

    1. _____ clase es ahora.

    2. _____ cuadernos son de los estudiantes.

    3. _____ señorita Márquez es profesora.

    4. _____ bolis son de Juan.

    5. _____ computadoras son pequeñas.

    6. _____ libro de español es interesante.

D. Invitados. Rafael is describing the people he has invited to dinner tonight. Complete his description by putting the adjectives in parentheses in the proper form.

    1. Sofía es _____. (pequeño)

    2. Los chicos son _____. (activo)

    3. Arturo es _____. (gordito)

    4. Daniel y Laura son _____. (guapo)

    5. El profesor es _____. (peruano)

    6. Yo soy _____. (extrovertido)

E. ¿De qué nación? Tell what country these people are from based on the nationality provided.

    1. La señorita Blanco es panameña.
    2. Los profesores son salvadoreños.
    3. Elena y Margarita son puertorriqueñas.
    4. Las señoras altas son peruanas.
    5. El señor Avellano es argentino.
    6. José María Moreno es español.

F. ¿Cuántos? Tell how many items were purchased for class. Write out the numbers.

    1. (27) _____ cuadernos

    2. (21) _____ libros

    3. (15) _____ bolígrafos

    4. (25) _____ mochilas

    5. (11) _____ calculadoras

    6. (30) _____ sillas

Preguntas culturales
1. Who is an American?
2. Name several ways in which Mexican cultural influence is felt in the U.S.
3. Name at least one advantage enjoyed by Hispanic Americans in the U.S.

G. ¡Preguntas y más preguntas! Write the appropriate questions, using interrogative words.

1. ¿ _____ es? Es mi profesora.

2. ¿ _____ es? Es de México.

3. ¿ _____ es? Es alta y delgada.

4. ¿ _____ es la clase? Es mañana.

5. ¿ _____ clase es? Es la clase de español.

H. Presentaciones. Write the correct form in the space provided, choosing from **a, al, a la, a los, a las.**

1. Mario, quiero presentar _____ señor Miranda.

2. Señor Miranda, quiero presentar _____ Mario.

3. Quiero presentar _____ chicas.

4. Juan, quiero presentar _____ profesor Espinosa.

5. Clase, quiero presentar _____ mi amiga.

I. ¿De quién es? Complete the sentence with the correct form of **de, del, de la, de los, de las.**

1. ¿La mochila? Es _____ señorita Seldis.

2. ¿Las calculadoras? Son _____ mi amigo, Juanito.

3. ¿El boli? Es _____ profesor López.

4. ¿Los libros? Son _____ chicas.

5. ¿Las sillas? Son _____ estudiantes.

Querido Diario. Make a list of ten physical and personality characteristics of a person you admire and would like to know better. Using this list to organize your thinking, write a few (five to eight) sentences describing that person in your journal. You might start out: **Alfredo es alto y guapo...**

Grammar: use of **ser**, adjective agreement
Phrases: describing people
Vocabulary: personality

Vocabulario activo

Nombres

el/la amigo(a)	el día	la mañana	el señor
mi amigo(a)	el (la) estudiante	la noche	la señora
el (la) chico(a)	la fiesta	el papá	la señorita
la clase	la mamá	el (la) profesor(a)	la tarde

De la clase

el bolígrafo (boli)	el diccionario	el papel
la calculadora	el lápiz	la pluma
la computadora	el libro	la silla
el cuaderno	la mochila	

Verbo

ser

Adjetivos

activo	bueno	guapo	simpático
alegre	delgado	inteligente	tímido
alto	extrovertido	introvertido	tradicional
bonito	gordito	pequeño	

Nacionalidades

argentino (Argentina)	español (España)	puertorriqueño (Puerto Rico)
chileno (Chile)	mexicano (México)	salvadoreño (El Salvador)
colombiano (Colombia)	panameño (Panamá)	
cubano (Cuba)	peruano (Perú)	

Palabras interrogativas

¿Cómo?	¿De dónde?	¿Qué?
¿Cuál?	¿De quién?	¿Quién?
¿Cuándo?	¿Por qué?	

Artículos

el	los
la	las

Pronombres

yo	él	vosotros(as)	ellas
tú	ella	ustedes	
usted	nosotros(as)	ellos	

Otras palabras y expresiones

adiós	de	mucho gusto	quiero presentar a
ahora	gracias	muy	regular
buenas noches	hola	(no) muy bien	¿y tú?
buenas tardes	igualmente	porque no	¿y usted?
buenos días	mañana	porque sí	
chao	menos	¿Qué tal?	

Transparencies A–3, A–11: Cuba

CUBA

Nombre oficial: República de Cuba

Área: 110.922 km²

Población: 11.000.000

Capital: la Ciudad de La Habana

Moneda: peso

Idioma oficial: español

Fiesta nacional: 1 de enero, Día de la Liberación

Cuba y los cubanos

El centro de Habana que bordea el mar

In this chapter you will learn:

GRAMMAR POINTS
- Basic functions of **estar**
- Indefinite articles
- Infinitives
- **Ir**
- **Ir a** + infinitive
- **Tener**
- **Tener que** + infinitive
- **Hay**
- Possessive adjectives

COMMUNICATIVE FUNCTIONS
- Tell and ask how people are
- Describe location of things
- Tell where you are going and what you are going to do
- Tell what you have to do
- Describe the classroom

VOCABULARY
- Adjectives of condition
- Prepositions of location
- Familiar buildings and destinations
- Family members
- Common verbs (infinitives)
- Numbers 31–100

I. Cuba

LECTURA

La isla de Cuba **está** situada a unas noventa[1] millas del estado de Florida. La capital, La Habana, **está** en la costa norteña de la isla y es la ciudad[2] más grande. A causa del[3] gran número de cubanoamericanos que **están** en Miami, hay[4] una sección de la ciudad llamada[5] «La Pequeña Habana».

---

[1]**noventa:** *ninety* / [2]**ciudad:** *city* / [3]**a causa de:** *because of* / [4]**hay:** *there is* / [5]**llamada:** *called*

¿Comprendes?

1. How far is Cuba from the United States?
2. Where is "Little Havana" found?
3. Why is it called "Little Havana"?

■ El verbo *estar*

Like the verb **ser**, the verb **estar** has six forms, corresponding to the possible subjects.

estar			
yo	est**oy**	nosotros(as)	est**amos**
tú	est**ás**	vosotros(as)	est**áis**
Ud.		Uds.	
él	est**á**	ellos	est**án**
ella		ellas	

¿Cómo **estás**?	*How are you?*
Estoy bien, gracias.	*I'm fine, thank you.*
La Habana y Camagüey **están** en Cuba.	*Havana and Camaguey are in Cuba.*

The verb **estar** is used to express how someone is feeling or what state or condition something is in. Typical conditions following **estar** include:

aburrido	*bored*	horrible	*horrible, in bad shape*
bien	*well, fine*	mal	*bad, sick*
cansado	*tired*	ocupado	*busy*
contento	*happy*	regular	*OK*
enfermo	*sick, ill*	terrible	*terrible*
estupendo	*stupendous, fantastic*	triste	*sad*

Martita y Raúl **están** enfermos.
Mi carro **está** horrible.
Estoy contento.

*Martita and Raúl **are** ill.*
*My car **is** in bad shape.*
I'm happy.

Practiquemos

A. ¿Qué tal? Give the letter of the correct verb form to complete these sentences telling how people are.

MODELO: Rafaél __c.__ triste.

1. Nosotros _____ muy bien.   **a.** estoy

2. Mi primo Julio _____ cansado.   **b.** estás

3. Los abuelos _____ orgullosos.   **c.** está

4. ¿Tú _____ enferma?   **d.** estamos

5. Yo _____ perfectamente bien.   **e.** están

■ *Estar* to express location

The verb **estar** is also used to tell where something is situated. This may be expressed by a single word like the following:

aquí   *here*   cerca   *near*   lejos   *far*

Location may also be expressed with **estar** followed by the preposition **en** and a location such as:

en Cuba, México, Chicago,...	*in Cuba, Mexico, Chicago, . . .*
en la universidad	*at the university*
en casa	*at home*
en clase	*in class*
en la oficina	*at the office*
en el trabajo	*at work*
en el mercado	*at the market*
en la escuela	*at school*

¡Ah! **Estás aquí.**   *Oh! **You're here.***
Mi oficina **está cerca.**   *My office **is near.***
Estamos en la clase de español.   ***We are in** Spanish class.*
Muchas personas **están en el trabajo.**   *Many people **are at work.***

All of these locations answer the question **¿dónde?**

¿Dónde está tu oficina?   ***Where is** your office?*
Está cerca.   ***It's** nearby.*
¿Dónde están tus hijos?   ***Where are** your children?*
Están en la escuela.   ***They're at** school.*

Practiquemos

A. ¿Dónde? Select the proper verb form to complete the sentences that tell where people are at 10:30 in the morning.

MODELO: María (estás, *está*) en clase

1. Papá (están, está) en el trabajo.
2. Mis hermanas (estás, están) en clase.
3. Tú y yo (estoy, estamos) en la oficina.
4. Mi abuelo (estoy, está) en el café.
5. Mi mamá y mi abuelo (estás, están) en el mercado.
6. Yo (estoy, está) en el trabajo.
7. Mi abuelo y mi papá (estamos, están) lejos.
8. Tú y Mario (estás, están) cerca.

B. ¿Estamos todos? Complete the sentences with the proper form of **estar** to help your instructor take roll for the class.

MODELO: La Sra. Rosa *está* presente.

1. La Srta. Martin _____ ausente.

2. Los Sres. Gilbert _____ presentes.

3. Yo _____ presente.

4. El Sr. Walters y la Srta. Stone _____ presentes.

5. Maryann Calder _____ ausente.

6. Tú _____ presente.

7. El Sr. Hill _____ ausente.

8. Nosotros _____ presentes.

C. ¿Está cerca? Looking at the map of Cuba in the chapter opener, tell whether the places provided are near *(cerca)* or far *(lejos)* from La Habana.

> What restaurants are near the class? Which ones are far away?

MODELO: Mariel
          Mariel está cerca.

1. Santiago de Cuba
2. Santa Clara y Santo Domingo
3. Guantánamo
4. Matanzas y Cárdenas
5. Isla de la Juventud
6. nosotros
7. Manzanillo
8. San Francisco y Los Ángeles, California

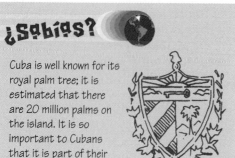

¿Sabías?

Cuba is well known for its royal palm tree; it is estimated that there are 20 million palms on the island. It is so important to Cubans that it is part of their coat of arms.

■ El artículo indefinido

Indefinite articles are used to talk about something nonspecific: *a* woman, *a* class, *an* article in the paper.

Spanish indefinite articles have four forms.

	Masculine	Feminine	
SINGULAR	un	una	*a, an*
PLURAL	unos	unas	*some*

Point out that **un** and **una** can also mean *one.*

Es **una** calculadora.	*It's **a** calculator.*
Unos estudiantes están aquí.	***Some** students are here.*
Un libro está en la mesa.	***A** book is on the table.*
Unas sillas están en la clase.	***Some** chairs are in the class.*

Practiquemos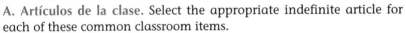

A. Artículos de la clase. Select the appropriate indefinite article for each of these common classroom items.

1. _____ cuadernos
2. _____ calculadora
3. _____ bolígrafo
4. _____ lápices
5. _____ diccionario
6. _____ sillas
7. _____ papeles
8. _____ computadora

a. un
b. una
c. unos
d. unas

B. Conocidos. Supply the appropriate indefinite article to match each class member listed below.

1. _____ profesor
2. _____ chicas
3. _____ estudiantes
4. _____ muchacha

5. _____ señor
6. _____ profesoras
7. _____ muchachos
8. _____ señora

■ Los infinitivos

The infinitive is sometimes called "the name of the verb"; it specifies an action or state of being. In English, the infinitive is preceded by *to: to run, to sleep, to study.*

In Spanish, all infinitives end in **-r**, and the infinitive is the form that appears in the dictionary.

Regular Verbs

The most common type of infinitive ends in **-ar**:

bail**ar**	*to dance*	estudi**ar**	*to study*
camin**ar**	*to walk*	habl**ar**	*to talk; to speak*
celebr**ar**	*to celebrate*	llam**ar**	*to call*
cocin**ar**	*to cook*	lleg**ar**	*to arrive*
descans**ar**	*to rest*	mir**ar**	*to look (at), to watch*
entr**ar**	*to enter, to go in*	trabaj**ar**	*to work*

Other infinitives end in **-er**:

aprend**er**	*to learn*	corr**er**	*to run*
beb**er**	*to drink*	hac**er**	*to do; to make*
com**er**	*to eat*	le**er**	*to read*
comprend**er**	*to understand*	sab**er**	*to know*

The third kind of infinitive ends in **-ir**:

dorm**ir**	*to sleep*	sal**ir**	*to go out, to leave*
escrib**ir**	*to write*	ven**ir**	*to come*
ir	*to go*	viv**ir**	*to live*

Practiquemos

A. Actividades. Write at least four verbs commonly associated with each place mentioned.

MODELO: **el parque**
caminar, leer, escuchar, mirar

Verbos: escuchar, leer, escribir, correr, caminar, aprender, comer, beber, dormir, cocinar, vivir, celebrar, trabajar, estudiar

1. el trabajo
2. la clase
3. la casa
4. la biblioteca *(library)*

B. Muy inteligente. Help Lucinda practice for a test by selecting a third infinitive that logically goes with the other two provided.

MODELO: estudiar, leer (hacer, *saber*)

1. escribir, leer, (beber, hablar)
2. salir, ir (llegar, llamar)
3. estudiar, aprender (correr, comprender)
4. beber, comer (celebrar, saber)
5. comer, beber (vivir, entrar)
6. escribir, hablar (estudiar, leer)
7. cocinar, comer (dormir, beber)
8. mirar, escuchar (aprender, salir)

II. Los turistas en Cuba

LECTURA

Los turistas en Cuba **van a** muchos sitios[1] interesantes. En La Habana, visitan La Plaza[2] de la Catedral, el Capitolio[3] Nacional y La Plaza de la Revolución. **Van a** restaurantes elegantes a **comer** y **van a** clubes para **escuchar** música y **bailar**. También **van al** teatro y otros sitios culturales. Casi todos **van** a la playa[4] y unas personas **van** a la Isla de la Juventud para **bucear**.[5] Y todos **tienen que visitar** la estatua[6] más antigua[7] de Cristobal Colón en las Américas.

---

[1]**sitio:** *site, place* / [2]**plaza:** *square, plaza* / [3]**capitolio:** *capitol building* / [4]**playa:** *beach* /
[5]**bucear:** *scuba dive* / [6]**estatua:** *statue* / [7]**antigua:** *old*

¿Comprendes?

1. What are some popular tourist sights in Cuba?
2. Of the sights mentioned above, which would you visit? Why?

■ El verbo *ir*

The verb **ir** means *to go* in Spanish. Like other verbs, it has six forms.

ir			
yo	**voy**	nosotros(as)	**vamos**
tú	**vas**	vosotros(as)	**vais**
Ud.		Uds.	
él	**va**	ellos	**van**
ella		ellas	

The forms of **ir** in the present tense can mean *go(es), am/is/are going,* or *do(es) go*.

Mi hermano **va** a la oficina.	My brother **is going (goes)** to the office.
Tú y yo **vamos** a clase cada noche.	You and I **go (are going)** to class every evening.
Tus primos **van** a Miami frecuentemente.	Your cousins **do go (are going)** to Miami often.

The verb **ir** is used with the preposition **a** to tell where someone or something is going (goes, does go).

El tren **va a** La Habana.   *The train **goes to** Havana.*
Mis amigas **van a**l mercado.   *My friends **are going to** the*
                                              market.

Todos **vamos a** Cuba.   *We **are all going to** Cuba.*
Voy a la biblioteca.   *I'm **going to** the library.*

Remember that **a** + **el** form the contraction **al**.

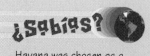

¿Sabías?

Havana was chosen as a convenient stopping point for treasure ships returning to Spain from Mexico and Peru because of its wide port.

To ask where something or someone is going, use the question word **¿adónde?**

¿Adónde va el tren?   *Where* does the train
                              go?
¿Adónde van los García?   *Where* are the Garcías
                              going?

Practiquemos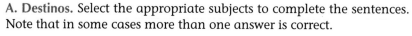

A. Destinos. Select the appropriate subjects to complete the sentences. Note that in some cases more than one answer is correct.

1. _____ voy al club.   **a.** yo   **f.** Susana y
2. _____ vas a la biblioteca. **b.** usted   Carlos
3. _____ va al café.   **c.** Marcos y yo   **g.** nosotros
4. _____ vamos a la clase.   **d.** mi mamá   **h.** ellas
5. _____ van al trabajo.   **e.** tú

B. Vacaciones. Select the proper verb form to complete the sentences and tell where these people are going on vacation.

MODELO: Lorenzo (*va, vas*) a Chile.

1. Yolanda y Tomás (vamos, van) a Lima, Perú.
2. Mi esposa y yo (vamos, van) a Santa Clara, Cuba.
3. La familia Rodríguez (va, van) a Barcelona, España.
4. Yo (voy, va) a Guantánamo, Cuba.
5. Ellas (vas, van) a Bogotá, Colombia.
6. Mario (voy, va) a Santiago, Cuba.
7. Nosotros (vamos, van) a Buenos Aires, Argentina.
8. ¿Y tú? ¿Adónde (vas, van)?

C. ¿Adónde vas? A neighbor child is always asking **¿Adónde vas?** Formulate responses using the cues provided. Be sure to use the contraction **al** when necessary.

MODELO: el mercado
          Voy al mercado.

1. el trabajo	5. el centro
2. la clase de español	6. la oficina
3. el cine	7. la biblioteca
4. la casa de mi amigo	8. el café

D. Después del trabajo. Using the subjects and places indicated, write sentences to tell where people are going today after work.

MODELO: Elena / la universidad
          Elena va a la universidad.

1. Isabel y Alfredo / el cine
2. yo / la casa de Norberto
3. Hortensia / el gimnasio
4. Norberto y yo / la clase de español
5. ustedes / el teatro
6. mi esposo y mi mamá / el centro
7. mi papá / el doctor
8. tú / el mercado

¿Adónde vas tú después del trabajo?

■ *Ir a* + infinitivo

The verb **ir** is also used to tell what someone *is going to do* in the immediate future. This expression uses a form of the verb **ir** followed by the preposition **a** and the infinitive of a verb.

Alicia y José **van a trabajar.**	*Alicia and José are going to work.*
Tú **vas a estudiar.**	*You are going to study.*
Yo **voy a comer.**	*I'm going to eat.*
Mi papá **va a descansar.**	*My dad is going to rest.*

To ask what someone is going to do, Spanish uses **¿qué?** + **ir a hacer.**

¿Qué vas a hacer?	*What are you going to do?*
¿Qué va a hacer Jacinto?	*What is Jacinto going to do?*
¿Qué voy a hacer?	*What am I going to do?*

Words used to talk about the future include the following:

mañana	*tomorrow*
mañana por la mañana	*tomorrow morning*
esta tarde	*this afternoon*
esta noche	*tonight*
la semana que viene	*next week*
el año que viene	*next year*

Practiquemos

A. Esta noche. Choose the appropriate subject(s) for each of the activities mentioned. Note that in some cases there is more than one correct answer.

MODELO: __a.,g.__ va a estudiar.

1. _____ va a mirar la tele *(TV).*
2. _____ vamos a la clase de español.
3. _____ van a comer en un café.
4. _____ voy a aprender mucho.
5. _____ vas a descansar.

a. Lucas
b. Alicia y yo
c. tú
d. mis padres
e. yo
f. tú y Rita
g. Fausto

B. El sábado. Complete the sentences to describe what the Gómez family is going to do tomorrow morning, according to Jaime Gómez.

MODELO: Mario / correr
Mario va a correr mañana por la mañana.

1. mi papá / trabajar
2. Quique y Sara / mirar televisión
3. abuelita Carmen / escribir cartas *(letters)*
4. Mamá y Araceli / cocinar
5. mi novia y yo / salir
6. mi abuelo José / leer
7. mis padres / caminar
8. tú / estudiar

Have students work in pairs and make lists of three things they will do tomorrow and three things they will do next week. Then have them compare their lists with those of another pair.

C. Lugares distintos. Everyone is going to a different place next week. Write at least three activities they will do at their destinations.

MODELO: Mis padres van al teatro la semana que viene.
a. *Van a escuchar.*
b. *Van a mirar.*
c. *Van a aprender.*

1. Vamos al trabajo la semana que viene.
a.
b.
c.
2. Voy al centro la semana que viene.
a.
b.
c.
3. Vas al club la semana que viene.
a.
b.
c.

4. Mi amiga va a la clase la semana que viene.
a.
b.
c.
5. Mis amigos van a Cuba la semana que viene.
a.
b.
c.

III. La familia cubana

LECTURA

La familia cubana, como otras familias latinas, es muy unida.[1] Muchas veces viven[2] juntos[3] abuelos y tíos con la «familia nuclear» (el padre, la madre y los hijos) típica[4] de los Estados Unidos. Las familias cubanas **tienen** muchas celebraciones y fiestas[5] para toda la familia. También **tienen** sus comidas[6] juntos y **tienen** conversaciones largas.[7]

---

[1]**unida:** *united, close* / [2]**viven:** *they live* / [3]**juntos:** *together* / [4]**típico:** *typical* / [5]**fiesta:** *party* / [6]**comida:** *meal, dinner* / [7]**largo:** *long*

¿Comprendes?

1. What characterizes the typical Cuban family?
2. How does the Cuban family differ from the typical American family? How are they similar?

■ El verbo *tener*

The verb **tener** is used to express ownership or to tell about things you have, like family members and friends, that are not really owned.

Here are the six forms of the verb **tener**:

tener			
yo	**tengo**	nosotros(as)	**tenemos**
tú	**tienes**	vosotros(as)	**tenéis**
Ud., él, ella	**tiene**	Uds., ellos, ellas	**tienen**

Tengo cuatro cuadernos.	*I have four notebooks.*
Paloma **tiene** muchas clases.	*Paloma has a lot of classes.*

Practiquemos

A. En el trabajo. Tell what people have with them at work by selecting the appropriate form of **tener** to match the subject of each sentence.

1. La Srta. Martínez y el Sr. Arena _____ calculadoras.

2. Samuel Cuevas _____ una mochila grande.

3. Yo _____ muchos bolígrafos.

4. Tú y yo _____ sillas pequeñas.

5. Tú _____ una computadora muy buena.

a. tengo

b. tienes

c. tiene

d. tenemos

e. tienen

⊃

6. Uds. _____ muchos lápices.

7. Nosotros _____ unos documentos importantes.

8. Ud. y Manuel Ortega _____ teléfonos complicados.

❖ Para hablar de la familia

Los miembros de la familia

el/la abuelo(a)	*grandfather/grandmother*
el padre, papá, papi	*father, dad*
la madre, mamá, mami	*mother, mom*
el/la hijo(a)	*son/daughter*
el/la hermano(a)	*brother/sister*
el/la tío(a)	*uncle/aunt*
el/la primo(a)	*cousin (male and female)*
el/la nieto(a)	*grandson/granddaughter*
el/la sobrino(a)	*nephew/niece*
el/la cuñado(a)	*brother-in-law/sister-in-law*
el/la esposo(a)	*husband/wife*

The masculine plural of these kinship terms can be used for both genders. **Los padres** may mean *parents* as well as *fathers,* **los tíos** may mean *uncles and aunts,* etc.

Students may be interested in more words for family members: **suegro(a)** *(father-in-law/mother-in-law),* **yerno** *(son-in-law),* **nuera** *(daughter-in-law),* **padrastro** *(stepfather),* **madrastra** *(stepmother),* **hermanastros** *(stepbrothers and stepsisters),* **hijastros** *(stepchildren),* **compañero(a)** *(partner, companion),* **padrino** *(godfather),* **madrina** *(godmother),* **ahijados** *(godchildren),* **ex-esposo(a)** *(ex-husband, ex-wife).*

Have students ask each other the names of five friends and/or family members and then report to the class.

Practiquemos

A. ¡Qué familia! You have discovered a "large family chat room" on the Internet. Tell the size of people's families by filling in the blanks with the proper form of the verb **tener.**

MODELO: Elena Montero *tiene catorce* tías. (14)

1. Aurora de la Oca _____ primos. (18)

2. Juan y Joaquín Montes de Oca _____ sobrinos. (23)

3. Mi hermana y yo _____ tíos. (19)

4. Tú _____ primas. (13)

5. Uds. _____ hijos. (12)

6. Yo _____ hermanas. (7)

7. Florentino y Ana Castellán _____ nietos. (30)

8. Berta Ruiz _____ sobrinas. (20)

B. Yo tengo… From the list of objects below write at least five sentences that indicate things you have with you. Then make a similar series describing what your instructor or your friend has with him or her. Have students share their answers with a partner.

MODELO: *Yo tengo un cuaderno.*

Objetos: un bolígrafo, un lápiz, un cuaderno, un libro, una calculadora, una pluma, una mochila, unos papeles, unas fotos, unos dólares

■ *Tener que* + **infinitivo**

To express obligation or to tell what *you have to do,* Spanish uses a form of the verb **tener** followed by **que** and the infinitive of a verb.

Tengo que trabajar.	*I have to work.*
Manuela **tiene que practicar** el piano.	*Manuela **has to practice** the piano.*
Lorenzo está cansado. **Tiene que dormir.**	*Lorenzo is tired. **He has to sleep.***

To ask what someone has to do, Spanish uses **¿qué?** + **tener que hacer.**

¿Qué tienes que hacer?	*What do you have to do?*
¿Qué tienen que hacer tus hijos?	*What do your children **have to do?***

Practiquemos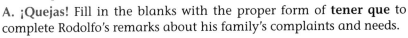

A. ¡Quejas! Fill in the blanks with the proper form of **tener que** to complete Rodolfo's remarks about his family's complaints and needs.

MODELO: Mamá *tiene que* cocinar.

1. Papá _____ trabajar.

2. Yo _____ estudiar.

3. Mis hermanas _____ practicar el piano.

4. Mi hermano y yo _____ correr.

5. Mi mamá y mi papá _____ dormir más.

6. Y tú, ¿qué _____ hacer?

¿Sabías?

Cuba is the largest of the Caribbean islands. Along with Hispaniola and Puerto Rico, it is part of the Greater Antilles.

B. El fin de semana. Complete Maribel's description of what she and her family have to do this weekend by supplying the correct form of **tener que.**

MODELO: mi hermano / leer un artículo
          Mi hermano tiene que leer un artículo.

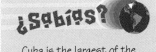

Y tú, ¿qué tienes que hacer?

1. mi esposo / trabajar
2. mi hijo y su amiga / salir
3. mi hija Martina y yo / cocinar

4. yo / descansar
5. mis hijas / estudiar
6. Y Ud., ¿qué / hacer?

C. De negocios. Everyone has to travel on business. Tell which capital and country these people must visit. (Check the map in the front of the book.)

MODELO: el señor Flores / Santiago
          El señor Flores *tiene que ir a* Santiago, Chile.

1. Alberto Coto / Madrid
2. yo / Buenos Aires
3. Verónica Llano y Horacio Luna / La Habana
4. tú y Marcela / México, D.F.
5. Gilberto Márquez y yo / Lima
6. tú / San Salvador

■ El verbo *hay*

The verb form **hay** (from **haber**) means *there is* or *there are*. It is used with one subject (singular) or more than one (plural).

Hay muchos estudiantes en la clase.	***There are** a lot of students in the class.*
Hay un libro en la mesa.	***There is** a book on the table.*
Hay unas sillas en la clase.	***There are** some chairs in the class.*

Practiquemos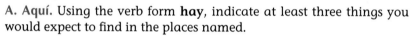

A. Aquí. Using the verb form **hay**, indicate at least three things you would expect to find in the places named.

MODELO: En la librería *(bookstore) hay bolígrafos, papel y libros.*

1. En la oficina _____.

2. En la biblioteca _____.

3. En la clase _____.

4. En una mochila _____.

B. En la clase. Using the verb form **hay**, name at least five things that are in your classroom or your office.

MODELOS: *En la clase hay unas sillas.*
            En la clase hay muchos estudiantes.

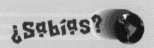 **¿Sabías?**

Baseball is the Cuban national sport. Soccer, the usual Latin favorite, comes in second, behind baseball, in Cuba.

IV. José Martí

LECTURA

Hay un cubano muy importante en la historia de **su** patria. Se llama José Martí y es poeta, escritor[1] y revolucionario, recordado[2] como un patriota que sacrificó[3] **su** vida por la independencia de **su** país. Entre[4] **sus** poemas más famosos, están los *Versos sencillos*[5] de donde viene[6] la canción "Guantanamera." Vamos a leer una estrofa[7] muy famosa.

Yo soy un hombre[8] sincero

de donde crece[9] la palma,

y antes de morirme[10] quiero[11]

echar[12] mis versos del alma.[13]

---

[1]**escritor:** writer / [2]**recordado:** remembered / [3]**sacrificó:** sacrificed / [4]**entre:** among / [5]**Versos sencillos:** Simple lines / [6]**viene:** comes / [7]**estrofa:** verse (strophe) / [8]**hombre:** man / [9]**crece:** grows / [10]**morirme:** to die / [11]**quiero:** I want / [12]**echar:** cast out (shout out) / [13]**alma:** heart, soul

¿Comprendes?

1. Why is José Martí important in Cuban history?
2. What does the line **"de donde crece la palma"** refer to?

■ Los adjetivos posesivos

Possessive adjectives identify owners (or relationships, in the case of people).

Possessive Adjectives			
mi(s)	*my*	**nuestro(a, os, as)**	*our*
tu(s)	*your (fam. sing.)*	**vuestro(a, os, as)**	*your (fam. pl.)*
su(s)	*your (form. sing.),*	**su(s)**	*your (form. pl.),*
	his, her		*their*

Like other adjectives, possessive adjectives agree with the nouns they modify.

Manuel tiene **sus** notas.   *Manuel has **his** notes.*
¿Quién es **tu** prima?   *Who is **your** cousin?*
Nuestra tía va a llegar tarde.   ***Our** aunt is going to arrive late.*

Note that the forms **su** or **sus** can mean *your, his, her,* or *their.* The meaning is usually clear from the context, but it may need to be clarified by adding **de** and the name of the owner(s).

Es **su** casa.	*It's **their** house.*
Es la casa **de Felipe y Clara.**	*It's **Felipe's and Clara's** house.*
Son **sus** documentos.	*They are **his** documents.*
Son los documentos **del profesor Sánchez.**	*They are **Professor Sánchez's** documents.*

Practiquemos

A. Nuestras familias. Identify people's family relationships, making each possessive adjective agree with the family member it modifies. Then give the meaning(s) of the phrase.

MODELO: mi / tías
          mis tías   *my aunts*

1. nuestro / abuelo
2. tu / hermanos
3. su / padres
4. mi / primo
5. su / sobrina
6. nuestro / hijas
7. tu / madre
8. nuestro / familia

B. ¿De quién? Using the information given, identify the owner of the objects.

MODELOS: Tomás tiene un carro.
           Es su carro.

           Tengo dos cuadernos muy grandes.
           Son mis cuadernos.

1. Verónica y yo tenemos muchos bolígrafos.
2. Laura tiene una casa grande.
3. Everardo y Lisa tienen unos libros de arte.
4. Tú tienes una computadora avanzada.
5. Yo tengo unos papeles importantes.
6. Inés y Marisa tienen una oficina muy bonita.
7. Tú y Alberto tienen un trabajo muy bueno.
8. Nosotros tenemos una clase interesante.

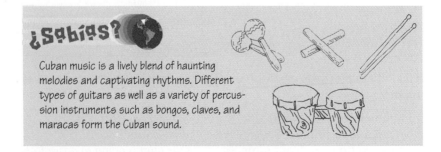

¿Sabías?

Cuban music is a lively blend of haunting melodies and captivating rhythms. Different types of guitars as well as a variety of percussion instruments such as bongos, claves, and maracas form the Cuban sound.

C. No comprendo. Clarify the following potentially ambiguous sentences.

MODELO: Es su casa. (David y Lisa)
Es la casa de David y Lisa.

1. Son sus libros. (Carlos)
2. Es su oficina. (Alicia)
3. Es su carro. (Mario y su hermano)
4. Son sus papeles. (el señor González)
5. Son sus sillas. (Mamá y Papá)
6. Es su cuaderno. (Juanito)

❖ Los números de 31–100

31	treinta y uno	50	cincuenta
32	treinta y dos	51, …	cincuenta y uno, …
33	treinta y tres	60	sesenta
34	treinta y cuatro	61, …	sesenta y uno, …
35	treinta y cinco	70	setenta
36	treinta y seis	71, …	setenta y uno, …
37	treinta y siete	80	ochenta
38	treinta y ocho	81, …	ochenta y uno, …
39	treinta y nueve	90	noventa
40	cuarenta	91, …	noventa y uno, …
41, …	cuarenta y uno, …	100	ciento, cien

Like **uno** and **veintiuno**, other numbers containing **uno** drop -o immediately before a masculine noun; before a feminine noun, **uno** becomes **una**. When counting, **uno** does not change.

Treinta y **un** hombres.	*Thirty-**one** men.*
Setenta y **una** calculadoras.	*Seventy-**one** calculators.*
cincuenta, cincuenta y **uno**, cincuenta y dos	*fifty, fifty-**one**, fifty-two*

The number **ciento** must be shortened before nouns. It is also frequently shortened when counting.

Cien personas.	***One hundred** people.*
Cien estudiantes.	***One hundred** students.*
noventa y nueve, cien (ciento)	*ninety-nine, **one hundred***

Practiquemos

A. A practicar. Count by fives from 30 to 100 with a partner. Then have your partner count by threes from 30 to 99. Switch roles so that both partners practice counting.

MODELO: treinta, treinta y cinco, cuarenta, …

Students may be interested in knowing *minus* (**menos**), *divided by* (**dividido por**), and *times* (**por**).

B. Problemas. Your neighbor in the second grade needs help with his addition problems. Write out the problems and answers to the following problems in words. Remember that **más** means *plus.* **Son** means *equals.*

Popular singers Gloria Estefan, Celia Cruz, and Jon Secada are Cuban.

M O D E L O :
46 + 13 = *Cuarenta y seis más trece son cincuenta y nueve.*

1. 53 + 24 =   **5.** 49 + 4 =
2. 66 + 30 =   **6.** 35 + 60 =
3. 89 + 11 =   **7.** 93 + 4 =
4. 71 + 7 =   **8.** 29 + 3 =

C. Inventario. Help the secretary of your children's school take inventory of the school supplies in the cabinet.

M O D E L O :   64 bolígrafos
Hay sesenta y cuatro bolígrafos.

1. 35 lápices finos
2. 82 bolígrafos azules *(blue)*
3. 51 plumas
4. 96 bolígrafos rojos *(red)*

5. 41 libros de arte
6. 77 lápices rojos
7. 99 cuadernos
8. 58 paquetes *(packages)* de papel

A ver si sabes

Use this self-test to see if you know the material presented in Chapter 2.

A. ¡Hola! Complete the following conversation with the appropriate forms of the verb **estar.**

JUAN: Lola, ¿cómo _____ ?

LOLA: _____ muy bien, gracias, ¿y tú?

JUAN: Regular. Tengo un examen en mi clase de español. ¿Tú _____ ocupada?

LOLA: Ay, sí. ¿Dónde _____ Linda? Ella es muy buena en la clase de español.

JUAN: Ah, sí. Linda y Ramón _____ en la cafetería.

LOLA: Pues, nosotros _____ muy cerca. ¿Vamos a la cafetería?

B. En la lista hay... Complete Arturo's list of school supplies with the verb **hay** and the appropriate form of the indefinite article.

1. _____ plumas.   **3.** _____ calculadora.

2. _____ cuaderno.   **4.** _____ lápices.

C. Planes. This weekend everyone has different plans. Complete these sentences with the appropriate form of the verb **ir** and any other word(s) required.

1. Marcos y Guillermina _____ teatro.

2. Araceli _____ casa de sus padres.

3. Yo _____ trabajo.

4. Benjamín y yo _____ cafetería.

5. ¿Tú _____ universidad?

D. Actividades. Choose an appropriate activity and tell what people will be doing in the places mentioned in **Actividad C**.

Actividades: leer, estudiar, entrar, mirar, hablar, beber

1. En el teatro, Marcos y Guillermina _____ una comedia.

2. En casa de sus padres, Araceli _____ con su familia.

3. En el trabajo, yo _____ unos papeles.

4. En la cafetería Benjamín y yo _____ café.

5. En la universidad, ¿tú _____ español?

E. El estrés. Everyone always has to do something. Fill in the blanks to indicate what people have to do in the places mentioned.

1. En la clase los estudiantes _____ estudiar.

2. En el trabajo Jorge _____ trabajar.

3. En casa, Papa y yo _____ cocinar.

4. En la cafetería yo _____ comer muy rápido.

5. En la biblioteca tú _____ leer muchos libros.

F. ¿De quién? Based on the information given, indicate whose things have been left behind after a class party.

1. Yo tengo una calculadora.   Es _____.

2. Tú tienes un bolígrafo.   Es _____.

3. Soledad tiene unos lápices.   Son _____.

4. Ustedes tienen unos papeles.   Son _____.

5. Pablo y yo tenemos unas mochilas.   Son _____.

6. Ellos tienen un diccionario.   Es _____.

G. Cuentas y más cuentas. Several invoices need to be paid right away. Write out the amount owed in words.

1. $71.00 _____ dólares   **5.** $57.00 _____ dólares

2. $33.00 _____ dólares   **6.** $42.00 _____ dólares

3. $94.00 _____ dólares   **7.** $85.00 _____ dólares

4. $69.00 _____ dólares   **8.** $78.00 _____ dólares

Preguntas culturales

1. What is the relationship between Havana and Little Havana?

2. Name at least three cultural attractions found in Cuba.

3. How are customs in the Cuban family different from the customs in a typical U.S. family?

Querido Diario. Write a journal entry describing how you plan to spend next weekend. To organize your thoughts, write three or four things you have to do and three or four other things you are going to do. Now write several sentences (five to six) telling what you have to do and what you are going to do. You might start out: **Tengo que trabajar y estudiar. Voy a escuchar música...**

Grammar: use of **tener**; future with **ir**; verbs: infinitives
Phrases: expressing compulsion and obligation
Vocabulary: leisure; food: restaurant; house: household chores; sports; traveling

Vocabulario activo

Adjetivos y adverbios

aquí	cerca	estupendo	ocupado
bien	contento	horrible	regular
cansado	en casa	lejos	terrible
casado	enfermo	mal	triste

Sustantivos (nombres)

la biblioteca	la escuela	el trabajo
el carro	el mercado	la universidad
la casa	la oficina	
el centro	el parque	

Preposiciones

a

en

La familia

el/la abuelo(a)	la madre	el/la primo(a)
el/la esposo(a)	la mamá	el/la sobrino(a)
el/la hermano(a)	el padre	el/la tío(a)
el/la hijo(a)	el papá	

Artículos indefinidos

un, una

unos, unas

Verbos (infinitivos)

aprender	comprender	estudiar	mirar
bailar	correr	hablar	saber
beber	descansar	hacer	salir
caminar	dormir	ir	tener
celebrar	entrar	leer	trabajar
cocinar	escribir	llamar	venir
comer	estar	llegar	vivir

Adverbios

mañana
mañana por la mañana
esta tarde
esta noche
la semana que viene
el año que viene

Posesivos

mi
tu
su
nuestro(a)
vuestro(a)

Verbo

hay

Web site:
http://spanishforlife.heinle.com

Transparencies A–2, A–7: México

Tijuana
Mexicali
Ensenada
Baja California Norte
Puerto Peñasco
San Quintín
Nogales
Ciudad Juárez
Sonora
Hermosillo
Chihuahua
Ojinaga
Chihuahua
Piedras Negras
Guaymas
Delicias
Coahuila
Nuevo Laredo
Santa Rosalía
Ciudad Obregón
Hidalgo del Parral
Monclova
Nuevo León
Loreto
Los Mochis
Durango
Torreón
Saltillo
Monterrey
Matamoros
Baja California Sur
Culiacán
La Paz
Sinaloa
Durango
Zacatecas
Tamaulipas
Ciudad Victoria
Cabo San Lucas
Mazatlán
Zacatecas
San Luis Potosí
Ciudad Mante
San Luis Potosí
Tampico
MÉXICO
Nayarit
Aguascalientes
Tepic
Aguascalientes
Guanajuato
Querétaro
Hidalgo
México
Guanajuato
Poza Rica
Distrito Federal
Guadalajara
Querétaro
Pachuca
Tlaxcala
Jalisco
Morelos
Morelia
México
Xalapa
Colima
Colima
Toluca
Tlaxcala
Veracruz
Manzanillo
Michoacán
Puebla
Orizaba
Cuernavaca
Puebla
Veracruz
Lázaro Cárdenas
Guerrero
Coatzacoalcos
Chilpancingo
Oaxaca
Acapulco
Oaxaca
Salina Cruz
Puerto Escondido
Uxmal
Progreso
Mérida
Chichén Itzá
Yucatán
Campeche
Quintana Roo
Chetumal
Campeche
Villahermosa
Chiapas
Tuxtla Gutiérrez
Comitán
Tapachula

MÉXICO

Nombre oficial: Estados Unidos Mexicanos

Área: 1.958.201 km^2

Población: 105.000.000

Capital: México, D.F. (Distrito Federal)

Moneda: peso

Idioma oficial: español

Fiesta nacional: 16 de septiembre,
Día de la Independencia

México y los mexicanos

Trozo antiguo reservado en la Ciudad de México

In this chapter you will learn:

GRAMMAR POINTS

- Regular present-tense verbs: **-ar**
- Stem-changing verbs (o→**ue**, u→**ue**)
- Stem-changing verbs (**e→ie**)
- Introduction to **gustar** and **encantar** + infinitive
- Direct object and personal **a**

COMMUNICATIVE FUNCTIONS

- Describe typical activities
- Tell the date
- Tell your favorite activities
- Describe the weather

VOCABULARY

- Numbers 101– . . .
- Hundreds, thousands, millions
- Days of the week, months of the year, seasons
- Formulas for telling the date
- Weather terms

I. Sobre México y los mexicanos

LECTURA

En los Estados Unidos, el grupo más numeroso de inmigrantes que hablan español es de México. Estas personas viven[1] principalmente en el suroeste del país[2] (Texas, Nuevo México, Arizona, Colorado y California), pero[3] también[4] en las ciudades[5] grandes como Chicago y Detroit.

La gente[6] de México también es diversa. La población **refleja**[7] la historia del país; incluye europeos, indígenas y mestizos (una mezcla de europeos y nativos). Los mexicanos **hablan** varias lenguas,[8] principalmente el español (casi todos los mexicanos hablan español), el nahuatl (la lengua de los aztecas) y el maya.

Los mexicanos tienen una dieta variada. Mucha comida mexicana es popular también en los Estados Unidos. Por ejemplo, muchos norteamericanos **preparan** tortillas, frijoles, arroz,[9] guacamole, tacos, tamales y tostadas en muchas partes de nuestro país.

---

[1]**vivir:** *to live* / [2]**el país:** *country* / [3]**pero:** *but* / [4]**también:** *also* / [5]**la ciudad:** *city* / [6]**la gente:** *people* / [7]**refleja:** *reflects* / [8]**la lengua:** *language, tongue* / [9]**el arroz:** *rice*

¿Comprendes?

Answer the following questions about the reading.

1. In traveling through the U.S., where would you expect to find people of Mexican heritage?
2. How would you characterize the people of Mexico?
3. What foods typical of Mexico do you eat?

■ El tiempo presente

The present tense is used to talk about situations that are happening now, events that generally happen, or things that will happen in the near future.

Hablas y no **escuchas**.	*You are talking and not **listening**.*
Como a las 2:00 de la tarde.	*I eat at 2:00 in the afternoon.*
Vamos al cine mañana.	*We're going to the movies tomorrow.*

Verbos con el infinitivo *-ar*

In Spanish, **-ar** verbs have a different verb form that corresponds to each subject, as you have seen with the verbs **ser** and **estar**. The six verb endings follow a pattern. Regular **-ar** verbs follow the pattern of the verb **mirar** *(to look [at])*.

mirar			
yo	mir**o**	nosotros(as)	mir**amos**
tú	mir**as**	vosotros(as)	mir**áis**
Ud.		Uds.	
él	mir**a**	ellos	mir**an**
ella		ellas	

Trabajo con una mexicana.	*I **work** with a Mexican woman.*
Tú **preparas** tacos.	*You **make** tacos.*
Manuel **organiza** los trabajadores.	*Manuel **organizes** the workers.*
Julia y yo **contamos** los pesos.	*Julia and I **count** the pesos.*
Uds. **trabajan** aquí, ¿no?	*You **work** here, don't you?*

Other **-ar** verbs include:

cantar	*to sing*	practicar	*to practice*
cenar	*to eat dinner*	preguntar	*to ask (a question)*
desayunar	*to eat breakfast*	preparar	*to prepare*
descansar	*to rest*	terminar	*to end, finish (terminate)*
desear	*to want, desire*	tocar	*to play (an instrument)*
escuchar	*to listen (to)*	tomar	*to drink*
pasar	*to spend, pass (time)*	visitar	*to visit*

Remind students of other **-ar** verbs they know from Chapter 2: **bailar, caminar, cocinar, entrar, estudiar, hablar, llamar, llegar, trabajar.**

Practiquemos

A. De México. You get a letter from a prospective correspondent from Mexico. Fill in the blanks with the appropriate verb form to find out what she says.

MODELO: Yo _____ *(estudio, estudia)* por la noche.
                      estudio

¡Hola!

Soy Xochitl y soy de Guadalajara. Mi vida es típica. Por la mañana yo (1) _____ (practico, practican) el piano mientras mis hermanos (2) _____ (desayunamos, desayunan) cereal con fruta y café. Yo no (3) _____ (desayuno, desayunas) porque *(because)* (4) _____ (deseo, desea) llegar temprano *(early)* al trabajo. (5) _____ (Trabajo, Trabaja) en el Banco Banamex todo el día.

Generalmente, mi papá (6) _____ (preparas, prepara) una cena deliciosa y toda la familia (7) _____ (cena, cenan) junta. Por la noche mis amigos y yo (8) _____ (miramos, miran) un vídeo o (9) _____ (bailamos, bailan) en un club.

¿Dónde (10) _____ (trabajas, trabaja) tú? ¿(11) _____ (Toco, Tocas) un instrumento musical? Escríbeme pronto.

B. Mi rutina. Berta is describing her weekly routine. To find out what she says, fill in the blanks with the approriate form of the verb.

Estoy muy ocupada. Todos los días *(Everyday),* (1) _____ (trabajar, yo) por la mañana. Frecuentemente (2) _____ (hablar, yo) con mi hermana. Ella (3) _____ (llamar) por teléfono y nosotras (4) _____ (hablar). Dos días de la semana, mi esposo (5) _____ (preparar) la comida y yo no tengo que cocinar. Los fines de semana *(On weekends)* mi esposo y yo (6) _____ (escuchar) música y (7) _____ (bailar). Mis papás (8) _____ (visitar) y (9) _____ (cenar) con nosotros los domingos. Después *(Afterward),* todos (10) _____ (descansar, nosotros) y (11) _____ (mirar) un partido de fútbol en la tele. Y tú, (12)¿ _____ (mirar) los partidos de fútbol?

C. Los fines de semana. Complete this conversation about weekend activities, using the appropriate form of the verb in parentheses that best completes the sentence.

> Tell your partner what you do on weekends. And on your day off?

EDUARDO: ¡Hola, Beatriz! ¿Qué tal?

BEATRIZ: Estupendo, gracias, porque es el fin de semana.

EDUARDO: ¿Cómo _____ (visitar, pasar) los fines de semana?

BEATRIZ: Bueno, los sábados _____ (tomar, terminar) café en la Peña Roca. A veces, _____ (preparar, tocar) la guitarra y _____ (cantar, visitar).

EDUARDO: Mi esposa y yo _____ (escuchar, terminar) música y _____ (mirar, bailar). Mis hijos solamente *(only)* _____ (tocar, mirar) la tele. Claro, los domingos por la tarde yo _____ (trabajar, desayunar).

BEATRIZ: ¡Qué lástima! *(What a shame!)* Los domingos yo _____ (estudiar, visitar) a mis padres y _____ (terminar, cenar) en casa de mis hermanos.

D. Un día típico. Complete what Cristina says about a typical day on campus with the correct form of the verbs given.

¡Hola! Yo me (1) _____ (llamar) Cristina Márquez y (2) _____ (ser) estudiante en la Universidad Nacional Autónoma de México (UNAM). Mis amigos y yo (3) _____ (estudiar) mucho porque (4) _____ (desear) sacar muy buenas notas. A veces *(Sometimes),* mis amigos Gloria y Carlos (5) _____ (desayunar) en mi casa y entonces nosotros (6) _____ (preparar) nuestra tarea de español. Nuestro amigo Enrique (7) _____ (llegar) a la UNAM temprano y (8) _____ (terminar) su tarea de biología en el laboratorio. Después de clase, Sara y yo (9) _____ (tomar) una coca en la cafetería y Carlos y Gloria (10) _____ (terminar) sus experimentos de la clase de física. Luego, mis amigos (11) _____ (descansar) después de trabajar mucho. Y tú, ¿(12) _____ (descansar) también después de las clases?

E. Entrevista. Ask your partner the following questions and then switch roles.

1. ¿Qué estudias?
2. ¿Qué comida mexicana preparas?
3. ¿Qué música escuchas?
4. ¿Qué programas de televisión miras?
5. ¿Tocas un instrumento musical? ¿Qué instrumento?

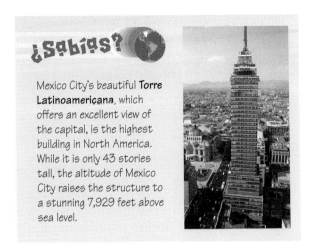

¿Sabías?

Mexico City's beautiful **Torre Latinoamericana**, which offers an excellent view of the capital, is the highest building in North America. While it is only 43 stories tall, the altitude of Mexico City raises the structure to a stunning 7,929 feet above sea level.

❖ Los números 101–...

101	ciento uno		700	setecientos
102	ciento dos		800	ochocientos
103,...	ciento tres,...		900	novecientos
200	doscientos		1.000	mil
300	trescientos		2.000	dos mil
400	cuatrocientos		1.000.000	un millón
500	quinientos		2.000.000	dos millones
600	seiscientos			

Where English uses a comma to divide hundreds from thousands and thousands from millions, Spanish uses a period: 6.000 (6,000); 3.498.000 (3,498,000). And where English uses a period to mark decimals, Spanish uses a comma: 5,32 (5.32); 49,99 (49.99).

NOTA:
The forms **quinientos, setecientos,** and **novecientos** do not follow the pattern of the others.

In Chapters 1 and 2 you learned that **un(a)** and numbers ending in -**ún(una)** use the feminine singular form when modifying a feminine noun (**una silla, veintiuna mujeres, veintiún lapices,** etc.). The same is true for numbers over 100. The feminine form of the number is used when modifying a feminine noun.

Ciento **una** personas trabajan aquí.

One hundred **one** people work here.

Ochocientas mujeres asisten al congreso.

Eight hundred women attend the congress.

Pedro tiene **doscientas** treinta y cinco pesetas.

Pedro has **two hundred** thirty-five pesetas.

Mil is invariable (singular and plural). When expressing one thousand in Spanish, the indefinite article is never used.

Necesito tres **mil** dólares.

I need three **thousand** dollars.

¿Tienes **mil** dólares?

Do you have **one (a) thousand** dollars?

Multiples of **un millón** are written in the plural form. When followed by a noun, **de** is used.

3.000.000	tres millones
10.000.000 pesos	diez millones de pesos

When the date is written or said, the year is expressed as one thousand nine hundred, etc., not nineteen hundred, etc.

1999	mil novecientos noventa y nueve
1492	mil cuatrocientos noventa y dos
2025	dos mil veinticinco

Practiquemos

A. ¡La lotería! Tell how much money you won during your week in México.

MODELO: $1.496 (pesos)
          mil cuatrocientos noventa y seis pesos

1. día 1: $4.000
2. día 2: $66.000
3. día 3: $1.000.985
4. día 4: $9.452
5. día 5: $55.000

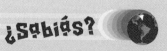
Tell how many people live in your home town or country. Put the figures on the board and compare them with those of other members of the class.

B. ¿Cuántos boletos? Now tell how many tickets were purchased each day.

MODELO: 64.000 boletos
          sesenta y cuatro mil boletos

1. día 1: 23.000 boletos
2. día 2: 1.477.124 boletos
3. día 3: 98.544 boletos
4. día 4: 5.000.000 boletos (¡Ojo!)
5. día 5: 89.657 boletos

■ Verbos con cambio en la vocal radical (*o→ue, u→ue*)

The vowel immediately preceding the verb endings in Spanish is called the stem vowel. In some Spanish verbs the stem vowel -o- becomes -ue- in all forms but **nosotros(as)** and **vosotros(as)** in the present tense. These verbs must be memorized. They are marked with (-ue-) in the Glossary at the end of the book and in some dictionaries.

almorzar *(to eat lunch)*			
yo	almuerzo	nosotros(as)	almorzamos
tú	almuerzas	vosotros(as)	almorzáis
Ud.		Uds.	
él	almuerza	ellos	almuerzan
ella		ellas	

Because of the shape of the conjugation pattern, these verbs are sometimes called *boot verbs*. It may help some students to bear this shape in mind when learning which forms change.

Nosotros **almorzamos** en el trabajo.   ***We eat lunch*** *at work.*
Ellos **almuerzan** en casa.   ***They eat lunch*** *at home.*

Other verbs that follow this pattern include:

contar	*to tell; to count*	recordar	*to remember*
costar	*to cost*	volar	*to fly*
encontrar	*to find*		

The verb **jugar** *(to play [a sport])* undergoes the same stem change, even though the stem vowel is **-u-** rather than **-o-**.

jugar			
yo	juego	nosotros(as)	jugamos
tú	juegas	vosotros(as)	jugáis
Ud.		Uds.	
él	juega	ellos	juegan
ella		ellas	

El equipo de fútbol **juega** todos los sábados.   *The soccer team **plays** every Saturday.*
Gabriela **juega** al tenis muy bien.   *Gabriela **plays** tennis very well.*

Practiquemos

A. ¿Cuánto tienes? At the end of the day, the store employees count the money. Fill in the blanks with the appropriate form of **contar**. Then write out the numbers. Remember that $ means **pesos** in México.

   1. Todos _____ el dinero.

   2. Yo _____ $979,00.

   3. Manuel _____ $986,00.

   4. Julia y Marta _____ $1.027,00.

   5. El jefe *(The boss)* _____ $1.585,00.

   6. ¿Cuánto _____ tú?

B. Vamos a jugar. Using the appropriate form of **jugar**, complete what Diego says about the sports he and his friends participate in after work.

MODELO: Mis amigos y yo *jugamos* después del trabajo.

Divide the class into teams and have each team make ten flashcards with numbers. Then have one student from each team compete to see who can say the number correctly first.

1. Yo _____ al tenis con mi novia, Yolanda.

2. Roberto y Tomás _____ al golf.

3. Alicia _____ al voleibol.

4. Todos nosotros _____ al fútbol.

5. Gloria y Susana _____ al béisbol.

6. Gonzalo _____ al ping-pong con Paula.

7. ¡Todos _____ muy bien!

8. Y tú, ¿a qué _____?

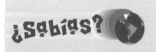
¿Sabías?

Mexicans celebrate Independence Day on September 16. On that day in 1810 Father Miguel Hidalgo, leading a group of willing but poorly armed insurgents, launched the Mexican rebellion against the oppression of the Spanish government. He shouted his **Grito de Dolores** in the town of Dolores, Guanajuato, now known as Dolores de Hidalgo in his honor.

■ Para hablar de los días de la semana

The days of the week in Spanish are all masculine and are not capitalized. Spanish calendars start the week on Monday and end on Sunday.

lunes   martes   miércoles   jueves
viernes   sábado   domingo

On Monday, on Tuesday, etc. is expressed as **el lunes, el martes**, etc. To form the plural, put **los** before the name of the day: **los lunes, los martes**, etc.

Voy al dentista **el martes**.

*I'm going to the dentist **on Tuesday**.*

Muchos mexicanos van a misa **los domingos**.

*Many Mexicans go to Mass **on Sundays**.*

As in English, the weekend days are Saturday and Sunday.

el fin de semana   *weekend*

los fines de semana   *weekends*

¿Qué vas a hacer este **fin de semana**?

*What are you going to do this **weekend**?*

Me encantan **los fines de semana**.   *I love **weekends**.*

On the weekend is expressed as **el fin de semana**; *on weekends* is expressed as **los fines de semana**.

| **El fin de semana** voy a estudiar. | *On the weekend I'm going to study.* |
| Trabajo **los fines de semana**. | *I work on weekends.* |

Practiquemos

A. Actividades típicas. Working with a partner, describe your typical activities for each day of the week.

MODELO: *Los lunes voy a mis clases.*

1. los lunes
2. los martes
3. los miércoles
4. los jueves

5. los viernes
6. los sábados
7. los domingos

■ Para hablar de los meses del año y las estaciones

As in English, the Spanish calendar begins with January and ends with December.

enero	febrero	marzo	abril	mayo
junio	julio	agosto	septiembre	octubre
noviembre	diciembre			

While the names of the months in Spanish, like the days of the week, are all masculine, they are rarely used with an article. In most countries, they are not capitalized.

| Mi cumpleaños es en **junio**. | *My birthday is in **June**.* |
| **Febrero** tiene 28 días. | ***February** has 28 days.* |

As in English, the Spanish calendar year consists of four seasons. The months that comprise each season depend on where you are in the Spanish-speaking world.

North of the Equator

La primavera consiste en los meses de marzo, abril y mayo.

El verano consiste en los meses de junio, julio y agosto.

El otoño consiste en los meses de septiembre, octubre y noviembre.

El invierno consiste en los meses de diciembre, enero y febrero.

South of the Equator

La primavera consiste en los meses de septiembre, octubre y noviembre.

El verano consiste en los meses de diciembre, enero y febrero.

El otoño consiste en los meses de marzo, abril y mayo.

El invierno consiste en los meses de junio, julio y agosto.

Practiquemos

Transparencies
H–1: **Las estaciones del año,**
H–3: **La hora y la temperatura,**
H–5: **El tiempo**

A. Meses y estaciones. Complete the following sentences with the month and season in which each holiday falls.

MODELO: El día de los Inocentes es el primero de *abril.*
Es en *la primavera.*

1. El día de la Independencia de los Estados Unidos es el 4 de
   _____. Es en _____.

2. El día de San Valentín es el 14 de _____. Es en _____.

3. El día de Labor es el primer lunes de _____. Es en _____.

4. El cumpleaños *(birthday)* de Jorge Washington es el 22 de
   _____. Es en _____.

5. El cumpleaños de Martin Luther King es el 15 de _____. Es en
   _____.

6. La Navidad es el 25 de _____. Es en _____.

7. El día de San Patricio es el 17 de _____. Es en _____.

8. El día de la Raza *(Columbus Day)* es el 12 de _____. Es en
   _____.

9. El día de la Independencia de México es el 16 de _____. Es en
   _____.

10. Mi cumpleaños es el _____ de _____. Es en _____.

■ Para hablar de las fechas

Spanish has two ways of expressing the date: **Estamos al** + number + **de** + month and **Hoy es** + day + **el** + number + **de** + month.

Estamos al 31 de marzo.   *It's March 31.*
Hoy es sábado, el 14 de marzo.   *Today is Saturday,*
                                      March 14.

To ask what the date is, two forms may be used: **¿A cuántos estamos?** and **¿Cuál es la fecha hoy?**

¿A cuántos estamos?   **Estamos al 22 de octubre.**
¿Cuál es la fecha hoy?   **Hoy es sábado, el 30**
                              de mayo.

Dates are expressed in cardinal numbers, except for *the first,* which is expressed as **el primero** rather than **el uno.**

el primero de marzo   *the first of March*
el cinco de junio   *the fifth of June*
el veintiséis de noviembre   *the twenty-sixth of*
                              November

To say the year after the day and month, add **de** + year.

México declaró independencia el
   16 de septiembre **de mil
   ochocientos diez.**

*Mexico declared indepen-
dence on September 16, 1810.*

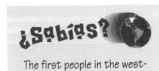

When writing out abbreviated dates in Spanish, the
order is day, month, and year (the same way it is said),
in contrast to the English practice of writing month,
day, and year.

   2-12-75 (2 de diciembre de 1975)
   12-2-75 (December 2, 1975)

Practiquemos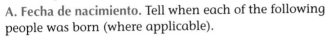

A. **Fecha de nacimiento.** Tell when each of the following
people was born (where applicable).

1. yo
2. mi mamá
3. mi gato
4. mi hermano(a)
5. mi hijo(a)
6. mi esposo(a)
7. mi amigo(a)
8. mi tío(a)

B. **Fechas memorables.** Match each event with the correct date. Then
say and write out the date in Spanish.

1. Ludvig von Beethoven is born.
2. Mexico declares independence from
   Spain.
3. Princess Diana (of Wales) dies.
4. Neil Armstrong walks on the moon.
5. Mexicans are victorious at the
   Alamo.
6. The U.S. Civil War ends.
7. The U.S. Declaration of Independence is signed.
8. The last episode of Seinfeld is aired.

a. July 4, 1776
b. March 6, 1836
c. July 21, 1969
d. May 14, 1998
e. April 9, 1865
f. August 31, 1997
g. September 16, 1810
h. December 16, 1770

C. **¿Cuándo?** Practice saying these dates aloud with a partner.

1. 2-18-82
2. 7-14-93
3. 12-1-72
4. 4-26-69
5. 8-12-57
6. 1-15-29
7. 9-23-40
8. 5-5-38

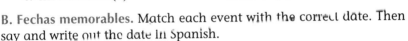

Think of three other significant
dates and ask a partner to say
why they are important.

II.   La ciudad de México

LECTURA

La Ciudad de México, la ciudad más grande[1] del mundo, tiene una población de 30 millones de habitantes. En esta ciudad enorme hay de todo: museos, cines, teatros, salones,[2] el Palacio de Bellas Artes, centros de estudio, muy buenos restaurantes de todo tipo, centros comerciales e industriales y mucho más. Muchos turistas y mexicanos **piensan** que esta ciudad es un centro de actividad y oportunidad.

El Zócalo es el centro de esta ciudad. Es una plaza muy grande rodeada de edificios históricos como la Catedral, el Templo Mayor, el Palacio Nacional y el Palacio de Gobierno. Muchas personas **comienzan** su visita en esta plaza y **terminan** en la anciana capital azteca de Tenochtitlán que ocupaba el mismo sitio del Zócalo.

La Ciudad de México nunca **cierra** sus puertas. Aquí la gente experimenta[3] la rica historia mexicana y aprecia[4] la importancia del pasado y la promesa[5] del futuro de México.

---

[1]**más grande:** largest / [2]**salones:** large halls / [3]**experimentar:** to experience / [4]**apreciar:** to appreciate / [5]**promesa:** promise

Transparency F–6: **Mapas de Madrid, San Juan, México, D.F.**

¿Comprendes?

1. Why is Mexico City considered the center of activity and opportunity?
2. What is the Zócalo and where is it situated?
3. What occupied the same site as the Zócalo?

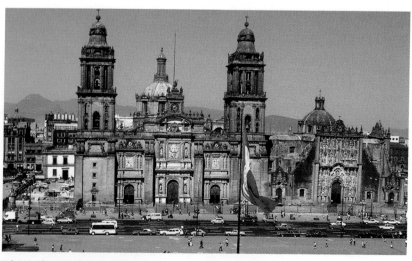

El Zocálo, Ciudad de México

■ Verbos con cambio en la vocal (e→ie) radical

In some Spanish verbs the stem vowel -e- becomes -ie- in all present tense forms except **nosotros(as)** and **vosotros(as)**. Just as with o→ue verbs, these verbs must be memorized.

pensar *(to think)*		**comenzar** *(to begin)*	
pienso	pensamos	comienzo	comenzamos
piensas	pensáis	comienzas	comenzáis
piensa	piensan	comienza	comienzan

Pienso que es importante.	*I think that it is important.*
La clase **comienza** a las 6:00.	*Class begins at 6:00.*

Other verbs that follow this pattern include: **cerrar** *(to close)* and **empezar** *(to begin)*.

Practiquemos

A. Un día típico. Using the appropriate form of **comenzar**, complete what Elenita says about what time she and her family begin their various daily activities.

Have students describe their typical day, first as a whole class and then in pairs.

MODELO: Mamá *comienza* a preparar el desayuno a las 7:30.

1. Mamá _____ a tomar café a las 8:00.

2. Papá y Alberto _____ a trabajar a las 9:00.

3. Mis hermanos _____ a estudiar a las 9:00 también.

4. Mi familia y yo _____ a almorzar a la 1:00.

5. Cristina _____ a preparar la tarea a las 4:00.

6. Yo _____ a jugar al fútbol a las 4:30.

7. Mamá y papá _____ a descansar a las 6:00.

8. Toda la familia _____ a cenar a las 8:00.

B. En la clase de español. Complete the following description of a Spanish class with the appropriate form of each verb.

La clase (1) _____ (empezar) a las 8:00. La profesora (2) _____ (cerrar) la puerta y (3) _____ (comenzar) la lección. Ella explica las formas de los verbos. Los estudiantes (4) _____ (pensar) mucho durante la clase. Ramón es un buen estudiante; (5) _____ (recordar) todas las formas. ¡Qué lástima! Yo no (6) _____ (recordar) mucho aunque *(although)* estudio todos los días. Todos nosotros (7) _____ (pensar) que los verbos son difíciles. ¿Y tú? ¿ (8) _____ (Recordar) todas las formas?

III. La salud mexicana

taco

tostada

torta

Transparency
B–5: **Comida
mexicana**

LECTURA

Los mexicanos, como todas las personas contemporáneas, se preocupan[1] por la salud.[2] Caminan, toman mucha agua y practican deportes. Pero los mexicanos también tienen una solución única:[3] la vitamina T. ¿Qué es la vitamina T? Tiene tres ingredientes: tacos, tostadas y tortas. ¿Te gusta tomar la vitamina T?

[1]**preocupado:** *worried, concerned* / [2]**la salud:** *health* / [3]**único:** *unique*

¿Comprendes?

1. What concern do Mexicans share with other people?
2. Do you think that "vitamin T" is serious or tongue-in-cheek? Why?

■ Introducción a *gustar, encantar: me gusta, te gusta, me encanta, te encanta*

Only **me gusta** and **te gusta** + infinitive are presented here. The complete use of the verb will be presented in Chapter 10. Indirect object pronouns are introduced in Chapter 7.

To say *I like to (do something)* in Spanish you use the phrase **me gusta** + infinitive.

Me gusta estudiar.	*I like to study.*
Me gusta comer.	*I like to eat.*

To say what you don't like, put **no** before **me gusta**.

No me gusta estudiar en la biblioteca.	*I don't like to study* in the library.
No me gusta cocinar.	*I don't like to cook.*

To tell or ask a friend what he/she likes to do, use **te gusta** + infinitive.

¿Te gusta jugar al béisbol?	*Do you like to play* baseball?
No te gusta cenar temprano.	*You don't like to eat dinner* early.

To say that you really like or love to do something, use **me encanta +** infinitive.

Me encanta ir al cine.   *I love to go to the movies.*
Me encanta comer comida   *I love to eat Mexican food.*
   mexicana.

Practiquemos

A. ¡Me gusta! Tell what you like or don't like to do in the various seasons. Then compare your answers with a partner.

MODELO: En invierno *no me gusta* nadar.
             o En invierno *me gusta* nadar.

1. En invierno _____ esquiar.

2. En otoño _____ estar en casa con mi familia.

3. Después del trabajo en primavera _____ tomar café al aire libre *(outdoors)*.

4. Los fines de semana en verano _____ ir a fiestas.

5. Los sábados en verano _____ ir a la discoteca.

6. Después de clases en primavera _____ trabajar en mi jardín *(garden)*.

7. En las noches en otoño _____ tomar chocolate.

8. En invierno _____ mirar la tele y descansar.

> **NOTA:**
> These expressions (**me gusta, me encanta,** etc.) do not use the subject pronouns **yo** or **tú.** They are similar to the English verbs to interest, to appeal, to disgust.
>
> That interests me.
> Sewing doesn't appeal to me.
> Eating squid disgusts me.

B. Es mi favorito. Tell how you feel about the following after-work activities.

MODELO: cenar en un restaurante mexicano
             Me gusta cenar en un restaurante mexicano.
             o *Me encanta cenar en un restaurante mexicano.*
             o *No me gusta cenar en un restaurante mexicano.*

1. mirar la tele
2. preparar la comida
3. caminar
4. hablar con los amigos
5. tomar café
6. escuchar música
7. descansar
8. tomar vino

Transparency
G–5: **Pasatiempos**

As a follow-up activity, have students ask a partner if he/she shares the same preferences.

C. Mis actividades favoritas. Describe yourself by writing at least eight things you like or don't like to do. You may select activities from the vocabulary list or choose other activities. Share your list with a partner.

> Write a list of at least eight questions, asking what your partner likes (or doesn't like) to do. Then ask the questions.

MODELO: *Me gusta mirar la tele.*
             o *No me gusta mirar la tele.*

mirar la tele
escuchar música
caminar
bailar
preparar la comida
estudiar
trabajar

cenar en un restaurante
cantar en público
tomar vino
hablar con mis amigos
ir a una fiesta
tomar café
¿ ?

¿Sabías?

Mole, a typical Mexican sauce, consists of a variety of condiments and **chiles picantes** (hot peppers). It is usually put in stews or used to marinate meats. **Mole poblano** calls for the unusual combination of chocolate with spices and chilis. This type of **mole** is frequently served over poultry.

■ El complemento directo

The direct object of a verb tells who or what is affected by the action of the verb. In the sentence *I read that book last week*, the phrase *that book* tells *what* was read. In the sentence *I saw Cynthia again*, the word *Cynthia* tells *who* was seen.

Estudio **español**.
Toman **mucho café**.

*I study **Spanish**.*
*They drink **a lot of coffee**.*

Practiquemos

A. Los Pérez. Identify the direct object in the following sentences that describe the Pérez family's typical activities.

MODELO: Miran *la televisión* todas las noches.

1. Pepe y Cristina tienen una clase a las 2:00 de la tarde.
2. Elena escucha discos de música rock después de las clases.
3. Papá toca la guitarra en un club los viernes y sábados.
4. Papá termina su trabajo a las 2:00 de la mañana.
5. Los hijos preparan el desayuno los fines de semana.

■ La *a* personal

In Spanish the preposition **a** is placed before a direct object that refers to specific people or to a pet.

¿Invitas **a mi hermano**?
Amo **a mi perro**, Gordito.

*Will you invite **my brother**?*
*I love **my dog**, Chubby.*

The personal **a** is not used before direct objects that refer to things or to nonspecific people.

Escucho **discos compactos** de México.
Buscan **la información**.

Buscamos **una profesora** de francés.

*I listen to **CDs** from Mexico.*

*They are looking for **the information**.*

*We are looking for **a French professor**.*

Practiquemos 🖉

A. La clase de español. Read the following sentences and insert **a** before the direct object where appropriate. Be sure you can explain your answers.

MODELOS: Mario canta _____ una canción bonita.
(no **a** because **canción** isn't a person)

La profesora saluda *a* los estudiantes.
(**a** needed because **estudiantes** are specific people)

1. Escuchamos _____ español en la clase.

2. Estudio _____ muchas palabras nuevas.

3. Alicia mira _____ su compañero de clase.

4. La profesora prepara _____ un examen.

5. Los estudiantes tienen que escribir _____ informes.

6. En casa, Alicia llama _____ su compañero de clase.

7. Ella no empieza _____ la tarea.

8. Su compañero prepara _____ todas las respuestas.

9. Alicia invita _____ su compañero a estudiar en su casa.

10. El compañero visita _____ Alicia.

¿Sabías? 🌐

In many parts of the Spanish-speaking world, the word **torta** means cake. In Mexico, however, a **torta** is a sandwich consisting of a bread roll, a creamy condiment, and sandwich filling such as meat or cheese, frequently accented with avocado and sauces.

IV. La geografía y el clima de México

LECTURA

México es un país muy variado. La geografía es muy variada: hay montañas muy altas, mesetas, costas, selvas[1] tropicales y desiertos. El clima cambia[2] de región en región. En las selvas **hace calor** y **hay mucha humedad**. En los desiertos **hace mucho calor** y es muy árido. En las montañas y las mesetas el clima es templado.[3] El clima también varía según las estaciones del año: la primavera y el verano son húmedos con **lluvias**[4] frecuentes. El otoño y el invierno son más secos.[5]

[1]**la selva:** jungle / [2]**cambiar:** change / [3]**templado:** temperate / [4]**la lluvia:** rain / [5]**seco:** dry

Transparency
A–2: **México y La América Central**

¿Comprendes?

1. What geographic features does Mexico share with the United States?
2. Assuming that Mexico City enjoys the climate described in the article, how does the weather of Mexico City differ from that of New York City?

■ El tiempo

Spanish uses the third-person singular of the verb **hacer** + noun to describe most weather conditions.

¿Qué **tiempo hace** hoy?	*What **is the weather like** today?*
Hace (mucho) frío.	*It's (very) cold.*
Hace fresco.	*It's cool.*
Hace (mucho) calor.	*It's (very) hot.*
Hace sol.	*It's sunny.*
Hace (mucho) viento.	*It's (very) windy.*
Hace mal/buen tiempo.	*It's bad/good weather.*

There are also some other verbs that describe the weather. They are used only in the third-person singular form.

Llueve.	*It's raining.*
Va a llover.	*It's going to rain.*
Llovizna.	*It's drizzling.*
Va a lloviznar.	*It's going to drizzle.*
Nieva.	*It's snowing.*
Va a nevar.	*It's going to snow.*
Hay neblina.	*It's foggy.*

> ¿Qué tiempo hace esta semana? Y, ¿qué tiempo hace en tu estación favorita?

Practiquemos

A. ¡Qué tiempo! Make drawings of the following weather phenomena. (Use your imagination to depict the weather or the effects of the weather. Drawing ability doesn't count.) Ask a classmate to identify the weather conditions. Then identify your classmate's drawings.

1. rain or drizzle
2. snow falling
3. leaves blowing

4. a cold scene
5. the sun shining
6. a very hot day

B. ¿Y tú? Ask what your partner likes to do in various weather conditions, using **¿Te gusta... ?** Then tell whether or not you enjoy the same activity.

MODELO:
Tú: Cuando llueve ¿*te gusta* nadar?
COMPAÑERO(A): *No me gusta nadar.*
o Me gusta nadar.

TÚ.   *No me gusta nadar tampoco* (either).
       o *Me gusta nadar también* (too).

1. Cuando hace buen tiempo, ¿ _____ estudiar?

2. Cuando hace calor, ¿ _____ tomar café?

3. Cuando llueve, ¿ _____ trabajar en el jardín *(garden)*?

4. Cuando nieva, ¿ _____ esquiar en las montañas?

C. ¿En qué estación hace… ? Describe the typical weather in the season indicated and write an activity that you might do in that weather. Then ask a classmate what he/she does in that season.

M O D E L O :   En el verano *hace calor* y yo *nado.*

1. En el invierno, _____ y yo _____.

2. En el otoño, _____ y yo _____.

3. En la primavera, _____ y yo _____.

4. En el verano, _____ y yo _____.

D ¿   y en Chicago? A Mexican tourist wants to know about the weather in the United States. What does he/she ask you? How do you reply?

As a follow-up activity, have students work in pairs to ask and answer the questions.

M O D E L O :   San Francisco / verano
                 ¿Qué tiempo hace en San Francisco en el verano?

1. Miami / invierno
2. Phoenix / verano
3. Kansas City / otoño
4. Seattle / verano

5. Fargo / invierno
6. Boston / primavera
7. Washington, D.C. / otoño
8. Memphis / primavera

A ver si sabes

Use this self-test to see if you know the material presented in Chapter 3.

A. ¡De viaje! Write out the altitude of these Mexican tourist destinations in Spanish.

1. Querétaro: 1.836 metros (3.000 pies)
2. Pico de Orizaba: 5.700 metros (18.700 pies)
3. Uxmal: 12 metros (39 pies)
4. Ciudad de México: 2.240 metros (7.349 pies)

B. Fechas de nacimiento. Write out these birth dates in Spanish and tell in which season they occur.

1. Laura Pérez García: Saturday, February 26, 1911
2. Jorge Ramón López Bustos: Tuesday, April 18, 1952
3. Anita Ester Huerta Chávez: Thursday, July 23, 2079
4. Pedro Vázquez Soler: Wednesday, September 29, 2014

Preguntas culturales
1. How is life in the U.S. similar to and different from life in Mexico?
2. Describe the Zócalo and explain how it represents both old and modern aspects of Mexico.

C. Después de las clases. Fill in the blank with the appropriate form of the verb in parentheses to describe typical after-class activities.

1. Esteban y Elena _____ (trabajar) en la cafetería.
2. Yo _____ (preparar) una torta de jamón.
3. Tú y yo _____ (tomar) té.
4. Alicia _____ (cocinar) la comida.
5. Tú _____ (estudiar) la lección.

D. En el parque Chapultepec. Write the appropriate form of the verb in parentheses.

1. Mario _____ (recordar) dónde está el Parque Chapultepec.
2. Las actividades _____ (comenzar) a las 11:00.
3. Todos _____ (jugar) al fútbol.
4. Paulina _____ (pensar) que _____ (jugar) bien.
5. Yo _____ (contar) los puntos.
6. Nosotros _____ (almorzar) a la 1:00.
7. El parque se _____ (cerrar) a las 9:00.

E. ¿A quién? Add the personal **a** to the sentences where necessary to complete this conversation about an upcoming party.

1. Busco _____ las invitaciones.
2. ¿Vas a invitar _____ Pedro?
3. No, porque visita _____ su tía en Monterrey.
4. ¿Vamos a escuchar _____ música?
5. No, vamos a mirar _____ un vídeo.

F. ¡Qué tiempo! Describe at least two typical weather conditions for each season in your area and tell what you like to do in that weather. Use the verbs **gustar** or **encantar** in each sentence.

1. en el invierno
2. en la primavera
3. en el verano
4. en el otoño

Querido Diario. Write a journal entry that includes today's date, today's weather conditions, and what you like to do in that type of weather. To organize your thoughts, write today's weather conditions and then cluster around them all the activities possible in this weather. Then select your favorites and write about them in your journal. You might start out: **Hoy es el...., Hace... y...., Cuando hace... me gusta...**

Grammar: verbs: present
Phrases: describing weather, stating a preference
Vocabulary: leisure

Vocabulario activo

Verbos

almorzar (o→ue)	desayunar	pasar	terminar
cantar	descansar	pensar (e→ie)	tocar
cenar	desear	practicar	tomar
comenzar (e→ie)	escuchar	preguntar	visitar
contar (o→ue)	jugar (u→ue)	preparar	

Días

el lunes	el jueves	el domingo
el martes	el viernes	el fin de semana
el miércoles	el sábado	todos los días

Otro sustantivo

la gente

Meses

enero	abril	julio	octubre
febrero	mayo	agosto	noviembre
marzo	junio	septiembre	diciembre

Otras palabras

a veces	hoy	por la mañana/	también
ayer	luego	tarde/noche	tarde
casi	mañana	siempre	temprano
después	mientras	solamente (sólo)	todavía

El tiempo

hace calor	hace sol	nieva
hace fresco	hace viento	
hace frío	llueve	

Transparencies:
A–3: **El Caribe**; A–11: Country Profiles,
Cuba, La República Dominicana

REPÚBLICA DOMINICANA

Monte Cristi · Luperón · Puerto Plata · Cabarete

Dajabón · Mao · Esperanza · Río San Juan

Santiago Rodríguez · Santiago · Pimentel · Villa Riva

HAITÍ

· Tocino · La Vega · San Francisco de Macorís · Los Robalos · Samana

Constanza · Bonao · Cotui

San Juan · San José de Ocoa · Santo Domingo · San Pedro de Macorís · Cabo Engaño

Lago Enriquillo · Neiba · Azua · San Cristóbal · Andrés

Port au Prince · Vicente Noble · Bajos de Haina

Cabral · Barahona · Baní

Pedernales · La Cienaga

Manuel Golla

▲ Parque Nacional del Este
ISLA SAONA

ISLA ESPAÑOLA

LA REPÚBLICA DOMINICANA

Nombre oficial: la República Dominicana

Área: 48.308 km^2

Población: 8.000.000

Capital: Santo Domingo

Moneda: peso ($RD)

Idioma oficial: español

Fiesta nacional: 27 de febrero,
Día de la Independencia

La República Dominicana y los dominicanos

Adolescentes bailando al ritmo de la música de músicos de calle en la Plaza mayor

In this chapter you will learn:

GRAMMAR POINTS

- Regular present-tense verbs: **-er**
- Regular present-tense verbs: **-ir**
- Verbs with an irregular first person
- The verb **oír**
- **Saber** vs. **conocer**
- **Me gustaría, te gustaría**

COMMUNICATIVE FUNCTIONS

- Discuss your daily schedule
- Make plans
- Extend, accept, and reject an invitation
- Tell time

VOCABULARY

- Entertainment and pastimes
- Time vocabulary

I. El deporte más popular

LECTURA

En la mayoría[1] de los países de habla española,[2] el deporte[3] más popular es el fútbol.[4] Pero en la República Dominicana no es así. Allí el béisbol es mucho más popular. Los niños **aprenden** a jugar al béisbol cuando **aprenden** a andar.[5] Hay ligas profesionales, y muchos jugadores norteamericanos pasan el invierno jugando al béisbol en la República Dominicana. Los aficionados[6] de béisbol **saben** que algunos de los jugadores de béisbol en las Grandes Ligas[7] de los Estados Unidos son dominicanos. En los periódicos[8] **leemos** frecuentemente sobre Pedro Martínez, el ganador[9] del Premio[10] Cy Young, y también de Sammy Sosa, que tiene más jonrones[11] que Roger Maris en una sola temporada:[12] en la temporada de 1998, Sosa pegó 66 jonrones. ¡Viva[13] el béisbol!

---

[1]**mayoría:** *majority* / [2]**de habla española:** *Spanish speaking* / [3]**deporte:** *sport* / [4]**fútbol:** *soccer* / [5]**andar:** *to walk* / [6]**aficionados:** *fans* / [7]**ligas:** *leagues* / [8]**periódicos:** *newspapers* / [9]**ganador:** *winner* / [10]**premio:** *award, prize* / [11]**jonrones:** *homeruns* / [12]**temporada:** *season* / [13]**¡Viva!:** *long live, hurray for*

¿Comprendes?

1. How are sports preferences in the Dominican Republic different from those in other Latin American countries?
2. What connections exist between the Dominican Republic and the United States?
3. Who are Pedro Martínez and Sammy Sosa?

■ Tiempo presente de los verbos *-er*

Spanish verbs whose infinitives end in **-er** have the following forms in the present tense:

comer *(to eat)*			
yo	como	nosotros(as)	comemos
tú	comes	vosotros(as)	coméis
Ud.		Uds.	
él	come	ellos	comen
ella		ellas	

Como can mean *I eat, I am eating,* or *I do eat,* according to the context.

Other **-er** verbs include:

aprender (a)	*to learn (how to)*	creer	*to believe*
beber	*to drink*	deber	*to owe; to ought to, should*
comprender	*to understand*	leer	*to read*
correr	*to run*	romper	*to break; to tear*

¿**Aprendes a** bucear en Cabarete?   ***Are you learning (how)** to scuba dive in Cabarete?*

Norma **corre** mucho cerca de la playa.   *Norma **runs** a lot near the beach.*

Comprendo un poco de español.   ***I understand** a little (bit of) Spanish.*

Bebemos muchos refrescos.   ***We drink** a lot of soft drinks.*

Practiquemos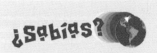

A. ¡A leer! On the way to work on the bus, everyone is reading something. Tell what people are reading by supplying the appropriate form of the verb **leer**.

1. Lorenzo y Elena _____ artículos científicos.

2. Yo _____ el periódico *(newspaper)*.

3. La profesora _____ la lección.

4. Tú _____ una novela.

5. Manuel y yo _____ las noticias *(news)*.

6. Ud. _____ el libro de español.

7. Mi hermana y sus amigas _____ revistas.

8. Todos nosotros _____ algo interesante.

¿Sabías?

The highest and lowest points in the Caribbean are both in the Dominican Republic. The highest point is **Pico Duarte** (Duarte Peak), which measures 3,175 meters (more than 10,000 feet) and the lowest point is a saltwater lake, **Lago Enriquillo**, at 27 meters below sea level.

Lago Enriquillo

❖ Para hablar de los pasatiempos

asistir a un concierto	*to attend a concert*
asistir a un partido de béisbol/ fútbol/fútbol americano/ basquetbol/voleibol	*to attend a baseball/soccer/football/ basketball/volleyball game*
bucear	*to scuba dive*
cantar en un coro	*to sing in a chorus*
comer en un restaurante	*to eat in a restaurant*

Transparencies:
G–5: **Pasatiempos**,
G–6: **Deportes (1)**,
G–7: **Deportes (2)**,
G–8: **En el lago**,
G–9: **En la playa**

dar un paseo	*to go for a stroll, walk, drive*
escuchar música	*to listen to music*
ir a la ópera	*to go to the opera*
ir a un club	*to go to a (night)club*
ir al cine	*to go to the movies*
ir al teatro	*to go to the theater*
ir de compras	*to go shopping*
leer (revistas, libros, periódicos)	*to read (magazines, books, newspapers)*
mirar un espectáculo	*to see a show*
nadar	*to swim*
navegar la red	*to surf the web*
practicar deportes (jugar al tenis, golf, etc.)	*to participate in sports (to play tennis, golf, etc.)*
tocar en una orquesta/banda	*to play in an orchestra/a band*
tocar la guitarra, el piano, etc.	*to play the guitar, the piano, etc.*
ver televisión (mirar televisión)	*to watch television*
ver un ballet	*to see a ballet*
ver un vídeo/una película	*to watch a video/a film (movie)*
visitar museos	*to visit museums*

> ¿Qué te gusta hacer en tu tiempo libre?

Practiquemos

A. Los deberes. This weekend, the following people have something they must do and something they like to do. Describe their obligations and intentions by making sentences from the three columns.

> ¿Qué debes hacer hoy?
> ¿Qué vas a hacer?

MODELO: *Elena **debe** estudiar español pero **va a** ir al cine.*

A	B	C	D	E
Paco y Lucía		estudiar español		ir al cine
Elena		preparar la comida		asistir a un concierto
Florentino y yo	deber	trabajar	ir a	dar un paseo
Uds.		practicar el piano		bucear
yo		terminar la tarea		ir de compras
María		visitar al médico		navegar la red
tú		escribir un reporte		leer una novela
tú y Federico		leer la lección		nadar

B. Algo nuevo. What new activity are these people learning how to do? Fill in the blanks with the appropriate form of **aprender + a**.

1. El señor Carrera _____ bailar merengue.

2. Mi esposo y yo _____ preparar una comida dominicana.

3. La señorita Luna y su hija _____ bucear.

4. La hija de mi jefe *(boss)* _____ leer griego *(Greek)*.

5. La profesora y los estudiantes _____ cantar una nueva canción.

6. Yo _____ tocar la guitarra.

7. Mi amiga y yo _____ cocinar bien.

8. Y tú, ¿qué _____ hacer?

C. Una carta. Finish Tina's letter to her friend, which describes her vacation at her cousin's home, by filling in the blanks with the appropriate verb form.

> You are Berta. Write back to Tina.

Querida Berta,

Estoy tan contenta aquí. Cada día en la República Dominicana (1) _____ (comprender) más. Los otros estudiantes y yo (2) _____ (aprender) mucho en clase, pero yo (3) _____ (aprender) más en casa. La familia (4) _____ (comer) a las 2:00 de la tarde y todos (5) _____ (beber) vino con la comida, hasta yo *(even I)*. Después de comer, yo (6) _____ (deber) hacer mi tarea, pero muchas veces (7) _____ (leer) novelas o mi prima y yo (8) _____ (correr) cerca de la playa. Me encanta estar aquí.

Recibe un abrazo,

Tina

II. El alcalde de Santo Domingo

LECTURA

Santo Domingo, una ciudad donde **viven** unos dos millones de personas, es muy diversa. **Existen** barrios[1] viejos y modernos, sectores ricos[2] y pobres.[3] Y en todas partes la gente **discute** la política de la ciudad y espera[4] que el alcalde[5] resuelva[6] sus problemas. ¿Y quién es el alcalde? Es el famoso músico Johnny Ventura, estrella[7] de 100 álbumes de merengue. El merengue es una canción bailable[8] muy popular en el Caribe, y uno de los merengueros[9] más importantes es Johnny Ventura. Pero Johnny también es político y conoce los problemas de Santo Domingo. Ahora trata de **dirigir** la ciudad como **dirige** su orquesta, y espera **salir** con una ciudad que es la bella unión de muchas voces[10] distintas.

---

[1]**barrios:** *neighborhoods* / [2]**rico:** *rich* / [3]**pobre:** *poor* / [4]**esperar:** *hopes, waits, expects* / [5]**alcalde:** *mayor* / [6]**resolver:** *resolves* / [7]**estrella:** *star* / [8]**canción bailable:** *dance song* / [9]**merengueros:** *musicians who produce the merengue* / [10]**voces:** *voices*

¿Comprendes?

1. Who is the mayor of Santo Domingo?
2. What is the mayor's other job?
3. How might one consider his two jobs to be similar?

■ Tiempo presente de los verbos *-ir*

Spanish verbs whose infinitives end in -ir have the following forms in the present tense:

decidir *(to decide)*			
yo	decid**o**	nosotros(as)	decid**imos**
tú	decid**es**	vosotros(as)	decid**ís**
Ud.		Uds.	
él }	decid**e**	ellos }	decid**en**
ella		ellas	

Note that only the endings of the **nosotros(as)** and **vosotros(as)** forms of **-ir** verbs are different from the present-tense endings of **-er** verbs.

Decido can mean *I decide, I am deciding,* or *I do decide,* according to the context.

Other **-ir** verbs include:

abrir	*to open*
asistir (a)	*to attend (school, a concert)*
describir	*to describe*
dirigir	*to direct (a program, an orchestra)*
discutir	*to argue; to discuss*
escribir	*to write*
existir	*to exist*
ocurrir	*to happen, occur*
recibir	*to receive*
vivir	*to live*

> **NOTA:**
> The verb **ocurrir** is used only in the forms **ocurre** and **ocurren** because only events can occur.

Vivimos en los Estados Unidos.	*We **live** in the United States.*
Mís padres no **escriben** muchas cartas.	*My parents do not **write** many letters.*
Ahora la gente **vive** a través del Internet.	*Now people **live** through the Internet.*
Los estudiantes **asisten a** clases electrónicas.	*Students **attend** electronic classes.*
Esto **ocurre** ahora mismo.	*This **is happening** right now.*

Practiquemos

A. En mi clase... Use the appropriate form of the verbs given to write sentences describing what happens in a Spanish class.

MODELO: ¿Qué *ocurre* (ocurrir) en la clase?

1. Todos nosotros _____ (asistir) a clase.

2. La profesora _____ (dirigir) la clase.

3. Los estudiantes _____ (escribir) los párrafos.

4. Yo _____ (describir) a los otros estudiantes.

5. La profesora y los estudiantes _____ (discutir) los puntos difíciles.

6. Tú _____ (escribir) un poema.

¿Sabías?

The national currency of the Dominican Republic is the **peso**, but many merchants prefer to do business in American currency. You can pay for your hotel, your meals, and your souvenirs in dollars.

B. ¿Y tu dirección? Ask five classmates for their addresses. Then write at least five sentences that describe where people live, including the street, area, town, etc. Use as many forms of the verb **vivir** as possible.

C. Típicamente... Choose two verbs from the list for each sentence that describes things that people typically do in the places mentioned. (A verb may be used more than once, but use each one at least once.)

leer   comer   beber   escribir   correr   aprender   vivir   discutir

MODELO: En la biblioteca yo *leo y escribo.*

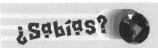

¿Sabías?

1. En casa mamá _____.

2. En el trabajo los trabajadores _____.

3. En el restaurante nosotros(as) _____.

4. En la clase tú _____.

5. En el parque yo _____.

Dominican cuisine features brown beans (**habichuelas**), rice dishes, chicken, pork, beef, and goat. Only mild spices are used in food preparation. Don't expect to find hot chilis used in Dominican cuisine!

D. ¿Qué vamos a hacer? You and a group of friends are going to spend the weekend in Cabarete, the Dominican Republic. Combine elements from the three columns to tell what two things each person will do for entertainment. Note that not all verbs can be used with all activities.

MODELO: *Yo decido ir a la discoteca y bailar el merengue.*

A	B	C
los hermanos Pérez		correr en la playa
Marta, Alma y yo		mirar un espectáculo
tú y Salvador	decidir	ir a la discoteca
Alicia y sus amigas	ir a	bailar el merengue
yo	pensar	ver una película
tú	discutir	ir al parque
Lalo	aprender a	ver un partido de béisbol
Mariana y su novio		bucear

III. La naturaleza en la República Dominicana

LECTURA

La República Dominicana está en la parte oriental[1] de la Isla Española. En el oeste[2] está Haití. Los turistas que van a la República Dominicana **conocen** un país maravilloso, no sólo por sus 870 millas de playas sino también[3] por la naturaleza de la isla que ven alrededor,[4] sobre todo en los parques nacionales. Los parques **dan** al turista una variedad de experiencias. En el Parque del Este los visitantes **ven** bosques[5] y mamíferos[6] marinos como el manatí y el delfín.[7] Otros parques incluyen lagos[8] y lagunas de agua fresca y agua salada,[9] islas, montañas y una variedad de plantas y animales raros y a veces[10] casi[11] extinguidos.[12] Los turistas que **vienen** a casa después de pasar tiempo en la República Dominicana **saben** que ya **conocen** todo un mundo tropical.

[1]**oriental:** *eastern* / [2]**oeste:** *west* / [3]**no sólo... sino también:** *not only . . . but also* / [4]**alrededor:** *around* / [5]**bosques:** *forests* / [6]**mamíferos:** *mammals* / [7]**delfín:** *dolphin* / [8]**lagos:** *lakes* / [9]**agua salada:** *salt water* / [10]**a veces:** *at times* / [11]**casi:** *almost* / [12]**extinguidos:** *extinct*

¿Comprendes?

1. What are two reasons that the Dominican Republic is a good place to visit?
2. Name at least five natural phenomena that visitors will find in the national parks.

■ Algunos verbos con formas irregulares de *yo*

Some verbs have irregular **yo** forms in the present tense. Some forms change because of Spanish spelling rules. These changes affect any verb whose infinitive ends in **-ger, -gir**. In Spanish, the letter **g** is pronounced with an **h** sound before **e** or **i** but has a hard **g** sound (as in *go*) before the letters **a**, **o**, and **u**. In order to maintain the sound of the infinitive, the **yo** form must be spelled **-jo**, not **-go**.

Other verbs of this type include **fingir** *(to pretend),* **coger** *(to get),* and **recoger** *(to pick up).*

escoger *(to choose)*			
yo	escojo	nosotros(as)	escogemos
tú	escoges	vosotros(as)	escogéis
Ud.		Uds.	
él	escoge	ellos	escogen
ella		ellas	

dirigir *(to direct)*			
yo	dirijo	nosotros(as)	dirigimos
tú	diriges	vosotros(as)	dirigís
Ud.		Uds.	
él	dirige	ellos	dirigen
ella		ellas	

Dirijo la banda de la universidad.   *I direct the university band.*
Yo **escojo** chocolate y tú **escoges** vainilla.   *I choose chocolate and you choose vanilla.*

Likewise, **c** before **e** and **i** is pronounced with an **s** sound, whereas **c** before **a**, **o**, and **u** has a **k** sound. In verbs whose infinitives end in a consonant and -**cer**, the **yo** form must end in -**zo**, not -**co**, to maintain the **s** sound of the infinitive. (Infinitives ending in a vowel and -**cer** are conjugated like **conocer**, explained below.)

vencer *(to defeat)*			
yo	ven**zo**	nosotros(as)	ven**c**emos
tú	ven**c**es	vosotros(as)	ven**c**éis
Ud.		Uds.	
él	ven**c**e	ellos	ven**c**en
ella		ellas	

Other verbs of this type include **ejercer** *(to practice [a profession])* and **coercer** *(to coerce).*

Yo siempre **venzo** a mis rivales.   *I always **defeat** my rivals.*

Other verbs with **yo** form irregularities do not follow a pattern and must be memorized:

conocer *(to know, meet)*				**dar** *(to give)*				**saber** *(to know)*			
yo	cono**zco**	nosotros(as)	conocemos	yo	doy	nosotros(as)	damos	yo	sé	nosotros(as)	sabemos
tú	conoces	vosotros(as)	conocéis	tú	das	vosotros(as)	dais	tú	sabes	vosotros(as)	sabéis
Ud.		Uds.		Ud.		Uds.		Ud.		Uds.	
él	conoce	ellos	conocen	él	da	ellos	dan	él	sabe	ellos	saben
ella		ellas		ella		ellas		ella		ellas	

salir *(to go out)*				**venir** *(to come)*				**ver** *(to see)*			
yo	sal**go**	nosotros(as)	salimos	yo	ven**go**	nosotros(as)	venimos	yo	ve**o**	nosotros(as)	vemos
tú	sales	vosotros(as)	salís	tú	vienes	vosotros(as)	venís	tú	ves	vosotros(as)	veis
Ud.		Uds.		Ud.		Uds.		Ud.		Uds.	
él	sale	ellos	salen	él	viene	ellos	vienen	él	ve	ellos	ven
ella		ellas		ella		ellas		ella		ellas	

No **conozco** al señor alto.   *I don't **know** the tall man.*

Sé que es de la República Dominicana.   *I **know** that he is from the Dominican Republic.*

Veo a muchas personas que **conozco**.   *I see many people I **know**.*

Practiquemos

A. Una carta a casa. Finish the letter that Enrique is writing to his wife from a large sales meeting by filling in the blanks with the **yo** form of each verb in parentheses.

Hola, mi querida,

Aquí todo está muy bien. (1) _____ (Ver) muchas presentaciones cada día y (2) _____ (aprender) mucho pero todavía no lo (3) _____ (saber) todo. (4) _____ (Asistir) a muchas reuniones *(meetings)* y (5) _____ (conocer) a muchas personas interesantes. Mañana (6) _____ (dar) mi presentación y luego (7) _____ (salir) con el jefe a comer muy bien en un restaurante famoso. El miércoles (8) _____ (regresar *[to return]*) a casa y te (9) _____ (ver). (10) _____ (Llegar) a las 9:00. Hasta entonces, mi amor.

Te quiero mucho, Enrique

B. Cada día. Lorenza is musing over the opportunities life presents. Finish her thoughts by filling in the blanks with the **yo** form of the appropriate verb in parentheses.

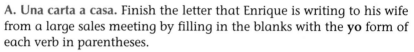
¿Cuáles son algunas cosas que tú haces todos los días? ¿Son diferentes durante la semana y el fin de semana?

Cada día...

1. _____ (comprender, comer) más español.

2. _____ (ver, venir) más cosas interesantes.

3. _____ (conocer, dar) a más personas simpáticas.

4. _____ (dar, saber) una sonrisa *(smile)* a todo el mundo.

5. _____ (saber, salir) más cosas interesantes.

6. _____ (vencer, venir) otro obstáculo.

7. _____ (salir, conocer) con mi novio guapo.

8. _____ (venir, dar) a casa cansada.

■ El verbo *oír* y verbos que terminan en *-uir*

The verb **oír** also has an irregular **yo** form along with other irregularities.

oír *(to hear)*			
yo	**oigo**	nosotros(as)	**oímos**
tú	**oyes**	vosotros(as)	**oís**
Ud.		Uds.	
él	**oye**	ellos	**oyen**
ella		ellas	

Oigo mi música favorita todos los días.	*I hear my favorite music every day.*
¿Qué **oyes**?	*What do you hear?*

The form **oye** is also used as a way of calling the attention of friends and family.

Oye, ¿tienes cinco dólares?	*Listen, do you have five dollars?*
Oye, Pepe. ¿Cómo estás?	*Hey, Pepe. How are you?*

Verbs whose infinitives end in -**uir** share the irregularities of **oír**.

construir *(to build)*			
yo	construy**o**	nosotros(as)	construimos
tú	construy**es**	vosotros(as)	construís
Ud.		Uds.	
él	construy**e**	ellos	construy**en**
ella		ellas	

Verbs ending in -**uir** include:

destruir *to destroy*   incluir *to include*   instruir *to instruct*

Los profesores **instruyen** a sus clases.	*The professors **instruct** their classes.*
Construyen muchas casas en la R. D.	*They **are building** a lot of houses in the D. R.*

Practiquemos

A. **¿Qué oyen?** What do these people hear at work and at home? Complete the sentences that describe what people hear by inserting the appropriate form of the verb **oír** and a logical word from the list.

música clásica	la televisión	la radio
música rock	un libro en casete	un programa
una conversación	una presentación	un disco compacto

MODELO: Ella *oye un libro en casete.*

1. Mi compañera y su amigo _____.
2. Yo _____.
3. El jefe _____.

4. Manuel y yo _____.
5. Tú _____.
6. Todos _____.

B. ¿Oyes algo interesante? What are people listening to? Form sentences by using items from each column and the appropriate form of the verb **oír**.

MODELO: *Mi madre oye su música favorita.*

mi madre	la televisión
yo	su música favorita
mi esposo(a)	a la profesora
mis compañeros(as)	la banda más popular
tú	una conferencia *(lecture)*
nosotros(as)	un libro en casete
mis amigos(as)	la radio

C. ¿Qué pasa? Complete the partial sentences with an appropriate verb according to the context.

construir   destruir   incluir   instruir   oír

1. Mi familia _____ a los tíos y los abuelos.

2. Los tíos _____ a mis hijos a jugar con legos.

3. Yo _____ mi música favorita y ellos juegan.

4. Mis hijos _____ una casa con legos.

5. Hijita, ¿tú _____ su casa de legos?

6. ¿Por qué no _____ todos nosotros su casa otra vez *(again)*?

IV. Sammy Sosa, un gran dominicano

LECTURA

Muchas personas **conocen** el nombre de Sammy Sosa. ¿Pero también **saben** que, además[1] de ser un famoso jardinero derecho[2] y un gran bateador,[3] es un altruista?[4] Da donaciones de dinero y equipo a hospitales y escuelas de San Pedro de Macorís, su pueblo natal.[5] Sammy Sosa **conoce** la pobreza[6] y quiere[7] ayudar[8] a otros a escaparla. Es un hombre que **sabe** pegar[9] la pelota,[10] pero también es un hombre que **sabe** ser generoso.

---

[1]**además:** *besides* / [2]**jardinero derecho:** *right fielder* / [3]**bateador:** *batter* / [4]**altruista:** *altruistic* / [5]**pueblo natal:** *home town* / [6]**pobreza:** *poverty* / [7]**querer:** *wants, loves* / [8]**ayudar:** *to help* / [9]**pegar:** *to hit* / [10]**pelota:** *ball*

¿Comprendes?

1. Why is Sammy Sosa famous?

2. Why do the people in San Pedro de Macorís appreciate him?

3. Explain what the word *altruista* means. (Do not say *altruistic*.)

■ *Saber* vs. *conocer*

Both **saber** and **conocer** mean *to know,* but they are distinct from one another.

The verb **saber** means *to know facts.*

Verónica **sabe** tu número de teléfono.	Veronica **knows** *your phone number.*
Saben mucho de la República Dominicana.	**They know** *a lot about the Dominican Republic.*

Saber also means *to know how to do something.*

Teresa **sabe** tocar el violín.	Teresa **knows how** *to play the violin.*
¿Quién **sabe** esquiar?	Who **knows how** *to ski?*

Conocer means *to know, meet,* or *to be familiar with* people, things, and places. If a *person* is known, **a** must precede the noun.

Fausto, ¿**conoces a** Susana López?	Fausto, **do you know** *Susana López?*
Conozco a la profesora Santiago.	**I know** *Professor Santiago.*
¿Uds. **conocen** Santo Domingo?	**Are you familiar with** *Santo Domingo?*

Practiquemos

A. ¿Qué saben de la RD? Tell what the following students know about the Dominican Republic.

1. Nosotros(as) _____ que se habla español en la República Dominicana.

2. Tú _____ cuál es la capital del país.

3. Yo _____ quién es el presidente.

4. Teodoro y Pablo _____ mucho sobre *(about)* la geografía.

5. ¿Quién _____ el nombre de un dominicano famoso?

6. Marta _____ el nombre. Es Sammy Sosa.

7. Marta y Pedro _____ cuál es su profesión.

8. Todos _____ que es un excelente jugador de béisbol.

B. ¿Qué saben hacer? Complete the sentences to tell what the members of the Spanish Club know how to do.

> ¿Qué sabes hacer tú que no sabe hacer tu compañero(a)?

A	B	C
Juan Carlos y Celia		tocar la guitarra
Felipe		jugar al fútbol
todos		hablar bien
Francisco y María	saber	usar la computadora
yo		bailar salsa
tú		bucear

C. Nuevos estudiantes. These new students in the university say they know certain people and places on campus. Complete the sentences as shown. Remember to use **a** with people.

MODELO: Francisco / Ana
Francisco conoce a Ana.

1. Gloria / la profesora Díaz
2. todos los estudiantes / el laboratorio de ciencias
3. ¿Uds. / el gimnasio?
4. Eva y Tomás / Oscar Pérez
5. yo / la cafetería
6. tú / el Dr. Sánchez
7. nosotros(as) / el laboratorio de lenguas
8. Alicia Uribe / la librería

Ask your classmates if they know anyone important. Find out who it is and why this person is important.

D. Buscando información. Complete the short dialogues, using the appropriate forms of **saber** or **conocer** to answer the questions. Remember to use **a** with **conocer** and people.

1. ROBERTO: Santiago, ¿ _____ cuál es la capital de la República Dominicana?
   SANTIAGO: Yo no _____ pero Gloria sí _____.
   ROBERTO: No _____ Gloria pero dicen que ella _____ mucho.

2. CLARA: Tina, ¿ _____ mi amigo, Manuel?
   TINA: Sí, yo _____ Manuel. Es muy simpático.
   CLARA: ¿ _____ tú su número de teléfono?
   TINA: No, yo no lo _____ pero Silvia sí _____.

3. RAÚL Y MARÍA ELENA: David y Paulina, ¿ _____ Uds. la ciudad de Santo Domingo?
   DAVID Y PAULINA: Sí, _____ muy bien la ciudad. ¿ _____ Uds. que está en la costa?
   RAÚL Y MARÍA ELENA: ¿De veras? *(Really?)* Debemos _____ más sobre la República Dominicana y debemos _____ todos los lugares interesantes.

❖ La hora en español

Transparency H–2: **La hora y la temperatura**

The following expressions are used when telling time in Spanish. To say the hour, use **son las** + the hour.

Son las tres.	*It's 3:00.*
Son las nueve.	*It's 9:00.*

To say the time between the hour and the half hour, say the hour + **y** + the minutes.

Son las cinco **y** veinte.	*It's 5:20.*
Son las once **y** cinco.	*It's 11:05.*

It is common to use **cuarto** and **media** for the quarter and half hours respectively.

Son las dos y **cuarto**.	*It's 2:15.*
Son las diez y **media**.	*It's 10:30.*

When telling time after the half hour, subtract the minutes from the next hour using **menos** *(minus)*.

Son las seis **menos** diez.	*It's 5:50.*
Son las diez **menos** cuarto.	*It's 9:45.*

Note that when talking about 1:00, **es** is used instead of **son**.

Es la una y cuarto.	***It's** 1:15.*
Es la una menos veinte.	***It's** 12:40.*

To say *noon,* use **mediodía** and to say *midnight,* use **medianoche**.

La clase comienza a **mediodía**	*The class starts at **noon**.*
El baile termina a **medianoche**.	*The dance ends at **midnight**.*

To express A.M. use **de la mañana**; P.M. is expressed as **de la tarde** (12:00 noon to sunset) and **de la noche** (after sunset). To say *in the morning, afternoon,* or *evening* without a specific time mentioned, use **por la mañana**, **por la tarde**, and **por la noche**.

In many countries, schedules for buses, planes, trains, theaters, museums, and the like use the twenty-four hour clock. After 12:00 noon, 13:00–24:00 are used.

El tren sale a las **catorce**.	*The train leaves at **fourteen-hundred hours** (2:00 P.M.).*
El teatro abre a las **veinte**.	*The theater opens at **twenty-hundred hours** (8:00 P.M.).*

Because of the use of digital watches and clocks, it is also common to tell time in the following manner without using **y**.

Son **las dos cuarenta**.	*It's 2:40.*
Es la **una cincuenta**.	*It's 1:50.*

To ask the time, use **¿Qué hora es?** To ask at what time something takes place, use **¿A qué hora?**

¿Qué hora es? Son las cinco y media.	***What time is it?** It's 5:30.*
¿A qué hora comes? A las siete.	*(At) **What time** do you eat? At 7:00.*

Transparency
O–2: **En la agencia de viaje**

Practiquemos

A. ¿Qué hora es? Express the following times in Spanish.

MODELO: 7:15 A.M.
          Son las siete y cuarto de la mañana.

1. 6:00 A.M.	**3.** 12:00 noon	**5.** 1:28 A.M.	**7.** 5:05 A.M.
2. 2:30 P.M.	**4.** 3:25 P.M.	**6.** 12:00 midnight	**8.** 4:45 P.M.

B. ¿A qué hora? Tell at what time you generally do the following. Give the hour and time period of the day (**de la mañana, de la tarde, de la noche**).

MODELO: eat breakfast
          a las seis y media de la mañana

1. eat lunch	**4.** study
2. get up on Saturdays	**5.** go to your first class
3. go to bed	**6.** go to work

C. Horarios. Complete the following dialogue between Samuel and Linda, using the correct time expressions.

SAMUEL: Hola, Linda. ¿Qué tal?
LINDA: Bastante bien. Oye, ¿qué hora _____?
SAMUEL: _____ (9:25).
LINDA: ¿A qué hora tienes tu clase de español?
SAMUEL: _____ (2:00 P.M.) ¿Y tú?
LINDA: ¿Yo? _____ (1:00 P.M.)
SAMUEL: ¿A qué hora es el baile mañana?
LINDA: _____ (8:00 P.M.).
SAMUEL: ¿Sabes si Julia y Ramón van al baile?
LINDA: Sí. Llegan a mi casa _____ (7:20).
SAMUEL: ¡Qué bueno! Vamos a comer algo después del baile _____ (1:00 A.M.).
LINDA: Ay, es muy tarde. Tengo que salir con Mario mañana _____ (9:00 A.M.).
SAMUEL: Está bien. Comprendo. _____ (9:35) ahora. Tengo que irme. Hasta mañana.
LINDA: Adiós. Hasta mañana.

V. Cabarete, pueblo encantador

LECTURA

Cabarete es un pueblo[1] pequeño en la costa del norte de la República Dominicana. La playa exquisita atrae[2] un turismo[3] internacional a este lugar, el cual les **encanta** a todos. El clima es encantador[4] y perfecto para todo tipo de deportes acuáticos. También Cabarete es un centro ecológico para la flora y fauna de la región.

De noche, los restaurantes, clubes y discotecas están vivos con la música del Caribe. Allí,[5] la gente baila merengue, bachata y salsa. La música es una mezcla de rock, "tecno" y reggae con los ritmos populares de las islas. **¿Te gustaría** ir a Cabarete? A mí, **me encantaría**.

---

[1]**pueblo:** *town* / [2]**atraer:** *attracts* / [3]**turismo:** *tourist trade* / [4]**encantador:** *charming, enchanting* / [5]**allí:** *there*

¿Comprendes?

1. Where is Cabarete?
2. Besides water activities, what other activities of interest does Cabarete offer?
3. If you were in Cabarete, what would you do?

■ *Me gustaría, te gustaría:* extender y aceptar o no aceptar una invitación

Spanish uses the following expressions to make requests, extend invitations, and respond politely.

Me gustaría…	*I would like to . . .*
No me gustaría…	*I wouldn't like to . . .*
(Sí) **Me encantaría…**	*(Yes)* **I would love to . . .**
Sí, **encantado(a).**	*Yes,* **I would be delighted.**
Me encantaría, pero…	**I would love to,** *but . . .*
No, gracias…	**No, thanks . . .**

Luci, ¿**te gustaría** ir al cine?	*Luci,* **would you like** *to go to the movies?*
Sí, **me encantaría** pero tengo que estudiar.	**I'd love to,** *but I have to study.*
Mario, ¿**te gustaría** bailar?	*Mario,* **would you like** *to dance?*
Encantado.	**I'd be delighted.**
No, gracias. Tengo una clase.	**No, thanks.** *I have class.*

Practiquemos

A. ¿Qué te gustaría hacer? Juan Tomás wants to know what Amalia would like to do this weekend. How does Amalia respond?

JUAN TOMÁS: Amalia, ¿te gustaría ir al baile conmigo?

AMALIA: _____.

JUAN TOMÁS: Amalia, ¿te gustaría ir al restaurante a las 7:00?

AMALIA: _____.

JUAN TOMÁS: Amalia, ¿te gustaría ir al teatro mañana?

AMALIA: _____.

JUAN TOMÁS: Amalia, ¿te gustaría ir al cine el sábado?

AMALIA: _____.

JUAN TOMÁS: Amalia, ¿te gustaría ir al parque el domingo?

AMALIA: _____.

JUAN TOMÁS: Amalia, ¿te gustaría ser mi novia?

AMALIA: _____.

B. ¡Me gustaría! Ask your partner if he/she would like to do the following. Your partner will answer.

MODELO: bailar ahora

TÚ: *¿Te gustaría bailar ahora?*
COMPAÑERO(A): *Me encantaría.*
o Me gustaría mucho.
o Me gustaría pero...

1. ir a la playa
2. vivir en Hawai
3. visitar la República Dominicana
4. aprender a bailar salsa
5. conocer al presidente de los Estados Unidos

This activity may be done in pairs. Have students compare their preferences with those of another pair.

C. Preferencias. From the list below, state three things that you would like to do and three that don't interest you, using one of these expressions: **Me gustaría, Me encantaría, No me gustaría**, and phrases from the list below.

comer pizza
tener clases difíciles
ver un vídeo
viajar al Caribe
tener mucha tarea
(homework)

comer en un restaurante elegante
ser el/la presidente(a) de los Estados Unidos
ser el/la profesor(a) de esta clase
ir a la luna *(moon)*

MODELOS: *No me gustaría tener clases difíciles.*
Me encantaría ir a la luna.

D. Sobre Cabarete. Answer the questions, based on the information you learned in the reading about Cabarete.

1. ¿Te gustaría visitar Cabarete?
2. ¿Qué te gustaría hacer allí?
3. ¿Cómo es el clima de Cabarete?
4. ¿Qué tipo de música oye la gente?
5. ¿Qué música te gustaría oír?
6. ¿Qué baile te gustaría bailar?
7. ¿Te gustaría aprender a bucear?
8. ¿Qué te gustaría ver en Cabarete?

A ver si sabes

Use this self-test to see if you know the material presented in Chapter 4.

A. El examen. Tell what the following students do to prepare for their Spanish exam. Fill in each blank with the appropriate form of the verb in parentheses.

1. Lola no _____ (comprender) muchos verbos y _____ (tener) que estudiar mucho.

2. Pepe y Santa _____ (correr) a la casa de Miguel donde todos _____ (preparar) las tareas.

3. Tú _____ (beber) una coca *(cola)* mientras _____ (aprender) los verbos.

4. Pablo y yo _____ (creer) que _____ (saber) mucho, pero la verdad *(truth)* es que _____ (tener) mucho que aprender.

5. Mariana está tan frustrada con los verbos irregulares que _____ (romper) su lápiz.

6. Y tú, ¿qué _____ (hacer) para aprender bien los verbos?

B. ¡Qué día! It is 4:00 in the afternoon and the Spanish exam is over. Tell what the students are doing now.

1. Pablo y yo _____ (escribir) la tarea para otra clase.

2. Mariana _____ (decidir) tomar una siesta.

3. Pepe y Santa _____ (describir) el examen a sus amigos.

4. Lola _____ (discutir) sus planes contigo.

5. Yo _____ (asistir) a mi otra clase.

C. ¿Qué debo hacer? Xochi is thinking about her class. Complete the sentences with the **yo** form of the verbs indicated.

1. _____ (Saber) que _____ (tener) mucho que hacer en esta clase.

2. _____ (Ver) que hay muchos detalles en este capítulo.

3. Esta clase es difícil, pero _____ (vencer) mi frustración y estudio más.

4. _____ (Oír) que los exámenes no son muy difíciles.

5. _____ (Dar) al profesor mis tareas más tarde.

6. _____ (Conocer) al amigo de Petra. Él tiene la información que necesito.

7. Siempre _____ (venir) a clase preparada y _____ (salir) contenta.

D. Todo el día. What do people hear all day? Complete the sentences with the appropriate form of the verb **oír**.

1. Carlos _____ las noticias *(news)* por la mañana.

2. Rosa y Griselda _____ la radio en el trabajo.

3. Gregorio y yo _____ música latina en clase.

4. Tú _____ la televisión por la noche.

5. Yo _____ mi programa favorito por la radio.

E. ¿Qué saben? What do the following students answer when they are asked for specific information? Use the appropriate forms of **saber** or **conocer (a)**.

1. Yo _____ su hermano pero no _____ su nombre.

2. Adela y yo _____ la ciudad de Santo Domingo pero no _____ llegar.

3. Tú no _____ cómo se llama este libro.

4. Beto _____ México y _____ cuáles son las playas más bonitas.

5. Muchos estudiantes no _____ presidente de la universidad.

F. Me gustaría pero… Complete the conversation between Tino and María, using the appropriate polite expressions to extend, accept, or decline an invitation at the times indicated.

TINO:	¿Te _____ ir a la fiesta conmigo _____ (8:00 P.M.)?
MARÍA:	Sí, me _____ pero necesito salir _____ (9:00 P.M.).
TINO:	¿Te _____ estudiar conmigo mañana _____ (1:30)?
MARÍA:	Ay, _____ encantaría pero voy a jugar al tenis _____ (2:15) con Jorge.
TINO:	Está bien. Oye, ¿qué _____ es?
MARÍA:	_____ (4:20). Ay, tengo que irme. Hasta luego.
TINO:	Adiós, María.

Querido Diario. What person (famous or not) would you like to know? What would you like to invite that person to do with you? To organize your thoughts, make a list of activities you like. Then make a list of the things you believe the other person enjoys. Now write an invitation to that person. Invite him or her to spend a day (or evening) with you and tell when you would like to do each activity. You might start out: **Querida Mariana, Me gustaría conocerte. ¿Te gustaría… ?**

Grammar: verbs: present
Phrases: inviting, accepting, declining
Vocabulary: leisure

Vocabulario activo

Verbos

abrir	dar	escribir	saber (+ *inf.*)
aprender (a)	deber	existir	salir
asistir	decidir	gustaría	vencer
beber	describir	leer	ver
comer	dirigir	ocurrir	vivir
conocer	discutir	oír	
correr	ejercer	recibir	
creer	encantaría	romper	

Otras palabras y expresiones

de la mañana	por la noche
de la noche	por la tarde
de la tarde	es la…
por la mañana	son las…

Sustantivos

la medianoche
el mediodía
la República
    Dominicana

Adjetivos

dominicano
encantado

Pasatiempos

el baile	el coro	la ópera	la película
el ballet	dar un paseo	la orquesta	el periódico
la banda	el espectáculo	el partido de	practicar deportes
bucear	ir de compras	béisbol	el restaurante
el cine	el museo	(básquetbol/fútbol/	la revista
el club	nadar	fútbol americano/	el teatro
el concierto	navegar la red	voleibol)	el tenis

Web site:
http://spanishforlife.heinle.com

Transparencies:
A–3: **El Caribe**
A–10: Country Profile: **Puerto Rico**

San Sebastián

Mayagüez

Castaner

PUERTO RICO

San Juan ★

Bayamón

Comerio

Loiza
Aldea

El Yunque ▲

Ponce

Guayama

ISLA VIEQUES

PUERTO RICO

Nombre oficial: Estado Libre Asociado de Puerto Rico

Área: 8.897 km^2

Población: 3.800.000

Capital: San Juan

Moneda: dólar de los EE.UU.
(llamado el peso)

Idioma oficial: español

Fiestas nacionales: 4 de julio, Día de la Independencia
(EE.UU.), 25 de julio, Día de la Constitución

Puerto Rico y los puertorriqueños

Vendedor ambulante con un Coca-Cola paraguas sobre su carrito en Puerto Rico

In this chapter you will learn:

GRAMMAR POINTS

- Stem-changing verbs **o→ue**
- Stem-changing verbs **e→ie**
- Stem-changing verbs **e→i**
- **Ser** vs. **estar**
- Comparatives (equality/inequality)
- Superlatives
- Indefinite and negative words

COMMUNICATIVE FUNCTIONS

- Order food
- Discuss food
- Compare things and people

VOCABULARY

- Food vocabulary

105

I. Puerto Rico: Estado Libre Asociado

LECTURA

¿Cuál es la situación política entre los Estados Unidos y Puerto Rico? Puerto Rico no es un estado de los EE.UU.[1] No es una nación independiente. Puerto Rico **tiene** otra situación: es el Estado Libre Asociado[2] de Puerto Rico. Los puertorriqueños son ciudadanos de los EE.UU. Si **quieren** viajar al continente, no necesitan ni pasaporte ni visa. Aunque[3] son ciudadanos, no pagan impuestos[4] federales. **Pueden** votar en elecciones locales, pero no en las elecciones federales. Un punto curioso[5] es que los puertorriqueños **sirven** en las fuerzas militares estadounidenses, y cuando el servicio militar es obligatorio, también **tienen** que servir.

Muchos puertorriqueños están satisfechos[6] con la situación política de la isla y **quieren** que Puerto Rico siga siendo Estado Libre Asociado. Otros **prefieren** que el país se convierta[7] en estado número 51 de los Estados Unidos. Y hay otro grupo que **prefiere** la independencia total del país. ¿Cuál es la mejor solución? Los puertorriqueños **tienen** que decidir.

---

[1]**EE.UU:** Estados Unidos / [2]**Estado Libre Asociado:** *Commonwealth* / [3]**aunque:** *although* / [4]**impuestos:** *taxes* / [5]**curioso:** *curious, interesting* / [6]**satisfechos:** *satisfied* / [7]**se convierta:** *becomes*

The comprehension questions as well as the *¿Sabías?* sections and instructions for the activities appear for the first time in Spanish in Chapter 5. If students cannot answer the questions in Spanish, then permit them to answer in English. They also may need help understanding the *¿Sabías?* sections and the instructions.

¿Comprendes?

1. ¿Cuál es la relación política entre los Estados Unidos y Puerto Rico?
2. ¿Cuáles son los «privilegios» que tienen los ciudadanos que viven en Puerto Rico?
3. ¿Están contentos los puertorriqueños de su situación política? Explica.

■ Verbos con cambios en la vocal radical (o→ue)

In the present tense of some Spanish -er and -ir verbs, the stem vowel **o** becomes **ue** in all forms but the **nosotros/as** and **vosotros/as** forms. These verbs are indicated in the dictionary and must be memorized.

poder *(to be able)*				**dormir** *(to sleep)*			
yo	puedo	nosotros(as)	podemos	yo	duermo	nosotros(as)	dormimos
tú	puedes	vosotros(as)	podéis	tú	duermes	vosotros(as)	dormís
Ud.		Uds.		Ud.		Uds.	
él	puede	ellos	pueden	él	duerme	ellos	duermen
ella		ellas		ella		ellas	

Duermo ocho horas todos los días.	*I sleep eight hours every day.*		The verbs **doler**,
¿Cuántas horas **duermes** tú?	*How many hours **do you sleep?***		**morder**, **oler**, and
Yo no **puedo** dormir más de seis.	*I can't sleep more than six.*		**torcer** are included to provide variety. They need not be memorized as active vocabulary.

Other **-er** verbs of this type include:

cocer*	*to cook*	oler‡	*to smell*
doler†	*to hurt, ache*	torcer*	*to twist*
morder	*to bite*	volver	*to return*

An **-ir** verb of this type is:

morir	*to die*

Practiquemos

A. La invitación. Nadie va con Anita al Restaurante Plaza Ponce. ¿Por qué? Llena los espacios en blanco con la forma adecuada del verbo **poder**.

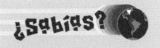

Los taínos vivían en Puerto Rico antes de la llegada de Cristóbal Colón. Eran pacíficos y cultivaban la tierra. Ya no existen hoy porque, además de morir en guerras *(wars)*, no tenían resistencia a las enfermedades *(diseases)* europeas.

1. Mario no _____ ir porque trabaja por la noche.

2. Jorge y Susana no _____ ir porque tienen otros planes.

3. Nani y yo no ___ ir porque nuestra clase termina tarde.

¿Qué puedes hacer tú? Compara tus talentos con los de tu compañero(a) de clase.

4. El novio de Anita no _____ ir porque tiene que trabajar.

5. Tú no _____ ir porque tienes que estudiar.

6. Yo no _____ ir porque asisto a la clase de español.

B. ¿Vamos a comer? Esta semana Carlota y Miguel preparan la comida en el restaurante Burgers San Juan. ¿Qué pasa? Llena los espacios en blanco con la forma adecuada del verbo indicado.

1. Carlota y Miguel _____ (cocer) las hamburguesas el miércoles.

2. La comida _____ (oler) sabrosa *(delicious)*.

3. Pero yo _____ (morder) algo duro *(something hard)*.

---

* The verbs **cocer** and **torcer** have z in the **yo** form like **vencer: cuezo, tuerzo.** The other forms have **c: cueces, cuece, cocemos, cocéis, cuecen.**

† The verb **doler** functions like the verb **gustar:**

    Me **duele** la cabeza.   *I have a headache (My head **hurts**).*
    Me **duelen** los pies.   *My feet **hurt**.*

‡ The verb **oler** means both *to emit* and *to perceive a smell.* It also has a spelling change: **h** is added before **ue:**

oler *(to smell)*	
yo **h**uelo	nosotros(as) olemos
tú **h**ueles	vosotros(as) oléis
él, ella, Ud. **h**uele	ellos, ellas, Uds. **h**uelen

4. Me _____ (doler) dos dientes *(teeth)*. (¡Ojo! **doler** must agree with **dientes**.)

5. Nadie _____ (morir) pero todos tomamos una decisión.

6. Mis amigos y yo no _____ (volver) a Burgers San Juan si Carlota y Miguel _____ (cocer) las hamburguesas.

C. Un accidente. Completa la conversación entre Carlitos y Rita con la forma adecuada de los verbos indicados.

CARLITOS: ¡Ay, mi tobillo *(ankle)*!

RITA: ¡Ay, Carlitos! Siempre _____ (torcer, tú) el tobillo. ¿_____ (poder) moverlo? ¿Te _____ (doler) el tobillo?

CARLITOS: Sí, _____ (poder, yo) moverlo, pero me _____ (doler) [el tobillo] muchísimo.

RITA: Pues, los doctores _____ (poder) ayudarte *(help you)*. Nadie _____ (morir) de un tobillo torcido.

CARLITOS: ¡Ay, me _____ (doler)!

RITA: Si _____ (dormir, tú) ahora, yo _____ (cocer) algo que va a calmarte.

CARLITOS: Bien, Mamá.

RITA: _____ (Volver, yo) en seguida *(right away)*.

❖ Para comer bien

Los alimentos			
el arroz	*rice*	el pan tostado	*toast*
el cereal	*cereal*	el pescado	*fish*
la ensalada	*salad*	el sándwich	*sandwich*
el huevo	*egg*	la sopa de tomate	*tomato soup*
la lechuga	*lettuce*	la sopa de pollo	*chicken soup*
el pan	*bread*	el tomate	*tomato*

Las verduras *(Vegetables)*			
el brócoli	*broccoli*	la papa (la patata)	*potato*
las habichuelas verdes	*green beans*	el plátano	*plantain*
el maíz	*corn*		

Las carnes *(Meats)*			
el bistec	*steak*	el jamón	*ham*
la chuleta de cerdo	*pork chop*	el pollo	*chicken*

Las frutas *(Fruit)*

el guineo	*banana*	la naranja (la china)	*orange*
la manzana	*apple*	la piña	*pineapple*
el melón	*melon (canteloupe type)*		

Postres *(Desserts)*

el flan de caramelo	*carmelized custard*
el helado	*ice cream*
la torta	*cake*

> **NOTA:** **Guineo** is the name of only one kind of banana, the type that is eaten raw in the U.S. In the tropics there are many words for the many varieties of bananas grown and eaten there.

Las bebidas *(Drinks)*

el agua mineral	*mineral water*	el refresco	*soft drink*
el café	*coffee*	el té	*tea*
el vino (tinto, blanco)	*(red, white) wine*	la leche	*milk*

Vocabulario suplemental

el ajo	*garlic*	el jugo de naranja	*orange juice*
la cebolla	*onion*	el mango	*mango*
la cerveza	*beer*	la papaya	*papaya*
la fresa	*strawberry*	el pepino	*cucumber*
la galleta	*cookie*	el queso	*cheese*
los guisantes	*peas*	la toronja	*grapefruit*
el helado de chocolate	*chocolate ice cream*	la zanahoria	*carrot*
el helado de vainilla	*vanilla ice cream*		

Practiquemos

A. A ver. ¿Cuál prefieres comer? Elige los alimentos que prefieres y forma oraciones completas.

Have students compare their preferences with a partner.

MODELO: Para el almuerzo: ¿pescado o pollo?
Prefiero pollo para el almuerzo.

Transparencies
B–2: **El desayuno y la merienda**
B–1: **Bebidas calientes y frías**

Para el desayuno:

1. ¿jugo de toronja o jugo de naranja?
2. ¿cereal o huevos?
3. ¿café o chocolate?

Para el almuerzo:

4. ¿ensalada o postre?
5. ¿vino o leche?
6. ¿pan o arroz?

Para la cena:

7. ¿sopa o ensalada?
8. ¿zanahorias o guisantes?
9. ¿bistec o jamón?
10. ¿frutas o torta?

B. El menú. Escribe un menú para el desayuno, el almuerzo y la cena. Incluye cuatro o cinco alimentos para cada comida.

DESAYUNO	ALMUERZO	CENA
_____	_____	_____
_____	_____	_____
_____	_____	_____
_____	_____	_____
_____	_____	_____

Compara tu menú con un(a) compañero(a) de clase. ¿Quién tiene la comida más nutritiva?

■ Verbos con cambios en la vocal radical *(e→ie)*

In the present tense of some Spanish -**er** and -**ir** verbs, the stem vowel **e** beomes **ie** in all but the **nosotros(as)** and **vosotros(as)** forms.

entender *(to understand)*			
yo	ent**ie**ndo	nosotros(as)	entendemos
tú	ent**ie**ndes	vosotros(as)	entendéis
Ud.		Uds.	
él	ent**ie**nde	ellos	ent**ie**nden
ella		ellas	

sentir *(to feel [sorry])*			
yo	s**ie**nto	nosotros(as)	sentimos
tú	s**ie**ntes	vosotros(as)	sentís
Ud.		Uds.	
él	s**ie**nte	ellos	s**ie**nten
ella		ellas	

querer *(to want, to wish)*			
yo	qu**ie**ro	nosotros(as)	queremos
tú	qu**ie**res	vosotros(as)	queréis
Ud.		Uds.	
él	qu**ie**re	ellos	qu**ie**ren
ella		ellas	

No **entiendo** tus ideas.	*I don't **understand** your ideas.*
Lo **siento** mucho.	*I'm very **sorry**.*

Other verbs of this type include **tener** and **venir**, which you already know, and the following:

Other **-er** verbs with this stem change include **ascender**, **descender**, and **encender**; other **-ir** verbs include **convertir** and **divertir**.

-er

| defender | *to defend* |
| perder | *to lose* |

-ir

diferir	*to differ, be different*
hervir	*to boil*
mentir	*to lie*
sugerir	*to suggest*

¿Sabías?

La china, un tipo de naranja, es muy popular en Puerto Rico. Es una fruta cítrica que llegó a Puerto Rico desde China. Por eso, se llama «china».

Practiquemos

A. Muchos idiomas. En la vida de hoy es importante saber otras lenguas. ¿Qué entienden estas personas? Forma oraciones con la forma apropiada del verbo **entender**.

M O D E L O :   Mario / árabe
Mario entiende árabe.

1. yo / portugués
2. nosotros(as) / chino
3. los estudiantes / español
4. el profesor / francés
5. y tú, ¿qué / tú?
6. yo / italiano

B. ¡Ay! Lo siento. Forma oraciones con un elemento de cada columna.

el presidente		dar exámenes
Mike Tyson		no trabajar mucho
los profesores		estar ausente
los estudiantes		no estudiar mucho
mis compañeros	sentir	mentir
de trabajo y yo		ofender a la gente
yo		hablar sin pensar
tú		¿…?

C. Un caso triste. Un amigo describe a su amigo Manuel. Completa su descripción con la forma adecuada de los verbos. Tienes que usar uno de los verbos dos veces.

> ¿Qué piensas tú? ¿Qué persona famosa debe pedir perdón por alguna ofensa? ¿Por qué?

defender   entender   mentir   perder
preferir   tener   venir

Manuel (1) _____ a clase sin estudiar. Siempre (2) _____ sus libros pero (3) _____ y dice que no (4) _____ tiempo para estudiar. Nosotros(as) (5) _____ a Manuel pero (6) _____ el tiempo *(we're wasting our time)*. Él (7) _____ no cambiar. Manuel no (8) _____ que no puede continuar así.

D. En la Casa Colón. Contesta las preguntas del mesero sobre la comida que tú y tu compañero(a) de clase van a pedir.

MODELO: Señores, ¿quieren una mesa?
Sí, queremos una mesa pequeña.

1. Señorita, ¿quiere una bebida?
2. Señor, ¿prefiere vino tinto o vino blanco?
3. Señores, ¿prefieren sopa o ensalada?
4. Señorita, ¿qué quiere comer?
5. Señorita, ¿prefiere arroz o papas?
6. Señor, ¿quiere el mismo plato?
7. Señores, ¿qué van a pedir de postre?
8. Señor, ¿prefiere el café ahora o más tarde?

As a follow-up activity, have students role-play their conversations.

II. Sabor a Puerto Rico

LECTURA

La comida de Puerto Rico es muy parecida a la comida de Cuba y la República Dominicana. **Sirven** platos con arroz, frijoles o habichuelas y carne. **Sirven** muchas especies[1] de plátano: el guineo, que comen crudo[2] cuando está maduro[3] y muchas variedades de plátano verde que **fríen**,[4] **hierven**[5] o preparan en el horno.[6] Los puertorriqueños comen un plato que se llama "pastel", que tiene yautía (una verdura tropical) y plátano verde. Todo **se envuelve**[7] en hojas[8] de guineo o plátano, como el tamal de México y Centroamérica. La dieta de Puerto Rico incluye muchas frutas y verduras tropicales. Es muy sana y ¡es riquísima!

---

[1]**especies:** *species, types* / [2]**crudo:** *raw* / [3]**maduro:** *mature, ripe* / [4]**fríen:** *they fry* /
[5]**hierven:** *they boil* / [6]**el horno:** *oven* / [7]**se envuelve:** *is wrapped* / [8]**hojas:** *leaves*

Guineos

Plátanos

¿Comprendes?

1. ¿Qué comidas son típicas en Puerto Rico?
2. ¿Cómo son diferentes los plátanos y las bananas?
3. ¿Por qué es sana la dieta de Puerto Rico?

■ Verbos con cambios en la vocal radical *(e→i)*

In the present tense of some Spanish **-ir** verbs, the stem vowel **e** becomes **i** in all forms but **nosotros(as)** and **vosotros(as)**. This change affects only **-ir** verbs. These verbs are indicated in the dictionary and must be memorized.

pedir *(to ask for; to order)*				**reír** *(to laugh)*			
yo	pido	nosotros(as)	pedimos	yo	río	nosotros(as)	reímos
tú	pides	vosotros(as)	pedís	tú	ríes	vosotros(as)	reís
Ud.		Uds.		Ud.		Uds.	
él	pide	ellos	piden	él	ríe	ellos	ríen
ella		ellas		ella		ellas	

Note that although the verb **reír** looks different, it is conjugated like the verb **pedir**, except for the accents.

> Yo siempre **pido** arroz con pollo.　　*I always **order** rice and chicken.*
> Mis amigos **ríen** mucho.　　*My friends **laugh** a lot.*

The verb **decir** belongs to this same class of verbs, but it also has an irregular **yo** form:

decir *(to say; to tell)*			
yo	digo	nosotros(as)	decimos
tú	dices	vosotros(as)	decís
Ud.		Uds.	
él	dice	ellos	dicen
ella		ellas	

¿Sabías?

La palabra inglesa **hurricane** viene de la palabra española **huracán**. La palabra española **huracán** viene de la palabra taína *hurakan*.

> Te **digo**, chico...　　*I'm telling you, man . . .*
> ¿Qué **dicen**?　　*What **are they saying**?*

Other verbs of this type include:

despedir	to send off; to fire
elegir	to choose
freír	to fry
repetir	to repeat
seguir + *present participle*	to continue (doing something)
seguir	to follow
servir	to serve
sonreír	to smile

Remind students that the **taínos** lived in Puerto Rico when the Europeans arrived.

Other verbs of this type include **conseguir** *(to get)* and **impedir** *(to impede)*. Point out that the **u** of **seguir** is only to assure the pronunciation of the hard **g**. In the yo form it is not needed, so the **yo** form is **sigo**.

Practiquemos ✎

A. ¿Qué vamos a comer? ¿Qué deciden pedir todos cuando salen al Restaurante El Dorado? Forma oraciones completas con la forma adecuada del verbo **pedir**.

> Pregunta a tres compañeros qué piden de postre en un restaurante y reporta sus respuestas a la clase. ¿Qué postre prefiere la clase?

1. papá / la sopa de pollo y arroz con pollo
2. mamá y Susana / un plato de frutas
3. mi esposa y yo / carne con verduras y una ensalada
4. para el postre, Enriquito y Paulita / flan de caramelo
5. yo / helado de chocolate
6. Y tú, ¿qué / ?

B. La despedida. Salimos a un restaurante elegante porque el jefe va de viaje por dos semanas. ¿Qué pasa? Llena los espacios en blanco con la forma adecuada de los verbos indicados.

1. Hoy nosotros(as) _____ (despedir) al jefe en el restaurante.

2. El jefe _____ (seguir) al mesero a la mejor mesa del restaurante.

3. El comité social _____ (conseguir) la mejor comida de la casa.

4. Nos _____ (servir, ellos) muy elegantemente.

5. Todos _____ (repetir [have seconds]).

6. El jefe _____ (reír) mucho y se divierte *(has a good time)*.

7. Los empleados _____ (decir) «buen viaje».

8. Todos nosotros(as) nos _____ (despedir) del jefe.

C. El Restaurante El Dorado. Completa la conversación con las formas adecuadas de los verbos indicados.

Have students role-play a restaurant scene.

RAQUEL: Ay, la comida puertorriqueña es tan sabrosa. ¿Qué _____ (querer) yo?

NORMA: Yo no _____ (entender) muy bien algunas palabras. ¿Qué _____ (sugerir), Daniel? ¿_____ (Poder) tú interpretar este plato? ¿El pastel no es postre?

DANIEL: No, el pastel _____ (tener) plátano verde y otra verdura envueltos en hojas de guineo o plátano. Pero si tú _____ (querer) comer bien ¿por qué no _____ (elegir) carne frita con plátano? Yo siempre _____ (pedir) ese plato.

NORMA: Raquel, ¿_____ (seguir) nosotros estudiando el menú? No me gusta mucho la carne.

RAQUEL: No _____ (entender, yo) los precios. Parecen muy diferentes.

DANIEL: Bueno, claro, algunos platos son más económicos que otros y algunos incluyen sopa, postre y café. Hay para todos los gustos *(tastes)*.

RAQUEL: Pues, yo _____ (creer) que el restaurante El Dorado es magnífico.

NORMA: ¿Listos? ¿_____ (Pedir, nosotros) ahora? Yo me _____ (morir) de hambre.

DANIEL: Sí. ¡A comer!

> Pregunta a tu compañero(a) qué comida pide en su restaurante favorito. Contesta las preguntas de tu compañero(a).

III. San Juan

Transparency: F–6: **Mapas de Madrid, San Juan y México, D.F.**

El Castillo de San Cristóbal

LECTURA

La capital de Puerto Rico, San Juan, **está** en el norte de la isla. **Es** el centro político y cultural del país, pero también **es** muy popular con los turistas por sus playas y casinos. San Juan **es** conocido por su Centro de Bellas Artes Luis A. Ferré, donde se presentan obras[1] de teatro, música y baile.

Viejo San Juan, un sector histórico, **está** en una pequeña isla situada en el puerto[2] de San Juan. Hay puentes[3] que conectan la isla con el resto de la ciudad.

Viejo San Juan **es** una ciudad amurallada[4] (rodeada[5] de murallas[6]) y **es** un lugar de mucho interés turístico. Las calles **son** de adoquines[7] y **son** muy angostas.[8] A los dos lados[9] de las calles **están** edificios coloniales de importancia histórica y arquitectónica.

Uno de los sitios más interesantes **es** El Morro, un castillo[10] construido[11] en el siglo[12] XVI para proteger[13] a los habitantes de los piratas y los invasores. Los muros[14] de El Morro **son** de 15 pies de grueso[15] y 150 pies de alto.[16] Dentro de los muros hay túneles para poder escapar a otro lugar **más** seguro. ¿Vamos a San Juan?

---

[1]**las obras:** *works* / [2]**el puerto:** *port* / [3]**puentes:** *bridges* / [4]**amurallada:** *walled* / [5]**rodeada de:** *surrounded by* / [6]**murallas:** *walls (of a city), ramparts* / [7]**adoquines:** *cobblestones* / [8]**angostas:** *narrow* / [9]**lados:** *sides* / [10]**el castillo:** *castle* / [11]**construido:** *constructed* / [12]**el siglo:** *century* / [13]**proteger:** *to protect* / [14]**los muros:** *walls* / [15]**15 pies de grueso:** *15-feet thick* / [16]**150 pies de alto:** *150-feet tall*

¿Comprendes?

1. ¿Dónde está la capital de Puerto Rico?
2. Describe tres características de Viejo San Juan.
3. ¿Cuántos años tiene *(How old is)* El Morro?

■ *Ser* vs. *estar*

You have learned the verbs **ser** and **estar** separately and no doubt have noticed that they both mean *to be*. Their functions, however, are quite distinct.

The verb *ser*

Defines or identifies things, people, or ideas

Puerto Rico **es** un Estado Libre Asociado.	*Puerto Rico **is** a Commonwealth.*
Puerto Rico **es** una isla.	*Puerto Rico **is** an island.*
San Juan **es** la capital.	*San Juan **is** the capital.*

Describes inherent characteristics

Puerto Rico **es** hermoso.	*Puerto Rico **is** beautiful.*
Los borinqueños **son** muy simpáticos.	*The Puerto Ricans **are** very nice.*
La isla **es** tropical.	*The island **is** tropical.*

Is used with *de* to indicate origin, material, and possession

Los puertorriqueños **son de** Puerto Rico.	*Puerto Ricans **are from** Puerto Rico.*
La isla **es de** roca y tierra.	*The island **is made of** rock and earth.*
La decisión **es de** la gente.	*The decision **belongs to** the people.*

Is used to tell time

Son las ocho y cuarto.	*It's eight-fifteen.*
Es la una menos diez.	*It's ten to one.*

The verb *estar*

Indicates the location of people or things

Puerto Rico **está** en el Caribe.	*Puerto Rico **is** in the Caribbean.*
San Juan **está** en el norte.	*San Juan **is** in the north.*

Tells the condition of people or things

Los turistas en Puerto Rico **están** contentos.	*The tourists in Puerto Rico **are** very happy.*
Todos **están** listos para todo.	*They **are** all ready for anything.*

Describes food or drink being consumed.

Esta sopa **está** sabrosa.	*This soup is tasty.*
Los frijoles **están** ricos.	*The beans are delicious.*
El café **está** horrible.	*The coffee is horrible.*

Ser vs. *estar*

When describing a person or thing, if the characteristic is inherent or defining, use **ser**. If the characteristic describes a condition or a state, use **estar**.

Susita **es** loca.	*Susita is crazy (fun, does silly things).*
La pobre **está** loca.	*The poor thing is crazy (mentally ill).*

Ser may be used to describe a particular kind of food, dish, or beverage in general, but if you are eating it, **estar** is used. If you can substitute *tastes* for *is,* you should use **estar**.

Me encanta el café. **Es** rico.	*I love coffee. It is delicious.*
Este café **está** rico. ¿Cómo lo haces?	*This coffee is/tastes delicious. How do you make it?*

 ¿Cómo se llama Puerto Rico? Para los taínos, el nombre de la isla era Borinquen (Borinken). Cristóbal Colón le dio el nombre de San Juan Bautista. Por fin, Ponce de León le dio el nombre de Puerto Rico. Los puertorriqueños de hoy todavía llaman su país Borinquen.

Practiquemos

A. Borinquen. Completa esta descripción con la forma adecuada de los verbos **ser** o **estar**.

Puerto Rico (1) _____ una isla. (2) _____ muy bonito. La isla (3) _____ en el Mar Caribe a unas 1000 millas de Miami y a unas 550 millas de Caracas, Venezuela. San Juan (4) _____ una ciudad interesante. (5) _____ la capital del país. Viejo San Juan (6) _____ en una isla pequeña en el puerto de San Juan. Las calles (7) _____ de piedras *(stones)* y (8) _____ angostas. El castillo de El Morro (9) _____ en el oeste de la isla de Viejo San Juan. (10) _____ muy cerca del mar. El Morro (11) _____ viejo pero (12) _____ en muy buenas condiciones. El castillo (13) _____ muy popular con los turistas.

B. Turistas. Jorge y Luisa están en Puerto Rico. Completa el párrafo con la forma adecuada de **ser** o **estar**.

Jorge y Luisa (1) _____ en Puerto Rico de vacaciones y el día (2) _____ perfecto. Hoy ellos (3)_____ en el Hotel Princesa. El hotel (4) _____ muy hermoso. Las habitaciones (5) _____ grandes y cómodas *(comfortable)*. Pronto (6) _____ las 2:00 de la tarde y Jorge y Luisa deciden

Have students in groups of four think of five attractions that they would like to visit in the world. Have them tell where the sites are located and describe them.

almorzar. El restaurante que (7) _____ en el
hotel (8) _____ muy elegante y la comida que
se sirve allí (9) _____ típica de Puerto Rico.
Jorge y Luisa (10) _____ muy contentos porque
Puerto Rico (11) _____ un país tan encantador.
Sus vacaciones (12) _____ fantásticas.

> ¿Qué te gustaría hacer en Puerto Rico?

C. La invitación. Los Gómez invitan a Manuel Yáñez a comer en su casa. Completa los comentarios con la forma adecuada de los verbos **ser** o **estar**.

MAMÁ: _____ tarde.

ANITA: ¿Todo _____ en la mesa?

MAMÁ: ¿Dónde _____ Daniel? _____ las 7:00 y él no _____ aquí.
          Todos los otros hijos _____ en casa.

ANITA: Todo _____ bien, Mamá.

MANUEL: ¡Ah! ¡Su casa _____ muy bonita! Y la mesa _____ muy
          grande.

MAMÁ: Aquí _____ la sopa.

MANUEL: ¡Qué rica _____ la sopa!

PAPÁ: Lo siento, mi amor, pero mi sopa _____ fría.

SARITA: ¿Dónde _____ la sal? Esta carne _____ muy sosa.

MANUEL: ¡Qué delicioso _____ este platillo! Me encanta.

MAMÁ: Este plato _____ de plátano verde con carne frita. Se llama
          carne frita con mofongo y _____ muy típica.

MANUEL: Pues, tengo que decirlo. Ud. _____ muy buena cocinera.

D. En la tienda de artesanías. Completa la conversación entre Jorge y la dependienta, usando la forma adecuada de los verbos **ser** o **estar**.

JORGE: ¿De dónde _____ esta caja *(box)*?

DEPENDIENTA: Es de la Isla Vieques.

JORGE: ¿Dónde _____ Vieques?

DEPENDIENTA: _____ al este de esta isla.

JORGE: ¿De qué _____ la caja?

DEPENDIENTA: Creo que _____ de abulón *(abalone)*
              de alguna otra concha *(shell)*.

JORGE: _____ muy bonita. ¿Cuál _____ el precio?

DEPENDIENTA: Para Ud., _____ un precio muy especial.

JORGE: Ud. _____ muy amable.

> Describe a ti mismo(a). Incluye características inherentes y tu estado físico y mental.

❖ Para describir la comida

caliente	*hot (temperature)*
frío	*cold*
rico (riquísimo)	*delicious*

Vocabulario suplemental

de chuparse los dedos	*extra delicious (finger-licking good)*
delicioso	*delicious*
picante	*hot (spicy)*
sabroso	*tasty*
salado	*salty*
soso	*tasteless, bland*

Practiquemos

A. ¡Qué comida! Termina los comentarios sobre la comida con un término adecuado.

1. Me encanta esta sopa. Está _____.
2. ¡Uf! El café está _____.
3. Mmmm. ¡Qué _____ están las verduras!
4. Pásame la sal. La carne está _____.
5. ¡Ay, ay! La salsa está muy _____.
6. Quiero más flan. Está _____.
7. Pásame el agua. Los plátanos están muy _____.
8. Mmmm. Este pollo está _____.

IV. ¿Es latino Puerto Rico?

LECTURA

Puerto Rico es **más** pequeño **que** las otras islas de habla española,[1] y está densamente poblado de ciudadanos que son muy orgullosos de su identidad. Muchas personas creen que Puerto Rico es **más** americanizado **que** otros países hispanoamericanos, pero los puertorriqueños tienen **tanto** orgullo de su herencia[2] latina **como** los otros latinos. Aunque muchas personas hablan inglés, todos hablan español, la lengua oficial. Y a pesar de[3] la situación política de la isla, ¡sí, Puerto Rico es latino!

---

[1]**de habla española:** *Spanish speaking* / [2]**herencia:** *heritage* / [3]**a pesar de:** *in spite of*

¿Comprendes?

1. ¿Qué idea tienen muchas personas de Puerto Rico?
2. ¿Cuál es la actitud *(attitude)* de los puertorriqueños?
3. ¿Qué idea tienes tú?

■ Comparisons of superiority

When making comparisons, Spanish uses the following forms.

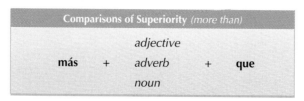

Comparisons of Superiority *(more than)*		
más +	adjective adverb noun +	**que**

Puerto Rico es **más** pequeño **que** Cuba.

*Puerto Rico is **smaller than** Cuba.*

Su casa está **más** cerca **que** mi casa.

*His house is **closer than** my house.*

Hay **más** borinqueños en la Ciudad de Nueva York **que** en San Juan.

*There are **more** more Puerto Ricans in New York City **than** in San Juan.*

Transparencies:
J–1: **Las descripciones**
J–4: **El carácter**

Practiquemos

A. Mis amigos. Mira a las personas en la clase de Felipe. Compara a sus compañeros de clase, usando **más que** y el adjetivo dado.

M O D E L O :   Raúl, Jaime (alto)
Raúl es más alto que Jaime.

1. Lorena, sus amigos (ocupado)
2. Elvira, Juan (entusiástico)
3. tú, profesor (bajo)
4. libro de español, libro de biología (corto)
5. la ensalada, el postre (grande)
6. Nené, Maribel (viejo)

■ Comparisons of inferiority

Comparisons of Inferiority *(less than)*		
menos +	*adjective* *adverb* *noun* +	**que**

Puerto Rico tiene **menos** gente que Cuba.

Mario corre **menos** rápido **que** su hija.

El Sr. Delgado pesa **menos que** su esposa.

*Puerto Rico has **fewer** people **than** Cuba.*

*Mario runs **less fast than** his daughter.*

*Mr. Delgado weighs **less than** his wife.*

Practiquemos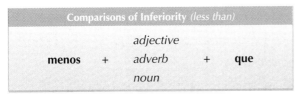

A. Comparaciones. Celia Gómez compara a su familia con la familia Sánchez. Forma comparaciones, usando **menos... que.**

M O D E L O :   casa
La casa de la familia Sánchez es menos grande que nuestra casa.

1. hijos
2. fiestas
3. personas
4. horas de trabajo

5. mascotas *(pets)*
6. plantas
7. carro
8. problemas

■ Comparisons of equality

Comparisons of Equality *(as . . . as, as much/many as)*		
tan +	*adjective* *adverb* +	**como**
tanto (a/os/as) +	*noun* +	**como**

In comparisons of nouns, **tanto** must agree with the gender and number of the noun compared. The expression **tanto como** *(as much as)* is used when no nouns are mentioned or are understood from the context of the sentence.

Ella es **tan** simpática **como** tú.	*She's **as** nice **as** you are.*
Esta película es **tan** larga **como** la otra.	*This movie is **as** long **as** the other one.*
Marta no tiene **tantos** exámenes **como** yo.	*Marta doesn't have **as many** exams **as** I do.*
Tú sabes **tanto como** yo.	*You know **as much as** I do.*

As a follow-up to the different types of comparatives, have groups of three or four students write six sentences comparing pairs of celebrities; for example they might compare Arnold Schwarzenegger and Danny DeVito, Roseanne Barr and Cindy Crawford, Michael Jordan and Michael Jackson, etc. Then read the descriptions aloud in class.

Practiquemos

A. Países bonitos. Compara la República Dominicana y Puerto Rico, usando comparativos de igualdad de las palabras indicadas.

MODELO: (simpático) La gente de la República Dominicana es *tan simpática como la gente de Puerto Rico.*

1. (bonito) La República Dominicana es _____.

2. (interesante) Puerto Rico es _____.

3. (sitios turísticos) La República Dominicana tiene _____.

4. (grande) Puerto Rico no es _____.

5. (playas bonitas) Puerto Rico tiene _____.

6. (viejo) La ciudad de San Juan no es _____.

■ Comparisons with numbers

Before a number, **más de** and **menos de** are used instead of **más que** and **menos que**.

Hay **más de** 15 estudiantes en la clase.	*There are **more than** 15 students in the class.*
Tengo **menos de** cinco dólares.	*I have **less than** five dollars.*

NOTA:
Mayor and menor are used only to indicate age of people and animals, not buildings, cities, etc.

Irregular comparisons

Some adjectives have irregular forms to express comparisons of superiority:

mejor	*better*	mayor	*older*
peor	*worse*	menor	*younger*

Esta clase es **mejor que** la otra.	*This class is **better than** the other one.*
El tiempo es **peor** hoy **que** ayer.	*The weather is **worse** today **than** yesterday.*

■ Superlatives *(most, -est)*

In Spanish the superlative is expressed by the following:

Superlatives
el (la, lo, los, las) + **más** + *adjective* (+ **de**)

Martina es **la más** inteligente de la clase.

Martina is **the smartest** of the class.

Nuestro grupo es **el mejor de** todos.

Our group is **the best of** all.

The **de** phrase may not always be expressed.

Jorge es **el más alto.**

Jorge is **the tallest.**

Lo más means *the most . . . part, the most . . . thing.*

Lo más interesante es esto.

The most interesting **thing** is this.

> **NOTA:**
> Spanish has no equivalent to **it** to refer to nouns. When referring to nouns **el, la, los,** or **las** must be used depending on the gender of the noun.

Practiquemos

A. El Caribe. Describe las islas caribeñas, formando oraciones de los elementos indicados, usando el superlativo con **de.**

> Compara tu pueblo natal (hometown) con Nueva York, Dallas, San Francisco o Seattle.

MODELO: Hispaniola / ser / isla / grande
Hispaniola es la isla más grande de todas.

1. béisbol / ser / deporte / popular
2. Puerto Rico / ser / isla / pequeño
3. islas / tener / playas / bonito
4. playas / tener / la arena (sand) / blanco
5. Santo Domingo / ser / ciudad / antiguo
6. Cuba / ser / isla / cerca de Miami

■ "Absolute" superlatives

Adjectives and adverbs that end in the suffix **-ísimo** express a superlative concept: "to a very high degree, extremely."

El mar Caribe está **tranquilísimo.**

The Caribbean Sea is **very quiet.**

La isla es **angostísima.**

The island is **very narrow.**

These superlatives are formed by removing the final vowel of an adjective and adding **-ísimo** (a/os/as).

alt**o**	*tall*	alt**ísimo**	*very tall*
hermos**a**	*beautiful*	hermos**ísima**	*most/very beautiful*
trist**e**	*sad*	trist**ísimo**	*extremely sad*

When the **-ísimo** ending is added to adjectives that end in **-co** and **-go,** they are spelled **-quísimo** and **-guísimo,** respectively.

El jugo de tamarindo está **riquísimo.**

The tamarind juice is **most delicious.**

Esta playa es **larguísima.**

This beach is **extremely long.**

Practiquemos

A. Más comparaciones. Combina los elementos de las columnas A, B y C con un adjetivo adecuado y una forma del verbo **ser**. Hay varias combinaciones posibles.

MODELO: *La comida mexicana es más picante que la comida puertorriqueña.*

Algunos adjetivos útiles:

agradable, bonito, denso, diferente, grande, importante, interesante, pequeño, picante, pintoresco, popular, sabroso

A	B	C
Los Angeles, California	más [adjetivo] que	los deportes de Cuba
el clima de Puerto Rico	menos [adjetivo] que	el clima en Cuba
Cabarete, la República Dominicana	tan [adjetivo] como	las playas de Cuba
la comida mexicana		el béisbol en Cuba
los deportes en los Estados Unidos		la comida puertorriqueña
las playas de la República Dominicana		San Juan, Puerto Rico
el béisbol en la República Dominicana		las junglas de la República Dominicana
las junglas de México		el béisbol en los Estados Unidos

B. Orgullo borinqueño. Nani es muy orgullosa de Puerto Rico. Completa su descripción, usando la forma **-ísimo(a/os/as)**.

1. Puerto Rico es _____. (hermoso)

2. El clima es _____. (bueno)

3. La gente es _____. (simpático)

4. El Castillo del Morro es _____. (interesante)

5. La comida es _____. (rico)

6. Es una isla _____. (precioso)

■ Palabras indefinidas y negativas

In a negative sentence, there must always be a negative element before the verb. As you have learned, the most common way to make a sentence negative is to put **no** before the verb.

Julia **no** quiere salir esta noche. *Julia **doesn't** want to go out tonight.*

La clase **no** repite las palabras. *The class **doesn't** repeat the words.*

In a negative sentence, indefinite words must be in the negative form. The following indefinite words have opposite negative forms.

Affirmative	**Negative**
algo *(something)*	nada *(nothing, not anything)*
alguien *(someone, anyone)*	nadie *(nobody, no one, not anyone)*
algún, alguno(a/os/as) *(some, any)*	ningún, ninguno(a) *(none, not any)*
a veces, algunas veces *(sometimes, at times)*	nunca, jamás *(never, not ever)*
siempre *(always)*	nunca, jamás *(never, not ever)*
o… o *(either . . . or)*	ni… ni *(neither . . . nor)*
también *(also, too)*	tampoco *(neither, not either)*

Alguno and **ninguno** must agree with the words they modify since they are adjectives. The ending **-uno** shortens to **-ún** when it precedes a masculine singular noun.

No tengo **ningún** amigo puertorriqueño.	I *don't* have *any* Puerto Rican friends.
¿Tienen **algunos** libros interesantes?	Do they have *any* good books?
—**No** quiero **ninguna** verdura.	I don't want *any* vegetables.
—**Ni** yo **tampoco**.	Me *neither*.

Double negative constructions are common in Spanish. Note that when the negative word precedes the verb, **no** is not necessary.

Nunca voy al parque. **No** voy **nunca** al parque.	I *never* go to the park.
Nadie vive en esta zona. **No** vive **nadie** en esta zona.	*Nobody* lives in this area.

Note the uses of **nadie**, **ningún**, **ninguno(a)** to make comparisons:

Esta playa es más hermosa que **ninguna** otra playa.	This beach is more beautiful than *any* other beach.
Juanita es más bonita que **nadie**.	Juanita is prettier than *anybody*.
Ponce es más interesante que **ningún** otro lugar.	Ponce is more interesting than *any* other place.

Practiquemos

A. Novios. Julián habla con su novia para estar seguro de su relación con ella. Llena los espacios en blanco con estas palabras: **nadie, algo, siempre, nunca, nada, también, alguien.**

JULIÁN: ¿Hay _____ que quieres decirme?

MÓNICA: No, no hay _____ .

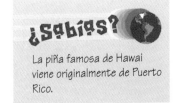

¿Sabías?

La piña famosa de Hawai viene originalmente de Puerto Rico.

JULIÁN: Creo que hay _____ en tu vida. ¿Ramón? ¿Paco?

MÓNICA: No, Julián. No hay _____ más en mi vida excepto tú, mi amor.

JULIÁN: Mónica, quiero estar contigo para _____ .

MÓNICA: Yo _____ , Julián. ¡ _____ te voy a abandonar!

B. En el café. Marta y Carolina conversan en el café antes de hacer ejercicio aeróbico. Completa las oraciones con una palabra indefinida o negativa.

CAROLINA: Marta, ¿quieres leche o café?

MARTA: Gracias, pero no quiero _____ leche _____ café. Prefiero una coca.

CAROLINA: Pero Marta, tú _____ tomas coca. ¿Qué te pasa?

MARTA: Voy a hacer _____ cambios *(changes)* en mi vida. Empiezo con la coca.

CAROLINA: Buena idea. Oye, quisiera comer _____ fruta. ¿Hay frutas en el menú?

MARTA: No, no veo _____ fruta. Lo siento.

CAROLINA: ¿Quieres _____ más, Marta?

MARTA: No, no quiero _____ más. _____ me gusta comer _____ antes de hacer ejercicio.

CAROLINA: Ni yo _____ .

MARTA: Bueno, vamos a hacer ejercicio.

C. ¡Contradicciones! Pablito siempre contradice lo que dice su hermano, Juanito. Completa su conversación con palabras negativas.

JUANITO: Pablito, ¿por qué juegas siempre con mis jugetes *(toys)*?

PABLITO: Oye, yo _____ juego con tus juguetes. Ves, no tengo _____ juguete tuyo *(of yours)*.

JUANITO: ¡Ay, cómo eres, Pablito! O tienes mi pelota *(ball)* o tomas mis canicas *(marbles)*.

PABLITO: No es verdad. Mira, aquí no tengo _____ tu pelota _____ tus canicas.

JUANITO: ¡Ay, Pablito! ¡Eres imposible! _____ *(No one)* quiere jugar contigo *(with you)*.

PABLITO: ¡Mamá! ¡No voy a jugar con Juanito _____ más!

JUANITO: ¡No voy a jugar contigo _____ , Pablito!

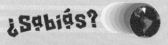

¿**Sabías?**

Vive en Puerto Rico una especie de rana o sapo *(frog)* que se llama **coquí** por su canto. Dice «coquíiii...». Los coquíes son muy pequeños y no viven en ninguna otra parte del mundo.

A ver si sabes

Use this self-test to see if you know the material presented in Chapter 5.

A. Estoy cansado. Completa las oraciones sobre las horas de descanso con la forma adecuada de los verbos indicados.

1. Yo _____ (dormir) ocho horas cada noche.

2. Mi hermano no _____ (poder) dormir toda la noche.

3. Siempre le _____ (doler) los ojos porque lee mucho. *(verb must agree with ojos)*

4. ¿Cuántas horas _____ (dormir) tú?

B ¡Qué platillo! María y Cristina discuten una receta. Completa las oraciones con la forma adecuada de los verbos indicados.

1. No _____ (entender, yo) esta receta *(recipe)*.

2. _____ (Tener, nosotras) que estudiar los ingredientes.

3. Primero _____ (hervir, tú) el agua.

4. ¿Y el arroz? ¿Qué _____ (sugerir) la receta?

C. ¡Silencio! Los estudiantes no estudian siempre. Completa las oraciones con la forma adecuada de los verbos indicados.

1. Mariana _____ (decir) buenos chistes *(jokes)*.

2. Todos _____ (reír) mucho.

3. La profesora _____ (pedir) silencio.

4. Pero yo _____ (seguir) riendo *(laughing)*.

D. ¡Qué divertido! La clase de español tiene una fiesta. Completa los comentarios con la forma adecuada de los verbos **ser** o **estar**.

1. esta clase / divertida

2. ya / las 8:00

3. ¿dónde / el profesor?

4. este platillo / riquísimo

5. ¿de quién / este cuchillo *(knife)*?

6. ¿Manuel / enfermo?

7. Sí, tiene gripe. Manuel / en casa

8. ¡Qué lástima! Esta fiesta / muy buena

E. La clase. Los estudiantes hablan de su clase de español. Completa las oraciones con la forma adecuada de las palabras negativas.

1. Berta y Raúl no estudian _____.

2. Tú, Felipe, no comprendes _____ los verbos _____ las palabras negativas.

3. ¿Y sabes qué? ¡ _____ yo _____ !

⊃

Preguntas culturales

1. Explica la relación política entre Puerto Rico y los Estados Unidos.
2. Explica como difieren la comida puertorriqueña y la comida mexicana.
3. Nombra al menos tres características del Viejo San Juan.

4. El profesor dice que los estudiantes no hacen _____ en clase.

5. Y es verdad. En nuestra clase _____ comprende todo. ¡Tenemos que estudiar más!

F. Compañeros de clase. Los estudiantes describen a sus compañeros de clase. Completa las oraciones con las formas comparativas adecuadas.

1. Arnoldo es alto y Felipe es bajo. Arnoldo es _____ alto _____ Felipe.

2. Marta tiene 25 años. El profesor tiene 46. Marta es _____ _____ el profesor.

3. Yo estudio muchísimo pero Ricardo nunca estudia. Yo estudio _____ _____ Ricardo.

4. Tú eres extrovertido pero tu amiga Gloria es muy tímida. Gloria es _____ extrovertida _____ tú.

5. Uds. son inteligentes; nosotros(as) también. Nosotros(as) somos _____ inteligentes _____ Uds.

6. Enrique tiene cinco dólares; Elena también. Enrique tiene _____ dólares _____ Elena.

G. ¡Sobresaliente! Llena los espacios en blanco con una forma superlativa para describir Puerto Rico.

1. Puerto Rico es un país hermoso. Los puertorriqueños dicen que es la isla _____ hermosa _____ todas.

2. Las playas de Puerto Rico son las _____ largas _____ todas.

3. La comida puertorriqueña es muy, muy rica; es _____.

4. La música de Puerto Rico es muy, muy bonita; es _____.

5. Para los turistas, Puerto Rico es muy, muy interesante; es _____.

Querido Diario. ¿Cuál es tu restaurante favorito? ¿Cuál es la mejor comida que comes ulli? Para organizar tus ideas haz una lista de los puntos positivos de la comida: el menú, (¿qué comes?), el servicio (¿puntual?, ¿cortés?), el ambiente del restaurante (el decoro, los otros clientes, música). Ahora escribe una descripción de la comida, diciendo por qué es buena.

Grammar: comparisons (all categories)
Phrases: appreciating food, comparing and contrasting, comparing and distinguishing
Vocabulary: food (all categories)

Vocabulario activo

Verbos

cocer (o→ue)
decir (e→i)
defender (e→ie)
doler (o→ue)
dormir (o→ue)

entender (e→ie)
freír (e→i)
hervir (e→ie)
morir (o→ue)
oler (o→ue)

pedir (e→i)
poder (o→ue)
querer (e→ie)
reír (e→i)
seguir (e→i)

seguir + *present*
   participle
sentir (e→ie)
servir (e→i)
torcer (o→ue)

Los alimentos

el arroz
el cereal
la ensalada
la galleta
el helado de
   chocolate
el helado de vainilla
el huevo

el pan
el pan tostado
el pescado
el queso
el sándwich
la sopa (de tomate,
   de pollo)

Las verduras

el ajo
el brócoli
la cebolla
las habichuelas
   verdes
la lechuga
el maíz
la papa (la patata)

el pepino
el plátano
el tomate
la zanahoria

Las frutas

la fresa
el guineo
el mango
la manzana

el melón
la naranja (la
   china)
la papaya

la piña
la toronja

Las carnes

el bistec
la chuleta de cerdo
el jamón
el pollo

Los postres

el flan de caramelo
el helado
la torta

Las bebidas

el agua mineral
el café
la cerveza
el jugo de naranja

la leche
el refresco
el té
el vino (tinto, blanco)

Para describir la comida

caliente
frío
rico (riquísimo)

Comparativos

más... que
mayor
mejor
menor
menos... que

peor
tan... como
tanto(a/os/as)...
   como

Palabras indefinidas

a veces, algunas
   veces
algo
alguien

algún,
   alguno(a/os/as)
o... o
siempre

Palabras negativas

nada
nadie
ni... ni

ningún, ninguno(a)
nunca, jamás
tampoco

Otras palabras y expresiones

el (la) mesero(a)

Web site:
http://spanishforlife.heinle.com

Transparencies:
A–2: La América Central
A–16: Country Profile, El Salvador

EL SALVADOR

Nombre oficial: República de El Salvador

Área: 20.752 km²

Población: 5.900.000

Capital: San Salvador

Moneda: el colón

Idioma oficial: español

Fiesta nacional: 15 de septiembre,
    Día de la Independencia

El Salvador y los salvadoreños

Medicinas herbales en un mercado en San Salvador

In this chapter you will learn:

GRAMMAR POINTS

- Present progressive verb forms
- Present participle of stem-changing verbs
- Direct object pronouns
- Affirmative **tú** commands
- Negative **tú** commands
- Direct objects with commands, progressives, and infinitives

COMMUNICATIVE FUNCTIONS

- Tell what is going on right now
- Ask and order friends and family to do something

VOCABULARY

- Chores
- House
- Furniture

131

I. Mirando hacia el futuro

Una vista del aire del volcán de Santa Ana

LECTURA

El Salvador es un pequeño país de volcanes y montañas, de valles y de playas. Su pasado reciente es triste pero ahora, muchas cosas **están cambiando**[1] y el futuro parece mucho más prometedor.[2] Con la guerra[3] civil de los años 80 en el pasado, hoy en día[4] El Salvador **está haciendo** mucho progreso en la reconstrucción del país. Muchas naciones **están ayudando** en este proyecto. Por ejemplo, los japoneses **están construyendo**[5] pozos[6] para proveer[7] agua en las zonas donde escasea.[8] Los Estados Unidos y varios países europeos **están aconsejando**[9] a los salvadoreños en los campos de la educación, la salud[10] y la agricultura. Gracias a los grandes esfuerzos[11] de los salvadoreños mismos y la cooperación internacional, el futuro de El Salvador parece mucho más positivo que el pasado reciente.

---

[1]**están cambiando:** *changing* / [2]**prometedor:** *promising* / [3]**la guerra:** *war* / [4]**hoy en día:** *nowadays* / [5]**están construyendo:** *are building, constructing* / [6]**pozos:** *wells* / [7]**proveer:** *to provide* / [8]**escasea:** *is scarce* / [9]**están aconsejando:** *are advising* / [10]**la salud:** *health* / [11]**esfuerzos:** *efforts*

¿Comprendes?

1. ¿Por qué es triste el pasado de El Salvador?
2. ¿Qué evidencia hay del progreso en El Salvador?
3. ¿Crees que es importante la colaboración internacional? ¿Por qué?

◼ Presente progresivo

The progressive form of the verb is used to tell what *is happening* at the moment of speaking. The progressive forms of Spanish verbs consist of a form of the verb **estar** and the present participle of the verb.

The present progressive consists of the present tense of **estar** + present participle.

Estoy estudiando.	*I am studying.*
Estamos escribiendo en español.	*We are writing in Spanish.*

-ar verbs

The present participle of **-ar** verbs is formed by adding **-ando** to the verb stem:

hab**lar**	hab**lando**
traba**jar**	traba**jando**

Pasan mucho tiempo **trabajando.**	*They spend a lot of time working.*
Hablando del trabajo…	*Speaking of work . . .*

-er and *-ir* verbs

The present progressive of **-er** and **-ir** verbs is formed by adding **-iendo** to the verb stem:

com**er**	com**iendo**
escrib**ir**	escrib**iendo**
v**er**	v**iendo**

If the stem of the verb ends in a vowel, the present participle ending is **-yendo**:

constru**ir** *(to build, construct)*	constru**yendo**
leer	le**yendo**
traer *(to bring)*	tra**yendo**
oír	o**yendo**

Practiquemos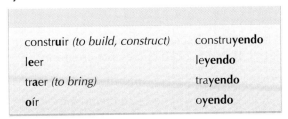

A. El sábado por la mañana. ¿Qué están haciendo estas personas hoy?

MODELO: Francisca / practicar el piano
          Francisca está practicando el piano.

1. Marco / jugar al fútbol
2. mamá y Anita / preparar el almuerzo
3. abuelito / mirar televisión
4. yo / trabajar

5. mi tío Roberto / practicar la tuba
6. el jefe y yo / hablar por teléfono
7. Jaime y Catalina / bailar merengue
8. ¿tú / estudiar español?

> ¿Qué están haciendo tus amigos y tu familia ahora?

❖ Los quehaceres de la casa

arreglar	*to straighten, make (the bed), fix*
barrer	*to sweep*
cortar el césped	*to cut the grass*
doblar	*to fold*
guardar	*to put away*
ir de compras	*to go shopping*
lavar el carro	*to wash the car*
lavar el piso	*to wash the floor*
lavar los platos	*to wash the dishes*
lavar la ropa	*to wash the clothes*
limpiar	*to clean*
pasar la aspiradora	*to vacuum*
planchar	*to iron*
poner en orden	*to straighten up (to put in order)*
poner la mesa	*to set the table*
sacar la basura	*to take out the garbage*
sacudir	*to dust*

NOTA:
The verb **poner** (*to put, place, set*) has an irregular **yo** form in the present tense: **pongo**. The other forms are regular.

> ¿Cuál es tu quehacer favorito? ¿menos favorito?

Practiquemos

A. ¿Quién puede… ? El jefe necesita alguien para hacer un trabajo muy difícil. ¿Por qué no puede ayudar nadie? Usa el presente progresivo.

1. La señorita Alfonso _____ (escribir) un informe.
2. Mariano Ortega y Raúl Bátiz _____ (leer) un memo importante.
3. Tú _____ (hacer) una llamada.
4. Inés García _____ (oír) las noticias.
5. Carla Pedrasco y yo _____ (comer) el almuerzo.
6. Yo _____ (beber) coca con el almuerzo.

¿Sabías? El Salvador es el país más pequeño de América Central. Sin embargo, es una de las naciones más industrializadas de la región. Producen comida procesada, textiles y drogas farmacéuticas. El producto agricultural más importante es el café. Mucha de la riqueza del país viene de la producción del café.

B. ¡Visitas! Tenemos visitas para cenar. ¿Qué están haciendo todos en preparación? Forma oraciones usando elementos de las tres columnas.

A	B	C
	poner	
	limpiar	cena
mi esposo(a)	sacudir	basura
los hijos	barrer	mesa
yo	cocinar	aspiradora
mi mamá y yo	pasar	cuarto
tú	arreglar	piso
toda la familia	lavar	ropa
	sacar	la casa

■ Present participle of stem-changing verbs

In -**ir** stem-changing verbs that undergo the present tense change o→ue, the stem vowel becomes **u** in the present participle.

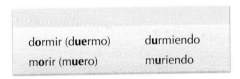

dormir (d**ue**rmo)	d**u**rmiendo
morir (m**ue**ro)	m**u**riendo

Manuel todavía está **durmiendo**.   *Manuel is still **sleeping**.*

In stem-changing -**ir** verbs that undergo the present tense change e→i, the stem vowel becomes **i** in the present participle.

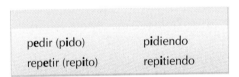

pedir (p**i**do)	p**i**diendo
repetir (rep**i**to)	rep**i**tiendo

Estoy **repitiendo** la dirección.   *I am **repeating** the address.*

In the case of **reír** and **freír**, the present participle has only one **i**.

freír (fr**í**o)	fr**i**endo
reír (r**í**o)	r**i**endo

Marta está **friendo** los frijoles.   *Marta is **frying** the beans.*

empezar (emp**ie**zo)	empezando
entender (ent**ie**ndo)	entendiendo
contar (c**ue**nto)	contando
volver (v**ue**lvo)	volviendo

Practiquemos

A. ¿Qué están haciendo, Mami? Explicas a tu hija Susita qué está pasando en el restaurante donde trabajas. ¿Qué dices?

1. Los meseros _____ (poner) las mesas.

2. El jefe _____ (repetir) sus instrucciones.

3. Algunos clientes _____ (pedir) su comida.

4. Yo _____ (freír) las papas.

5. Todos nosotros _____ (reír) mucho.

6. Y tú, ¿por qué no _____ (dormir), mi hija?

■ The use of the present progressive

In contrast with English, in which the present progressive may be used to talk about future activities, the Spanish present progressive is used to talk only about the here and now. Spanish uses the simple present or **ir a** + infinitive to talk about the future.

¿Qué **estás haciendo** (ahora)?	What **are you doing** (now)?
¿Qué **haces** esta noche?	What **are you doing** tonight?
¿Qué **vas a hacer** mañana?	What **are you doing (going to do)** tomorrow?

The present progressive of the verb *ir*

The present participle of **ir** is **yendo**. It may be used by itself.

Yendo al aeropuerto, ves muchas vistas bonitas.	**Going** to the airport, you see a lot of pretty sights.

However, the verb **ir** is not normally used in the present progressive. The simple present is used instead:

¿Adónde **vas**?	Where **are you going**?
Voy al centro.	**I'm going** downtown.

Practiquemos

Have students explain their answers.

A. ¿Cómo se dice? Indica la mejor manera de expresar las oraciones *(sentences)* en español.

1. I'm reading a whole book next week.
   a. Estoy leyendo todo un libro la semana que viene.
   b. Voy a leer todo un libro la semana que viene.

2. Elena travels to El Salvador in the summer.
   a. Elena va a viajar a El Salvador en verano.
   b. Elena está viajando a El Salvador en verano.

3. What are you doing now?
   a. ¿Qué vas a hacer ahora?
   b. ¿Qué estás haciendo ahora?

4. I'm studying all day tomorrow.
   a. Voy a estudiar todo el día mañana.
   b. Estoy estudiando todo el día mañana.

5. We're eating dinner. Can you call back later?
   a. Vamos a cenar. ¿Puedes llamar más tarde?
   b. Estamos cenando. ¿Puedes llamar más tarde?

6. I'm going to class.
   a. Estoy yendo a clase.
   b. Voy a clase.

B. ¡Ay! Es Águeda. Cuando llama Águeda, tu amiga entrometida *(nosy)*, quiere saber exactamente qué están haciendo todos hoy. Forma oraciones con los elementos dados.

MODELO: Susana y Roberto / beber café
            Susana y Roberto están bebiendo café.

1. mamá / hacer / comida
2. papá y José / ver / partido de fútbol
3. Susana y Roberto / estudiar
4. mi amiga y yo / leer revistas
5. la tía Eva / barrer en el garaje
6. yo / oír música latina
7. el tío Mario y Raúl / cortar el césped
8. papá / comer papas fritas

C. El lunes por la mañana. ¿Qué están haciendo estas personas a las 7:00 el lunes?

MODELO: *Mamá está haciendo el café.*

A	B	C
mamá	preparar	un artículo
los chicos	comer	español
papá y yo	leer	desayuno
tú	escribir	café
yo	dormir	la lección
la doctora	beber	la tele
el profesor	mirar	jugo de naranja
	hacer	una prescripción

Have students imagine that they are at work, at home after dinner, or on vacations, and then tell a partner what everyone is doing. This could also be brainstormed by a group of three or four.

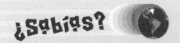

¿Sabías?

Una comida favorita de los salvadoreños se llama «papusas». Las papusas consisten en masa de harina de maíz *(corn flour dough)* rellena de requesón *(farmer's cheese)*, frijoles o chicharrón *(cracklings, fried pork rinds)*. ¡Son riquísimas!

II. ¿Quiénes son los salvadoreños?

LECTURA

¿Quiénes son los salvadoreños? Para contestar esta pregunta debemos investigar un poco la historia de la región. Antes de la llegada de los europeos al país, **lo** habitaban[1] varios grupos de indios: primero **lo** dominaban los olmecas y después los mayas. Luego, **lo** habitaban los pipil, descendientes de los aztecas y toltecas de México. En 1525 llegaron los españoles y allí comenzó la mezcla[2] de sangre[3] india con sangre europea, una mezcla que continúa hoy en día. La población **la** refleja: son 94% mestizos (indios con europeos) con sólo 5% indios y 1% europeos. Por eso las caras[4] de los salvadoreños son muy similares a las caras de los mexicanos y muchos otros centroamericanos.

---

[1]**habitaban:** *inhabited* / [2]**la mezcla:** *mixture* / [3]**sangre:** *blood* / [4]**caras:** *faces*

¿Comprendes?

1. ¿Cómo son similares los salvadoreños y los mexicanos?

2. ¿Hay similaridades entre la población de El Salvador y la población de los Estados Unidos?

■ Complementos directos

The direct object of a sentence tells *who* or *what* is affected by the verb.

Loren saw *Mary* yesterday.   (Who was seen?)
Henry reads many *books*.   (What is being read?)

The direct object may be a noun *(Mary, books)*, as above, or a pronoun *(them, her)*.

> **NOTA:** Remember that if the direct object is a person, the preposition **a** must precede it.

Loren saw *her* yesterday.
Henry is reading *them*.

Enrique lee **muchos libros**.   *Henry reads **many books**.*
Loren ve a **María**.   *Loren sees **Mary**.*

Spanish direct object pronouns have eight forms.

Direct Object Pronouns			
me	*me*	**nos**	*us*
te	*you (fam.)*	**os**	*you (fam.)*
lo	*you (form.), him, it*	**los**	*you (form.), them*
la	*you (form.), her, it*	**las**	*you (form.), them*

Lo, la, los, and **las** must agree with the gender of the noun they stand for. For example, **la** may take the place of **Cristina**, **casa**, or **usted** (when **usted** is a woman). **Lo** can replace **David**, **lápiz**, or a male **usted**.

Elena llama a **Cristina** todos
   los días.   *Elena calls **Cristina** every day.*

Elena **la** llama todos los días.   *Elena calls **her** every day.*

No conozco a **David**.   *I don't know **David**.*
No **lo** conozco.   *I don't know **him**.*

Buscamos las **notas**.   *We are looking for the **notes**.*
Las buscamos.   *We are looking for **them**.*

Claro que recuerdo a **usted**.   *Of course I remember **you**.*
Claro que **lo** recuerdo.   *Of course I remember **you**.*

As you can see, Spanish direct object pronouns are placed immediately before the present tense verb. Nothing may come between the pronoun and the verb.

> **NOTA:**
> Common verbs that take direct objects include olvidar *(to forget)*, **recordar (o→ue)** *(to remember)*, and mover **(o→ue)** *(to move).*

❖ Para hablar de la casa

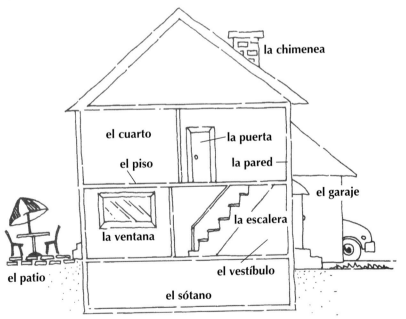

la chimenea
el cuarto
el piso
la puerta
la pared
el garaje
la escalera
la ventana
el vestíbulo
el patio
el sótano

Transparencies:
C–1: La casa/El transporte
C–2: En los cuartos
C–3: Los artículos personales
C–4: La sala/El dormitorio
C–5: El cuarto de baño/La cocina

Los cuartos	The rooms
el cuarto de baño	*bathroom*
el cuarto de familia	*family room*
los muebles	*furniture*

En la sala	In the living room	En la cocina	In the kitchen
la alfombra	carpet	la cafetera	coffee maker
el estéreo	stereo	el congelador	freezer
la lámpara	lamp	la estufa (cocina)	stove
el radio	radio	el fregadero	(kitchen) sink
el sillón	easy chair	el gabinete	cabinet
el sofá	sofa, couch	el horno	oven
el televisor	TV set	el lavaplatos	dishwasher
		la licuadora	blender
En el comedor	**In the dining room**	el microondas	microwave
la mesa	table	la plancha	iron
la silla	chair (dining room chair, straight chair)	el refrigerador	refrigerator
		la tabla de planchar	ironing board
En el dormitorio	**In the bedroom**	la tostadora	toaster
la cama	bed	**En el cuarto de baño**	**In the bathroom**
la cómoda	chest of drawers		
el escritorio	desk	el inodoro	toilet
el estante	shelf	la tina	bathtub
la mesita	small table	el lavabo	lavatory
la mesita de noche	nightstand		
En el garaje	**In the garage**		
la lavadora	washing machine		
la secadora	dryer		

Describe tu casa a tu compañero(a) de clase. Dile qué cuartos tiene, y qué cuarto es tu favorito. ¿Qué muebles tiene tu cuarto favorito?

NOTA:

The radio station is **la radio**; the electronic apparatus through which the sound is played is **el radio**. A similar distinction between waves and furniture occurs between **televisor** (TV set) and **televisión** (TV broadcast waves). There are many words for bedroom: The words **recámara**, **habitación**, **cuarto**, and **alcoba** are used in different countries to mean bedroom, but **dormitorio** is universally understood. Both **habitación** and **cuarto** mean room. Although family rooms are not common in Spanish-speaking countries, that vocabulary is included here to allow you to talk about your own home.

Practiquemos

A. No puedo ver. Hay un desfile *(parade)* con mucha gente y tu compañero(a) de clase no puede ver a su amiga Elena. Completa la conversación entre tú y tu compañero(a) de clase.

MODELO: Tú: ¿Ves a este señor alto con un sombrero?
COMPAÑERO(A): *Sí, lo veo.*

Tú: ¿Ves la banda de la escuela?

COMPAÑERO(A):   Sí, _____ _.

Tú: ¿Ves a las dos chicas bailando?

COMPAÑERO(A):   Sí, _____.

Tú: ¿Ves el carro muy grande?

COMPAÑERO(A):   Sí, _____.

Tú: ¿Ves a los señores cantando?

COMPAÑERO(A):   Sí, _____.

Tú: Pues, Elena está con ellos.

COMPAÑERO(A):   Sí, sí, _____.

B. ¡Con salsa! Ezequiel y Sara no comen nada sin salsa. ¿Qué comen con salsa?

MODELO: ¿El pescado?
           Lo comen con salsa.

1. ¿Las papas?
2. ¿Los vegetales?
3. ¿Las enchiladas?
4. ¿La carne?
5. ¿El bistec?
6. ¿Las papusas?
7. ¿El pan?
8. ¿Los huevos?
9. ¿El arroz?
10. ¿La sopa?

C. ¿Quién lo hace? Todos tienen que ayudar en los quehaceres. ¿Qué hacen? Completa las oraciones y luego convierte los complementos directos en pronombres.

MODELO: Marta arregla *la cama.*
           Marta la arregla.

1. Jorge y Loreto lavan _____.

2. Yo _____ la aspiradora.

3. Tú y Susana _____ la basura.

4. Mamá pone _____.

5. Loreto y yo _____ los platos.

6. Tú sacudes _____.

7. Papá barre _____.

8. Jorge y papá _____ el césped.

D. En mi familia. Contesta las preguntas con los nombres de tus familiares o tus amigos. Si nadie hace la actividad, escribe eso. Luego, haz estas preguntas a un(a) compañero(a) de clase y contesta las preguntas de tu compañero(a).

This activity can be done aloud by the whole class, in small groups or in pairs.

As a follow-up activity, distribute a series of familiar objects (classroom supplies, foods) among the students. Then ask **¿Quién tiene la calculadora?** Students may answer about themselves (**Yo la tengo. / Yo no la tengo.**) or about others (**Olga la tiene.**).

Have students make a list of the chores that must be done in each room. Then have them share with a partner which ones they don't mind and which ones they hate. Ask them to decide how they would divide the housework if they lived together.

⊃

MODELO: ¿Quién siempre come pan?
Mi esposo lo come. o *Nadie lo come.*

1. ¿Quién escucha música clásica?
2. ¿Quién estudia español?
3. ¿Quién mueve los muebles?
4. ¿Quién ve películas de horror?
5. ¿Quién prepara la comida?
6. ¿Quién limpia la casa?
7. ¿Quién usa la red (el Internet)?
8. ¿Quién escribe muchas cartas?
9. ¿Quién bebe café todos los días?
10. ¿Quién lava la ropa?

> Dile a tu compañero(a) de clase los quehaceres que tú tienes que hacer en tu casa, oficina o residencia. ¿Quién tiene más?

III. Disfruta de[1] El Salvador

LECTURA

¿Quieres saber más sobre El Salvador? Entonces, **toma** un avión y **visita** el país que te ofrece una experiencia inolvidable.[2] Primero, **ve** a la capital, San Salvador, y **visita** la Catedral Metropolitana, el Teatro Nacional y el Jardín[3] Botánico La Laguna. Luego, **viaja** más al oeste del país para conocer la segunda ciudad en importancia de El Salvador, Santa Ana. **Explora** sus calles coloniales, **admira** los jardines llenos de flores y **habla** con la gente que es amable y trabajadora. **No dejes** de[4] visitar la famosa Catedral de Santa Ana. Para completar tu visita, **no salgas** del país sin explorar la Costa del Sur. **Pasa** tiempo en las bonitas playas de El Cuco y el Espino. Hay mucho que ver, así que **toma** tu tiempo para conocer bien este país fascinante.

---

[1]**Disfruta de:** *Enjoy* / [2]**inolvidable:** *unforgettable* / [3]**el Jardín:** *Garden* / [4]**No dejes de:** *Don't fail to*

San Salvador, El Slavador

¿Comprendes?

1. ¿Qué sitios de interés hay en San Salvador?
2. ¿Dónde queda (está) Santa Ana?
3. ¿Qué te gustaría hacer en El Salvador?

■ Los mandatos familiares *(tú)*

Commands are used to tell someone to do something. In English commands, the subject *you* is not expressed in the sentence but is "understood."

(You) Take out the garbage.   *(You) Tell the truth.*

Spanish uses special forms of the verb to express commands. The **tú** command, or familiar command, is used with a friend or family member whom you would address as **tú**.

The affirmative familiar command (**tú**) of regular verbs is formed by removing the **s** from the **tú** form of the present tense.

Infinitive	Form of *tú*	Command
preparar	prepara**s**	prepara
comer	come**s**	come
escribir	escribe**s**	escribe

Prepara la comida.   ***Prepare*** *the food.*
Come estos vegetales.   ***Eat*** *these vegetables.*
Escribe estos ejercicios.   ***Write*** *these exercises.*

Irregular **tú** commands must be memorized.

Infinitive	Command	Infinitive	Command
decir	**di**	salir	**sal**
hacer	**haz**	ser	**sé**
ir	**ve**	tener	**ten**
poner	**pon**	venir	**ven**

Hijo, **ven** aca, por favor.   *Son,* ***come*** *here, please.*
Pepe, **pon** la mesa, por favor.   *Pepe,* ***set*** *the table, please.*

Note that, as in English, commands may be softened by using **por favor** *(please)* with them.

Practiquemos

A. La fiesta. Sandra Méndez, la presidenta del Círculo Español, está organizando una fiesta para los socios y necesita ayuda. Llena los espacios con la forma adecuada del mandato familiar (**tú**).

1. Ana María, _____ (comprar) las bebidas.

2. Julia, _____ (escribir) las invitaciones.

3. Ramón, _____ (arreglar) las sillas y las mesas.

4. Santiago, _____ (buscar) las decoraciones que vamos a usar.

5. Tomás, _____ (pedir) ayuda a Tina y Jorge.

6. Andrea, _____ (hablar) con Felipe para ver si nos ayuda.

7. Félix, _____ (leer) la lista de los invitados.

8. También _____ (ver) si todos los nombres están.

9. Susana, _____ (llamar) a los profesores para invitarlos.

10. Todos los otros dicen: Y tú, Sandra, ¡ _____ (preparar) la comida para todos!

As a follow-up activity, have students role-play roommates with an apartment to clean. Have them give each other commands about the housework that must be done. A list of chores can be put on the board.

B. Mucho que hacer. Es sábado por la mañana y mamá le da una serie de mandatos a Pablito. ¿Qué dicen?

> Da cinco mandatos a tus compañeros(as) de clase. (Ellos tienen que hacer lo que tú haces.)

MAMÁ: Ay, Pablito, ¿qué estás haciendo?
PABLITO: Uh, estudiando, mamá.
MAMÁ: Hijo, _____ (decir) la verdad.
PABLITO: ¡Ay! Estoy escuchando mi música.
MAMÁ: Por favor, _____ (salir) de tu cuarto y _____ (hacer) lo que te digo. _____ (Venir) acá, hijo.
PABLITO: ¡Ay, mamá!
MAMÁ: Primero, _____ (poner) en orden toda la sala y _____ (tener) cuidado *(be careful)* con las lámparas. Luego _____ (ir) a la cocina y _____ (poner) la mesa.
PABLITO: Pero mi hermana...
MAMÁ: _____ (Ser) bueno y _____ (tener) paciencia *(be patient)*. Mañana tu hermana me ayuda.

C. Mensajes. El señor Sánchez manda un mensaje por correo electrónico a su esposa, Liliana. Completa las oraciones con mandatos familiares.

De: sanchezrg@usaga.com.ca
Fecha: martes, 20 Oct 23:14:54 UMT
Para: sanchezlt@esol.com.ca
Mime-Versión: 1.0
Asunto: por favor

> Tú eres Liliana. ¿Qué dices a Roberto?

----Message Text----

Oye, Liliana. Voy a llegar muy tarde hoy. ¿Me puedes hacer estos favores, mi amor? Por favor, _____ (ir) al banco y _____ (sacar) los 200 dólares que necesito para mi viaje. Luego _____ (lavar) mi ropa y _____ (poner) la ropa en mi maleta *(suitcase)* grande. Después, _____ (llamar) a Jorge León para decirle que voy a llegar tarde. _____ (Poner) mis papeles importantes sobre mi escritorio y _____ (hacer) mi agenda para mañana. Finalmente, _____ (comer) sin mí porque tampoco puedo comer contigo. ¿Está bien, mi amor? Hasta más tarde.

Roberto

■ Los mandatos negativos

Negative commands tell someone *not* to do something. To form negative **tú** commands, add the following endings to the stem of the verb:

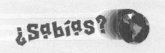

Cuando Cristóbal Colón llegó a la isla Guanahani, la bautizó con el nombre de San Salvador, bajo el patronato (protection) del Divino Salvador del Mundo (Jesucristo). Luego, en 1824, se constituyó un estado federal con el nombre oficial de El Salvador.

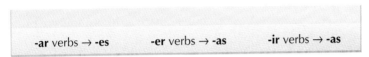

-ar verbs → **-es**	**-er** verbs → **-as**	**-ir** verbs → **-as**

Infinitive	Root	Negative Command
habl**ar**	habl-	no habl**es**
pon**er**	pong-	no pong**as**
dorm**ir**	duerm-	no duerm**as**

No tomes la leche.   *Don't drink the milk.*
No leas el periódico ahora.   *Don't read the paper now.*
No duermas en clase.   *Don't sleep in class.*
No salgas con ella.   *Don't go out with her.*

Some verbs have irregular negative command forms, which must be memorized.

dar	no **des**		ir	no **vayas**
estar	no **estés** (triste)		ser	no **seas**

Ana, **no estés** triste.   *Ana, don't be sad.*
Hijo, **no seas** malo.   *Son, don't be naughty.*

For verbs that end in -**gar**, add a **u** before the **e** to maintain the original sound of the infinitive. For verbs that end in -**car**, add **qu** before the **e**.

Infinitive	Command
llegar	no lle**gues**
sacar	no sa**ques**

Por favor **no llegues** tarde.   *Please don't get there late.*
No saques fotos aquí.   *Don't take photos here.*

Practiquemos 🖊

A. ¡Ten cuidado! El hermano de Mario recibe recomendaciones de su hermano mayor para su vida en la universidad. Forma mandatos negativos, usando las frases indicadas.

MODELO: no venir a casa tarde
No vengas a casa tarde.

1. no tomar mucho café
2. no beber mucho vino
3. no escuchar música fuerte *(loud)*
4. no salir todas las noches
5. no ir a clase sin preparar
6. no comer mucha grasa *(fat)*
7. no tomar drogas
8. no ser flojo *(lazy)*

B. En clase. Tu compañero(a) te dice que Roberto es un estudiante muy malo. ¿Qué dices tú a Roberto?

MODELO: COMPAÑERO(A): llegar tarde
Roberto llega tarde.
TÚ: *Roberto, no llegues tarde.*

1. COMPAÑERO(A): hablar inglés
2. COMPAÑERO(A): beber en clase
3. COMPAÑERO(A): comer en clase
4. COMPAÑERO(A): no copiar los exámenes de otros
5. COMPAÑERO(A): abrir el libro en un examen
6. COMPAÑERO(A): estar ausente
7. COMPAÑERO(A): dormir en clase
8. COMPAÑERO(A): salir temprano *(early)* de clase

> Dile a tu compañero(a) qué debe y no debe hacer si quiere sacar buenas notas.

IV. La Isla Montecristo

LECTURA

Un sitio muy atractivo en El Salvador es la Isla Montecristo. ¿Vamos a visitar**la**? Para llegar allí, tomamos el autobús en San Salvador y después de un par[1] de cambios,[2] llegamos a la desembocadura[3] del Río Lempa y el Océano Pacífico. Desde allí vamos en canoa a la isla. Al llegar allí vamos a presenciar[4] una naturaleza[5] pura, casi extinguida[6] en otras partes. **La** vamos a encontrar[7] en los animales y la rica vegetación de la isla. También vamos a ver**la** en los niños que dan la bienvenida[8] a las visitas. ¿Quieres ir? Piénsa**lo**. Es un pequeño rincón[9] del paraíso.[10]

---

[1] **un par:** couple / [2] **cambios:** changes / [3] **la desembocadura:** mouth (of a river) / [4] **presenciar:** to witness, be in the presence of / [5] **una naturaleza:** nature / [6] **extinguida:** extinct, extinguished / [7] **encontrar:** to find, encounter / [8] **bienvenida:** welcome / [9] **un rincón:** corner / [10] **el paraíso:** paradise

Para ir a la Isla Montecristo, es necesario viajar en canoa desde la Playa El Zunza.

¿Comprendes?

1. ¿Por qué es tan atractiva esta isla para los turistas?
2. ¿Conoces otra isla que conserve la naturaleza?

■ Complementos directos con el progresivo y los mandatos

Direct object pronouns follow present participles. When they are written, the pronouns are attached to the end of the present participle and an accent must be added to keep the original stress.

Point out that, unlike the English *-ing* form, the Spanish **-ndo** form is never used as a noun. *Reading is fun* is not **Leyendo es divertido** but rather **El leer es divertido**.

Leyéndolo, uno comprende la idea.	***Reading it***, one understands the idea.
Pensándolo bien, parece buena idea.	***Thinking it over***, it seems like a good idea.

When direct object pronouns are used with progressive forms, the pronoun may follow the present participle. When written, the pronoun is attached to the present participle and requires an accent to retain the original stress.

Estoy leyendo **la novela**.	*I'm reading **the novel**.*
Estoy **leyéndola**.	*I'm **reading it**.*
¿Quién está usando **el bolígrafo**?	*Who is using **the ballpoint**?*
¿Quién está **usándolo**?	*Who is **using it**?*

Direct object pronouns may also be placed before the verb **estar**.

Estamos escuchando **la canción**.	*We are listening to **the song**.*
La estamos escuchando.	*We are listening to **it**.*

Practiquemos

A. Actividades. Di lo que estas personas están haciendo, usando un pronombre en cada oración. Recuerda los acentos.

MODELO: La profesora está preparando sus lecciones.
La profesora está preparándolas. La profesora las está preparando.

⊃

1. Miguel está estudiando los verbos.
2. Los chicos están mirando un vídeo.
3. Están comiendo una ensalada.
4. Tú estás escuchando la radio.
5. Mariela está lavando los platos.
6. Javier y yo estamos escribiendo una carta.
7. Pablito está haciendo los quehaceres.
8. Yo estoy preparando mis tareas.

■ Complementos pronominales con infinitivos

When a direct object pronoun is used with an infinitive, the pronoun follows the infinitive. When written, the pronoun is attached to the infinitive, but here no accent is needed.

¿Comer **la pizza** ahora?	*Eat **the pizza** now?*
¿Comer**la** ahora?	*Eat **it** now?*

When an infinitive is used with a conjugated verb, the direct object pronoun may be attached to the infinitive or precede the conjugated verb as shown.

Van a preparar **la lección**.	*They are going to prepare **the lesson**.*
Van a preparar**la**.	
La van a preparar.	*They are going to prepare **it**.*
¿Puedes repetir **las palabras**?	*Can you repeat **the words**?*
¿Puedes repetir**las**?	
¿**Las** puedes repetir?	*Can you repeat **them**?*
Pienso estudiar **los verbos**.	*I plan to study **the verbs**.*
Pienso estudiar**los**.	
Los pienso estudiar.	*I plan to study **them**.*

Practiquemos

A. Más quehaceres. La familia Domínguez está planeando sus quehaceres para el fin de semana. Di lo que van a hacer, según el modelo.

MODELO: ¿El cuarto? Paco / limpiar
          Paco va a limpiarlo. Paco lo va a limpiar.

1. ¿El carro? papá / lavar
2. ¿Los muebles? Tina / sacudir
3. ¿La basura? Silvia / sacar
4. ¿El césped? Mario / cortar
5. ¿La sala? mamá / poner en orden
6. ¿La cocina? Marta y Pedro / barrer
7. ¿Los dormitorios? Jaime / limpiar
8. ¿El café? abuelita / preparar

B. El viaje. Unos amigos van a El Salvador a estudiar. ¿Qué tienen que hacer? Escribe oraciones, combinando los elementos de cada columna. Luego repite las oraciones usando un pronombre.

MODELO: *Flora va a arreglar los documentos. Flora va a arreglarlos.*
o Flora los va a arreglar.

A	B	C	D
Flora			libros de español
Ramona		consultar	calculadora
Lupe	ir a	estudiar	papel
Rafael y Gema	tener que	preparar	lápices
María y yo	poder	comprar	documentos
tú y Martín	pensar	conseguir	mochila
yo		arreglar	cuadernos
tú			diccionario

■ Complementos directos con mandatos afirmativos

Direct object pronouns are attached to affirmative command forms. Note that a written accent mark is necessary to maintain the original stress of verbs of more than one syllable. The accent is written on the next-to-the-last syllable of the verb.

Lava la ropa.	Lávala.	*Wash* **it.**
Escribe las cartas.	Escríbelas.	*Write* **them.**
Haz el café.	Hazlo.	*Make* **it.**
Di las palabras.	Dilas.	*Say* **them.**
Llama.	Llámame.	*Call* **me.**

Practiquemos

A. Limpiando la casa. La Sra. Ortiz está limpiando la casa con sus hijos. ¿Qué mandatos les da ella a sus hijos?

MODELO: Pon en orden la sala.
Ponla en orden.

1. Barre el piso.
2. Limpia tu dormitorio.
3. Pon los platos aquí.
4. Pasa la aspiradora.
5. Saca la basura.
6. Sacude los estantes.
7. Corta el césped.
8. Termina los quehaceres ahora.

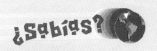

¿Sabías?

Agustín Farabundo Martí, héroe de muchos salvadoreños, fue líder de una sublevación (uprising) de campesinos e indios para mejorar el estándard de vida. Otro héroe es el arzobispo Óscar Romero, quien trabajó hasta su muerte para conseguir una mejor vida para los pobres.

B. Una amiga enferma. Tienes unas recomendaciones para un(a) compañero(a), quien está enfermo(a). Con tu compañero(a) de clase, escribe mandatos usando pronombres.

MODELO: COMPAÑERO(A): Escucha esta música bonita.
Escúchala.

Tú: *No quiero escucharla.*

1. COMPAÑERO(A): Cierra la ventana.
2. COMPAÑERO(A): Bebe muchos líquidos.
3. COMPAÑERO(A): Come esta sopa.
4. COMPAÑERO(A): Prepara un té caliente más tarde.
5. COMPAÑERO(A): Toma dos aspirinas ahora.
6. COMPAÑERO(A): Si no estás bien mañana, llama al doctor López.

■ Complementos pronominales con mandatos negativos

Object pronouns precede negative command forms:

No tomes **esta leche**.	No **la** tomes.	*Don't drink **it**.*
No leas **el periódico** ahora.	No **lo** leas ahora.	*Don't read **it** now.*
No pongas **las mesas**.	No **las** pongas.	*Don't set **them**.*
No olvides **los anuncios**.	No **los** olvides.	*Don't forget **them**.*

Practiquemos

A. ¿Qué dice tu amigo? Estás trabajando con un amigo. ¿Qué te dice? Usa pronombres en las respuestas.

1. ¿Los libros? No _____ _____ (poner) aquí.

2. ¿La lámpara? No _____ _____ (limpiar) ahora.

3. ¿Tus tareas? No _____ _____ (hacer) ahora.

4. ¿Tu novio? No _____ _____ (llamar) ahora.

5. ¿Tu ropa? No _____ _____ (lavar) ahora.

6. ¿La basura? No _____ _____ (sacar) ahora.

B. La dieta. Tu compañero(a) de clase quiere seguir una dieta estricta. ¿Qué sugieres *(do you suggest)*?

MODELO: COMPAÑERO(A): comer caramelos *(candy)*
Me gusta comer caramelos.

Tú: *No los comas.*

1. COMPAÑERO(A): comer la grasa *(fat)*
2. COMPAÑERO(A): beber las margaritas
3. COMPAÑERO(A): fumar
4. COMPAÑERO(A): beber café
5. COMPAÑERO(A): comer carne roja
6. COMPAÑERO(A): beber chocolate

¿Qué haces tú cuando debes estudiar y no quieres?

C. El examen. Tienes un examen de español mañana. Quieres hacer todo menos *(except)* estudiar. ¿Qué mandatos te da tu compañero(a) de clase?

MODELO: Tú: ver un vídeo
                      Quiero ver un vídeo.
        COMPAÑERO(A):   *No lo veas ahora.*

1. mirar la tele
2. leer una novela
3. escribir cartas electrónicas

4. salir al cine
5. escuchar música
6. llamar a mis amigos

Have students make a list of things they do to avoid an unpleasant task. Have them role-play a person trying to avoid something unpleasant and another trying to advise the first.

A ver si sabes

Use this self-test to see if you know the material presented in Chapter 6.

A. ¿Quieres ir al cine? ¿Por qué no puede salir nadie con Alicia hoy? Usa una forma progresiva para describir lo que están haciendo todos.

1. papá / trabajar en su oficina
2. mamá y la tía Julia / limpiar la casa
3. Laura y Esteban / lavar los platos
4. Enrique / estudiar para un examen
5. yo / pasar la aspiradora
6. tú / sacudir la sala
7. Mario / barrer el garaje
8. abuelito / dormir

B. ¿Recuerdas? Elena asiste a la reunión de su clase después de 20 años ¿Qué pasa? Sustituye los complementos directos por pronombres.

1. Elena ve al señor Gibson.
2. Roberto García no recuerda a Elena.
3. Elena no bebe los refrescos.
4. Elena y su amiga comen mucha torta.
5. Todos miran un vídeo.
6. Elena no conoce a las nuevas profesoras de español.
7. Elena no saluda a sus viejos novios.
8. Después de la reunión, Elena llama a sus amigas.

C. Y ahora, ¿qué? El señor Millán tiene preguntas para sus hijos. ¿Cómo responden? Escribe las respuestas de dos maneras, poniendo los pronombres en las dos posiciones posibles.

MODELO: Felipe, ¿vas a hacer los quehaceres?
                      Sí, Papá, voy a hacerlos. / Sí, Papá, los voy a hacer.

1. Sara, ¿puedes arreglar la sala?
2. Pepe, ¿estás sacando la basura?
3. Nacho, ¿puedes cortar el césped?
4. Silvia, ¿estás lavando la ropa?
5. Martita, ¿vas a poner en orden tus cosas?

Preguntas culturales

1. ¿Cómo está reforzando El Salvador un mejor futuro?

2. ¿Por qué se parecen los salvadoreños a los mexicanos y otros centroamericanos?

3. ¿Cuáles son tres lugares de El Salvador que son interesantes para muchos turistas? ¿Cómo son?

D. En clase. ¿Qué mandatos afirmativos da tu profesora?

1. (Escuchar) a la profesora.
2. (Sacar) tu lápiz.
3. (Abrir) el libro de español.
4. (Hacer) los ejercicios escritos.
5. (Estudiar) la lección.
6. (Hablar) español en clase.
7. (Escribir) las palabras en tu papel.
8. (Practicar) los mandatos.

Ahora, escribe estos mandatos de arriba con pronombres.

1. _____   5. _____

2. _____   6. _____

3. _____   7. _____

4. _____   8. _____

E. ¡Más mandatos! Paula quiere tonificar *(to tone up)* su cuerpo. ¿Qué sugieres? Escribe mandatos afirmativos o negativos con pronombres.

1. (Tomar) vitaminas.
2. (Hacer) mucho ejercicio.
3. (Comer) muchos postres.
4. (Practicar) los deportes.
5. (Seguir) una buena dieta.
6. (Beber) mucho alcohol.
7. (Buscar) un lugar para correr.
8. (Fumar) cigarillos.

Querido Diario. ¿Estás enojado(a) con alguien? ¿Quizás con tu compañero(a), amigo(a), jefe(a), un miembro de tu familia? ¿Te gustaría darle unos mandatos? Vas a escribir una lista de mandatos para esa persona en tu diario. Para organizar tus pensamientos, escribe los aspectos de tu interacción con esa persona: por ejemplo, en casa, en el trabajo, en clase o en la vida personal o social. ¿Qué hace la persona que te molesta *(bothers)*? Ahora escribe lo que te gustaría decir a esa persona.

Grammar: imperative, imperative (**tú**)
Vocabulary: house (all groups), office, school, working conditions

Vocabulario activo

Los quehaceres

arreglar
barrer
cortar el césped
doblar
guardar

ir de compras
lavar el carro
lavar el piso
lavar los platos
lavar la ropa

limpiar
pasar la aspiradora
planchar
poner en orden
poner la mesa

regar (e→ie) las
  plantas
sacar (qu) la basura
sacudir

La casa

la chimenea
el cuarto
el cuarto de baño
el cuarto de familia
la escalera

el garaje
los muebles
la pared
el piso
la puerta

el sótano
la ventana
el vestíbulo

Más verbos

mover (o→ue)
olvidar
recordar (o→e)

En la sala

la alfombra
el estéreo
la lámpara

el radio
el sillón
el sofá

el televisor

En el comedor

la mesa
la silla

En la cocina

la cafetera
el congelador
la estufa (cocina)
el fregadero

el gabinete
el horno
el lavaplatos
la licuadora

el microondas
la plancha
el refrigerador
la tabla de planchar

la tostadora

En el dormitorio

la cama
la cómoda
el escritorio

el estante
la mesita
la mesita de noche

En el garaje

la lavadora
la plancha
la secadora

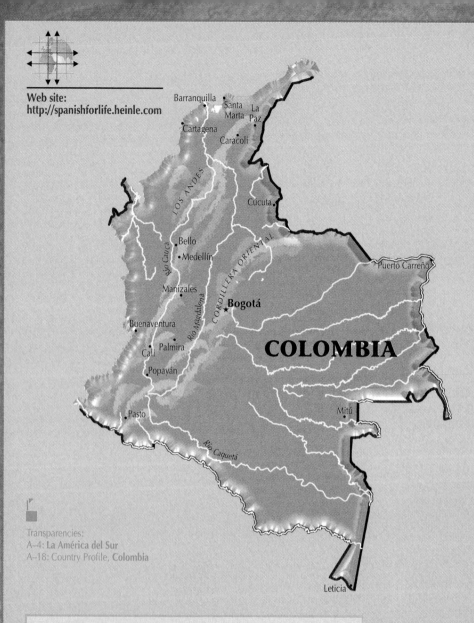

Web site:
http://spanishforlife.heinle.com

Barranquilla
Santa Marta
La Paz
Cartagena
Caracoli
Cúcuta
LOS ANDES
Bello
Medellín
Río Cauca
CORDILLERA ORIENTAL
Manizales
Bogotá
Buenaventura
Río Magdalena
Palmira
Cali
Popayán
COLOMBIA
Puerto Carreño
Pasto
Mitú
Río Caquetá
Leticia

Transparencies:
A–4: La América del Sur
A–18: Country Profile, Colombia

REPÚBLICA DE COLOMBIA

Nombre oficial: República de Colombia

Area: 1.141.748 km^2

Población: 36.200.000

Capital: Bogotá

Moneda: el peso

Idioma oficial: español

Fiesta nacional: 20 de julio, Día de la Independencia

CAPÍTULO

7

Colombia y los colombianos

Una vista del aire de Mompox, Colombia

In this chapter you will learn:

GRAMMAR POINTS

- Preterite tense of regular **-ar** verbs
- Preterite tense of regular **-er** and **-ir** verbs
- Indirect object pronouns with conjugated verbs
- Indirect object pronouns with other verb forms
- Indirect object pronouns in sentences with conjugated and non-conjugated verbs
- Preterite tense of the verbs **ir**, **ser**, **dar**, **hacer**, **decir**
- Time expressions with **hace** + present
- Time expressions with **hace** + preterite

COMMUNICATIVE FUNCTIONS

- Tell what you did yesterday
- Narrate an event in the past

VOCABULARY

- Travel vocabulary
- Past travel experiences

I. ¡Viajamos a Colombia!

LECTURA

¿Qué nos ofrece Colombia? Como estudiantes en la clase de español de la profesora Magdalena Oregón, tuvimos la oportunidad de pasar las vacaciones estudiando y viajando por Colombia. Antes de salir, mis cuatro compañeros y yo **estudiamos** un mapa de Colombia y unas guías turísticas. **Aprendimos** que Colombia es el único[1] país del continente sudamericano con costas en el Pacífico y el Atlántico (el Caribe). También, es un país famoso por su rico café y otros productos —bananas y caña de azúcar.

Cuando **llegamos** a Bogotá, la capital de Colombia, **notamos** que es una ciudad moderna con hoteles elegantes, tiendas y restaurantes excelentes y muchos lugares de importancia cultural. **Visitamos** la muy bella Catedral de Sal y algunas personas **sacaron** muchas fotos. Un día, **visitamos** el Museo del Oro donde **admiramos** los tesoros[2] de oro y muchos artefactos precolombinos. Una noche, **miramos** un ballet folklórico; ¡**resultó** estupendo! También pasamos una semana al pie de los Andes y hasta **nadamos** en el Río Magdalena. ¡Nos **encantó** nuestro viaje!

---

[1]**único:** *only* / [2]**tesoros:** *treasures*

¿Comprendes?

1. ¿Qué característica geográfica **única** tiene Colombia?
2. ¿Qué productos agriculturales cultivan en Colombia?
3. ¿Cuáles son tres sitios de interés cultural y turístico en Bogotá?

■ El tiempo pasado: el pretérito con verbos *-ar*

The imperfect tense will be presented in Chapter 10.

Until now, you have been able to talk about present or future activities. In this chapter you will learn how to tell what happened in the past. To narrate activities and events from the past, Spanish uses the preterite tense. Regular **-ar** verbs have the following preterite endings:

viajar *(to travel)*			
yo	viaj**é**	nosotros(as)	viaj**amos**
tú	viaj**aste**	vosotros(as)	viaj**asteis**
Ud.		Uds.	
él	viaj**ó**	ellos	viaj**aron**
ella		ellas	

Viajé a Colombia el año pasado.	*I traveled to Colombia last year.*
Visitamos muchos museos.	*We visited many museums.*
Los niños **probaron** platillos típicos.	*The children tasted typical dishes.*

Note that the only difference between the **yo** form of the present tense and the **Ud., él, ella** form of the preterite is the accent in the preterite form.

Yo **hablo** poco español.	*I speak just a little Spanish.*
Ud. **habló** muy bien.	*You spoke very well.*

The **nosotros(as)** form of **-ar** verbs is the same in the present and the preterite. The context clarifies the meaning.

Miramos la tele todos los días.	*We watch TV every day.*
Miramos un buen programa anoche.	*We watched a good program last night.*

Verbs ending in **-car** spell the **yo** form of the preterite **-qué**.

Practiqué dos horas.	*I practiced two hours.*
Busqué mi libro por todas partes.	*I looked for my book everywhere.*

Verbs ending in **-gar** spell the **yo** form of the preterite **-gué**.

Yo **pagué** por todos.	*I paid for everyone.*
Llegué ayer por la tarde.	*I arrived yesterday afternoon.*

Verbs ending in **-zar** spell the **yo** form of the preterite **-cé**.

Almorcé ayer con Claudia.	*I had lunch yesterday with Claudia.*
Empecé el trabajo esta mañana.	*I started the job this morning.*

Practiquemos

A. En la cocina. ¿Qué pasó antes de la comida ayer? Forma oraciones de los elementos indicados.

MODELO: Esteban / olvidar / papas
          Esteban olvidó las papas.

1. la Sra. Martínez / preparar / comida
2. Manuel / hablar con / amigos
3. Luci y yo / limpiar / cocina
4. Germán y sus amigos / jugar fútbol
5. mamá / llamar / papá
6. Pamela y yo / tomar café
7. Pamela y Norma / lavar / platos
8. yo / cocinar / carne

¿Sabías?

Colombia tiene más de 1.550 especies de pájaros (birds) — más que Norteamérica y Europa juntas.

Transparencies:
O–2: **En la agencia de viajes**
O–3: **En el aeropuerto**
O–4: **En el avión**
O–5: **El horario de tren**

❖ **Para viajar**

hacer un viaje	*to take a trip*
viajar	*to travel*
volar (o→ue)	*to fly*

Antes de viajar

la agencia de viajes	*travel agency*
el (la) agente de viajes	*travel agent*
confirmar las reservaciones	*to confirm reservations*
empacar (c→que) las maletas	*to pack the bags*
hacer las reservaciones (por la red)	*to make reservations (on the Internet)*
la inyección	*shot*
el itinerario	*itinerary*

Modos de transporte

el autobús	*bus*
el avión	*plane*
el tren	*train*

Para llegar al aeropuerto o a la estación

el coche alquilado	*rented car*
el permiso de conducir	*driver's license*
el taxi	*taxi*

En el aeropuerto o la estación

la aduana	*customs*
despedirse	*to say good-bye*
el destino	*destination*
la inmigración	*immigration*
el (la) inspector(a)	*inspector*
mejorar el vuelo	*to upgrade the flight*
el número del vuelo	*flight number*
el pasaporte	*passport*
la puerta	*gate*
recoger (g→j) los boletos	*to pick up the tickets*
la visa	*visa*

En el viaje

el (la) aeromozo(a)	*flight attendant*
el (la) conductor(a)	*driver*
el (la) piloto	*pilot*

El alojamiento (Lodging)

el albergue	*hostal*
el ascensor	*elevator*

Point out that many people say **hacer las maletas** instead of **empacar**. **Omnibús, guagua,** and **camión** are used in addition to **autobús**. Other words for *flight attendant* include **sobrecargo** and **azafata** *(stewardess)*.

To practice the vocabulary, have pairs of students pick out at least ten things they do (or imagine they might do) when they travel and write sentences describing those activities. Then have each pair compare their list with the list of another pair. The four should compile a list of shared activities and then, by comparing all lists, the class can decide which are the most common activities. As a second activity, students can practice **tú** command forms by writing a list of ten suggestions for a friend who is taking a trip, e.g., **Saca muchas fotos, Mándame una postal, Visita los museos,** etc.

el botones	*bellhop*
la cama matrimonial	*double bed*
la cama sencilla	*single bed*
la habitación (doble, sencilla)	*(double, single) room*
el hotel	*hotel*
la propina	*tip*
la recepción	*reception desk*
el servicio de habitación	*room service*
En el destino	
la cámara	*camera*
dar una vuelta	*to take a walk, ride*
el (la) guía	*guide*
la guía	*guidebook*
mandar	*to send*
la postal	*postcard*
el recuerdo	*souvenir; memory*
sacar (qu) fotos	*to take photos*
el sello	*stamp*
Al pagar	
cambiar dinero	*to change money*
el cheque de viajero	*traveler's check*
cobrar un cheque	*to cash a check*
pagar (gu) en efectivo	*to pay cash*
la tarjeta de crédito	*credit card*

B. El viaje. Manuel está dando un reporte sobre el viaje de su familia a Colombia. Completa las oraciones con la forma adecuada del pretérito.

1. Yo _____ (empacar) mi propia maleta.

2. Nuestra familia _____ (viajar) a Colombia en un avión de Avianca.

3. Mis padres _____ (comprar) los boletos muy temprano.

4. Papá _____ (pagar) con su tarjeta de crédito.

5. Mi hermana y yo _____ (llegar) al hotel muy cansados.

6. Mamá y Papá _____ (visitar) todos los museos.

7. Yo _____ (sacar) muchas fotos con mi nueva cámara.

8. Mamá le _____ (preguntar) a mi papá: "¿ _____ (Comenzar, tú) a escribir las postales?"

9. Papá _____ (contestar): "Sí, ya las _____ (comenzar, yo)."

C. Antes del viaje. Tu compañero(a) de viaje te preguntó muchas cosas. ¿Qué preguntó? ¿Qué contestaste?

M O D E L O :   COMPAÑERO(A):   *¿Terminaste (Terminar)* las preparaciones?
                            TÚ: Sí, las *terminé.*

1. COMPAÑERO(A):   ¿ _____ (Recordar) los boletos?

   TÚ: Sí, los _____.

2. COMPAÑERO(A):   ¿ _____ (Pagar) toda la cuenta *(bill)*?

   TÚ: Sí, la _____.

3. COMPAÑERO(A):   ¿ _____ (Reservar) el cuarto del hotel?

   TÚ: Sí, lo _____.

4. COMPAÑERO(A):   ¿ _____ (Sacar) las fotos para los pasaportes?

   TÚ: Sí, las _____.

5. COMPAÑERO(A):   ¿ _____ (Empacar) las maletas?

   TÚ: Sí, las _____.

6. COMPAÑERO(A):   ¿ _____ (Comprar) las guías turísticas?

   TÚ: Sí, las _____.

> En los últimos diez años, ¿adónde viajaste? ¿Cuándo? ¿Con quién?

7. COMPAÑERO(A):   ¿ _____ (Llamar) al agente de viajes?

   TÚ: Sí, lo _____.

8. COMPAÑERO(A):   ¿ _____ (Buscar) la dirección del hotel?

   TÚ: Sí, la _____.

II. Los chibcha

LECTURA

Alonso de Ojeda, un compañero de Cristobal Colón, **descubrió** el país que hoy es Colombia en 1499. Él y sus compañeros **vieron** la riqueza de los indios y unos años después, otros españoles **volvieron** para explotarla. Encontraron entre otras tribus a los indios chibcha, una confederación de tribus en las montañas centrales. Los chibcha **vivieron** de la agricultura, produciendo maíz, papas, manioca y otros productos. El centro cultural de estas tribus fue Bogotá. Los españoles atacaron a los chibcha y los indios se

⊃

defendieron, pero los invasores los **vencieron** porque los cinco caciques[1] de los cinco grupos de chibcha no se **unieron**[2] en su defensa.

Hoy en día quedan unos pocos descendientes de los chibcha en América Central. Sin embargo, aspectos de la cultura chibcha perduran[3] en la cultura de Colombia, y los colombianos consideran la aportación[4] de los chibcha un aspecto muy importante de la historia del país.

[1] **el cacique:** *chieftain* / [2] **se unieron:** *united* / [3] **perduran:** *last, remain* / [4] **la aportación:** *contribution*

¿Comprendes?

1. ¿Quién es Alonso de Ojeda?
2. ¿Cómo vivieron los indios chibcha?
3. ¿Por qué vencieron los españoles a los chibcha?
4. ¿Qué importancia tienen los chibcha para los colombianos modernos?

■ El pretérito de los verbos *-er, -ir*

Regular **-er** and **-ir** verbs have these forms in the preterite:

comer

yo	comí	nosotros(as)	comimos
tú	comiste	vosotros(as)	comisteis
Ud. / él / ella	comió	Uds. / ellos / ellas	comieron

discutir

yo	discutí	nosotros(as)	discutimos
tú	discutiste	vosotros(as)	discutisteis
Ud. / él / ella	discutió	Uds. / ellos / ellas	discutieron

One-syllable verbs do not require a written accent in the first- and third-person forms.

ver

yo	vi	nosotros(as)	vimos
tú	viste	vosotros(as)	visteis
Ud. / él / ella	vio	Uds. / ellos / ellas	vieron

Decidimos hacer un viaje.	*We decided to take a trip.*
Marta **escogió** el itinerario.	*Marta chose the itinerary.*
Yo **recogí** los boletos.	*I picked up the tickets.*

In verbs whose stem ends in a vowel, **y** replaces **i** in the third-person forms. For example, the verb **leer**.

yo	leí	nosotros(as)	leímos
tú	leíste	vosotros(as)	leísteis
Ud.		Uds.	
él }	leyó	ellos }	leyeron
ella		ellas	

Norman **leyó** muchos libros.	*Norman read a lot of books.*
Leyeron los periódicos locales.	*They read the local newspapers.*
Oyeron un sonido extraño.	*They heard a strange sound.*

Practiquemos

A. Congreso internacional. ¿Qué experiencias nuevas encontraron los empleados de la oficina en un congreso profesional en Bogotá?

1. Rose Green _____ (aprender) mucho español.
2. El jefe y su esposa _____ (beber) aguardiente.
3. Yo _____ (asistir) a un ballet folklórico.
4. Y tú, ¿qué _____ (ver)?
5. Jorge García _____ (escribir) muchas postales a su novia.
6. Martín Delgado y yo _____ (comer) ajiaco.
7. Jorge y Martín _____ (describir) nuestro negocio a los colombianos.
8. Y nosotros _____ (oír) muchas cosas de los negocios en Colombia.
9. Los colombianos y nosotros _____ (recibir) información muy útil.
10. Todos _____ (salir) contentos del congreso.

B. Correspondencia electrónica. Completa la carta electrónica que mandó Leticia Rojas de la reunión en Bogotá a su esposo.

A: Roberto Moreno RMorenoGar@col.com
Fecha: 18 de marzo
De: Leticia Badéa Moreno
Sujeto: Saludos

Querido Roberto, ¿Cómo estás, mi amor? Como puedes ver, (1) _____ (aprender, yo) a usar una computadora colombiana. Ayer Martín, Rosa y yo (2) _____ (asistir) a unas sesiones muy interesantes. Los participantes (3) _____ (discutir) temas de mucho interés y yo (4) _____ (oír) unas ideas muy buenas. En el almuerzo, todos (5) _____ (comer, nosotros) comida típica y (6) _____ (beber) café colombiano. ¡Qué rico! Por la tarde, Rosa (7) _____ (leer) unos reportes en su cuarto y luego ella y yo (8) _____ (salir) a un restaurante excelente. Después (9) _____ (ver) un espectáculo de bailes y canciones colombianos. Al llegar al hotel, yo (10) _____ (escribir) unas postales. Pronto nos vemos, mi amor. Recibe un abrazo de tu esposa que te quiere mucho.

Leti

C. Ayer. ¿Qué pasó ayer en la clase de español de la señorita Arrabal? Forma oraciones en el pretérito con los elementos indicados.

1. por la mañana Elaine / estudiar / lecciones
2. Rob y Jane / trabajar
3. la Srta. Arrabal / escribir / planes
4. Anita / leer / reporte
5. yo / hablar / teléfono con otros estudiantes
6. Laura y Martha / oír / cintas
7. ¿tú / preparar / tarea?
8. Peter y yo / comer / cafetería
9. yo / buscar artículos / biblioteca por mucho tiempo
10. por eso yo / llegar tarde / clase de español

D. Otro fin de semana. ¿Cómo pasaron los Martínez el sábado pasado? Forma diez oraciones, usando un elemento de cada columna en cada oración y las formas apropiadas del pretérito.

MODELO: *Enriqueta lavó la ropa.*

> ¿Cómo pasaste tú el fin de semana pasado?

A	B	C
Enriqueta	barrer	garaje
Lorenzo	limpiar	película
mamá y papá	cortar	baño
mi novio y yo	sacudir	café
tú	preparar	césped
todos	lavar	abuelos
el perro	ver	ropa
yo	comer	carro
los chicos	jugar	casa
Enriqueta y yo	llamar	comida

Have students write an e-mail letter describing their last week.

Have students share their weekends with a partner and then decide who had the most interesting weekend.

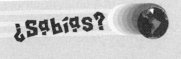

¿Sabías?   Un plato favorito de los colombianos es el ajiaco bogotano. Lo comen tanto los bogotanos como los turistas. El ajiaco es una sopa que tiene pollo, papas, maíz y a veces también carne.

III. Gabriel García Márquez, autor extraordinario

Gabriel García Márquez

LECTURA

Gabriel García Márquez es uno de los autores más famosos de Sudamérica. Nació en el año 1928 en el pequeño pueblo de Aracataca, Colombia. Estudió leyes y después trabajó como periodista[1] en Colombia y en otros países latinos. Pero en el año 1954, se dedicó totalmente a escribir. Una de sus obras[2] más importantes y conocidas es *Cien años de soledad.* En esta obra, **nos** describe Macondo, un pueblo olvidado por la civilización. En otras obras, Márquez **nos** cuenta historias que **nos** permiten participar en su mundo narrativo. También, nos lleva a diferentes planos de realidad e irrealidad. A Márquez **le** preocupan mucho el nacionalismo latinoamericano, sus orígenes y tradiciones; son algunos temas que **les** ofrece a sus lectores.

En el año 1982, **le** concedieron[3] el Premio Nóbel de Literatura. Es verdad que las obras de Gabriel García Márquez **nos** encantan.

---

[1]**periodista:** *journalist* / [2]**obra:** *work* / [3]**concedieron:** *awarded, gave*

¿Comprendes?

1. ¿Cuántos años tiene Gabriel García Márquez?
2. Además de escribir ficción, ¿qué otra profesión ejerció?
3. ¿Cuáles son tres características de las obras de García Márquez?
4. ¿Qué importancia tiene Gabriel García Márquez en el mundo literario hispanoamericano?

■ Los complementos indirectos con verbos conjugados

Indirect objects tell who is affected by the action of a verb: *to whom* or *for whom* something is done. In the sentences *I gave my boss the report, I gave the report to my boss,* the phrase *(to) my boss* tells to whom the report was given.

Indirect objects may be pronouns as well as nouns.

*I gave **her** the report.*
*I gave the report **to her**.*

In Spanish, indirect objects may be nouns . . .

Le di el informe **a mi jefa.**   *I gave the report **to my boss**.*

or they may be pronouns. There are six Spanish indirect object pronouns:

Indirect Object Pronouns			
me	*to, for me*	**nos**	*to, for us*
te	*to, for you (fam.)*	**os**	*to, for you (fam.)*
le	*to, for you (form.), him, her*	**les**	*to, for you (form.), them*

Le di el informe.   *I gave **her** the report.*
Te escribimos una postal.   *We wrote **you** a postcard.*
Les mandaron un paquete.   *They sent **them** a package.*

Since **le** and **les** may refer to more than one person, a clarifying phrase with the preposition **a** and a noun may be added. This structure may also be used for emphasis.

Le mandaron la carta **a Ema.**   *They sent the letter **to Ema**.*
Les preguntaron **a Susi y a Mando.**   *They asked **Susi and Mando**.*
Le di la composición **al profesor.**   *I gave the composition **to the professor**.*

Unambiguous pronouns, too, may be made emphatic with an added phrase.

Me dio el artículo **a mí.**   *He gave the article **to me**.*
¿**Te** dijo eso **a ti**?   *He said that **to you**?*

The placement of indirect object pronouns is the same as that of direct object pronouns. Indirect object pronouns precede conjugated verbs and negative commands, and nothing may come between the pronoun and the verb.

Me hizo muchos favores.   *He did many favors **for me**.*
Nos prepara comida deliciosa.   *She prepares delicious food **for us**.*

No **me** digas nada.   *Don't say anything **to me**.*
No **me** sirvas sopa fría.   *Don't serve **me** cold soup.*

Practiquemos

A. De regreso. Los abuelos volvieron de Colombia con recuerdos para todos. ¿Qué les dieron?

1. A mamá _____ dieron una figurina.

2. A mí _____ dieron un CD.

3. A ti _____ dieron un libro.

4. A Beto y a mí _____ dieron una guitarra.

5. A Andrés y a Elena _____ dieron unas maracas.

6. A todos nosotros _____ dieron muchas fotos.

7. A papá _____ dieron un sombrero típico de los Andes.

8. A ti y a José _____ dieron un tambor *(drum)*.

B. Esta mañana. ¿Qué hicieron todos esta mañana? Completa las oraciones con el pronombre adecuado.

MODELO: Los niños *le* hicieron muchas preguntas (a la profesora).

> Dile a tu compañero(a) tres cosas interesantes y dos cosas aburridas que hiciste esta mañana.

1. Enrique _____ mandó una carta (a mí).

2. Yo _____ compré unos boletos de avión (a mis amigos).

3. Evis y Rosita _____ prepararon una comida especial (a ti).

4. Mi esposa _____ compró un regalo (a mí y a los hijos).

5. Los hijos y yo _____ dijimos gracias (a mi esposa).

6. La profesora de español _____ preparó un examen (a nosotros).

7. Norma _____ hizo un favor (a mí).

8. El jefe _____ escribió un memo (a los empleados).

¿Sabías? Amazonia (la región del Río Amazonas de Colombia y otros países sudamericanos) se conoce como "el pulmón *(lung)* del mundo". Se llama así a causa de todo el oxígeno que producen los árboles de la selva. Además de ser responsable por el aire del mundo, esa región sostiene una increíble diversidad de especies de plantas y animales.

■ El complemento indirecto con otras formas verbales

Indirect object pronouns are attached to infinitives, present participles, and affirmative commands. Written accents are necessary to maintain the original stress of present participles and affirmative commands of more than one syllable.

Es importante decir**me** la verdad.	*It's important to tell **me** the truth.*
Contándo**nos** el cuento, rió.	*Telling **us** the story, he laughed.*
¡Di**me**!	*Tell **me**!*
Pása**le** la sal **a tu hermana**.	*Pass **your sister** the salt.*

Practiquemos

A. Juanito, por favor. Escribe la lista de mandatos que tú le diste a Juanito cuando fuiste al trabajo.

MODELO: mandar / carta a tu abuela
Mándale una carta a tu abuela.

1. preparar / almuerzo a tus hermanitos
2. pedir / dinero a tu padre
3. decir / planes a tu madre
4. preguntar / tarea a tus profesores
5. leer / cuento a tu hermanita
6. escribir / lista de tus actividades (a mí)

Have students role-play a scene between roommates or family members, in which one of the students is going out with friends and the other(s) give(s) instructions for the night.

■ El complemento indirecto en oraciones con verbos conjugados y no conjugados

In phrases that contain both a conjugated verb and an infinitive or present participle, the pronoun may either precede the conjugated verb or be attached to the infinitive or present participle.

Voy a contar**te** una historia.	*I'm going to tell **you** a story.*
Te voy a contar una historia.	
Estamos preparándo**les** ajiaco.	*We're preparing ajiaco **for them**.*
Les estamos preparando ajiaco.	

Nota: The verbs **gustar** and **encantar** (Chapter 3) require indirect object pronouns. (The English translations do not require indirect objects since the Spanish subject corresponds to what is "liked" or "enjoyed" in English.)

Me gustan los platos típicos.	*I like typical dishes. (Typical dishes are pleasing **to me**.)*
¿**Te** gusta este restaurante?	*Do you like this restaurant? (Is this restaurant pleasing **to you**?)*
Les encanta viajar.	*They love to travel. (Traveling is pleasing **to them**.)*

The verb **parecer** *(to seem [like]; to like)* also employs indirect object pronouns.

Me parece muy buena idea.	*It seems like a good idea **to me**.*
¿Qué **te** parecen los bailes?	*How do you like the dances? (How do they seem **to you**?)*
Les pareció bien.	*It seemed all right **to them**.*

Practiquemos

A. De viaje. ¿Qué dicen estos turistas en el autobús? Escribe las oraciones de dos formas.

MODELO: (a ti) Voy a pagar mañana.
Voy a pagarte mañana.
Te voy a pagar mañana.

1. (a Manuel) Estamos escribiendo una carta.
2. (a nosotros) Van a preparar una comida especial.
3. (a ella) Puedo conseguir una visa de estudiante.
4. (a mí) ¿Vas a comprar la guía?
5. (a Lorenzo y a Felipe) Puedo decir el itinerario.
6. (a Leona y a mí) Están sirviendo un café especial.

B. ¡Magnífico! ¿Cuál es la reacción de estos turistas en Colombia? Forma oraciones con los elementos dados.

MODELO: Martín / encantar / Barranquilla
A Martín le encanta Barranquilla.

1. Susana y Jorge / gustar / las cervezas colombianas
2. ¿Ud. / gustar / ajiaco?
3. Alicia / encantar / el Monserrat
4. nosotros / gustar / el jardín botánico
5. ¿tú / gustar / los museos?
6. yo / encantar / el Mercado de las Pulgas

> ¿Qué comidas te encantan? ¿Qué comidas no te gustan?

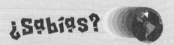

¿Sabías?

A muchas personas en los Estados Unidos les gusta un postre llamado «isla flotante». Pues, este plato también es un postre popular en Colombia. Consiste en una «isla» de merengue que flota sobre un «mar» de crema. La receta es antigua y evidentemente es popular en muchas partes del mundo.

IV. El Dorado

LECTURA

La leyenda de El Dorado[1] probablemente originó con los indios chibcha de Colombia. Al llegar al poder[2] un nuevo jefe, la tribú lo cubría[3] de polvo de oro.[4] Ese jefe cubierto de oro **fue** "el dorado" original. Creció[5] la fama de "el dorado" y los españoles creyeron[6] que existía todo un país, lleno de oro y piedras[7] preciosas, llamado "El Dorado". Montaron expediciones para encontrar el país mágico. **Fueron** desde las altas montañas hasta los valles de los Ríos Orinoco y Amazonas buscando riquezas.[8] Aunque nunca encontraron el país legendario, sus expediciones **dieron** forma al norte de Sudamérica en la forma de mapas e información geográfica. Tan conocida es la leyenda de El Dorado que Edgar Allan Poe y John Milton **hicieron** mención del país tan buscado y deseado.

[1]**dorado:** *golden* / [2]**el poder:** *power* / [3]**cubría:** *covered* / [4]**el polvo de oro.** *gold dust* / [5]**Creció:** *It grew* / [6]**creyeron:** *believed* / [7]**la piedra:** *stones* / [8]**las riquezas:** *riches*

¿Comprendes?

1. ¿Fue un mito «El Dorado» original?
2. ¿Cómo fue «El Dorado» que buscaron los españoles?
3. ¿Cuál fue un resultado positivo de las exploraciones de los españoles?

■ Verbos irregulares en el pretérito

The verbs **ir, ser, dar, hacer,** and **decir** are irregular in the preterite tense and must be memorized. **Ser** and **ir** share the same forms. The context clarifies the meaning of these verbs.

ir/ser			
yo	**fui**	nosotros(as)	**fuimos**
tú	**fuiste**	vosotros(as)	**fuisteis**
Ud.		Uds.	
él	**fue**	ellos	**fueron**
ella		ellas	

Fue necesario comprar los boletos hoy.	***It was*** *necessary to buy the tickets today.*
Ella **fue** al museo primero.	***She went*** *to the museum first.*

dar			
yo	**di**	nosotros(as)	**dimos**
tú	**diste**	vosotros(as)	**disteis**
Ud. él ella	**dio**	Uds. ellos ellas	**dieron**

hacer			
yo	**hice**	nosotros(as)	**hicimos**
tú	**hiciste**	vosotros(as)	**hicisteis**
Ud. él ella	**hizo**	Uds. ellos ellas	**hicieron**

decir			
yo	**dije**	nosotros(as)	**dijimos**
tú	**dijiste**	vosotros(as)	**dijisteis**
Ud. él ella	**dijo**	Uds. ellos ellas	**dijeron**

¿Qué **dijo** ese hombre?	*What **did** that man say?*
Ellos **hicieron** las maletas.	*They **packed** the suitcases.*
¿Qué le **diste**?	*What **did you give** her?*
¿Adónde **fuiste**?	*Where **did you go**?*

Compound verbs ending in **-decir** have the same preterite endings as **decir**. These verbs include **maldecir** *(to curse)* and **bendecir** *(to bless)*.

Los **maldijeron** y se fueron.	*They **cursed** them and left.*
El cura los **bendijo** a todos.	*The priest **blessed** them all.*

Practiquemos

A. Un mensaje. Margarita dejó este mensaje telefónico para su novio, David. ¿Qué dijo ella? Completa las oraciones con la forma adecuada del pretérito.

Hola, David. Soy yo, Margarita. Quiero decirte lo que (1) _____ (hacer) hoy. (2) _____ (Ir) a la agencia de viajes y (3) _____ (hablar) con nuestro agente de viajes. Me (4) _____ (decir) que hoy es el último día de un precio especial. (5) _____ (Ser) necesario comprar los boletos para el viaje a Colombia hoy. Así que, le (6) _____ (dar) mi tarjeta de crédito y los (7) _____ (comprar).

También yo (8) _____ . (hacer) otras compras en el centro. Aquí estoy en casa esperándote. Te veo más tarde, amor mío.

B. ¿Y ayer? Di lo que hizo la familia Menéndez ayer, formando oraciones con los elementos dados.

MODELO: Rosita / ir / escuela
          Rosita fue a la escuela.

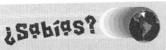

¿Qué hiciste tú ayer?

1. la Sra. Menéndez / ir / agencia de viajes
2. Robert y Cecilia / hacer / quehaceres
3. la tía Rosa y yo / dar una vuelta / parque
4. el Sr. Menéndez / hacer / llamadas telefónicas
5. Princesa, la perra / ir / oficina del veterinario
6. la abuelita Carmen / hacer / pastel
7. yo / ir / supermercado
8. todos / decir: / "ser un buen día"

C. Un fracaso. Completa la conversación entre Manuel y Elena con el pretérito del verbo apropiado. Puedes usar los verbos más de una vez si es necesario.

Distribute classroom objects among students. Then ask the students: ¿A quién (le) di la calculadora? They should answer: Dio la calculadora a ____.

dar   decir   hacer   ir   parecer   resultar *(to turn out)*

MANUEL: ¿Adónde _____ Uds. después de clase?

ELENA: _____ a ver una película.

MANUEL: ¿Cuál _____?

ELENA: _____ *El ogro del monte.*

MANUEL: ¿Qué tal les _____ la película? _____ que es muy buena.

ELENA: ¡Qué va! *(Nonsense!)* ¡ _____ tonta! El ogro _____ (resultar) ser muy bueno. _____ muchos favores y _____ mucha comida y ropa y le trajo *(brought)* prosperidad a la gente del monte... tú sabes. La película _____ un verdadero desastre.

¿Sabías?

Colombia produce más del 95% de las esmeraldas del mundo. También es el productor más importante de oro en América Latina.

V. El café en Colombia

LECTURA

Hace más de doscientos años que el primer café llegó a Colombia del norte de África. Desde entonces, el café es un producto de mucha importancia económica. ¿Cómo se produce el café? Primero el agricultor planta los granos[1] de café. Cuando germinan, el agricultor transplanta las pequeñas plantas. Cuando **hace seis meses que** están en el invernadero,[2] el agricultor las mueve[3] a la plantación. En tres o cuatro años, los árboles[4] empiezan a producir granos maduros de café. Cada árbol produce aproximadamente una libra[5] de café al año. El agricultor cosecha[6] los granos de café y luego los lleva a la fábrica[7] donde los trabajadores los lavan, los tuestan[8] y los mandan al mercado. Allí nosotros compramos el café, lo molemos,[9] le agregamos[10] agua caliente y pronto estamos probando[11] café. ¡Qué rico! ¿Quieres un café?

[1]**los granos:** *beans* / [2]**el invernadero:** *greenhouse* / [3]**mueve:** *moves* / [4]**los árboles:** *trees* / [5]**la libra:** *pound* / [6]**cosecha:** *harvests* / [7]**la fábrica:** *factory* / [8]**los tuestan:** *toast them* / [9]**molemos:** *we grind* / [10]**agregamos:** *we add* / [11]**estamos probando:** *we are tasting, trying*

¿Comprendes?

1. ¿Es el café una planta nativa de Colombia?
2. ¿Cuántos años tienen los árboles de café cuando producen sus primeros granos maduros?
3. ¿Qué les pasa a los granos de café entre el árbol y nuestra taza de café?

■ Las expresiones de tiempo con *hace* + presente

In Spanish, this construction is used to describe an action that began in the past and continues in the present.

hace + *time* + **que** + verb in the present

Hace tres horas que esperas el avión. — *You have been waiting for the plane for three hours.*

Hace mucho tiempo que vivo aquí. — *I've been living here for a long time.*

To ask a question, use the following construction:

¿Cuanto tiempo hace que + *verb in the present tense* **?**

¿Cuánto tiempo hace que estudias?	*How long have you been studying?*
¿Cuánto tiempo hace que vive Ud. aquí?	*How long have you been living here?*

Practiquemos

A. Esperando. ¿Cuánto tiempo hace que estas personas esperan el avión en el aeropuerto? Primero, haz la pregunta y luego, contéstala usando la información que sigue.

MODELO: Antonio: cinco minutos
¿Cuánto tiempo hace que Antonio espera? Hace cinco minutos que espera.

1. la familia Alarcón: dos horas
2. Ernesto y su novia: 25 minutos
3. yo: una hora y 20 minutos
4. Silvia y su mamá: 45 minutos
5. tú: media hora
6. Hector y yo: diez minutos
7. Javier y tú: tres horas
8. los socios del Club de Golf: una hora y media

B. ¿Cuánto tiempo hace que... ? Carmen les hace estas preguntas a sus amigos. ¿Cómo contestan?

MODELO: María Elena, / vivir en Bogotá / dos años
—*María Elena, ¿cuánto tiempo hace que vives en Bogotá?*
—*Hace dos años que vivo en Bogotá.*

1. Raúl, / conducir *(to drive)* su carro nuevo / (un mes)
2. Gloria y Ester, / asistir a la Universidad de Bogotá / (un año)
3. Fernando, / leer las novelas de Gabriel García Márquez / (un semestre)
4. profesor Guzmán, / enseñar en la Universidad de Bogotá / (diez años)
5. Margarita, / recibir cartas por correo electrónico / (dos semanas)
6. José y Lulú, / ir frecuentemente a Cartagena / (muchos años)

Have students make up five questions about how long a classmate has been engaging in certain activities, e.g., living in your town, studying Spanish, driving a car, working at a current job, etc. Then have pairs ask and answer questions.

■ Las expresiones de tiempo con *hace* + pretérito

To indicate time that has passed since an event took place, these constructions are used.

NOTA:
Hace in these constructions means ago.

Hace + *time* + **que** + *verb in the preterite*

Verb in the preterite + **hace** + *time*

Hace dos días que llegué.	*I arrived two days ago.*
Comieron hace 20 minutos.	*They ate 20 minutes ago.*

Practiquemos

A. ¿Cuánto tiempo hace que... ? Cuánto tiempo hace que hiciste las siguientes cosas? Responde usando la expresion **hace que** y el verbo en el pretérito.

MODELO: ¿Cuánto tiempo hace que diste unas flores a alguien?
          —*Hace cuatro años que di unas flores a alguien.*

1. ¿Cuánto tiempo hace que hiciste las tareas de español?
2. ¿Cuánto tiempo hace que fuiste a una fiesta?
3. ¿Cuánto tiempo hace que hablaste con un miembro de tu familia?
4. ¿Cuánto tiempo hace que viste una buena película?
5. ¿Cuánto tiempo hace que comiste algo?

B. ¿Cuántos años hace... ? ¿Cuánto tiempo hace que ocurrieron estos eventos? Escribe las preguntas. Luego hazle las preguntas a un(a) compañero(a) de clase.

MODELO: Tú: los Juegos Olímpicos / tener lugar
                           en Los Ángeles
                           ¿Cuánto tiempo hace que los Juegos
                           Olímpicos tuvieron lugar en Los Ángeles?
          COMPAÑERO(A):   en 1984
                           Hace 15 años que los Juegos Olímpicos
                           tuvieron lugar en Los Ángeles.

1.   Tú: los estadounidenses / llegar a la luna
   COMPAÑERO(A):   en 1969

2.   Tú: Gabriel García Márquez / recibir el Premio
                      Nóbel
   COMPAÑERO(A):   en l982

3.   Tú: Fidel Castro / tomar control del gobierno
                      cubano
   COMPAÑERO(A):   en 1958

4.   Tú: los Estados Unidos / proclamar su
                      independencia
   COMPAÑERO(A):   en 1/76

5.   Tú: tú / nacer
   COMPAÑERO(A):   en ¿ ?

> ¿Cuánto tiempo hace que viajaste la última vez *(last time)*? Describe tu viaje.

A ver si sabes

Use this self-test to see if you know the material presented in Chapter 7.

A. El diario de Anita. Completa el diario de Anita con el pretérito de los verbos indicados.

Hoy mi clase de biología (1) _____ (visitar) el Jardín Botánico. (2) _____ (Mirar, nosotros) muchas plantas y flores interesantes. Yo (3) _____ (sacar) una foto de un árbol de café. Después (4) _____ (almorzar) en la cafetería con Pamela y yo (5) _____ (pagar) por las dos. Después de las clases, mis padres me (6) _____ (llamar). ¡ (7) _____ (Hablar, nosotros) por una hora! Luego (8) _____ (llegar) Antonio, y él y yo (9) _____ (estudiar) para un examen de español. Bueno, es todo por ahora. Escribo más mañana.

B. Las vacaciones. Norma y Martín hablan de sus vacaciones. Completa su conversación con el pretérito de los verbos indicados.

NORMA: ¿Dónde _____ (pasar) Uds. las vacaciones?

MARTÍN: _____ (Decidir, nosotros) hacer un viaje a Sudamérica. Raquel _____ (leer) en una guía que Colombia es fantástica y así la _____ (escoger, nosotros) para nuestras vacaciones. Y Uds., ¿ _____ (viajar) también?

NORMA: No. Yo _____ (asistir) a una clase para mi trabajo. _____ (Aprender) mucho pero José y yo no _____ (viajar) a ninguna parte. En Colombia, ¿ _____ (ver, tú) cosas interesantes?

MARTÍN: Sí, muy interesantes. También _____ (comer, nosotros) comida muy rica. Y claro, estando en Colombia, Raquel _____ (beber) mucho café. _____ (Conocer, nosotros) a unos amigos colombianos. Ellos nos _____ (invitar) a su casa y nos _____ (servir) un café riquísimo.

NORMA: ¡Qué envidia! Bueno, José y yo ya lo _____ (discutir). ¡El año que viene *(next year)* vamos a viajar!

C. En el trabajo. ¿Qué pasa hoy en la oficina? Haz oraciones con los pronombres indirectos.

1. (a Carlos) Voy a escribir un memo.
2. (a ti) Están preguntando sobre tus planes.
3. (a María y a mí) El jefe dice algo importante.
4. (al jefe) Puedo preparar un informe esta tarde.
5. (a Horacio y a Elena) ¿Piensas leer tu carta?
6. (a mí) Antonio pide un favor.

Preguntas
culturales
1. ¿Cuáles son
tres atracciones
de Bogotá?
2. ¿Qué pasó
entre los chibcha
y los españoles?
3. ¿Quién es
Gabriel García
Márquez y por qué
es importante?

D. En Colombia. Todos fueron impresionados por diferentes cosas en Colombia. Escribe oraciones con los pronombres indirectos y los elementos indicados.

1. (a mí) gustar los platillos típicos
2. (a José) encantar la gente
3. (a María y a mí) gustar el café
4. (a ti) gustar las montañas
5. (a todos nosotros) encantar las playas
6. (a ellas) encantar todo el país

E. De vacaciones. Completa el párrafo con la forma adecuada de estos verbos, según el contexto: dar, decir, hacer, ir, ser.

¡Qué buenas vacaciones! Hace un año que mi amiga Tina y yo (1) _____ a Colombia. Antes de salir, mi papá me sorprendió y nos (2) _____ $2.000 para nuestro viaje. ¡Qué sorpresa! Mi mamá le (3) _____: "¡Benjamín, tú eres tan generoso!" Mi papá respondió que lo (4) _____ porque le dio mucho gusto. Claro que nuestro viaje (5) _____ maravilloso, ¡gracias a mi papá!

F. Una familia ocupada. ¿Cuánto tiempo hace que la familia Rojas hace lo siguiente?

1. los señores Rojas / dos años / trabajar la universidad
2. Lucía / dos años / tomar lecciones de piano
3. Anamaría y Beto / tres meses / tener su perro, Chico
4. yo, la hija mayor / cinco semanas / trabajar en el banco
5. y tú, Joselito / una semana / jugar al fútbol con tus amigos

G. ¿Qué pasó y cuándo? ¿Cuánto tiempo hace que estas personas hicieron lo siguiente?

1. Norma y Arnoldo visitaron Colombia en 1991.
2. Mis amigos y yo fuimos a Puerto Rico en 1996.
3. Uds. comenzaron sus estudios en 1989.
4. Hablé con mi hermana a las 3:00 y ahora son las 8:00.
5. Hiciste las tareas de español el viernes y hoy es domingo.
6. Planeaste tu viaje a Cuba el año pasado.

Querido Diario. ¿Hiciste un viaje interesante o fuiste a un evento (fiesta, campamento, congreso [convention]) muy bueno? Dile a tu diario qué pasó en esa experiencia. Para organizar tus ideas, haz un esquema con los puntos más positivos: por ejemplo, las actividades, los sitios o la gente. Ahora describe tu experiencia a tu diario.

Grammar: preterite, preterite (irregular)
Phrases: talking about past events
Vocabulary: camping, travel, beach

Vocabulario activo

Antes de viajar

la agencia de viajes
el (la) agente de viajes
confirmar las reservaciones
empacar (c→qu) las maletas

hacer las reservaciones (por la red)
la inyección
el itinerario

Los viajes

hacer un viaje
viajar
volar (o→ue)

En el aeropuerto o la estación

la aduana
despedirse
el destino
la inmigración

el (la) inspector(a)
mejorar el vuelo
el número del vuelo
el pasaporte

la puerta
recoger (g→j) los boletos
la visa

Modos de transporte

el autobús
el avión
el tren

Para llegar al aeropuerto o la estación

el coche alquilado
el permiso de conducir
el taxi

En el viaje

el (la) aeromozo(a)
el (la) conductor(a)
el (la) piloto

El alojamiento

el albergue
el ascensor
el botones
la cama matrimonial

la cama sencilla
la habitación (doble, sencilla)
el hotel

la propina
la recepción
el servicio de habitación

En el destino

la cámara
dar una vuelta
el (la) guía
la guía
mandar

la postal
el recuerdo
sacar (qu) fotos
el sello

Al pagar

cambiar dinero
el cheque de viajero
cobrar un cheque
pagar (gu) en efectivo
la tarjeta de crédito

Otras palabras y verbos

bendecir
buscar (c→qu)
el (la) jefe(a)
maldecir

parecer
probar (o→ue)
reservar

Web site:
http://spanishforlife.heinle.com

Transparencies:
A–2: México y La América Central
A–16: Country Profile, Guatemala

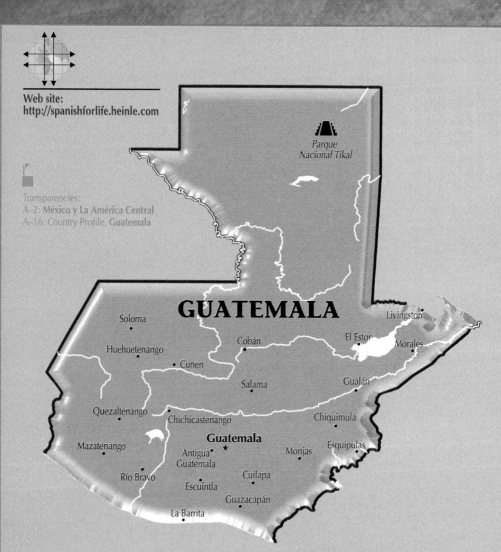

Parque
Nacional Tikal

GUATEMALA

Soloma

Livingston

Huehuetenango

Cobán

El Estor

Morales

Cunen

Quezaltenango

Salama

Gualán

Chichicastenango

Chiquimula

Guatemala
★

Mazatenango

Antigua
Guatemala

Monjas

Esquipulas

Río Bravo

Cuílapa

Escuintla

Guazacapán

La Barrita

REPÚBLICA DE GUATEMALA

Nombre oficial: República de Guatemala

Área: 108,889 km²

Población: 11.000.000

Capital: Ciudad de Guatemala

Moneda: el quetzal

Idioma oficial: español

Fiesta nacional: 15 de septiembre,
Día de la Independencia

178

Guatemala y los guatemaltecos

Pirámides mayas en Tika, Guatemala

In this chapter you will learn:

GRAMMAR POINTS

- Irregular verbs in the preterite
- Stem-changing verbs in the preterite (o→u, e→i)
- Direct and indirect object pronouns
- Direct and indirect object pronouns in the third person
- Expressions with the verb **tener**

COMMUNICATIVE FUNCTIONS

- Tell what you did on vacation
- Narrate past events

VOCABULARY

- Vacation vocabulary
- Adverbs that refer to the past

179

I. Rigoberta Menchú

LECTURA

Rigoberta Menchú, indígena maya-quiché, luchadora por los derechos humanos y defensora de la gente indígena, ganó el Premio Nóbel de la Paz en 1992.

Esta mujer extraordinaria nació el 9 de enero de 1959 al norte de Guatemala en un pueblito que se llama Chinel. Ella viene de una familia pobre. Comenzó a trabajar desde muy niña en los campos[1] donde **tuvo** que ayudar a sus papás con la cosecha[2] de café y algodón. De jovencita se **despidió** de su familia y se fue a la capital para trabajar como sirvienta en las casas de la gente rica.

Hubo un evento que cambió la vida de Rigoberta: la muerte violenta de sus padres y su hermano durante la guerra civil que duró muchos años. Ella **supo** más tarde que el gobierno guatemalteco fue responsable y, desde entonces,[3] **quiso** cambiar la situación horrible de la gente indígena y se dedicó a una labor infatigable para mejorar[4] su condición social. Escribió unos libros y muchos ensayos describiendo las atrocidades que se cometieron contra su gente y **expuso** la corrupción de los líderes guatemaltecos. Con el dinero que ganó Rigoberta del Premio Nóbel, ella **pudo** establecer una fundación para continuar su campaña para los derechos humanos.[5]

---

[1]**los campos:** *fields* / [2]**la cosecha:** *harvest* / [3]**desde entonces:** *from then on* / [4]**mejorar:** *to improve, to make better* / [5]**los derechos humanos:** *human rights*

¿Comprendes?

1. ¿Qué hizo Rigoberta Menchú para ayudar a la gente pobre de su país?
2. Haz una lista de otras personas famosas que lucharon —y siguen luchando por los derechos humanos. ¿Cómo caracterizas a este tipo de gente?
3. Compara tu lista con la de un(a) compañero(a) de clase y comparte *(share)* tus ideas.

■ Unos verbos irregulares en el pretérito

You have already learned that **ir, ser, dar, decir,** and **hacer** are irregular verbs in the *preterite* tense. The following verbs are irregular as well. Note that they have irregular stems and unstressed first and third person singular endings.

i-Stem Verbs			
querer	**quis**	**-e**	**-imos**
		-iste	**-isteis**
venir	**vin**	**-o**	**-ieron**

Mario **quiso** ayudarme.	Mario **wanted** to help me.
¿A qué hora **vinieron** tus primos?	At what time **did** your cousins **come?**

u-Stem Verbs			
andar	**anduv**		
estar	**estuv**	**-e**	**-imos**
haber	**hub**	**-iste**	**-isteis**
poder	**pud**	**-o**	**-ieron**
poner	**pus**		
saber	**sup**		
tener	**tuv**		

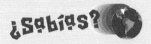

¿Sabías?

En nuestra época más de dos millones de mayas viven en el territorio tradicional maya (México, Guatemala, Belize, El Salvador y Honduras) y hablan 21 lenguas diferentes. Estas lenguas no son más similares que el español y el italiano. También se habla garífuna, una lengua hablada por los negros que son descendientes de esclavos (slaves) que escaparon de Belize y otros lugares.

Hubo un accidente ayer en la capital.	**There was** an accident yesterday in the capital.
Ella **tuvo** la oportunidad de visitar Guatemala.	**She had** the opportunity to visit Guatemala.

j-Stem Verbs			
conducir	**conduj**	**-e**	**-imos**
		-iste	**-isteis**
traer	**traj**	**-o**	**-eron**

¿Quién **trajo** la comida guatemalteca?	Who **brought** the Guatemalan food?

Other verbs that are conjugated like **conducir** and **traer** include:

decir	to say; to tell	atraer	to attract
traducir	to translate	distraer	to distract
reducir	to reduce	contraer	to contract
producir	to produce		

Some verbs have special meanings in the preterite:

poder:	pude, pudiste...
	I was able (and succeeded in doing something), you were able…
no poder:	no pude, no pudiste...
	I didn't succeed (failed), you didn't succeed . . .

These verbs will be discussed and practiced further in Chapter 10.

querer:	quise, quisiste...
	I tried, intended (to do something), you tried...
no querer:	no quise, no quisiste...
	I refused (to do something), you refused . . .
saber:	supe, supiste...
	I found out, you found out . . .
conocer:	conocí, conociste...
	I met, you met . . .

Por fin nuestro equipo **pudo** ganar.   *Finally our team **was able to** win (succeeded in winning).*

Me invitaron, pero no **pude** ir.   *They invited me, but **I couldn't** (failed to) go.*

Quise hablar con ella, pero ella **no quiso**.   *I tried to talk with her, but **she refused**.*

¿**Supiste** los resultados?   *Did you find out the results?*

Lo **conocí** ayer.   *I met him yesterday.*

Practiquemos

A. El terremoto. Completa el párrafo siguiente con la forma adecuada del verbo entre paréntesis.

Ayer (1) _____ (haber) un terremoto en la Ciudad de Guatemala. Muchos turistas (2) _____ (querer) salir de la ciudad pero no (3) _____ (poder). Rosa (4) _____ (estar) en el Hotel Palma con su esposo, Ricardo. Cuando oyeron el ruido a la 1:00 de la mañana, se levantaron y se (5) _____ (poner) la ropa y (6) _____ (ir) rápidamente a la puerta de la habitación. Ricardo y Rosa (7) _____ (tener) que calmar a los otros vecinos muy agitados. Después de unos minutos, todos salieron del hotel. Más tarde, todos (8) _____ (saber) que el terremoto registró cinco en la escala Richter. ¡Qué experiencia!

B. ¡Un buen restaurante Guatemalteco! Mis amigos y yo fuimos al restaurante Sol ayer. Completa las oraciones con la forma adecuada del verbo indicado.

1. El mesero nos _____ (traer) unos platos muy ricos.
2. Tú _____ (poder) leer el menú, ¿verdad?
3. Unos turistas _____ (andar) por 20 minutos buscando este restaurante.
4. Felipe _____ (venir) con su novia.
5. Una niña _____ (no querer) comer sus verduras.
6. Yo_____ (conducir) mi coche al restaurante.
7. Nosotros _____ (estar) muy contentos con nuestra comida.
8. _____ (Haber) mucha gente en el restaurante.

Cuenta a tu compañero(a) una experiencia inolvidable en un restaurante.

C. El accidente. De las tres posibilidades, escoge la forma del verbo que mejor complete la oración.

1. La semana pasada en la ciudad de Antigua _____ un accidente.

a. estuvo **b.** hubo **c.** tuvo

2. Víctor y Mary, unos turistas norteamericanos, _____ en el accidente.

a. hubieron **b.** anduvieron **c.** estuvieron

3. Víctor _____ con mucho cuidado pero no _____ evitar *(to avoid)* el accidente.

a. condujo **b.** estuvo **c.** vino

a. quiso **b.** tuvo **c.** pudo

4. Después del accidente, el chófer del autobús llamó a la policía y los oficiales _____ inmediatamente.

a. anduvieron **b.** vinieron **c.** estuvieron

5. Después de una investigación, Víctor y Mary _____ que el chófer del autobús _____ la culpa.

a. supieron **b.** pudieron **c.** quisieron

a. hubo **b.** pudo **c.** tuvo

D. De vacaciones. Describe las actividades de un grupo de turistas en Guatemala el verano pasado. Forma ocho oraciones con elementos de las tres columnas, usando el tiempo del pretérito.

A	B	C
		de inglés a español
la guía		cansado
Manuel y Susana	andar	por la playa
los niños	conducir	por toda Guatemala
yo	traducir	por los museos
tú	estar	para los otros turistas
Manuel y yo	traer	muchas maletas
todo el grupo		de casa a Antigua
el director		muy contentos
		una mochila

❖ **Para hablar de las vacaciones**

Al pasar las vacaciones en casa

reponer el techo

pintar la casa

organizar (c) el garaje

ordenar los gabinetes

arreglar el coche

trabajar en el jardín

Transparencies:
F–5: **El campo**
G–8: **En el lago**

Remind students that many other vacation activities are found in Chapters 2, 3, and 7. In Mexico, **carpa** means *tent*. In Spain, **una bombona** means a *propane or butane cannister*, and **sartén** is feminine, not masculine.

Al acampar

armar la tienda

la hielera

la fogata

la tienda

el colchón de aire

el saco de dormir

la mochila

la estufa para acampar

la leña

el abrelatas	can opener	el propano	propane
la cuchara	spoon	el sartén	frying pan
el cuchillo	knife	el tanque de gas	gas canister
la linterna	flashlight	el tenedor	fork
la navaja universal	Swiss army knife	los utensilios de cocina	cooking utensils
la olla	pot, sauce pan		

Otros pasatiempos

Transparencies:
G–6: **Deportes (1)**
G–7: **Deportes (2)**

la red

el voleibol

el esquí acuático

correr las olas

pescar (qu)

el (la) veleador(a)

velear

el árbitro	referee	patinar	to skate
el badminton	badminton	el ping-pong	ping-pong
esquiar (esquío)	to ski	la raqueta	racket
hacer la tabla de nieve	to snowboard	la raquetilla	paddle
hacer la tabla de vela	to sail	el vuelo libre	hang gliding

Practiquemos ✎

Mis vacaciones. Contesta las preguntas.

Al acampar

1. ¿Qué preparaciones hay que hacer para dormir?
2. ¿Qué usas para preparar la comida?
3. ¿Qué haces después de comer?

En casa

4. ¿Qué debes hacer en tu casa? (reparaciones *[repairs]*, organización)
5. ¿Qué te gusta hacer en tu casa durante las vacaciones?

Los pasatiempos

6. Si puedes viajar, ¿qué te gusta hacer para pasar el tiempo durante las vacaciones?

> Dile a tu compañero(a) cómo pasaste tus últimas vacaciones.

II. Miguel Ángel Asturias

LECTURA

Miguel Ángel Asturias es la figura más destacada de la literatura guatemalteca. Nació en 1899 en la Ciudad de Guatemala. **Murió** en 1974. Fue poeta y novelista, pero fue más. Estudió leyes y **sirvió** a su país como representante en el Congreso y diplomático en México, Argentina, Francia y El Salvador. Fundó[1] y dirigió el *Diario del Aire*.

En su obra literaria **siguió** técnicas muy modernas. Estuvo preocupado por la justicia social, la suerte[2] de los mayas y el destino de su país, y **repitió** estas preocupaciones en los temas de sus obras. Escribió *El señor presidente*, su obra maestra, en 1946. Esta novela es muy conocida en todas partes[3] porque fue traducida a 16 lenguas extranjeras.

En 1968, Miguel Ángel Asturias recibió el Premio Nóbel de Literatura. Los compatriotas de Asturias sienten mucho orgullo por este héroe de las letras guatemaltecas.

---

[1]**Fundó:** *He founded* / [2]**suerte:** *luck, fate* / [3]**en todas partes:** *everywhere*

¿Comprendes?

1. ¿Cuántos años vivió Miguel Ángel Asturias?
2. ¿Sobre qué temas escribió Asturias?
3. ¿Qué otras figuras latinoamericanas recibieron el Premio Nóbel?

¿Sabías?

En los países de cultura maya, los chicos modernos juegan fútbol en canchas muy antiguas. El Popol Vuh, un poema épico de los mayas, menciona juegos de pelota que tienen importancia ritual en la religión maya. Aunque el fútbol moderno no es importante en la religión contemporánea, es la continuación de una costumbre antigua.

■ Los verbos con cambios en la raíz en el preterito (o→u, e→i)

Stem-changing verbs whose infinitives end in **-ar** or **-er** undergo *no* changes in the preterite tense.

Asturias **empezó** a estudiar en Paris en 1923.	*Asturias **began** to study in Paris in 1923.*
Defendió a los pobres en sus obras.	*He **defended** the poor in his works.*

Stem-changing verbs whose infinitives end in **-ir** do undergo the following changes in the preterite tense.

The stem change *o→u*

The stem vowel **o** changes to **u** in the third person singular and plural. This change affects verbs whose stem vowel **o** changes to **ue** (**dormir**→**duermo**) in the present tense.

dormir *(to sleep)*			
yo	dormí	nosotros(as)	dormimos
tú	dormiste	vosotros(as)	dormisteis
Ud. ⎫ él ⎬ ella ⎭	durmió	Uds. ⎫ ellos ⎬ ellas ⎭	durmieron

morir *(to die)*			
yo	morí	nosostros(as)	morimos
tú	moriste	vosotros(as)	moristeis
Ud. ⎫ él ⎬ ella ⎭	murió	Uds. ⎫ ellos ⎬ ellas ⎭	murieron

Mario **durmió** más que yo.	*Mario **slept** more than I did.*
Muchos soldados **murieron** en la guerra.	*Many soldiers **died** in the war.*

The stem change e→i

The stem vowel e changes to i in the third person singular and plural in the preterite. This change affects verbs whose stem vowel **e** changes to **ie** (**sugerir**→**sugiero**) in the present tense as well as those whose stem vowel **e** changes to **i** (**seguir**→**sigo**).

sugerir *(to suggest)*			
yo	sugerí	nosotros(as)	sugerimos
tú	sugeriste	vosotros(as)	sugeristeis
Ud. } él } ella }	sugirió	Uds. } ellos } ellas }	sugirieron

seguir *(to follow)*			
yo	seguí	nosotros(as)	seguimos
tú	seguiste	vosotros(as)	seguisteis
Ud. } él } ella }	siguió	Uds. } ellos } ellas }	siguieron

Other verbs like **sugerir** include:

diferir	*to differ*		mentir	*to lie*
divertir	*to amuse*		sentir	*to feel (sorry)*
hervir	*to boil*			

Other verbs like **seguir** include:

despedir	*to say good-bye*		reír	*to laugh*
freír	*to fry*		repetir	*to repeat*
pedir	*to ask (for); to order*			

Practiquemos

A. La comida. Marta y Pablo invitaron a Ernesto a comer a su casa. ¿Qué pasó? Llena los espacios en blanco con el pretérito de los verbos indicados.

1. Cuando _____ (llegar) Ernesto, Marta _____ (servir) los cócteles.

2. Pablo _____ (freír) la carne y Marta _____ (hervir) agua para el arroz.

3. Ernesto y Marta _____ (seguir) a Pablo a la mesa.

4. Marta y Pablo _____ (servir) la comida.

5. Ernesto _____ (pedir) más carne.

6. Todos _____ (repetir) todos los platos.

7. Ernesto _____ (divertir) a Marta y Pablo con cuentos de su viaje a Guatemala.

8. Marta y Pablo _____ (despedir) a Ernesto y _____ (sentir) mucha satisfacción.

B. Ayer. ¿Qué pasó ayer en la clase de español del Profesor Arvizu? Forma oraciones con los elementos indicados.

M O D E L O :   María Elena / pedir / otro / explicación
María Elena pidió otra explicación.

1. estudiantes / repetir / palabras / nuevo
2. nosotros / seguir / instrucciones del profesor
3. yo / sugerir / actividad / nuevo
4. Paco / dormir / todo / hora
5. tú / reír / todo / clase
6. profesor / divertir / estudiantes

C. ¿Quién mintió? Con un(a) compañero(a) de clase, repite lo que dijeron las personas indicadas sobre Miguel Ángel Asturias y luego indica si las personas mintieron o no.

Escribe diez oraciones, algunas ciertas y otras falsas. (Las frases deben ser sobre cosas familiares.) Luego lee las oraciones a tu compañero(a) de clase y pregúntale si mentiste o si dijiste la verdad.

M O D E L O :   Tú: Carolina dijo: Miguel Ángel Asturias / seguir / técnicas antiguas
Miguel Ángel Asturias siguió técnicas antiguas.
Compañero(a):   Carolina *mintió.* o Carolina *dijo la verdad.*

Tú: Yo dije: Asturias / nacer / 1946
Compañero(a):   Tú _____.

Tú: Roberto dijo: Asturias / recibir / Premio Nóbel / 1968
Compañero(a):   Roberto: _____.

Tú: Mónica y Arnoldo dijeron: Asturias / ser / agricultor
Compañero(a):   Mónica y Arnoldo _____.

Tú: Nosotros dijimos: Asturias / escribir / poemas
Compañero(a):   Uds. _____.

Tú: Tú dijiste: Asturias / morir / 1968
Compañero(a):   Yo _____.

Tú: Uds. dijeron: Asturias / estudiar / medicina
Compañero(a):   Nosotros _____.

III. Los mayas

LECTURA

S.G. Morley, un estudioso[1] de la cultura hispanoamericana, llamó a los mayas «los griegos[2] de América». Lo dijo porque los mayas inventaron un sistema matemático basado en el número 20. Con este sistema numérico inventaron el famoso calendario. También desarrollaron[3] un sistema jeroglífico de escritura para recordar su historia, sus ritos religiosos, sus estudios astronómicos y matemáticos. **Nos los** dejaron[4] en códices, libros hechos de la corteza[5] de los árboles, en sus esculturas y su cerámica.

La cultura maya empezó a decaer[6] antes de la llegada de los europeos, pero sufrió más decadencia en sus manos. El Padre Bartolomé de las Casas escribió una protesta y **se la** llevó a la corona[7] española. Aunque el rey limitó los abusos de los indígenas, los españoles les quitaron[8] muchos de los códices de los mayas y **se los** quemaron[9] diciendo que no tenían nada de valor.[10] Sólo recientemente descubrimos el verdadero valor de estas obras maravillosas.

---

[1]**un estudioso:** *scholar* / [2]**los griegos:** *Greeks* / [3]**desarrollaron:** *they developed* / [4]**dejaron:** *they left (something)* / [5]**la corteza:** *bark* / [6]**decaer:** *to weaken* / [7]**la corona:** *crown* / [8]**quitaron:** *they took away* / [9]**quemaron:** *they burned* / [10]**el valor:** *value*

¿Comprendes?

1. ¿Cómo es diferente el sistema numérico de los mayas del nuestro?
2. ¿Qué es un códice?
3. ¿Sobre qué protestó el Padre Bartolomé de las Casas?
4. ¿Por qué cree S. G. Morley que los mayas son similares a los griegos?

■ Los complementos directos e indirectos

Many sentences have both a direct object and an indirect object. In the sentence *I gave her a necklace*, the word *necklace* is the direct object and *her* is the indirect object. The *necklace* is given and it is given *to her*.

Le di un **collar**.   *I gave **her** a **necklace**.*

- In Spanish, when both the direct and indirect objects are pronouns, the indirect object precedes the direct object and both are placed before conjugated verbs.

Estela **me** lo enseñó.   *Stella showed **it to me**.*
¿**Te la** dieron?   *Did they give **it to you**?*

- When the action is made up of both a conjugated verb with an infinitive or a present participle, the pronouns may either precede the conjugated verb or be attached to the infinitive or present participle.

¿Puedes explicár**melo**?
¿**Me lo** puedes explicar?

*Can you explain **it to me?***

Estoy buscándo**telos**.
Te los estoy buscando.

*I'm looking for **them for you**.*

- Double object pronouns must be placed before negative commands and after affirmative commands. When placed after, the verb may need an accent to retain the original stress.

No **me lo** digas.
Lée**noslo**.

*Don't tell **me (it)**.*
*Read **it to us**.*

- Double object pronouns must follow infinitives and present participles that stand alone (without a conjugated verb). An accent must always be added when two pronouns are added to a verb form.

Al mencion**ármelo**, rió.

*When he mentioned **it to me**, he laughed.*

Practiquemos

A. Dámelo. Tú necesitas muchas cosas y las pides a tu compañero(a). Tu compañero(a) te contesta que tú ya tienes las cosas.

MODELO:
TÚ: dar / papel / a mí
Dáme el papel. Dámelo.

COMPAÑERO(A): *Ya te lo di.*

Have students repeat the activity or switch roles halfway through so that each partner practices each part.

1. TÚ: pasar / calculadora / a mí
COMPAÑERO(A):

2. TÚ: dar / diccionario / a mí
COMPAÑERO(A):

3. TÚ: pasar / bolígrafos / a mí
COMPAÑERO(A):

4. TÚ: alcanzar *(to reach)* / cartas / a mí
COMPAÑERO(A):

5. TÚ: dar / el memo del jefe / a mí
COMPAÑERO(A):

6. TÚ: pasar / pluma / a mí
COMPAÑERO(A):

Pídele a tu compañero(a) cinco cosas que sabes que tiene. Tu compañero(a) responde a tus peticiones.

B. Promesas. Todos prometieron hacer favores para otras personas. ¿Qué hicieron todos? Cambia los nombres a pronombres.

MODELO: Me dio una novela.
Me la dio.

1. Nos diste unos vídeos.
2. Elena me regaló una pluma.
3. Emilio y José te escribieron una postal.
4. Yo te leí un cuento interesante.
5. Pepe nos preparó una comida deliciosa.
6. El jefe nos dio un día libre.

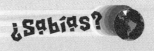

¿Sabías?

Tikal es un famoso centro ceremonial maya. Este lugar está situado en la jungla y allí se puede visitar muchas ruinas mayas que incluyen pirámides, templos, unas plazas y un museo. El contraste entre la jungla viva y densa y las ruinas tan antiguas es impresionante, sobre todo a la hora del amanecer (cuando sale el sol).

C. La comida cooperativa. Todos cooperaron en preparar una comida especial. ¿Qué pasó? Cambia los complementos directos e indirectos a pronombres.

MODELO: Miguel nos preparó un postre magnífico.
Miguel nos lo preparó.

1. Cecilia me trajo unas bebidas sabrosas.
2. Elena y Paco te hicieron una salsa para la carne.
3. Jorge y Memo nos mandaron platos y vasos.
4. Tú nos cocinaste una rica carne.
5. Yo te serví todos los platos.

Have each student select a favorite food and write it and a date on a piece of paper. Then ask: ¿Qué nos va a traer Susita? The class will look at Susita's paper and answer: Nos va a traer ensalada. Then ask ¿Cuándo? The class should answer: Nos la va a traer el jueves, el 28 de febrero.

■ Los complementos directos e indirectos en la tercera persona

When both the direct and indirect object pronouns are third person (when both begin with **l**) the indirect object pronoun becomes **se.**

le or **les** + **la** → **se la**	**le** or **les** + **las** → **se las**
le or **les** + **lo** → **se lo**	**le** or **les** + **los** → **se los**

It is customary to include a redundant indirect object pronoun in the sentence even when the indirect object noun to which the pronoun refers is present in the sentence. This is particularly true in writing.

Le dimos las notas **a Roberto.**
Se las dimos.

*We gave the notes **to Roberto.***
*We gave **them to him.***

Les dije la verdad **a mis padres.**
Se la dije.

*I told **my parents** the truth.*
*I told **it to them.***

Le mandó las cartas **a Patricia.**
Se las mandó.

*She sent the letters **to Patricia.***
*She sent **them to her.***

Les enseñaron los informes **a los jefes.**   *They showed the reports **to the bosses.***

Se los enseñaron.   *They showed **them to them**.*

Since the indirect object of these sentences may be ambiguous (se can refer to **le** or **les,** meaning *to him, her, you, it,* or *them*), they may be clarified with an explanatory phrase. English does not include both the pronoun and the noun in this type of construction.

Se las dimos **a Roberto.**   *We gave **them to Roberto**.*
Se la dije **a mis padres.**   *I told **it to my parents**.*

Practiquemos

A. El viaje. Trini va a ayudar a varias personas a prepararse para viajar a Guatemala. ¿Qué debe hacer? Forma mandatos con los verbos indicados.

MODELO: Los hermanos Peña buscan cheques de viajero. (traer)
Tráeselos.

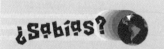

Para los mayas, como para otras antiguas culturas americanas, el «santo padre» es el sol y la «santa madre» es la luna. Algunos mayas conservan las creencias y los ritos tradicionales, pero muchos de los mayas modernos son católicos. Sin embargo, su catolicismo es una mezcla de prácticas antiguas y católicas.

1. Ricardo necesita una visa. (conseguir)
2. Mariana quiere comer comida guatemalteca. (preparar)
3. Eduardo y Patricia prefieren boletos de primera clase. (comprar)
4. Carolina tiene que encontrar su raqueta de badminton. (buscar)
5. Enrique y Leonardo desean cuartos sencillos *(single).* (reservar)
6. Carmen necesita una blusa. (empacar)
7. Loreto y Benito quieren ver unas guías turísticas. (traer)
8. Las familias quieren recibir postales. (mandar)

B. ¿Quién lo hizo? Muchas cosas inexplicadas pasan en la oficina y la jefa quiere saber quién es responsable. Contesta sus preguntas usando complementos pronominales (directos e indirectos).

MODELO: ¿Quién le escribió la carta a Luis? (nosotros)
Nosotros se la escribimos.

1. ¿Quién le compró flores a la secretaria? (yo)
2. ¿Quién me mandó el informe sobre Guatemala? (Gerardo)
3. ¿Quién nos organizó los escritorios? (la Srta. Flores)
4. ¿Quién nos mandó chocolates a todos nosotros? (su esposo)
5. ¿Quién me hizo reservaciones para el Palacio? (todos nosotros)
6. ¿Quién les dio más dinero a Uds? (Ud.)

❖ Para hablar del pasado

Si quieres decir cuándo algo ocurrió en el pasado, puedes usar estas palabras.

el año pasado	*last year*
anoche	*last night, last evening*
anteayer	*day before yesterday*
ayer	*yesterday*
el fin de semana pasado	*last weekend*
el mes pasado	*last month*
la semana pasada	*last week*

Practiquemos

A. ¿Cuándo? Manuela no puede recordar el orden de los eventos. Contesta sus preguntas con las respuestas indicadas.

> Haz una lista de ocho actividades comunes. Pregunta a tu compañero(a) de clase cuándo hizo las actividades. Contesta las preguntas de tu compañero(a).

MODELO: ¿Cuándo me mandó Ignacio el paquete? (ayer)
Te lo mandó ayer.

1. ¿Cuándo te escribió Laura la carta? (anteayer)
2. ¿Cuándo nos dieron los informes? (esta mañana)
3. ¿Cuándo les dijimos las noticias *(news)* a los jefes? (el viernes pasado)
4. ¿Cuándo me pintaron la casa? (el mes pasado)
5. ¿Cuándo le compraron el escritorio a Ernesto? (el lunes)
6. ¿Cuándo nos mencionó el jefe el nuevo proceso? (la semana pasada)
7. ¿Cuándo te expliqué yo todo esto? (ayer)
8. ¿Cuándo le traje café al jefe? (nunca)

B. En la oficina. Contesta las preguntas de tu amiga sobre la fiesta de la oficina. Después de terminar las respuestas, dile a tu compañero(a) de clase las respuestas, poniendo los pronombres después de los infinitivos.

MODELO: ¿Tú vas a traer café a Carlos?
No, *no se lo voy a traer.*
(a tu compañero[a]): *No voy a traérselo.*

1. ¿Marcos va a escribir la invitación a la jefa?

   Sí, _____.

   (a tu compañero[a]):

2. ¿Elena puede comprar el regalo para el Sr. López?

   No, _____.

   (a tu compañero[a]):

3. ¿La Srta. García puede preparar la torta para todos?

Sí, _____.

(a tu compañero[a]):

4. ¿Nosotros tenemos que escribir informes al comité hoy?

No, _____.

(a tu compañero[a]):

5. ¿El Sr. Marques y la señorita Ames van a traer helado a nosotros?

Sí, _____.

(a tu compañero[a]):

6. ¿Tú puedes mandar las invitaciones a los invitados?

Sí, _____.

(a tu compañero[a]):

IV. El Popol Vuh

LECTURA

El *Popol Vuh* o «libro de la comunidad» es un libro maya que contiene la mitología quiché que se expresa en una poesía[1] misteriosa y mágica. La palabra «quiché» significa «bosque»,[2] el lugar donde vivían los mayas. Muchas personas dicen que el *Popol Vuh* es la biblia maya porque describe cómo los dioses **tienen ganas de** crear hombres para que éstos les den alabanzas[3] y honor; ésta es la primera parte del libro. La segunda parte del *Popol Vuh* trata de la concepción de los gemelos[4] Hunahpú e Ixbalanqué en el vientre[5] de la virgen Ixquic.

La prosa narrativa describe el anciano mundo maya con sus dioses, leyendas[6] y héroes. Un franciscano español, Francisco Ximénez, tradujo el libro a una versión en español para poder compartir la riqueza de la lengua y las historias. La traducción **tuvo mucho éxito** e inspira a las personas que la leen. El *Popol Vuh* inmortaliza a la gente maya y nos ayuda a comprender esta civilización fascinante.

---

[1]**una poesía:** *poetry* / [2]**el bosque:** *forest* / [3]**alabanzas:** *praise* / [4]**los gemelos:** *twins* / [5]**el vientre:** *womb* / [6]**leyendas:** *legends*

¿Comprendes?

1. ¿Qué significa el Popol Vuh?
2. ¿Por qué dicen que es la biblia maya?
3. ¿Qué representa el Popol Vuh para nosotros?

◼ Expresiones con *tener*

An idiom consists of a group of words whose meaning is not predictable from the meaning of its parts. For example, *to pull someone's leg* has nothing to do with *pulling* or with *legs*. An idiom may also be defined as a group of words that makes perfect sense in one language but cannot be translated literally to another.

The following Spanish idioms are formed with **tener** + noun. They are frequently equivalent to English *to be* + adjective.

tener calor	*to be hot, warm*	tener paciencia	*to be patient*
tener celos	*to be jealous*	tener prisa	*to be in a hurry*
tener cuidado	*to be careful*	tener razón	*to be right*
tener éxito	*to succeed*	no tener razón	*to be wrong*
tener frío	*to be cold*	tener sed	*to be thirsty*
tener hambre	*to be hungry*	tener sueño	*to be sleepy*
tener miedo de	*to be afraid of*	tener suerte	*to be lucky*
tener... ___ años	*to be . . . ___ years old*		

Other idioms with **tener** include:

tener ganas de + *inf.*	*to feel like (doing something)*
tener la culpa	*to be to blame, be at fault*
tener que + *inf.*	*to have to (do something)*

No almorcé. **Tengo hambre.** *I didn't have lunch. **I'm hungry.***
Por favor, **ten paciencia.** *Please **be patient.***
Olga no **tiene la culpa.** *Olga is not **to blame.***
¿**Tienes ganas de** ir al cine? ***Do you feel like** going to a movie?*

Practiquemos 🖊

A. ¿Qué tienen? Escribe la expresión con **tener** que mejor complete cada idea.

1. ¡Ya es muy tarde!
   Yo _____.

2. Ramón tiene que estar en la oficina del médico ahora.
   Él _____.

3. Tú no dormiste bien anoche.
   Tú _____.

4. Mariana va al restaurante.
   Ella _____.

5. La temperatura está a -10 centígrados.
   Todos _____.

6. Ema y yo encontramos 50 dólares.
   Nosotros _____.

7. Felipe dice que la capital de Guatemala es San José.
   Él _____.

8. Mamá está enferma.
   Ella no _____ comer.

B. ¿Cómo respondes? ¿Qué expresión con **tener** va con las siguientes ideas? Usa la forma **tú** en tus respuestas.

1. Digo que 6 y 6 son 13.
2. Es la 1:00 de la mañana.
3. Quiero comer ahora.
4. Tengo un examen hoy.
5. ¡La temperatura está a 110° F!
6. Quiero un vaso de agua fría.
7. Estudié mucho y saqué una «A».
8. ¡Encontré 50 dólares!
9. Hace una hora que espero.
10. Mi clase comienza en un minuto.

Haz ocho dibujos que reflejan expresiones con *tener*. Enséñalos a un(a) compañero(a) de clase para ver si puede identificar la expresión.

C. En el café. Unos amigos están en el café Luna. ¿Qué dicen? Completa el diálogo con una expresión con **tener**.

ANTONIO: Ay, quiero una limonada porque _____.

CAROLINA: Primero, quiero un café. _____ y no tengo energía. No dormí bien anoche.

ISABEL: ¿Qué hora es? Hace 20 minutos que esperamos y yo _____. Tengo que estar en casa a las 3:00.

ANTONIO: Ay, tú, Isabel. Siempre _____.

CAROLINA: Oí que el profesor de español ganó 500 dólares en la lotería. _____, ¿verdad?

ISABEL: Sí. Yo nunca gano nada. Qué mala _____ tengo.

CAROLINA: ¿Ven esa hamburguesa? Quiero una. _____.

ANTONIO: Amigos, está lloviendo. ¿Uds. no _____? Estamos a 15 grados hoy.

CAROLINA: Antonio, no _____. Estamos a 20 grados hoy.

ISABEL: ¡Qué bueno! Ya viene el mesero.

D. Una clase típica. ¿Qué tienen estos estudiantes? Completa la oración con una expresión con **tener**. Luego, haz la pregunta correspondiente a un(a) compañero(a) de clase. Tu compañero(a) va a contestar la pregunta.

MODELO: **Tú:**   Cuando tengo que esperar mucho tiempo no *tengo mucha paciencia.*
¿Y tú? ¿Cuándo (no) tienes mucha paciencia?

Compañero(a):   *Yo no tengo mucha paciencia cuando mis compañeros hablan en clase.*

1. Cuando conduzco mi coche a la universidad siempre _____.

   ¿Y tú? _____

2. Los estudiantes siempre _____ después de sus clases y van al café.

   ¿Y tú? _____

3. Cuando nosotros estudiamos mucho, _____ en los exámenes.

   ¿Y tú? _____

4. Roberto siempre _____ despues de sus clases y toma una siesta.

   ¿Y tú? _____

5. Durante las vacaciones, yo _____ jugar al voleibol.

   ¿Y tú? _____

6. A veces, el profesor _____. Olvida la lección.

   ¿Y tú? _____

7. En contraste, los estudiantes preparan bien sus lecciones porque _____ cometer errores.

   ¿Y tú? _____

8. Si las mujeres en la clase sacan buenas notas, ¡los hombres nunca _____!

   ¿Y tú? _____

¿Sabías?

Antigua es una de las ciudades más viejas y más bellas de las Américas. Está rodeada de (surrounded by) tres volcanes magníficos —Agua, Fuego y Acatenango. Antigua fue la capital de Guatemala por 233 años, de 1543 a 1776, cuando cambiaron la capital a la Ciudad de Guatemala.

A ver si sabes

Use this self-test to see if you know the material presented in Chapter 8.

A. ¿Enfermo? ¿Qué pasó ayer en la familia López? Completa el párrafo para saber.

Ayer, (1) _____ (haber) un problema en la casa de los López. Miguelito no (2) _____ (querer) ir a la escuela porque (3) _____ (estar) enfermo. Entonces, su mamá le tomó la temperatura y le (4) _____ (traer) una aspirina. Su papá le (5) _____ (poner) una buena película en su videograbadora. Después, llegó su hermana mayor, Sara, para pasar el día con Miguelito; ella no (6) _____ (tener) que asistir a clases en la universidad. Todos (7) _____ (querer) ayudar al pobre enfermo. Pero, más tarde, toda la familia (8) _____ (saber) por qué Miguelito (9) _____ (estar) enfermo: ¡(10) _____ (Haber) un examen en su clase de matemáticas!

B. Correo electrónico. Guillermo tuvo que ir a una exposición comercial con su jefe. Termina la carta electrónica que le escribe a su esposa.

Fecha: jueves, 15 nov 2000 13:41:57
De: Guillermo González <ggonz48@gol.com>
A: lbarrgonz4@bedel.net
Sujeto: Buenas noches

Hola, mi amor,

Anoche salí con el jefe a comer a un restaurante que él conoce. ¡Uf! (1) _____ (Servir, ellos) una comida horrible. Creo que (2) _____ (hervir) mucho todos las verduras. (3) _____ (Freír) toda la carne. Yo no (4) _____ (repetir) nada —¡y bien sabes cuánto me gusta comer! El jefe (5) _____ (pedir) de todo y (6) _____ (sugerir) el mismo restaurante para mañana. Yo le (7) _____ (pedir) permiso de comer con otros amigos mañana. (8) _____ (Mentir, yo) porque no tengo otros amigos, ¡¡¡pero no puedo volver allí!!!

C. Buenos amigos. Recientemente cuando muchos estuvimos enfermos, Diana y Quico nos trataron muy bien. Explica cuándo pasaron los eventos mencionados, según *(according to)* los tiempos mencionados, y cambia a pronombres los complementos directos e indirectos.

1. Diana me escribió una carta. (ayer)
2. Diana y Quico nos mandaron tarjetas. (anteayer)

3. Quico te preparó una comida especial. (anoche)
4. Quico y Diana nos compraron regalitos a todos. (el lunes pasado)
5. Quico me repuso el techo. (la semana pasada)
6. Diana me trajo unos libros bonitos. (el fin de semana pasado)

D. Fiesta de Memo. ¿Qué hizo la familia de Martín para celebrar el cumpleaños de su hermano Memo? Cambia los nombres a pronombres.

1. Margarita le dio un libro a su hermano.
2. Mamá le preparó la comida favorita a la familia.
3. Yo le mandé una tarjeta a Memo.
4. Papá les preparó un ponche delicioso a todos.
5. Los abuelos le mandaron unos paquetes a Memo.
6. Los vecinos *(neighbors)* le compraron un fútbol a Memo.

E. En la universidad. ¿Qué les pasa a estos estudiantes universitarios? Completa las oraciones con expresiones apropiadas de la lista. No es necesario usar todas.

tener calor   tener suerte   tener sed   tener sueño   tener razón
tener frío   tener celos   tener hambre   no tener razón   tener cuidado

1. Voy a comer esta hamburguesa.

   Yo _____.

2. Ellos tienen un coche nuevo.

   Tú _____.

3. Hace mucho calor hoy.

   Julia y Sara _____.

4. Queremos velear pero tenemos que esperar media hora.

   Nosotros _____.

5. Patricio dice que Guatemala es un país mágico.

   Él _____.

6. María Isabel está en Alaska.

   Ella _____.

7. Ya son las 11:00 de la noche.

   Uds. _____.

8. Voy a hacer un viaje a Antigua.

   Yo _____.

Preguntas culturales
1. ¿Cuáles fueron las preocupaciones de Rigoberta Menchú?
2. ¿Cuáles fueron las profesiones de Miguel Ángel Asturias?
3. ¿Qué inventaron los mayas?
4. ¿Qué es el *Popol Vuh?*

F. ¿Qué pasó? ¿Cómo reaccionaron estas personas en las siguientes situaciones? Llena los espacios en blanco con la forma adecuada del pretérito y una expresión con **tener.**

1. _____ (Haber) un accidente terrible en la ciudad.

   Ahora Felipe _____.

2. Rita y Paulina _____ (andar) cuatro millas.

   Ahora _____.

3. Samuel no _____ (conducir) muy rápido.

   Siempre _____.

4. Uds. _____ (poder) comprar el boleto que ganó la lotería.

   Uds. _____.

5. Yo _____ (querer) comprar una coca pero no _____ (poder).

   Yo todavía (still) _____.

Querido Diario. Vas a describir unas vacaciones especiales a tu diario. Para organizar tus pensamientos, haz una lista de las cosas que hiciste y divídelas en categorías: experiencias muy positivas, experiencias negativas y experiencias neutrales. Luego escribe por qué las experiencias positivas o negativas te dieron unas vacaciones especiales.

Grammar: preterite, preterite (irregular)
Phrases: talking about past events
Vocabulary: beach, traveling, sports, leisure

Vocabulario activo

Verbos en el pretérito

conocer
poder (preterite)
no poder (preterite)
querer (preterite)
no querer (preterite)
saber (preterite)

Verbos

diferir
divertir
fréir
hervir
mentir
reír

repetir

Pronombre

se *(indirect object pronoun)*

Al acampar

el abrelatas
armar la tienda
el colchón de aire
la cuchara
el cuchillo
la estufa para acampar
la fogata

la hielera
la leña
la linterna
la navaja universal
la olla
el propano
el saco de dormir

el sartén
el tanque de gas
el tenedor
la tienda
los utensilios de cocina

Al pasar las vacaciones en casa

arreglar el coche
ordenar los gabinetes
organizar(c) el garaje
pintar la casa
reponer el techo
trabajar en el jardín

Otros pasatiempos

el árbitro
el badminton
correr las olas
el esquí acuático
esquiar (esquío)
hacer la tabla de nieve
hacer la tabla de vela
patinar
pescar(qu)

el ping-pong
la raqueta
la raquetilla
la red
el (la) veleadora
velear
el voleibol
el vuelo libre

Expresiones con *tener*

tener calor
tener celos
tener cuidado
tener éxito
tener frío
tener hambre
tener miedo de
tener paciencia
tener prisa

tener razón
no tener razón
tener sed
tener sueño
tener suerte
tener... ___ años
tener la culpa
tener ganas de + *inf.*
tener que + *inf.*

Adverbios de tiempo

el año pasado
anoche
anteayer
ayer
el fin de semana pasado
el mes pasado
la semana pasada

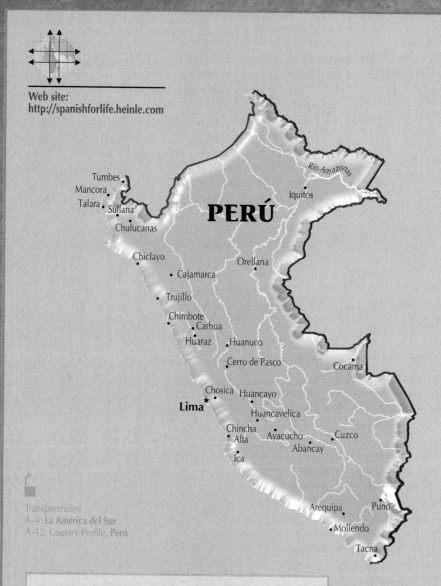

Tumbes
Mancora
Talara
Sullana
Chulucanas

Río Amazonas

Iquitos

PERÚ

Chiclayo

Orellana

Cajamarca

Trujillo

Chimbote
Carhua
Huaraz

Huanuco

Cerro de Pasco

Cocama

Chosica
Huancayo

Lima

Huancavelica

Chincha
Alta

Ayacucho

Cuzco

Abancay

Ica

Arequipa

Puno

Mollendo

Tacna

REPÚBLICA DEL PERÚ

Nombre oficial: República del Perú

Área: 1.285.215,6 km^2

Población: 23.400.000

Capital: Lima

Moneda: el nuevo sol

Idiomas oficiales: español,
quechua, aymará

Fiesta nacional: 28 de julio,
Día de la Independencia

Perú y los peruanos

Machu Picchu

In this chapter you will learn:

GRAMMAR POINTS

- Reflexive verbs and pronouns
- Prepositions
- Pronoun objects of preposi-
  tions; **conmigo**, **contigo**,
  consigo
- Demonstratives

COMMUNICATIVE
FUNCTIONS

- Describe your daily routine

VOCABULARY

- Daily routine
- The face
- Clothes
- Colors

I. Los peruanos

LECTURA

Todos los peruanos **se despiertan**[1] y **se duermen**[2] en el mismo país y todos **se consideran** peruanos. Sin embargo, hay muchos diversos grupos de peruanos. Muchos peruanos urbanos de ciudades como Lima y Arequipa **se levantan**,[3] **se visten**[4] de ropa elegante y van a trabajar en oficinas, tiendas, bancos y otros negocios. Van de compras en supermercados y pequeñas tiendas especializadas. Por la noche asisten al cine, a conciertos o a dramas. La vida es rápida y agitada.[5]

En las ciudades, la línea entre los ricos o la clase media y los pobres es muy clara. Los pobres viven en casas de cartón o desamparados[6] en las afueras[7] de la ciudad y **se ganan** la vida[8] con mucha dificultad. Algunos venden chicle[9] o dulces[10] en la calle, otros son criados[11] en las casas de los ricos.

La gente del pueblo o del campo tiene una vida más tradicional. **Se viste** ropa tradicional, trabaja en el campo o vende sus productos en el mercado tradicional. En general, estas personas **se levantan** y **se acuestan**[12] más temprano y prácticamente no hay vida nocturna. La vida del pueblo es tranquila y segura.

En el campo la división entre rico y pobre no es tan marcada. En general, los habitantes de los pueblos no tienen tanto dinero como la gente de la ciudad, **se viste** de una forma más simple y humilde y todos **se sienten**[13] más iguales.

Los habitantes de la costa peruana **se consideran** muy diferentes de las personas que viven en la sierra.[14] Estos dos grupos no **se confunden**[15] y no quieren confusión. Además de la diversidad geográfica, hay diferencias étnicas y culturales. Más del 50% de la población es de herencia indígena, sea quechua o aymará, y los demás son mestizos, europeos, negros y asiáticos (como el presidente Fujimori). Aunque la mayoría sabe hablar español, algunos hablan sólo quechua[16] o aymará.[17]

---

[1]**se despiertan:** *they wake up* / [2]**se duermen:** *they fall asleep* / [3]**se levantan:** *they get up* / [4]**se visten:** *they get dressed* / [5]**agitada:** *hectic, busy* / [6]**desamparados:** *homeless* / [7]**las afueras:** *outskirts* / [8]**se ganan la vida:** *they earn their living* / [9]**el chicle:** *chewing gum* / [10]**los dulces:** *sweets, candy* / [11]**los criados:** *servants* / [12]**se acuestan:** *they go to bed, lie down* / [13]**se sienten:** *they feel* / [14]**la sierra:** *mountain, sierra* / [15]**no se confunden:** *they don't get confused* / [16]**la quechua:** *Andean language* / [17]**el aimará:** *Andean language*

¿Comprendes?

1. ¿Cuáles son tres diferencias entre los peruanos ricos y pobres que viven en las ciudades?
2. Menciona tres diferencias entre los peruanos de la ciudad y los peruanos del campo.
3. ¿Existen estas diferencias en los Estados Unidos?
4. ¿Cuáles de las otras diferencias mencionadas en la lectura también se encuentran en los Estados Unidos? ¿Cuáles son exclusivas del Perú?

■ Construcciones reflexivas

Verbos y pronombres reflexivos

Reflexive constructions are those constructions whose subject and object are the same.

Subject		Object
I	cut	*myself.*

In this sentence *I* refers to the same person as *myself*. In English, reflexive constructions are characterized by the action of the verb to -*self* or -*selves*.

In Spanish, reflexive constructions are characterized by the presence of reflexive pronouns, which agree with the subject of the sentence: for example, a **yo** subject takes the reflexive pronoun **me**, **tú** goes with **te**, etc.

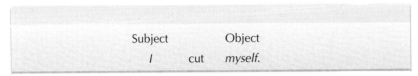

Reflexive Pronouns			
me	*myself*	**nos**	*ourselves*
te	*yourself (fam.)*	**os**	*yourselves (fam.)*
se	*yourself (form.), himself, herself, itself*	**se**	*yourselves (form.), themselves*

Spanish has more reflexive verbs than English. They are marked in the dictionary by *refl.* or another indicator; in this book they are presented with the pronoun **se** attached to the infinitive, for example, **levantarse**.

The placement of reflexive pronouns is the same as for direct and indirect objects; before conjugated verbs and negative commands, and after affirmative commands, infinitives, and gerunds.

In combinations of conjugated verb + infinitive or gerund, the reflexive pronoun may be placed before the conjugated verb or after the other form.

Many verbs that express daily activities are reflexive.

Me levanto a las 6:00.	*I get up at 6:00.*
¿**Te bañas** todos los días?	*Do you bathe every day?*
Nos acostamos temprano.	*We go to bed early.*

❖ Para hablar de tus actividades diarias

acostarse	*to go to bed, lie down*
afeitarse	*to shave*
bañarse	*to bathe (oneself), take a bath*
despertarse (e→ie)	*to wake up*
desvestirse (e→i)	*to get undressed*

dormirse (o→ue, u)	*to fall asleep*
lavarse (el pelo, las manos)	*to wash (your hair, your hands)*
levantarse	*to get up*
peinarse	*to comb your hair*
pintarse/maquillarse la cara	*to put on makeup*
ponerse (ropa)	*to put on (clothes)*
vestirse (e→i)	*to get dressed*

Practiquemos

A. Fuera de la oficina. Cada trabajador de la compañía Andetour tiene un horario diferente. Completa las oraciones con el verbo indicado para descubrir información sobre sus hábitos.

1. La jefa _____ (bañarse) por la noche.

2. La Sra. Gutiérrez y su familia _____ (levantarse) tarde frecuentemente.

3. Tú _____ (lavarse) el pelo todos los días.

4. Los señores del departamento de relaciones públicas _____ (peinarse) muy bien.

5. Manuel Ponce y yo _____ (ponerse) ropa informal.

6. Pedro García _____ (afeitarse) dos veces al día.

7. Yo _____ (acostarse) temprano.

8. Las secretarias _____ (dormirse) muy tarde.

B. Al campamento. Hablas con tu hijo(a) acerca del campamento donde va a pasar dos semanas. Tu compañero(a) de clase va a hacer el papel *(role)* de tu hijo(a). ¿Qué dicen Uds.?

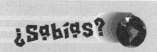

Dile tu rutina diaria a tu compañero(a) de clase y luego escucha la rutina de él (ella).

MODELO: (despertarse) temprano
TÚ: *Despiértate temprano.*
HIJO(A): *Sí, mamá (papá). Me despierto.*

1. (levantarse) inmediatamente
2. (bañarse) cada día
3. (peinarse) con cuidado
4. (ponerse) ropa limpia todos los días
5. (lavarse las manos) antes de comer
6. (acostarse) temprano

¿Sabías?

Un plato muy popular en el Perú es «cui» o «cuy». La palabra «cui» viene del idioma quechua. Es un conejillo de Indias *(guinea pig)* que se fríe o que se prepara a la parrilla *(grilled).*

❖ Para hablar de la cara

la cara	*face*	las mejillas	*cheeks*
las cejas	*eyebrows*	el mentón	*chin*
los dientes	*teeth*	la nariz	*nose*
la frente	*forehead*	los ojos	*eyes*
los labios	*lips*	las orejas	*ears*

NOTA: In some countries, **el cachete** is used instead of **la mejilla**, and **la barbilla** is used in place of **el mentón**.

Practiquemos

A. ¡Qué hermosas! Todos los modelos de la compañía La Belleza sin Bestia se preparan con mucho cuidado todos los días. ¿Cómo se preparan? Completa las oraciones con el verbo o la parte de la cara que falta.

MODELO: Mariana *se pinta* los labios.

afeitarse lavarse pintarse

1. Susana _____ la frente.

2. Mario y Federico se afeitan _____ pero no _____.

3. Todas las mujeres _____ las cejas.

4. Fabiano _____ los dientes muy bien.

5. Catalina y yo _____ los labios.

6. Sara y Berta se pintan _____.

¿Cuánto tiempo necesitas para prepararte en la mañana? Discútelo con tres compañeros(as) y luego informa a la clase.

To practice these words, bring in pictures of models or other people and have students identify parts of their faces and heads. It can also be entertaining for students to identify people known for their characteristics, for example, Elizabeth Taylor's eyes, Jimmy Durante's or Jamie Farr's nose, etc.

Have students tell what they do to their faces every morning.

■ Verbos usados solamente como reflexivos

A few verbs in Spanish must always be used reflexively (like the English verb *to perjure oneself*).

Se arrepintió de sus acciones.
Ellos **se quejaron** de todo.

He repented of his actions.
They complained about everything.

Verbs of this type include:

acurrucarse (c→qu)	*to snuggle up*
arrepentirse de (e→ie, i)	*to repent*
atreverse a	*to dare*
quejarse de	*to complain about*

Some plural reflexive expressions can also be *reciprocal,* that is, they involve two or more persons doing something to *each other.*

No **nos hablamos**.	***We don't speak to each other.***
Se **abrazaron**, se **besaron** y se **casaron**.	***They hugged (each other), kissed, and got married.***

Practiquemos

A. ¿Reflexivo o no? Decide según el contexto si es necesario usar la forma reflexiva del verbo o no. Pon el pronombre reflexivo apropiado en el espacio si es necesario.

> Escribe un cuento romántico y léelo a tu compañero(a) de clase.

1. José y Anita _____ conocieron

2. Ricardo _____ habló por teléfono.

3. Todo el tiempo mi abuelo _____ queja de sus vecinos.

4. ¡Yo no _____ acosté hasta las 2:00 de la mañana! ¡Estoy cansada!

5. Mi hermano necesita lavar_____ el perro hoy después de las clases.

6. El bebé _____ acurruca a su padre por la noche.

7. ¡Es increíble! ¡Elena y Jorge _____ casaron!

■ Verbos usados como reflexivos o no reflexivos

Many reflexive verbs may be used reflexively or nonreflexively.

Acuesto a los hijos después de la cena.	***I put** the children **to bed** after supper.*
Yo **me acuesto** más tarde.	***I go to bed** later.*
El papá **viste** al bebé.	*The dad **dresses** the baby.*
El papá **se viste** rápidamente.	*The dad **dresses (gets dressed)** quickly.*

Verbs of this type include:

	Reflexive Meaning	Nonreflexive Meaning
acostar(se)	*to go to bed, lie down*	*to put to bed*
afeitar(se)	*to shave*	*to shave*
bañar(se)	*to bathe (oneself), take a bath*	*to bathe*
casar(se)	*to get married*	*to marry (perform the ceremony)*
despedir(se)	*to say good-bye*	*to send off; to fire*
despertar(se)	*to wake up*	*to wake up*
desvestir(se) (e→i)	*to get undressed*	*to undress*
divertir(se) (e→ie, i)	*to have a good time*	*to entertain*
lavar(se)	*to wash*	*to wash*

	Reflexive Meaning	Nonreflexive Meaning
levantar(se)	*to get up*	*to lift*
peinar(se)	*to comb one's hair*	*to comb hair*
pintar(se)	*to put on makeup*	*to put makeup on (someone)*
poner(se) (ropa)	*to put on (clothes)*	*to put (clothes) on (someone)*
sentar(se) (e→ie)	*to sit down*	*to seat*
vestir(se) (e→i)	*to get dressed*	*to dress*

❖ Para describir la ropa

el anillo	*ring*	las medias	*(panty)hose*
los aretes	*earrings*	el reloj	*watch (clock)*
los calcetines	*socks*	la ropa interior	*underwear*
la chaqueta	*jacket*	el traje de baño	*bathing suit*
el collar	*necklace*		

Practiquemos

A. En el hospital. Los pacientes están muy enfermos cuando llegan al hospital. Primero, escribe lo que hicieron los enfermeros para los pacientes cuando llegaron al hospital. Luego, escribe lo que hacen los pacientes cuando se sienten mejor.

MODELO: enfermero / desvestir / el Sr. Molino
El enfermero desvistió al Sr. Molino.
Ahora el Sr. Molino se desviste.

1. enfermera / lavar / la Sra. Peña
2. enfermero / afeitar / el Sr. Gómez
3. enfermero / peinar / te
4. enfermera / despertar / las niñas
5. enfermera / vestir / me
6. enfermeros / acostar / los hermanos Herrera

B. El orden. Cada persona se viste de una forma individual. ¿Qué se ponen al final estas personas?

MODELO: Marta

Marta se pone la camisa al final.

1. José

2. yo

3. Paulina y Susana

4. tú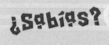

5. Norberto y yo

6. tú y Enrique

7. Ernesto y Sandra

8. Elena

¿Sabías?

Un profesor de historia de la Universidad de Yale en los Estados Unidos, Hiram Bingham, descubrió las ruinas de Machu Picchu en 1911.

■ Verbos que cambian el sentido en el reflexivo

Some verbs have a different meaning when used reflexively.

Voy al mercado.	*I'm going to the market.*
Después del concierto, **me voy**.	*After the concert, I'm leaving.*
Rita **duerme** profundamente.	*Rita sleeps deeply.*
Rita **se duerme** inmediatamente.	*Rita falls asleep immediately.*

Verbs like this include:

	Nonreflexive	Reflexive
dormir(se)	*to sleep*	*to fall asleep*
ir(se)	*to go*	*to leave*
poner(se)	*to put, place*	*to become (sad, furious, etc.)*
sentir(se)	*to regret*	*to feel (happy, well, etc.)*

Practiquemos

A. Apagón. ¿Cómo se pusieron todos cuando se apagó *(shut off)* la electricidad? Usa la forma apropiada de **ponerse** y un adjetivo adecuado para completar cada oración. Las respuestas pueden variar.

> aburrido   alegre   cansado   contento   enfermo
> enojado   nervioso   triste

MODELO: Todo estuvo oscuro.
Tú *te pusiste cansado.*

1. No hubo clases. Juanito _____.

2. No pude ver a mis amigos. Yo _____.

3. Los autobuses no funcionaron. María _____.

4. No hubo programas de televisión. Tú _____.

5. No pudieron estudiar. Lorenzo y Elena _____.

6. No tuvimos que trabajar. Mis amigos y yo _____.

II. Mario Vargas Llosa

LECTURA

Uno de los grandes escritores peruanos **de** este siglo es Mario Vargas Llosa. Nació[1] **en** Arequipa, Perú, **en** el año 1936. **En** su juventud,[2] estudió **en** Perú, Bolivia y, finalmente, se doctoró[3] **en** la Universidad **de** Madrid. También pasó muchos años viviendo **en** Barcelona, París y Londres.

Vargas Llosa es un autor prolífico. **Entre** sus muchas novelas, la que le trajo más fama fue *La ciudad y los perros.* Esta novela recibió mucha aclamación y fue traducida[4] a muchos idiomas. **Con** la publicación **de** sus obras literarias, Vargas Llosa recibió unos premios[5] prestigiosos como el Premio **de** la Crítica **en** 1963 y 1966. También ganó el Premio Internacional **de** Literatura Rómulo Gallegos **en** 1967.

Sin abandonar su carrera literaria, este autor **de** inmenso talento participa activamente **en** la vida política **de** su país. **Con** su gran interés **en** el futuro político **de** su país, en 1990 Mario Vargas Llosa fue candidato **a** la presidencia pero perdió. No obstante,[6] sigue escribiendo obras **con** temas profundos mientras viaja por todo el mundo. **De** estas experiencias variadas, Vargas Llosa seguramente saca las ideas para sus libros.

---

[1]**Nació:** *He was born* / [2]**la juventud:** *youth* / [3]**se doctoró:** *he got a doctorate (Ph.D)* / [4]**traducida:** *translated* / [5]**unos premios:** *prizes* / [6]**No obstante:** *Nevertheless*

¿Comprendes?

1. En tu opinión, ¿qué contribuye al éxito literario de un gran autor como Mario Vargas Llosa?
2. Muchos autores hispanoamericanos tienen un gran interés en la vida política de su país, participando activamente en ella. ¿Puedes explicar por qué? Comparte tu opinión con un(a) compañero(a) de clase.

■ Las preposiciones: *a, sin, con, de, en, entre, sobre*

Prepositions are words that indicate relationships between parts of a sentence. They frequently indicate material, time, place, direction, or possession, but the relationship is arbitrary and must be learned. Prepositions introduce phrases with nouns or pronouns.

*I found my keys **in** my backpack.*
*I left them **on** the table **under** the newspaper **behind** the books.*

Remind students of the contractions **al** and **del**. The following simple (one-word) prepositions are key prepositions in Spanish:

a	to, at		**entre**	between, among
con	with		**sin**	without
de	of, from, about		**sobre**	on, above
en	in, at			

Mis amigos salieron **sin** sus libros.	*My friends left **without** their books.*
Estamos **entre** la pared y la espada.	*We're **between** a rock and a hard place (literally, the wall and the sword).*

Practiquemos

A. ¡Me encanta Perú! Alfredo le escribió una postal a su familia, describiendo sus aventuras en Perú. Llena los espacios en blanco con una de las siguientes preposiciones. Haz contracciones (**al**, **del**) cuando sea necesario.

a   sin   de   con   en   sobre   entre

El 16 de octubre

Mi querida familia,

Aquí estoy en Perú. Es un país fascinante. La semana pasada, mis amigos y yo fuimos (1) _____ Arequipa y exploramos el mercado y otros sitios interesantes. (2) _____ allí, nos fuimos (3) _____ el Lago Titicaca y (4) _____ allí para Cuzco y Machu Picchu (5) _____ otros turistas (6) _____ el tren; fue una experiencia increíble. (7) ____ Machu Picchu, vimos templos, casas y otras construcciones incaicas. (8) _____ las ruinas, descubrimos muchos elementos de esta cultura mágica. Unos amigos nos dijeron: «No se vayan *(Don't leave)* (9) _____ ver un convento donde se guardan artefactos religiosos. Supimos que Machu Picchu fue construido como centro religioso a una altura impresionante (10) _____ el mar. Pensamos pasar dos semanas más en este país maravilloso. ¡Saludos a todos!

Alfredo

B. La rutina diaria. Escoge la preposición que mejor complete la oración.

1. María se lava la cara (con, sin) _____ jabón y agua.
2. Tú te levantas (sin, de) _____ mirar el reloj.
3. Nos acostamos (de, a) _____ las 10:00.
4. Me preparo la sopa (a, en) _____ la cocina.
5. Domingo y su esposa van a la oficina (en, de) _____ su papá muy temprano.
6. Tú y yo nunca salimos de casa (con, sin) _____ nuestros libros y un poco de dinero.
7. Cuando todos llegan en la tarde, mamá nos prepara una buena comida (en, de) _____ la cocina.

Cerca de Nazca, Perú, hay unas figuras geométricas trazadas (formed, sketched) en la tierra. Las figuras son enormes y algunas son animales. La mejor manera de verlas es desde (from) un avión. Se formaron por quitar piedras oscuras y exponer la tierra más blanca debajo. ¿Quién hizo estas líneas de Nazca? Hay varias teorías, pero la explicación sigue siendo un misterio.

■ Preposiciones adicionales

In addition to simple prepositions, these compound prepositions (more than one word) are useful in describing the whereabouts of nouns and pronouns.

a la derecha de	*to the right of*
a la izquierda de	*to the left of*
al lado de	*alongside, next to, beside*
antes de	*before*
cerca de	*near, close to*
debajo de	*behind*
delante de	*in front of*
después de	*after*
detrás de	*behind*
encima de	*on top of, on*
enfrente de	*facing, opposite*
lejos de	*far from*

Practiquemos

A. ¿Qué ven? Completa el párrafo con las preposiciones adecuadas para saber qué ven los estudiantes en Cuzco.

Cuzco, la capital del imperio inca, está (1) _____ (lejos de, después de) Lima. (2) _____ (Después de, Antes de) la llegada de los conquistadores españoles, los incas construyeron su capital (3) _____ (al lado de, encima de) las mesetas andinas. La capital era difícil de alcanzar *(to reach);* había bastante protección para sus habitantes. (4) _____ (Cerca de, Lejos de) la fortaleza hay un sinnúmero de ruinas incaicas. En la ciudad, (5) _____ (enfrente de, debajo de) la catedral, hay calles llenas de turistas y descendientes de los incas. Es una mezcla de lo moderno y lo antiguo.

B. Mi dormitorio. Usando la puerta de tu dormitorio como punto de orientación, describe dónde están los muebles. Tu compañero(a) de clase va a dibujar *(to draw)* tu dormitorio tal como lo describes. Luego, mirando el dibujo, vas a evaluar tu descripción.

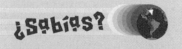 **¿Sabías?**

El Lago Titicaca, a unos 3.820m (12.530 pies) sobre el nivel del mar, es el lago navegable más alto del mundo. También se conoce como el lago más largo de Sudamérica.

III. Los tesoros del Perú

LECTURA

Además de ser un país fascinante que le ofrece mucho al turista, Perú es para **nosotros** un tesoro[1] **de** sitios arqueológicos. Para los arqueólogos que estudian las ruinas y artefactos incaicos, es una entrada a un mundo misterioso. Para **ellos**, es una oportunidad de conocer el imperio inca. Hay reliquias[2] como las decoraciones de oro y turquesa[3] encontradas en las Tumbas Reales de Sipán. También, se sacaron de **ellas** objetos de oro, cerámica y herramientas.[4] Con estos descubrimientos,[5] sabemos que los incas tenían una sociedad muy avanzada.

En Lima, la capital de Perú, hay muchos sitios de importancia donde se conservan numerosos artefactos de oro, plata y piedras preciosas:[6] el Museo de Oro del Perú, el Museo Nacional de Antropología y las iglesias de San Francisco y Santo Domingo.

Otro tesoro de Perú es su geografía diversa. La impresionante cordillera[7] de los Andes, con sus valles verdes y sus picos cubiertos de nieve atrae a miles de turistas cada año. También hay desiertos altos y bajos, selvas con una gran variedad de animales salvajes[8] y una infinidad de plantas exóticas. Uno de los ríos más importantes y misteriosos es el Amazonas que nace **en** la provincia Cayolloma de Arequipa. El Amazonas está reconocido como el segundo río más largo del mundo.

[1]**el tesoro:** *treasure* / [2]**las reliquias:** *relics* / [3]**la turquesa:** *turquoise* / [4]**las herramientas:** *tools* / [5]**los descubrimientos:** *discoveries* / [6]**las piedras preciosas:** *precious stones* / [7]**la cordillera:** *mountain range* / [8]**salvajes:** *wild, savage*

¿Comprendes?

1. ¿Qué tipos de artefactos se conservan en los museos e iglesias del Perú?
2. ¿Puedes nombrar otros sitios arqueológicos importantes en las Américas?
3. ¿Qué tesoros geográficos tiene Perú?

■ Los pronombres preposicionales

The following pronouns are used as objects of prepositions. Note that they are identical to the subject pronouns with the exceptions of **mí** and **ti**. The word **mí** has a written accent to distinguish it from the possessive adjective **mi**.

Prepositional Pronouns			
mí	*me*	**nosotros(as)**	*us*
ti	*you (fam.)*	**vosotros(as)**	*you (fam.)*
Ud.	*you (form.)*	**Uds.**	*you (form.)*
él	*him, it*	**ellos**	*them*
ella	*her, it*	**ellas**	*them*

The preposition **con** has special forms that are combined with **mí, ti,** and **si** to form the following irregular forms:

conmigo   *with me*

contigo   *with you*

consigo   *with oneself, himself, herself, itself, yourself (form.), themselves*

Julia estudió **conmigo** toda la noche.	*Julia studied **with me** all night long.*
Vamos a ir **contigo**.	*We are going to go **with you**.*

Note an exception: After the preposition **entre**, the proper pronouns are **tú** and **yo**, rather than the expected **ti** and **mí**.

Entre **tú** y **yo**...	*Just between **you** and **me** . . .*
¿Qué pasó entre **tú** y **ella**?	*What happened between **you** and **her**?*

Practiquemos

A. ¿Con quién? Di con quién van estas personas al Museo de Arqueología. Usa los pronombres preposicionales.

MODELO: Mario va con *él*. (Roberto)

1. Tú vas con _____. (yo)

2. La familia Salas va con _____. (ellos)

3. Lidia y Juan van con _____. (tú)

4. Héctor va con _____. (nosotros)

5. Los turistas van con _____. (Ángela y Ramona)

6. Todos van con _____. (Ud. y Memo)

7. El tío Raúl va con _____. (abuelita)

B. Contestando preguntas. Contesta estas preguntas, usando una preposición y el pronombre preposicional apropiado.

MODELO: ¿De quién es este sombrero? Es de Silvia. Es *de ella*.

1. ¿De quién es esta camisa? Es de José. Es _____.

2. ¿De quiénes son estos zapatos? Son de ti y Felipe. Son _____.

3. ¿A quién le regalas esta blusa? Se la regalo a Miguelina y a Susana. Se la regalo _____.

4. ¿A quiénes les regalan estos pantalones? Nos los regalan a ti y a mí. Nos los regalan _____.

5. ¿La blusa no va bien sin la falda azul? No va bien _____.

6. ¿El sombrero elegante no va bien sin los guantes? No va bien _____.

7. ¿Mamá, con quién vas a la tienda de ropa? Voy _____, hija.

8. Muy bien, mamá. Voy contigo y tú vas _____.

C. ¿Qué llevas? Di **adónde vas, con quién vas** y **qué vas a llevar**. Combina elementos de las tres columnas para formar oraciones. Luego, compara tus oraciones con las de un(a) compañero(a) de clase. Hay muchas posibilidades.

¿Adónde fuiste recientemente? ¿Cuándo? ¿Tuviste que llevar ropa especial? ¿Qué ropa llevaste?

MODELO:

TÚ: *Voy a la playa con mis amigos. Voy a llevar unos pantalones cortos y un traje de baño. ¿Y tú?*

TU COMPAÑERO(A): *Voy al mercado con ellos. Voy a llevar unos pantalones azules y una camiseta.*

Destinos	Compañeros	Ropa
a la playa	con mis papás	un traje de baño
a una fiesta elegante	con Julián	una falda bonita
al museo	con la profesora	una blusa blanca
al campo	con mis hermanos	una chaqueta
a la universidad	con mi novio(a)	una camiseta
a las montañas Andes	con mis hijos(as)	un vestido elegante
al Río Amazonas	contigo	un traje con una corbata
a la iglesia	con nuestra tía	unos pantalones cortos y
a la discoteca	con mis amigos(as)	unas sandalias
		una camisa elegante

IV. Los incas

LECTURA

Muchas personas creen que la civilización de los incas fue la más grande de América. **Ésta** no fue una cultura construida a base de invenciones propias de los incas, porque **éstos** inventaron muy poco. Los incas se destacaron[1] en aprovechar[2] y mejorar las

Ruinas incas, Perú

ideas de otras culturas indígenas y en aplicar estas ideas a su eficiente organización social.

La civilización inca floreció y dominó gran parte de Sudamérica durante los siglos XIV y XV, y **por eso**[3] los españoles encontraron **esta** gran sociedad cuando llegaron al continente. A causa de divisiones internas del Imperio inca y la fuerza superior de los españoles, el gobierno inca fue derribado[4] en pocos años.

Los incas eran arquitectos maravillosos y construyeron edificios de pura piedra,[5] sin cemento de ningún tipo. **Estos** edificios todavía quedan en pie[6] mientras otros edificios, construidos con ideas y materiales europeos, han caído con los temblores[7] típicos de la región. Las piedras que forman las estructuras son enormes, pesando toneladas[8]—una piedra en las ruinas de Sacsayhuaman pesa 300 toneladas. Los edificios más importantes y sagrados tenían piedras y metales preciosos incrustados.[9]

Las famosas ruinas de Machu Picchu son los restos no de una fortaleza sino de un centro religioso. Machu Picchu está escondido en los Andes y por eso los españoles nunca lo descubrieron. En **este** centro religioso vivieron los sacerdotes[10] que adoraron el sol, el dios principal de los incas. El templo más importante en todas partes es el templo del sol. Los incas pensaban que el Inca, el emperador de todos, era el hijo del sol. Pero también adoraron la luna, la lluvia, los relámpagos[11] y otros elementos naturales que controlan la vida y la prosperidad de todas las civilizaciones. **Estos** elementos forman una parte central de la vida de los descendientes de los incas, los quechuas que todavía viven en el altiplano de Perú.

---

[1]**se destacaron:** *they stood* / [2]**aprovechar:** *to take advantage of* / [3]**por eso:** *therefore* / [4]**derribado:** *overturned, brought down* / [5]**la piedra:** *stone* / [6]**en pie:** *standing* / [7]**los temblores:** *earthquakes* / [8]**pesando toneladas:** *weighing tons* / [9]**incrustados:** *embedded* / [10]**los sacerdotes:** *priests* / [11]**los relámpagos:** *lightning bolts*

¿Comprendes?

1. ¿En qué sobresalieron *(excelled)* los incas?
2. ¿Cómo son distintos de nuestros edificios los edificios de los incas?
3. ¿Qué es Machu Picchu?
4. ¿Qué importancia tiene el sol para los incas?

◼ Los demostrativos: *este, ese, aquel*

Demonstratives are words that point things out, like the English *this, that, these,* and *those. This* and *these* refer to nouns near the speaker in space or time, while *that* and *those* refer to nouns far from the speaker.

In Spanish, demonstratives have three points of reference:

> **Este** refers to nouns near the speaker, in space or time.
>
> **Ese** refers to those near the person spoken to.
>
> **Aquel** refers to things far from both the speaker and the listener.

Demonstrative adjectives have four forms to agree with the number and gender of the noun they modify, just like regular adjectives.

Demonstrative Adjectives					
este	*this*	ese	*that*	aquel	*that (over there)*
esta		esa		aquella	
estos	*these*	esos	*those*	aquellos	*those (over there)*
estas		esas		aquellas	

Point out that *this* and *that* vary depending on the person speaking; what is *this* for me is *that* for you, and vice versa.

Point out that, historically, English had the form *yon,* which referred to things far from the speaker and listener. It may be helpful to see *this* and **este** as relating to *here* and **aquí,** *that* and **ese** relating to *there* and **ahí,** and *yon* and **aquel** referring to *yonder* and **allí.**

Point out that in Latin America there is a tendency to use the **este** and **ese** series much more than **aquel,** and Spaniards prefer **este** and **aquel,** assigning a pejorative tone to **ese.**

Practiquemos

A. ¿Cuál? ¿Qué demostrativos usamos en español para expresar las siguientes relaciones espaciales?

MODELO: El vestido que está ahí.
          ese vestido

1. El reloj que está aquí.
2. Las blusas que están allí.
3. La falda que está ahí.
4. Los zapatos que están aquí.
5. Las camisetas que están ahí.
6. El traje que está ahí.
7. La corbata que está aquí.
8. Los calcetines que están allí.

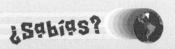

¿Sabías?

En Cuzco, el 24 de julio de cada año se celebra el Inti Raymi —un festival en veneración del sol. Hay canciones y danzas, y muchos grupos presentan ofrendas al sol. En el pasado se realizaron sacrificios, pero hoy en día solamente hacen representaciones de los viejos ritos.

B. Comprando regalos. Escoge la forma adecuada de los demostrativos para completar la conversación entre Silvia y la dependienta.

SILVIA: Es el cumpleaños de mi esposo y necesito un regalo. ¿Puedo ver (este, esta, esa) camisa?

DEPENDIENTA: ¿(Esta, Esa, Este) blanca aquí?

SILVIA: No, (esa, ese, esta) amarilla.

DEPENDIENTA: Sí, aquí tiene. Mire Ud., combina muy bien con (estos, aquellos, esas) pantalones verdes allí en la mesa cerca de la puerta.

SILVIA: Bien. ¿Cuánto vale (esta, esa, este) corbata que tengo aquí?

DEPENDIENTA: Es muy económica. ¿Vio Ud. (aquellos, estas, aquellas) chaquetas verdes allí, cerca de los pantalones? Son muy bonitas y económicas.

SILVIA: Ah, sí. ¡Qué bien va la chaqueta con (esas, estos, aquellas) pantalones! Me llevo todo. ¡Qué guapo va a estar mi esposo en toda (este, ese, esta) ropa!

❖ Los colores

amarillo	*yellow*	marrón, café	*brown*
anaranjado	*orange*	morado	*purple*
azul	*blue*	negro	*black*
azul marino	*navy blue*	oscuro	*dark*
beige	*beige*	rojo	*red*
blanco	*white*	rosado	*pink*
castaño, moreno	*brown*	verde	*green*
claro	*light*	violeta	*violet*
gris	*gray*		

NOTA:

Café and **marrón** (Mexico, Central America, Chile) are used for eye color and clothing, and **castaño** is used when referring to hair color. **Moreno** describes someone with dark features.

Practiquemos

A. Colores típicos. ¿De qué color son estos objetos comunes?

1. El limón es _____.

2. La bandera de los Estados Unidos es _____, _____ y _____.

3. La lechuga y las habichuelas son _____.

4. La leche es _____.

5. Los elefantes son _____.

6. Las naranjas son _____.

7. El chocolate es _____.

8. El asfalto es _____.

9. La violeta es _____.

10. El uniforme de los marineros es _____.

B. En la tienda. Escoge entre **este(a/os/as)** y **ese(a/os/as)** para señalar la ropa que quieres probarte. Si la ropa está cerca de tu amigo, tienes que pedírsela. Si está cerca de ti, puedes probártela sin problema.

M O D E L O :   Me gusta *esa* camisa amarilla. Pásamela.
Me encanta *este* vestido verde. Voy a probármelo.

1. Me gustan _____ pantalones negros. Dámelos.

2. Me encanta _____ blusa blanca. Voy a probármela.

3. Prefiero _____ sombrero rojo. ¿Puedes pasármelo?

4. _____ traje azul es muy bonito. Voy a probármelo.

5. Me gustan _____ medias grises. ¿Me las quieres pasar?

6. Prefiero la falda _____ marrón. Voy a probármela ahora mismo.

7. ¡Ay! ¡Qué bonitos son _____ zapatos negros! ¿No me los quieres pasar?

8. Quiero probarme _____ camiseta anaranjada. Dámela.

Describe la ropa y las características físicas de un(a) compañero(a) de clase sin decir su nombre. La clase va a identificar a la persona.

¿Sabías?

La alpaca y la vicuña son animales cuya lana *(wool)* se usa para hacer tejidos muy finos. Las alpacas son abundantes y es fácil encontrar suéteres y bufandas *(scarves)* de su lana. La vicuña, por otro lado, es más rara y durante años fue ilegal vender o comprar productos de su lana tan fina. Ahora el número de vicuñas es mayor y podemos encontrar unos cuantos artículos de vicuña de venta legalmente.

■ Pronombres demostrativos

Demonstrative pronouns take the place of nouns, like pronouns. An accent mark must be written over the stressed vowel to distinguish demonstrative pronouns from demonstrative adjectives.

Demonstrative Pronouns					
éste **ésta**	this (one)	**ése** **ésa**	that (one)	**aquél** **aquélla**	that (one) (over there)
éstos **éstas**	these (ones)	**ésos** **ésas**	those (ones)	**aquéllos** **aquéllas**	those (ones) (over there)

Me gusta **este** suéter, no **ése**.
¿Qué bolígrafo prefieres, **éste**
    o **aquél**?

*I like **this** sweater, not **that one**.*
*Which pen do you prefer, **this**
    one or **that one**?*

Practiquemos

A. ¡Qué bonito! Toda tu ropa es especial y les gusta mucho a tus amigos. ¿Qué dicen ellos y qué respondes tú?

MODELO: Me gustan mucho esos pantalones.
                    ¿Éstos? ¡Qué amable!

1. Me encanta _____ traje.

¿ _____? Gracias, es mi favorito.

2. ¡Qué bonita es esa blusa!

¿ _____? No es nueva.

3. Me gusta mucho tu suéter.

¿ _____? Gracias, ¡qué simpático!

4. ¡Qué llamativo es _____ collar!

¿ _____? Fue un regalo de mi esposo.

5. ¡Qué elegante es ese sombrero!

¿ _____? Gracias, es nuevo.

6. ¡Me encantan tus zapatos!

¿ _____? Los compré ayer.

B. Dame, dame. Tu compañero(a) no tiene las cosas que necesita para trabajar y te las pide. ¿Qué dicen Uds.?

MODELO: bolígrafo
                    COMPAÑERO(A):   *Dame ese bolígrafo.*
                            TÚ: *¿Éste? No, no puedo dártelo.*
                                    o ¿Éste? Sí, aquí tienes.

1. calculadora
2. diccionario
3. documentos

4. lápices
5. notas
6. disco

Have students write
out negative
answers to practice
written accents.

■ Demostrativos neutros

Neuter demonstratives are used to refer to a situation
or to an unspecified object. Neuter demonstratives
never require a written accent. The neuter demonstratives are **esto**, **eso**, and **aquello**.

¿Qué es **esto**?   *What is **this**?*
Mira todo **aquello**.   *Look at all **that (mess)**.*
¿Oíste **eso**?   *Did you hear **that**?*

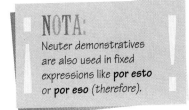

NOTA:
Neuter demonstratives
are also used in fixed
expressions like **por esto**
or **por eso** (*therefore*).

Practiquemos

A. ¿Qué es? Con un(a) compañero(a) de clase, pregunta sobre objetos
de la clase. Tu compañero(a) te va a contestar.

Have students con-
tinue with the activ-
ity, selecting other
items from those
objects available in
the classroom, items
of clothing, or other
personal items.

MODELO: ¿Qué es *esto* aquí?
           ¿Eso? Es un bolígrafo.

1. ¿Qué es _____ allí?

   ¿ _____? Es el escritorio de la profesora.

2. ¿Qué es _____ aquí?

   ¿ _____? Es tu mochila.

3. ¿Qué es _____ ahí?

   ¿ _____? Es mi cuaderno de biología.

4. ¿Qué es _____ allí?

   ¿ _____? Es la pizarra.

5. ¿Qué es _____ ahí?

   ¿ _____? Es un calendario.

6. ¿Qué es _____ aquí?

   ¿ _____? Es un lápiz.

En casa, escoge tres objetos y
escribe tres oraciones que describan
cada objeto. Incluye el color, el
tamaño (grande o pequeño) y el uso
(lo uso para...). Luego en clase,
cuando tu compañero(a) de clase te
pregunta «¿Qué es eso?», tú vas a
describir el objeto y tu
compañero(a) tiene que adivinar
(*to guess*) qué es.

A ver si sabes

Use this self-test to see if you know the material presented in Chapter 9.

A. De vacaciones. En el trabajo de Carlota, todos están de vacaciones. Completa su rutina diaria con la forma adecuada del verbo reflexivo.

1. Anita y Martín _____ (dormirse) a las 2:00 de la mañana.
2. Carlota _____ (levantarse) al mediodía.
3. La jefa y su familia _____ (bañarse) en el mar.
4. Tú y Carlota no _____ (peinarse) nunca.
5. Inés y yo _____ (despertarse) y luego _____ (dormirse) otra vez.
6. Yo _____ (acostarse) por la tarde.
7. Jorge no _____ (afeitarse) en toda la semana.
8. Tú _____ (ponerse) ropa vieja o no _____ (vestirse).

B. Los pensamientos. La mamá y la hija tienen ideas muy diferentes. Completa sus pensamientos con la forma reflexiva o no reflexiva del verbo indicado.

1. levantar(se)

   MAMÁ: Tengo que _____ a mi hija.

   HIJA: Yo misma quiero _____.

2. bañar(se)

   MAMÁ: Tengo que _____ a mi hija.

   HIJA: Yo misma quiero _____.

3. lavar(se) el pelo

   MAMÁ: Voy a _____ a mi hija.

   HIJA: Yo misma voy a _____.

4. peinar(se)

   MAMÁ: Debo _____ a mi hija.

   HIJA: Yo misma prefiero _____.

5. vestir(se)

   MAMÁ: Tengo que _____ a mi hija.

   HIJA: Yo misma _____.

C. Noticias. Di cómo se pusieron todos al oír las noticias. Usa la forma apropiada de **ponerse** y los siguientes adjetivos:

aburrido   contento   enfermo   enojado   nervioso   triste

1. La novia de Carlos salió con otro. Carlos _____.
2. Toda tu familia se enfermó. Tú también _____.

3. Manuel supo que mañana hay examen de español. _____.

4. Victoria y Susana salieron bien en el examen de inglés. _____.

5. Mi hermano no me esperó después del trabajo. Yo _____.

6. El profesor empezó a leer en voz alta *(aloud)*. Todos _____.

D. ¡Cómo se divierten! Llena los espacios en blanco con una preposición o un pronombre preposicional, según el contexto.

Cuando Benjamín sale (1) _____ Margarita y van a la discoteca Luna en Lima, siempre se visten bien. (2) _____ él le gusta llevar sus pantalones favoritos, una camisa blanca (3) _____ una corbata especial. Como *(Since)* Margarita siempre tiene frío, ella nunca sale (4) _____ la casa (5) _____ su suéter; lo lleva (6) _____ y se lo pone cuando es necesario. Dice a su amigo: «Una camiseta no es bastante (7) _____ (8) _____». Sus amigos Tina y Julián también van a la discoteca Luna. A veces, Julián le pregunta (9) _____ Margarita: «Margarita, quieres bailar (10) _____?» Ella responde, como siempre: «Sí, claro, (11) _____ mí me gusta bailar (12) _____, Julián.» Los jóvenes se divierten mucho (13) _____ problemas porque son muy buenos amigos y (14) _____ ellos les gusta estar juntos.

E. En la tienda. Usa las siguientes preposiciones para completar el diálogo.

a   con   de   en   entre

DEPENDIENTA: ¿ _____ qué puedo servirle?

PETRA: Me interesa esta falda ya que va _____ esta blusa. ¿Cuánto cuestan?

DEPENDIENTA: El precio es muy razonable —55 dólares. _____ Ud. y yo, es casi un regalo.

PETRA: Gracias. Dígame, por favor, ¿dónde puedo probar la falda y la blusa? No me gusta comprar ropa _____ probarla.

DEPENDIENTA: Tiene razón, señorita. Pase por aquí mismo.

PETRA: Señora, Ud. es muy amable. A propósito *(By the way)*, ¿ _____ dónde es Ud.? Tiene un acento interesante.

DEPENDIENTA: Soy _____ Lima, Perú. Y usted, señorita, ¿ _____ dónde es?

PETRA: Soy _____ Guadalajara, México.

F. En la joyería. Escoge la forma adecuada del demostrativo para completar el diálogo.

CLIENTE: ¿Cómo se llama (este, ese, esa) piedra preciosa?

DEPENDIENTA: ¿(Ésta, Esta, Éste) o (ésta, ese, éste)?

CLIENTE: (Ésa, Esta, Ése) ahí. La roja.

DEPENDIENTA: ¡Ah! (Esta, Éste, Ésta) piedra es un rubí.

CLIENTE: ¿Puede Ud. poner (este, ese, esta) rubí en un collar para mi esposa?

DEPENDIENTA: Sí, señor. (Esta, Ese, Este) rubí va a estar muy elegante en un collar. Con mucho gusto se lo hago.

Querido Diario. Tienes un día muy ocupado mañana. Para prepararte, vas a escribir tu horario tentativo en tu diario. Primero, haz una lista de cosas que tienes que hacer y cuándo. ¿A qué hora vas a levantarte? ¿Qué ropa vas a ponerte? ¿Cuándo tienes que salir de tu casa?, etc. Es importante incluir unas actividades agradables (*pleasant*) además de los quehaceres y obligaciones. Luego describe tu horario de mañana en tu diario.

Grammar: verbs: future with **ir**, verbs: use of **tener**, verbs: present
Phrases: expressing compulsion and obligation, expressing intention
Vocabulary: clothing, colors; house: household chores, leisure

Vocabulario activo

Verbos

acostar(se)
acurrucarse (c→qu)
afeitar(se)
arrepentirse
atreverse a
bañar(se)
casar(se) (con)
despedir(se) (e→i)

despertar(se) (e→ie)
desvestir(se) (e→i)
divertir(se) (e→ie, i)
dormir(se) (o→ue, u)
ir(se)
lavar(se)
levantar(se)
peinar(se)

pintar(se)/maquillar(se)
poner(se) (ropa)
ponerse
quejarse de
sentar(se) (e→ie)
sentir(se) (e→ie, i)
vestir(se) (e→i)

Preposiciones

a
con
de
en
entre
sin
sobre

Pronombres

conmigo
consigo
contigo
mí
ti

Adjetivos demostrativos

aquel
ese
este

Para describir la ropa

la blusa
los calcetines
la camisa
la camiseta
la corbata
la falda
las medias
los pantalones

la ropa interior
el saco
el sombrero
el suéter
el traje
el vestido
los zapatos

Para hablar de la cara

la cara
las cejas
los dientes
la frente
los labios
las mejillas
el mentón
la nariz

los ojos
las orejas

Los colores

amarillo
anaranjado
azul
azul marino
beige
blanco
claro
gris

marrón
morado
negro
oscuro
rojo
rosado
verde
violeta

Pronombres demostrativos

aquél, aquélla
aquéllos, aquéllas
ése, ésa
ésos, ésas
éste, ésta
éstos, éstas

Web site:
http://spanishforlife.heinle.com

Transparencies:
A–4: La América del Sur
A–8: Country Profile, Argentina

San Salvador
Salta
San Miguel de Tucuman
Resistencia
Córdoba
Mendoza
Rosario
San Rafael
Buenos Aires
ARGENTINA
Mar del Plata
Neuquen
Bahía Blanca
San Carlos de Bariloche
Rawson
Comodoro Rivadavia
Puerto Santa Cruz
Río Gallegos
Ushuaia

REPÚBLICA ARGENTINA

Nombre oficial: República Argentina

Área: 2.776.653 km^2

Población: 34.000.000

Capital: Buenos Aires

Moneda: el peso

Idioma oficial: español

Fiesta nacional: 9 de julio, Día de la Independencia

Argentina y los argentinos

Cataratas del Iguazú, Argentina

In this chapter you will learn:

GRAMMAR POINTS

- Imperfect tense: regular verbs
- Imperfect tense: irregular verbs
- Changes in meaning: preterite vs. imperfect
- The verb **gustar** and verbs that have the same structure

COMMUNICATIVE FUNCTIONS

- Recount childhood memories
- Talk about likes and dislikes, aches and pains

VOCABULARY

- Human body
- Health

I. «No llores por mí, Argentina»

LECTURA

Una de las figuras más controversiales en la historia argentina fue Eva Perón o «Evita», el nombre cariñoso[1] que le dio el pueblo[2] argentino. Esta ex-actriz se enamoró del presidente Juan Perón pero fue rechazada[3] por la alta sociedad a causa de su vida escandalosa y sus orígenes humildes. Sin embargo, Evita se alió[4] con las mujeres, los pobres y los trabajadores. Se dedicó a muchas causas sociales para proteger los derechos humanos de sus paisanos. **Reconocía** las muchas injusticias prevalentes de la época y le **dolía** la miseria que **se encontraba** en su país.

Se dice que Juan Perón no **compartía** la preocupación[5] por los pobres tanto como su esposa; ni **era** tan popular como ella. Él ganó la presidencia en 1946 y de nuevo en 1952. Perón **era** coronel militar con una posición menor en el Departamento de Labor pero sus habilidades políticas tanto como su carisma le **servían** muy bien. Junto con[6] su esposa, Evita, inició muchas reformas económicas e insistió en el concepto de auto-determinación. Todas estas reformas les **parecían** positivas a muchos argentinos en aquella época.

Para muchos argentinos, Evita Perón **era** (y todavía es) una santa responsable por grandes cambios sociales. De hecho,[7] las mujeres obtuvieron el derecho al voto en 1947 debido a la intervención de Evita. No obstante,[8] les **fastidiaba**[9] a otros argentinos porque ellos la **consideraban** una oportunista escandalosa. **Protestaban** diciendo que a Evita le **faltaban** la experiencia, la educación formal y la posición social para ser la esposa del presidente Juan Perón.

En fin, la verdad es que Evita Perón sigue siendo la causa de mucha controversia histórica entre los argentinos.

---

[1]**cariñoso:** *affectionate* / [2]**el pueblo:** *people* / [3]**rechazada:** *rejected* / [4]**se alió:** *allied herself* / [5]**preocupación:** *concern* / [6]**Junto con:** *Together with* / [7]**De hecho:** *In fact* / [8]**No obstante:** *Nevertheless* / [9]**fastidiaba:** *bothered, annoyed*

¿Comprendes?

1. ¿Qué hicieron Juan y Evita Perón para su país?
2. ¿Viste la película *Evita* que salió en 1998 con Madonna en el papel de Evita? ¿Qué opinas? ¿Te gustó?

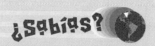

¿Sabías?

Cuando el presidente Juan Perón murió en 1975, su segunda esposa, María Isabel Perón, que era la vice-presidenta, asumió la presidencia. Ella fue una de las muy pocas mujeres de toda Latinoamérica que ha ocupado una posición política de tanta importancia.

■ Tiempo imperfecto: verbos regulares que terminan en -*ar*

The other functions of the imperfect as well as the other functions of the preterite will be covered in Chapter 11, where the two tenses are contrasted.

In Chapter 5 you learned about the preterite tense, which is used to tell what things happened in the past. Spanish has another past tense, the imperfect tense, which is used to describe what things were like and to reminisce about the past. It is used to tell how things used to be or what would happen in the past. For describing things you used to do, the imperfect is the appropriate tense to use.

De niño, **vivía** en Argentina.	As a child, **I lived** in Argentina.
Mi familia **se levantaba** temprano.	My family **would get up** early.
Todos **trabajábamos** en el rancho.	We all **used to work** on the ranch.

In the imperfect, -**ar** verbs follow the pattern of **bailar**.

bailar (to dance)			
yo	bail**aba**	nosotros(as)	bail**ábamos**
tú	bail**abas**	vosotros(as)	bail**abais**
Ud.		Uds.	
él }	bail**aba**	ellos }	bail**aban**
ella		ellas	

NOTA: The **nosotros** form requires an accent: -**ábamos**.

Mi hermana **cantaba** milonga.	Mi sister **used to sing** the milonga.
Yo **tocaba** la guitarra.	**I played** the guitar.
Mis padres **bailaban** tango.	My parents **would dance** the tango.

Practiquemos

A. Las vacaciones de verano. Martín recuerda su niñez y cómo pasaba las vacaciones de verano. Termina sus pensamientos con la forma adecuada del imperfecto del verbo indicado.

1. Mi familia _____ (visitar) a mis abuelos en su rancho.

2. Nosotros _____ (levantarse) tarde y _____ (desayunar) fuerte.

3. Luego mi abuelo y mi papá _____ (montar) a caballo.

4. Mi hermana _____ (hablar) con mis primas.

5. Mis hermanos y yo _____ (jugar) al fútbol.

6. Por la noche mi mamá y mi abuelo _____ (preparar) la cena.

7. Después de la cena yo _____ (tocar) la guitarra y mis hermanos _____ (cantar).

8. Y tú, ¿cómo _____ (pasar) tus vacaciones?

B. Hace cinco años. Todos recuerdan su vida de hace cinco años. ¿Qué hacías? Forma oraciones con un elemento de cada columna.

> Dile a tu compañero(a) cómo pasabas las vacaciones de niño(a).

A	B	C
		todo el día
	mirar	la fábrica *(factory)*
yo	estudiar	proyecto importante
Elena	trabajar	música rock
Norman y Clara	escuchar	sólo verduras
tú	terminar	alemán
tú y yo	viajar	mucha televisión
¿ ?	probar	mucho
		por todo el mundo

■ Tiempo imperfecto: verbos regulares que terminan en *-er* o *-ir*

-Er and **-ir** verbs share the same set of endings in the imperfect tense.

hacer *(to do; to make)*			
yo	hacía	nosotros(as)	hacíamos
tú	hacías	vosotros(as)	hacíais
Ud.		Uds.	
él	hacía	ellos	hacían
ella		ellas	

escribir *(to write)*			
yo	escribía	nosotros(as)	escribíamos
tú	escribías	vosotros(as)	escribíais
Ud.		Uds.	
él	escribía	ellos	escribían
ella		ellas	

Mis primos **vivían** en Buenos Aires.	*My cousins **lived** in Buenos Aires.*
Me divertía mucho con ellos.	*I **had a** really **good time** with them.*
Comíamos en restaurantes italianos.	*We **would eat** in Italian restaurants.*

Practiquemos

A. Los sábados. ¿Cómo pasaban Fernanda y su familia los sábados hace 20 años? Completa su descripción con la forma apropiada del imperfecto de los verbos apropiados.

barrer   comer   creer   deber   divertirse   escribir
hacer   leer   preferir   sacudir   salir   tener

¿Qué hacías tú los sábados cuando eras niño(a)?

Por la mañana, mi mamá y yo (1) _____ muchos quehaceres. (2) _____ que lavar la ropa y los platos. Luego
yo (3) _____ los pisos mientras mi mamá (4) _____ los muebles. Mi
hermana (5) _____ limpiar los cuartos de baño, pero ella (6) _____
dormir. Mi papá generalmente (7) _____ informes para su trabajo y
mis hermanos mayores (8) _____ sus lecciones. Mis padres, mis hermanos y yo casi siempre (9) _____ a almorzar — (10) _____ en una
pizzería muy buena. Y luego por la tarde (11) _____ mucho. Todos
nosotros (12) _____ que éramos muy afortunados.

B. Hace diez años. ¿Qué hacían estas personas
hace diez años? Escribe oraciones sobre tus actividades y las actividades de tus amigos y tu familia.

Dile a tu compañero(a) algunas cosas que hacías hace diez años.

M O D E L O :   yo
Yo comía comida argentina.

1. mis padres
2. yo
3. mi amiga
4. mis amigos y yo
5. tú

6. Uds.
7. mi familia
8. mis hermanos(as)
9. mi mamá y yo
10. mi novio(a)

C. La señora Perón. Termina la descripción de Evita Perón con el
imperfecto de los verbos apropiados.

adorar   compartir   considerar   defender   gobernar
pensar   reconocer   recordar   sentir   servir

Evita Perón, esposa del presidente de Argentina, (1) _____ las injusticias y (2) _____ los derechos del pueblo argentino. (3) _____ su pasado humilde y (4) _____ compasión por los pobres. Algunos argentinos
la (5) _____ y la (6) _____ una santa. Otras personas (7) _____ que
era oportunista. Su esposo, Juan, que (8) _____ el país, no (9) _____
la popularidad de Evita, pero (10) _____ a su país con una capacidad
política extraordinaria.

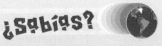

¿Sabías?

Las Madres de la Plaza de Mayo son
un grupo de mujeres (madres y abue-
las) que se reúnen cada jueves para
recordar a sus hijos, parientes y amigos que desaparecieron durante la
dictadura militar en Argentina.

■ Tiempo imperfecto: verbos irregulares

Only three verbs are irregular in the imperfect tense:

ir *(to go)*				**ser** *(to be)*			
yo	iba	nosotros(as)	íbamos	yo	era	nosotros(as)	éramos
tú	ibas	vosotros(as)	ibais	tú	eras	vosotros(as)	erais
Ud.		Uds.		Ud.		Uds.	
él	iba	ellos	iban	él	era	ellos	eran
ella		ellas		ella		ellas	

ver *(to see)*			
yo	veía	nosotros(as)	veíamos
tú	veías	vosotros(as)	veíais
Ud.		Uds.	
él	veía	ellos	veían
ella		ellas	

Era profesora de literatura.	***She was*** *a literature professor.*
Veíamos muchas películas argentinas.	***We saw*** *many Argentine movies.*
Ibas a la playa en el verano.	***You went*** *to the beach in the summer.*

Practiquemos

A. Los cuentos de abuelito. Completa la historia de abuelo con **ser**, **ir** o **ver** en el imperfecto.

¿Cómo era diferente la vida cuando tú eras niño(a)?

La vida ahora es muy fácil. Uds. tienen mucha suerte. Cuando yo (1) _____ niño, el mundo (2) _____ muy diferente. Mis amigos y yo (3) _____ muy felices, pero la vida (4) _____ un poco dura. Todos los días mis hermanos y yo (5) _____ diez millas a pie *(on foot)* a la escuela. (6) _____ cosas interesantes en el camino pero en el invierno el viaje (7) _____ difícil a causa de la profunda nieve. La nieve (8) _____ tan profunda que nadie (9) _____ a mi perro cuando nos acompañaba a la escuela. Un día, cuando yo (10) _____ a la escuela...

B. Mi niñez. Describe tu niñez escribiendo tres oraciones para cada sujeto. Usa los verbos **ir**, **ser** y **ver**. Luego escribe tres preguntas para un(a) compañero(a) de clase. Luego hazle las preguntas a tu compañero(a).

MODELO: Mi mamá...
Mi mamá era enfermera.
Ella iba al hospital para trabajar.
No veía mucha televisión.

1. Yo…

2. Mis padres…

3. Mis amigos y yo…

4. Mi mejor amigo(a)…

5. ¿Tú…?

II. El laberinto literario de Jorge Luis Borges

LECTURA

Uno de los más grandes escritores hispanoamericanos de nuestro tiempo fue Jorge Luis Borges, un argentino que nació en Buenos Aires en 1899. Vino de una familia culta[1] en la cual se cultivaba un gran aprecio para la literatura y las bellas artes.[2] Desde muy niño, Borges leía constantemente; a los siete años comenzó a escribir y a los diez años publicó su primera obra. De joven, Borges vivió con su familia en Europa: Italia, Suiza y España. Allí **conoció** a muchos escritores de la época y **pudo** seguir perfeccionando su arte literaria con mucho éxito. Regresó a Buenos Aires en 1921, donde su fama como ensayista,[3] cuentista y poeta brillante creció rápidamente.

Una vez en Buenos Aires, Borges se opuso al primer gobierno de Juan Perón; **no quiso** aceptar las prácticas políticas de los peronistas y siguió denunciándolos en sus ensayos. Logró[4] una fama universal con sus muchas obras literarias. Aunque fue nombrado para el Premio Nóbel varias veces, fue rechazado injustamente por razones políticas.

En los años 50, Borges empezó a perder la vista y ya en 1956 perdió la vista completamente. Pero **pudo** seguir escribiendo con la ayuda de su madre y otros amigos fieles.[5]

El tono poético, el carácter filosófico y el esceptisismo caracterizan las obras de Borges. De sus argumentos[6] salen figuras fantásticas y abstractas. Para él, el mundo es un laberinto absurdo en donde todos se pierden y no pueden trazar[7] su destino y gobernarse bien. Sus temas metafísicos son envueltos[8] en la idea del tiempo circular, y su estilo es limpio,[9] preciso y poderoso.[10]

Las obras de Jorge Luis Borges siguen siendo reconocidas[11] universalmente y para los argentinos, él es un ícono literario.

---

[1]**culta:** *cultured* / [2]**bellas artes:** *fine arts* / [3]**ensayista:** *essayist* / [4]**Logró:** *He obtained, acquired* / [5]**fieles:** *faithful, loyal* / [6]**argumentos:** *plots* / [7]**trazar:** *trace* / [8]**envueltos:** *entangled* / [9]**limpio:** *neat, clean* / [10]**poderoso:** *powerful* / [11]**reconocidas:** *recognized, known*

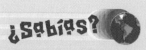

En Argentina y otros países en Sudamérica y Centroamérica se usa el pronombre **vos** en lugar de **tú**. Esta práctica se llama el «voseo». La gente dice: «¿Cómo estás vos? Vos hablás muy bien el español».

¿Comprendes?

1. ¿Qué caracteriza las obras de Jorge Luis Borges?
2. Aunque totalmente ciego en sus últimos años, Borges no quiso dejar de escribir. ¿Qué nos dice eso de su carácter?

In South America, the **voseo** is used in Argentina, Uruguay, Paraguay, parts of Bolivia, Chile, Ecuador, Colombia, and Venezuela. In Central America, it is found in all countries except Panama.

Remind students that they learned the special meanings of these verbs in the preterite in Chapter 8.

■ Verbos con un significado especial en el pretérito e imperfecto

The following verbs have special meanings in the preterite and imperfect. These changes in meaning focus on the fact that the preterite indicates the completion of an action while the imperfect stresses repetitive or habitual action.

Pregúntales a dos compañeros(as) tres cosas que supieron recientemente.

Infinitive	Imperfect	Preterite
saber	*knew* (facts, information)	*found out*
conocer	*knew* (person, place), *was acquainted with*	*met*
poder	*was able*	*managed to, succeeded in*
no poder	*could not, was not able to*	*failed, did not succeed*
querer	*wanted, wished*	*tried*
no querer	*did not want*	*refused*
tener	*had*	*received, got*
tener que	*had to*	*had to (and did)*

Yo **conocía** bien a Ángela.   *I knew Angela well.*
Yo **conocí** a su hermana ayer.   *I met her sister yesterday.*
Emilia siempre **sabía** la verdad.   *Emily always knew the truth.*
Ramón **supo** la verdad hoy.   *Raymond found out the truth today.*

Practiquemos

A. ¡Buenas noticias! Ayer el señor Garza fue a ver al médico. ¿Qué supo él? Escoge el pretérito o imperfecto de los verbos, según el contexto.

1. El señor Garza (no quiso / no quería) ir a ver al médico pero (supo / sabía) que (tuvo / tenía) que hacerlo.
2. Le dolía mucho la rodilla y (no podía / no pudo) andar bien.
3. Finalmente, (podía / pudo) conseguir una cita con la doctora Rivas.

4. Él (conocía / conoció) a la doctora el año pasado.

5. La doctora examinó su rodilla, y pronto, el señor Garza (supo / sabía) que le iba a ayudar.

6. Al día siguiente, (tenía / tuvo) buenas noticias de la doctora Rivas.

7. (Sabía / Supo) que, con unos medicamentos y unos ejercicios, no iba a sufrir más.

B. Escritor. Completa el párrafo sobre Jorge Luis Borges con los verbos indicados en el imperfecto o el pretérito, según el contexto.

La familia de Jorge Luis era importante y (1) _____ (conocer) a gente en todas partes del mundo y (2) _____ (saber) hablar muchas lenguas. En Europa, Borges (3) _____ (conocer) a muchos escritores famosos. Jorge Luis (4) _____ (saber) que (5) _____ (tener) que estudiar, pero era inteligente y (6) _____ (poder) publicar su primer libro a los diez años. Jorge Luis Borges (7) _____ (saber) que se volvía ciego pero los doctores no (8) _____ (poder) detener el progreso de la enfermedad.

C. En el gimnasio. Catalina y Mónica platican en el gimnasio mientras hacen su ejercicio. Completa su diálogo con el pretérito o imperfecto de estos verbos, según el contexto.

Transparencies:
K–1: El cuerpo
K–2: Las enfermedades
K–3: La nutrición
K–4: Una visita al médico
K–5: Los consejos del médico

saber   conocer   poder   querer   tener

CATALINA: ¿Qué tal, Mónica? Oye, yo _____ noticias de tu hermano ayer. Me dijo algo interesante de ti. ¿Qué pasa, mujer?

MÓNICA: Pues, ayer _____ a un hombre muy simpático y guapo; se llama Julio.

CATALINA: ¿En serio? ¿Dónde lo _____?

MÓNICA: Lo _____ en mi clase de ejercicio aeróbico.

CATALINA: ¿Cómo _____ conocerlo?

MÓNICA: Bueno, yo conversaba con la instructora cuando él se acercó.

Pregúntale a tu compañero(a) dos cosas que supo recientemente y dos cosas que pudo hacer esta semana.

CATALINA: ¿Y…?

MÓNICA: La instructora me lo presentó y así _____ su nombre.

CATALINA: Entonces, ¿qué pasó? ¡Dime!

MÓNICA: ¡Ay! Fíjate que la instructora tuvo que salir y me dejó con Julio.

CATALINA: ¿Y él _____ continuar la conversación?

MÓNICA: ¡Sí, cómo no! Platicamos por lo menos diez minutos. ¡Qué suerte tuve yo!

CATALINA: ¿Y después…?

MÓNICA: Julio me pidió mi número de teléfono y, claro, yo no _____ decirle que no. Bueno, me llamó y fuimos al Club Gaucho para bailar tango.

CATALINA: ¡Qué romántico, Mónica!

MÓNICA: Pero, ahora tengo un problema. Es mi amigo, Lorenzo.

CATALINA: Ah, sí, Lorenzo.

MÓNICA: Él _____ que yo salí con Julio y no _____ llamarme anoche.

CATALINA: ¡Ay, qué celos tiene Lorenzo!

Remind students that vocabulary relating to the face was presented in Chapter 9.

❖ Para hablar del cuerpo humano y la salud

Partes del cuerpo

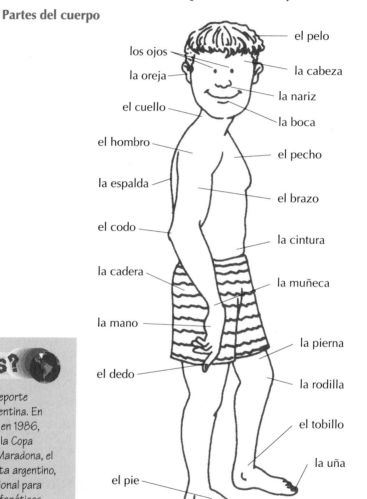

el pelo
la cabeza
la nariz
la boca
el pecho
el brazo
la cintura
la muñeca
la pierna
la rodilla
el tobillo
la uña
el dedo (de pie)

los ojos
la oreja
el cuello
el hombro
la espalda
el codo
la cadera
la mano
el dedo
el pie

El fútbol es el deporte nacional de Argentina. En 1978 y también en 1986, Argentina ganó la Copa Mundial. Diego Maradona, el famoso futbolista argentino, es un héroe nacional para millones de sus fanáticos.

Órganos internos	Internal organs		
el cerebro	*brain*	la garganta	*throat*
la columna vertebral	*backbone*	la lengua	*tongue*
el corazón	*heart*	el oído	*ear*
el esqueleto	*skeleton*	el pulmón	*lung*
el estómago	*stomach*		

Para tener buena salud	To have good health	la pierna rota	broken leg
brincar	to hop	tener dolor de cabeza, estómago	to have a headache, stomachache
estirarse	to stretch		
hacer ejercicio	to exercise	tener fiebre	to have a fever
hacer footing	to jog	tener gripe	to have the flu
levantar pesas	to lift weights	tener resfriado	to have a cold
saltar	to jump	torcerse el tobillo (o→ue)	to sprain, twist your ankle
Condiciones médicas	**Medical conditions**	toser (tener tos)	to cough
el brazo roto	broken arm	**Curas**	**Cures**
la contusión	bruise	comer bien	to eat well/ healthy
dolerle la cabeza	to have one's head hurt, ache	descansar	to rest
dolerle el estómago (o→ue)	to have one's stomach hurt, ache	seguir las instrucciones del doctor (de la doctora)	to follow the doctor's orders
dolerle la garganta	to have one's throat be sore	tomar aspirina	to take aspirin
		tomar pastillas	to take pills
enfermarse	to get sick	usar muletas	to use crutches
lastimarse	to hurt oneself		

NOTA:

In Argentina and Spain, **hacer footing** means *to jog*; other countries use **trotar**. **Un catarro** as well as **un resfriado** mean *a cold*. **Oreja** (Chapter 9) refers to the outer portion of the ear. **Oído** is the internal hearing organ.

Have students think of other healthy practices, like sleeping enough, drinking lots of water, exercising, eating well, etc.

Practiquemos

A. ¿Qué te pasa? Contesta las siguientes preguntas y luego compara tus respuestas con las de otros estudiantes.

1. ¿Cuáles son los síntomas de un catarro? ¿de la gripe?
2. ¿Qué te pasa cuando haces ejercicio por cuatro horas?
3. ¿Qué te pasa cuando te caes?
4. ¿Cómo te sientes cuando estudias o trabajas toda la noche?
5. ¿Qué dice el médico cuando tienes catarro? ¿Qué instrucciones te da?
6. ¿Qué debes hacer cuando tienes gripe?
7. ¿Qué haces cuando te duele la cabeza? ¿el estómago? ¿la garganta?
8. ¿Qué haces para mantener la buena salud?

Describe a una persona que admires, usando las partes del cuerpo. ¿Tiene hombros anchos? ¿Tiene una cintura pequeña? Lee tu descripción a un(a) compañero(a) y pregúntale si sabe quién es. Si no sabe, dile más características.

III. Una carta de Argentina

LECTURA

Queridos compañeros,

Quería compartir[1] con Uds. unas experiencias de mi estancia[2] en Argentina. Puedo explicar los semenarios y talleres de trabajo[3] al regresar, pero quiero contarles mis otras experiencias.

Al llegar, mis primos de Buenos Aires me recibieron en el aeropuerto e hicimos un recorrido por la ciudad. Buenos Aires me recordó[4] un poco a París con sus museos, teatros, avenidas anchas,[5] sus tiendas elegantes y, claro, el Río de la Plata. La ciudad **me encantó**. Tiene restaurantes excelentes —sobre todo los italianos y los que se especializan en preparar carne argentina. Por eso, al segundo día, me hice miembro de un club atlético para hacer ejercicio y levantar pesas[6] y así poder comer más. El próximo día empezaron los seminarios.

El primer fin de semana, salí de Buenos Aires para ver las famosas pampas. Fui al Parque Nacional Liahué Calel, donde vi animales indígenas y raros, como el puma, la rhea y la vizcacha.[7] El segundo fin de semana visité el Parque Nacional Iguazú donde están las famosas cataratas.[8] ¡Qué maravilla! **Me gustó** muchísimo. El tercer fin de semana fue cuando todo se vino para abajo.[9]

A algunos compañeros del seminario también **les gusta** esquiar y decidimos ir a los Andes a esquiar. El sábado por la mañana, subimos la montaña por góndola y cuando yo bajaba la pista para principiantes sentí que me caía. De repente, perdí el conocimiento y cuando me volví en mí,[10] me llevaban al hospital. ¡Cuánto **me dolía** la pierna! Pensaba que me moría. También me **dolían** los brazos. En el hospital, me sacaron radiografías[11] y el médico me dijo que no tenía la pierna rota —solamente había torcido el tobillo. Pero tengo que caminar con muletas. Imagínense. ¡Yo con muletas! ¡Cuánto me **fastidian**! Los brazos están magullados[12] y sólo **me falta** tomar aspirina para aliviarme.

Regresé a Buenos Aires, cancelé mi membrecía[13] en el club atlético y cancelé el viaje que iba a hacer a las Islas Malvinas. Ahora tengo que seguir las instrucciones del médico, tomar mis pastillas y, sobre todo, seguir una buena dieta y hacer el poco ejercicio que puedo. ¡Adiós, restaurantes italianos! Pero tengo buenas noticias. La pierna va a estar completamente curada[14] para mi regreso a Estados Unidos.

Hasta pronto, compañeros. Les manda saludos su amigo, Mario

---

[1]**compartir:** *to share* / [2]**la estancia:** *stay* / [3]**talleres de trabajo:** *workshops* / [4]**recordó:** *reminded* / [5]**anchas:** *wide* / [6]**levantar pesas:** *lift weights* / [7]**la vizcacha:** *type of chinchilla* / [8]**cataratas:** *waterfalls* / [9]**se vino para abajo:** *went wrong, fell apart* / [10]**me volví en mí:** *I regained consciousness, came to* / [11]**radiografías:** *X-rays* / [12]**magullados:** *bruised* / [13]**membrecía:** *membership* / [14]**curada:** *healed, cured*

¿Comprendes?

1. ¿Cómo son parecidos Buenos Aires y París?
2. ¿Por qué es famoso el Parque Nacional Iguazú?
3. ¿Por qué fueron Mario y sus compañeros a los Andes?

Cuenta a tu compañero(a) de una vez que te enfermaste o te lastimaste. ¿Tuviste que cambiar tus planes?

■ *Gustar* **y otros verbos similares**

You have already learned that the verbs **gustar** and **encantar**, which mean *to like* and *to love,* are conjugated differently from regular verbs. The forms of these verbs are always preceded by an indirect object pronoun. Therefore, what is liked will always be the *subject* of the sentence. If the subject is plural, add an **-n** to the verb.

Transparencies:
G–5: Pasatiempos
G–6: Deportes (1)
G–7: Deportes (2)

gustar *(to like)*			
(a mí)	**me gusta(n)**	(a nosotros[as])	**nos gusta(n)**
(a ti)	**te gusta(n)**	(a vosotros[as])	**os gusta(n)**
(a Ud.)		(a Uds.)	
(a él)	**le gusta(n)**	(a ellos)	**les gusta(n)**
(a ella)		(a ellas)	

¿**Te gustan** los postres?   *Do you like desserts?*
De niños, **no nos gustaba** estudiar.   *As children, **we didn't like** to study.*

A los estudiantes **les gustó** su viaje.   *The students **liked** their trip.*

You may use **a** + emphatic pronoun for emphasis and clarification.

A mí no **me gustan** las zanahorias.   *I don't like carrots.*
A ella le gusta esquiar.   *She likes to ski.*

Other verbs like **gustar**:

convenir	*to suit*
doler	*to hurt, ache*
encantar	*to be very fond of, really like*
faltar	*to lack, be lacking*
fastidiar	*to annoy, bother, bore*
importar	*to matter, be important*
interesar	*to interest*
parecer	*to seem*
sorprender	*to surprise, startle*

NOTA:
If what follows **gustar** is an infinitive, then the verb is singular. **Les gusta comer postres.**

Pregúntale a tu compañero(a) tres cosas que le gustaba hacer de niño.

Practiquemos

A. Gustos. ¿Qué les gusta y no les gusta a estas personas? Combina los elementos para describir sus gustos y disgustos *(dislikes).*

⊃

	Sí	No
a mi mejor amigo	esquiar	hacer los quehaceres
a Cecilia y a Alicia	ir de compras	estudiar
a Tina y a mí	los deportes	limpiar la casa
a ti	leer	las verduras
a mamá	ver películas	ir de compras
a mí	la naturaleza	leer novelas
a los argentinos	tener éxito	la polución
a todos	¿ ?	fracasar *(to fail)*
		¿ ?

B. Somos diferentes. Este grupo de personas compara sus diferencias. ¿Qué dicen? Combina las tres columnas, usando tu imaginación.

A	B	C
a ti	molestar	la cabeza
a los estudiantes	encantar	pagar con tarjetas de crédito
a Ceci	faltar	los pacientes difíciles
a la familia Saranillo	convenir	las vacaciones en Argentina
a los enfermos	gustar	viajar
a la profesora	doler	los juguetes
a Pablo y a mí	fastidiar	sacar buenas notas
a la Dra. Orihuela	importar	las preguntas ridículas
a mí	interesar	la música argentina
a todos	sorprender	esquiar en los Andes

¿Sabías?

El tango es un aspecto muy típico de la vida social de Argentina. Tanto la música como el baile son populares con todas las generaciones y todas las clases. Es posible bailar toda la noche en muchos clubes. El tango es muy apreciado no solamente en Argentina sino también en muchos países donde hay organizaciones en que los «tangueros» aprenden y practican su querido baile.

C. Problemas. Felipe necesita los consejos de «Pachita», la mujer que les da consejos a sus correspondientes en el periódico *Diario*. Completa la carta de Felipe con los pronombres de objeto indirecto y la forma adecuada de los verbos indicados.

Querida Pachita:

Mi novia, Teresa, es muy simpática pero a veces a mí (1) _____ (molestar) sus acciones. Creo que a ella (2) _____ (faltar) la sensibilidad que yo necesito. Pero, no es decir que no nos divertimos mucho. A nosotros (3) _____ (encantar) bucear *(to swim)*, hacer ejercicio y esquiar. También (4) _____ (gustar) ir al cine y comer en restaurantes elegantes. Sin embargo, todavía tenemos unos problemas. Por ejemplo, a Teresa (5) _____ (importar) mucho llegar puntualmente cuando tenemos una cita; a ella (6) _____ (fastidiar) cuando yo llego tarde o si no me visto bien. ¡También (7) _____ (molestar) si yo no pago todo! ¿Qué me aconseja, Pachita? ¿Qué debo hacer para no tener más problemas con mi novia?

Desesperado,
Felipe

D. Respuesta. Ahora, ¿qué le contesta Pachita? Escribe la carta y ¡usa tu imaginación!

E. Después del accidente. ¿Cómo se sentía Mario después de su accidente en la montaña? Completa las oraciones con los verbos adecuados en el imperfecto y los pronombres apropiados.

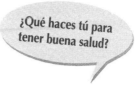

¿Qué haces tú para tener buena salud?

doler   encantar   fastidiar   interesar

A Mario (1) _____ el tobillo y (2) _____ mucho tener que caminar con muletas. Las muletas (3) _____ los brazos, y ¡los brazos ya (4) _____ de todas las contusiones! Mario decidió que aunque (5) _____ las montañas, ya no (6) _____ esquiar.

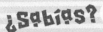

¿Sabías?   El té más popular de Argentina es el mate. Viene del árbol yerba mate que crece en las selvas subtropicales del norte de Argentina. Con las hojas de este árbol, se prepara este té refrescante y sabroso.

A ver si sabes

Use this self-test to see if you know the material presented in Chapter 10.

A. Una carta. Elena describe sus seis meses de estudios en Buenos Aires en una carta electrónica a su amigo Ricardo. Completa su descripción con el imperfecto de los verbos adecuados.

asistir   caminar   divertirse   empezar   estudiar
hacer   pasar   salir   terminar   vivir   volver

De: ECabreraMontenegro11@uar.edu
A: RicardoFG13@mexnet.net
Sujeto: Mi viaje

Hola Ricardo,
Quiero contarte de mis experiencias en Buenos Aires. (1) _____ en casa de una familia muy simpática. Mi compañera y yo (2) _____ a las clases cada día. En el camino (3) _____ la Casa Rosada, la residencia del presidente de la República. Las clases (4) _____ a las 9:00 y (5) _____ a las 2:00 para el almuerzo. Yo siempre (6) _____ a casa para comer. Por las tardes, (7) _____ a laboratorios o (8) _____ en la biblioteca y luego mis amigos y yo (9) _____ a tomar café y a charlar. Y tú, ¿que (10) _____ durante esos meses? ¿Tú también (11) _____ ?
Escríbeme pronto.
Recibe un abrazo de tu amiga,
Elena

Preguntas culturales
1. Explica por qué Evita Perón es tan importante en la Argentina.
2. ¿Por qué se juntan las Madres de la Plaza de Mayo?
3. Describe la actitud de Jorge Luis Borges hacia los peronistas.

B. Los fines de semana de niño. Cuando Ernesto era niño, él y sus amigos tenían una rutina fija. Termina su descripción con los verbos **ir, ser** o **ver** en el imperfecto.

De niño, yo (1) _____ al cine cada sábado por la tarde. Mis amigos y yo siempre (2) _____ películas de aventura —a veces (3) _____ modernas y a veces viejas. ¡Qué buenas (4) _____! Mi amiga Carlota a veces (5) _____ al cine los domingos también y (6) _____ películas románticas. ¡Uf! No me gustaban nada. ¿Tú (7) _____ mucho al cine de niño? ¿Qué películas (8) _____?

C. Conociendo Argentina. ¿Qué hicieron estos turistas en Argentina? Escoge la forma correcta de los verbos, según el contexto.

1. Los turistas (supieron / sabían) hablar español antes de viajar a Argentina.
2. Emilia y yo (conocíamos / conocimos) a Mario Pinelli en la Península Valdés.
3. Durante el viaje, yo siempre (pude / podía) hacer lo que quería porque hacía buen tiempo.
4. Cuando estábamos en Buenos Aires, nosotros (sabíamos / supimos) que el Museo Histórico Provincial Marqués de Sobremonte es uno de los más importantes del país.
5. Sandra (no quería / no quiso) esquiar en los Andes con Tim; quería esquiar con su novio, Brian.
6. Tú (quisiste / querías) abordar el tren para Patagonia pero ya salía cuando llegaste.
7. El día antes de salir, Marianela y Josefina no tenían mucho dinero pero (pudieron / podían) hacer más compras en Buenos Aires.
8. Antes de salir de Argentina, el grupo (tenía / tuvo) noticias de sus familiares.

D. El viaje. Tú y tus amigos pasaron tres semanas viajando por Argentina. Haz unas preguntas combinando los siguientes elementos y luego escribe las respuestas.

MODELO: ¿A Mariana?
¿A Mariana le gustó la ciudad de Buenos Aires?
Sí, a ella le encantó esa ciudad.

A: encantar, faltar, gustar, doler, interesar, fastidiar

B: bailar el tango, el té mate, los platos argentinos, el clima, las discotecas, la historia argentina, los edificios históricos, las ciudades

1. ¿A ti?
2. ¿A Juan y su novia?
3. ¿A Patricia y a mí?
4. ¿A Flora?
5. ¿A mí?
6. ¿A Rafael y a ti?
7. ¿A todo el grupo?
8. ¿A Petra?

Querido Diario. Vas a compartir con tu diario unos recuerdos de tu niñez. Para organizar tus pensamientos, haz una lista en tres columnas de tus actividades *habituales:* 1) durante el año escolar, 2) durante las vacaciones y 3) los días feriados (cumpleaños, el día de acción de gracias, la Navidad, Chanukka, etc). Luego escribe tres párrafos de tus recuerdos de tus actividades cuando asistías a la escuela, de cuando tenías vacaciones y los aspectos de los días feriados que te gustaban más. Puedes comenzar diciendo: Cuando yo era niño(a) siempre...

Grammar: verbs: imperfect
Phrases: describing the past; talking about habitual actions
Vocabulary: camping; clothing; foods (all categories); health; leisure; religious holidays; sports; travel; upbringing

Vocabulario activo

Verbos

convenir	faltar	interesar	parecer
doler	fastidiar	molestar	sorprender
encantar	importar	montar a caballo	

Partes del cuerpo

La cabeza	El tronco	el dedo	Órganos internos
la boca	la cadera	el dedo (de pie)	la columna vertebral
el cerebro	la cintura	la mano	el corazón
el cuello	la espalda	la muñeca	el esqueleto
la lengua	el hombro	el pie	el estómago
la nariz	el pecho	la pierna	la garganta
los ojos		la rodilla	el oído
la oreja	**Las extremidades**	el tobillo	el pulmón
el pelo	el brazo	la uña	
	el codo		

Para tener buena salud

brincar		
estirarse		
hacer ejercicio		
hacer footing		
levantar pesas		
saltar		

Condiciones médicas

la contusión	tener dolor de cabeza,
dolerle la cabeza	estómago
dolerle el estómago	tener fiebre
dolerle la garganta	tener gripe
enfermarse	tener resfriado
lastimarse	torcerse el tobillo
la pierna rota, el brazo roto	toser (tener tos)

Curas

comer bien	tomar aspirina
descansar	tomar pastillas
seguir las instrucciones del doctor (de la doctora)	usar muletas

Otras palabras

la niñez
de niño(a)

Web site:
http://spanishforlife.heinle.com

Transparencies:
A–2: **México y la América Central**
A–15: Country Profile, **Costa Rica**
A–17: Country Profile, **Honduras**

REPÚBLICA DE COSTA RICA

Nombre oficial: República de Costa Rica

Área: 51.100 km²

Población: 3.500.000

Capital: San José

Moneda: el colón

Idioma oficial: español

Fiesta nacional: 15 de septiembre, Día de la Independencia

REPÚBLICA DE HONDURAS

Nombre oficial: República de Honduras

Área: 112.492 km²

Población: 5.800.000

Capital: Tegucigalpa

Moneda: el lempira

Idioma oficial: español

Fiesta nacional: 15 de septiembre, Día de la Independencia

Costa Rica y los costarricenses
Honduras y los hondureños

Taxi acuático con pasajeros costarricenses sobre el Lago de Nicaragua

In this chapter you will learn:

GRAMMAR POINTS

- Preterite tense: review of uses
- Imperfect tense: review of uses
- Preterite vs. imperfect
- The verbs **acabar de**, **acabar**, **acabarse**, **acabar con**

COMMUNICATIVE FUNCTIONS

- Describe and narrate in the past
- Tell a story in past
- Recount a past incident

VOCABULARY

- Ecology
- Animals

I. Costa Rica y un líder sin igual, Óscar Arias Sánchez

LECTURA

Costa Rica tiene la distinción de ser un país democrático progresista. Es un pequeño país de 2,8 millones de habitantes que mantiene su identidad como una república pacífica y próspera. Costa Rica tiene fama de ser el «país de la paz».

Óscar Arias, ex-presidente de Costa Rica

En 1948, el presidente de Costa Rica **fue** José Figueres Ferrer. Con el apoyo de todo el pueblo costarricense, **depusieron**[1] al entonces presidente Rafael Calderón Guardia y sus títeres.[2] Lo más importante e interesante de aquella acción **fue** la abolición del ejército y todos los cuerpos militares de la época. El nuevo presidente, «Don Pepe», como la gente lo llamaba, **estableció** un sistema de seguros,[3] sanidad,[4] educación fuerte y un banco nacional.

Luego, en 1979, con sus esfuerzos antimilitaristas, Costa Rica **tuvo** éxito en resistir la presión antidemocrática de sus vecinos que se **encontraron** en sus propias revoluciones e inestabilidad política económica. En particular, los problemas de Nicaragua **pusieron** en peligro la paz delicada de la cual gozaban los costarricenses.

Cuando Óscar Arias Sánchez **llegó** a ser presidente, **siguió** el movimiento de paz y prosperidad que había iniciado Don Pepe. En 1987, Óscar Arias **presentó** su Plan de Pacificación para solucionarse los problemas económicos de Costa Rica causados por la guerra en los países vecinos. Este Plan **tuvo** como objetivo la eliminación del terrorismo y de la violencia promoviendo, en contraste, una paz fuerte, los derechos humanos y una estabilidad económica para todos.

Óscar Arias **fue** un presidente sin igual. Por eso, en 1987, **recibió** el Premio Nóbel de la Paz por su Plan de Pacificación, un plan firmado por cinco naciones centroamericanas. Los costarricenses están muy orgullosos[5] de su progreso democrático, su economía estable y la seguridad de sus ciudades y pueblos. Gracias a la previsión[6] de Óscar Arias, Costa Rica ha logrado un bienestar que es la envidia[7] de sus vecinos militarizados.

---

[1]**depusieron:** *they deposed, removed from office* / [2]**títeres:** *puppets* / [3]**seguros:** *insurance* / [4]**sanidad:** *public health* / [5]**orgulloso:** *proud* / [6]**previsión:** *foresight* / [7]**envidia:** *envy*

¿Comprendes?

1. ¿Qué es lo que distingue a Costa Rica de las otras naciones centroamericanas?
2. ¿Qué tipo de líder fue Don Pepe?
3. ¿Cómo se distinguió el presidente Óscar Arias Sánchez?

■ El tiempo pretérito: repaso de los usos

Remember that the preterite tense is the simple past tense in Spanish that focuses on (1) the beginning or end of an action, (2) events that began in the past and were completed in the past, and (3) narrations.

¿Qué **hiciste** ayer?	*What **did you do** yesterday?*
Los turistas **mandaron** sus postales.	*The tourists **sent** their postcards.*
El año pasado, **viajamos** a Costa Rica.	*Last year, **we traveled** to Costa Rica.*

Practiquemos

A. Explorando la ciudad. Ayer, Sara y Julieta fueron a San José, Costa Rica. Completa el párrafo para saber lo que hicieron.

Ayer, Sara y Julieta (1) _____ (levantarse) muy temprano para explorar San José. (2) _____ (Desayunar) a las 7:00 y luego (3) _____ (irse) para la ciudad. Cuando (4) _____ (llegar) al centro, (5) _____ (tomar) un taxi a la Avenida Central donde (6) _____ (encontrarse) con José Luis y Mariela. Mariela, quien conoce muy bien la ciudad, los (7) _____ (llevar) al Parque Central y al Teatro Nacional. Después, los amigos (8) _____ (ir) a la Plaza de la Democracia y (9) _____ (almorzar) en un restaurante muy bueno que está cerca. Entonces, José Luis (10) _____ (tener) que ir a trabajar a las 3:00, así que los otros amigos (11) _____ (salir) para ir de compras en el centro comercial «El Pueblo». ¡Cómo (12) _____ (divertirse) todos!

B. ¿Qué aprendieron? Los estudiantes prepararon un informe sobre un presidente hondureño, Francisco Morazán. Para saber lo que aprendieron, completa las oraciones con un verbo de la lista, usando el pretérito.

asistir a   autorizar   dirigir *(to lead)*
educarse   iniciar   matar   morir   nacer
regresar   ser

> Con tu compañero(a), narra una visita que hiciste a una ciudad. Incluye por lo menos ocho cosas que viste e hiciste. Luego comparte lo que hiciste con un(a) compañero(a) diferente.

1. Francisco Morazán _____ en 1792 y _____ en 1842 en Honduras.

2. Nunca _____ la escuela; _____ él mismo.

3. En 1825, _____ elegido presidente de la Asamblea Legislativa de Honduras.

4. _____ muchas reformas para limitar el poder de la Iglesia Católica y _____ muchos cambios para mejorar la situación económica del país.

5. En 1829, Morazán _____ el ejército hondureño en una guerra civil para derrotar a las facciones conservadoras.

6. Después de otra guerra civil en 1840, Morazán _____ exiliado pero _____ para restaurar la Federación.

7. Desafortunadamente, uno de sus propios soldados lo _____.

II. Tegucigalpa

LECTURA

Tegucigalpa, la capital de Honduras, es una mezcla de lo viejo y lo moderno. Su nombre se derivó de la lengua náhuatl y significa «montaña de plata».[1] Durante la época colonial, Tegucigalpa **era** un centro de la industria minera centroamericana.

Esta ciudad fascinante, que es la puerta a la costa pacífica, está ubicada en un valle pintoresco[2] con un clima muy agradable. El centro comercial de la ciudad es un distrito animado que también se conoce como «la zona viva». Allí hay muchos restaurantes, oficinas, hoteles y tiendas.

Al otro lado de la ciudad, se encuentra un centro histórico que es también muy interesante. Allí se encuentran muchos edificios antiguos como la muy famosa catedral dedicada al santo patrón de Tegucigalpa, San Miguel Arcángel. Esta catedral contiene un altar barroco hecho de joyas[3] y metales preciosos de la época cuando Tegucigalpa **era** el centro minero y **tenía** estas riquezas a su alcance.[4] La gente **trabajaba** en las minas y lo que no se **usaba** en el adorno de los famosos edificios, como la Universidad Nacional de Honduras (hoy es el Museo del Hombre Hondureño), la casa presidencial y otros museos, se **exportaba** a otros países.

Saliendo de la ciudad central, se puede visitar unos parques magníficos como el Parque de la Leona, el Parque de las Naciones Unidas y el Parque de la Concordia donde hay reproducciones de templos mayas en miniatura.

Tegucigalpa mantiene la gloria de su pasado pero también es una ciudad moderna y dinámica que ofrece mucho a todos que la visitan.

---

[1]**la plata:** *silver* / [2]**pintoresco:** *picturesque* / [3]**joyas:** *jewels, gems* / [4]**a su alcance:** *within reach, at hand*

¿Comprendes?

1. ¿Cómo era Tegucigalpa en la época colonial?

2. ¿Cuáles son algunos lugares interesantes en la ciudad?

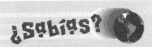

¿Sabías?

Lempira fue uno de los líderes nativos hondureños que tuvo éxito en resistir la dominación de los españoles, en 1530. Desafortunadamente, su movimiento de resistencia fracasó con su muerte. Para honrar su memoria, el gobierno de Honduras nombró su moneda nacional el «lempira».

■ El tiempo imperfecto: repaso de los usos

As you learned in Chapter 10, the imperfect is one of two past tenses in Spanish. It has several well-defined functions:

■ *to describe the past as it was happening, emphasizing the progression of the event. For this reason it is used in descriptions to set the stage.*

Los hondureños **consideraban** a Lempira un héroe.	*Hondurans **considered** Lempira a hero.*
Tegucigalpa **era** un centro industrial.	*Tegucigalpa **was** an industrial center.*

■ *to describe repeated or habitual actions in the past*

Los mineros **iban** a las minas.	*The miners **went/used to go** to the mines.*
Honduras **exportaba** oro y plata.	*Honduras **exported/used to export** gold and silver.*

■ *to tell time or age in the past*

Eran las 2:00 de la tarde.	*It **was** 2:00 in the afternoon.*
Cristóbal Colón **tenía** 51 años en 1502.	*Christopher Columbus **was** 51 in 1502.*

■ *to describe mental, physical, or emotional states in the past*

Yo **tenía** mucho estrés con mi trabajo.	*I **was** very stressed with work.*
Estábamos emocionados al ver a nuestra abuela.	*We **were** excited to see our grandmother.*

Practiquemos

A. Una noche en Tegucigalpa. Completa la descripción con verbos en el imperfecto y otras palabras necesarias. Luego compara tu descripción con la de un(a) compañero(a).

Describele a tu compañero(a) una tarde muy especial que recuerdas.

La noche _____.

Dentro de la casa _____.

En la sala, una mujer _____.

Los niños _____.

Toda la familia _____.

B. La escuela. ¿Qué hacían tu familia y tus amigos cuando estabas en la escuela primaria? Forma oraciones de los elementos de las tres columnas.

> ¿Cómo eras de niño(a)? Dile a tu compañero(a) algunas cosas que hacías regularmente cuando eras niño(a) o joven.

A	B	C
yo	dormir	a los niños
mis padres	jugar	la ropa
mi hermano(a)	leer	al cine
mi tío(a)	trabajar	el periódico
mis amigos y yo	hacer	mucho
mi papá	estudiar	a la escuela
mi mamá	asistir	después de las clases
¿ ?	ir	poco
	cuidar	la casa
	¿ ?	¿ ?

C. ¿A qué hora? ¿Qué hora era cuando hiciste estas cosas ayer?

MODELO: Cuando me levanté *eran las 6:00 de la mañana.*

1. Cuando me bañé
2. Cuando salí de la casa
3. Cuando almorcé
4. Cuando fui al trabajo (a la clase)
5. Cuando volví a casa
6. Cuando descansé
7. Cuando cené
8. Cuando me acosté

❖ Para hablar de la ecología

el abono	*fertilizer*	la energía nuclear	*nuclear energy*
el aire	*air*	la erosión	*erosion*
el bióxido de carbono	*carbon dioxide*	el herbicida	*herbicide*
el bosque (lluvioso)	*(rain) forest*	el monóxido de carbono	*carbon monoxide*
el calentamiento	*warming*	el oxígeno	*oxygen*
la capa de ozono	*ozone layer*	el pesticida	*pesticide*
el combustible	*fuel*	la pureza	*purity*
la combustión	*combustion*	la química	*chemical, chemistry*
la contaminación	*contamination, pollution*	el químico	*chemist*
contaminar	*to contaminate, pollute*	el residuo	*residue, by-product*
la deforestación	*deforestation*	la selva tropical	*tropical jungle*
la ecología	*ecology*	la tierra	*earth, ground*
el ecosistema	*ecosystem*		

> ¡NOTA:
> La capa de ozono también se llama **la ozonósfera**; **la jungla** también se usa para **la selva**; **el bosque** también se llama **la floresta**; y **el abono** también se conoce como **el fertilizante**.

Practiquemos ✎

A. Protección del planeta. Contesta las siguientes preguntas y luego compara tus respuestas con las de un(a) compañero(a).

1. ¿Qué necesitamos para respirar?
2. ¿Qué sustancia gaseosa producen las plantas?
3. ¿Qué sustancia gaseosa exhalamos?
4. ¿Qué agentes contaminan el aire?
5. ¿Qué protege la tierra del calentamiento global?
6. ¿Cuál es la importancia del bosque lluvioso y las selvas?
7. ¿Qué agentes contaminan el agua?
8. ¿Qué matan *(kill)* los herbicidas?
9. ¿Qué función tiene la capa de ozono?
10. En tu opinión, ¿cuál es el mejor tipo de combustible? ¿Por qué?

III. Informe: la ubicación[1] de la nueva planta

LECTURA

Memo

A: Presidente de NaturaTela

De: Comité exploratorio (Manuel Gómez, Elena Costa,
             Rubén García Poole)   MG EC RGP

Sujeto: Informe sobre Honduras y Costa Rica

Como usted sabe, **fuimos** a dos países centroamericanos para evaluarlos como sitio para la ubicación de la nueva fábrica.[2] Primero **visitamos** la República de Honduras. **Notamos** que la capital, Tegucigalpa, que afortunadamente los habitantes **llamaban** Tegus, **tenía** dos sectores principales: la ciudad de Tegucigalpa, al lado oriental[3] del Río Choluteca, y la ciudad de Comayagüela, al lado occidental.[4] «Tegus» **era** la parte más viva y próspera, pero Comayagüela **parecía** mejor y más económica para la fábrica. Allí **había** mucha necesidad de empleo.

Fuera de la capital, **visitamos** varios sitios de interés cultural. **Vimos** las ruinas en Copán donde **vivían** los mayas hace mil años. La marca de los mayas todavía **era** evidente en las caras de los hondureños —el 90% **eran** mestizos. También **fuimos** a varios pueblos y unas islas tranquilas y muy bonitas. Los mayas también **ocupaban** las islas y Colón también **llegó** allí. Se ven muchos recuerdos de la civilización maya y la europea.

⊃

No vimos mucho desarrollo industrial en Honduras y por eso nos **interesó**, pero el país está muy vulnerable a huracanes. Nos **impresionó** mucho la destrucción del huracán «Mitch» de 1998.

Costa Rica nos **impresionó** como país mucho más europeo que Honduras. La población **era** el 96% europea y el país no **manifestaba** la cultura indígena de Honduras. La capital, San José, **parecía** una ciudad norteamericana. **Tenía** algunas atracciones culturales como museos y teatros de que **disfrutamos**.

Lo que más nos **impresionó** de Costa Rica **fue** su fuerte programa de protección de recursos naturales y de su biodiversidad. **Salimos** varias veces de la capital, siempre a un parque nacional u otra reserva natural. A causa de la vigorosa protección del ambiente, creemos que nuestros productos naturales van a encontrar una acogida⁵ en Costa Rica y por eso recomendamos este país como el preferido sitio de la nueva empresa.

---

¹**ubicación:** *placement, location* / ²**fábrica:** *factory* / ³**oriental:** *eastern* / ⁴**occidental:** *western*
⁵**acogida:** *welcome*

¿Comprendes?

1. Compara Honduras y Costa Rica culturalmente.
2. ¿Qué ventajas tienen los dos países para la ubicación de la fábrica?
3. ¿Cuáles son las desventajas?

■ El pretérito vs. el imperfecto

When talking about the past, it is necessary to use both the imperfect and the preterite. The choice of tense depends on which aspect of the past is emphasized. Many times both tenses may be correctly used, but the focus is different.

■ If a speaker wishes to focus on the beginning or end of an action, or wishes to emphasize a completed unit of time in the past, the preterite is the correct choice.

Los españoles **llegaron** a Costa Rica en 1502.	*The Spaniards **arrived** in Costa Rica in 1502.*
Colón **llamó** el país «Costa Rica».	*Columbus **called** the country "Costa Rica."*

■ If it is important to emphasize the continuation of a situation or the repeated nature of an action in the past, the imperfect is required.

Los indígenas **vivían** de la agricultura.	*The natives **lived** from agriculture.*
Los norteamericanos **exportaban** mucha fruta de Centroamérica.	*North Americans **used to export** a lot of fruit from Central America.*

■ The imperfect is the only tense used to tell time and age in the past.

Colón **tenía** 51 años cuando llegó a Honduras.

Columbus **was** 51 when he got to Honduras.

Era muy tarde cuando salimos de San José.

It was very late when we left San José.

■ The imperfect is used for background description and for physical and mental states.

Era una tarde de marzo y **caía** una lluvia fría. Lorenzo **se sentía** un poco triste. **Estaba** solo en su cuarto y sus pensamientos **volvían** una y otra vez a Susana.

It was an afternoon in March and a cold rain *was falling*. Lorenzo *felt* a little sad. *He was* alone in his room and his thoughts *returned* again and again to Susana.

¿Sabías?

Costa Rica es un país sin armas, es decir que no existe ni un ejército ni un sistema militar. En 1948 el ejército fue eliminado y se creó un país no militarizado.

■ When one action interrupts another, the ongoing action is expressed in the imperfect and the interrupting action is in the preterite.

Los indígenas **vivían** tranquilamente cuando **llegaron** los españoles.

The natives **were living** peacefully when the Spaniards **arrived**.

Los turistas **admiraban** el paisaje cuando **oyeron** el avión.

The tourists **were admiring** the countryside when **they heard** the plane.

■ The imperfect is used to describe; the preterite is used to narrate.

El bosque **estaba** todo tranquilo. Los animales **dormían** o **comían** bajo la densa sombra de los árboles. De repente todos **oyeron** un ruido muy fuerte y luego **vieron** a unos hombres con escopetas. Los hombres **apuntaron** las armas y los animales **empezaron** a correr.

*The forest **was** all quiet. The animals **were sleeping** or **eating** beneath the dense shade of the trees. Suddenly **they** all **heard** a very loud noise and then **they saw** some men with shotguns. The men **aimed** their weapons and the animals **began** to run.*

NOTA:
While the preterite is frequently compared to a snapshot, which captures a single moment, a capsule of time in the past, the imperfect is more like a video or a movie, which can depict the ongoing nature of a scene.

Practiquemos

A. Una visita. Completa esta conversación entre Pablo y Laura. Escoge entre el imperfecto y el pretérito para terminar las oraciones. Debes estar preparado(a) para explicar tus respuestas.

PABLO: Hola, Laura. ¿Qué hay de nuevo?

LAURA: Hola, Pablo. Pues, fíjate, ayer por la tarde (pasaba / pasó) algo completamente inesperado.

PABLO: ¿Sí? ¿Qué (pasaba / pasó)?

LAURA: Pues, (era / fue) tarde y yo (leía / leí) un artículo aburrido
        cuando (sonaba / sonó) *(rang)* el teléfono. (Contestaba /
        Contesté) y ¿sabes quién me (hablaba / habló)?
PABLO: ¡Claro que no! ¿Quién te (llamaba / llamó)?
LAURA: ¿Recuerdas al profesor Pelayo? Pues él y su esposa (estaban /
        estuvieron) aquí en Tegucigalpa y (decidían / decidieron) lla-
        marme. Me (invitaban / invitaron) a comer y todos nos
        (divertíamos / divertimos) mucho.
PABLO: Pues, ¿por qué no me (invitabas / invitaste)? No (hacía /
        hice) nada en toda la noche.
LAURA: Quizás la próxima vez...

B. Una historia romántica. Completa
la historia con los verbos indicados en
el pretérito o el imperfecto.

> Escribe una breve historia romántica y luego cuéntalo a tu compañero(a).

Simón y Clara (1) _____ (trabajar) en
la misma compañía. Cada uno (2) _____ (ir) a su tra-
bajo en el autobús, (3) _____ (hacer) su trabajo, (4) _____ (almorzar)
en la cafetería y (5) _____ (volver) a su casa. Los dos (6) _____ (sentirse)
muy solos y tristes. Su trabajo (7) _____ (ser) satisfactorio pero Clara y
Simón (8) _____ (necesitar) un amigo especial. Un día, por casualidad
(by chance), (9) _____ (tomar) el mismo autobús y (10) _____ (bajar)
(got off) juntos en la parada de la compañía. (11) _____ (Saludarse) y
(12) _____ (entrar) en la fábrica. En la cafetería (13) _____ (verse) otra
vez y (14) _____ (comer) juntos. Por la tarde, Simón (15) _____ (esperar) a Clara en la parada del autobús y la (16) _____ (invitar) al cine.
Ella (17) _____ (decir) que sí y así (18) _____ (comenzar) una bonita
amistad que todavía dura después de 50 años de matrimonio.

C. Una diferencia. Explica la diferencia de enfoque *(focus)* entre las oraciones que tienen el pretérito y las oraciones que tienen el imperfecto.

1. Fue a Nueva York (en 1979).
   Iba a Nueva York (cada verano).
2. Estudié por dos años en Cincinnati.
   Estudiaba en Cincinnati durante esos años.
3. Anoche leyeron el artículo y escribieron el informe.
   Escribían el informe mientras leían el artículo.
4. No supiste la verdad.
   No sabías la verdad.
5. Tuvimos que trabajar.
   Teníamos que trabajar.

D. Eloísa. En grupos de cuatro personas, inventen la historia de Eloísa.
La primera persona del grupo escribe la primera oración, la segunda
persona escribe la segunda oración y así continúan las otras dos personas. Cada persona debe escribir un mínimo de tres oraciones.

Hace diez años, Eloísa vivía en Chicago en una calle tranquila y
aparentemente aburrida...

❖ Para hablar de los animales

Las especies	*Species*
el anfibio	*amphibian*
el ave (f.)	*fowl*
el mamífero	*mammal*
el pájaro	*bird*
el pez	*fish*
el reptil	*reptile*

Animales domésticos y mascotas	*Farm animals and pets*
el burro	*donkey*
el caballo (la yegua)	*horse (mare)*
el canario	*canary*
el cerdo	*pig*
el chivo (la cabra)	*(billy) goat (nanny goat)*
el conejo	*rabbit*
la gallina (el gallo)	*chicken (rooster)*
el gato (la gata)	*cat*
la oveja (el carnero)	*sheep (ram)*
el periquito	*parakeet*
el perro (la perra)	*dog*
la vaca (el toro)	*cow (bull)*

Animales salvajes	*Wild animals*
la ardilla	*squirrel*
la cebra	*zebra*
el elefante	*elephant*
el hipopótamo	*hippopotamus*
la iguana	*iguana*
el jaguar	*jaguar*
la jirafa	*giraffe*

el león	*lion*
el leopardo	*leopard*
el loro	*parrot*
la mariposa	*butterfly*
el mono	*monkey*
el murciélago	*bat*
el oso	*bear*
la pantera	*panther*
el puma	*mountain lion*
la serpiente	*snake*
el tigre	*tiger*
la tortuga	*turtle, tortoise*

Vocabulario suplemental	
la almeja	*clam*
la ballena	*whale*
el canguro	*kangaroo*
el caracol	*snail*
el conejillo de indias	*guinea pig*
el delfín	*dolphin*
el insecto	*insect*
la lechuza (el buho)	*owl*
el manatí	*manatee*
el mejillón	*mussel*
el ocelote	*ocelot*
el perezoso	*sloth*
la piraña	*piranha*
el rinoceronte	*rhinoceros*
el tiburón	*shark*
el venado	*deer*

Practiquemos

A. Nuestros compañeros. Contesta las siguientes preguntas.

1. ¿Qué animal se asocia con el Jardín de Edén?
2. Hay una famosa película que se llama *La noche de la* _____. (hecha en Puerto Vallarta, México, con Elizabeth Taylor y Richard Burton) ⟶

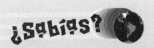

¿Sabías?

Los costarricenses son conocidos como «ticos» porque usan mucho el diminutivo **-ico**. Comen su «comidica» (comida) y se acuestan en su «pequeñica camica» (pequeña cama).

3. ¿Qué animales típicamente son mascotas?
4. El famoso «Porky» es un _____.
5. ¿Qué animales pueden «hablar»?
6. ¿Qué animales viven en el agua?
7. ¿Qué animales vuelan?
8. ¿Qué animales comemos?
9. ¿Qué animal tiene fama de economizar y de ahorrar *(save)* comida para el futuro?
10. ¿Qué animal se puede montar?
11. ¿Qué animal tiene fama de comer de todo, inclusive las latas *(tin cans)*?
12. ¿Qué pez tiene fama de ser el más feroz?
13. ¿Quién es el «rey de los animales»?
14. ¿Qué animal tiene el cuello más largo?
15. ¿Qué animal(es) produce(n) huevos que comemos?
16. ¿Qué animales producen leche que bebemos?

> Dibuja tu primera mascota. Luego cuéntale a tu compañero(a) tus experiencias con esa mascota.

IV. La biodiversidad de Costa Rica

LECTURA

Costa Rica es un país de increíble diversidad ecológica. Se divide en varias regiones —montañas, valles, costas— y cada región tiene su ambiente[1] distinto y sus parques y reservas nacionales. En lugar de[2] **acabar con** los recursos[3] naturales, los costarricenses los protegen y los conservan.

Tomemos la Zona Sur como ejemplo. Allí encontramos una variedad de ecosistemas que incluyen los bosques lluviosos[4] o selvas de las tierras bajas y bosques montañosos que llegan a las nubes.[5] A causa de la protección del ambiente que asegura el gobierno, se encuentran muchas especies ya **acabadas** o raras en otras partes del mundo, además de las especies más comunes. Allí viven jaguares, tapires, monos, pecaríes, armadillos, perezosos, venados, ardillas y murciélagos, entre otros mamíferos. También se encuentran muchos reptiles, como la iguana, el cocodrilo y varias especies de lagarto.[6]

Los bosques también abundan en plantas. Como el 70% de la tierra consiste en bosques lluviosos, los costarricenses tienen una relación muy especial con la naturaleza. Casi todo el mundo conoce las plantas tradicionalmente consideradas medicinales. También los «ticos» saben identificar los animales y conocen sus hábitos —por eso pueden ayudar a los turistas a comprender su país.

El ecoturismo es muy importante para la economía de Costa Rica. Algunos grupos de comerciantes[7] y ciudadanos **acaban de** fundar reservas privadas en todas partes del país, como por ejemplo, en la Península de Osa. El motivo de estas reservas y parques particulares es atraer[8] el ecoturismo y así reunir fondos para la protección del ambiente en el futuro. Tanto el gobierno como estos grupos privados y todos los costarricenses reconocen el tesoro natural que es la biodiversidad del país, y todos se esfuerzan a[9] guardar este tesoro para el futuro de Costa Rica y del mundo.

[1]**ambiente:** *atmosphere, environment* / [2]**En lugar de:** *Instead of* / [3]**recursos:** *resources* / [4]**bosques lluviosos:** *rain forests* / [5]**nubes:** *clouds* / [6]**lagarto:** *lizard* / [7]**comerciantes:** *businesspersons* / [8]**atraer:** *to attract* / [9]**se esfuerzan a:** *try*

¿Comprendes?

1. ¿Cuáles son algunos rasgos *(features)* de la Zona Sur de Costa Rica?
2. ¿Cómo se comparan las especies de animales en Costa Rica con las de otros países? ¿Cómo se explica esto?
3. ¿Cómo es posible que Costa Rica conserve los recursos naturales de su país?

> Cuéntale a un(a) compañero(a) una experiencia que tuviste de joven con un animal doméstico o salvaje.

■ Los verbos *acabar de, acabar, acabarse* y *acabar con*

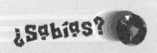
¿Sabias?

Many verbs in Spanish are used idiomatically and cannot be translated literally. Note the special meanings of the following words and expressions.

En Costa Rica hay 12.000 variedades de plantas, 237 especies de mamíferos, 848 tipos de pájaros y 361 diferentes anfibios. Todos son naturales de Costa Rica.

> **acabar de** + infinitive = *to have just (done something)*

■ Although the idea conveyed refers to the recent past, the verb **acabar** is conjugated in the present tense.

Acaban de visitar Tegucigalpa.	They **have just visited (just visited)** *Tegucigalpa.*
Julián me **acaba de llamar.**	*Julian* **has just called (just called)** *me.*
Acabo de comer.	**I have just eaten (I just ate).**

■ When **acabar** + infinitive is conjugated in the imperfect, it means *had just* (done something).

Rita **acababa de ver** la Catedral.	*Rita* **had just seen** *the Cathedral.*
Acabábamos de llegar a Costa Rica.	*We* **had just arrived** *in Costa Rica.*
Acabaron de comer a las 6:00.	***They finished*** *eating at 6:00.*

NOTA:
Acabar de conjugated in the preterite means to finish [doing something]. As you know, when conjugated in the present, it means to have just [done something].

Note the meaning and use of these verbs:

acabar = *to finish*
acabarse = *to finish up, run out of*
acabar con = *to do away with, get rid of*

Samuel **acabó** su tarea y luego salió.	*Samuel **finished** his homework and then went out.*
Se acabaron los boletos.	***They ran out of** tickets.*
Se acabó todo el postre.	*The dessert **was all finished up**.*
La gente **acabó con** la contaminación.	*The people **got rid of** the pollution.*

Practiquemos

A. Recién llegados. ¿Qué acaban de hacer estos turistas recién llegados a Tegucigalpa? Completa cada oración con la forma adecuada de **acabar de.**

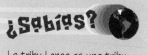

¿Sabías?

La tribu Lenca es una tribu hondureña con parentesco a los chibchas de Colombia. Lempira era de esa tribu y todavía vive esta gente indígena en una zona aislada de Honduras.

1. El avión _____ aterrizar.

2. Los turistas _____ reclamar su equipaje.

3. Lorenzo _____ hablar con su hermano por teléfono.

4. Tú y yo _____ comprarnos un mapa de Tegucigalpa.

5. Tú _____ saludar a tu primo hondureño.

6. Marisela y tú _____ (imperfecto) despedirse cuando Flora recibió una llamada de los EE.UU.

7. Todos _____ tomar una Coca.

B. Visitando Tegucigalpa. Los turistas describen su primer día en Honduras. Completa el párrafo con las formas adecuadas de estos verbos:

acabar de   acabarse   acabar con

Nosotros (1) _____ (imperfecto) llegar a Tegucigalpa cuando tomamos la decisión de visitar el centro comercial de la capital. En «la zona viva», Cristina y Pablo comieron en un buen restaurante. Nuestra compañera, Alicia, fue de compras en una de las tiendas que la ciudad (2) _____ (imperfecto) abrir; ella se divirtió haciendo muchas compras. Mario y yo fuimos al Teatro Nacional para ver una obra de teatro, pero cuando llegamos (3) _____ todos los boletos y no pudimos entrar. ¡Qué lástima! Luego, llegó Amelia. Ella nos dijo: «Oigan, ellos (4) _____ el otro edificio *(building)* y (5) _____ abrir un cine cerca de la Catedral. ¡Vengan conmigo!» Entonces, aceptamos la invitación y fuimos al cine con Amelia. Después de la película, decidimos ir al café Tortuga para tomar algo. Al día siguiente, vimos otros sitios como el Museo del Hombre Hondureño; ¡fue una maravilla! Después de recorrer la ciudad, (6) _____ nuestras compras y regresamos al hotel.

C. Y tú, ¿qué haces cuando… ? Contesta estas preguntas con las expresiones que acabas de aprender.

Dile a un(a) compañero(a) de clase qué haces cuando acabas de conocer a una persona muy simpática. Pregúntale a tu compañero(a) qué hace cuando acaba de sacar una A en un examen.

1. ¿Qué haces cuando se acaba tu dinero? ¿tu energía? ¿tu paciencia? ¿tu tiempo libre?
2. ¿Qué haces cuando acabas tus tareas? ¿tus quehaceres? ¿un examen? ¿tus ejercicios en un gimnasio?
3. ¿Qué haces cuando acabas de comer un plato sabroso? ¿de dormir ocho horas? ¿de ver una película buena?

A ver si sabes

Use this self-test to see if you know the material presented in Chapter 11.

A. ¡Saludos de Costa Rica! María Elena acaba de escribir una tarjeta postal a su familia en México. Usando el pretérito, completa su tarjeta.

Mamá, Papá y Sandra,

Aquí estoy en Puntarenas, Costa Rica. Nosotros (1) _____ (llegar) anoche a las 8:00. (2) _____ (Pasar) por la aduana y luego (3) _____ (ir) a nuestro hotel. Allí, yo (4) _____ (conocer) a unos amigos costarricenses, Dolores, Ricardo y Rogelio. Ellos me (5) _____ (decir) que iban a llevarme a San José, la capital. Bueno, al día siguiente, todos nosotros (6) _____ (salir) temprano y (7) _____ (ver) muchas cosas interesantes. (8) _____ (Divertirse) mucho. Una vez en San José, (9) _____ (comer) en un buen restaurante y luego (10) _____ (ir) a un club. Yo (11) _____ (bailar) toda la noche con Rogelio. ¡Es tan guapo y simpático!

Les mando muchos saludos. Hasta la próxima.

María Elena

B. ¡Ah, la juventud! Mateo recuerda sus experiencias de joven. Completa sus pensamientos con verbos en el imperfecto.

asistir   ayudar   caminar   divertirse   hablar   hacer   ir
jugar   leer   levantarse   sentarse   ser

Cuando yo (1) _____ joven, (2) _____ a una escuela cerca de mi casa. Cada día mis amigos y yo (3) _____ a la escuela. Antes de las clases (4) _____ al básquetbol y (5) _____ con las chicas. En las clases, mis amigos Jorge y Martín (6) _____ en el fondo *(at the back)* y (7) _____ tiras cómicas *(comics)*.

Durante las vacaciones mi familia (8) _____ a visitar a mis abuelos. En su casa todos nosotros (9) _____ temprano y (10) _____ con los animales.

Yo (11) _____ mucho de joven. ¿Qué (12) _____ tú?

Preguntas culturales.
1. ¿Quién fue don Pepe?
2. Describe «la zona viva». ¿Dónde está y qué hace la gente allí?
3. ¿Qué mezcla de civilizaciones forma la cultura hondureña?
4. ¿Qué caracteriza la geografía de Costa Rica?

C. Mi primera gata. Escoge el tiempo correcto para completar la historia.

Cuando yo (tenía / tuve) seis años siempre (quería / quise) una mascota. A cada rato les (pedía / pedí) un perro o un gato a mis padres, pero ellos me (respondían / respondieron) que nuestra calle (tenía / tuvo) demasiado tráfico y que yo (tenía / tuvo) que esperar.

Un día (comprábamos / compramos) una nueva casa. Inmediatamente les (pedía / pedí) un gatito a mis padres —la gata de los vecinos (tenía / tuvo) cinco bellos gatitos dos días antes. Por fin mis padres (decían / dijeron) que sí y todos (pasábamos / pasamos) muchos años felices con la pequeña Penélope.

D. Los bosques. Escoge entre el tiempo imperfecto o el pretérito para completar estos párrafos.

Hace muchos años los indígenas (1) _____ (vivir) tranquilamente en los bosques. (2) _____ (Comer) las frutas y los animales que (3) _____ (encontrar) allí y todo (4) _____ (continuar) pacíficamente.

Un día (5) _____ (llegar) unos hombres modernos y "civilizados". (6) _____ (Cortar) los bosques y (7) _____ (plantar) bananales *(banana plantations)*. Los animales (8) _____ (empezar) a morir y los indígenas (9) _____ (perder) la comida.

Por fin el gobierno (10) _____ (entrar) y (11) _____ (pasar) leyes. Así (12) _____ (comenzar) la protección del ambiente y del futuro del país.

E. Más noticias de Costa Rica. Una semana más tarde, María Elena habló con su mamá por teléfono. ¿Qué dijo? Usa las formas apropiadas de **acabar de, acabarse, acabar** y **acabar con** para completar la conversación.

María Elena: Mamá, ¿cómo estás?

Sra. Sánchez: Oh, hija, nosotros _____ recibir tu postal. Gracias.

María Elena: Todo está bien aquí. Ayer, vi a Rogelio. Él _____ unos proyectos e hicimos planes para ir a a San Pedro.

Sra. Sánchez: Qué bueno, hija. Oye, ¿_____ tu dinero? Dime, eh.

María Elena: No, todavía tengo bastante. Gracias, mamá.

Sra. Sánchez: Pues, cuéntame de tu viaje.

María Elena: El jueves Rogelio me llevó a un parque ecológico en San José. Era interesante ver cómo los costarricenses _____ la contaminación del río y limpiaron el parque. Ellos _____ abrir el parque al público.

Sra. Sánchez: El año próximo, tú y yo podemos regresar a Costa Rica, ¿eh?

María Elena: Sí, mamá. Bueno, tengo que decirte adiós; es larga distancia y ¡tú estás pagando! Además, Rogelio _____ llegar.

Sra. Sánchez: ¡Qué gusto me da oír tu voz, hija!

María Elena: Besos y abrazos, mamá. Saludos a todos. Adiós.

Querido Diario. Hoy recordaste un incidente de tu pasado. Para no olvidar-lo, vas a contarle el incidente a tu diario. Para organizar tus ideas, (1) pien-sa en un incidente divertido o impresionante con animales o con la naturaleza, (2) describe varios aspectos del fondo *(background)* y (3) luego escribe los eventos que ocurrieron. Ahora combina los elementos descrip-tivos y narrativos y cuenta el incidente en tu diario. Puedes empezar así: Hoy recordé un incidente que pasó cuando…

Grammar: verbs: imperfect; preterite; preterite and imperfect
Phrases: describing the past; talking about habitual actions; talking about past events
Vocabulary: animals: domestic; animals: wild; plants: trees; plants: flowers

Vocabulario activo

Los animales
Las especies
el anfibio
el ave (f.)
el mamífero
el pájaro
el pez
el reptil

Animales domésticos y mascotas
el burro
el caballo (la yegua)
el canario
el cerdo
el chivo (la cabra)
el conejo
la gallina (el gallo)

el gato (la gata)
la oveja (el carnero)
el periquito
el perro (la perra)
la vaca (el toro)

Verbos
acabar
acabar de
acabar con
acabarse
contaminar

La ecología
el abono
el aire
el bióxido de carbono
el bosque (lluvioso)
el calentamiento
la capa de ozono

el combustible
la combustión
la contaminación
la deforestación
el ecosistema
la energía nuclear

la erosión
el herbicida
el monóxido de
    carbono
el oxígeno
el pesticida

la pureza
la química
el químico
el residuo
la selva tropical
la tierra

Animales salvajes
la ardilla
la cebra
el elefante
el hipopótamo
la iguana

el jaguar
la jirafa
el león
el leopardo
el loro

la mariposa
el mono
el murciélago
el oso
la pantera

el puma
la serpiente
el tigre
la tortuga

Vocabulario suplemental
la almeja
la ballena
el canguro
el caracol

el conejillo de indias
el delfín
el insecto
la lechuza (el búho)

el manatí
el mejillón
el ocelote
el perezoso

la piraña
el rinocerante
el tiburón

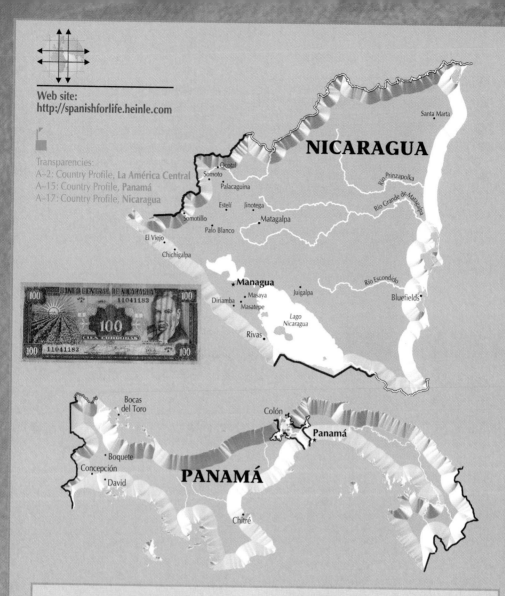

REPÚBLICA DE NICARAGUA

Nombre oficial: República de
Nicaragua

Área: 130.700 km²

Población: 4.500.000

Capital: Managua

Moneda: el córdoba

Idioma oficial: español

Fiesta nacional: 15 de septiembre,
Día de la Independencia

REPÚBLICA DE PANAMÁ

Nombre oficial: República de
Panamá

Área: 77.082 km²

Población: 2.800.000

Capital: Ciudad de Panamá

Moneda: el balboa

Idioma oficial: español

Fiesta nacional: 3 de noviembre,
Separación de Colombia

Nicaragua y los nicaragüenses
Panamá y los panameños

Una escena panameña

In this chapter you will learn:

GRAMMAR POINTS

- Formal commands: **usted** and **ustedes**
- The subjunctive mood: Present-tense forms
- Impersonal expressions and the subjunctive mood
- Changes required by the first syllable of the following word

COMMUNICATIVE FUNCTIONS

- Ask (Order) someone to do something
- Express attitudes

VOCABULARY

- Impersonal expressions
- World of work: skills, professions, duties, activities, personnel

265

I. ¡A Panamá! Unos consejos

LECTURA

Queridos Gloria y Luis,

Me da tanto gusto[1] que ustedes **vayan** a Panamá por fin. Ya saben cuánto me gusta el país y pueden imaginarse que voy a darles unos consejos.[2]

Primero, **vuelen** directamente de Dallas a la Ciudad de Panamá. Al llegar, **vayan** directamente al hotel sin cambiar dinero ya que[3] el balboa es igual al dólar. ¡Sí! **Salgan** en seguida[4] para visitar el distrito colonial San Felipe, llamado Casco Viejo, y **admiren** los edificios del siglo XVI. **Den** un paseo por la ciudad y **vayan** de compras en la Avenida Central donde tienen de todo. Luego, **vean** la Universidad de Panamá y el Parque Natural Metropolitano. Y no **se pierdan** el Canal de Panamá. Antes de ir, **lean** un poco de la historia de la construcción del canal, porque es fascinante. Y después, **vayan** al canal y **miren** las grandes naves al pasar por las esclusas[5] del canal que las mueven del Pacífico al Atlántico o viceversa.

Si pueden hacer reservaciones, **visiten** la Isla Barro Colorado donde el Smithsonian tiene su Instituto de Investigaciones Tropicales. Es una excursión fabulosa. **Visiten** también los magníficos parques que tiene Panamá. Hay parques marinos en las dos costas. En el Caribe, **pasen** Uds. varios días en Bocas del Toro donde pueden nadar, bucear y visitar varias islas del archipiélago Bocas del Toro. De allí, **viajen** al interior a la provincia de Chiriquí, al Volcán Barú. **Suban** al volcán para ver una densa selva, muchos animales y plantas y, en la cima,[6] una vista magnífica de las costas del Pacífico y del Caribe. Para la diversidad, **viajen** al Parque Nacional del Darién en la frontera[7] de Colombia. Es una reserva de la biosfera y allí pueden observar muchísimas especies de plantas y animales.

En mi primera visita a Panamá un agente de viajes me dijo: «Señorita, **vaya** Ud. a las Islas de San Blas.» Y tenía razón el señor. Allí viven los indios Kuna que todavía conservan sus trajes y sus costumbres tradicionales y su modo de vivir.[8] **Hagan** el esfuerzo y **vayan** allí. Pueden quedarse allí varios días y olvidarse del mundo frenético de otras partes.

Pues, con lo que me encanta Panamá, podría escribirles un libro, pero voy a dejarlos en paz y sólo quiero decir: «¡**Mánden**me muchas postales!»

Reciban un abrazo cariñoso de su hermana

Evangelina

---

[1]**me da tanto gusto:** *it makes me so happy* / [2]**consejos:** *advice* / [3]**ya que:** *since* / [4]**en seguida:** *immediately* / [5]**esclusas:** *locks* / [6]**cima:** *top, summit* / [7]**frontera:** *border, frontier* / [8]**modo de vivir:** *lifestyle*

¿Comprendes?

1. ¿Cuáles son dos atracciones de la Ciudad de Panamá?
2. ¿Qué hacen las esclusas?
3. ¿Por qué crees que hay tan pocos grupos indígenas que conservan sus antiguas costumbres y sus trajes típicos?

■ Mandatos formales: *usted* y *ustedes*

As you learned in Chapter 6, commands are used to tell someone to do or not to do something. Remember that the subject *you*, though not expressed in English, may be expressed in Spanish for emphasis.

■ To form **usted** commands, personal endings are added to the stem of the **yo** form of the present indicative. These forms take the "opposite" vowel endings (not the vowel of the infinitive) as shown in the chart below: for -**ar** verbs, the "opposite" vowel is -**e**; for -**er** and -**ir** verbs, the "opposite" vowel is -**a**.

Point out to students that there is also a command form for vosotros. The affirmative command is formed by dropping the -**r** from the infinitive and adding -**d**:

cantar   cantad
comer   comed
escribir   escribid

The negative command form is the **vosotros** form of the *present subjunctive:*

No digáis esas palabras.
No comáis tanta grasa.

Infinitive	Yo Form	Ud. Command	Meaning
cantar	cant**o**	**Cante** (Ud.).	*Sing.*
comer	com**o**	**Coma** (Ud.).	*Eat.*
salir	salg**o**	**Salga** (Ud.).	*Leave.*

■ To form **ustedes** commands, add an -**n** to the **usted** form.

Hablen (Uds.) español en clase.   ***Speak*** *Spanish in class.*
Salgan (Uds.) ahora.   ***Leave*** *now.*

■ You may use the expression **por favor** to soften commands.

Mírenme, por favor.   ***Look at me, please.***

El canal de Panamá es una vía fluvial de suma importancia para todo el mundo. La construcción del canal comenzó en 1904. Más de 75.000 trabajadores laboraron por diez años, enfrentándose con enfermedades, mosquitos, desastres y otras dificultades horrendas, pero tuvieron éxito. El primer barco pasó por el canal el 15 de agosto de 1914.

■ Some irregular command forms must be learned.

	dar	estar	hacer	ser	ir	saber
usted	dé	esté	haga	sea	vaya	sepa
ustedes	den	estén	hagan	sean	vayan	sepan

Estén aquí a las 6:00, por favor.　　*Please **be** here at 6:00.*
Clase, **sepan** estos verbos para　　*Class, **know** these verbs by*
　mañana.　　　　　　　　　　　　　*tomorrow.*

■ Note that verbs ending in **-car**, **-gar**, and **-zar** also have special forms to maintain the original sound of the infinitive.

Saque las fotos.　　　　　　　*Take the pictures.*
No me **juzgue**.　　　　　　　　*Don't **judge** me.*
Comiencen Uds.　　　　　　　*Start.*

Practiquemos

A. El nuevo empleo. La señora Guzmán acaba de conseguir un empleo en una empresa panameña. Su jefa le da unos mandatos. ¿Qué le dice? Cambia el infinitivo a un mandato.

Señora Guzmán, haga lo siguiente, por favor.

1. _____ (Escribir) esta carta.

2. _____ (Hacer) estas llamadas.

3. _____ (Llevar) esta correspondencia al Sr. Luz.

4. _____ (Preparar) estos paquetes para el correo.

5. _____ (Arreglar) las citas para mañana.

6. _____ (Mandar) este memorándum a estas secretarias.

7. _____ (Traducir) esta carta al inglés.

8. _____ (Comer) su almuerzo a la 1:00.

B. ¡Ejercicios! En la empresa donde trabaja la señora Guzmán, hay un gimnasio para los empleados. Allí van todos los días para hacer sus ejercicios. ¿Qué mandatos les da la instructora Salinas a **sus estudiantes** en la clase de ejercicios aeróbicos? Combina las ideas que siguen.

A	B
relajar	las piernas
respirar	el cuerpo
saltar	las manos
levantar	los brazos
dar vuelta	profundamente
estirar	diez veces en un pie
subir	los hombros
tomar	cinco minutos de descanso

> Reúnete con *dos compañeros(as)* de clase y dales *diferentes ejercicios físicos* que puedan hacer en la clase. Usa el mandato plural *ustedes.*

■ When using command forms, remember that object pronouns always *precede the negative command* but are *added to the end of the affirmative command.* In the latter case, an accent mark is added to maintain the original stress.

Prepare la comida.	***Prepare** the food.*
Prepárela.	***Prepare it.*** *(the food)*
¡Acuéstense Uds.!	***Get to bed!***
No se duerman en clase.	***Don't fall asleep*** *in class.*

Practiquemos

A. En Panamá. ¿Qué consejos reciben Gloria y Luis? Escribe estos mandatos usando pronombres.

M O D E L O :   visitar el canal
Visítenlo.
no omitir las esclusas
No las omitan.

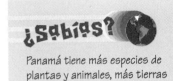

¿Sabías?

Panamá tiene más especies de plantas y animales, más tierras protegidas y menos turistas que Costa Rica.

1. leer la historia del canal
2. ver la Isla Barro Colorado
3. visitar los parques nacionales
4. subir el Volcán Barú
5. sacar muchas fotos
6. mandar tarjetas postales
7. no comprar boletos caros
8. no gastar *(to spend)* mucho dinero
9. no olvidar las Islas de San Blas
10. no perder los indios Kuna

B. En clase. ¿Qué mandatos les da la profesora Luz a sus estudiantes en la clase de español? Primero, escribe los mandatos **Uds.** y luego escríbelos utilizando el pronombre complemento directo e indirecto cuando sea posible.

sacar	no hablar	leer	no escribir	tomar
no comparar	pasarme	sentarse	hacer	

1. Clase, _____ en las sillas, por favor.

2. _____ sus libros.

3. _____ apuntes.

4. _____ inglés.

5. _____ la Actividad B.

6. _____ sus respuestas.

7. _____ con cuidado.

8. _____ los papeles.

Con un(a) compañero(a) de clase, haz una lista de diez mandatos que su profesor(a) usa frecuentemente en clase.

❖ Para expresar actitudes

Para expresar emociones	To express emotions
Es espantoso.	It's frightening.
Es sorprendente.	It's surprising.
Es triste.	It's sad.
Es una lástima.	It's a pity.

Para expresar un juicio	To express a judgment
Es bueno.	It's good.
Es curioso.	It's curious, interesting.
Es deseable.	It's desirable.
Es horrible (terrible).	It's horrible (terrible).
Es importante.	It's important.
Es interesante.	It's interesting.
Es loco.	It's crazy.
Es lógico.	It's logical.
Es malo.	It's bad.
Es mejor.	It's better.
Es necesario.	It's necessary.
Es ridículo.	It's ridiculous.

Para expresar duda o certeza	To express doubt or certainty
Es cierto.	It's certain, true.
Es dudoso.	It's doubtful.
Es evidente.	It's evident, obvious.
Es obvio.	It's obvious.
Es verdad.	It's true.

Para expresar probabilidad	To express probability
Es imposible.	It's impossible.
Es posible.	It's possible.
Es probable.	It's probable.

Practiquemos

A. Mi opinión. Expresa tu opinión sobre estas actividades usando expresiones impersonales: es bueno, es malo, es loco, es interesante, es necesario, es triste, es espantoso, es horrible.

MODELO: *Es interesante* ver películas internacionales.

1. _____ hacer ejercicio.

2. _____ tomar café.

3. _____ estudiar poco.

4. _____ dormir mucho.

5. _____ trabajar duro.

6. _____ hablar varias lenguas.

7.   estar enfermo.

8. _____ visitar otros países.

9. _____ ver violencia.

10. _____ beber mucha agua.

> Can you think of other words that can be used to make impersonal expressions?

II. Violeta Chamorro y la política nicaragüense

LECTURA

Violeta Barrios de Chamorro nació en 1930. De joven, se interesaba mucho en la política y por eso se alió con[1] los nicaragüenses que se oponían a la dictadura de la familia Somoza que controló el país desde 1937 hasta 1978. El esposo de Violeta, Pedro Chamorro, el famoso editor del periódico *La Prensa*, fue asesinado en 1978. Fue en aquella época que Violeta Chamorro, con su

extensa experiencia en el mundo político, prestó su energía al movimiento revolucionario que tomó el poder desde julio de 1979 hasta abril de 1980. En 1984, cuando Daniel Ortega fue elegido presidente de Nicaragua, Violeta Chamorro seguía su lucha para el bien de su país.

Es sorprendente que esta mujer de carácter fuerte **esté** en un nivel de mucho poder político en su país. También es interesante que sus paisanos[2] **acepten** a una mujer en una posición de honor y poder. Violeta Chamorro fue elegida presidenta de la repúbilica en 1990; derrotó a[3] Daniel Ortega, el candidato sandinista. Es importante que la gente **se dé cuenta de**[4] que Violeta Chamorro fue la primera mujer elegida presidenta de Nicaragua en su historia.

La presidenta Chamorro hizo mucho para mejorar su país durante su presidencia. Por ejemplo, reestableció relaciones positivas con los Estados Unidos y tuvo éxito en reconciliar a las diferentes facciones políticas en su país. Pero también sufrió muchas desilusiones en cuanto a sus planes y proyectos económicos para Nicaragua. Es esencial que todos **recuerden** que Violeta Chamorro es una mujer latina extraordinaria que sigue luchando por el bienestar de su país.

---

¹**se alió con:** *she allied herself with* / ²**paisanos:** *compatriots* / ³**derrotó a:** *she defeated* / ⁴**se dé cuenta de:** *realize*

¿Comprendes?

1. ¿Por qué es Violeta Chamorro una mujer extraordinaria?
2. ¿Qué logró *(achieved)* Violeta Chamorro cuando era presidenta?
3. ¿Es común en Latinoamérica tener una mujer como presidenta del país? ¿Cuántas hay?

> **NOTA:**
> The subjunctive mood in English exists only in such set phrases as "I move that the meeting be adjourned," "If I were you," etc. The English way of expressing the Spanish subjunctive varies.

■ El modo subjuntivo: formas del presente

Up to now, you have been using verb forms in the *indicative mood.* The indicative mood is used to express facts and to relay information in an objective way without revealing anything about how the speaker feels about the statement.

Llueve fuerte.	*It's raining hard.*
Carlos **llega** mañana.	*Carlos arrives tomorrow.*

But as speakers, we may have doubts about what we say or we may want to state a value judgment or express our reaction to something. To express our subjective feelings toward what we are saying, we use the *subjunctive mood* in Spanish.

Es bueno que **llueva.**	*It's good that it's raining.*
Es importante que Carlos **llegue** mañana.	*It's important for Carlos to arrive tomorrow.*

■ Like formal commands, the present tense forms of the subjunctive mood are based on the **yo** form of the present tense (indicative mood):

yo form (present) + the opposite vowel (**-e** for **-ar** verbs and **-a** for **-er** and **-ir** verbs) + the personal endings

	hablar	aprender	describir
	habl -ø→-**e**	aprend -ø→-**a**	describ -ø→-**a**
yo	habl- **e**	aprend- **a**	describ- **a**
tú	habl- **es**	aprend- **as**	describ- **as**
Ud. él ella	habl- **e**	aprend- **a**	describ- **a**

➲

	hablar	aprender	describir
nosotros(as)	habl- **emos**	aprend- **amos**	describ- **amos**
vosotros(as)	habl- **éis**	aprend- **áis**	describ- **áis**
Uds. ellos(as)	habl- **en**	aprend- **an**	describ- **an**

■ The same verbs that have irregular command forms also have *irregular present subjunctive forms.*

dar				estar			
yo	**dé**	nosotros(as)	**demos**	yo	**esté**	nosotros(as)	**estemos**
tú	**des**	vosotros(as)	**déis**	tú	**estés**	vosotros(as)	**estéis**
Ud. él ella	**dé**	Uds. ellos(as)	**den**	Ud. él ella	**esté**	Uds. ellos(as)	**estén**

ir			
yo	**vaya**	nosotros(as)	**vayamos**
tú	**vayas**	vosotros(as)	**vayáis**
Ud. él ella	**vaya**	Uds. ellos(as)	**vayan**

saber				ser			
yo	**sepa**	nosotros(as)	**sepamos**	yo	**sea**	nosotros(as)	**seamos**
tú	**sepas**	vosotros(as)	**sepáis**	tú	**seas**	vosotros(as)	**seáis**
Ud. él ella	**sepa**	Uds. ellos(as)	**sepan**	Ud. él ella	**sea**	Uds. ellos(as)	**sean**

Es importante que visites Managua.	*It's important for you to visit* Managua.
Es necesario que veas el canal.	*It's necessary for you to see* the canal.
Es mejor que sepas las respuestas.	*It's better for you to know* the answers.
Ojalá saque una buena calificación.	*I hope I get* a good grade.
Ojalá que lleguemos pronto.	*I hope we get there soon.*

NOTA:
The word **ojalá [que]**... means roughly *I hope (that)* ... and always requires the subjunctive mood. It is derived from the Arabic *May Allah grant that* ...

Practiquemos

A. Los preparativos. Susana está pensando en el viaje que su familia va a hacer a Panamá. Completa sus pensamientos con el presente del subjuntivo.

1. Ojalá que Manuel _____ (llamar) al agente de viajes.

2. Ojalá que mis padres _____ (empacar) todo lo que necesitan.

3. Ojalá que mi esposo y yo no _____ (llegar) tarde al aeropuerto.

4. Ojalá que tú _____ (comprar) bastante película para la cámara.

5. Ojalá que yo _____ (recordar) los boletos.

6. Ojalá que toda la familia _____ (terminar) su trabajo antes de salir.

B. Examen mañana. Completa los pensamientos de Nacho con los verbos en paréntesis.

1. Ojalá que Ester y Alicia _____ (ir) a la biblioteca a estudiar.

2. Es mejor que Manuel _____ (dar) bastante tiempo a los estudios.

3. Es importante que nosotros _____ (saber) las respuestas.

4. Ojalá que yo _____ (estar) muy bien descansado.

5. Es deseable que todos _____ (ser) estudiantes brillantes mañana.

C. Nuevo empleado. Manuela está pensando en el nuevo contador que va a empezar su trabajo en la compañía esta semana. Usa los verbos de la lista para terminar sus pensamientos: aprender, hacer, interrumpir *(to interrupt),* ayudar, hablar, tener.

1. Es importante que nosotros le _____ cortésmente.

2. Es necesario que él _____ rápidamente.

3. Es mejor que Susana y Pamela no lo _____ demasiado.

4. Es importante que él _____ buen trabajo.

5. Es necesario que tú _____ tiempo para enseñarle.

6. Es deseable que yo le _____ a acostumbrarse.

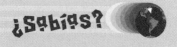

Nicaragua es el país más grande de Centroamérica pero, con Belice, es el menos poblado.

D. Esperanzas. ¿Qué esperanzas tienes para tu familia en el próximo año? Forma oraciones con **Ojalá que**, elementos de las tres columnas y cualquier otro elemento que sea necesario.

Dile a tu compañero(a) de clase lo que esperas para ti y después escucha sus deseos.

M O D E L O : *Ojalá que mi esposo encuentre un buen trabajo.*

A	B	C
yo	levantarse	trabajo
mi esposo(a)	conseguir	muchas clases
mis padres	estudiar	un viaje
mis hijos	sacar	una buena persona
mi compañero(a)	casarse con	cocinar
tú	hacer	la casa
toda la familia	asistir a	buenas notas
	aprender a	más temprano
	encontrar	muchos conciertos

❖ Para hablar de los trabajos

En la oficina

el (la) programador(a)	*programmer*
el (la) secretario(a)	*secretary*
el (la) técnico(a)	*technician*

En la corte

el (la) abogado (licenciado[a])	*lawyer*
el (la) intérprete	*interpreter*
el (la) juez	*judge*

En la clínica

el (la) dentista	*dentist*
el (la) doctor(a) (médico)	*doctor*
el (la) enfermero(a)	*nurse*

En el taller

el (la) alfarero(a)	*potter*
el (la) carpintero	*carpenter*
el (la) joyero(a)	*jeweler*
el (la) mecánico(a)	*mechanic*

En el restaurante

el (la) cocinero(a)	*cook, chef*
el (la) mesero(a)	*server*

En el sitio de la construcción

el (la) albañil	*bricklayer*
el (la) constructor(a)	*builder*
el (la) electricista	*electrician*
el (la) ingeniero(a)	*engineer*
el (la) plomero	*plumber*

En los negocios

el (la) banquero(a)	*banker*
el (la) comerciante	*business-person*
el (la) contador(a)	*accountant*
el (la) dependiente(a)	*clerk*
el (la) peluquero(a)	*hairdresser*
el (la) vendedor(a)	*salesperson*

En los medios de comunicación

el (la) fotógrafo(a)	*photographer*
el (la) locutor(a)	*announcer*
el (la) periodista	*journalist*

En la universidad

el (la) escritor(a)	*writer*
el (la) músico	*musician*
el (la) profesor(a)	*professor*

Remind students to think of other professions that they have learned previously.

En las fuerzas armadas		El trabajo	
el (la) marinero(a)	*sailor*	ayudar	*to help*
el (la) soldado	*soldier*	construir	*to construct*
Otras profesiones		cuidar	*to take care of*
el (la) deportista	*athlete*	enseñar	*to teach*
el (la) diplomático(a)	*diplomat*	juzgar	*to judge*
el (la) portero(a)	*janitor, doorperson*	representar	*to represent*

Practiquemos

A. Mi trabajo es... ¿Qué hacen estas personas? Comparte tus respuestas con tu compañero(a) de clase.

> Piensa en un mínimo de cinco profesiones más y describe el trabajo que hacen las personas que tienen esas profesiones. Comparte tu lista con un(a) compañero(a) de clase.

MODELO: La doctora *ayuda a los enfermos.*

1. El carpintero _____.
2. La juez _____.
3. El portero _____.
4. El deportista _____.
5. El comerciante _____.
6. La aeromoza _____.

7. El electricista _____.
8. La periodista _____.
9. El contador _____.
10. La cocinera _____.
11. El dentista _____.
12. La diplomática _____.

III. ¡Y tú vas a Nicaragua!

LECTURA

Queridísima Evangelina,

Nos encantó Panamá —seguimos tus consejos y nos divertimos a las mil maravillas.[1] Y ahora nos toca[2] darte nuestros mejores consejos, como vas a Nicaragua —¡nuestro destino favorito!

Primero, **es mejor que vayas** durante enero y febrero, en parte porque es la temporada seca.[3] Pero también el 20 de enero puedes presenciar[4] una costumbre muy antigua y muy curiosa, el Toro Guaco. El Toro Guaco consiste en una serie de festivales que tienen lugar en los pueblos de Jinotepe, Diriamba y San Marcos y que representa la antigua rivalidad y relación entre los pueblos. Es divertido ver las sátiras de los españoles y el «Güegüense», una figura que representa a los nicaragüenses.

Claro, también **es importante que visites** la capital, Managua, y **que veas** el Palacio Nacional y el Teatro Rubén Darío en la Plaza de la República. **Es indispensable que vayas** al Museo de Huellas[5] de Acahualinca donde puedes ver las huellas de pie de seres humanos que vivían en Nicaragua hace 6.000 años.

Después de Managua, **es importante que veas** el Lago de Nicaragua (también llamado «Cocibolca» y «La Mar Dulce»), que es el lago más grande de Centroamérica. Si tienes suerte, puedes ver los únicos tiburones[6] de agua dulce. Puedes ir a las Isletas (un grupo de 356 pequeñas islas volcánicas), a la Isla Zapatera —donde se encuentra el mejor sitio arqueológico de Nicaragua— o a la Isla de Ometepe, que conecta dos volcanes (uno activo) y tiene pocos turistas y una riqueza natural de vegetación y animales. Y tienes que ir a San Juan de Oriente, que no está lejos. Es un pueblo conocido por sus cerámicas. Puedes comprar artículos fabulosos en una cooperativa o en talleres de alferrería —¡y puedes traernos un bonito regalo!

Es absolutamente **necesario** también **que visites** la Costa de Miskitos *(Mosquito Coast),* la costa caribeña que los españoles nunca colonizaron pero que los ingleses habitaron por mucho tiempo. Todavía viven allí los indios miskitos.

¡Ay, hermana! Ni mencionamos Granada, León, Masaya, Matagalpa, Estelí y otros muchos sitios que son fascinantes. Pero estamos aquí si tienes alguna pregunta.

Por ahora, recibe un abrazo de

Gloria   Luis

---

[1]**a las mil maravillas:** *fabulously* / [2]**nos toca:** *it's our turn* / [3]**temporada seca:** *dry season* / [4]**presenciar:** *to witness, be present for* / [5]**Huellas:** *Tracks* / [6]**tiburones:** *sharks*

¿Comprendes?

1. ¿Qué evento especial ocurre en Nicaragua en enero?
2. ¿Por qué es famoso San Juan de Oriente?
3. En tu opinión, ¿por qué se llama la costa caribeña de Nicaragua la «Costa de Miskitos»?

■ El uso del subjuntivo con expresiones impersonales

As you have learned in this chapter, there are many impersonal expressions used in Spanish. They are called *impersonal* because they do not have a specific subject and the second verb in the sentence is in the infinitive form.

Es importante ver la capital.   *It's important to see the capital.*

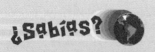

¿Sabías?

La ciudad de Managua no tiene letreros para anunciar los nombres de las calles. Las direcciones que los nicaragüenses dan para guiarte son «al sur», «al lago» (al norte), «arriba» (al este) y «abajo» (al oeste). Para un turista puede ser muy confuso encontrar un edificio en particular.

Impersonal expressions, however, may be followed by a conjugated verb. In this case, the impersonal expression will be followed by **que** and the subjunctive mood if it expresses any of the following:

- doubt
- necessity
- personal judgment or opinion
- emotion
- (im)possibility or probability

Es dudoso que llueva hoy.	*It's doubtful that it will rain today.*
Es necesario que te vistas bien.	*It's necessary for you to dress well.*
Es mejor que hagas ejercicio antes de comer.	*It's better for you to exercise before you eat.*
Es triste que Uds. no **salgan** más.	*It's sad that you don't go out more.*
Es posible que salgamos hoy.	*It's possible that we're going out today.*
Es imposible que yo llegue a la hora.	*It's impossible for me to be on time.*

■ Note that with expressions of *certainty,* the subjunctive is *not* used.

Es cierto que hay mucho que ver.	*It's certain that there is a lot to see.*
Es evidente que les gusta viajar.	*It's obvious that you like to travel.*

When there is a change of subject, **me parece** can be used instead of **es** in these expressions, especially to express opinions or judgments.

Me parece absurdo que él hable así.	*It seems absurd (to me) that he talks that way.*
Me parece increíble que no sepas.	*It seems incredible that you don't know.*

Practiquemos

A. En la oficina. Ramón Valdéz y sus colegas tienen mucho que hacer hoy en la oficina. Completa las oraciones con la forma adecuada del verbo.

1. Es dudoso que la correspondencia _____ (llegar) antes de las 2:00.

2. Me parece curioso que María no _____ (saber) usar la computadora.

3. Es mejor que Cintia y Pablo _____ (hacer) las llamadas telefónicas.

4. Es necesario que nosotros _____ (completar) estos archivos ahora.

5. Es sorprendente que _____ (haber) tanto que hacer hoy.

6. Es importante que los técnicos _____ (reparar) las computadoras.

7. Es bueno que hoy _____ (ser) viernes.

8. Es esencial que tú me _____ (esperar) hasta las 5:00.

B. El memo. El gerente de la tienda les manda a todos sus empleados el memorándum siguiente. ¿Qué les dice? Completa las oraciones con la forma correcta del verbo en paréntesis.

MEMORÁNDUM

A: Todos los empleados de Video Circo

Del: Gerente Juan Tomás Sender   JTS

Atención:

Quiero avisarles que es urgente que todos (1) _____(preparar) el inventario para mañana. Es importante que nosotros (2) _____(estar) listos para la visita del gerente general la semana próxima. Es posible que (3)_____(hay) unos cambios de responsabilidades y es obvio que yo, el gerente de esta tienda, (4) _____(tener) que revisar el inventario y preparar la lista de nuevas adquisiciones. Me parece dudoso que todo se (5) _____(poder) terminar pronto, pero es bueno que Uds. (6) _____(reconocer) la necesidad de cumplir con este deber.

Gracias por su atención a este asunto.

Juan Tomás Sender

C. ¿Qué piensas? Completa las oraciones de acuerdo con *(according to)* tus pensamientos.

1. Es importante que mi familia _____.

2. Es deseable que mi trabajo _____.

3. Es lógico que mis amigos y yo _____.

4. Es triste que las personas _____.

5. Es necesario que yo _____.

6. Es verdad que los seres humanos _____.

7. Es interesante que mi jefe _____.

8. Es obvio que mi esposo(a)/compañero(a) y yo _____.

9. Es curioso que tú _____.

10. Ojalá que mi profesor(a) _____.

> Usando estas expresiones impersonales, hagan en grupos de dos una lista de lo que es importante hacer para prepararse para una entrevista. Luego, compartan su lista con otro grupo. Expresiones: *Es importante, necesario, bueno, lógico, mejor, probable, evidente...*

IV. La pluma mágica de Rubén Darío

LECTURA

Entre los grandes escritores hispanoamericanos surge el nombre de Félix Rubén García Sarmiento. Nació en la pequeña aldea[1] de Metapa, Nicaragua, en 1867. «De esa "aldehuela" de Nicaragua, rincón[2] de la América española, casi nada en el mundo» (así la describió Darío mismo), salió este genio literario de quien los nicaragüenses están muy orgullosos.

De niño, Darío no tuvo la oportunidad de crecer con sus padres (**u** otros miembros de familia) ya que se separaron antes de su nacimiento;[3] posteriormente fue a vivir con su tío-abuelo paterno.[4] Aunque era un niño enfermo y bastante tímido, poseía una gran imaginación, sensibilidad y una facilidad increíble para la literatura, en especial la poesía; antes de cumplir los 14 años, publicó sus primeros versos. De joven, Darío estudió las letras hispánicas en Chile y luego fue a España donde conoció y pasó tiempo con los grandes autores de las letras **e** inició su carrera larga y brillante. Viajó por toda Europa conociendo a autores y desarrollando su técnica literaria. Él describió esos años como su época de «gloria y bohemia».

El alma de Darío, a veces triste y atormentada debido a su vida intensa, se puede percibir en sus obras. Su libro capital, *Cantos de vida y esperanza*, se publicó en 1905 y fue aclamado por esa intensidad y profundidad del tema. A Rubén Darío también se le conoce por su uso del término «modernismo», un movimiento de renovación literaria que él comenzó. Quería transformar la prosa y el verso de su tiempo, hacer de la belleza el primer fin de la poesía y fusionar las diferentes escuelas literarias. Lo que caracteriza las obras de Darío es su uso de cultismos,[5] palabras que inventó él, nuevos ritmos, verso libre y muchas licencias poéticas. Esta estrofa de su *Prosa profana* ejemplifica la pluma mágica del príncipe de la literatura hispanoamericana.

> El olímpico cisne[6] de nieve
> con **el ágata**[7] rosa del pico[8]
> lustra **el ala** eucarística[9] y breve
> que abre al sol como un casto[10] abanico.[11]

---

[1]**aldea (aldehuela):** *village* / [2]**rincón:** *corner* / [3]**nacimiento:** *birth* / [4]**tío-abuelo paterno:** *paternal great-uncle* / [5]**cultismos:** *learned words, words derived from Latin* / [6]**cisne:** *swan* / [7]**ágata:** *agate* / [8]**pico:** *beak, bill* / [9]**eucarística:** *Eucharistic, having to do with Holy Communion* / [10]**casto:** *pure, chaste* / [11]**abanico:** *fan*

¿Comprendes?

1. ¿Cómo era la vida temprana de Rubén Darío?
2. ¿Qué caracteriza las obras de Rubén Darío?
3. Explica el término «modernismo».

■ Formas especiales a causa de la primera sílaba de la próxima palabra

y (y→e)

■ As you know, the Spanish word for *and* is **y**. However, if the word following **y** begins with **i-** or **hi-**, **y** becomes **e**.

Ana estudia química **e** historia.	*Ana studies chemistry **and** history.*
Él es guapo **e** ingenioso.	*He is good-looking **and** clever.*

o (o→u)

■ Like the Spanish word for *and,* the Spanish word for *or* (**o**) has an alternate spelling. The Spanish word **o** becomes **u** before words that begin with **o-** or **ho-**.

Hay que estudiar escritura **u** ortografía.	*You must study penmanship **or** spelling.*
Encontré siete **u** ocho.	*I found seven **or** eight.*

a tónica y el artículo definido

■ Feminine singular words that begin with stressed **a** or **ha** require the singular definite article **el** instead of **la**. Remember that if a word has two syllables and ends in a vowel, **-n**, or **-s**, it is stressed on the first syllable: **el arma** *(weapon)*. Words of more than two syllables that are stressed on the first syllable have a written accent: **el ánima** *(spirit)*. Other feminine words that begin with **a-** or **ha-** and are not stressed on the first syllable have the normal feminine article: **la ansiedad** *(anxiety).*

The plural definite article of these feminine nouns as well as all others is **las**. Adjectives that modify them are in the feminine form.

El agua aquí es muy pura.	*The water here is very pure.*
Las aguas son profundas.	*The waters are deep.*
La habitación es muy grande.	*The lodging is very big.*
Las habitaciones son feas.	*The lodgings are ugly.*

Practiquemos

A. Pares. Escribe **y** o **e** en el espacio en blanco, según el sonido de la sílaba que sigue.

1. Manuel es doctor _____ ingeniero.

2. Su descubrimento es nuevo _____ importante.

3. Estudió matemáticas _____ español.

4. Dice que respiramos oxígeno _____ hidrógeno.

5. También dice que el universo es viejo _____ infinito.

6. Manuel es francés _____ italiano.

7. Le gusta beber Coca-cola _____ agua.

8. Es complicado _____ interesante.

B. El nuevo apartamento. Escribe **o** o **u** en el espacio en blanco, según el sonido de la sílaba que sigue.

1. El apartamento viene con refrigerador _____ horno.

2. Es el número siete _____ ocho.

3. Está en el piso tres _____ el cuatro.

4. Está cerca de un centro médico, clínica _____ hospital.

5. El dueño se llama Hugo _____ Homero.

6. Es de Noruega _____ Holanda.

7. Quiere alquilar el apartamento hoy _____ mañana.

8. No le importa si la nueva persona es mujer _____ hombre.

¿Sabías?

En noviembre de 1998, el Huracán Mitch casi destruyó Nicaragua. Fue una de las tormentas más fuertes del siglo XX, dejando destrucción por todas partes. La comunidad internacional llegó a la ayuda de los nicaragüenses para comenzar la restauración de su país.

C. Al comienzo del alfabeto. Escribe los artículos definidos apropiados para estos nombres.

1. ___ águila   _____ águilas   *eagle(s)*
2. _____ almeja   _____ almejas   *clam(s)*
3. _____ aria   _____ arias   *aria(s)*
4. _____ hada   _____ hadas   *fairy(-ies)*
5. _____ antena   _____ antenas   *antenna(s)*
6. _____ anguila   _____ anguilas   *eel(s)*
7. _____ arpa   _____ arpas   *harp(s)*
8. _____ amenaza   _____ amenazas   *threat(s)*
9. _____ ancla   _____ anclas   *anchor(s)*
10. _____ ala   _____ alas   *wing(s)*

> Escribe un poema usando estas palabras: *arpa, ala, ancla, águila, agua* y algunas otras necesarias.

A ver si sabes

Use this self-test to see if you know the material presented in Chapter 12.

A. Turistas. ¿Qué les dice el director de viaje a los turistas que acaban de llegar a Managua, Nicaragua? Usa las formas del mandato para **Ud.** o **Uds.**

Buenas tardes, amigos. Aquí estamos en el centro de la ciudad de Managua. (1) _____ (Mirar) las estatuas impresionantes aquí enfrente del Palacio Nacional. Ahora, ya que tenemos tiempo, (2) _____ (ir) a la Plaza de Compras y (3) _____ (buscar) unos recuerdos de su visita. (4) _____ (Recordar) que mañana vamos al Centro Cultural Managua. Vamos a tener más de tres horas allí, así que (5) _____ (sacar) muchas fotos de los artefactos que van a ver. Y Ud., señor Domingo, (6) _____ (visitar) las playas Pochomil y la Boquita; ¡yo sé que a Ud. le gusta correr las olas y tomar el sol! Y a todos Uds. les digo que no (7) _____ (dejar) de experimentar la belleza de estos lugares. Y ahora, vamos a continuar nuestro recorrido. (8) ¡_____ (Venir) conmigo!

B. Este fin de semana. Juanita está pensando en este fin de semana. Completa sus pensamientos con la forma adecuada del presente del subjuntivo.

1. Ojalá que no _____ (llover).

2. Es mejor que yo no _____ (tener) que trabajar.

3. Es necesario que Rubén y Raquel me _____ (llamar).

Preguntas culturales
1. ¿Por qué es famoso e interesante el Parque Nacional del Darién?
2. ¿Cómo eran las relaciones políticas entre EE.UU. y Nicaragua durante la presidencia de Violeta Chamorro?
3. ¿Cómo se llama el lago más grande de Centroamérica y qué mamífero se encuentra en sus aguas?
4. ¿Qué características se pueden percibir en las obras de Darío?

4. Es deseable que nosotros _____ (poder) salir.

5. Ojalá que tú _____ (divertirse) también.

6. Es importante que tú y yo _____ (descansar).

C. Observaciones. Usando las expresiones impersonales, expresa unas observaciones sobre lo que hacen estos profesionales.

1. no ser bueno / el deportista comer comida grasosa
2. ser evidente / tú trabajar mucho como fotógrafo
3. ser ridículo / los locutores decir cosas absurdas
4. ser importante / el piloto dormir bien antes de su viaje
5. ser mejor / la diplomática saber hablar varios idiomas
6. ser una pena / nosotros los vendedores no poder ofrecer descuentos
7. ser posible / yo no recibir un buen sueldo
8. ser necesario / todos los empleados descansar después de trabajar todo el día

D. Una fiesta fracasada. Completa la descripción del desastre de Claudia con estas palabras: **y, e, o, u, el, la, los, las**.

¡Ay! Alguien ofreció traer helado, pero no recuerdo si fue Jorge (1) _____ Homero. No pude preparar (2) _____ almejas *(clams)* porque no funcionaba la estufa y (3) _____ agua estaba fría. ¡Qué horror! Esteban invitó a Marta (4) _____ Inés porque le encanta bailar con ellas, pero la banda canceló al último momento. Y Anita iba a tocar (5) _____ arpa *(harp)* pero estaba enferma. Todos estábamos enojados (6) _____ irritados porque queríamos bailar (7) _____ oír la música de (8) _____ arpa.

Querido Diario. Vas a compartir con tu diario algunas cosas que te gustaría decir a personas con quienes tienes contacto. Haz una lista de personas, por ejemplo, tu jefe(a), tu instructor(a), tu compañero(a) de trabajo, el (la) dependiente(a) en una tienda, tu doctor(a) o dentista, tu esposo(a), tus hijos o hermanos. Luego dile a tu diario lo que te gustaría decirles. Puedes empezar así: «Me gustaría decir a mi jefe...»

Grammar: verbs: imperative, imperative **tú**
Phrases: requesting or ordering
Vocabulary: professions

Vocabulario activo

Para expresar emociones
Es espantoso.
Es sorprendente.
Es triste.
Es una lástima.

Para expresar un juicio
Es bueno.
Es curioso.
Es deseable.
Es horrible (terrible).
Es importante.
Es interesante.
Es loco.
Es lógico.
Es malo.
Es mejor.
Es necesario.
Es ridículo.

Para expresar duda o certeza
Es cierto.
Es dudoso.
Es evidente.
Es obvio.
Es verdad.

Para expresar probabilidad
Es imposible.
Es posible.
Es probable.

Los trabajos

En la oficina
el (la) programador(a)
el (la) secretario(a)
el (la) técnico(a)

En la corte
el (la) abogado
  (licenciado[-a])
el (la) intérprete
el (la) juez

En la clínica
el (la) dentista
el (la) doctor(a) (médico)
el (la) enfermero(a)

En el taller
el (la) alfarero(a)
el (la) carpintero(a)
el (la) joyero(a)
el (la) mecánico(a)

En el restaurante
el (la) cocinero(a)
el (la) mesero(a)

En el sitio de la construcción
el (la) albañil
el (la) constructor(a)
el (la) electricista
el (la) ingeniero(a)
el (la) plomero

En los negocios
el (la) banquero(a)
el (la) comerciante
el (la) contador(a)
el (la) dependiente(a)
el (la) peluquero(a)
el (la) vendedor(a)

En los medios de comunicación
el (la) fotógrafo(a)
el (la) locutor(a)
el (la) periodista

En la universidad
el (la) escritor(a)
el (la) músico(a)
el (la) profesor(a)

En las fuerzas armadas
el (la) marinero(a)
el (la) soldado

Otras profesiones
el (la) deportista
el (la) diplomático(a)
el (la) portero(a)

El trabajo
ayudar
construir (y)
cuidar
enseñar
juzgar (g→gu)
representar

Coro
Maracaibo
Cabimas
Barquistimento
Valencia
★ **Caracas**
Carúpano
Cumaná
Barcelona
Valera
Maturín
Tucupita
LA CORDILLERA DE MÉRIDA
Mérida
▲ PICO
BOLÍVAR
San Fernando
de Apure
El Tigre
Río Orinoco
Ciudad
Bolívar
Cuidad
Guayana
Arauca
VENEZUELA
Canaima
Puerto Ayacucho
RORAIMA
Santa Elena
de Uarén
Río Orinoco
San Carlos
de Río Negro

Transparencies:
A–4: La América del Sur
A–14: Country Profile: Venezuela

REPÚBLICA DE VENEZUELA

Nombre oficial: República de Venezuela

Área: 912.050.700 km^2

Población: 21.051.000

Capital: Caracas

Moneda: el bolívar

Idiomas oficial: español

Fiesta nacional: 5 de julio, Día de la
Independencia

Venezuela y los venezolanos

CAPÍTULO
13

Salto Ángel, Venezuela

In this chapter you will learn:

GRAMMAR POINTS

- Subjunctive mood: verbs of volition, will, prohibition
- Subjunctive mood: verbs of reaction and anticipation (emotion)
- Verbs like **gustar** to express reaction
- **Estar** + adjective to express emotion

COMMUNICATIVE FUNCTIONS

- Express desired outcomes
- Express feelings with regard to a situation

VOCABULARY

- Goals: Work and money, family, personal life

287

I. Un hombre renacentista, Andrés Bello

LECTURA

Entre los muchos autores venezolanos bien conocidos, surge el nombre de Andrés Bello. Nació en Caracas el 29 de noviembre de 1781. De niño, le encantaba leer los clásicos, lo cual se nota definitivamente en sus obras. Bello era muy amigo del viajero y naturalista alemán Alexander Von Humboldt y con esta amistad creció su interés en la geografía y las ciencias naturales. También es importante notar que Bello fue amigo y maestro del libertador Simón Bolívar. Debido a esta amistad, fue enviado a Londres en misión política en 1810 por la junta revolucionaria venezolana.

Bello **quiere que** sus obras **caractericen** las circunstancias de su tiempo. La nueva cultura de América, la fuerza independentista y el amor a la realidad hispanoamericana son temas constantes que trata este autor en sus obras; es la entrega humanista de poeta, filósofo, gramático,[1] legislador y político.

Junto con su amor a las letras, Andrés Bello alababa[2] la tranquilidad y la belleza del campo. En muchos de sus poemas, desprecia el lujo[3] y la vida de la ciudad. **Sugiere que** la gente **busque** y **disfrute** la paz en el campo.

Entre todo lo que contribuyó Andrés Bello a la literatura hispanoamericana, es indispensable destacar[4] que fue su pasión por su idioma lo que le distingue. **Quiere que** los pueblos de Hispanoamérica **conserven** la unidad del idioma. En su *Gramática de la lengua español,* escrita en 1847, es evidente su erudición en cuestiones de filología,[5] su análisis de los tiempos verbales, las diferentes conjugaciones y las complejidades del idioma. Muchos profesores de español hoy en día **quieren que** sus estudiantes **estudien** esta obra de Andrés Bello.

Así escribió: «Juzgo importante la conservación de la lengua de nuestros padres en su posible pureza, como medio providencial de comunicación y un vínculo[6] de fraternidad entre las varias naciones de origen español derramados[7] sobre los dos continentes». (*Gramática,* p. 24)

---

[1]**gramático:** *grammarian* / [2]**alababa:** *praised* / [3]**lujo:** *luxury* / [4]**destacar:** *to point out, show* / [5]**filología:** *linguistics* / [6]**vínculo:** *bond, tie* / [7]**derramados:** *spread out, running over*

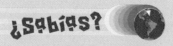

¿Sabías?

El Salto Ángel es la cascada más alta del mundo. Tiene una caída de más de media milla, 16 veces más alta que la cascada de Niágara.

¿Comprendes?

1. ¿Qué caracteriza las obras de Andrés Bello?
2. Describe una de sus contribuciones a la lengua española.
3. ¿Qué creía Bello que era importante para la unificación de hispanoamérica?

■ Usos del subjuntivo: Verbos de voluntad

In Chapter 12 you learned that impersonal expressions with certain meanings require the next conjugated verb to be in the subjunctive mood. Other types of expressions also require the use of the subjunctive. One of these consists of verbs of "volition," which are used when one party tries to influence the behavior of another. These verbs, when followed by **que** and another conjugated verb with a new subject, require that the second verb be in the subjunctive.

Quiero que lo **llames.**   *I want you to call him.*

Verbs of preference, want, need

■ Common verbs of this type include expressions of preference, wants, and needs.

necesitar	*to need*
preferir (e→ie)	*to prefer*
querer (e→ie)	*to want*

> **NOTA:**
> If there is no new subject, the infinitive rather than a conjugated verb is used.

Necesito que tú me **ayudes.**   *I need for you to help me.*
Prefiere que **veamos** Caracas   *She prefers that we see*
  primero.   *Caracas first.*
Preferimos empezar ahora.   *We prefer to begin now.*
Quiero salir afuera.   *I want to go outside.*

Point out again that the way English expresses the Spanish subjunctive varies.

¿Sabías?

El Río Orinoco es el tercer río más largo de Sudamérica, cubriendo 2.150 kilómetros (1.333 millas) de su origen cerca de la frontera brasileña en el sur de Venezuela hasta la delta en la costa del noreste.

Practiquemos

A. A Venezuela. Tu familia tiene planes para ir de vacaciones a Venezuela. ¿Qué deben hacer todos para completar los preparativos? Completa las oraciones con las formas apropiadas de los verbos indicados.

1. Yo quiero que todos _____ (empacar) sus propias maletas.

2. Los niños prefieren que sus padres _____ (hacer) todo.

3. Mis padres necesitan que mi esposo y yo _____ (llamar) al agente de viajes.

4. Mi cuñado quiere que nosotros le _____ (mandar) una postal.

5. Mi esposo y mi hijo prefieren que yo _____ (recoger) los boletos.

6. Hija, necesito que tú me _____ (ayudar).

7. Todos queremos que mis suegros nos _____ (llevar) al aeropuerto.

8. Yo prefiero que la familia _____ (tener) una fiesta de despedida.

B. En la oficina. En el trabajo todos quieren algo distinto. Completa las oraciones con la forma correcta de uno de los siguientes verbos.

ayudar   dar   estar   hacer   llegar   ser

1. El jefe prefiere que los empleados _____ a las 8:00.

2. Las secretarias quieren que otra persona _____ el café.

3. Yo necesito que mi compañero me _____ los informes hoy.

4. Los empleados quieren que el almuerzo _____ más largo.

5. El portero prefiere que la oficina _____ bastante limpia y arreglada.

6. ¿Cómo quieres que yo te _____?

C. El viaje del fin de semana. Tienes que ir a otra ciudad este fin de semana. Escribe una lista de ocho cosas que deben hacer para ti las otras personas de tu casa. Usa **necesitar**, **preferir** o **querer** en cada oración.

MODELO: *Necesito que los niños se acuesten temprano.*

1. _____   5. _____
2. _____   6. _____
3. _____   7. _____
4. _____   8. _____

Con un(a) compañero(a), escriban una lista de cosas que Uds. prefieren que hagan los otros compañeros de clase. Luego compartan la lista con la clase.

■ Verbos de persuasión

Other verbs that indicate that one individual (or group) is attempting to influence the behavior of another include verbs of "suasion": persuading, asking, and recommending.

aconsejar	*to advise*
insistir en	*to insist on*
pedir (e→i)	*to ask (for)*
persuadir	*to persuade*
recomendar (e→ie)	*to recommend*
rogar (o→ue)	*to beg*
sugerir (e→ie)	*to suggest*

Te pido que no **hables** más.

I'm asking you not to talk any more.

¿Me sugieres que lo **llame** ahora?

Are you suggesting that I call him now?

Point out that **preguntar** *(to ask a question)* is followed by the indicative mood, whereas **pedir** *(to ask for [a favor])* is followed by the subjunctive.

Practiquemos

A. En la agencia de viajes. ¿Qué recomendaciones les da el agente de turismo a los turistas que van a Venezuela? Completa las oraciones con la forma del subjuntivo de un verbo apropiado. (Usa distintos verbos en cada oración.)

1. Recomiendo que todos Uds. _____ el Río Orinoco.

2. Sugerimos que las mujeres _____ solas a los clubes.

3. El gobierno venezolano aconseja que los turistas _____ inyecciones.

4. Cuando voy a Caracas, siempre me recomiendan que _____ varios días allí.

5. En los restaurantes piden que les _____ comida típica como arepas o pabellón criollo.

6. Y yo les ruego que _____ mucho cuidado y también que se _____ mucho.

7. Y al regresar, Uds. pueden persuadirme que yo _____ a Venezuela otra vez.

B. La buena salud. ¿Qué recomiendan los expertos para mantener la buena salud? Haz recomendaciones usando elementos de las cuatro columnas. Las recomendaciones pueden ser afirmativas o negativas.

¿Qué recomendaciones tienes para tu compañero(a) si él (ella) va a lograr sus metas personales?

A	B	C	D
el médico	recomendar	nosotros(as)	comer carne
las enfermeras	aconsejar	todos(as)	hacer ejercicio
la profesora de	pedir	tú	beber agua
aeróbicos	sugerir	Ud.	beber café
los especialistas	insistir en	Uds.	comer grasa *(fat)*
en nutrición	rogar		dormir
el especialista	persuadir		tomar alcohol
en dietética			fumar *(to smoke)*
yo			comer frutas y
tú			verduras

C. Digo yo. Usando los verbos de abajo, dales sugerencias a tu familia, tus amigos y tus conocidos *(acquaintances).*

aconsejar   insistir en   necesitar   pedir   preferir   querer
recomendar   rogar   sugerir

MODELOS: *Quiero que mis sobrinos estudien mucho.*

Prefiero que nadie me llame después de las 10:00.

1. _____   5. _____

2. _____   6. _____

3. _____   7. _____

4. _____   8. _____

■ Verbos de permiso, prohibición, mandato

A third group of verbs of "volition" include verbs of permitting, prohibiting, and commanding.

decir	*to tell*
dejar	*to let, allow*
impedir (e→i)	*to impede, keep from*
mandar	*to order (command)*
permitir	*to permit*
prohibir	*to prohibit*

No **dejan que entremos** en el museo.

*They don't **let us go into** the museum.*

Permiten que yo lo **visite** los jueves.

*They **permit me to visit** on Thursdays.*

No **nos dejan entrar** en el museo.	*They don't **let us go into** the museum.*
Me **permiten visitar** los jueves.	*They **permit me to visit** on Thursdays.*
Te **prohiben hablar** aquí.	*They **prohibit you to talk** here.*

You may wish to point out that the verbs **dejar**, **permitir**, and **prohibir** may be used with an infinitive but only if the direct object pronoun is present in the sentence.

NOTA:

The verb **decir** may be used either to communicate information or to tell someone to do something. When you are simply conveying a message, use the indicative mood. When telling someone to do something, use the subjunctive.

Te **digo que es** importante.	*I'm telling you that it is important.*
Me **dice que me vaya** ahora.	*He's telling me to leave now.*

Practiquemos

A. Mi casa / tu casa. Los hijos de tus vecinos y tus hijos comparan su situación —en una casa los padres son estrictos y en la otra casa son más liberales. Completa los comentarios de los hijos de una forma apropiada.

Padres estrictos

1. Mis padres prohiben que yo _____.
2. No permiten que nosotros _____.
3. No dejan que mis hermanos _____.
4. Impiden que nosotros _____.
5. Nos dicen que _____.

Padres liberales

6. Mis padres dejan que los hijos _____.
7. No prohiben que nosotros _____.
8. Permiten que yo _____.
9. Nos mandan que _____.
10. No impiden que los niños _____.

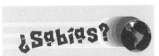

¿Sabías?

Alonso de Ojeda y Américo Vespuci le dieron el nombre «Venezuela» a este país que parecía la pequeña Venecia porque los indígenas vivían en casas sobre pilotes (stilts) en el agua.

B. En mi trabajo. ¿Cuáles son las limitaciones de tu trabajo? Completa las oraciones de acuerdo con tu situación. Usa estos verbos.

decir   dejar   impedir   mandar   permitir   prohibir

1. Mi jefe(a) _____.
2. Todos(as) _____.
3. Mi compañero(a) _____.
4. Los otros _____.
5. Tú _____.
6. Y yo _____.

C. La carta. Rosa le escribe una carta a su amiga Tina. ¿Qué le dice de su experiencia en Venezuela? Llena los espacios en blanco con la forma adecuada de uno de los verbos de abajo.

Escribe un párrafo en que describes una situación personal difícil, e.g., problemas con los hijos, el (la) esposo(a), un(a) compañero(a) o un(a) amigo(a). Luego dale tu carta a un(a) compañero(a) para que esa persona te dé recomendaciones. Tú vas a darle recomendaciones a tu compañero(a).

verbos de voluntad: insistir en, querer, recomendar, sugerir

verbos de acción: decir, haber (hay), hacer, pasar, ver, visitar

Querida Tina,

Aquí estamos en Caracas. Todo es tan bonito. Elisa y yo (1) _____ que tú y Benjamín nos (2) _____ aquí. Es la ciudad de la eterna primavera. Mañana vamos a visitar Valencia. Catalina Pérez y sus papás (3) _____ que nosotros (4) _____ la parte colonial. También, ellos (5) _____ que yo (6) _____ unos días con sus familiares en Mérida porque saben cuánto me gusta hacer caminatas en las montañas.

Otra cosa. Felipe (7) _____ que Ramón, su primo y yo (8) _____ un recorrido de Maracaibo. Ojalá que (9) _____ tiempo para hacerlo todo. Yo (10) _____ que tú me (11) _____ lo que tú (12) _____ en Mérida.

Un fuerte abrazo,
Rosa

❖ Para hablar de las metas

El trabajo y el dinero

acumular una fortuna	to amass a fortune
cambiar de trabajos	to change jobs
conseguir un trabajo mejor pagado	to get a better paid job
ganar la lotería (sacarse el gordo)	to win the lottery (to get the grand prize)
invertir más dinero	to invest more money
pedir un ascenso	to ask for a raise

La familia

ahorrar para la educación de los hijos	to save for the children's education
ayudar a los padres	to help your parents
criar a los hijos	to raise your children
pasar más tiempo en casa	to spend more time at home
salir más con mi esposo(a), compañero(a)	to go out more with my spouse, partner

La vida personal

aprender a...	*to learn to . . .*
jugar al golf	*play golf*
tocar el piano	*play the piano*
usar mejor la computadora	*use the computer better*
asistir a la universidad	*to go to college*
casarse (divorciarse)	*to get married (to get divorced)*
escribir mis memorias	*to write my memoirs*
hacer más ejercicio	*to do more exercise*
organizar mis fotos	*to organize my photos*
viajar	*to travel*
vivir una vida sana	*to live a healthy life*
volver a la universidad	*to go back to college*

¿Sabías?

¿Recuerdas que en Managua las calles no tienen nombres? Pues también en la vieja parte central de Caracas las direcciones son curiosísimas. Para decir dónde está un edificio no se usan números ni nombres de calles sino los nombres de las esquinas (corners). Todas las esquinas tienen nombre y para decir que un edificio está situado entre la esquina Maderero y la esquina Glorieta, la gente dice «Maderero a Glorieta». Si el edificio está en la esquina misma, la dirección es Esquina Glorieta. En las partes modernas de la ciudad, las calles tienen nombres y los edificios tienen números.

Practiquemos

A. Mis metas. Haz una lista de diez metas personales. Luego, compara tu lista con un(a) compañero(a). Entre los dos, identifiquen dos metas que tengan en común, y luego busquen a dos otras personas que también compartan estas mismas metas.

II.   ¡Viva la música!

LECTURA

¿A quién no le encanta la música sudamericana y, en particular, la de Venezuela con sus melodías vivas y su ritmo característico, el joropo? Este joropo, que fue desarrollado en Los Llanos, poco a poco[1] cautivó al pueblo venezolano. El joropo se interpreta en canciones, acompañado del arpa, el cuatro y las maracas.

También hay una forma de baile que se llama el joropo. Los **venezolanos se alegran de que puedan** jactarse de[2] su propio ritmo y de que el resto del mundo **tenga** la oportunidad de apreciar su música también.

Un instrumento muy popular y a la vez³ muy venezolano es el cuatro. Es una guitarra pequeña de cuatro cuerdas⁴ que los músicos usan para tocar las melodías características venezolanas. En casi todos los conjuntos,⁵ el uso del cuatro es notable.

También es fascinante que haya otros ritmos regionales. En el este del país, **le complace** a la gente **que** los músicos **toquen** el estribillo, el polo margariteño, las malagueñas y las jotas. En Maracaibo en el oeste, **les gusta** a todos que las bandas **interpreten** la gaita zuliana, otro ritmo típico de Venezuela. En la costa central **les gusta** todos que se **toque** música con tambores africanos debido a la gran población africana que allí se encuentra.

Sin duda, Caracas ha absorbido todas las influencias locales, regionales e internacionales. La ciudad vibra con esta variedad de sonido y ritmo. ¡Qué **viva**⁶ la música venezolana!

---

¹**poco a poco:** *little by little* / ²**jactarse de:** *to boast of* / ³**a la vez:** *at the same time* / ⁴**cuerdas:** *strings* / ⁵**conjuntos:** *bands, musical groups* / ⁶**¡Que viva... !:** *Hooray for . . ., Up with . . .*

¿Comprendes?

1. ¿Qué es el joropo?
2. ¿Qué influencia tiene la música de la costa central?
3. ¿Qué es el cuatro?

■ Usos del subjuntivo: Expresiones de reacción y anticipación

In Chapter 12 you learned that impersonal expressions like **Es triste** *(It's sad)*, **Es una lástima** *(It's a shame)*, **Es sorprendente** *(It's surprising)*, and the like require the subjunctive mood in the verb that follows. Other expressions of emotion reacting to or anticipating an action also require the subjunctive when there is a change of subject.

subject + verb + direct object

alegrarse de	*to be happy*	temer	*to fear*
esperar	*to hope*	tener miedo	*to be afraid*
sentir (e→ie)	*to regret, feel sorry*		

Me alegro de que trabajes aquí.   *I'm happy that you work here.*

Sentimos que no vayas a Amazonas.   *We're sorry that you are not going to Amazonas.*

Although the expression **¡Que... !** plus a verb does not contain an actual verb that expresses anticipation, it implies anticipation and thus the verb must be in the subjunctive mood. Many verbs may be used in this way with the meaning *I hope* or *Let . . .*

¡**Que vengan** pronto!	*I hope they come soon!*	Remind students that if there is no change of subject, the infinitive is used.
¡**Que traiga** María la comida!	*Let María **bring** the food!*	

Practiquemos

A. En Caracas. Completa el párrafo con la forma adecuada del verbo en paréntesis.

Me alegro de que (1) _____ (ir, nosotros) a visitar Caracas. Espero que nuestra visita (2) _____ (empezar) en la parte vieja de la ciudad donde están la Catedral, la Plaza Bolívar con su estatua y otros edificios históricos. La Universidad Central de Venezuela es muy interesante. Espero que (3) _____ (ver, tú) una protesta estudiantil, porque los estudiantes son muy activos políticamente. Y tenemos que caminar por la Sabana Grande, donde podemos ver muchas tiendas, restaurantes y hoteles. Y tenemos que ver las Torres (dos edificios muy altos) en el Parque Central. Tengo miedo de que no (4) _____ (tener, nosotros) tiempo para verlo todo, pero espero que (5) _____ (visitar) por lo menos el Parque los Caobos, donde están los museos. Temo que mi profesor de español me (6) _____ (matar *[to kill]*) si no vemos el Museo de Arte Contemporáneo y el Complejo Cultural Teresa Carreño y el Ateneo (donde tienen conciertos). Mis compañeros sienten que no (7) _____ (poder, yo) invitarlos a acompañarme pero esperan que yo les (8) _____ (mandar) por lo menos una tarjeta postal.

B. En mi casa. Forma oraciones usando elementos de todas las columnas. El sujeto del segundo verbo tiene que ser diferente del sujeto del primer verbo.

A	B	C	D	E
mi mejor amigo(a)			hijos(as)	poder graduarse
mis compañeros(as)	esperar		vecinos(as)	cambiar de trabajos
mi esposo(a)	temer		nosotros(as)	aprender otra lengua
yo	alegrarse de	que	mejor amigo(a)	no saber esquiar
tú	sentir		mascotas	hacer mucho ruido
mi papá	tener miedo		secretario(a)	trabajar el sábado
mi mejor amigo(a) y yo			profesor(a)	irse temprano
Uds.			tú	no venir hoy

C. Mis emociones. Completa las oraciones de una forma adecuada.

1. Me alegro de que mis padres _____.

2. Espero que mi hijo(a) _____.

3. Siento que mañana mi jefe(a) _____.

4. Temo que mis compañeros de trabajo _____.

5. Tengo miedo de que _____.

6. Espero que tú _____.

Compara tu lista de emociones con la lista de un(a) compañero(a). Luego, identifiquen dos emociones adicionales que Uds. dos tengan en común.

■ Usos del subjuntivo: Verbos como *gustar* para expresar reacciones

Some verbs that express emotional reaction function like **gustar** (indirect object + verb + subject).

indirect object + verb + subject

alegrar	*to make happy*	fastidiar	*to annoy*
chocar (c→qu)	*to annoy, tick off*	gustar	*to like, please*
complacer (c→zc)	*to please, gratify*	molestar	*to bother*
disgustar	*to displease*	sorprender	*to surprise*
enojar	*to irritate*		

Me fastidia que el museo **esté** cerrado.

It annoys me that the museum is closed.

Nos complace que estudies mucho.

It pleases us that you study a lot.

Me sorprende que no te **guste** el Lago Maracaibo.

I'm surprised that you don't like Lake Maracaibo.

Practiquemos

A. Vamos a Mérida. Completa la carta con las formas correctas de los siguientes verbos. Hay que usar los verbos **poder** y **tener** dos veces.

poder   prometer   ser   subir   tener   terminar   ver

Queridos tíos,

Nuestro grupo de cinco amigos está en Mérida de vacaciones. Nos alegra mucho que Venezuela (1) _____ picos muy altos para escalar y que no (2) _____ necesario salir del país. Me sorprende que todos nosotros (3) _____ ir de vacaciones al mismo tiempo. Empezamos con el Pico Humboldt y nuestro amigo Jesús se cayó y torció el tobillo. Le fastidia mucho que los demás *(the rest)* (4) _____ al Pico Bolívar y él no (5) _____. Pero le complace que Susana le (6) _____ acompañarlo en Mérida en el Teleférico —el tranvía *(cable car)* más largo y alto del mundo. Nos enoja a todos que después del Pico Bolívar (7) _____ nuestras vacaciones y (8) _____ que volver a casa. Pero me complace mucho que Uds. y yo nos (9) _____ otra vez en pocos días.

Un abrazo de su sobrino,
Rafael

B. Mi clase de español. ¿Qué reacción tienes a tu clase de español? Describe tu reacción a (1) el (la) profesor(a), (2) tus compañeros, (3) los estudiantes excelentes, (4) los estudiantes malos, (5) la hora de la clase, etcétera. Usa ocho de los verbos siguientes. Cuando termines, compara tus oraciones con las de un(a) compañero(a).

MODELOS: *Me choca que los estudiantes malos hablen durante la clase.*

Me encanta que la clase sea a las 5:30 de la tarde.

alegrar chocar complacer disgustar encantar enojar
fastidiar gustar molestar sorprender

1. _____   5. _____

2. _____   6. _____

3. _____   7. _____

4. _____   8. _____

■ Usos del subjuntivo: *Estar* + adjetivo para expresar emoción

estar + adjective

The verb **estar** combined with adjectives that express emotions is also followed by the subjunctive mood.

estar alegre	*to be happy*
estar contento	*to be happy, content*
estar desilusionado	*to be disappointed*
estar enojado	*to be irritated, annoyed*
estar sorprendido	*to be surprised*
estar triste	*to be sad*

Raúl **está contento que** Sara **cante** ahora.	*Raúl is happy that Sara is singing now.*
Estamos tristes que tengan que irse.	*We're sad that you have to leave.*

Practiquemos

A. ¿Cómo te sientes? Suponte *(Suppose)* que estas cosas son ciertas. ¿Cómo reaccionas? Usa **estar** + un adjetivo para formar tus respuestas.

MODELO: Mi compañero de trabajo busca trabajo en otra empresa.

Estoy triste que mi compañero busque trabajo en otra empresa.

1. Tus padres viajan a Acapulco.
2. Tu hija saca malas notas.
3. No puedes ir a un concierto de tu grupo favorito.
4. Tu profesor(a) de español no viene a clase.
5. Tu jefe te da más dinero.
6. Tu familia no va de vacaciones.
7. Tienes que trabajar más horas.
8. Tu mejor amiga vive en otra ciudad y no te escribe nunca.

B. En mi vida… Vas a describir aspectos de tu vida que te causan sentir emociones. Completa las oraciones para describir tu vida.

1. Estoy contento(a) que _____.

2. Estoy enojado(a) que _____.

3. Estoy desilusionado(a) que _____.

4. Estoy sorprendido(a) que _____.

5. Estoy triste que _____.

6. Estoy alegre que _____.

> Habla con un(a) compañero(a) de las cosas que les hacen alegres. ¿Son las mismas cosas?

C. ¿Cuál es tu opinión? Vas a dar una pequeña presentación sobre tres temas en tu clase de español. ¿Qué vas a decir? Escribe cuatro oraciones sobre cada tema empleando (1) expresiones de **voluntad** y (2) expresiones de **emoción**. Luego compara tus oraciones con dos compañeros(as) de clase.

MODELOS: *Recomiendo que lean las obras de Andrés Bello.*

Me complace que Uds. vayan a ver el Pico Humboldt.

Andrés Bello y sus obras

1. _____   3. _____

2. _____   4. _____

La música venezolana

5. _____   7. _____

6. _____   8. _____

¡Uds. van a Venezuela!

9. _____   11. _____

10. _____   12. _____

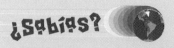

¿Sabías?

Las arepas son una comida muy popular en Venezuela. Se hacen de maíz y se rellenan de mantequilla, carne, pollo o queso. Los venezolanos las sirven fritas u horneadas.

A ver si sabes

Use this self-test to see if you know the material presented in Chapter 13.

A. El mensaje. ¿Qué mensaje telefónico le deja Carla a su novio, Memo, acerca de su anticipado luna de miel *(honeymoon)*? Llena los espacios en blanco con la forma adecuada del subjuntivo.

Memo. Soy yo, Carla. Oye, mi amor, quiero que nosotros (1) _____ (cambiar) nuestros planes para la luna de miel. Mira, muchos novios van a la cascada de Niágara; por eso quiero que nosotros (2) _____ (ir) al Salto Ángel. ¿Qué piensas, mi vida? Yo sé que prefieres que (3) _____ (visitar) Nueva York pero sugiero que lo (4) _____ (pensar, tú) bien. Pues, mi papá prefiere que (5) _____ (pasar) dos semanas con ellos en Cancún. No sé... Otra cosa: Mi abuela ruega que tú le (6) _____ (escribir) una nota diciéndole lo que quieres para la boda. Prefiero que ella nos (7) _____ (regalar) dinero. ¿Qué te parece? Necesito que tú me (8) _____ (llamar) mañana. Espero oír tu voz. Te hablo mañana.

B. Otras ideas. ¿Qué dicen estas personas? Escribe frases con lo que sigue.

1. el profesor de español / decirme / que yo tomar dos clases más
2. tu amiga Sara / sugerirte / que tú no vivir lejos de la universidad
3. mi hermana / decirnos / que no ver la nueva película
4. Jorge / impedir / que sus amigos manejar su coche
5. su jefa / permitir / que él salir temprano
6. yo / recomendarte / que seguir las instrucciones

C. ¿Cómo reaccionan? Combina **estar** con los elementos de las cuatro columnas para saber cómo reaccionan estas personas en estas circunstancias.

A	B	C	D
Ellos	triste que	Gloria	sacarse el gordo
Delia y Tonio	alegre que	tú	cambiar de empleo
Yo	molesto que	tu jefe	viajar a Cuba
Sus amigos	enojado que	Pedro y yo	tener que irse
Nosotros	desilusionado que	Uds.	manejar bien
Tú	sorprendido que	yo	estar enfermo
Carmen	contento que	el taxista	decir mentiras

D. ¡Qué emoción! El equipo de fútbol venezolano juega en el campeonato hoy. ¿Cómo reaccionan estas personas?

1. Eduardo _____ (alegrarse) de que los jugadores _____ (estar) bien entrenados.
2. Mario y yo _____ (temer) que _____ (ir) a llover.

⊃

**Preguntas
culturales**
1. ¿Por qué fue a
Londres Andrés
Bello?
2. ¿Qué conexión
tenía Andrés
Bello con Simón
Bolívar?
3. ¿Cómo es la
música típica de
Caracas?

3. El capitán del equipo _____ (esperar) que sus compañeros _____ (jugar) bien.

4. Los entrenadores _____ (decir) que los equipos _____ (estar) listos.

5. Al árbitro le _____ (chocar) que los fanáticos _____ (interrumpir) la acción.

6. Nosotros _____ (sentir) que Morales no _____ (jugar) hoy.

7. Tú _____ (estar) triste que (tú) no _____ (poder) jugar como ellos.

8. ¡Nos _____ (fastidiar) que nosotros no _____ (tener) boletos para el partido!

Querido Diario. Vas a abrir tu corazón a tu diario. Para empezar, nombra cuatro emociones y escríbelas en una línea horizontal. Luego, bajo cada emoción escribe los aspectos de tu vida que provocan esa emoción. Luego, comparte tus sentimientos con tu diario. Puedes empezar así: "Me alegro tanto que..."

Grammar: verbs: subjunctive with **que**, subjunctive with **ojalá**
Phrases: expressing a wish or desire, expressing irritation, persuading
Vocabulary: emotions: positive, emotions: negative

Vocabulario activo

Verbos de voluntad

aconsejar	insistir en	permitir	querer (c →ie)
decir	mandar	persuadir	recomendar (e→ie)
dejar	necesitar	preferir (e→ie)	rogar (o→ue)
impedir (e→i)	pedir (e→i)	prohibir	sugerir (e→ie)

Verbos de emoción

alegrar	enojar	estar enojado	molestar
alegrar(se) (de)	esperar	estar sorprendido	sentir (e→ie)
chocar (c→qu)	estar alegre	estar triste	sorprender
complacer (c→zc)	estar contento	fastidiar	temer
disgustar	estar desilusionado	gustar	tener miedo

Para hablar de las metas

El trabajo y el dinero
acumular una fortuna
cambiar de trabajos
conseguir (e→i) un trabajo
  mejor pagado
ganar la lotería
invertir más dinero
pedir (e→i) un ascenso
sacarse el gordo

La familia
ahorrar para la educación
  de los hijos
ayudar a los padres
criar a los hijos
pasar más tiempo en casa
salir con mi esposo(a),
  compañero(a)

La vida personal
aprender a...
  jugar al golf
  tocar el piano
  usar mejor la computadora
asistir a la universidad
casarse (divorciarse)
escribir mis memorias
hacer más ejercicio
organizar mis fotos
viajar
vivir una vida sana
volver a la universidad

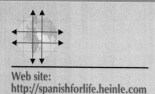

Transparencies:
A–1: España
A–5: Country Profile, España

La Coruña
Lugo
Pontevedra
Orense
Oviedo
Santander
Bilbao   San Sebastián
Vitoria   Pamplona
León
Palencia
Burgos
Logroño
Huesca
Gerona
Zamora
Valladolid
Soria
Zaragoza
Lleida
Barcelona
Tarragona
Salamanca
Segovia
ESPAÑA
Ávila
Guadalajara
Madrid
Teruel
Cuenca
Castellón
de la Plana
Toledo
MENO
Palma
ISLAS BALEARES
MALLORCA
PORTUGAL
Cáceres
Valencia
Badajoz
Albacete
IBIZA
Ciudad Real
FORMENTERA
Alicante
Córdoba
Murcia
Jaén
Huelva
Sevilla
Granada
Almería
Málaga
Cádiz

REINO DE ESPAÑA

Nombre oficial: Reino de España

Área: 504.788 km^2

Población: 39.200.000

Capital: Madrid

Moneda: la peseta

Idiomas oficiales: español, gallego (en Galicia), catalán (en Cataluña), vascüence o euskera (en el País Vasco), valenciano (en Valencia), mallorquín (en las Islas Baleares)

Fiesta nacional: 12 de octubre, Fiesta nacional y de la Hispanidad

España y los españoles

Paisaje de España

In this chapter you will learn:

GRAMMAR POINTS

- Subjunctive mood: expressions of doubt
- **Se:** impersonal use
- The prepositions **por** and **para**

COMMUNICATIVE FUNCTIONS

- Express doubt
- Give and understand directions
- Describe the use of something (**es para**)
- Describe the reason for something (**lo hizo por**)

VOCABULARY

- Directions
- Public locations

I. Ana María Matute: autora española del siglo XX

LECTURA

No es verdad que no haya muchas excelentes autoras españolas. De hecho, en los últimos 25 años, unas autoras españolas han sido reconocidas como las mejores y más notables del grupo moderno feminista. Ana María Matute es una de las mejores y más prolíficas escritoras de su generación por sus novelas y cuentos.

Ella nació en Barcelona, España, en 1926. Era una niña enfermiza,[1] de delicada sensibilidad, que le gustaba leer y escribir. Observaba a sus compañeros jóvenes, captada por sus travesuras,[2] juegos y deseos. Por eso, sus novelas y cuentos son estudios psicológicos infantiles escritos con ternura maternal y un conocimiento profundo del mundo de los jóvenes. Sus escrituras hacen sobresalir[3] los comentarios de los campesinos, pastores[4] y sus propios familiares.

Hay gente que **no cree que** Matute **sea** rebelde pero la verdad es que siempre escribe con un afán[5] de exponer y denunciar los valores superficiales de su época. Ella misma se considera una autora feminista que trata de apoyar las causas feministas del siglo XX.

Los temas que aparecen frecuentemente en las obras de Matute son la desolación, la tragedia, la tristeza y la autodenegración. Muchos de los protagonistas que crea son personas que **dudan que** una persona **pueda** escaparse de su propia realidad, su propio destino. Sus obras son realistas y sombrías.[6] La autora creó con su pluma el pueblo de Artámila, un lugar donde la gente languidece[7] sin la posibilidad de salir ni de su miseria ni de su vida aburrida.

Ana María Matute ha ganado muchos premios literarios prestigiosos como el Premio Planeta en 1958, el Premio Nacional de Literatura en 1959 y el Premio Nadal en 1961 entre otros. Sus obras más notables incluyen *Los Abel* (1948), *Fiesta al noroeste* (1958), *Primera memoria* (1960) e *Historias de la Artámila* (1961).

---

[1]**enfermiza:** *sickly* / [2]**travesuras:** *mischief* / [3]**hacen sobresalir:** *feature* / [4]**pastores:** *shepherds* /
[5]**afán:** *eagerness* / [6]**sombrías:** *somber, gloomy* / [7]**languidece:** *languish*

¿Comprendes?

1. ¿Por qué se dice que Ana María Matute es rebelde?
2. ¿Cómo era ella de niña?
3. ¿Cuáles son los temas típicos de sus obras?

■ Usos del subjuntivo: Expresiones de duda

You learned in Chapter 13 that the subjunctive mood follows verbs of volition and verbs of reaction or anticipation. Since human beings also express our subjective feelings when we express doubt, in Spanish expressions of doubt are followed by the subjunctive mood. Expressions of doubt include:

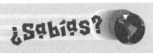
¿Sabías?

Entre 1936 y 1939 España fue devastada por una amarga guerra civil entre los Republicanos, el gobierno legítimo, y los Nacionalistas, encabezados por el general Francisco Franco, un fascista. Muchos soldados internacionales fueron a España para luchar, inclusive la Brigada Lincoln de EE.UU. Eventualmente triunfaron las tropas Nacionalistas y Franco fue caudillo (jefe) de España hasta su muerte en 1975.

dudar	to doubt
es dudoso	it's doubtful
no creer	not to believe
no es cierto	it's not true
no es verdad	it's not true

Dudo que vayan a Málaga.

I doubt that they are going to Málaga.

No creen que Matute ya **escriba** más.

They don't believe that Matute will write any more.

Use of the subjunctive or indicative after **No es cierto** and **No es verdad** varies somewhat according to dialect, personal preference, and degree of doubt.

Expressions of certainty are considered objective statements of fact and are followed by the indicative mood. Expressions of certainty include:

creer	to believe	es verdad	it's true
es cierto	it's true	no dudar	not to doubt
es indudable	it's indubitable (doubtless)	saber	to know

No dudo que están en España.

I don't doubt that they are in Spain.

Es verdad que Córdoba **es** interesante.

It's true that Córdoba is interesting.

Questions involving the verb **creer** *(to think, to believe)* are followed by the subjunctive mood.

¿Crees que sirvan cordero asado?

Do you think they will serve roast lamb?

Practiquemos

A. Tomás. Tomás y su familia no creen nada. ¿Cómo reaccionan a estos hechos de España? Usa las expresiones **no creer, dudar, es dudoso, no es cierto** y **no es verdad.**

M O D E L O : Madrid es la capital de España.
  Tomás dice: *No creo que Madrid sea la capital de España.*

1. La Alhambra está en Granada.
 La mamá de Tomás dice:
2. Los catalanes hablan catalán.
 Las hermanas de Tomás dicen:

3. El ceramicista Lladró vive en Valencia.
El hermano de Tomás dice:
4. Miles de turistas van a Sevilla cada año.
Tomás dice:
5. En Gibraltar puedes ver monos.
Los hermanos de Tomás dicen:
6. Los españoles comen mucho arroz y pescado.
Tomás dice:

B. ¿Cómo reaccionas tú? ¿Cuál es tu reacción a las siguientes oraciones? Usa las expresiones de abajo para expresar tu reacción. Debes estar preparado(a) a explicar tu opinión.

creer, no creer, dudar, no dudar, es verdad, no es verdad, es dudoso

> Inventa una lista de diez cosas probables e improbables (o ciertas y falsas) y luego pide a un(a) compañero(a) que reaccione a tu lista.

1. Muchas personas viven en la luna.
2. El 50% de la población del mundo habla español.
3. Hay 21 países de habla española.
4. El mundo produce suficiente comida para su población.
5. Más personas trabajan hoy que en el pasado.
6. La meta más importante en la vida es acumular una fortuna.
7. Las mascotas nos ayudan a vivir felizmente.
8. La gente debe comprar un carro nuevo cada cuatro años.

❖ Para dar y entender las direcciones

Transparencies:
F–1: Los lugares
        públicos
F–2: Un pueblo
F–3: ¿Dónde está?
F–4: La ciudad

Direcciones	Directions
a la derecha	to the right
a la izquierda	to the left
a mano derecha	on the right-hand side
a mano izquierda	on the left-hand side
adelante	forward
al lado de	beside
atrás	back
la cuadra	block
debajo de	underneath
delante de	ahead of
derecho	straight ahead
detrás de	behind
enfrente de	in front of, facing
la esquina	corner

> Usando mandatos, explica a un(a) compañero(a) de clase cómo ir (1) de tu casa a tu trabajo, (2) de tu casa a tu almacén favorito, (3) de tu casa a la clase de español y (4) de tu casa al correo principal.

El tránsito	**Traffic**
el alto	stop sign
el autobús	bus
el (la) conductor(a)	driver
el metro	subway
la parada	stop (bus)
el paso de peatones	pedestrian crosswalk
el (la) peatón/peatona	pedestrian
el semáforo	traffic signal (stop light)
el taxi	taxi

Las calles

la acera	sidewalk
la autopista	freeway, expressway
el camino	road
la carretera	highway
la senda	path

Los edificios

el almacén	department store
el banco	bank
la biblioteca	library
el capitolio	capitol building
la casa de bomberos	fire station
la comisaría de policía	police station
el correo	post office
la estatua	statue
la legislatura	legislature
el palacio	palace
el palacio de gobierno	government building
el palacio de justicia	courthouse

Los verbos

bajar	to get off (bus, subway, taxi)
cruzar (z→c)	to cross
doblar	to turn
pasar	to pass
retroceder	to go back
seguir (e→i)	to follow, stay on
subir	to get on
tomar	to take

¿Sabías?

Don Quijote de la Mancha, el famoso caballero andante, su amigo Sancho Panza, su caballo Rocinante y la muy bella Dulcinea son nombres de fama internacional en la literatura. En el siglo XVII Miguel de Cervantes escribió *Don Quijote de la Mancha*, una de las más grandes obras de ficción jamás escritas. Sigue siendo uno de los libros más leídos y apreciados de toda la literatura mundial.

Don Quixote y Sancho Panza por Pablo Picasso

NOTA:

Además de **la acera** se usan las palabras **la vereda** y **la banqueta**. También se dice **el subterráneo** o **«el subte»** para **el metro**. En España, **la cuadra** significa todo el rectángulo con sus cuatro lados. Para hablar de **un lado** del cuadrilátero, se dice **la manzana**. En España, la legislatura se llama **Las Cortes**.

II. España: Todo bajo el sol

LECTURA

El Alhambra

Si **se quiere** pasar unas vacaciones estupendas, **se tiene** que ir a España, un país donde **se puede** ver un poco de todo. Si **se va** a España durante el verano, es mejor empezar por el sur en junio, porque en julio y agosto hace un calor de mil demonios.[1]

En el sur, **se puede** empezar en Granada, donde **se encuentra** la Alhambra, el magnífico palacio construido por los árabes, y el Generalife, un enorme jardín hecho para los sultanes. También **se debe** explorar el Albaycín, la vieja zona árabe donde **se puede** encontrar buena comida y música flamenca —¡indispensable!

De Granada, **se viaja** a Sevilla para visitar su Alcázar, palacio construido en el siglo IX que todavía se usa. También hay que ver la Catedral de Sevilla con su Giralda, una torre que fue minarete durante la época árabe cuando la iglesia fue mezquita musulmana.[2] Y **se tiene** que ir de compras en la calle Sierpes, una calle para peatones. Al norte de Sevilla **se encuentra** Córdoba, otra ciudad de mucha influencia árabe que tiene una magnífica mezquita con arcos[3] y columnas en blanco y rojo. En Córdoba también **se debe** ver «la judería», la sección judía.[4]

Después de pasar por Toledo y visitar la casa del artista El Greco y la Sinagoga del Tránsito, **se va** a Madrid donde **se encuentra** todo lo que ofrece una capital moderna —museos, teatros, almacenes y tiendas, parques y un buen sistema de transporte público. Además, Madrid tiene unos habitantes poco comunes en la época actual:[5] una familia real.[6] El rey don Juan Carlos, la reina Sofía, el príncipe Felipe y las infantas Elena y Cristina residen en el Palacio Real. **Se puede** descansar en el Parque del Retiro o pasar el día en la Casa de Campo, un parque enorme que tiene zoo, lago y otras atracciones.

De Madrid, **se vuela** a Barcelona, que es una ciudad muy artística. No **se puede** visitar esa ciudad sin ver la arquitectura de Antoni Gaudí en iglesias, parques, viviendas[7] y oficinas. También **se puede** admirar las obras de Pablo Picasso y Joan Miró en los Museos de Picasso y Miró, respectivamente.

En la Costa Cantábrica es muy agradable pasar muchas horas en las playas, y en Puente Viesgo **se puede** apreciar el arte prehistórico en las Cuevas del Castillo.

En Galicia, hay que visitar Santiago de Compostela, el fin del famoso Camino de Santiago, donde **se dice** que están los restos[8] de Santiago, el santo patrón de España. Si **se dispone** de más tiempo, hay que visitar las ciudades de las otras provincias de la península y también las Islas Baleares y las Islas Canarias. Pero no importa qué parte de España **se visita** —**se lo va a pasar** estupendamente bien.[9] ¡España: todo bajo el sol!

---

[1]**de mil demonios:** devilish, very intense / [2]**musulmana:** Muslim / [3]**arcos:** arches / [4]**judía:** Jewish / [5]**actual:** current / [6]**real:** royal / [7]**viviendas:** dwellings / [8]**restos:** remains / [9]**se lo va a pasar estupendamente bien:** you will have a really good time

¿Comprendes?

1. ¿Qué se puede ver en el sur de España, específicamente en Granada, Sevilla y Córdoba?
2. ¿Cuál fue la profesión de Antoni Gaudí? ¿Dónde se encuentra su obra?
3. ¿Qué importancia tiene Santiago de Compostela?

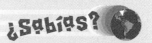

¿Sabías?

La música típica española es integral a la cultura de España. El flamenco de Andalucía, la jota de Aragón y los cantes sevillanos son bailes y estilos musicales que se reconocen internacionalmente. En esta música se notan las influencias árabes y gitanas. Los instrumentos más populares en la música folklórica de España son la guitarra, la bandurria (un tipo de mandolina), las castañuelas y la pandereta que sirven para acentuar el ritmo. Hay canciones alegres, enérgicas y melancólicas.

■ El uso impersonal de *se*

So far you have learned two uses for **se**, as a reflexive pronoun and as a replacement for an indirect object pronoun when two pronouns begin with **l**.

Manuel **se** sienta en la primera fila.	*Manuel sits in the first row.*
Se la mandaron ayer.	*They sent it **to them (him, her, you)** yesterday.*

The pronoun **se** is also used to speak impersonally. When we ask *How do you get to the library?* we are not asking specifically how *you* get to the library, but rather we are inquiring the way to the library. In this context, Spanish uses the pronoun **se** + *verb in the third-person singular.*

¿Cómo **se va** a la Plaza Mayor?	*How **do you (does one) get** to the Plaza Mayor?*
Se sigue por la calle Mayor.	*You stay (One stays) on the Calle Mayor.*
Se come muy bien allí.	*The food **is** good there. (**You can/One can eat** really well there.)*

Se cruza la plaza.	*You cross (One crosses) the plaza.*

Impersonal expressions are very common, and practically any Spanish verb may be used with **se** to make an impersonal statement or question. However, there is an important *exception*. Reflexive verbs in the third person already have a pronoun **se**. In order to use reflexive verbs impersonally, you may use **uno** *(one)* or the third-person plural of the verb *they*.

Uno se levanta temprano en el campo.	*One gets up early in the country.*
Se acuestan muy tarde en España.	*They go to sleep late in Spain.*

Practiquemos

A. ¿Adónde? ¿Cómo se llega a los lugares de interés turístico en Madrid? Escribe las instrucciones para llegar a los sitios indicados usando el plano de Madrid y siguiendo las calles indicadas.

MODELO: ¿Cómo se va de la Puerta del Sol a la Plaza Santa Cruz? (Calle Mayor, Calle Zaragoza, Plaza Mayor)

Se sigue por la Calle Mayor, se dobla a la izquierda en la Plaza Mayor y se dobla a la derecha en la Calle Zaragoza, se siga dos cuadras y allí está la Plaza Santa Cruz.

1. ¿Cómo se va de la Plaza de la Cibeles a la Plaza de las Cortes? (Paseo del Prado, Calle de los Madrazo, Calle del Marqués de Cubas)

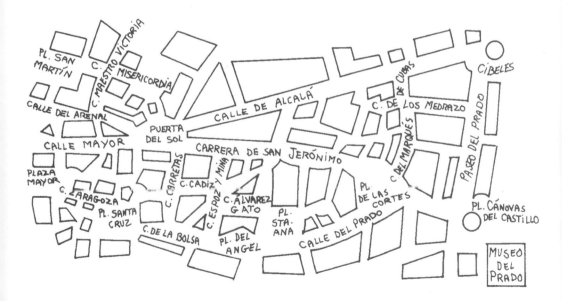

2. ¿Cómo se va de la Puerta del Sol a la Plaza San Martín? (Calle Misericordia, Calle Maestro Victoria, Calle de Arenal)

3. ¿Cómo se va de la Plaza Mayor al Museo del Prado? (Calle Zaragoza, Plaza Santa Cruz, Calle de la Bolsa, Plaza del Ángel, Calle del Prado, Plaza de las Cortes, Plaza Cánovas del Castillo, Paseo del Prado)

> Explica a tres compañeros(as) de clase cómo se va de cada una de sus casas a tu casa.

4. ¿Cómo se va de la Puerta del Sol a la Plaza Santa Ana? (Calle Carretas, Calle Cádiz, Calle Espoz y Mine, Calle Álvarez Gato)

B. En Madrid. ¿Qué se puede hacer en Madrid? Completa las oraciones de una forma lógica usando verbos en la forma impersonal.

MODELO: En los parques *se descansa y se lee muy felizmente.*

1. En los restaurantes _____.

2. En las discotecas _____.

3. En el Museo del Prado _____.

4. En las calles _____.

5. En los almacenes _____.

6. En el Teatro Real _____.

7. En el Palacio Real _____.

8. En la Puerta del Sol _____.

C. Una tortilla diferente. La tortilla española es un plato favorito en España. Completa la receta con formas impersonales para descubrir cómo se hace. (Sirve a siete u ocho personas.)

> Explica a un(a) compañero(a) de clase el proceso de planear una excursión y tu compañero(a) te va a explicar el proceso de planear una fiesta o una comida especial.

Ingredientes

1 docena de huevos	sal y pimienta
2 cebollas	aceite de oliva
1 kilo de papas	

(1) _____ (Picar *[To dice]*) la cebolla y (2) _____ (poner) a dorar *(to brown)*. (3) _____ (Pelar) y se pica el kilo de papas y, cuando esté dorada la cebolla, (4) _____ (freír) hasta estar suave *(tender)*. (5) _____ (Batir *[To beat]*) la docena de huevos y (6) _____ (poner) en la sartén con las papas y la cebolla. Cuando esté cocido un lado de la tortilla, (7) _____ (quitar) de la sartén y (8) _____ (poner) en un plato. (9) _____ (Agregar *[To add]*) un poco más aceite y luego (10) _____ (volver) a poner la tortilla en la sartén, pero con el lado crudo *(raw)* para abajo. (11) _____ (Cocinar) unos minutos más y (12) _____ (servir).

¿Sabías?  En España se come mucho pescado, arroz, mariscos y embutidos (*sausages*). Una deliciosa combinación de estos ingredientes con otros se llama la paella. Se sirve en muchas variaciones en todas partes de España. Otras comidas populares y famosas son el cordero asado (*roast lamb*) y lechón asado (*roast suckling pig*).

III. España: mosaico cultural

LECTURA

España es un mosaico de las influencias históricas y culturales que contribuyeron a su desarrollo como una nación. Situada en el extremo suroeste de Europa, separada de África **por** el Estrecho de Gibraltar y de Europa **por** los Pirineos, su posición geográfica permitió a muchos invasores llegar a sus fronteras. En el siglo III antes de Cristo llegaron los romanos y luego, en 409 de la era cristiana, las tribus germanas invadieron y dejaron su marca. En 711 los musulmanes cruzaron el Estrecho de Gibraltar y derrotaron al último Rey Godo, Rodrigo, y en 718 terminaron la conquista.

Durante la época musulmana, las artes y las ciencias florecieron, nuevas técnicas de agricultura fueron introducidas y muchos palacios, mesquitas,[1] escuelas y jardines fueron construidos.

En el año 722, el godo Pelayo y su ejército iniciaron la Reconquista **por** los cristianos y a fines[2] del siglo XV, Fernando e Isabel unificaron toda España e iniciaron la Edad de Oro de España. Con la derrota[3] de Granada en 1492, la Reconquista se acabó y los grupos no cristianos fueron expulsados **por** los cristianos.

Ahora bajo el mando de Fernando e Isabel, España inició exploraciones en el Nuevo Mundo **para** extender su imperio. Cristóbal Colón y otros conquistadores proclamaron las nuevas colonias bajo el reino español y regresaron **para** España con oro, plata y piedras preciosas, así estableciendo España como la nación más poderosa de la tierra.

Después de una serie de guerras en que el imperio español fue muy reducido, España pudo lograr una época pacífica y establecer un reino democrático bajo el rey don Juan Carlos.

Hoy en día, España es un país de muchos contrastes donde son evidentes todas las características de su rica historia.

---

[1]**mesquitas:** *mosques* / [2]**a fines:** *at the end* / [3]**derrota:** *defeat*

¿Comprendes?

1. ¿Cuáles son las grandes influencias culturales que se notan en España?
2. ¿Qué hicieron Fernando e Isabel para España?
3. ¿Quién es don Juan Carlos?

■ Las preposiciones *por* y *para*

Prepositions are used to relate the elements of a sentence, and while they may have the same uses in other languages, they often do not. The prepositions **por** and **para** may correspond to English *for,* but they are also used to convey specific ideas and are not synonyms.

Note the following meanings and uses:

A. *Para* indicates the purpose, objective, or finality of an action.

In order to

Estudio mucho **para** sacar buenas notas.	*I study a lot **in order to** earn good grades.*
Para llegar a Madrid, hay que tomar el tren.	***In order to** get to Madrid, one must take a train.*
Estudia **para** (ser) profesor de español.	*He's studying **to be** a professor of Spanish.*

For, as in relation to others, compared with others

Para Diego, es mejor que salga temprano.	*It's better **for** Diego to leave early.*
Eso no es bueno **para** ti.	*That's not good **for** you.*
Para un niño, es muy alto.	*He's tall **for** a child.*

For, as in intended for, given to

Este regalo es **para** ella.	*This gift is **for** her.*
¿Qué hiciste **para** mí?	*What did you do **for** me?*

For, as in the direction of, toward, destination

Salimos **para** Segovia.	*We left **for** Segovia.*
Caminan **para** el parque.	*They are walking **toward** the park.*

For, to, as to express an opinion

Para mí, es importante.	*It's important **to me**.*

For, or by a certain date, due

Esta composición es **para** el martes.	*This composition is **for (due on)** Tuesday.*

Estar para to indicate that an action is about to occur

El avión está **para** salir.	*The plane is **ready to (about to)** leave.*

B. *Por* indicates the motive, reason, or cause of an action.

Through, along, on, by

Ayer, caminamos **por** el parque central.	Yesterday, we walked **through** the central park.
Voy **por** esa avenida.	I go **along** this avenue.

By means of

Nos gustaba viajar **por** tren.	We liked to travel **by** train.
Prefieres viajar **por** avión.	You prefer to travel **by** plane.

During, in

Me puedes ver **por** la tarde.	You can see me **in** the afternoon.

For, as in a period of time

Estudiaron **por** dos horas.	They studied **for** two hours.

In exchange for as in price or equivalency

Ella pagó 300 pesetas **por** la blusa.	She paid 300 pesestas **for** the blouse.
Cambié la manzana **por** otra fruta.	I exchanged the apple **for** another fruit.

For, as in place of

¿Quiénes jugaron **por** ellos?	Who played **in place of (for)** them?

On account of, because of

Lo hice **por** ti.	I did it **on account of** you.

For the sake of

Lo hice **por** mis padres.	I did it **for** my parents.

To express per

El coche se da a siete **por** ciento.	The car is offered at seven **per**cent.
Iba a 70 millas **por** hora.	He was going 70 miles **per** hour.

To indicate the object of an action or the reason for an errand as with the verbs ir, venir, preguntar, mandar, and enviar

Envió los libros **por** correo.	**He sent** the books **by** mail.
Mario **preguntó por** ti.	Mario **asked about (for)** you.
Mamá **fue por** los niños.	Mother **went for** the children.

To indicate preference for someone or something

Voté **por** el mejor candidato.	I voted **for** the best candidate.
Somos **por** la igualdad en todo.	We are **for** equality in everything.

To indicate multiplication

Dos **por** seis son doce.	Two **times** six equals twelve.

Estar por to indicate to be about to do something, at the point of

Elena **estuvo por** decirle la verdad.	Elaine **was about to** tell him the truth.

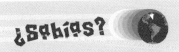

¿Sabías?

You are already familiar with a number of expressions using **por**:

¿Por qué? porque por favor por ejemplo

The preposition **por** is used with many exclamations and expressions.

por ahora	*for the time being*
por casualidad	*by chance*
por cierto	*in fact*
por consiguiente	*therefore*
¡Por Dios!	*For Heaven's (goodness') sake!*
por el estilo	*something like that*
por eso	*that's why, therefore*
por fin	*finally*
por lo general	*in general*
por lo menos	*at least*
por lo pronto	*for the moment*
por lo visto	*apparently*
por otra parte	*on the other hand*
por si acaso	*just in case*
por suerte	*luckily*
por supuesto	*of course*

Practiquemos

A. Preguntas y más preguntas. Luis quiere respuestas a sus preguntas. Usa **por** o **para** para hacer la pregunta y contestarla.

LUIS: ¿ _____ qué vas a la tienda?

FELIPE: _____ comprar unos recuerdos de Toledo.

LUIS: ¿Cuándo vas? ¿ _____ la mañana o _____ la tarde?

FELIPE: Creo que voy a ir _____ la tarde, después de mis clases.

LUIS: ¿ _____ quién son los recuerdos?

FELIPE: Bueno, son _____ mí y _____ Simón y Tina, mis hermanos.

LUIS: _____ lo menos, piensas en tus hermanos.

FELIPE: Bueno, ya me voy. Tengo mucho que hacer _____ mañana.

LUIS: Hasta luego, Felipe. Oye, ¡no olvides de comprar algo _____ tu amigo, Luis!

B. El Museo del Prado. Sara y sus amigos piensan ir al Museo del Prado. Completa el párrafo con **por** o **para** según el contexto.

Hoy es un día muy especial (1) _____ Sara y sus amigos que están (2) _____ salir de la casa (3) _____ encontrarse con sus otros amigos que los acompañan al Museo. (4) _____ llegar, tienen que tomar el autobús que pasa (5) _____ su casa; es muy conveniente (6) _____ ellos. El Museo es tan grande y tan bello. (7) _____ muchas personas, es una experiencia inolvidable poder admirar las obras de arte de muchos artistas españoles famosos como Goya, Velázquez, Dalí y Picasso. Diego estudia (8) _____ ser artista y (9) _____ consiguiente está muy entusiasmado con esta oportunidad. Fernando tiene ganas de ver las Meninas (10) _____ primera vez. Los amigos van a estar en España (11) _____ tres semanas y esperan pasar más tiempo en el Museo (12) _____ poder verlo todo.

C. Una visita a Toledo. Unos turistas están en Toledo. ¿Qué comentarios hacen? Completa las oraciones con una de las expresiones con **por**.

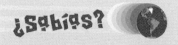

Con un(a) compañero(a), escribe una breve conversación usando *por lo menos tres expresiones con por* y tres oraciones que emplean *para*. Luego, preséntenla a la clase.

SANDRA: Amigos, _____ llegamos a Toledo. ¡Es magnífico!

SUSITA: Tienes razón. _____ se dice que es un monumento histórico.

TOMÁS: ¿Ven la Catedral? Es enorme y _____ ocupa un espacio grande en el centro de la ciudad.

JUAN: _____, hay muchos turistas que la visitan.

SUSITA: _____ llegamos temprano y no hay tanta gente aquí. Bueno, _____ tenemos mucha suerte.

SANDRA: Oigan, yo quiero ver el Alcázar. _____ estoy aquí.

TOMÁS: Sandra, ¡ _____! Tenemos todo el día. ¡Cálmate!

SANDRA: Bueno, _____ tengo mucha paciencia pero es que hoy me emociono con todo.

¿Sabías?

El arte florece en España. Entre los grandes artistas se reconocen nombres como Velázquez, Goya y El Greco. Sus obras influyeron a otros artistas de su época y los museos están llenos de sus pinturas famosas.

A ver si sabes

Use this self-test to see if you know the material presented in Chapter 14.

A. Opuestos. Cristina y Pablo siempre tienen opiniones contrarias. Basando tu respuesta en la opinión de Cristina, da la opinión de Pablo.

1. Cristina no cree que importe hacer mucho ejercicio.

   Pablo _____.

2. Cristina no duda que es importante trabajar todos los días.

   Pablo _____.

3. Cristina cree que los hombres deben pagar siempre cuando salen con las mujeres.

   Pablo _____.

4. Cristina dice que no es dudoso que la tecnología siempre representa el progreso.

   Pablo _____.

5. Cristina duda que la comida en España sea deliciosa.

   Pablo _____.

6. Cristina dice que es indudable que ella es más inteligente que Pablo.

   Pablo _____.

B. La sopa de ajo. Otro plato favorito en España es la sopa de ajo. Completa la receta para saber cómo se hace.

Ingredientes

2 dientes *(cloves)* de ajo
4 rebanadas *(slices)* de pan francés
2 cucharadas de aceite de oliva
sal y pimienta

(1) _____ (Quitar) la corteza *(crust)* del pan. (2) _____ (Picar) o (3) _____ (machacar *[to mash, pound]*) el ajo y (4) _____ (freír) en el aceite. Cuando esté dorado el ajo, (5) _____ (poner) el pan en la sartén y (6) _____ (freír) un poco. (7) _____ (Agregar *[to add]*) sal y pimienta al gusto. Luego (8) _____ (poner) la mezcla en un litro de agua fría y (9) _____ (hervir) por diez minutos. Si (10) _____ (querer), (11) _____ (poder) freír cuatro tomates con el pan y el ajo y agregar las yemas *(yolks)* de tres huevos inmediatamente antes de servir. Sirve a cuatro.

Preguntas culturales

1. ¿Cómo se puede caracterizar a Ana María Matute?

2. ¿Qué tipo de gobierno distingue a España de otras naciones de habla española?

3. ¿Por qué se dice que España es un mosaico de culturas?

C. Por fin. La profesora Santiago está planeando un viaje a España con un grupo de estudiantes. Completa la carta que escribió la profesora con **por** o **para**.

El 23 de mayo

Queridos estudiantes:

Pronto vamos a salir (1) _____ España y (2) _____ eso, tengo ganas de darles más información sobre el viaje. Necesito todos sus documentos (3) _____ el día 5 de junio (4) _____ poder finalizar nuestros planes. (5) _____ favor, tengan todo listo antes del viaje. (6) _____ suerte, tenemos un vuelo temprano (7) _____ no llegar tan cansados a Madrid. Primero, vamos a quedarnos en la capital (8) _____ poder disfrutar de todo lo que hay que ver en esta ciudad impresionante. Luego, vamos a viajar (9) _____ tren (10) _____ Sevilla (11) _____ visitar el Alcázar, el Parque de María Luisa y otros sitios importantes. Entonces, vamos (12) _____ tren a Barcelona (13) _____ admirar la iglesia Sagrada Familia, el Museo Picasso y la Fundación Joan Miró.

(14) _____ lo menos pueden descansar (15) _____que, (16) _____ supuesto, no tienen clases y pueden prepararse (17) _____ nuestra aventura. (18) _____ si acaso, les dejo mi número de teléfono.

Un fuerte abrazo,

Profesora Santiago

Querido Diario. Oíste un rumor que en tu trabajo piensan despedir *(to fire)* a muchas personas y se va a eliminar tu trabajo. Vas a explicar a tu diario por qué crees que tu puesto es indispensable y por qué dudas que se pueda hacer el trabajo de la compañía sin tu contribución. Para organizar tus pensamientos, haz una lista de todas tus contribuciones y otra lista de lo que va a perder la compañía sin tu presencia. Luego explica tus creencias y dudas a tu diario. Puedes empezar diciendo «Dudo que verdaderamente quieran despedirme».

Grammar: verbs: subjunctive with **que**
Phrases: expressing a wish or desire, expressing irritation, persuading
Vocabulary: emotions: positive, emotions: negative

Vocabulario activo

Direcciones

a la derecha	adelante	debajo de	enfrente de
a la izquierda	al lado de	delante de	la esquina
a mano derecha	atrás	derecho	
a mano izquierda	la cuadra	detrás de	

El tránsito   ## Las calles

El tránsito		Las calles
el alto	el paso de peatones	la acera
el autobús	el (la) peatón/	la autopista
el (la) conductor(a)	peatona	el camino
el metro	el semáforo	la carretera
la parada	el taxi	la senda

Los edificios

el almacén	la casa de bomberos	la legislatura
el banco	la comisaría de policía	el palacio
la biblioteca	el correo	el palacio de gobierno
el capitolio	la estatua	el palacio de justicia

Los verbos   ## La familia real

Los verbos			La familia real
bajar	(no) creer	retroceder	el (la) infante(a)
cruzar (z→c)	(no) dudar	saber	la princesa
doblar	(no) es cierto	seguir (e→i)	el príncipe
es dudoso	(no) es verdad	subir	la reina
es indudable	pasar	tomar	el rey

Las preposiciones y expresiones

para	por consiguiente	por lo general	por si acaso
por	¡Por Dios!	por lo menos	por suerte
por ahora	por el estilo	por lo pronto	por supuesto
por casualidad	por eso	por lo visto	
por cierto	por fin	por otra parte	

Web site:
http://spanishforlife.heinle.com

Transparencies:
A–4: **América del Sur**
A–13: Country Profile, **Chile**

Arica

Iquique

Antofagasta

CHILE

Valparaíso

Santiago

Concepción

Valdivia

Puerto
Montt

**ISLA
CHILOÉ**

Coihaique

Puerto
Natales

Punta
Arenas

REPÚBLICA DE CHILE

Nombre oficial: República de Chile

Área: 736.903 km^2

Población: 14.700.000

Capital: Santiago

Moneda: el peso

Idioma oficial: español

Fiesta nacional: 18 de septiembre,
Día de la Independencia

Chile y los chilenos

Los canotieres costarricences fondean las montañas del Parque Nacional Nicaragua-Chileno

In this chapter you will learn:

GRAMMAR POINTS

- Subjunctive with nonexistent and indefinite antecedents
- Passive voice with **se** and with **ser** + past participle
- Adverbs
- Ordinal numbers

COMMUNICATIVE FUNCTIONS

- State desired characteristics
- Describe things, people, jobs

VOCABULARY

- World of work
- Hunting for a job

I. Chile: un país de contrastes deportivos

LECTURA

Mucha gente **no quiere visitar ciudades que tengan** museos o mercados sino que[1] **busca lugares que ofrezcan** una variedad de actividades deportivas **o lugares que tengan** oportunidades para disfrutar de la naturaleza. De hecho, Chile les ofrece a todos muchas oportunidades para satisfacer cualquier interés deportivo.

La gran variedad geográfica chilena atrae a miles de turistas anualmente. **A los que les guste** dar una caminata o acampar, el Parque Nacional del Paine en Magallanes y el Parque Nacional Lauca son ideales. También el Parque Nacional Laguna San Rafael en Patagonia tiene unos terrenos montañosos que atraen a los alpinistas expertos. A causa de la cantidad y variedad, los parques nacionales en Chile son perfectos para **las personas que quieran encontrar** oportunidades para montar a bicicleta terreno y a caballo.

Para los **esquiadores que necesiten** la inclinación[2] perfecta para probar sus destrezas,[3] hay muchos sitios invernales populares como el Valle Nevado. La Isla de Pascua tiene excelentes oportunidades para esquiar. Además,[4] se dice que es más económica y hay menos gente.

Finalmente, para **los turistas que tengan interés** en correr las olas del río en balsa[5] **no hay lugar que ofrezca** el desafío último como los Ríos Maipo, Claro y Biobío.

---

[1]**sino que:** *but rather* / [2]**inclinación:** *slope* / [3]**destrezas:** *skills* / [4]**Además:** *Besides* / [5]**correr las olas del río en balsa:** *to go river rafting*

¿Comprendes?

1. ¿Adónde va la gente para esquiar en Chile?
2. ¿Qué oportunidades ofrece la Isla de Pascua?

■ Usos del subjuntivo: antecedentes indefinidos

To describe a noun, an adjective is sometimes used.

Compré un libro **interesante**.   *I bought an **interesting** book.*

Other times, a group of words is used to describe a noun. A group of words that functions like an adjective and includes a conjugated verb is called an *adjective clause*. The noun described by such a clause is known as the *antecedent*.

Compré el **libro que me interesaba**.   *I bought the **book that interested me**.*

In this sentence **libro** is the antecedent and **que me interesaba** is the adjective clause that modifies it.

Antecedentes indefinidos

English has no way of distinguishing between a definite, existing antecedent and one that is indefinite or unknown. In the sentence "My cousin wants to marry a woman who is beautiful," we have no clue as to whether he has found a specific woman who is beautiful or wants to find a beautiful woman who will marry him. Spanish, on the other hand, can distinguish between these two meanings by using the indicative or subjunctive mood.

Mi primo quiere casarse con **una mujer que es** hermosa.

The indicative mood in the sentence above indicates that the intended bride is a real person who is beautiful.

Mi primo quiere casarse con **una mujer que sea** hermosa.

The subjunctive mood above indicates that the cousin's ideal bride is beautiful, but he hasn't found her yet.

The subjunctive mood is frequently used in clauses that follow such verbs as **buscar**, **necesitar**, and **querer**, which are used when a goal is sought.

Se busca secretaria que **sepa** mecanografía.	*(We are) Seeking a secretary who knows typing.*
Quiero ver una película que me **entretenga**.	*I want to see a movie that will entertain me.*

However, these verbs are not always associated with the subjunctive mood. If you are familiar with what you are *looking for,* then you need to use the indicative mood.

Necesito el informe que **está** en mi escritorio.	*I need the report that is on my desk.*
Buscan la pluma que **tiene** tinta azul.	*They are looking for the pen that has blue ink.*

Los antecedentes que son complementos directos

Normally, when a definite person is the direct object of a sentence, it is preceded by the personal **a**.

Conocí **a** un poeta.	*I met a poet.*
Vi **a** una señora muy distinguida.	*I saw a very distinguished woman.*

However, an indefinite, unknown human direct object is not preceded by **a**.

Se necesita cocinero.	*Cook needed.*

If these indefinite, unknown nouns are described by a clause, the verb in that clause is in the subjunctive mood.

Se necesita **cocinero** que **sepa**   *Cook needed who knows*
cocina francesa.   *French cuisine.*

¿Conoces una **persona** que **hable**   *Do you know a person who*
quechua?   *speaks quechua?*

An exception to this rule is the indefinite pronoun **alguien** *(anyone)*, which always requires the personal **a** when it is the direct object of a sentence.

¿Conoces **a alguien** que **sepa**   *Do you know anyone who*
quechua?   *knows quechua?*

Of course, nonhuman direct objects are not preceded by **a**.

Practiquemos

A. En el restaurante. Todos los empleados del Lobo Marino renunciaron *(resigned)* sus puestos recientemente. ¿Qué tipo de personal *(personnel)* se busca ahora en el restaurante? Combina **Se busca** con los elementos indicados para describir los empleados deseados.

MODELO: portero / limpiar bien
               Se busca portero que limpie bien.

1. cocinero / conocer / cocina indígena
2. contador / tener / experiencia
3. meseros / hablar / varias lenguas
4. maitre d' / ser / amable
5. gerente / planear / un menú interesante

B. Vamos a Chile. Tenemos planes para ir a Chile y necesitamos varias cosas para realizar nuestros planes. Completa cada oración con una de las terminaciones abajo en la forma correcta: **incluir unos días en los Andes, ir a la Isla de Pascua, saber mucho del país, ser divertido, ser lujoso** *(luxurious)*, **ser muy atento** *(attentive)*.

MODELO: *Todos queremos un viaje que sea divertido.*

1. Buscamos un hotel que _____.
2. Tenemos una agencia de viajes que _____.
3. Queremos encontrar un guía que _____.
4. Mi compañero encontró una excursión que _____
5. Otros compañeros tienen interés en un viaje que _____.

C. Mi ideal. ¿Cuáles son tus ideales? ¿Qué deseas? Describe tu ideal de cada categoría.

MODELO: película
               Busco una película que
               sea interesante y divertida,
               que tenga actores muy
               buenos y que me dé información.

Explica a tu compañero(a) tus ideales y compáralas con los de tu compañero(a). ¿Qué tienen en común? ¿Cómo difieren?

1. casa _____

4. amigo(a) _____

2. carro _____

5. trabajo _____

3. compañero(a)/esposo(a) _____

■ Usos del subjuntivo: antecedentes indefinidos y negativos

Antecedentes negativos

When we negate or deny the existence of a noun, we remove it from the objective, real world and we assign it to the world of unreality, part of the subjunctive world. When a negated or denied noun is the antecedent described by a clause, then the verb of that clause is in the subjunctive mood.

No hay cocinero que **sepa** cocina francesa.

There is no cook who ***knows*** *French cuisine.*

Dudo que existan estudiantes que **puedan** entender esto.

I doubt that students exist who ***can*** *understand this.*

Antecedentes indefinidos que son complementos directos

Like **alguien, nadie** *(nobody)* requires the personal **a** when it functions as the direct object. The indefinite adjective **ningún, ninguno(a)**, also requires **a** when it modifies a direct object noun.

No conozco **a nadie** que **hable** quechua.

*I don't know **anybody** who speaks quechua.*

No conozco **a ningún chileno** que **viva** en Atacama.

*I don't know **any Chilean** who lives in Atacama.*

Other human direct objects that are negated or denied are *not* preceded by **a**. Note also that the indefinite article (**un[a]**) is often omitted before negated nouns, both human and nonhuman.

No hay secretaria que sepa taquigrafía.

There is no secretary who *knows shorthand.*

Practiquemos

A. En mi trabajo. Combina los elementos de las cuatro columnas para saber cuáles son los deseos y las necesidades de mi oficina.

A	B	C	D
		secretario	cobrar poco
yo	buscar	gerente	ser económico
el jefe	necesitar	empleo	pagar bien
mis compañeros	querer	computadora	estar cerca
tú y yo	(no) tener	contador	ser justo
tú	(no) encontrar	carro	saber bien su
	(no) conocer	restaurante	trabajo
			funcionar bien

Transparency:
M–4: **Buscar empleo**

B. Sobre Chile. Contesta estas preguntas sobre Chile. Algunas respuestas van a ser negativas y otras afirmativas.

MODELO: ¿Buscan Uds. un sitio que tenga la oportunidad de
esquiar?
No, no buscamos sitio que tenga la oportunidad de
esquiar. **o**
No, ya conocemos un sitio que ofrece la oportunidad de
esquiar. **o**
Sí, buscamos un sitio que tenga la oportunidad de esquiar.

1. ¿Hay una isla donde se pueda esquiar en Chile?
2. ¿Conoces una región donde haga mucho frío?
3. ¿Dónde hay un puerto chileno que tenga mucho tráfico internacional?
4. ¿Necesitas un mapa que enseñe la geografía de Chile?
5. ¿Se puede encontrar un libro que hable de Chile en tu biblioteca?

❖ Para hablar de los trabajos

Antes de conseguir el empleo

el/la candidato(a)	*candidate*
la cita (previa)	*(previous) appointment*
el contrato (contratar)	*contract (to contract, hire)*
la cualificación	*qualification*
el/la director(a) de personal	*personnel director*
la entrevista (entrevistar)	*interview (to interview)*
la exigencia	*requirement, demand*
la experiencia	*experience*
la referencia	*reference*
solicitar (la solicitud)	*to apply (application)*

En el trabajo

el cheque semanal	*weekly check*
el comité	*committee*
contratar (emplear)	*to hire*
despedir (e→i, i)	*to fire*
los días laborales	*work days*
el/la gerente	*manager*
el pago mensual	*monthly pay*
renunciar	*to resign*
el sueldo anual	*annual salary*

¿Cuáles son las características de tu trabajo actual *(current)*? ¿Cuáles son negativas y cuáles son positivas? ¿Cuáles son las características de tu trabajo ideal?

Las prestaciones	Benefits
los días de vacaciones	*vacation days*
el seguro de salud	*health insurance*
el seguro social	*social security*

Relaciones laborales	Labor Relations
el acuerdo	*agreement*
el desempleo	*unemployment*
estar de acuerdo con	*to agree with*
la huelga	*strike*
el paro	*lockout, layoff*
el sindicato	*union*

Practiquemos

A. Se busca trabajo. Cuando se busca un trabajo, ¿qué características son deseables? Comenta sobre las características siguientes e indica si cada una es algo que se busca o no se busca.

MODELO: seguro social
          No se busca seguro social.

1. seguro de salud
2. sindicato
3. mucho trabajo en comité
4. cheque semanal
5. historia de huelgas

¿Sabías?

Aunque parezca extraño para un país hispanoamericano, se asocia el nombre de Bernardo O'Higgins con uno de los grandes líderes chilenos. O'Higgins, irlandés de nacimiento, fue el héroe nacional de la independencia de Chile en 1818.

II. Chile: país único

Los moai de la Isla de Pascua

LECTURA

Chile tiene rasgos típicos de otros países latinos pero también ofrece características únicas. Chile, con Argentina, linda[1] el Estrecho de Magallanes, un pasaje del Océano Atlántico al Pacífico que permite que las naves eviten pasar por el Cabo de Hornos. El Estrecho de Magallanes separa la isla de Tierra del Fuego del resto de América de Sur. En esta isla, conocida por sus fuertes vientos casi constantes, **se crían**[2] ovejas[3] y ganado[4] y los turistas pueden ver la esquila[5] de ovejas. Aquí **se encuentra** el Parque Nacional Torres de Paine, donde **se pueden admirar** bosques, ríos, lagos, glaciares y muchos animales.

Otra faceta interesante de Chile es un número de islas que están por la costa. Chiloé y las Islas de Juan Fernández que **fueron estudiadas por** Charles Darwin son las más famosas. Las especies de plantas y animales que son similares, pero también distintas de otras especies del continente, ayudaron a Darwin a desarrollar su teoría de evolución.

Un tercer punto de mucho interés es la Isla de Pascua o Rapa Nui. Está situada lejos de Chile en medio del Océano Pacífico, y la mayor parte de la población actual es polinesia. Pero unos habitantes anteriores ocupaban la isla y hasta hoy **se pueden ver** las pruebas de su estancia:[6] los *moai*. Son estatuas enormes de piedra (50–200 metros) que **son** muy **estudiadas** pero no **comprendidas** completamente, y todavía **se encuentran** allí. **Se sabe** muy poco de los creadores de estos monolitos, pero los podemos admirar hoy en día.[7]

---

[1]**linda:** borders on / [2]**se crían:** are raised / [3]**ovejas:** sheep / [4]**ganado:** cattle / [5]**esquila:** sheering / [6]**estancia:** stay / [7]**hoy en día:** nowadays

¿Comprendes?

1. ¿Por qué es importante el Estrecho de Magallanes?
2. ¿Qué interés tienen las Islas de Juan Fernández y la Isla de Pascua?

◼ La voz pasiva

Spanish and English both have two voices: *active* and *passive*. In the active voice, the subject of the sentence is the *agent* (or actor) and the topic of the sentence; the direct object of the verb is the *patient* (receiver of the action).

(Yo) Leo **muchos libros**.   *I read **a lot of books**.*

Here the agent is **yo** and the patient is **muchos libros**. This sentence is about what *I* do. But sometimes it is more important to focus on the patient, and this is what the *passive voice* does: it puts the focus of the sentence on the *patient*.

Spanish has two ways of forming the passive voice. One form, derived from the Latin passive, is formed like the English passive but is not very common in Spanish and will be examined later (on pp. 333–334). The more common passive constructions use the pronoun **se**.

La voz pasiva con *se*

In a passive sentence with **se**, **se** accompanies the verb and the subject is the *patient* rather than the agent. The verb is always in the third-person singular or plural, depending on the number of the subject (patient).

NOTA: Placement of the subject after the verb is much more common than placing it before the verb.

se + verb (*sing.* or *pl.*) + subject   or   subject + **se** + verb (*sing.* or *pl.*)

Se leen muchos libros.	A lot of books **are read**.
Se vendió la casa la semana pasada.	The house **was sold** last week.
No se puede ver el mar desde Santiago.	The sea **can't be seen** from Santiago.

The preceding construction is used when the subject is nonhuman. When the subject is a person, the following form is used:

se + singular verb + **a** + patient

Se invitó a María.	María **was invited**.
Se veía a Darwin en las islas.	Darwin **was seen** on the islands.

If saying the name of the patient would be repetitive, the direct object pronouns **lo/la** or **los/las** are used.

Se la invitó.	*She was (You [fem. sing.] were) invited.*
Se los ve frecuentemente.	*They are (You [pl.] were) seen frequently.*

Practiquemos

A. En Chile. ¿Cuáles son las atracciones de Chile? Forma oraciones pasivas con **se** y los elementos indicados.

MODELO: comprar muchos recuerdos
           Se compran muchos recuerdos.

1. ver volcanes activos
2. subir las montañas
3. comer comida rica
4. visitar museos interesantes
5. escuchar música popular

B. Fiesta familiar. Los preparativos para la fiesta de cumpleaños de la tía Consuelo ya se hicieron. ¿Qué se hizo? Usa los sustantivos con uno de los siguientes verbos para formar oraciones lógicas: **comprar, contratar, hacer, invitar, mandar, poner.**

MODELO: torta
           Se hizo la torta.

1. invitaciones
2. familia
3. comida

4. músicos
5. mesa

C. La casa. Estás listo(a) para divertirte porque ya se hicieron los quehaceres de la casa. ¿Qué se hizo? Usando cinco verbos diferentes, forma oraciones lógicas acerca de las cosas indicadas.

Compara con tu compañero(a) las cosas que se tienen que hacer en tu casa cada día.

Transparency:
C–6: **Los quehaceres de la casa**

MODELO: la ropa
Se planchó la ropa.

1. coche
2. pisos
3. césped

4. muebles
5. camas

■ El participio pasado (pasivo)

In order to form the other passive voice in Spanish (sometimes called the true passive), you need to know how to form the past participle (also called the passive participle). The past participles of regular Spanish verbs end in **-ado** (**-ar** verbs) or **-ido** (**-er**, **-ir** verbs).

-ar verbs: *infinitive* minus **ar** plus **ado**
-er, **-ir** verbs: *infinitive* minus **er**, **ir** plus **ido**

Past Participles		
hablar	habl-	**hablado**
viajar	viaj-	**viajado**
aprender	aprend-	**aprendido**
poder	pod-	**podido**
repetir	repet-	**repetido**
vivir	viv-	**vivido**

Some Spanish past participles are irregular and must be memorized.

abrir	**abierto**
cubrir	**cubierto**
decir	**dicho**
escribir	**escrito**
freír	**frito** (*also* **freído**)
hacer	**hecho** (satisfacer *[to satisfy]* **satisfecho**)
morir	**muerto**
poner	**puesto**
romper	**roto**
ver	**visto**
volver	**vuelto** (resolver *[to resolve]* **resuelto**)

The past participle of all -er and -ir verbs with stems ending in -a, -e, -o requires accented í:

creer **creído**   oír **oído**   traer **traído**

Practiquemos

A. Pares. Da los participios pasados de estas actividades asociadas.

1. discutir y resolver
2. escribir y leer
3. decir y hacer
4. ver y oír
5. abrir y cerrar

B. Mis asociaciones. Escribe una lista de cinco pares más de palabras que tú asocias y luego da los participios.

MODELO: *comer y beber*
            comido y bebido

1. _____   3. _____   5. _____
2. _____   4. _____

■ La voz pasiva con *ser*

The other Spanish passive form follows a construction similar to English:

English

subject (patient) + *to be* + past participle (+ *by* + agent)

These sonnets *were written by* Shakespeare.

Spanish

subject (patient) + **ser** + past participle (+ **por** + agent)

Don Quijote **fue escrito por** Miguel de Cervantes.

Don Quijote ***was written by*** Miguel de Cervantes.

The verb **ser** can be in any tense, but if it's in the past, the preterite is more commonly used than the imperfect.

Since the past participle in Spanish passive sentences follows **ser**, it agrees with the subject (patient) in number and gender.

La novela fue **escrita** por Cervantes.

*The novel was **written** by Cervantes.*

El poema fue **escrito** por Neruda.

*The poem was **written** by Neruda.*

Las novelas fueron **escritas** por Cervantes.

*The novels were **written** by Cervantes.*

Los poemas fueron **escritos** por Neruda.

*The poems were **written** by Neruda.*

This passive form with **ser** is used primarily in writing, especially in journalism, and very rarely in speech.

Practiquemos

A. Datos sobre Chile. Convierte las oraciones activas en oraciones pasivas.

MODELO: Pedro de Valdivia fundó Santiago en 1541.
Santiago fue fundado por Pedro de Valdivia en 1541.

1. Los indios diaguitos cultivaban Coquimbo.
2. Los españoles iniciaron los latifundios *(tenant farms)*.
3. Las vicuñas, animales en peligro, habitan las regiones altas.
4. En 1973, Augusto Pinochet derrocó *(overturned)* el gobierno constitucional de Salvador Allende.
5. Los chilenos eligieron a Patricio Aylwin en 1989.

Escribe una lista de cinco preguntas históricas (e.g., «¿Quién descubrió América?») y hazlas a un(a) compañero(a) de clase. Tu compañero(a) debe responder con la voz pasiva (e.g., «América fue descubierta por Colón.»).

III. Gabriela Mistral: tesoro nacional chileno

LECTURA

Gabriela Mistral se reconoce **principalmente** como maestra, amante de la humanidad y poeta.

Gabriela Mistral nació Lucila Godoy Alcayaga en 1889 en la provincia de Coquembo. De joven, se dedicaba a sus estudios; reconoció **temprano** la importancia de una buena educación. Tal era su dedicación al mundo académico que pasó muchos años educando a la juventud chilena. Enseñó en escuelas rurales, secundarias y primarias. Su fama como educadora creció **rápidamente** hasta el nivel internacional. **Indudablemente**, Mistral logró gran éxito en la reforma educacional chilena y mexicana; el Ministro de Educación Mexicana la invitó a participar en su reforma educacional en 1922.

Bajo su nombre literario, Gabriela Mistral, ella expresaba en su poesía su amor a la humanidad, a los niños, a los pobres y, **frecuentemente**, a la naturaleza. Publicó muchos libros de poesía en los cuales describía **profunda** e **íntimamente** su amor a todo lo creado.[1] Ganó el Premio Nóbel de Literatura en 1945.

De su mejor libro, *Desolación,* viene el poema «Los que no danzan».[2]

Una niña que es inválida
dijo: «Cómo danzo yo?»
Le dijimos que pusiera
a danzar su corazón…
Luego dijo la quebrada:[3]
«Cómo cantaría yo?»
Le dijimos que pusiera
a cantar su corazón…

---

[1]**todo lo creado:** *all creation* / [2]**danzan:** *dance* / [3]**quebrada:** *frail child*

¿Comprendes?

1. Describe a Gabriela Mistral la maestra.
2. ¿Cómo interpretas el poema «Los que no danzan»?

■ Los adverbios

Adverbs are words that modify verbs, adjectives, and other adverbs.
There are four types of adverbs:

Time (answers the question *when?*)	
ahora	*now*
anoche	*last night*
de noche	*at night*
por la mañana, etc.	*in the morning, etc.*
temprano	*early*

Manner (answers the question *how?*)	
bastante	*rather, enough*
bien	*well, fine*
felizmente, etc.	*happily, etc.*
mal	*badly*

Frequency (answers the question *how often?*)	
a veces	*sometimes*
generalmente	*generally*
siempre	*always*
todos los días	*every day*

Place (answers the question *where?*)	
ahí	*there*
allí, allá	*over there*
aquí	*here*
debajo, etc.	*beneath, etc.*

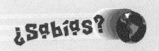

¿Sabías?

El nombre «chile» se deriva de la palabra aymará que significa «confines de la tierra». Se dice así porque Chile está casi totalmente aislado del resto de América del Sur por la cordillera de los Andes.

Para formar adverbios de adjetivos

Adverbs are also formed by adding -**mente** to the feminine singular form of the adjective. This is like adding *-ly* in English. If the adjective has an accent mark, then the adverb retains the accent.

Adjective	Adverb	English
tranquilo	tranquilamente	*calmly, tranquilly*
sospechoso	sospechosamente	*suspiciously*
rápido	rápidamente	*fast, rapidly*

Adjectives that do not have a separate feminine form add -**mente** to the singular.

feliz	felizmente	*happily*
cortés	cortésmente	*courteously*
triste	tristemente	*sadly*

> Con un(a) compañero(a) de clase, prepara una lista de tres cosas que haces rápida, lenta y cuidadosamente. Luego compartan su lista con la clase.

Adverbs are generally placed before adjectives or after the verb they modify.

Es **verdaderamente** imposible. *It's **really** impossible.*
Dormían **tranquilamente**. *They were sleeping **peacefully**.*

If two or more adverbs are used in a series, only the last takes the -**mente** ending.

Comían **lenta** y **felizmente**. *They were eating **slowly** and **happily**.*

Practiquemos

A. ¡A esquiar! Mateo y sus amigos pasan una semana esquiando en Valle Nevado, Chile. ¿Qué hacen? Primero, convierte los adjetivos de la siguiente lista en adverbios. Después, completa las oraciones con un adverbio adecuado.

a. exacto	**d.** rápido	**g.** regular
b. cuidadoso	**e.** lento	**h.** inteligente
c. tranquilo	**f.** feliz	**i.** inmediato

1. Mario y Mateo limpian _____ sus esquís.

2. Susita lee _____ delante de la chimenea.

3. Marta y yo esquiamos la inclinación _____.

4. Humberto y tú esquían _____. ¡Son expertos!

5. En una emergencia en las montañas, los amigos actúan _____ e _____.

B. De joven. ¿Qué hacías y con qué frecuencia hacías estas cosas de joven? Combina los siguientes elementos usando el imperfecto y un adverbio.

M O D E L O :   *Cuando era joven jugaba al tenis constantemente.*

Verbo	Adverbio
salir con amigos	nunca
jugar al tenis	de vez en cuando
hacer mis tareas	siempre
visitar a mis abuelos	generalmente
estudiar	todos los días
hacer ejercicio	frecuentemente
descansar	constantemente
hablar por teléfono	mensualmente

C. ¿Cómo? Contesta las preguntas que hacen los turistas en Chile. Usa los siguientes adverbios: **tranquilamente, constantemente, generalmente, intensamente, locamente, frecuentemente, felizmente, increíblemente**.

1. Los turistas consultan el diccionario _____.

2. Simón come _____.

3. Cambio mis cheques de viajero _____.

4. Magda y yo esquiamos _____ en Valle Nevado.

5. Tú dices que Chile es _____ bonito.

¿Sabías?

Salvador Allende, ex-presidente de Chile, trató de iniciar una transición positiva al socialismo, favoreciendo las clases bajas, pero fracasó. Murió el 11 de septiembre de 1973 durante un bombardeo de la casa de gobierno. Hasta hoy no se sabe si se suicidó o fue asesinado. En 1990 se trasladaron sus restos de una tumba anónima al panteón de su familia, donde los chilenos pueden darle el tributo que merece.

IV. Pablo Neruda: chileno esencial

LECTURA

Otro tesoro chileno es Pablo Neruda, nacido Neftalí Ricardo Reyes en 1904, escritor que ganó el Premio Nóbel de Literatura en 1971. Como los poemas de Mistral, Neruda escribía frecuentemente su amor por el mundo en que vivía en sus poemas profundos y románticos. Neruda escribió apasionadamente sus versos líricos.

En los poemas de Neruda, se nota principalmente una evolución dramática. En sus **primeros** libros, combinó sus creencias políticas e ideológicas con su arte poética. Más tarde, sus creaciones solían ser[1] más espirituales, enigmáticas y sutiles. Su poesía abarca[2] un mundo de símbolos e imágenes personales, así rompiendo las formas tradicionales de la poesía.

De su *Veinte poemas de amor y una canción desesperada,* una de sus **primeras** obras y publicada en 1924, viene la siguiente estrofa (del **décimoquinto** poema):

> Me gustas cuando callas porque estás como ausente,
> y me oyes desde lejos, y mi voz no te toca.
> Parece que los ojos se te hubieran volado
> y parece que un beso te cerrara la boca.

[1]**solían ser:** *tended to be* / [2]**abarca:** *encompasses*

¿Comprendes?

1. ¿Siguió siempre Pablo Neruda las formas tradicionales de la poesía?
2. ¿Cómo escribió Neruda sus versos líricos?

NOTA:

Primero and **tercero** drop the final **-o** before a masculine singular noun. Also, **primero** is the only ordinal number that can also be used as an adverb.

■ Los números ordinales

Ordinal numbers are used to place things, events, or people in a series. They may be used as pronouns or as adjectives.

primer, primero	*first*	sexto	*sixth*
segundo	*second*	séptimo	*seventh*
tercer, tercero	*third*	octavo	*eighth*
cuarto	*fourth*	noveno	*ninth*
quinto	*fifth*	décimo	*tenth*

As adjectives, ordinal numbers generally precede the nouns they modify and must agree in gender and number.

Hoy es el **primer** examen.	*Today is the **first** exam.*
Mañana leemos la **segunda** parte.	*Tomorrow we will read the **second** part.*
Primeramente, tenemos que estudiar.	***First of all (Firstly)**, we have to study.*

The equivalents of *secondly, thirdly,* etc., do not exist in Spanish; **segundo, tercero,** etc., are used instead.

When referring to royalty, the ordinal number follows the noun.

Carlos **V (Quinto)**	*Charles **the Fifth***
Isabel **II (Segunda)**	*Elizabeth **the Second***

Although cardinal numbers are often used to express ordinal numbers higher than ten, there are ordinal forms for these numbers. They vary in form, however. A rather complicated form may be used, but the form with the suffix **-avo** is simpler and used more frequently. All possible forms are presented here. You may recognize the **-avo** ending from the familiar word **centavo**, meaning both *hundredth* and *cent*.

> Con un(a) compañero(a), discute la primera, segunda, tercera y cuarta cosa que haces todos los días.

Ordinal Numbers			
onceavo (onceno, undécimo)	*eleventh*	dieciseisavo (décimosexto)	*sixteenth*
dozavo (duodécimo)	*twelfth*	diecisieteavo (decimoséptimo)	*seventeenth*
trezavo (décimotercio)	*thirteenth*	dieciochavo (décimoctavo)	*eighteenth*
décimocuarto	*fourteenth*	diecinueveavo (décimonono)	*nineteenth*
quinzavo (décimoquinto)	*fifteenth*	veintavo (vigésimo)	*twentieth*
treintavo (trigésimo)	*thirtieth*	setentavo (setegésimo)	*seventieth*
cuarentavo (cuadragésimo)	*fortieth*	ochentavo (octogésimo)	*eightieth*
cincuentavo (quincuagésimo)	*fiftieth*	noventavo (nonagésimo)	*ninetieth*
sesentavo (sexagésimo)	*sixtieth*	centavo (centésimo)	*one hundredth*

Practiquemos

A. ¿En qué orden? Pon en orden lo que hace una persona para prepararse para una entrevista para un nuevo empleo.

llenar la solicitud
vestirse bien
planear una fiesta para celebrar
estudiar las cualificaciones
pedir las referencias

hablar con el/la director(a)
    de personal
recoger la solicitud
hacer una cita
leer el anuncio del puesto
prepararse para la entrevista

MODELO: *La primera cosa que se hace es...*

1. _____   3. _____   5. _____   7. _____   9. _____

2. _____   4. _____   6. _____   8. _____   10. _____

B. En el estadio. ¿Dónde se sientan los fanáticos en el estadio? Usa los números ordinales para indicar sus asientos.

1. Pablo se sienta en la _____ fila, el _____ asiento. (*20th, 8th*)

2. Los novios se sientan en la _____ fila, el _____ asiento. (*17th, 10th*)

3. El papá del mejor jugador se sienta en la _____ fila, el _____ asiento. (*1st, 1st*)

4. Tú te sientas en la _____ fila, el _____ asiento. (*30th, 6th*)

5. Yo me siento en la _____ fila, el _____ asiento. (*40th, 2nd*)

Preguntas culturales
1. Si quieres hacer algo deportivo en Chile, ¿adónde vas según tus intereses?
2. ¿Qué rasgos distintivos tiene Chile?
3. ¿Cómo son los poemas de Gabriela Mistral?
4. ¿Cómo cambió la poesía de Pablo Neruda?

A ver si sabes

A. No encuentro. Completa las oraciones con la forma apropiada del subjuntivo o indicativo de los verbos que siguen: **escribir, parecer, perder, saber, terminar.**

1. Necesito encontrar mi bolígrafo que _____ la semana pasada.
2. No puedo trabajar si no tengo un bolígrafo que _____ bien.
3. ¿Dónde está ese informe que el comité _____ ayer?
4. En mi escritorio no hay nada que _____ ser informe.
5. ¿No hay nadie que _____ dónde está el informe o mi bolígrafo?

B. La comida. La familia Gómez ya terminó una cena especial para unos amigos íntimos. ¿Qué se hizo? Forma oraciones pasivas con **se** usando los siguientes verbos y los sustantivos dados: beber, lavar, poner, preparar, servir.

1. la mesa
2. unos platillos riquísimos
3. un postre especial
4. el café
5. los platos

C. En la oficina. ¿Cómo trabaja Elena? Llena cada espacio en blanco con el adverbio indicado.

1. _____ (Primero), Elena siempre llega _____ (puntual) a su oficina.
2. Escribe _____ y _____ (rápido, cuidadoso) en la computadora.
3. Sabe _____ (exacto) lo que tiene que hacer todos los días.
4. Piensa _____ y _____ (claro, lógico) en todo.
5. La jefa está _____ (completo, contenta) con el trabajo de Elena.

D. La familia. ¿Qué pasa en la familia Salas? Completa las oraciones con un número ordinal.

1. La familia acaba de comprar una casa. Es la _____ *(1ˢᵗ)* vez que no vive en un departamento.
2. La casa tiene dos pisos. La cocina está en el _____ *(1ˢᵗ)* piso y las recámaras están en el _____ *(2ⁿᵈ)* piso.
3. Hay tres baños. Las visitas usan el baño en el _____ *(1ˢᵗ)* piso y la familia suele usar el _____ *(2ⁿᵈ)* baño y el _____ *(3ʳᵈ)* baño en el _____ *(2ⁿᵈ)* piso.
4. La familia es muy grande. Ya tiene cuatro hijos y pronto la Sra. Salas va a dar a luz al _____ *(5ᵗʰ)* niño.
5. ¡Ésta es la _____ *(5ᵗʰ)* vez que los papás esperan a un niño!

Querido Diario. Vas a compartir con tu diario tus metas e ideales para el futuro. Primero, escoge tres o cuatro cosas que quieres tener como parte de tu vida en el futuro, por ejemplo, una familia, una carrera, una casa, un viaje, etc. Después, escribe en tu diario las características que quieres tener en cada categoría. Puedes empezar diciendo «En el futuro quiero un(a)... que... y... ».

Grammar: verbs: subjunctive in relative clauses
Phrases: describing health, objects, people, places; expressing a wish or desire
Vocabulary: house; family members; leisure; working conditions

Vocabulario activo

Antes de consequir el empleo

el/la candidato(a)
la cita (previa)
el contrato (contratar)
la cualificación

el/la director(a) de personal
la entrevista (entrevistar)
la exigencia
la experiencia

la referencia
solicitar (la solicitud)

En el trabajo

el cheque semanal
el comité
contratar (emplear)
despedir (e→i, i)
los días laborales
el/la gerente

el pago mensual
renunciar
el sueldo anual

Las prestaciones

los días de
  vacaciones
el seguro de salud
el seguro social

Relaciones laborales

el acuerdo
el desempleo
estar de acuerdo con
la huelga
el paro
el sindicato

Adverbios

de tiempo
ahora
anoche
de noche
por la mañana, etc.
temprano

de frecuencia
a veces
generalmente
siempre
todos los días

de manera
bastante
bien
felizmente
mal

de lugar
ahí
allí, allá
aquí
debajo, etc.

Los números ordinales   *See pp. 338–339.*

Transparencies:
A–4: La América del Sur
A–13: Country Profile, Bolivia

BOLIVIA

Río Beni

Trinidad

Lago Titicaca

★La Paz

Viacha

Colquiri Cochabamba

Oruro

Portachuelo •Montero

• Santa Cruz

San Ignacio de Velasco

San José de Chiquitos

CORDILLERA DE LOS ANDES

Vallegrande

Lago Poopó

★Sucre

Potosí

Tarija•

REPÚBLICA DE BOLIVIA

Nombre oficial: República de Bolivia

Área: 1.098.581 km^2

Población: 7.670.000

Capitales: Sucre (constitucional),
La Paz (sede de gobierno)

Moneda: el boliviano

Idiomas oficiales: español, quechua, aimará

Fiesta nacional: 6 de agosto, Día de la
Independencia

Bolivia y los bolivianos

El Lago Titicaca

In this chapter you will learn:

GRAMMAR POINTS

- **Nosotros** commands
- Perfect tenses: present perfect indicative and subjunctive; pluperfect indicative
- Nominalizations with **lo**

COMMUNICATIVE FUNCTIONS

- Describe living situations
- Make suggestions

VOCABULARY

- Find a house or apartment

I. ¡A Bolivia!

Una vendedora en su puesto en el Carnaval de Santa Cruz

LECTURA

Vamos a visitar Bolivia, pero **no vayamos** a los sitios turísticos típicos sino que **visitemos** a los indígenas: a los aymaras y los quechuas. Más del 50% de la población boliviana es india. Se cree que la civilización más antigua de esta región era la tihuanaca, que fue atacada por los collas o aymaras, cuya cultura floreció[1] por siglos. Luego el altiplano[2] boliviano (la región alta alrededor del Lago Titicaca) fue incorporado al Imperio inca, y cuando llegaron los españoles, los incas ocupaban el altiplano. Sus descendientes hoy se llaman los quechuas.

Viajemos al campo donde viven los aymaras y quechuas contemporáneos y hacen el trabajo que hacían sus antepasados[3] —la agricultura. Cultivan papas, quinoa (un cereal), maíz, cebada,[4] zapallo[5] y yuca,[6] o mandioca, un producto muy importante para la nutrición de los indígenas. Crían alpacas, llamas, ovejas y ganado[7] para usar su lana[8] y comer su carne. Muchos indígenas no son dueños de su propia tierra pero siguen trabajando en el campo.

Vamos a admirar la ropa multicolor y sus sombreros típicos y **comamos** su comida rica en papas, verduras y ají[9] picante. **Bailemos** la cueca y otros bailes populares y **escuchemos** la música de la quena[10] y las zampoñas.[11] **Probemos** la chicha, un tipo de cerveza hecha de maíz. Y **divertámonos** a las mil maravillas.[12]

---

[1]**floreció:** flourished / [2]**altiplano:** high plateau / [3]**antepasados:** ancestors / [4]**cebada:** barley / [5]**zapallo:** type of squash / [6]**yuca:** cassava / [7]**ganado:** cattle / [8]**lana:** wool / [9]**ají:** pepper / [10]**quena:** wooden flute / [11]**zampoñas:** panpipes / [12]**a las mil maravillas:** marvelously, greatly

¿Comprendes?

1. ¿Qué es el altiplano?
2. ¿Cuál es la profesión principal de la mayoría de los indios aymaras y quechuas?
3. ¿Cuáles son algunos elementos importantes en la dieta boliviana?

■ Los mandatos de *nosotros*

You learned in Chapters 6 and 12 how to form familiar (**tú**) and formal (**usted, ustedes**) commands. These are the only *logical* possibilities, since one can only give an order or suggestion to a person who is present. However, at times we want to make a suggestion about an activity and include ourselves in the activity. For this we use a "**nosotros**" command. English uses *"let's"* + verb for this purpose. Spanish has two forms for expressing affirmative **nosotros** commands.

Mandatos afirmativos *(ir a)*

You have already studied the first of these forms:

vamos a + infinitive

You learned that this form means *we are going to* + infinitive, but it also means *let's* + verb. The context will indicate which meaning is intended.

Vamos a visitar Oruro.	*Let's visit Oruro. (**We're going to . . .)**
Vamos a mandarle una postal.	*Let's send him (her) a post card. (**We're going to . . .)**

When a pronoun is used with **vamos a** + infinitive and the meaning is *let's . . .* , the pronoun must be attached to the infinitive. If the pronoun precedes **vamos**, however, then the meaning is *we're going to . . . .*

Vamos a visitarlo.	*Let's visit it.*
Lo vamos a visitar.	*We're going to visit it.*

Practiquemos ✎

A. Otra vez. Tú y tu amigo(a) quieren repetir un viaje que hicieron tus padres hace 30 años. A base de las acciones de tus padres, ¿qué sugieres?

> Tú y tu compañero(a) quieren divertirse este fin de semana. Cada uno debe hacer cinco sugerencias de posibles actividades.

MODELO: Pasaron tres semanas en Bolivia.
Vamos a pasar tres semanas en Bolivia.

1. Caminaron por el sendero inca.
2. Pasaron una semana en el Lago Titicaca.
3. Visitaron los parques nacionales.
4. Comieron platillos picantes y escucharon música popular.
5. Los comieron y la escucharon todos los días.

■ Mandatos afirmativos de *nosotros* (subjuntivo)

The second form of the **nosotros** commands uses the **nosotros** form of the *present subjunctive.*

Visitemos La Paz y Sucre.	***Let's visit*** *La Paz and Sucre.*
Crucemos el Lago Titicaca.	***Let's cross*** *Lake Titicaca.*

The only exception in which the *subjunctive is not used* in the **nosotros** command is the verb **ir**: the **nosotros** command of **ir** is **vamos**. This form can also mean *we're going to . . . .*

Vamos a Bolivia. ***Let's go*** *to Bolivia. (**We're going** to . . .)*

NOTA:
An accent must be added to the vowel before **-mos** to maintain the pronunciation of the command.

Pronouns must be attached to the end of **nosotros** subjunctive commands.

Visitémoslos.	***Let's visit them.***
Crucémoslo.	***Let's cross it.***

Reflexive verbs drop the final **-s** of the verb form in the **nosotros** affirmative command form.

Vámonos ahorita mismo.	***Let's leave*** *right now.*
Sentémonos aquí.	***Let's sit*** *here.*

Practiquemos

A. ¡Gol! Tú y tu familia son fanáticos del fútbol. ¿Qué te gusta hacer? Cambia las oraciones a sugerencias (mandatos de **nosotros**).

MODELO: Me gusta comprar nachos.
Compremos nachos.

1. Me gusta gritar mucho.
2. Prefiero sentarme cerca de la línea de medio campo *(midfield)*.
3. Me gusta beber muchos refrescos.
4. Me gusta vestirme en los colores de mi equipo.
5. Prefiero quedarme *(to stay)* hasta el final del juego.

B. Vamos de vacaciones. Vas de vacaciones a América del Sur. Haz una lista de sugerencias a tus compañeros(as) de viaje combinando un elemento de cada columna para formar oraciones completas. Tienes que agregar tus propias palabras.

A	B
	el Lago Titicaca
visitar	regalos folklóricos
viajar	comida indígena
subir	música popular
divertirse	varios países
probar	montañas altas
	mucho

Haz diez sugerencias de actividades que te gustaría hacer cuando vayas de vacaciones. Compara tu lista con la de tu compañero(a). ¿Qué actividades tienen en común?

Mandatos de *nosotros* negativos

In the negative, only one **nosotros** command form exists: the subjunctive form.

No visitemos la selva.	*Let's not visit the jungle.*
No subamos más alto.	*Let's not go up any higher.*

The negative **nosotros** command of **ir** is the present subjunctive form.

No vayamos a Oruro.   *Let's not go to Oruro.*

Like all other negative command forms, pronouns precede the **nosotros** negative command form. Reflexive verbs have no special form.

No la visitemos.	*Let's not visit it.*
No nos sentemos aquí.	*Let's not sit here.*

Practiquemos

A. ¿Casa? ¿Apartamento? Tú y tus compañeros(as) buscan una casa, pero no te gustan las sugerencias de tus compañeros(as). ¿Qué dices? Contéstales con mandatos negativos.

MODELO: Quiero buscar una casa cerca de mi trabajo.
           No busquemos una casa cerca de tu trabajo.

1. Quiero alquilar una casa grande.
2. Me gustaría vivir cerca del centro.
3. Yo prefiero buscar un apartamento con piscina.
4. Está bien pagar un alquiler alto.
5. Es importante pedir un contrato *(lease).*

B. ¿Quieres... ? Contesta estas preguntas con un mandato afirmativo o negativo, según tus preferencias.

MODELO: ¿Quieres ir a una fiesta?
           Sí, vamos a una fiesta. o
           No, no vayamos a una fiesta. o
           No, veamos una película.

1. ¿Quieres salir a bailar?
2. ¿Te gustaría ver una película?
3. ¿Quieres tomar un café?
4. ¿Prefieres nadar en el río o en el mar?
5. ¿Quieres comer en un restaurante sudamericano o chino?

Tú y tu compañero(a) van a limpiar la casa de tu profesor(a) de español. Hagan sugerencias (mandatos de nosotros) sobre cómo van a limpiarla.

❖ Para buscar una vivienda

Al buscar un apartamento

alquilar	*to rent*
el alquiler	*rent*
amplio	*large, roomy*
la cancha de tenis	*tennis court*
el/la dueño(a)	*owner*
el gimnasio	*gymnasium*
el/la inquilino(a)	*tenant*
la piscina (alberga)	*pool*

Al comprar una casa / un apartamento

los bienes raíces	*real estate*
la casa modelo	*model home*
la chimenea	*fireplace*
el/la comprador(a)	*buyer*
el dinero al contado	*cash*
el/la director(a) de préstamos	*loan officer*
el enganche	*down payment*
la hipoteca	*mortgage*
la inspección	*inspection*
los intereses	*interest*
pedir prestado	*to borrow*
pedir un préstamo	*to ask for a loan*
el porcentaje de ganancia	*percentage of profit*
la propiedad	*property*
la tasa de interés	*interest rate*
el terreno	*land*
el/la vendedor(a)	*seller*

> Conversa con tu compañero(a) sobre la casa o apartamento que los dos quieren buscar (juntos o individualmente).

¿Sabías?

Se dice que Bolivia es el Tibet de las Américas porque es la más alta y aislada de todas las repúblicas latinoamericanas.

Practiquemos

A. Mi casa. Escribe un párrafo que describa tu vivienda actual. Incluye un mínimo de diez características.

B. En el futuro. Ahora escríbele un párrafo a tu compañero(a) (real o ideal) describiendo tu casa ideal del futuro. Usa mandatos de **nosotros**.

MODELO: *Busquemos una casa que tenga piscina.*

II. La literatura boliviana

LECTURA

Bolivia **ha producido** unos grandes autores que **han contribuido** mucho al desarrollo de la literatura hispanoamericana. Tales nombres como Oscar Cerruto, Augusto Céspedes y Natanial Aguirre, entre otros, **han sido** reconocidos internacionalmente.

Entre las autoras bolivianas más conocidas surge[1] el nombre de Domitila Barrios de Chungara. Nació en Bolivia en 1937 de una buena familia, una familia que siempre **había tenido** grandes esperanzas[2] para su hija.

Domitila Barrios se distingue por su lucha constante por los derechos de la mujer y también por la igualdad del hombre y la mujer en la sociedad boliviana. Su libro, *¡Aquí también, Domitila!*, trata profundamente este tema. Su campaña la **ha llevado** a una posición de respeto entre todos los que creen en los derechos de la mujer. Ojalá que todos **hayan comprendido** la importancia de esta autora, las obras que **ha escrito** y su lucha por la humanidad.

[1]**surge:** *rises up* / [2]**esperanzas:** *hopes*

¿Comprendes?

1. ¿Cuál es un tema que siempre se nota en las obras de Domitila Barrios?
2. ¿Puedes pensar en otros autores hispanoamericanos que defiendan la igualdad de los hombres y las mujeres?

■ Los tiempos perfectos: El presente perfecto del indicativo

The present perfect tense is used to describe an action completed in the recent past but whose effects continue in the present. There are two components of the *present perfect:* the auxiliary verb **haber** *(to have)* and the *past participle.* Remember that the past participle is formed by dropping the -**ar**, -**er**, or -**ir** ending of the infinitive and adding -**ado** to -**ar** verbs and -**ido** to -**er** and -**ir** verbs. The two components of the present perfect are never separated and the past participle is invariable in form.

haber *(to have)*			
yo	**he**	nosotros(as)	**hemos**
tú	**has**	vosotros(as)	**habéis**
Ud.		Uds.	
él	**ha**	ellos	**han**
ella		ellas	

Ya **he comido.**	***I have** already **eaten.***
¿**Has viajado** a Bolivia?	***Have you traveled** to Bolivia?*
¿Qué **han hecho** aquí?	*What **have they done** here?*
Han traído toda la comida.	***They have brought** all the food.*

If there is a pronoun, it is placed before the auxiliary verb (**haber**).

Me he levantado tarde.	***I have gotten up** late.*
¿**Te han dado** los boletos?	***Have they given you** the tickets?*

Practiquemos

A. ¿Y hoy? Los estudiantes que llegaron a Bolivia con el profesor Santos dicen lo que han hecho hoy en La Paz. Completa las oraciones usando el presente perfecto.

1. Magda _____ (comprarse) muchos recuerdos en el mercado.

2. El profesor Santos _____ (volver) temprano al Hotel Estrella.

3. Yo _____ (ponerse) un sombrero típico.

4. Todos _____ (ver) la Catedral San Francisco.

5. Tú no _____ (conducir) un coche en la ciudad.

6. Santa y yo _____ (comer) un plato rico boliviano.

7. Marta _____ (acostarse) tarde.

8. Todos _____ (pasarlo) bien hoy.

B. Todavía no. Araceli y su familia tienen mucho que hacer antes de salir de Bolivia. Usa el presente perfecto para decir lo que todavía no han hecho.

1. Todavía / no visitar ellos / el Río Beni
2. Todavía / no ir su hermana Tina / a las Cuevas de Hielo
3. Todavía / no sacar fotos tú / de la playa
4. Todavía / no hacer compras nosotros / en el mercado al aire libre
5. Todavía / no asistir a una fiesta todos
6. Araceli todavía / no beber / chicha
7. Mamá y papá todavía / no comprar / sus recuerdos
8. Toda la familia todavía / no pasar / bastante tiempo en Bolivia

Con tu compañero(a) de clase, comparte una lista de cinco cosas que has hecho recientemente en tu vida.

■ Los tiempos perfectos: El presente perfecto del subjuntivo

The present perfect subjunctive is used in the subordinate clause when there is a need to express an action or idea in the past and the subjunctive mood is required. As in the present perfect indicative tense, which you have just learned, the present subjunctive form is composed of two components: the auxiliary verb **haber** and the past participle. In this case, however, **haber** is in the present subjunctive form:

Present Perfect Subjunctive			
...que yo	**haya**	...que nosotros(as)	**hayamos**
...que tú	**hayas**	...que vosotros(as)	**hayáis**
...que Ud.		...que Uds.	
...que él	**haya**	...que ellos	**hayan**
...que ella		...que ellas	

Espero que **hayan regresado** temprano.

Dudan que **hayas podido** hacerlo todo.

¡Ojalá que **hayamos ganado** la lotería!

*I hope that **they have returned** early.*

*They doubt that **you have been able** to do it all.*

*Let´s hope that **we have won** the lottery!*

Practiquemos

A. ¡Ojalá! Usando **Ojalá que**, combina los siguientes elementos para formar ocho oraciones completas.

A	B	C
Ojalá que	Carolina	comprar los nuevos muebles
	todos	escribir el anuncio en el periódico
	tú	terminar de limpiar la casa
	mi mamá	encontrar un apartamento nuevo
	sus primos	tener éxito en su búsqueda *(search)*
	nosotros(as)	gustar el vecindario
	yo	poder ahorrar el dinero necesario
	Juan Pablo	no mudarse esta semana

B. Mucho que hacer. Mateo y su esposa, Mariana, buscan una casa nueva para su familia y esperan poder mudarse pronto. Completa las oraciones con el presente perfecto de subjuntivo.

1. Mateo espera que Mariana _____ (estar) contenta con la idea de mudarse.

2. Sus hermanos dudan que Mateo _____ (poder) encontrar lo que buscaba.

3. La mamá de Mateo no cree que la familia _____ (considerar) todo.

4. Es lástima que los hijos _____ (tener) que despedirse de sus amigos.

5. Ojalá que la familia _____ (ahorrar) bastante dinero.

6. ¡Qué bueno es que Mateo _____ (tomar) sus propias decisiones!

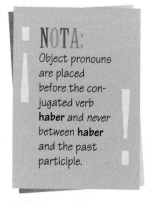

Dile a tu compañero(a) de clase cinco cosas que tú esperas que él o ella haya hecho esta semana.

■ Los tiempos perfectos: El pluscuamperfecto

You have already learned that the present perfect indicative is formed by combining the present indicative of the auxiliary verb **haber** with the *past participle*. The pluperfect indicative is formed in exactly the same way except that the verb **haber** is conjugated in the *imperfect tense*.

haber			
yo	**había**	nosotros(as)	**habíamos**
tú	**habías**	vosotros(as)	**habíais**
Ud.		Uds.	
él	**había**	ellos	**habían**
ella		ellas	

NOTA:
Object pronouns are placed before the conjugated verb **haber** and never between **haber** and the past participle.

The *pluperfect tense* **(pluscuamperfecto)** is used to refer to an action that has occurred prior to another action in the past: what *had* happened before something else occurred.

Cuando llegamos, ella ya **había salido**.	When we arrived, **she had already left**.
Tito ya **había visto** la película.	Tito **had already seen** the movie.
¿**Habías pensado** estudiar hoy?	**Had you planned** to study today?
Lisa ya **me lo había dado**.	Lisa **had already given it to me**.

Practiquemos

A. En La Paz. ¿Qué dicen estos turistas de su día en La Paz? Forma oraciones con las ideas siguientes usando el pluscuamperfecto.

1. Antes de salir del hotel / Simón consultar / el horario de los autobuses

2. Llegamos al café temprano pero / tú almorzar

3. Yo ya cambiar / mi dinero cuando llegaron mis amigos

4. Ellos querían salir con Manuela pero / ella hacer / otros planes
5. El taxista llegó a las 8:00 pero / nosotros tomar / otro
6. Elena quería ver el museo pero / sus amigos ya verlo

B. ¡Qué mañana! ¿Cómo fue esta mañana para Susana? Completa el párrafo con formas del pluscuamperfecto.

Cuando Susana se despertó, ya (1) _____ (salir) el sol. Se levantó y fue a la cocina para prepararse un buen desayuno pero su mamá ya (2) _____ (preparárselo). Entonces, fue a buscar el periódico, pero cuando llegó a la puerta vio que su hermano ya (3) _____ (recogerlo) y (4) _____ (ponerlo) en la mesa. Susana iba a leer su periódico pero no tuvo tiempo. Entonces, iba a pedirle un aventón *(a lift, a ride)* a su hermano pero descubrió que ya (5) _____ (irse).

> Con tu compañero(a) de clase, haz una lista de cinco cosas que habías pensado hacer antes de venir a clase. ¿Cuáles de estas cosas lograste hacer?

III. Aspectos curiosos de Bolivia

LECTURA

Bolivia tiene varias características especiales. **Lo más curioso y extraordinario** es que el país tiene dos capitales: Sucre y La Paz. Sucre es la capital establecida por la constitución y La Paz es la sede del gobierno. Otro dato interesante es que Bolivia es uno de dos países latinoamericanos que no tiene puertos, porque no tiene costas. Las importaciones llegan por tierra o aire, o por la buena voluntad de los países vecinos. **Lo importante** para Bolivia es hacer buenos acuerdos y mantener buenas relaciones con los vecinos.

¿Comprendes?

1. ¿Qué es lo curioso de las ciudades de La Paz y Sucre?
2. ¿Cómo recibe Bolivia sus importaciones?

■ Nominalizaciones con *lo*

Lo + adjetivo

You already know the word **lo** as a direct object pronoun meaning *you, him,* or *it.*

Lo vi ayer.   *I saw **it** (**him, you** [form.]) yesterday.*

But **lo** has another very useful function. It can combine with adjectives to form a noun-like (nominalized) phrase, equivalent to *the . . . part* or *the . . . thing.*

Por fin, Elena me dijo **lo bueno.**	*Finally Elena told me **the good part.***
Lo importante es ver el Lago Titicaca.	***The important thing** is to see Lake Titicaca.*

Lo is a neuter form that is neither masculine nor feminine. Thus, if a demonstrative pronoun is used in the same sentence as **lo**, the demonstrative must also be in the neuter form: **esto, eso,** or **aquello.**

Lo nuevo es **esto.**	*The new part is this.*
Eso es **lo triste.**	*That is the sad part.*

Lo + cláusula

Lo may also be combined with a clause that functions as a noun.

Lo que necesito es tu cooperación.	***What I need** is your cooperation.*
Lo que nos importa es saber la verdad.	***The thing that matters to us** is knowing the truth.*

As in the case of **lo** + adjective, demonstrative pronouns used in a sentence with **lo** + clause must be in the neuter form.

Lo que no comprendo es **esto.**	***What I don't understand** is **this.***
Esto es **lo que me gusta.**	***This** is what I like.*
Lo más probable es que no **llegue.**	***The most probable thing** is that he (she, you [form.]) won't come.*
Lo necesario es que **empecemos** ahora.	***The necessary thing** is for us to begin now.*
Lo que queremos es que tú **viajes.**	***What we want** is for you to travel.*

NOTA:
The concepts you have already studied in Chapters 12–14 that require the subjunctive also require the subjunctive in **lo** constructions.

Practiquemos

A. En busca. Tú y tu familia buscan una nueva casa. Usa los siguientes adjetivos para completar las oraciones de una forma lógica: **difícil, dudoso, importante, necesario, primero, triste.**

MODELO: *Lo triste es* tener que buscar una nueva casa.

1. _____ mirar el periódico para ver los anuncios.

2. _____ que la casa sea amplia.

3. _____ encontrar una casa económica.

4. _____ que podamos encontrar una casa cerca del trabajo.

5. _____ pedir un préstamo.

B. Necesito empleo. Buscas un nuevo trabajo. Completa las oraciones de una forma lógica.

Conversa con un(a) compañero(a) sobre lo que Uds. buscan y quieren en un trabajo.

M O D E L O :   Lo que necesito tener *es un sueldo más alto.*

1. Lo que yo quiero _____.

2. Lo que me importa _____.

3. Lo que buscan aquí _____.

4. Lo que considero ideal _____.

5. Lo que ofrecen en este trabajo _____.

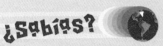

¿Sabías?

La Laguna Colorada, que se encuentra en un área remota en el suroeste de Bolivia, es un lago cuyas aguas son de un color rojo encendido. Está rodeado de un paisaje sin árboles y de colinas bajas. Allí viven los raros flamingos de San Diego.

A ver si sabes

Use this self test to see if you know the material presented in Chapter 16.

A. ¿Quieres salir? Quieres salir este fin de semana y tienes muchas ideas de posibles actividades. Sugiere a tus amigos(as) las actividades que siguen usando las dos formas de mandatos de **nosotros**.

1. ver una película
2. comer en un restaurante
3. asistir a un concierto
4. salir a un club
5. escuchar música
6. divertirnos toda la noche y acostarnos al amanecer *(dawn)*

B. No quiero… Tu amigo no quiere aceptar ninguna de tus sugerencias de la **Actividad A**. ¿Qué mandatos negativos de **nosotros** te da a ti?

1. no ver una película
2. no comer en un restaurante

Preguntas culturales
1. ¿Cuál es el estilo de vida de los indios bolivianos?
2. ¿Crees que se acepte fácilmente a una autora que se dedica a luchar por los derechos de la mujer?
3. En tu opinión, ¿cuál es el rasgo más interesante de Bolivia?

3. no asistir a un concierto
4. no salir a un club
5. no escuchar música
6. no divertirnos toda la noche y acostarnos al amanecer *(dawn)*

C. El alpinismo. Patricia está hablando con su vecino, el señor Aguirre. ¿Qué le pregunta? Usa los verbos de la lista en el presente perfecto de indicativo o subjuntivo: **atreverse, disfrutar, divertirse, escalar** *(to climb)*, **esquiar, ir, oír, pasar, poder, visitar.**

PATRICIA: Señor Aguirre, ¿cuánto tiempo _____ en Bolivia?
SR. AGUIRRE: Bueno, _____ varias veces. _____ muchos lugares y siempre _____ mucho.
PATRICIA: ¿ _____ Ud. Illimani, el pico más famoso de Bolivia? Ojalá que Ud. _____ hacerlo.
SR. AGUIRRE: Hasta mis amigos y yo _____ en esta montaña famosa.
PATRICIA: Yo nunca _____ a esquiar pero _____ que es divertidísimo.
SR. AGUIRRE: Debes hacerlo. Nosotros siempre _____ de estas experiencias.
PATRICIA: Voy a pensarlo.

D. Cita cancelada. Ibas a almorzar con tu jefe pero cuando llegas a su oficina, ya no está. ¿Qué te dice su secretaria? Completa sus comentarios con el presente perfecto de indicativo o subjuntivo.

1. Siento que el jefe _____ (irse) ya.
2. Parece que nosotros _____ (olvidar) la cita por completo.
3. Es una lástima que yo no _____ (escribir) nada en el calendario.
4. Es afortunado que Ud. _____ (venir) temprano.
5. Es triste que Uds. no _____ (hablar) por teléfono.

E. ¡Más sorpresas! El día de Susana continúa. Para saber cómo terminó, completa el párrafo con formas del pretérito y pluscuamperfecto.

Después de desayunar, Susana (1) _____ (salir) de la casa a las 9:00 para encontrarse con sus amigos en la esquina. Pero cuando (2) _____ (llegar), ella (3) _____ (descubrir) que sus amigos ya (4) _____ (irse) sin esperarla. (5) _____ (Esperar) el autobús pero nunca (6) _____ (llegar); ya (7) _____ (venir) y (8) _____ (salir). Finalmente, (9) _____ (llegar) a su clase de español pero el profesor (10) _____ (cancelarla).

F. Mi opinión. Completa las siguientes oraciones con nominalizaciones. Usa la palabra **lo** y adjetivos (e.g., **lo importante**) y cláusulas (e.g., **lo que importa**). Escoge de las siguientes palabras: **bueno, buscar, difícil, frustrante, gustar, importar, imposible, molestar, querer.**

1. En la vida, _____ es buscar la felicidad.

2. En la política, _____ es que los políticos no digan la verdad.

3. En cuanto al trabajo, _____ es encontrar un trabajo que te guste.

4. En la clase de español, _____ es aprender todo el material antes del examen.

5. En las relaciones amorosas, _____ es dar y recibir.

6. En la amistad, _____ es la comprensión y la lealtad.

Querido Diario. Vas a describir en tu diario tus ideas de la casa que quieres tener un día. Para organizar tus pensamientos, haz un diagrama con la palabra CASA en el centro y con líneas que salen como los rayos de una rueda (spokes of a wheel). En los rayos, escribe las posibles características de tu casa con las características esenciales más cerca del centro y las características deseadas más lejos del centro. Luego, dile a tu diario cómo va a ser tu casa del futuro. ¿Cómo y cuándo esperas tenerla? Puedes empezar diciendo: «Algún día, voy a tener una casa que... ».

Grammar: verbs: subjunctive in relative clauses
Phrases: describing objects, places; expressing a wish or desire
Vocabulary: house (all categories); family members; meals

Vocabulario activo

Al buscar un apartamento

alquilar	la cancha de tenis	el/la inquilino(a)
el alquiler	el/la dueño(a)	la piscina (alberga)
amplio	el gimnasio	

Al comprar una casa / un apartamento

los bienes raíces	el enganche	el porcentaje de ganancia
la casa modelo	la hipoteca	la propiedad
la chimenea	la inspección	la tasa de interés
el/la comprador(a)	los intereses	el terreno
el dinero al contado	pedir prestado	el/la vendedor(a)
el/la director(a) de préstamos	pedir un préstamo	

Web site:
http://spanishforlife.heinle.com

Transparencies:
A–4: La América del Sur
A–12: Country Profile, Ecuador

ECUADOR

Santo Domingo de los Colo

Quito

Tumbaco

Bahía de Caraquez
Chone
Calceta
Manta
Porto Viejo
Jipijapa

La Tacunga

Ambato

Guaranda

Ríobamba

Río Pastaza

Boliche

Guayaquil

CORDILLERA DE LOS ANDES

Azogues

Cuenca

Girón

Machala

Santa Rosa

Chacras

Loja

Catamayo

BANCO CENTRAL DEL ECUADOR
20000

Malabo

GUINEA
ECUATORIAL

CAMERÚN

GABÓN

REPÚBLICA DEL ECUADOR

Nombre oficial: República del Ecuador

Área: 275.830 km²

Población: 11.690.500

Capital: Quito

Moneda: el sucre

Idioma oficial: español

Fiesta nacional: 10 de agosto, Día de la Independencia

REPÚBLICA DE GUINEA ECUATORIAL

Nombre oficial: República de Guinea Ecuatorial

Área: 28.051 km²

Población: 442.500

Capital: Malabo

Moneda: el franco

Idioma oficial: español

Fiesta nacional: 5 de marzo, Día de la Independencia

Ecuador y los ecuatorianos
Guinea Ecuatorial y los guineanos

Estudiantes de una escuela agrícola, Guinea Ecuatorial

In this chapter you will learn:

GRAMMAR POINTS
- Future tense
- Subjunctive in adverb clauses

COMMUNICATIVE FUNCTIONS
- Talk about future plans

I. El ecuador, cinturón¹ del mundo

LECTURA

Si miramos los nombres «Ecuador» y «Guinea Ecuatorial», **veremos** que tienen en común la palabra «ecuador»— la línea geográfica que divide el planeta en dos hemisferios. En realidad, si miramos un mapa **notaremos** que Guinea Ecuatorial se encuentra un poco al norte del ecuador y así queda completamente en el hemisferio del norte. Pero nos **daremos** cuenta de que² Ecuador es partido por el ecuador; así que parte del país queda en el hemisferio del norte y parte en el hemisferio del sur.

---

¹**cinturón:** *belt* / ²**nos daremos cuenta de que:** *we will realize that*

¿Comprendes?

¿Cuál es la relación entre el ecuador y los países Ecuador y Guinea Ecuatorial?

■ El tiempo futuro

You have already learned in Chapter 2 that **ir a** + infinitive *(to be going to do something)* is used to refer to future activities. But, there is also a special future form, which is equivalent to *will do something* in English. The same set of endings is added to all verbs. Regular verbs form the future as follows:

Infinitive + -é, -ás, -á, -emos, -éis, -án					
hablar		**perder**		**dormir**	
hablaré	hablaremos	perderé	perderemos	dormiré	dormiremos
hablarás	hablaréis	perderás	perderéis	dormirás	dormiréis
hablará	hablarán	perderá	perderán	dormirá	dormirán

Visitaremos las Islas Galápagos.　　**We will visit** the Galapagos Islands.

Verás muchos animales exóticas.　　**You will see** many exotic animals.

Some verbs have an irregular future stem, although the same set of endings is attached to it:

Irregular Verbs in the Future Tense			
decir	**dir**	+	-é, -ás, -á, -emos, -éis, -án
hacer	**har**	+	-é, -ás, -á, -emos, -éis, -án
poder	**podr**	+	-é, -ás, -á, -emos, -éis, -án
poner	**pondr**	+	-é, -ás, -á, -emos, -éis, -án
querer	**querr**	+	-é, -ás, -á, -emos, -éis, -án
saber	**sabr**	+	-é, -ás, -á, -emos, -éis, -án
salir	**saldr**	+	-é, -ás, -á, -emos, -éis, -án
tener	**tendr**	+	-é, -ás, -á, -emos, -éis, -án
venir	**vendr**	+	-é, -ás, -á, -emos, -éis, -án

Saldremos el lunes que viene.   ***We will leave*** *next Monday.*
Querrán ver la Isla Bioko.   ***They will want*** *to see Bioko*
                                            Island.

Practiquemos

A. Nuestro viaje. Nuestra familia va a Guinea Ecuatorial frecuentemente y ahora vamos otra vez. ¿Qué harán todos? Cambia los verbos en las siguientes oraciones al futuro.

1. En Malabo visitamos el pueblo de Moka.
2. En Río Muni yo busco evidencia de la magia negra.
3. En Bata mis hermanos van a la playa.
4. En Mbini tú conoces a la gente local en los cafés.
5. En la Isla de Corisco mi esposo saca muchas fotos de las vistas preciosas.
6. En todas partes todos hacen cosas interesantes.

B. ¡Gracias a Dios que es viernes! ¿Qué planes tienen tú, tus amigos y tu familia para divertirse este fin de semana? Escribe seis oraciones usando algunos de los siguientes verbos: **comer, decir, hablar, hacer, ir, limpiar, mirar, poder, salir, tener, venir.**

1. _____   4. _____
2. _____   5. _____
3. _____   6. _____

> Dile a tu compañero(a) lo que harás mañana.

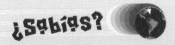

¿Sabías?

La República de Guinea Ecuatorial está dividida en dos provincias. La capital Malabo está situada en la Isla Bioko. La otra provincia, Río Muni, está en África continental, a unas 125 millas de Bioko. Varias tribus forman la población del país pero la más grande es la fang.

II. Las Islas Galápagos

LECTURA

Si vas de vacaciones, ¿por qué no visitas un sitio **donde puedas** ver un poco del paraíso,[1] por ejemplo, las Islas Galápagos? **Cuando vayas** a esas hermosas islas, vas a entrar en un paraíso natural donde vas a ver maravillosos animales. Pero no creas que vayas a ver las mismas Islas de antes, porque tan pronto como llegan muchos seres humanos a un sitio, empezamos a cambiarlo. Van a las Galápagos unas 60.000 turistas y dejan su huella[2] en el país. La población permanente de las Islas también crece, quitándoles[3] el hábitat a las tortugas, las iguanas marinas y los lobos marinos.[4] Todavía se pueden ver muchas especies de plantas y animales terrestres y marinos, pero han desaparecido muchos.

Cuando los seres humanos **aprendamos** a vivir sin alterar el ecosistema y **tan pronto como empecemos** a respetar todas las especies del mundo, los lugares idílicos como las Islas Galápagos no van a estar en peligro.

[1]**paraíso:** *paradise* / [2]**huella:** *track* / [3]**quitándoles:** *taking away* / [4]**lobos marinos:** *sea lions*

¿Comprendes?

¿En qué peligro están las Islas Galápagos?

■ Usos del subjuntivo: después de adverbios

The key to the use of the subjunctive mood after adverbs and adverbial conjunctions (phrases with an adverb and **que**) is distinguishing between the known or real versus the unknown or unreal. This division is similar to the one you saw in Chaper 15 between definite, real antecedents and those that are indefinite and unknown.

Certain adverbial phrases introduce concepts that do not yet exist and perhaps never will. These phrases are always followed by the subjunctive mood and must be memorized:

a menos que	*unless*	en caso (de) que	*in case*
antes (de) que	*before*	para que	*in order to*
con tal (de) que	*provided that*	sin que	*without*

Va a salir **antes de que** lo **salude** yo.

*He is going to leave **before I (can) say hi** to him.*

Irene va **con tal que** Mario **pague.**   *Irene is going **provided that** Mario **pays.***

Vu u salir **antes de saludarme.**   *He is going to leave **before saying hi to me.***

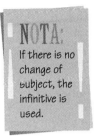

NOTA:
If there is no change of subject, the infinitive is used.

Adverbios de tiempo

When the following adverbs of time refer to a future action, the verb in that clause must be in the subjunctive mood since the action is unknown and unreal.

Adverbs that refer to time include:

cuando	*when*	mientras que	*while*
después (de) que	*after*	tan pronto como	*as soon as*
hasta que	*until*		

Cuando vayamos a Guinea Ecuatorial, pensamos visitar Malabo.
***When we go** to Equatorial Guinea, we plan to visit Malabo.*

Te vamos a llamar **tan pronto como lleguemos.**
*We are going to call you **as soon as we arrive.***

If the time referred to is habitual (what always happens) or past, then the indicative mood follows the adverb.

Cuando fuimos a Guinea Ecuatorial, visitamos Malabo.
***When we went** to Equatorial Guinea, we visited Malabo.*

Siempre te llamamos **tan pronto como llegamos.**
*We always call you **as soon as we arrive.***

Adverbios de lugar

Adverbs of place are similarly governed by the concepts of *known* versus *unknown.* If the place referred to is known, the indicative mood is used; if it is unknown, the subjunctive is the appropriate mood.

Vamos a comer **donde tú digas.**   *We'll eat **where(ever) you say.***
Siempre comemos **donde tú dices.**   *We always eat **where you say.***

In the first sentence, the person has not yet specified a place to eat. In the second sentence, the person always picks a specific place.

Practiquemos

A. ¡Qué viaje! Martina Ramos visita Guinea Ecuatorial y le escribe una carta a su esposo, quien va allí más tarde. Completa su carta con la forma adecuada de los verbos indicados.

Querido David,

¡Qué país más interesante! El viernes cuando (1) _____ (llegar), vine del aeropuerto en un minibús, una forma de transporte muy típica. Después de (2) _____ (comer) en el hotel, salí a investigar Malabo y ↪

encontré muchos cafés y clubes. Tan pronto como tú (3) _____ (llegar), quiero llevarte a un sitio donde (4) _____ (poder, nosotros) probar comida típica. Mientras que (5) _____ (estar, tú) aquí, quiero encontrar una playa donde (6) _____ (ser) posible nadar y descansar. ¡Estoy muy entusiasmada! ¡No puedo esperar hasta que (7) _____ (verse, nosotros)!

Con todo mi amor,

Martina

Escribe un párrafo sobre lo que hiciste cuando estabas de vacaciones el año pasado. Luego escribe otro párrafo sobre lo que piensas hacer cuando tengas vacaciones este año.

B. En Ecuador. Combina los elementos de las columnas para describir las vacaciones que van a pasar tú y tus amigos.

MODELO: *Yo voy a observar las iguanas marinas cuando nade bajo el agua.*

A	B	C	D
	ver tortugas		llegar a las Islas
tú	nadar en el Pacífico	cuando	visitar Guayaquil
yo	bailar toda la noche	tan pronto como	ir a Cuenca
Rita y yo	ver museos	mientras que	estar en Quito
Lalo y Lichi	comer en un restaurante	después que	servir comida típica
Pablo	observar iguanas marinas	donde	nadar bajo el agua
	ver la selva		encontrarse el Río Napo

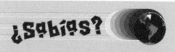

¿Sabías?

En Ecuador se habla español como idioma oficial pero muchas personas también hablan quechua. En Guinea Ecuatorial hay dos idiomas oficiales, el español y el francés. También se hablan fang, bubi e ibo.

A ver si sabes

Use this self test to see if you know the material presented in Chapter 17.

A. En el año 2100. ¿Cómo va a ser la vida del siglo XXII? Completa las oraciones con el futuro de los verbos indicados.

1. Nosostros _____ (tener) diferentes comunicaciones.

2. Yo _____ (leer) otros libros.

3. Tú _____ (hacer) muchas cosas nuevas.

4. Los científicos _____ (saber) más.

5. El transporte _____ (ser) muy diferente.

B. A Guinea Ecuatorial. Laura habla de un viaje que su familia va a hacer a Guinea Ecuatorial según las instrucciones de su amiga. ¿Qué van a hacer? Cambia estas oraciones en el presente al futuro. Recuerda que probablemente vas a tener que cambiar dos verbos.

1. Cuando llegamos a la capital vamos al hotel.
2. Esperas hasta que viene el guía.
3. Vamos adonde nos indica la guía turística.
4. Tan pronto como vamos a Malabo, tu esposo sube el volcán.
5. Cuando estamos en Evinayong, nado en las aguas cristalinas de los ríos.

Querido Diario. Vas a compartir con tu diario tus planes para el futuro y cuándo piensas realizarlos (*to carry them out*). Dividirás tus ideas en tres categorías: tu trabajo, tus diversiones y tus intenciones personales. Cuando tengas una lista de un mínimo de cinco aspiraciones, escribe tus planes en tu diario. Puedes empezar diciendo: «Algún día, cuando sea mayor, tendré… ».

Preguntas culturales
1. ¿Cómo han cambiado las Islas Galápagos desde la visita de Darwin en 1835?
2. ¿Qué tienen en común Ecuador y Guinea Ecuatorial?

Grammar: verbs: future; subjunctive with conjunction
Phrases: describing health, objects, people, places; expressing intention
Vocabulary: dreams and aspirations; house; family members; leisure; working conditions

Web site:
http://spanishforlife.heinle.com

Transparencies:
A–4: La América del Sur
A–9: Country Profiles, Paraguay, Uruguay

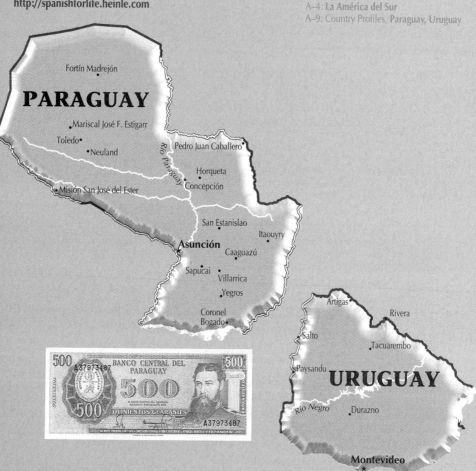

REPÚBLICA DEL PARAGUAY

Nombre oficial: República del Paraguay

Área: 406.752 km²

Población: 4.800.000

Capital: Asunción

Moneda: guaraní

Idioma oficial: español, guaraní

Fiesta nacional: 14 y 15 de mayo, Días de la Independencia

REPÚBLICA ORIENTAL DEL URUGUAY

Nombre oficial: República Oriental del Uruguay

Área: 176.215 km²

Población: 3.200.000

Capital: Montevideo

Moneda: nuevo peso

Idioma oficial: español

Fiesta nacional: 25 de agosto, Día de la Independencia

Paraguay y los paraguayos
Uruguay y los uruguayos

Río de la Plata, Uruguay

In this chapter you will learn:

GRAMMAR POINTS

- Conditional
- Imperfect subjunctive and conditional sentences
- Diminutives and augmentatives

COMMUNICATIVE FUNCTIONS

- Tell hopes
- Discuss hypothetical situations

I. Un cuentista uruguayo, Horacio Quiroga

LECTURA

¿**Querrías** leer un buen cuento en español? Bueno, se dice que Horacio Quiroga es uno de los mejores cuentistas de Hispanoamérica. Nació en 1878 en Uruguay y, de joven, le encantaba pasar su tiempo en la naturaleza salvaje debido al hecho de que vivió varios años en la provincia argentina de Misiones, un lugar conocido por sus selvas tropicales. Por eso, no nos **sorprendería** saber que muchos de sus cuentos se desarrollan en la naturaleza salvaje donde los personajes luchan contra la misma naturaleza que los destruye. La muerte, lo morboso,[1] lo fantástico y lo trágico caracterizan las obras de Quiroga. A todos les **gustaría** leer un buen cuento de Quiroga, ¿verdad?

[1] **lo morboso:** *the morbid*

¿Comprendes?

1. ¿Qué caracteriza los cuentos de Quiroga?
2. ¿Qué otros autores desarrollan temas de la muerte, lo morboso y lo fantástico?

■ El condicional

The conditional is used to indicate conditions under which an action is completed and is expressed as *would* in English. Most verbs form the conditional by adding the endings **-ía, -ías, -ía, -íamos, -íais, -ían** to the infinitive.

comprar		ser		escribir	
compraría	compraríamos	sería	seríamos	escribiría	escribiríamos
comprarías	compraríais	serías	seríais	escribirías	escribiríais
compraría	comprarían	sería	serían	escribiría	escribirían

Así **respondería** yo.
¿Qué **harías** en esa situación?

That is how **I would respond**.
What **would you do** in that situation?

Note that verbs that are irregular in the future tense have the same irregular stem in the conditional tense.

Conditional Verb Endings			
decir	dir-		
haber	habr-		
hacer	har-		
poder	podr-		
poner	pondr-	-ía	-íamos
querer	querr-	-ías	-íais
saber	sabr-	-ía	-ían
salir	saldr-		
tener	tendr-		
valer	valdr-		
venir	vendr-		

¿Cómo le **diríamos** eso?   How **would we tell** him that?
Yo **pondría** el sofá allí.   I **would put** the sofa there.

Practiquemos

A. ¿Y tú? ¿Qué harían tú y tus amigos en Paraguay la primera semana de vacaciones? Completa las oraciones usando el condicional.

1. Yo _____ (ir) a la Casa Viola, un museo muy bonito.

2. Tú _____ (comer) en un buen restaurante paraguayo en el centro.

3. Cristina _____ (visitar) el Jardín Botánico.

4. Memo y yo _____ (explorar) la Avenida Colón.

5. ¡Todos _____ (divertirse) mucho!

B. ¡Así lo haría yo! Estás buscando la casa de tus sueños. ¿Cómo sería? Escoge los elementos siguientes para describirla.

Haz una lista de por lo menos diez cosas que tú harías para tu mejor amigo(a) y luego compártela con dos compañeros(as).

La casa de mis sueños...

A
tener cinco recámaras
haber una piscina grande
estar en el campo
la cocina ser muy grande
haber mucho espacio para
   mis mascotas
estar cerca de un lago

B
tener dos pisos
tener una cocina my grande
haber un cuarto para una biblioteca
(no) estar cerca del centro comercial
tener...
ser...

■ Expresiones que usan el condicional

The conditional is often used to soften requests and to ask questions. Note the following examples:

¿**Podría** Ud. ayudarme, por favor?   *Could you help me, please?*
Me encantaría.   *I would be delighted.*
¿En qué **podría** servirle?   *How may I help you?*
Me gustaría ver estos aretes.   *I would like to see these earrings.*

Practiquemos

A. ¿Cómo? Enrique está en la ciudad de Itaguá, Paraguay, y quiere saber más de la región. ¿Cuáles de estas expresiones usaría?

podría   me encantaría   me gustaría

En la calle...

ENRIQUE: Señor, ¿ _____ decirme dónde yo _____ comprar ñanduti *(spiderweb lace—typical of Itaguá)*?

TAXISTA: _____. Siga derecho, derecho. Allí está una tienda donde se vende.

En la tienda...

DEPENDIENTA: Buenos días, señor. ¿En qué _____ servirle?

ENRIQUE: _____ comprar unos recuerdos de Paraguay. ¿ _____ enseñarme algunos?

DEPENDIENTA: ¡Cómo no! ¡_____! Sígame, por favor.

II. Paraguay y Uruguay

LECTURA

Paraguay y Uruguay son dos países **chiquitos**[1] en Sudamérica pero son joyas en ese continente. Paraguay, por ejemplo, fue política y económicamente aislado[2] por muchos años pero el gobierno paraguayo quería que **se abrieran** sus fronteras a otros sudamericanos y a los turistas. El país se jacta de[3] su bella capital, Asunción, las misiones jesuitas, unos parques nacionales exquisitas y un yermo[4] vasto.

Uruguay es el país más pequeño de la América del Sur. Tiene una bella costa que es la costa oriental de Sudamérica. Tiene una topografía variada de montañas bajas, la Cuchilla de Haedo y la Cuchilla Grande. También hay cinco ríos que cruzan el país hacia el oeste y desembocan en el Río Uruguay.

¿Quiénes no querrían visitar estos dos **paisitos** únicos si **tuvieran** la oportunidad?

---

[1] **chiquitos:** *very small* / [2] **aislado:** *isolated* / [3] **se jacta de:** *can boast about* / [4] **yermo:** *wilderness*

¿Comprendes?

1. ¿Cómo es la geografía de Paraguay?
2. Describe un aspecto de la geografía de Uruguay.

■ El imperfecto del subjuntivo

You have already learned the forms and uses of the present subjunctive. The imperfect subjunctive has the same uses as the present subjunctive, except that it refers to actions in the past.

The imperfect subjunctive of *all* verbs is formed by taking the *third-person plural* form of the *preterite,* removing the **-ron** ending, and adding the appropriate imperfect subjunctive endings.

cantar (cant*aron*)		comer (comi*eron*)		ir (fu*eron*)	
cantara	cant**á**ramos	comiera	comi**é**ramos	fuera	fu**é**ramos
cantaras	cantarais	comieras	comierais	fueras	fuerais
cantara	cantaran	comiera	comieran	fuera	fueran

> **NOTA:**
> The **nosotros** form requires an accent on the vowel preceding the ending.

Magda insistió en que **fuéramos.**	*Magda insisted that **we go.***
Era imposible que **comieras** tanto.	*It was impossible for **you to eat** so much.*
Si yo **tuviera** tiempo, te ayudaría.	*If **I had** time, I would help you.*

El subjuntivo en situaciones hipotéticas

The third sentence above is an example of a hypothetical situation. The *if* (**si**) clause construction used in combination with the conditional tense is used to describe hypothetical situations: *If I had time (but I don't), I would help you.*

Si yo **ganara** la lotería, **viajaría** mucho.	*If **I won** the lottery, **I would travel** a lot.*
Juan **pediría** un préstamo si **pudiera.**	*John **would ask for** a loan if **he could.***

There is also an alternate imperfect subjunctive form that is based on the third-person plural form of the preterite but uses the verb endings -se, -ses, -se, -semos, -seis, -sen. This form is used mostly in Spain and in literary texts.

Practiquemos

A. En un restaurante uruguayo. La familia Sender está de vacaciones en Uruguay y esta noche van a comer en un restaurante en Montevideo. Escribe oraciones usando los siguientes elementos.

1. El Sr. Sender quería que / sus hijos portarse bien
2. Catalina insistió en que / todos comer parrillada *(barbecue)*
3. Abuelita no permitió que / Ramón beber clericó (vino blanco con jugo de fruta)
4. El mesero sugirió que / la familia pedir un buen postre
5. La familia Sender estuvo contento que / la comida ser tan sabrosa

B. ¿La realidad o no? Todos tienen sueños. ¿Cómo expresan sus sueños estos estudiantes? Usa el imperfecto de subjuntivo y el condicional para terminar las oraciones.

> Prepara una lista de por lo menos ocho sueños que tienes y compártelos con dos miembros de tu clase.

1. Sonia y yo _____ (estudiar) en Hispanoamérica si _____.

2. Si los estudiantes no _____ (vivir) en las residencias estudiantiles, ellos _____.

3. Si Ernesto _____ (doctorarse) en la informática, él _____.

4. Y tú, ¿qué _____ (hacer) si _____?

5. Yo _____ si _____.

■ Los diminutivos y los aumentativos

In Spanish, certain endings are used to indicate size, affection, or a derogatory feeling about something.

Los diminutivos

The diminutive form is used to indicate smallness or affection. It is formed by adding -ito(a) or -cito(a) to nouns and adjectives. The -cito(a) ending is generally used with nouns and adjectives that end in **e, n,** or **r:**

-ito(a)		-cito(a)	
lago	**laguito** *(little lake)*	suave	**suavecito** *(very soft)*
papel	**papelito** *(bit of paper)*	madre	**madrecita** *(mommy)*
silla	**sillita** *(little chair)*	rincón	**rinconcito** *(little corner)*

Note that for words that end in **-co** or **-go**, the following spelling changes occur:

-co	**-qui**	poco	**poquito** *(tiny bit)*
-go	**-gui**	amigo	**amiguito** *(dear friend, little friend)*

There are other diminutive forms as well: **-illo, -ico, -clo.**

> chico **chiquillo, chiquito, chiquelo** *(little boy)*

A few one-syllable words add **e** before the ending: **panecillo, florecillo.**

Los aumentativos

To form the augmentative, which indicates a large size or gives a derogatory sense to something, use the following endings: **-ote(a),** **-azo(a), -ón(ona).**

casa   **casona** *(mansion, huge house)*
mujer   **mujerona** *(big/tough/mean woman)*
hombre   **hombrón** *(big man, tough/mean/bad man)*
muchacho   **muchachón** *(big/tough/mean boy)*

Practiquemos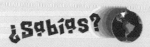

A. ¿Cómo son? ¿Cómo describe Esteban a estas personas y cosas? Usa el diminutivo o aumentativo según la indicación.

1. ¿Esa señora? Es mi _____ (madre).

2. ¿Ese pedazo de papel? Es un _____ (pedazo) de mi _____ (papel).

3. ¿Esa calle corta? Es mi _____ (calle).

4. ¿Este muchacho malo? Es un _____ (muchacho).

5. ¿Ese pan? Es un _____ (pan) rico.

6. ¿Ese _____ (niño) _____ (chico)? Es mi _____ (hermano).

¿Sabías?

Muchas recetas uruguayas incluyen carne. Uno de sus platos más populares es la parrillada, un plato de varias carnes asadas. Chivito es otro plato popular. Es un sándwich de bistec acompañado de verduras y papas. Clericó es una bebida nacional; es una mezcla de vino blanco y jugo de fruta.

A ver si sabes

Use this self test to see if you know the material presented in Chapter 18.

A. Buenos amigos. ¿Qué harían los amigos para ayudarse? Para saber, escribe oraciones usando el condicional.

1. Yo hacer / tus quehaceres si estuvieras enfermo
2. Felipa llevarle a Diego / unos regalos para su aniversario
3. Nosotros llamarte / con frecuencia si viajáramos al extranjero
4. Manuela ayudarles / con sus tareas si no comprendieran el concepto
5. Los buenos amigos sacrificarse / por los otros amigos si fuera necesario

B. Algo más... Lupita le manda a su esposo un mensaje electrónico antes de salir de su casa. ¿Qué le dice? Usa el imperfecto del subjuntivo y el condicional según el contexto.

A: luisv@computel.com
De: lupita17@computel.com

Preguntas culturales
1. Escribe cinco aspectos de la cultura y geografía de Paraguay y Uruguay que aprendiste en esta lección.
2. ¿Cuáles son las características de los cuentos de Horacio Quiroga?

Mi amor: Un mensaje rápidito para decirte lo que está pasando. Querías que yo (1) _____ (ir) a la oficina para tus archivos pero resultó que nuestra vecina me pidió que le (2) _____ (hacer) unos favores. Además, Juanito insistió en que sus amigos (3) _____ (venir) a la casa para hacer sus tareas y no tuve tiempo para hacer nada. Me (4) _____ (gustar) poder hacerlo todo pero a veces es imposible. Ahora, voy a la oficina. ¿Te (5) _____ (poder) pedir una cosita más? Tu mamá sugirió que tú (6) _____ (traerle) unas cosas del mercado y quería que la (7) _____ (llamar) más tarde. Nos vemos.

Un abrazo

Lupita

C. Sueños y más sueños. ¿Qué harías si pudieras realizar tus sueños? Completa las oraciones usando el imperfecto del subjuntivo y el condicional.

1. Si alguien (ofrecerme) un empleo en otro país, yo...
2. Si yo (ganar) un millón de dólares, yo...
3. Si yo (ser) un(a) artista famoso(a), yo...
4. Si (yo) (tener) más tiempo...
5. Si un amigo (regalarme) un nuevo coche, yo...

D. Dos países. Completa estas oraciones sobre Paraguay y Uruguay con formas diminutivas o aumentativas de las siguientes palabras: **casa, chico, chivo, cuento, país, plato.**

1. Son dos _____ muy _____.

2. Un _____ típico de Uruguay es _____.

3. Hay _____ grandes y espléndidas en las capitales.

4. Algunos _____ de Horacio Quiroga son breves pero trágicos.

Querido Diario. Vas a compartir con tu diario todas las cosas que harías si tuvieras la oportunidad de lograrlos. Primero, piensa en los sueños que parecen posibles. Luego, piensa en los sueños que parecen muy difíciles. Entonces, escribe en tu diario los sueños que son más importantes para ti. Puedes empezar así: «Si yo pudiera algún día... ».

Grammar: verbs: *If* clauses **(si)**
Phrases: expressing hopes and aspirations, a wish or desire; hypothesizing
Vocabulary: dreams and aspirations

Letra	Nombre	Ejemplos de nombres de personas y lugares		
a	a	Alfredo	Alicia	Argentina
b	be	Bernardo	Bárbara	Colombia
c	ce	Clemente	Cecilia	Chile
d	de	David	Ada	República Dominicana
e	e	Esteban	Estela	Guinea Ecuatorial
f	efe	Federico	Francisca	Islas Filipinas
g	ge	Guillermo	Gilberta	Guatemala
h	hache	Hugo	Honoria	Haití
i	i	Ignacio	Inés	Nicaragua
j	jota	José	Julieta	San Juan
k	ka	[no common Hispanic names]		Kentucky
l	ele	Lorenzo	Catalina	Brasil
m	eme	Miguel	Emilia	México
n	ene	Norberto	Ana	Honduras
ñ	eñe	Nuño	Toña	España
o	o	Óscar	Dolores	Costa Rica
p	pe	Pablo	Pilar	Panamá
q	cu	Enrique	Paquita	Querétaro
r	ere	Armando	Clara	Puerto Rico
rr	erre	(Roberto)	(Rebeca)	Navarra
s	ese	Samuel	Sara	El Salvador
t	te	Santiago	Teresa	Trinidad
u	u	Lucas	Lucía	Perú
v	uve	Víctor	Verónica	Veracruz
w	doble uve	[no common Hispanic names]		Williamsburg
x	equis	Maximiliano	Xochitl	Oaxaca
y	i griega	Reyes	Maya	Paraguay
z	zeta	Cruz	Zelia	Venezuela

If a Spanish word has no written accent, the stress is predictable. Words that end in a vowel, **n**, or **s** are stressed on the next-to-last (penultimate) syllable.

    ca-sa   *house*   a-*mi*-go   *friend*

Words that end in a consonant other than -**n** or -**s** are stressed on the last syllable.

    ver-dad   *truth*   **ha-*blar***   *to speak, talk*

Words whose spoken accent (stress) doesn't follow this pattern have a written accent to indicate the stressed syllable.

    na-***ción***   *nation*   **a-*ná*-li-sis**   *analysis*

La entonación en español

Spanish intonation resembles English intonation with one important difference: the voice rises higher and falls lower in English than in Spanish. To an English speaker, Spanish may appear to be monotonous. Spanish uses only three tones of voice: "1" being the lowest, "2" the middle tone, and "3" the highest.

Intonation pattern for declarative statements: 1 – 2 – 1

    La fiesta es mañana.   *The party is tomorrow.*
     1   2   1

Intonation pattern for yes-no questions: 1 – 2

    ¿Vas a la fiesta?   *Are you going to the party?*
     1   2

Intonation pattern for information questions: 1 – 2 – 1

    ¿Con quién vas a ir?   *Who(m) are you going with?*
     1   2   1

Intonation pattern for emphatic statements: 1 – 3 – 2

    ¡Yo no voy a ir!   *I am not going to go!*
     1 3   2

Present Infinitive	Indicative	Imperfect	Preterite	Future	Conditional	Present Subjunctive	Past Subjunctive	Commands
hablar	hablo	hablaba	hablé	hablaré	hablaría	hable	hablara	
to speak	hablas	hablabas	hablaste	hablarás	hablarías	hables	hablaras	habla (no hables)
	habla	hablaba	habló	hablará	hablaría	hable	hablara	hable
	hablamos	hablábamos	hablamos	hablaremos	hablaríamos	hablemos	habláramos	hablad
	habláis	hablabais	hablásteis	hablaréis	hablaríais	habléis	hablarais	(no habléis)
	hablan	hablaban	hablaron	hablarán	hablarían	hablen	hablaran	hablen
aprender	aprendo	aprendía	aprendí	aprenderé	aprendería	aprenda	aprendiera	
to learn	aprendes	aprendías	aprendiste	aprenderás	aprenderías	aprendas	aprendieras	aprende (no aprendas)
	aprende	aprendía	aprendió	aprenderá	aprendería	aprenda	aprendiera	aprenda
	aprendemos	aprendíamos	aprendimos	aprenderemos	aprenderíamos	aprendamos	aprendiéramos	aprended
	aprendéis	aprendíais	aprendisteis	aprenderéis	aprenderíais	aprendáis	aprendierais	(no aprendáis)
	aprenden	aprendían	aprendieron	aprenderán	aprenderían	aprendan	aprendieran	aprendan
vivir	vivo	vivía	viví	viviré	viviría	viva	viviera	
to live	vives	vivías	viviste	vivirás	vivirías	vivas	vivieras	vive (no vivas)
	vive	vivía	vivió	vivirá	viviría	viva	viviera	viva
	vivimos	vivíamos	vivimos	viviremos	viviríamos	vivamos	viviéramos	vivid
	vivís	vivíais	vivisteis	viviréis	viviríais	viváis	vivierais	(no viváis)
	viven	vivían	vivieron	vivirán	vivirían	vivan	vivieran	vivan

Compound tenses

Present progressive	estoy estás está estamos estáis están	hablando aprendiendo viviendo
Present perfect indicative	he has ha hemos habéis han	hablado aprendido vivido
Present perfect subjunctive	haya hayas haya hayamos hayáis hayan	hablado aprendido vivido
Past perfect indicative	había habías había habíamos habíais habían	hablado aprendido vivido

Infinitive / Present Participle / Past Participle	Present Indicative	Imperfect	Preterite	Future	Conditional	Present Subjunctive	Past Subjunctive	Commands
pensar *to think* **e → ie** pensando pensado	**pienso** **piensas** **piensa** pensamos pensáis **piensan**	pensaba pensabas pensaba pensábamos pensabais pensaban	pensé pensaste pensó pensamos pensasteis pensaron	pensaré pensarás pensará pensaremos pensaréis pensarán	pensaría pensarías pensaría pensaríamos pensaríais pensarían	**piense** **pienses** **piense** pensemos penséis **piensen**	pensara pensaras pensara pensáramos pensarais pensaran	**piensa** (no **pienses**) **piense** pensad (no **penséis**) **piensen**
acostarse *to go to bed* **o → ue** acostándose acostado	me **acuesto** te **acuestas** se **acuesta** nos acostamos os acostáis se **acuestan**	me acostaba te acostabas se acostaba nos acostábamos os acostabais se acostaban	me acosté te acostaste se acostó nos acostamos os acostasteis se acostaron	me acostaré te acostarás se acostará nos acostaremos os acostaréis se acostarán	me acostaría te acostarías se acostaría nos acostaríamos os acostaríais se acostarían	me **acueste** te **acuestes** se **acueste** nos acostemos os acostéis se **acuesten**	me acostara te acostaras se acostara nos acostáramos os acostarais se acostaran	acuéstate (no te acuestes) acuéstese acostaos (no os acostéis) acuéstense
sentir *to feel* **e → ie, i** **sintiendo** sentido	**siento** **sientes** **siente** sentimos sentís **sienten**	sentía sentías sentía sentíamos sentíais sentían	sentí sentiste **sintió** sentimos sentisteis **sintieron**	sentiré sentirás sentirá sentiremos sentiréis sentirán	sentiría sentirías sentiría sentiríamos sentiríais sentirían	**sienta** **sientas** **sienta** **sintamos** **sintáis** **sientan**	**sintiera** **sintieras** **sintiera** **sintiéramos** **sintierais** **sintieran**	siente (no sientas) sienta sentaos (no sintáis) sientan
pedir *to ask for* **e → i, i** **pidiendo** pedido	**pido** **pides** **pide** pedimos pedís **piden**	pedía pedías pedía pedíamos pedíais pedían	pedí pediste **pidió** pedimos pedisteis **pidieron**	pediré pedirás pedirá pediremos pediréis pedirán	pediría pedirías pediría pediríamos pediríais pedirían	**pida** **pidas** **pida** **pidamos** **pidáis** **pidan**	**pidiera** **pidieras** **pidiera** **pidiéramos** **pidierais** **pidieran**	pide (no pidas) pida pedid (no pidáis) pidan
dormir *to sleep* **o → ue, u** **durmiendo** dormido	**duermo** **duermes** **duerme** dormimos dormís **duermen**	dormía dormías dormía dormíamos dormíais dormían	dormí dormiste **durmió** dormimos dormisteis **durmieron**	dormiré dormirás dormirá dormiremos dormiréis dormirán	dormiría dormirías dormiría dormiríamos dormiríais dormirían	**duerma** **duermas** **duerma** **durmamos** **durmáis** **duerman**	**durmiera** **durmieras** **durmiera** **durmiéramos** **durmierais** **durmieran**	duerme (no duermas) duerma dormid (no durmáis) duerman

Apéndice E: Los verbos con cambios de ortografía

Infinitive / Present Participle / Past Participle	Present Indicative	Imperfect	Preterite	Future	Conditional	Present Subjunctive	Past Subjunctive	Commands
comenzar (e → ie) to begin z → c before e comenzando comenzado	comienzo comienzas comienza comenzamos comenzáis comienzan	comenzaba comenzabas comenzaba comenzábamos comenzabais comenzaban	**comencé** comenzaste comenzó comenzamos comenzasteis comenzaron	comenzaré comenzarás comenzará comenzaremos comenzaréis comenzarán	comenzaría comenzarías comenzaría comenzaríamos comenzaríais comenzaría	**comience** **comiences** **comience** **comencemos** **comencéis** **comiencen**	comenzara comenzaras comenzara comenzáramos comenzarais comenzaran	comienza (**no comiences**) **comience** comenzad (**no comencéis**) **comiencen**
conocer to know c → zc before a, o conociendo conocido	**conozco** conoces conoce conocemos conocéis conocen	conocía conocías conocía conocíamos conocíais conocían	conocí conociste conoció conocimos conocisteis conocieron	conoceré conocerás conocerá conoceremos conoceréis conocerán	conocería conocerías conocería conoceríamos conoceríais conocería	**conozca** **conozcas** **conozca** **conozcamos** **conozcáis** **conozcan**	conociera conocieras conociera conociéramos conocierais conocieran	conoce (**no conozcas**) **conozca** conoced (**no conozcáis**) **conozcan**
construir to build i → y, y inserted before a, e, o **construyendo** construido	**construyo** **construyes** **construye** construimos construís **construyen**	construía construías construía construíamos construíais construían	construí construiste **construyó** construimos construisteis **construyeron**	construiré construirás construirá construiremos construiréis construirán	construiría construirías construiría construiríamos construiríais construirían	**construya** **construyas** **construya** **construyamos** **construyáis** **construyan**	**construyera** **construyeras** **construyera** **construyéramos** **construyerais** **construyeran**	**construye** (**no construyas**) **construya** construid (**no construyáis**) **construyan**
leer to read i → y; stressed i → í **leyendo** leído	leo lees lee leemos leéis leen	leía leías leía leíamos leíais leían	leí leíste **leyó** leímos leísteis **leyeron**	leeré leerás leerá leeremos leeréis leerán	leería leerías leería leeríamos leeríais leerían	lea leas lea leamos leáis lean	**leyera** **leyeras** **leyera** **leyéramos** **leyerais** **leyeran**	lee (no leas) lea leed (no leáis) lean

Infinitive Present Participle Past Participle	Present Indicative	Imperfect	Preterite	Future	Conditional	Present Subjunctive	Past Subjunctive	Commands
pagar *to pay* **g → gu** **before e** pagando pagado	pago pagas paga pagamos pagáis pagan	pagaba pagabas pagaba pagábamos pagabais pagaban	**pagué** pagaste pagó pagamos pagasteis pagaron	pagaré pagarás pagará pagaremos pagaréis pagarán	pagaría pagarías pagaría pagaríamos pagaríais pagarían	**pague** **pagues** **pague** **paguemos** **paguéis** **paguen**	pagara pagaras pagara pagáramos pagarais pagaran	paga **(no pagues)** **pague** pagad **(no paguéis)** **paguen**
seguir **(e → i, i)** *to follow* **gu → g** **before a, o** siguiendo seguido	**sigo** sigues sigue seguimos seguís siguen	seguía seguías seguía seguíamos seguíais seguían	seguí seguiste siguió seguimos seguisteis siguieron	seguiré seguirás seguirá seguiremos seguiréis seguirán	seguiría seguirías seguiría seguiríamos seguiríais seguirían	**siga** **sigas** **siga** **sigamos** **sigáis** **sigan**	siguiera siguieras siguiera siguiéramos siguierais siguieran	sigue **(no sigas)** **siga** seguid **(no sigáis)** **sigan**
tocar *to play, to touch* **c → qu** **before e** tocando tocado toco	toco tocas toca tocamos tocáis tocan	tocaba tocabas tocaba tocábamos tocabais tocaban	**toqué** tocaste tocó tocamos tocasteis tocaron	tocaré tocarás tocará tocaremos tocaréis tocarán	tocaría tocarías tocaría tocaríamos tocaríais tocarían	**toque** **toques** **toque** **toquemos** **toquéis** **toquen**	tocara tocaras tocara tocáramos tocarais tocaran	toca **(no toques)** **toque** tocad **(no toquéis)** **toquen**

Infinitive / Present Participle / Past Participle	Present Indicative	Imperfect	Preterite	Future	Conditional	Present Subjunctive	Past Subjunctive	Commands
andar *to walk* andando andado	ando andas anda andamos andáis andan	andaba andabas andaba andábamos andabais andaban	**anduve** **anduviste** **anduvo** **anduvimos** **anduvisteis** **anduvieron**	andaré andarás andará andaremos andaréis andarán	andaría andarías andaría andaríamos andaríais andarían	ande andes ande andemos andéis anden	**anduviera** **anduvieras** **anduviera** **anduviéramos** **anduvierais** **anduvieran**	anda (no andes) ande andad (no andéis) anden
*caer *to fall* **cayendo** caído	**caigo** caes cae caemos caéis caen	caía caías caía caíamos caíais caían	caí **caíste** **cayó** **caímos** **caísteis** **cayeron**	caeré caerás caerá caeremos caeréis caerán	caería caerías caería caeríamos caeríais caerían	**caiga** **caigas** **caiga** **caigamos** **caigáis** **caigan**	**cayera** **cayeras** **cayera** **cayéramos** **cayerais** **cayeran**	cae (no caigas) **caiga** caed (**no caigáis**) **caigan**
*dar *to give* dando dado	**doy** das da damos dais dan	daba dabas daba dábamos dabais daban	**di** **diste** **dio** **dimos** **disteis** **dieron**	daré darás dará daremos daréis darán	daría darías daría daríamos daríais darían	**dé** **des** **dé** **demos** **deis** **den**	diera dieras diera diéramos dierais dieran	da (no des) **dé** dad (**no deis**) den
*decir *to say, tell* **diciendo** **dicho**	**digo** **dices** **dice** decimos decís **dicen**	decía decías decía decíamos decíais decían	**dije** **dijiste** **dijo** **dijimos** **dijisteis** **dijeron**	**diré** **dirás** **dirá** **diremos** **diréis** **dirán**	**diría** **dirías** **diría** **diríamos** **diríais** **dirían**	**diga** **digas** **diga** **digamos** **digáis** **digan**	**dijera** **dijeras** **dijera** **dijéramos** **dijerais** **dijeran**	**di (no digas)** **diga** decid (**no digáis**) **digan**
*estar *to be* estando estado	**estoy** **estás** **está** estamos estáis **están**	estaba estabas estaba estábamos estabais estaban	**estuve** **estuviste** **estuvo** **estuvimos** **estuvisteis** **estuvieron**	estaré estarás estará estaremos estaréis estarán	estaría estarías estaría estaríamos estaríais estarían	**esté** **estés** **esté** estemos estéis **estén**	estuviera estuvieras estuviera estuviéramos estuvierais estuvieran	está (**no estés**) **esté** estad (**no estéis**) **estén**

Infinitive Present Participle Past Participle	Present Indicative	Imperfect	Preterite	Future	Conditional	Present Subjunctive	Past Subjunctive	Commands
haber *to have* habiendo habido	he has ha [hay] hemos habéis han	había habías había habíamos habíais habían	hube hubiste hubo hubimos hubisteis hubieron	habré habrás habrá habremos habréis habrán	habría habrías habría habríamos habríais habrían	haya hayas haya hayamos hayáis hayan	hubiera hubieras hubiera hubiéramos hubierais hubieran	
*hacer *to make, do* haciendo **hecho**	**hago** haces hace hacemos hacéis hacen	hacía hacías hacía hacíamos hacíais hacían	**hice hiciste hizo hicimos hicisteis hicieron**	**haré harás hará haremos haréis harán**	**haría harías haría haríamos haríais harían**	**haga hagas haga hagamos hagáis hagan**	**hiciera hicieras hiciera hiciéramos hicierais hicieran**	**haz (no hagas) haga** haced (no hagáis) **hagan**
ir *to go* **yendo** ido	**voy vas va vamos vais van**	**iba ibas iba íbamos ibais iban**	**fui fuiste fue fuimos fuisteis fueron**	iré irás irá iríamos iréis irán	iría irías iría iríamos iríais irían	**vaya vayas vaya vayamos vayáis vayan**	**fuera fueras fuera fuéramos fuerais fueran**	**ve (no vayas) vaya** id (no vayáis) **vayan**
*oír *to hear* **oyendo** **oído**	**oigo oyes oye** oímos oís **oyen**	oía oías oía oíamos oíais oían	oí **oíste oyó** oímos oísteis **oyeron**	oiré oirás oirá oiremos oiréis oirán	oiría oirías oiría oiríamos oiríais oirían	**oiga oigas oiga oigamos oigáis oigan**	**oyera oyeras oyera oyéramos oyerais oyeran**	**oye (no oigas) oiga** oíd (no oigáis) **oigan**
poder (o → ue) *can, to be able* **pudiendo** podido	**puedo puedes puede** podemos podéis **pueden**	podía podías podía podíamos podíais podían	**pude pudiste pudo pudimos pudisteis pudieron**	**podré podrás podrá podremos podréis podrán**	**podría podrías podría podríamos podríais podrían**	**pueda puedas pueda** podamos podáis **puedan**	**pudiera pudieras pudiera pudiéramos pudierais pudieran**	

Infinitive / Present Participle / Past Participle	Present Indicative	Imperfect	Preterite	Future	Conditional	Present Subjunctive	Past Subjunctive	Commands
*poner to place, put poniendo **puesto**	**pongo** pones pone ponemos ponéis ponen	ponía ponías ponía poníamos poníais ponían	**puse** **pusiste** **puso** **pusimos** **pusisteis** **pusieron**	**pondré** **pondrás** **pondrá** **pondremos** **pondréis** **pondrán**	**pondría** **pondrías** **pondría** **pondríamos** **pondríais** **pondrían**	**ponga** **pongas** **ponga** **pongamos** **pongáis** **pongan**	**pusiera** **pusieras** **pusiera** **pusiéramos** **pusierais** **pusieran**	**pon** (no **pongas**) **ponga** poned (**no pongáis**) **pongan**
querer (e → ie) to want, wish queriendo querido	**quiero** **quieres** **quiere** queremos queréis **quieren**	quería querías quería queríamos queríais querían	**quise** **quisiste** **quiso** **quisimos** **quisisteis** **quisieron**	**querré** **querrás** **querrá** **querremos** **querréis** **querrán**	**querría** **querrías** **querría** **querríamos** **querríais** **querrían**	**quiera** **quieras** **quiera** queramos queráis **quieran**	**quisiera** **quisieras** **quisiera** **quisiéramos** **quisierais** **quisieran**	**quiere** (no **quieras**) **quiera** quered (no queráis) **quieran**
reír to laugh **riendo** **reído**	**río** **ríes** **ríe** **reímos** reís **ríen**	reía reías reía reíamos reíais reían	reí **reíste** **rió** **reímos** **reísteis** **rieron**	reiré reirás reirá reiremos reiréis reirán	reiría reirías reiría reiríamos reiríais reirían	**ría** **rías** **ría** **riamos** **riáis** **rían**	**riera** **rieras** **riera** **riéramos** **rierais** **rieran**	**ríe** (no **rías**) **ría** **reíd** (no **riáis**) **rían**
*saber to know sabiendo sabido	**sé** sabes sabe sabemos sabéis saben	sabía sabías sabía sabíamos sabíais sabían	**supe** **supiste** **supo** **supimos** **supisteis** **supieron**	**sabré** **sabrás** **sabrá** **sabremos** **sabréis** **sabrán**	**sabría** **sabrías** **sabría** **sabríamos** **sabríais** **sabrían**	**sepa** **sepas** **sepa** **sepamos** **sepáis** **sepan**	**supiera** **supieras** **supiera** **supiéramos** **supierais** **supieran**	sabe (**no sepas**) **sepa** sabed (**no sepáis**) **sepan**
*salir to go out saliendo salido	**salgo** sales sale salimos salís salen	salía salías salía salíamos salíais salían	salí saliste salió salimos salisteis salieron	**saldré** **saldrás** **saldrá** **saldremos** **saldréis** **saldrán**	**saldría** **saldrías** **saldría** **saldríamos** **saldrías** **saldrían**	**salga** **salgas** **salga** **salgamos** **salgáis** **salgan**	saliera salieras saliera saliéramos salierais salieran	**sal** (no **salgas**) **salga** salid (**no salgáis**) **salgan**

Infinitive Present Participle Past Participle	Present Indicative	Imperfect	Preterite	Future	Conditional	Present Subjunctive	Past Subjunctive	Commands
ser *to be* siendo sido	soy eres es somos sois son	era eras era éramos erais eran	fui fuiste fue fuimos fuisteis fueron	seré serás será seremos seréis serán	sería serías sería seríamos seríais serían	sea seas sea seamos seáis sean	fuera fueras fuera fuéramos fuerais fueran	sé (no seas) sea sed (no seáis) sean
*tener *to have* teniendo tenido	tengo tienes tiene tenemos tenéis tienen	tenía tenías tenía teníamos teníais tenían	tuve tuviste tuvo tuvimos tuvisteis tuvieron	tendré tendrás tendrá tendremos tendréis tendrán	tendría tendrías tendría tendríamos tendríais tendrían	tenga tengas tenga tengamos tengáis tengan	tuviera tuvieras tuviera tuviéramos tuvierais tuvieran	ten (no tengas) tenga tened (no tengáis) tengan
traer *to bring* trayendo traído	traigo traes trae traemos traéis traen	traía traías traía traíamos traíais traían	traje trajiste trajo trajimos trajisteis trajeron	traeré traerás traerá traeremos traeréis traerán	traería traerías traería traeríamos traeríais traerían	traiga traigas traiga traigamos traigáis traigan	trajera trajeras trajera trajéramos trajerais trajeran	trae (no traigas) traiga traed (no traigáis) traigan
*venir *to come* viniendo venido	vengo vienes viene venimos venís vienen	venía venías venía veníamos veníais venían	vine viniste vino vinimos vinisteis vinieron	vendré vendrás vendrá vendremos vendréis vendrán	vendría vendrías vendría vendríamos vendríais vendrían	venga vengas venga vengamos vengáis vengan	viniera vinieras viniera viniéramos vinierais vinieran	ven (no vengas) venga venid (no vengáis) vengan
ver *to see* viendo visto	veo ves ve vemos veis ven	veía veías veía veíamos veíais veían	vi viste vio vimos visteis vieron	veré verás verá veremos veréis verán	vería verías vería veríamos veríais verían	vea veas vea veamos veáis vean	viera vieras viera viéramos vierais vieran	ve (no veas) vea ved (no veáis) vean

*Verbs with irregular *yo*-forms in the present indicative

A ver si sabes Answer Key

Capítulo Preliminar

A. ¡Saludos a todos!
1. Buenos, tal, Bien, tú
2. Buenas, Quiero, Mucho gusto, Igualmente
3. Qué, muy bien, Muy, gracias, la vista

B. Parece familiar.
1. consideration
2. elevator
3. international
4. medicine
5. population
6. student
7. professor
8. hydrogen
9. capacity
10. generally

C. Juanito
1. [no written accent]
2. estúpido
3. lápiz
4. [no written accent]
5. [no written accent]
6. ambición
7. sabías
8. [no written accent]

Preguntas culturales
There are 21 Spanish-speaking countries (22 if you count the United States). They are found on four continents: Africa, Europe, North America, and South America.

Capítulo 1

A. ¿De quién hablas?
1. yo
2. nosotros
3. tú (usted)
4. tú
5. Usted
6. ustedes (vosotros)

B. Mis amigos y mi familia
1. son
2. es
3. es
4. somos

5. son
6. eres

C. ¿El? ¿La?
1. La
2. Los
3. La
4. Los
5. Las
6. El

D. Invitados
1. pequeña
2. activos
3. gordito
4. guapos
5. peruano
6. extrovertido / extrovertida

E. ¿De qué nación?
1. Es de Panamá.
2. Son de El Salvador.
3. Son de Puerto Rico.
4. Son de Perú.
5. Es de Argentina.
6. Es de España.

F. ¿Cuántos?
1. veintisiete
2. veintiún
3. quince
4. veinticinco
5. once
6. treinta

G. ¡Preguntas y más preguntas!
1. ¿Quién?
2. ¿De dónde?
3. ¿Cómo?
4. ¿Cuándo?
5. ¿Qué?

H. Presentaciones
1. al
2. a
3. a las
4. al
5. a

I. ¿De quién es?
1. de la
2. de
3. del
4. de las
5. de los

Preguntas culturales
1. An American is anyone who lives in the Americas.
2. Mexican culture is felt in the U.S. in music, food, and mural painting.
3. They have two different cultural backgrounds to enjoy.

Capítulo 2

A. ¡Hola!
JUAN: estás
LOLA: Estoy
JUAN: estás
LOLA: está.
JUAN: están
LOLA: estamos

B. En la lista hay...
1. hay unas
2. hay un
3. hay una
4. hay unos

C. Planes
1. van al
2. va a la
3. voy al
4. vamos a la
5. vas a la

D. Actividades
1. van a mirar
2. va a hablar
3. voy a leer / mirar
4. vamos a beber
5. vas a hablar / estudiar

E. El estrés
1. tienen que
2. tiene que
3. tenemos que
4. tengo que
5. tienes que

F. ¿De quién?
1. mi calculadora
2. tu bolígrafo
3. sus lápices
4. sus papeles
5. nuestras mochilas
6. su diccionario

G. Cuentas y más cuentas
1. setenta y un
2. treinta y tres
3. noventa y cuatro
4. sesenta y nueve
5. cincuenta y siete
6. cuarenta y dos
7. ochenta y cinco
8. setenta y ocho

Preguntas culturales
1. Little Havana is a section of Miami which is named after Havana because of all the Cubans who live there.
2. Cultural attractions found in Cuba include la Plaza de la Catedral, el Capitolio Nacional, and la Plaza de la Revolución.
3. Parties include all generations. Often aunts, uncles, and grandparents live with the family. The whole family eats together and they sit and chat afterwards.

Capítulo 3

A. ¡De viaje!
1. mil ochocientos treinta y seis metros (tres mil pies)
2. cinco mil setecientos metros (dieciocho mil setecientos pies)
3. doce metros (treinta y nueve pies)
4. dos mil doscientos cuarenta metros (siete mil trescientos cuarenta y nueve pies)

B. Fechas de nacimiento
1. sábado, el veintiséis de febrero de mil novecientos once
2. martes, el dieciocho de abril de mil novecientos cincuenta y dos
3. jueves, el veintitrés de julio de dos mil setenta y nueve
4. miércoles, el veintinueve de septiembre de dos mil catorce

C. Después de las clases
1. trabajan
2. preparo
3. tomamos
4. cocina
5. estudias

D. En el parque Chapultepec
1. recuerda
2. comienzan
3. juegan
4. piensa, juega
5. cuento
6. almorzamos
7. cierra

E. ¿A quién?
1. –
2. a
3. a
4. –
5. –

Preguntas culturales
1. Similarities include diet, the fact that the family is very important, the diversity of the population, and the fact that the ethnic mix reflects the history of the country. Differences include the ethnic composition of the population, and the fact that many Mexicans speak indigenous languages.
2. It is the center of both the ancient and the modern capitals and is surrounded by historic buildings.
3. The geography and climate of both countries are varied. Both countries have mountains, plains and deserts, and both have temperate and hot regions.

Capítulo 4

A. El examen
1. comprende, tiene
2. corren, preparan
3. bebes, aprendes
4. creemos, sabemos, tenemos

5. rompe
6. haces

B. ¡Qué día!
1. escribimos
2. decide
3. describen
4. discute
5. asisto

C. ¡Qué debo hacer?
1. Sé, tengo
2. Veo
3. venzo
4. Oigo
5. Doy
6. Conozco
7. vengo, salgo

D. Todo el día
1. oye
2. oyen
3. oímos
4. oyes
5. oigo

E. ¿Qué saben?
1. conozco a, sé
2. conocemos, sabemos
3. sabes
4. conoce, sabe
5. conocen al

F. Me gustaría pero...
TINO: gustaría, a las ocho de la noche
MARÍA: gustaría, a las nueve de la noche
TINO: gustaría, a la una y media
MARÍA: me, a las dos y cuarto
TINO: hora
MARÍA: Son las cuatro y veinte

Preguntas culturales
1. Some U.S. major league teams winter there, the Dominican Republic contributes excellent players to major U.S. ball clubs, and the children learn to play baseball as they learn to walk.
2. The other profession of the mayor of Santo Domingo is that he is a musician.

3. They are tropical and have plants and animals typical of the Dominican Republic (like the manatee) and not buffalo and bears.

Capítulo 5

A. Estoy cansado.
1. duermo
2. puede
3. duelen
4. duermes

B. ¡Qué platillo!
1. entiendo
2. tenemos
3. hierves
4. sugiere

C. ¡Silencio!
1. dice
2. reímos
3. pide
4. sigo

D. ¡Qué divertido!
1. es
2. son
3. está
4. está
5. es
6. está
7. está
8. es

E. La clase
1. nunca / nada
2. ni, ni
3. ni, tampoco
4. nada
5. nadie

F. Compañeros de clase
1. más…que
2. menor / más joven que
3. más que
4. menos…que
5. tan…como
6. tantos…como

G. ¡Sobresaliente!
1. más…de
2. más…de
3. riquísima
4. bonitísima
5. interesantísimo

Preguntas culturales
1. Puerto Rico es un Estado Libre Asociado de los Estados Unidos..
2. La comida mexicana es picante y la comida puertorriqueña no es. La gente de los dos países come frijoles y arroz.
3. Las calles son angostas, hay muchos edificios coloniales, es una ciudad amurallada, las calles son de adoquines, el Morro está allí.

Capítulo 6

A. ¿Quieres ir al cine?
1. está trabajando
2. están limpiando
3. están lavando
4. está estudiando
5. estoy pasando
6. estás sacudiendo
7. está barriendo
8. está durmiendo

B. ¿Recuerdas?
1. lo ve
2. no la recuerda
3. no los bebe
4. la comen
5. lo miran
6. no las conoce
7. no los saluda
8. las llama

C. Y ahora, ¿qué?
1. los voy a hacer, voy a hacerlos
2. la puedo arreglar, puedo arreglarla
3. la estoy sacando, estoy sacándola
4. lo puedo cortar, puedo cortarlo
5. la estoy lavando, estoy lavándola
6. las voy a poner en orden, voy a ponerlas en orden

D. En clase
1. Escucha
2. Saca
3. Abre
4. Haz

5. Estudia
6. Habla
7. Escribe en tu
8. Practica

Usando pronombres
1. Escúchala
2. Sácalo
3. Ábrelo
4. Hazlos
5. Estúdiala
6. Háblalo
7. Escríbelas
8. Practícalos

E. ¿Más mandatos?
1. Toma
2. Haz
3. No comas
4. Practica
5. Sigue
6. No bebas
7. Busca
8. No fumes

Preguntas culturales
1. Está construyendo un mejor futuro con cooperación internacional.
2. La gente de El Salvador, México y otros países es maya y otros indios indígenas.
3. Tres lugares de El Salvador que son interesantes para muchos turistas incluyen San Salvador, la capital, Santa Ana con sus calles coloniales y sus jardines bonitos, y las playas como El Cuco y el Espino.

Capítulo 7

A. El diario de Anita
1. Visitó
2. Miramos
3. saqué
4. almorcé
5. pagué
6. llamaron
7. Hablamos
8. llegó
9. estudiamos

B. Las vacaciones

Pasaron, decidimos, leyó, escogimos, viajaron, asistí, Aprendí, viajamos, viste, comimos, bebió, Conocimos, invitaron, sirvieron, discutimos

C. En el trabajo
1. Voy a escribirle un memo. Le voy a escribir un memo.
2. Están preguntándote sobre tus planes. Te están preguntando sobre tus planes.
3. El jefe nos dice algo importante.
4. Puedo prepararle un informe esta tarde. Le puedo preparar un informe esta tarde.
5. ¿Piensas leerles tu carta? ¿Les piensas leer tu carta?
6. Antonio me pide un favor.

D. En Colombia
1. A mí me gustan los platillos típicos.
2. A José le encanta la gente.
3. A María y a mí nos gusta el café.
4. A ti te gustan las montañas.
5. A todos nosotros nos encantan las playas.
6. A ellas les encanta todo el país.

E. De vacaciones
1. fuimos
2. dio
3. dijo
4. hizo
5. fue

F. Una familia ocupada
1. Hace dos años que los señores Rojas trabajan en la universidad.
2. Hace cinco años que Lucía toma lecciones de piano.
3. Hace tres meses que Anamaría y Beto tienen su perro, Chico.
4. Hace cinco semanas que trabajo en el banco.

5. Y tú, Joselito, hace una semana que juegas fútbol con tus amigos.

G. ¿Qué pasó y cuándo?
1. Hace…años que Norma y Arnoldo visitaron Colombia.
2. Hace…años que mis amigos y yo fuimos a Puerto Rico.
3. Hace…que Uds. comenzaron sus estudios.
4. Hace cinco horas que hablé con mi hermana.
5. Hace tres días que hice las tareas de español.
6. Hace un año que planeé mi viaje a Cuba.

Preguntas culturales
1. Las atracciones de Bogotá incluyen Catedral de Sal, el Museo de Oro y el Ballet Folklórico.
2. Los españoles invadieron y vencieron a los chibchas.
3. Es un autor colombiano que ganó el Premio Nóbel de Literatura.

Capítulo 8

A. ¿Enfermo?
1. hubo
2. no quiso
3. estuvo
4. trajo
5. puso
6. tuvo
7. quisieron
8. supo
9. estuvo
10. hubo

B. Correo electrónico
1. Sirvieron
2. hirvieron
3. frieron
4. repetí
5. pidió
6. sugirió
7. pedí
8. Mentí

C. Buenos amigos
1. Diana me la escribió ayer.

2. Diana y Quico nos las mandaron anteayer.
3. Quico te la preparó anoche.
4. Quico y Diana nos los compraron el lunes pasado.
5. Quico me lo repuso la semana pasada.
6. Diana me los trajo el fin de semana pasado.

D. Fiesta de Memo
1. Margarita se lo dio.
2. Mamá se la preparó.
3. Yo se la mandé.
4. Papá se lo preparó.
5. Los abuelos se los mandaron.
6. Los vecinos se lo compraron.

E. En la universidad
1. Yo tengo hambre.
2. Tú tienes celos.
3. Julia y Sara tienen calor.
4. Nosotros no tenemos paciencia.
5. tiene razón.
6. tiene frío.
7. Uds. tienen sueño.
8. Yo tengo suerte.

F. ¿Qué pasó?
1. Hubo, tiene miedo
2. tuvieron que, tienen sed, hambre
3. condujo, tiene cuidado
4. pudieron, tienen suerte
5. quise, pude, tengo ganas de comprarlo.

Preguntas culturales
1. Defiende los derechos humanos de la gente indígena.
2. Miguel Ángel Asturias fue autor, periodista, representante en el congreso y diplomático en varios países.
3. Los mayas inventaron un sistema matemático basado en 20.
4. El Popol Vuh es el libro de la comunidad, el libro sagrado de los mayas.

Capítulo 9

A. De vacaciones
1. se duermen
2. se levanta
3. se bañan
4. se peinan
5. nos despertamos
6. me duermo
7. se afeita
8. te pones, te vistes

B. Los pensamientos
1. levantar. levantarme
2. bañar, bañarme
3. lavarle el pelo, lavarme el pelo
4. peinar, peinarme
5. vestir, me visto

C. Noticias
1. se puso enojado
2. te pusiste enfermo / enferma
3. se puso nervioso
4. se pusieron contentas
5. me puse enojado / enojada
6. se pusieron aburridos

D. ¡Cómo se divierten!
1. con
2. A
3. con
4. de
5. sin
6. consigo
7. para
8. ella
9. a
10. conmigo
11. a
12. contigo
13. sin
14. a

E. En la tienda
DEPENDIENTA: En
PETRA: con
DEPENDIENTA: Entre
PETRA: sin
PETRA: De
DEPENDIENTA: de, de
PETRA: de

F. En la joyería
CLIENTE: esa
DEPENDIENTA: Ésta, ésta
CLIENTE: Ésa
DEPENDIENTA: Ésta
CLIENTE: ese
DEPENDIENTA: Este

Preguntas culturales
1. Perú tiene diversidad geográfica, étnica y cultural.
2. Mario Vargas Llosa es un autor famoso y fue candidato para presidente.
3. Los ricos tesoros de Perú incluyen artefactos de oro, plata y piedras preciosas, el Museo de Oro, el Museo Nacional de Antropología, las iglesias de San Francisco y Santo Domingo y su diversidad geográfica.
4. La arquitectura de los incas tiene piedras muy grandes y no tienen cemento. Duran más tiempo que los edificios construidos en la arquitectura moderna.

Capítulo 10

A. Una carta
1. Vivía
2. asistíamos
3. Pasábamos
4. empezaban
5. terminaban
6. volvía
7. asistía
8. estudiaba
9. salíamos
10. hacías
11. te divertías

B. Los fines de semana de niño
1. iba
2. veíamos
3. veíamos
4. eran
5. iba
6. veía
7. ibas
8. veías

C. Conociendo Argentina
1. sabían
2. conocimos
3. pude
4. supimos
5. no quiso
6. quisiste
7. pudieron
8. tuvo

D. El viaje
Answers will vary.

Preguntas culturales
1. Evita Perón es importante porque se dedicó a muchas causas sociales, defendió a la gente, luchó contra las injusticias, estableció programas de salud y programas sociales y políticos.
2. Jorge Luis Borges denunció a los peronistas en sus ensayos. No tenía confianza ni en los peronistas ni en sus programas políticos.
3. Los sitios de interés turístico en Argentina incluyen el Parque Nacional Iguazú, el Parque Nacional Liahué Calel, Buenos (con la Plaza de Mayo, los centros comerciales, restaurantes, el Río de la Plata), las Islas Malvinas y San Carlos Bariloche.

Capítulo 11

A. ¡Saludos de Costa Rica!
1. llegamos
2. Pasamos
3. fuimos
4. conocí
5. dijeron
6. salimos
7. vimos
8. nos divertimos
9. comimos
10. fuimos
11. bailé

B. ¡Ah, la juventud!
1. era
2. asistía
3. caminaban
4. jugábamos
5. hablábamos

B. ¡Ah, la juventud! *(cont.)*
6. se sentaban
7. leían
8. iba
9. nos levantábamos
10. ayudábamos
11. me divertía
12. hacías

C. Mi primera gata
tenía, quería
pedía, respondían, tenía,
   tenía
compramos
pedí, tuvo
dijeron, pasamos

D. Los bosques
1. vivían
2. Comían
3. encontraban
4. continúo
5. llegaron
6. Cortaron
7. plantaron
8. empezaron
9. perdieron
10. entró
11. pasó
12. comenzó

E. Mas noticias de Costa Rica
acabamos de, acabó,
te acabaste, acabaron con,
acaban de, acaba de

Preguntas culturales
1. Don Pepe (José Figueres Ferrer) fue presidente de Costa Rica. Estableció un sistema de seguros, sanidad y de educación fuerte y un banco nacional.
2. "La zona viva" está en Tegucigalpa el capital de Honduras. Es un centro comercial animado con muchos restaurantes, tiendas, hoteles y oficinas.
3. Las civilizaciones maya, y española forma la cultura hondureña. En la época colonial su capital, Tegucigalpa, fue un centro de la industria minera centroamericana.

4. La geografía de Costa Rica se caracteriza por una diversidad ecológica.

Capítulo 12

A. Turistas
1. Miren
2. vayan
3. busquen
4. Recuerden
5. saquen
6. visite
7. dejen
8. Vengan

B. Este fin de semana
1. llueva
2. tenga
3. llamen
4. podamos
5. te diviertas
6. descansemos

C. Observaciones
1. No es bueno que el deportista coma comida grasosa.
2. Es evidente que tú trabajas mucho como fotógrafo.
3. Es ridículo que los locutores digan cosas absurdas.
4. Es importante que el piloto duerma bien antes de su viaje.
5. Es mejor que la diplomática sepa hablar varios idiomas.
6. Es una pena que nosotros los vendedores no podamos ofrecer descuentos.
7. Es posible que yo no reciba un buen sueldo.
8. Es necesario que todos los empleados descansen después de trabajar todo el día.

D. Una fiesta fracasada
1. u
2. las
3. el
4. e
5. el
6. e, o

7. u, y
8. el (del)

Preguntas culturales
1. Es famoso por su diversidad y es una reserva de la biósfera donde hay muchísimas especies de plantas y animales.
2. Ella reestableció relaciones positivas con los EE.UU.
3. El lago se llama Lago de Nicaragua o Cocibolca o La Mar Dulce. Allí se encuentran tiburones de agua dulce.
4. Se puede percibir el alma triste y atormentada del autor.

Capítulo 13

A. El mensaje
1. cambiemos
2. vayamos
3. visitemos
4. pienses
5. pasemos
6. escribas
7. regale
8. llames

B. Otras ideas
1. El profesor de español me dice que yo tome dos clases más.
2. Tu amiga Sara te sugiere que no vivas lejos de la universidad.
3. Mi hermana nos dice que no veamos la nueva película.
4. Jorge impide que sus amigos manejen su coche.
5. Su jefa permite que él salga temprano.
6. Yo te recomiendo que sigas las instrucciones.

C. ¿Cómo reaccionan?
Answers will vary. Suggestions follow.
Ellos están molestos que tú estés enferma.
Nosotros estamos desilusionados que Gloria tenga que irse.

D. ¡Qué emoción!
1. se alegra, estén
2. tememos, vaya
3. espera, jueguen
4. dicen, están
5. choca, interrumpan
6. sentimos, juegue
7. estás, no puedas
8. fastidia, tengamos

Preguntas culturales
1. Andrés Bello fue a Londres en misión política en 1810 por la junta revolucionaria venezolana.
2. Andrés Bello fue amigo y maestro del libertador.
3. La música típica de Caracas muestra todas las influencias de la música local, regional e internacional.

Capítulo 14

A. Opuestos
1. Pablo cree que importa hacer mucho ejercicio.
2. Pablo duda que sea importante trabajar todos los días.
3. Pablo no cree que los hombres deban pagar siempre cuando salen con las mujeres.
4. Pablo dice que es dudoso que la tecnología siempre represente el progreso.
5. Pablo no duda que la comida en España es deliciosa.
6. Pablo dice que es dudoso que ella sea más inteligente que él.

B. La sopa de ajo
1. Se quita
2. Se pica
3. se machaca
4. se fríe
5. se pone
6. se fríe
7. Se agrega
8. se pone
9. se hierve
10. se quiere
11. se puede

C. Por fin
1. para
2. por
3. para
4. para
5. Por
6. Por
7. para
8. para
9. por
10. para
11. para
12. por
13. para
14. Por
15. por
16. por
17. para
18. Por

Preguntas culturales
1. Ana María Matute es una autora feminista, reconocida y prolífica.
2. España es un reino: tiene rey, reina y una familia real.
3. Se dice que España es un mosaico de culturas por las muchas influencias que forman la base de su cultura.

Capítulo 15

A. No encuentro
1. perdí
2. escriba
3. terminó
4. parezca
5. sepa

B. La comida
1. Se puso la mesa.
2. Se prepararon (sirvieron) unos platillos riquísimos.
3. Se sirvió (preparó) un postre especial.
4. Se bebió el café.
5. Se lavaron los platos.

C. En la oficina
1. Primeramente, puntualmente
2. rápida, cuidadosamente
3. exactamente
4. clara, lógicamente
5. completamente

D. La familia
1. primera
2. primer, segundo
3. primer, segundo, tercer, segundo
4. quinto
5. quinta

Preguntas culturales
1. *Answer will vary.*
2. Chile tiene el Estrecho de Magallanes, la Tierra del Fuego y un número de islas que estudió Darwin. También tiene la Isla de Pascua, que tiene unas estatuas grandes de piedra.
3. Los poemas de Gabriela Mistral son profundos. Describen su amor a la humanidad, a los niños, a los pobres y a la naturaleza.
4. Fue una evolución dramática. Primero combinó sus creencias políticas e ideológicas, y después su poesía era más simbólica y enigmática.

Capítulo 16

A. ¿Quieres salir?
1. Vamos a ver una película. Veamos una película.
2. Vamos a comer en un restaurante. Comamos en un restaurante.
3. Vamos a asistir a un concierto. Asistamos a un concierto.
4. Vamos a salir a un club. Salgamos a un club.
5. Vamos a escuchar música. Escuchemos música.
6. Vamos a divertirnos toda la noche y acostarnos al amanecer. Divirtámonos toda la noche y acostémonos al amanecer.

B. No quiero...
1. No veamos una película.
2. No comamos en un restaurante.
3. No asistamos a un concierto.

B. No quiero... *(cont.)*
4. No salgamos a un club.
5. No escuchemos música.
6. No nos divirtamos toda la noche y no nos acostemos al amanecer.

C. El alpinismo
ha pasado, he ido, He visitado, me he divertido, Ha escalado, haya podido, hemos esquiado, me he atrevido, he oído, hemos disfrutado

D. Cita cancelada
1. se haya ido
2. hemos olvidado
3. haya escrito
4. haya venido
5. hayan hablado

E. ¡Más sorpresas!
1. salió
2. llegó
3. descubrió
4. se habían ido
5. Esperó
6. llegó
7. había venido
8. salido
9. llegó
10. la había cancelado

F. Mi opinión
Answers will vary. Suggestions follow.
1. lo difícil, lo que importa
2. lo frustrante
3. lo difícil, lo imposible, lo que quiero
4. lo imposible, lo que busco, lo que quiero
5. lo bueno, lo que importa, lo que me gusta
6. lo que quiero, lo que busco, lo que me gusta

Preguntas culturales
1. Los indios bolivianos viven en el campo y producen verduras y cereales. También crían animales que usan para su lana y su carne. Comen muchas papas y su comida es picante. Llevan ropa típica con sombreros y tienen música que hacen con la quena y la zampoña. Bailan bailes populares.
2. Es muy difícil en una sociedad machista que se acepte a este tipo de autor. No todos reconocen los derechos de la mujer y muchos quieren suprimirlos. (Se aceptan otras respuestas.)
3. Dos aspectos curiosos de Bolivia son que el país tiene dos capitales y que no tiene costas. (Las respuestas van a variar.)

Capítulo 17

A. En el año 2100
1. tendremos
2. leeré
3. harás
4. sabrán
5. será

B. A Guinea Ecuatorial
1. Cuando lleguemos a la capital iremos (vamos a ir) al hotel.
2. Esperarás hasta que venga el guía.
3. Iremos (Vamos a ir) adonde nos indique la guía turística.
4. Tan pronto como vayamos a Malabo, tu esposo subirá el volcán.
5. Cuando estemos en Evinayong, nadaré en las aguas cristalinas de los ríos.

Preguntas culturales
1. Hay menos especies ahora y hay menos hábitates donde puedan vivir. También hay más contaminación y más seres humanos que visitan y viven en las islas.
2. Los dos países tienen la palabra **ecuador** en su nombre y los dos están muy cerca del ecuador.

Capítulo 18

A. Buenos amigos
1. haría
2. le llevaría
3. te llamaríamos
4. les ayudaría
5. se sacrificarían

B. Algo más...
1. fuera
2. hiciera
3. vinieran
4. gustaría
5. podría
6. le trajeras
7. llamaras

C. Sueños y más sueños
1. me ofreciera
2. ganara
3. fuera
4. tuviera
5. me regalara

D. Dos países
1. paisitos, chiquitos
2. platillo (platito), chivito
3. casonas
4. cuentitos

Preguntas culturales
1. Paraguay y Uruguay tienen una variedad de aspectos geográficos. La topografía varía pero hay ríos, montañas y Uruguay tiene una costa en el este también. Hay muchas comidas populares como la parrillada, bistecs, bebidas populares y otros platos indígenas. (Las respuestas varían.)
2. Sus cuentos son morbosos, fantásticos y trágicos. Describen la naturaleza salvaje y cómo la gente lucha contra la naturaleza.

Vocabulario español-inglés

A

a to, at
a mano derecha on the right-hand side
a mano izquierda on the left-hand side
a veces at times
abogado(a) lawyer
abono fertilizer
abrelatas *m.* can opener
abril *m.* April
abrir to open
abuelo(a) grandfather, grandmother
acabar to finish
acabar con to do away with, get rid of, finish off
acabar de + *inf.* to have just (done something)
acabarse to finish up, run out of
acampar to camp
acera sidewalk
aconsejar to advise
acostar(se) to put (go) to bed
activo active
actor *m.* actor
actriz *f.* actress
acuerdo agreement
acumular to accumulate
adelante forward
adiós good-bye
aduana customs
aeromozo(a) flight attendant
aeropuerto airport
afeitar(se) to shave
agencia agency
agente *m., f.* agent
agosto August
agua *f.* water
ahora now
ahorrar to save
aire *m.* air
al contado in cash
al lado de beside
alberga pool
albergue *m.* hostel
alegrar to make happy
alegrarse de to be happy

alegre happy
alfarero(a) potter
alfombra carpet
algo something
alguien someone, anyone
algunas veces sometimes, at times
algún, alguno some, any
alimento food
almacén *m.* department store
almorzar (o→ue) (z→c) to eat lunch
alojamiento lodging
alquilar to rent
alquiler *m.* rent
alto stop sign *(n.)*, tall *(adj.)*
amarillo yellow
amigo(a) friend
anaranjado orange
anfibio amphibian
animal doméstico *m.* a pet
año pasado last year
anoche last night, last evening
anteayer day before yesterday
anual annual
apartamento apartment
aprender (a) to learn (how to)
aquel that
aquí here
árbitro referee
ardilla squirrel
argentino Argentine, Argentinian
armar la tienda to put up the tent
arreglar to straighten, to fix
arroz *m.* rice
ascenso promotion
ascensor *m.* elevator
asistir to attend (e.g., school, a concert)
aspirina aspirin
atrás backward
autobús *m.* bus
autopista freeway
ave *f.* fowl
avión *m.* plane
ayer yesterday
ayudar to help
azul marino navy blue
azul blue

B

bádminton *m.* badminton
bailar to dance
baile *m.* dance
bajar to get off, out of (bus, car), to go down, to lower
bañar(se) to bathe
banco bank
banda band
banquero(a) banker
barrer to sweep
básquetbol *m.* basketball
basura garbage
beber to drink
bebida drink, beverage
beige beige
béisbol *m.* baseball
bendecir to bless
biblioteca library
bien well, fine
bienes raíces *m. pl.* real estate
bióxido de carbono carbon dioxide
bistec *m.* steak
blanco white
blusa blouse
boleto ticket
bolígrafo (boli) ballpoint pen
bonito pretty
bosque (lluvioso) *m.* (rain) forest
botones *m.* bell hop
brazo arm
brincar (c→qu) to hop
brócoli *m.* broccoli
bucear to scuba dive
buenas noches good night
buenas tardes good afternoon
bueno good
buenos días good morning
burro donkey
buscar (c→qu) to look for, seek

C

caballo (yegua) horse (mare)
cabeza head
cabra (nanny) goat
cadera hip
café *m.* coffee
cafetera coffee maker

calcetín *m.* sock
calculadora calculator
calentamiento warming
caliente hot (temperature)
calle *f.* street
cama matrimonial double bed
cama sencilla single bed
cama bed
cámara camera
cambiar (de) to change
caminar to walk
camino road
camisa shirt
camiseta T-shirt
canario canary
cancha de tenis tennis court
candidato(a) candidate
cansado tired
cantar to sing
capa de ozono ozone layer
capitolio capital building
cara face
carne *f.* meat
carpintero(a) carpinter
carretera highway
carro car
casa house, home
casa de bomberos firehouse
casa modelo model home
casado married
casar(se) (con) to marry, get married (to)
casi almost
cebra zebra
ceja eyebrow
celebrar to celebrate
cenar to eat supper
centro center, downtown
cerca near
cerdo pig
cereal *m.* cereal
cerebro brain
certeza certainty
chao bye
cheque de viajero *m.* traveler's check
chico(a) kid, child
chileno Chilean
chimenea fireplace
china orange
chivo (billy) goat

chocar (c→qu) to crash, to annoy
chuleta de cerdo pork chop
cierto certain, true
cine m. movie
cintura waist
cita appointment, date
claro light
clase f. class
clasificación f. classification
clínica clinic
club m. club
cobrar un cheque to cash a check
cocer (o→ue) to cook
coche m. car
coche alquilado m. rented car
cocina kitchen, stove
cocinar to cook
cocinero(a) cook, chef
codo elbow
colchón de aire m. air mattress
colchón de espuma m. foam rubber
    mattress
colombiano Colombian
columna vertebral backbone
combustible m. fuel
combustión f. combustion
comedor m. dining room
comenzar (e→ie) (z→c) to begin
comer to eat
comerciante m., f. business person
comisaría de policía police station
comité m. committee
cómo how
cómoda chest of drawers
complacer to please
comprador (a) buyer
comprender to understand
computadora computer
con with
concierto concert
conductor(a) driver
conejo rabbit
confirmar las reservaciones to confirm
    reservations
congelador m. freezer
conmigo with me
conocer to know, be familiar with
conseguir (e→i, i) (gu→g) to get
consigo with oneself

construcción f. building
constructor(a) builder
construir to build
contador(a) accountant
contaminación f. pollution
contaminar to pollute
contar (o→ue) to count, to tell
contento happy
contigo with you
contratar to hire
contrato contract
contusión f. bruise
convenir to suit, be suitable
corazón m. heart
corbata tie
coro chorus
correo post office
correr to run
correr las olas to surf
cortar el césped to cut the grass
corte court (f.), cut (m.)
creer to believe
criar (i→í) to raise (people, animals)
cruzar (z→c) to cross
cuaderno notebook
cuadra block
cuál which, what
cualificación f. qualification
cuándo when
cuarto de baño bathroom
cuarto de familia family room
cuarto room
cubano Cuban
cuchara spoon
cuchillo knife
cuello neck
cuidar to care for
cura cure
curioso curious, interesting

D

dar to give
dar un paseo to go for a stroll/walk/
    drive
dar una vuelta to take a walk/ride
de dónde from where
de la mañana in the morning
de la noche at night

de la tarde in the afternoon
de quién whose
de of, from, about
debajo de under
deber to owe, ought to, should
decidir to decide
decir (e→i) to say, to tell
dedo (de pie) finger (toe)
defender (e→ie) to defend
deforestación f. deforestation
dejar to leave
delante de in front of
delgado thin
dentista m., f. dentist
dependiente(a) clerk
deportista m., f. athlete
derecha right
derecho straight
desayunar to eat breakfast
descansar to rest
describir to describe
deseable desirable
desear to want, desire
desempleo unemployment
desilusionado disappointed
despedir(se) (e→i, i) to fire, to send off, to
  say goodbye
despertar(se) (e→ie) to wake up
después after(ward)
destino destination
desvestir(se) (e→i, i) to undress
detrás de behind
día m. day
diccionario dictionary
diciembre m. December
diente m. tooth
diferir (e→ie, i) to differ
dinero money
diplomático(a) diplomat
direcciones f. pl. directions
dirigir to direct
discutir to argue, to discuss
disgustar to displease
divertir(se) (e→ie, i) to amuse (to have a
  good time)
divorciarse to get divorced
doblar to turn, to fold
doble double
doctor(a) doctor

doler (o→ue) to hurt, ache
domingo Sunday
dominicano Dominican
dormir(se) (o→ue, u) to sleep (to fall
  asleep)
dormitorio bedroom
duda doubt
dudoso doubtful
dueño(a) owner

E

ecología ecology
ecosistema m. ecosystem
edificio building
el the
él he
electricista m., f. electrician
elefante m. elephant
ella she
ellas they (f.)
ellos they (m.)
empacar las maletas (c→qu) to pack the
  bags
emplear to employ
en in, at
en casa at home
encantado delighted
encantaría would love
energía nuclear nuclear energy
enero January
enfermarse to get sick
enfermero(a) nurse
enfermo sick, ill
enfrente de facing, in front of
enganche m. down payment
enojado annoyed
enojar to anger, annoy
ensalada salad
enseñar to teach
entender (e→ie) to understand
entrar to enter, go in
entre between, among
entrevista interview
entrevistar to interview
erosión f. erosion
escalera stairs
escoger (g→j) to choose
escribir to write
escritor(a) writer

escritorio desk
escuchar to listen (to)
escuela school
ese that
espalda back *(n.)*
español *m.* Spanish (language)
espantoso frightening
especie *f.* species
espectáculo show
esperar to hope, to wait (for), to expect
esposo(a) husband, wife
esqueleto skeleton
esquí acuático *m.* water skiing
esquina corner
estación *f.* station, season (of the year)
estante *m.* shelf
estar to be
estar de acuerdo con to agree with
estatua statue
este this
estéreo stereo
estirarse to stretch
estómago stomach
estudiante *m., f.* student
estudiar to study
estufa stove
estupendo great, stupendous
evidente evident, clear
exigencia demand, requirement
existir to exist
experiencia experience
extremidad *f.* extremity
extrovertido extroverted

F

fábrica factory
falda skirt
faltar to lack
fastidiar to bother, annoy, bore
febrero February
fiebre *f.* to have a fever
fiesta party
fin de semana (pasado) *m.* (last) week-end
flan de caramelo *m.* custard
fogata campfire
fortuna fortune
fotógrafo(a) photographer
fregadero (kitchen) sink

freír (e→i, i) to fry
frente *f.* forehead
frío cold
fruta fruit
fuerzas armadas armed forces
fútbol *m.* soccer
fútbol americano *m.* football

G

gabinete *m.* cabinet
gallina chicken (hen)
gallito shuttlecock
gallo rooster
ganancia earnings, profit
ganar to win, to earn
garaje *m.* garage
garganta throat
gato(a) cat
gente *f.* people
gerente *m., f.* manager
gimnasio gymnasium
golf *m.* golf
gordito chubby
gracias thank you
gripe f. flu
gris gray
guapo good looking, handsome
guardar to put away
guía *m., f.* guide (person)
guía *f.* guidebook
guineo banana
gustaría would like

H

habichuelas verdes green beans
habitación *f.* room
hablar to talk, speak
hace calor it's hot
hace fresco it's cool
hace frío it's cold
hace sol it's sunny
hace viento it's windy
hacer to do, to make
hacer ejercicio to exercise
hacer footing to jog
hacer las reservaciones to make reservations
hacer un viaje to take a trip
hay there is/are

helado ice cream
herbicida herbicide
hermano(a) brother, sister
hervir (e→ie, i) to boil
hielera cooler
hijo(a) son, daughter
hipopótamo hippopotamus
hipoteca mortgage
hola hi
hombro shoulder
horno oven
horrible horrible
hotel *m.* hotel
hoy today
huelga strike
huevo egg

I

igualmente likewise
iguana iguana
impedir (e→i, i) to impede, keep from
importante important
importar to matter
imposible impossible
infanta princess (not likely to ascend the
  throne)
infante *m.* prince (not likely to ascend
  the throne)
ingeniero(a) engineer
inmigración *f.* immigration
inquilino(a) tenant
insecto insect
insistir en to insist on
inspección *f.* inspection
inspector(a) inspector
inteligente intelligent
interés *m.* interest
interesar to interest
intérprete *m., f.* interpreter
introvertido introverted
inyección *f.* shot
ir (se) to go (to leave)
ir de compras to go shopping
itinerario itinerary
izquierda left

J

jaguar *m.* jaguar
jamás never

jamón *m.* ham
jardín *m.* garden
jefe(a) boss
joyero(a) jeweler
jueves *m.* Thursday
juez(a) judge
jugar (u→ue) (g→gu) to play (a sport)
juicio judgment
julio July
junio June
juzgar (g→gu) to judge

L

la the *(f., sing.)*
labio lip
laboral working, work *(adj.)*
lámpara lamp
lápiz *m.* pencil
las the *(f., pl.)*
lástima pity, shame
lastimarse to hurt oneself
lavadora washing machine
lavaplatos dishwasher
lavar(se) to wash
leche *f.* milk
lechuga lettuce
leer to read
legislatura legislature
lejos far
leña firewood
lengua tongue
león *m.* lion
leopardo leopard
levantar pesas to lift weights
levantar(se) to lift (to get up)
libro book
licenciado(a) lawyer
licuadora blender
limpiar to clean
linterna flashlight
llamar to call
llegar (g→gu) to arrive
llueve it's raining
loco crazy
locutor(a) announcer
lógico logical
loro parrot
los the *(m., pl.)*

lotería lottery
luego then
lunes *m.* Monday

M

madre *f.* mother
maíz *m.* corn
mal bad, sick
maldecir to curse
mamá mom, mama
mamífero mammal
mañana tomorrow, morning
mandar to order, command, to send
mano *f.* hand
manzana apple
marinero(a) sailor
mariposa butterfly
marrón brown
martes *m.* Tuesday
marzo March
más... que more . . . than
mascota pet
mayo May
mayor older
mecánico(a) mechanic
medianoche *f.* midnight
medias *pl.* hose
médico doctor
medio medium, means
mediodía *m.* noon
mejilla cheek
mejor better
mejorar el vuelo to upgrade the flight
melón *m.* melon
memorias memories
menor younger
menos less, minus
menos... que less . . . than
mensual monthly
mentir (e→ie, i) to lie
mentón *m.* chin
mercado market
mes pasado *m.* last month
mesa table
mesero(a) server, waitperson, waiter, waitress
mesita (de noche) small table, (nightstand)
meta goal

metro subway
mexicano Mexican
mi my
mí me
microondas *m.* microwave
mientras while
miércoles *m.* Wednesday
mineral mineral
mirar to look (at), watch
mochila backpack
molestar to bother, annoy
mono monkey
monóxido de carbono carbon monoxide
montar a caballo to ride a horse
morado purple
morir (o→ue, u) to die
mover (o→ue) to move
mucho gusto pleased to meet you
muebles *m.* pl. furniture
muleta crutch
muñeca wrist
murciélago bat
museo museum
músico(a) musician
muy very

N

nada nothing, not anything
nadar to swim
nadie nobody, no one
naranja orange
nariz *f.* nose
navaja universal Swiss army knife
navegar la red (g→gu) to surf the web
necesario necessary
necesitar to need
negocios *pl.* business
negro black
ni... ni neither . . . nor
nieva it's snowing
niñez *f.* childhood
ningún, ninguno *f.* none, not any
noche *f.* night
nosotros(as) we
noviembre *m.* November
nuestro our
número number
nunca never

O

o... o either . . . or
obvio obvious
octubre *m.* October
ocupado busy
ocurrir to happen, occur
oficina office
oído ear
oír to hear, to listen
ojo eye
oler (o→ue) to smell
olla pot, sauce pan
olvidar to forget
ópera opera
ordenar los gabinetes to put cabinets in order
oreja ear
organizar (z→c) to organize
órgano organ
orquesta orchestra
oscuro dark
oso bear
oveja (carnero) sheep (ram)
oxígeno oxygen

P

padre *m.* father
pagado paid
pagar en efectivo (g→gu) to pay cash
pago pay
pájaro bird
palacio palace
palacio de gobierno government building
palacio de justicia hall of justice
pan (tostado) bread (toast)
panameño Panamanian
pantalones *m. pl.* pants
pantera panther
papá dad, pop, papa
papa potato
papel *m.* paper
parada stop (bus, taxi)
parecer to seem (like)
pared *f.* wall
paro work stopage, lock out
parque *m.* park
partido game

pasado last
pasaporte *m.* passport
pasar to spend, pass
pasar la aspiradora to vacuum
pasar tiempo to spend time
paso de peatones crosswalk
pastilla pill
patata potato
patio patio, yard
peatón *m.* pedestrian
pecho chest
pedir prestado to borrow
pedir (e→i, i) to ask for, to order
peinar(se) to comb (your hair)
película movie
pelo hair
peluquero(a) hairdresser
pensar (e→ie) to think
peor worse
pequeño small
periódico newspaper
periodista *m., f.* journalist
periquito parakeet
permiso de conducir driver's license
permitir to permit
perro dog
personal personal *(adj.)*, personnel *(n. m.)*
persuadir to persuade
peruano Peruvian
pescado fish (food)
pescar (c→qu) to fish
pesticida pesticide
pez *m.* fish (live)
pie *m.* foot
pierna leg
piloto pilot
piña pineapple
ping pong *m.* ping pong
pintar(se) to paint (to put make-up on)
piscina pool
piso floor
plancha iron
planchar to iron
plátano plantain
plato dish
plomero plumber
pluma pen
poder to be able

pollo chicken
poner en orden to straighten up
poner la mesa to set the table
ponerse to become
ponerse (ropa) to put on (clothes)
por la mañana in (during) the morning
por la noche at (during the) night, in the
   evening
por la tarde in (during the) afternoon
por qué why
porcentaje m. percent
porque sí just because
portero(a) consierge, janitor
posible possible
postal m. postcard
postre m. dessert
practicar (c→qu) to practice
practicar deportes (c→qu) play sports
preferir (e→ie, i) to prefer
preguntar to ask (a question)
preparar to prepare
prestación f. benefit (work)
préstamo loan
previo previous
primo(a) cousin
princesa crown princess
príncipe m. crown prince
probabilidad f. probability
probable probable
probar (o→ue) to taste, to try
profesión f. profession
profesor(a) professor
programador(a) programmer
prohibir to prohibit
propano propane
propiedad f. property
propietario(a) owner
propina tip
puerta door, gate
puertorriqueño Puerto Rican
pulmón m. lung
puma mountain lion
pureza purity

Q

¿qué tal? how is it going?
qué what
quehacer m. chore
querer to want, to love

quién who
química n. chemical
químico adj. chemical

R

radio m., f. radio
raqueta racket
raquetilla paddle
real royal, real
recepción f. reception desk
recibir to receive
recoger (g→j) to pick up, collect
recomendar (e→ie) to recommend
recordar (o→e) to remember
recuerdo souvenir (memory)
red f. net, Internet
referencia reference
refresco soft drink
refrigerador refrigerator
regar las plantas (e→ie) (q→qu) to
   water the plants
regular OK, normal
reina queen
reír (e→i, i) to laugh
relaciones f. pl. relations
renunciar to resign
repetir (e→i, i) to repeat
reponer to replace
representar to represent, to play a role
reptil m. reptile
República Dominicana Dominican
   Republic
reservar to reserve
resfriado cold (illness)
residuo residue, by-product
restaurante m. restaurant
retroceder to back up
revista magazine
rey m. king
rico delicious
ridículo ridiculous
rodilla knee
rogar (o→ue) (g→gu) to beg
rojo red
romper to break, to tear
ropa interior underwear
ropa clothes
rosado pink
roto broken

S

sábado Saturday

saber to know, to know how to, to discover (preterite)

sacar (c→qu) to take

sacar fotos (c→qu) to take photos

sacarse el gordo (c→qu) to win the grand prize (lottery)

saco de dormir sleeping bag

saco jacket, blazer

sacudir to dust

sala living room

salir to go out, leave

saltar to jump

salud f. health

salvadoreño Salvadoran

salvaje wild

sándwich m. sandwich

sano healthy

sartén f. frying pan

se (indirect object pronoun) to you (**usted**, **ustedes**), him, her, them; is also a reflexive pronoun

secadora dryer

secretario(a) secretary

seguir (e→i, i) (gu→g) to follow, to continue

seguro insurance

seguro social social security

sello stamp

selva jungle

semáforo traffic signal

semana week

semanal weekly

sencilla single

senda path, trail

señor Mr., man

señora Mrs., woman

señorita Miss, woman

sentar(se) (e→ie) to sit down

sentir(se) (e→ie, i) to feel sorry, to feel

septiembre m. September

ser to be

serpiente f. snake

servicio de habitación room service

servir (e→i, i) to serve

siempre always

silla chair (dining room chair, straight chair)

sillón m. easy chair

simpático nice

sin without

sindicato union (labor)

sobre on, above

sobrino(a) nephew, niece

sofá m. sofa, couch

solamente (sólo) only

soldado soldier

solicitar to apply

solicitud f. application

sombrero hat

sopa soup

sorprendente surprising

sorprender to surprise, startle

sorprendido surprised

sorpresa surprise

sótano basement

su your (form.), his, her, their

subir to get on/in

sueldo salary

suéter m. sweater

sugerir (e→ie, i) to suggest

T

tabla de planchar ironing board

taller m. workshop

también also, too

tan... como as . . . as

tanque de gas m. gas cannister

tanto... como as much (many) . . . as

tarde afternoon (n.f.), late (adv.)

tarjeta de crédito credit card

tasa rate

taxi m. taxi

té m. tea

teatro theater

techo roof

técnico(a) technician

televisor m. TV set

temer to fear

temprano early

tenedor fork

tener (e→ie) to have

tener calor to be hot/warm

tener celos to be jealous

tener cuidado to be careful

tener éxito to succeed

tener frío to be cold (to do something)
tener ganas de + *inf.* to really want, to feel like (doing something)
tener hambre to be hungry
tener la culpa to be to blame/at fault
tener miedo de to be afraid of
tener paciencia to be patient
tener prisa to be in a hurry
tener que + *inf.* to have to (do something)
(no) tener razón to be wrong/to be right
tener sed to be thirsty
tener sueño to be sleepy
tener suerte to be lucky
tener... años to be . . . years old
tenis *m.* tennis
terminar to end, finish (terminate)
terreno land, terrain
terrible terrible
ti you *(fam.)*
tienda tent
tierra earth, ground
tigre *m.* tiger
tímido shy
tío(a) uncle, aunt
tobillo ankle
tocar (c→qu) to play (an instrument)
todavía still, yet
todos los días every day
tomar to take, to drink
tomate *m.* tomato
torcer (o→ue) (c→z) to twist
torta cake
tortuga turtle, tortoise
tos *f.* cough
toser to cough
tostadora toaster
trabajar to work
trabajo work
tradicional traditional
traje *m.* suit
tránsito traffic
transporte *m.* transportation
tren *m.* train
triste sad
tronco trunk
tu your *(fam. sing.)*
tú you *(fam. sing.)*

U

un, una a, an
uña nail (finger or toe)
universidad *f.* university
unos some
usted you *(form. sing.)*
ustedes you *(form. pl.)*
utensilio utensil

V

vaca (toro) cow (bull)
veleadores *m. pl.* wind surfers
velear to wind surf
vencer (c→z) to defeat
vendedor(a) seller, salesperson
venir to come
ventana window
ver to see
verdad *f.* truth *(n.)*, true *(adj.)*
verde green
verduras vegetables
vestíbulo entry hall, vestibule
vestido dress
vestir(se) (e→i, i) to dress (to get dressed)
viajar to travel
viaje *m.* trip, travel
viernes *m.* Friday
vino (tinto, blanco) (red, white) wine
violeta violet
visa visa
visitar to visit
vivienda dwelling
vivir to live
vivo alive
volar (o→ue) to fly
voleibol *m.* volleyball
voluntad *f.* will, volition
vosotros(as) you *(fam. pl.)*
vuelo flight
vuelo libre hang gliding
vuestro(a) your *(fam. pl.)*

Y

yo I

Z

zapato shoe
zoológico zoo

Vocabulario inglés-español

A

a, an un
about de, sobre
accountant contador(a)
accumulate acumular
ache doler (o→ue)
active activo
actor actor *m.*
actress actriz *f.*
advise aconsejar
after(ward) después
afternoon tarde *f.*
agree with estar de acuerdo con
agreement acuerdo
air aire *m.*
air mattress colchón de aire *m.*
airplane avión *m.*
almost casi
also, too también
always siempre
amphibian anfibio
amuse divertir (e→ie, i)
anger, annoy enojar
ankle tobillo
announcer locutor(a)
annoy fastidiar, enojar
annoyed enojado
annual anual
apartment apartamento
apple manzana
application solicitud *f.*
apply solicitar
appointment cita
April abril *m.*
Argentine (Argentinian) argentino
argue, discuss discutir
arm brazo (anatomy), arma *f.* (weapon)
armed forces fuerzas armadas
arrive llegar (y→gu)
as . . . as tan... como
as much (many) . . . as tanto... como
ask (a question) preguntar
ask for, order pedir (e→i, i)
aspirin aspirina
at a, en
at (during the) night por la noche
at home en casa
at night de la noche
at times a veces

athlete deportista *m., f.*
attend asistir (a la escuela, un concierto)
August agosto
aunt tía

B

back espalda
back up retroceder
backbone columna vertebral
backpack mochila
backward atrás
bad mal, malo
badminton bádminton *m.*
ballpoint pen bolígrafo (boli)
banana guineo, banana
band banda
bank banco
banker banquero(a)
baseball béisbol *m.*
basement sótano
basketball básquetbol *m.* (balóncesto)
bat *n.* murciélago, bate *m.* (baseball)
bat *v.* batear
bathe bañar(se)
bathroom cuarto de baño
be estar, ser
be . . . years old tener... años
be able poder (o→ue)
be afraid of tener miedo de
be careful tener cuidado
be cold tener frío
be happy alegrarse de
be hot, warm tener calor
be hungry tener hambre
be in a hurry tener prisa
be jealous tener celos
be lucky tener suerte
be patient tener paciencia
be right (be wrong) (no) tener razón
be sleepy tener sueño
be thirsty tener sed
be to blame, at fault tener la culpa
bean frijol *m.* (dry), habichuela (green)
bear *n.* oso(a)
become ponerse
bed cama
bedroom dormitorio
beg rogar (o→ue)
begin comenzar (e→ie) (z→c)
behind detrás de

beige beige
believe creer
bellhop botones *m.*
benefit (work) prestación *f.*
beside al lado de
better mejor
between, among entre
billy goat chivo
bird pájaro
black negro
blender licuadora
bless bendecir
block cuadra
blouse blusa
blue azul
boil hervir (e→ie, i)
book libro
borrow pedir prestado (e→i, i)
boss jefe(a)
bother molestar
brain cerebro
bread pan *m.*
break romper
breakfast desayuno
broccoli brócoli
broken roto
brother hermano
brown marrón, castaño
bruise contusión *f.*
build construir
builder constructor(a)
building edificio, construcción *f.*
bull toro
bus autobús *m.*
business negocios *pl.*
businessperson comerciante *m., f.*
busy ocupado
butterfly mariposa
buy vender
buyer comprador(a)
bye chao

C

cabinet gabinete *m.*
cake torta
calculator calculadora
call llamar
camera cámara
camp stove estufa para acampar
campfire fogata
can opener abrelatas *m.*
canary canario(a)
candidate candidato(a)

capital (city) capital *f.*
capital building capitolio
car carro, coche *m.*
carbon dioxide bióxido de carbono
carbon monoxide monóxido de carbono
care for cuidar
carpet alfombra
carpenter carpintero(a)
cash (a check) cobrar (un cheque)
cat gato(a)
celebrate celebrar
center centro
cereal cereal *m.*
certainty certeza
chair (straight chair) silla
change money cambiar dinero
change cambiar de
cheek mejilla
chemical *adj.* químico
chemical *n.* química
chemist químico(a)
chest pecho
chest of drawers cómoda
chicken (food) pollo
chicken (hen) gallina
child niño(a), chico(a)
childhood niñez *f.*
Chilean chileno
chin mentón *m.*
choose escoger (g→j)
chore quehacer *m.*
chorus coro
chubby gordito
class clase *f.*
classification clasificación *f.*
clean limpiar
clerk dependiente(a)
clinic clínica
clothes ropa
club club *m.*
coffee café *m.*
coffee maker cafetera
cold (illness) resfriado
cold (temperature) frío
Colombian colombiano
comb your hair peinar(se)
combustion combustión *f.*
come venir
committee comité *m.*
computer computadora
concert concierto
confirm confirmar

consierge (janitor) portero(a)
construction construcción f.
continue seguir, continuar
contract contrato
cook (chef) cocinero(a)
cook v. cocer (o→ue) (c→z), cocinar
cooking utensils utensilios de cocina
cooler hielera
corn maíz m.
corner esquina
couch sofá m.
cough n. tos f.
cough v. toser
count, tell contar (o→ue)
court corte f.
cousin primo(a)
cow vaca
crash chocar (c→qu)
crazy loco
credit card tarjeta de crédito
cross cruzar (z→c)
crosswalk paso de peatones
crown prince príncipe m.
crown princess princesa
crutch muleta
Cuban cubano
cure cura
curious curioso
curse maldecir
custard flan de caramelo m.
customs (immigration) aduana
cut n. corte m.
cut v. cortar

D

dad papá m., papi m.
dance n. baile m.
dance v. bailar
dark oscuro
date cita
daughter hija
day día m.
day before yesterday anteayer
December diciembre m.
decide decidir
defeat vencer (c→z)
defend defender (e→ie)
deforestation deforestación f.
delicious rico (riquísimo)
delighted encantado
demand n. exigencia
dentist dentista m., f.
department store almacén m.

describe describir
desirable deseable
desire desear
desk escritorio
dessert postre m.
destination destino
dictionary diccionario
die morir (o→ue)
differ diferir (e→ie, i)
difficult difícil
dining room comedor m.
diplomat diplomático(a)
direct v. dirigir (g→j)
direction dirección f.
disappointed desilusionado
dish plato
dishwasher lavaplatos m.
displease disgustar
do hacer
doctor médico m., f., doctor(a)
dog perro(a)
Dominican dominicano
Dominican Republic República
    Dominicana
donkey burro(a)
door puerta
double doble
double bed cama matrimonial
doubt duda
doubtful dudoso
down payment enganche m.
downtown centro
dress n. vestido
dress v. vestir(se) (e→i, i)
drink n. bebida
drink v. beber, tomar
driver conductor(a)
driver's license permiso de conducir
dryer secadora
dust v. sacudir
dwelling vivienda

E

ear (external organ) oreja
ear (hearing) oído
early temprano
earnings ganancia
earth tierra
easy fácil
easy chair sillón m.
eat comer
eat breakfast desayunar
eat lunch almorzar (o→ue) (z→c)

eat supper cenar
ecology ecología
ecosystem ecosistema m.
egg huevo
either . . . or o... o
elbow codo
electrician electricista m., f.
elephant elefante m.
elevator ascensor m.
employ emplear
engineer ingeniero(a)
enter entrar
entry hall vestíbulo
erosion erosión f.
every day todos los días
evident evidente
exercise ejercicio
exist existir
experience experiencia
extremity extremidad f.
extroverted extrovertido
eye ojo
eyebrow ceja

F

face cara
facing, in front of enfrente de
factory fábrica
fall asleep dormirse (o→ue, u)
family room cuarto de familia
far lejos
farm animal animal doméstico m.
father padre m.
fear n. miedo
fear v. temer
February febrero
feel sentir(se) (e→ie, i)
feel (sorry) sentir (e→ie, i)
feel like (doing something) tener ganas
    de + inf.
fertilizer abono
fever fiebre f.
finger dedo
finish acabar, terminar
finish off acabar con
finish up acabarse
fire n. incendio, fuego
fire v. despedir (e→i, i)
firehouse casa de bomberos
fireplace chimenea
firewood leña
fish (food) pescado
fish (live) pez m.

fish v. pescar (c→qu)
fix arreglar
flashlight linterna
flight attendant aeromozo(a)
floor piso
flu gripe f.
fly v. volar (o→ue)
foam rubber mattress colchón de
    espuma m.
fold v. doblar
follow seguir (e→i, i)
food alimento
foot pie m.
football fútbol americano m.
forehead frente f.
forest bosque m.
forget olvidar
fork tenedor m.
fortune fortuna
forward adelante
found out, discovered saber (preterite)
fowl ave f.
freeway autopista
freezer congelador m.
Friday viernes m.
friend amigo(a)
frightening espantoso
from de
fruit fruta
fry freír (e→i, i)
frying pan sartén m., f.
fuel combustible m.
furniture muebles m. pl.

G

game partido
garage garaje m.
garden jardín m.
gas cannister tanque de gas m.
gate puerta
get conseguir (e→i, i)
get divorced divorciarse
get dressed vestir(se) (e→i, i)
get married casarse
get off, out of (bus, car) bajar
get on, in subir
get sick enfermarse
get up levantar(se)
give dar
go ir
go (put) to bed acostar(se) (o→ue)
go for a stroll, walk, drive dar un paseo
go in entrar

go out salir
go shopping ir de compras
goal meta
goat cabra (nanny goat), chivo (billy goat)
golf golf *m.*
good bueno
good afternoon buenas tardes
good looking guapo
good morning buenos días
good night buenas noches
good-bye adiós
government building palacio de gobierno
grandfather abuelo
grandmother abuela
grass césped *m.*
gray gris
great grande (large), estupendo *(exclamation)*
green verde
guide (person) guía *m., f.*
guidebook guía
gymnasium gimnasio

H

hair pelo
hair dresser peluquero(a)
hall of justice palacio de justicia
ham jamón *m.*
hand mano *f.*
handsome guapo
hang gliding vuelo libre
happen ocurrir
happy alegre, contento
hat sombrero
have tener
have a good time divertir(se) (e→ie, i)
have just acabar de
have to (do something) tener que + *inf.*
he él
head cabeza
headache dolor de cabeza *m.*
health salud *f.*
healthy sano
hear oír
heart corazón *m.*
heat *v.* calentar (e→ie)
help ayudar
her *adj.* su
herbicide herbicida *m.*
here aquí
hi hola

highway carretera
hip cadera
hippopotamus hipopótamo
hire contratar
his *adj.* su
hop *v.* brincar (c→qu)
hope esperar
horrible horrible
horse caballo
hose (clothing) medias
hostel albergue *m.*
hot (temperature) caliente
hotel hotel *m.*
house casa
how cómo
how is it going? ¿qué tal?
hurt doler (o→ue)
hurt oneself lastimarse
husband esposo

I

I yo
ice cream helado
iguana iguana
ill enfermo
immigration inmigración *f.*
impede impedir (e→i, i)
important importante
impossible imposible
in en
in (during) the afternoon por la tarde
in (during) the morning por la mañana
in front of delante de
insect insecto
insist on insistir en
inspection inspección *f.*
inspector inspector(a)
insurance seguro
intelligent inteligente
interest *n.* interés *m.*
interest *v.* interesar
interpreter intérprete *m., f.*
interview *n.* entrevista
interview *v.* entrevistar
introverted introvertido
iron (appliance) plancha
iron *v.* planchar
ironing board tabla de planchar
itinerary itinerario

J

jacket saco
jaguar jaguar *m.*

January enero
jeweler joyero(a)
jog hacer footing, trotar
journalist periodista m., f.
judge n. juez(a)
judge v. juzgar (g→gu)
judgment juicio
July julio
jump saltar
June junio
jungle selva
just because porque sí

K

kid (child) chico(a)
king rey m.
kitchen cocina
knee rodilla
knife cuchillo
know conocer (be familiar with), saber
    (know facts, know how to)

L

lack faltar
lamp lámpara
land terreno
last month el mes pasado
last night anoche
last week la semana pasada
last weekend fin de semana pasado m.
last year el año pasado
late tarde
laugh reír (e→i, i)
lawyer abogado(a), licenciado(a)
learn (how to) aprender (a)
leave ir(se), salir, dejar (leave behind)
left n. izquierda
leg pierna
legislature legislatura
leopard leopardo
less menos
less . . . than menos... que
lettuce lechuga
library biblioteca
lie mentir (e→ie, i)
lift weights levantar pesas
light claro
likewise igualmente
lion león(a)
lip labio
listen (to) escuchar
live adj. vivo
live v. vivir

living room sala
loan n. préstamo
lock out (labor) paro
logical lógico
look (at) mirar
look for buscar (c→qu)
love querer
lunch almuerzo
lung pulmón m.

M

magazine revista
make hacer
make (the bed) arreglar
make happy alegrar
mammal mamífero
manager gerente m., f.
March marzo
mare yegua
market mercado
married casado
marry casar(se) (con)
matter importar v.
May mayo
me mí, me
meat carne f.
mechanic mecánico(a)
medium medio
melon melón m.
memories memorias
Mexican mexicano
microwave microondas m.
midnight medianoche f.
milk leche f.
mineral adj. mineral
minus menos
Miss señorita
model home casa modelo
mom mamá f., mami f.
Monday lunes m.
money dinero
monkey mono
monthly mensual
more . . . than más... que
morning mañana
mortgage hipoteca
mother madre f.
mountain lion puma m.
move mover (o→ue)
movie cine m., película (film)
Mr. señor m.
Mrs. señora
museum museo

musician músico(a)
my mi

N

nail (finger or toe) uña
navy blue azul marino
near cerca
necessary necesario
neck cuello
need necesitar
neither . . . nor ni... ni
nephew sobrino
net red *f.*
never nunca, jamás
newspaper periódico
nice simpático
niece sobrina
night noche *f.*
nightstand mesita de noche
none, not any ningún, ninguno
noon mediodía *m.*
normal regular, normal
nose nariz *f.*
notebook cuaderno
nothing nada
November noviembre *m.*
now ahora
nuclear energy energía nuclear
nurse enfermero(a)

O

obvious obvio
October octubre *m.*
of de
office oficina
OK bien, está bien, regular
older mayor
on sobre
on the left-hand side a mano
    izquierda
on the right-hand side a mano derecha
only solamente (sólo)
open *adj.* abierto
open *v.* abrir
opera ópera *f.*
orange (color) anaranjado
orange (fruit) naranja, china
orchestra orquesta
order (command) mandar
organ órgano
organize organizar (z→c)
ought to deber

our nuestro
oven horno
owe deber
owner dueño(a), propietario(a)
oxygen oxígeno
ozone layer capa de ozono

P

pack *v.* empacar (c→qu)
paddle (ping pong) raquetilla
paid pagado
paint pintar
palace palacio
Panamanian panameño
panther pantera
pants pantalones *m. pl.*
paper papel *m.*
parakeet periquito(a)
park parque *m.*
parrot loro
party fiesta
pass pasar
passport pasaporte *m.*
path senda
pay pago
pay cash pagar en efectivo (g→gu)
pedestrian peatón(a)
pen pluma
pencil lápiz *m.*
people gente *f.*
percent por ciento
percentage porcentaje *m.*
permit *n.* permiso
permit *v.* permitir
personal personal
personnel personal *m.*
persuade persuadir
Peruvian peruano
pesticide pesticida *m.*
pet mascota *m.*
photographer fotógrafo(a)
pick up recoger (g→j)
pig cerdo(a)
pill pastilla
pilot piloto
pineapple piña
ping pong ping pong *m.*
pink rosado
pity lástima
plantain plátano
play tocar (c→qu)(music), jugar (g→gu)
    (game), practicar (c→qu) (sports)
please complacer

pleased to meet you mucho gusto
plumber plomero *m., f*
police station comisaría de policía
pollute contaminar
pollution contaminación *f.*
pool piscina, alberca
pork chop chuleta de cerdo
possible posible
postcard postal *f.*
post office correo
pot olla
potato papa, patata
potter alfarero(a)
practice practicar (c→qu)
prefer preferir (e→ie, i)
prepare preparar
pretty bonito
previous previo
prince infante *m.*
princess infanta
probability probabilidad *f.*
probably probable
profession profesión *f.*
professor profesor(a)
profit ganancia
programmer programador(a)
prohibit prohibir
promotion ascenso
propane propano
property propiedad *f.*
Puerto Rican puertorriqueño
purity pureza
purple morado
put away guardar
put in order ordenar
put make-up on pintar(se)
put on (clothes) poner(se) (la ropa)
put up the tent armar la tienda

Q

qualification cualificación *f.*
queen reina

R

rabbit conejo(a)
racquet raqueta
radio radio *m., f.*
rain *v.* llover (o→ue)
raise (people, animals) criar
ram carnero
rate tasa
read leer

real estate bienes raíces *m. pl.*
receive recibir
reception desk recepción *f.*
recommend recomendar (e→ie)
red rojo
referee árbitro
reference referencia
refrigerator refrigerador *m.*
regret sentir (e→i, i)
regular regular
relations relaciones *f. pl.*
remember recordar (o→ue)
rent *n.* alquiler *m.*
rent *v.* alquilar
rented alquilado
repeat repetir (e→i, i)
replace the roof reponer el techo
represent representar
reptile reptil *m.*
reservation reservación *f.*, reserva
reserve reservar
residue, by-product residuo
resign renunciar
rest descansar
restaurant restaurante *m.*
rice arroz *m.*
ride a horse montar a caballo
ridiculous ridículo
right *n.* derecha
road camino
room cuarto, habitación *f.*
room service servicio de habitación
rooster gallo
royal, real real
run correr

S

sad triste
sailor marinero(a)
salad ensalada
salary sueldo
salesperson vendedor(a)
Salvadoran salvadoreño
sandwich sándwich *m.*
Saturday sábado
save ahorrar
say decir
say good-bye despedir (e→i, i)
school escuela
scuba dive bucear
secretary secretario(a)
see ver
seem (like) parecer

sell vender
seller vendedor(a)
send mandar
September septiembre m.
serve servir (e→i, i)
server mesero(a)
set the table poner la mesa
shave afeitar(se)
she ella
sheep oveja
shelf estante m.
shirt camisa
shot (medical) inyección f.
should deber
shoulder hombro
show espectáculo
shuttlecock gallito
shy tímido
sick enfermo, mal, malo
sidewalk acera
sing cantar
single bed cama sencilla
sink (kitchen) fregadero
sister hermana
sit down sentar(se) (e→ie)
skeleton esqueleto
skirt falda
sleep dormir (o→ue, u)
sleeping bag saco de dormir
small pequeño
small table mesita
smell oler (o→ue)
snake serpiente f.
snow v. nevar (e→ie)
soccer fútbol m.
social security seguro social
sock (stocking) calcetín m.
sofa sofá m.
soft drink refresco
soldier soldado
some (any) algún, alguno, unos
someone (anyone) alguien
something algo
sometimes algunas veces
son hijo
soup sopa
souvenir recuerdo
Spanish español
species especie f.
spend time pasar tiempo
spoon cuchara
squirrel ardilla
stairs escalera

stamp sello
statue estatua
steak bistec m.
stereo estéreo
still, yet todavía
stocking media, calcetín m.
stomach estómago
stop (bus, taxi) parada
stop sign alto
stove estufa (cocina)
straight derecho
straighten arreglar
street calle f.
stretch estirarse
strike huelga
student estudiante m., f.
study estudiar
subway metro
succeed tener éxito
suggest sugerir (e→ie, i)
suit n. traje m.
suit v. convenir (be suitable)
suitcase maleta
Sunday domingo
supper cena
surf correr las olas
surf the web navegar la red (g→gu)
surprise n. sorpresa
surprise v. sorprender
surprised sorprendido
surprising sorprendente
sweater suéter m.
sweep barrer
swim nadar
Swiss army knife navaja universal

T

table mesa
take tomar
take a trip hacer un viaje
take a walk, ride dar una vuelta
take out the garbage sacar la basura
  (c→qu)
take photos sacar fotos (c→qu)
talk hablar
tall alto
taste probar (o→ue)
taxi taxi m.
tea té m.
teach enseñar
tear romper
technician técnico(a)
tell decir, contar (o→ue)

tenant inquilino(a)
tennis tenis *m.*
tennis court cancha de tenis
terrible terrible
thank you gracias
that *adj.* aquel, aquella, aquello
(distant), ese, esa, eso
that *conj.* que
the el *(m. sg.)*, la *(f. sg.)*, los *(m. pl.)*,
las *(f. pl.)*
theater teatro
their su
them luego
there is/are hay
there allí (distant), ahí
they ellos, ellas
thin delgado
think pensar (e→ie)
this este, esto
throat garganta
Thursday jueves *m.*
tie (clothing) corbata
tiger tigre *m.*
tip propina
tired cansado
to a
toast pan tostado *m.*
toaster tostadora
today hoy
toe dedo (de pie)
tomato tomate *m.*
tomorrow mañana
tongue lengua
tooth diente *m.*
traditional tradicional
traffic tránsito
traffic signal semáforo
train tren *m.*
travel *v.* viajar
travel agency agencia de viajes
travel agent agente de viajes *m.*
traveler's check cheque de viajero *m.*
tropical tropical
true cierto
trunk tronco
truth verdad *f.*
T-shirt camiseta
Tuesday martes *m.*
turn doblar
turtle tortuga
TV set televisor *m.*
twist torcer (o→ue)

U

uncle tío
under debajo de
understand comprender, entender (e→ie)
underwear ropa interior
undress desvestir(se) (e→i, i)
unemployment desempleo
union (labor) sindicato
university universidad *f.*
upgrade the flight mejorar el vuelo

V

vacuum pasar la aspiradora
vegetable verdura
very muy
violet violeta
visa visa
visit visitar
volleyball voleibol *m.*

W

waist cintura
wait esperar
waiter (waitress) mesero(a)
wake up despertar(se) (e→ie)
walk caminar
wall pared *f.*
want querer
warming calentamiento
wash lavar(se)
washing machine lavadora
watch mirar, ver
water *v.* regar (e→ie) (g→gu)
water *n.* agua
water skiing esquí acuático *m.*
we nosotros(as)
Wednesday miércoles *m.*
weekend fin de semana *m.*
weekly semanal
well, fine bien
what qué, cuál
when cuándo
which cuál
while mientras
white blanco
who quién
whose de quién
why por qué
wife esposa
wild salvaje
will (volition) voluntad *f.*

win ganar
win the grand prize (lottery) sacarse el
  gordo (c→qu)
win the lottery ganar la lotería
wind surf velear
wind surfer veleador(a)
window ventana
wine (red, white) vino (tinto, blanco)
with con
with me conmigo
with oneself consigo (form.)
with you contigo (fam.)
without sin
work adj. laboral
work n. trabajo
work v. trabajar
work stopage paro
workshop taller m.

worse peor
wrist muñeca
write escribir
writer escritor(a)

Y

yard patio
yellow amarillo
yesterday ayer
you tú, usted, vosotros(as), ustedes
younger menor
your tu, su, vuestro

Z

zebra cebra
zoo zoológico, zoo m.

Índice

Photo Credits

Photos provided by Corbis:
Pages: 29 (three photos), 39, 53, 65, 83, 85, 131, 132, 164, 178, 179, 186, 213, 235, 229, 233, 247, 265, 267, 271, 278, 287, 289, 323, 329, 334, 337, 343, 344, 367

Other sources:
Cover illustration: Christie's Images/Superstock, *Centralus* by Emilio Pettoruti

74 tostada, Mike and Carol Werner/Stock Boston

142 San Salvador, David Simson/Stock Boston

147 El Zunza, Isla Montecristo, David Simson/Stock Boston

248 Oscar Arias, former president of Costa Rica, Milton C. Toby/DDB Stock Photo

309 *Don Quijote y Sancho Pancho* por Pablo Picasso, Scala/Art Resource, N.Y.

359 Estudiantes de une escuela agricola, Guinea Ecuatorial, © Sean Spraguel/Stock Boston

The other photos in the book were taken by Jonathan Stark for the Heinle & Heinle Image Resource Bank.

Notas

Notas